Justifying Genocide

Stefan Ihrig

Justifying Genocide

Germany and the Armenians
from Bismarck to Hitler

Harvard University Press

Cambridge, Massachusetts, and London, England   2016

Second Printing

Cataloging-in-Publication Data available from the Library of Congress
ISBN: 978-0-674-50479-0 (alk. paper)

Stefan Ihrig

Justifying Genocide

Germany and the Armenians
from Bismarck to Hitler

Harvard University Press

Cambridge, Massachusetts, and London, England   2016

Second Printing

Cataloging-in-Publication Data available from the Library of Congress
ISBN: 978-0-674-50479-0 (alk. paper)

To my wonderful wife, Roni, with whom everything makes a little bit more sense

Contents

13 Racial Discourse and the Armenians   301

14 The Nazis' New Turkey   320

15 No Smoking Gun   333

    Epilogue: Armenian Writings on the Wall   359

    Notes   373
    Acknowledgments   449
    Index   451

Contents

Justifying Genocide

Prologue

Franz Werfel Meets Adolf Hitler

A crowded hotel lobby in Breslau in late 1932. People waited there to see "the man of the hour," Adolf Hitler. Hitler was touring Germany in his final bid for power. In the crowd at the hotel was one of our story's main protagonists and his wife. And, remembering the moment when the soon-to-be annihilator of peoples walked past the spectators who had waited just to see him, our protagonist's wife recorded in her diary, "A face that has conquered 30 million people; it has to be quite a face. And yes . . . it was a face! Clutching eyes . . . a young, scared face . . . no Duce! Rather a youngling, who will never find old age or wisdom."[1] These words seem to have been heavily edited after 1945. In her husband's memoirs it all sounds different. When asked by his wife what his first personal impression of Hitler had been, he had reluctantly admitted, "Unfortunately, not so bad."[2] And this only made his current project all the more urgent.

The spectator in the Breslau Hotel lobby was Franz Werfel. Werfel was a German writer, born in Prague to a Jewish family. He was part of the Prague Circle, a friend of Franz Kafka and Max Brod, but he was to become a famous writer in his own right. His most successful novel, *The Forty Days of Musa Dagh*, is a literary monument to the Armenians and their fate in the Armenian Genocide that had taken place during World War I. It was widely read all over the world, especially by German-language speakers and Armenians. It follows the fate of Armenian communities in southern Turkey who fled to the high mountains around Moses Mountain (Musa Dagh), from where they fought against the advancing Ottoman army. They knew the fate that awaited them in the Ottoman Empire: genocide. They held out for forty days (in Werfel's version; in reality it was fifty-three days) and were eventually rescued by French and British warships, just as

1

ammunition and food supplies were running out, and were then evacuated to Port Said, Egypt. This lengthy novel, often published in two volumes, is a story of murder, desolation, and suffering, but it is also one of hope.

Werfel had decided to write such a book while traveling in the Middle East in the late 1920s. In Damascus he had met Armenian orphans who had survived the war.[3] A few years later, the threats of Nazism and of Hitler made the book project ever more pressing for Werfel. Now, he was writing this novel in order to warn Germany of Hitler. Werfel said about the book that the Armenians were his "stand-in Jews" (Ersatzjuden).[4] He assumed that his readers would understand the parallels between the Young Turk dictatorship and the Nazi dictatorship, and between the Turks' anti-Armenianism and the Nazis' anti-Semitism, and so would see the genocide of the Armenians as something that could be in store for Germany and the Jews there. It is a common assumption that Germany did not and could not know in 1932/1933 that Hitler's rise to power could mean genocide. Werfel and, as we shall see, others begged to differ. They recognized the language of systematic hate as well as the dark dimensions of Nazi "policy options" and political goals.

Werfel started writing in 1932. In the same year, he gave his first readings from his unfinished manuscript—which, in fact, is why he was in Breslau when he saw Hitler in the lobby. Hitler was there to rally Germany behind him and his ideas for the country, while Werfel was there to read from his book to *warn* Germany of Hitler and his ideas. That evening, he had read the chapter of his book in which, in the midst of the genocide, the German champion of the Armenians, the pastor Johannes Lepsius, another of our protagonists, meets Enver Pasha, the Ottoman minister of war, to intervene for the Armenians (see Chapter 7).[5] Werfel was writing against Hitler, and against the clock; and he lost against both. Hitler was appointed chancellor already in early 1933, merely a few weeks after they crossed paths in Breslau. In May 1933, books were burning in Germany. Overeager Nazis (students, Nazi storm troopers, librarians, and others) had piled up books of "un-German" authors and set them ablaze to celebrate the victory of a "new spirit." This signaled many things, one among them, of course, that the ideas represented by the authors and by these books were no longer welcome in Germany. Werfel's books were among those burned. And his grand warning against Hitler, his *Forty Days,* was still not even finished, let alone published. Now it seemed improbable if not impossible that his Armenian novel would ever reach its German target audience. Werfel worked in a frenzy and finished the book in the same year. And surprisingly, in late 1933, it was published in Germany, and more surprisingly, it was not even seized immediately by the Third Reich authorities. Those who had subscribed to the publishing house's series in which it appeared, and probably some other nonsubscribing customers as well, were able to get their copy of *Forty Days* before the book was outlawed in early 1934, and the rest of the copies were seized.

It is now something of academic legend, repeated again and again, that the book was only banned at the insistence and after the intervention of the Turkish ambassador in Germany. However, this legend heavily underestimates the "intellectual" capacities of the Nazis, the power of the novel itself, as well as the "iconic" role of the Armenian Genocide for the Nazis. Indeed, when the novel was banned, the chief publication of the SS—the paramilitary SS having been proclaimed the future (racial) elite of the new Reich—the *Schwarze Korps,* denounced Werfel as well as the "American Armenian Jews" promoting the book in the United States.[6] This fusion of Armenians and Jews not only involuntarily validates Werfel's usage of the Armenians as "stand-in Jews," but also betrays the racial view the Nazis held of the Armenians. For the Nazis, the Armenians were quasi-Jews, or indeed über-Jews, as this book will show.

Introduction

Questions of Genocide?

F ranz Werfel's *Forty Days* was indeed a powerful warning—against genocide, against extreme racial policies and stereotypes, but especially a warning against Hitler and the Nazis. And to get his warning across, Werfel made use of the Armenian Genocide. Why would a German (-language) author use the Armenian Genocide to warn Germany of Hitler and the Nazis? How could he think this was an effective narrative and use of his time? And how come this usage of the Armenian Genocide never took on an important role in our history of the Holocaust? After all, it did produce one of the most important German novels of the twentieth century, as well as one of the most important novels of genocide ever. In a way, it is the present book's humble mission to explain just that. I argue that, so far, the Armenian Genocide has received too little attention in the study of German history, the Nazis, and the Holocaust because it has been relegated to a place distant from all this, and thus to a place of partial relevance only (or, inversely, partial irrelevance). The absence or merely peripheral mentioning of the Armenian Genocide in histories of Nazism and the Holocaust has solidified this position of the Armenian Genocide over time as distant in both time and place. It was in fact neither, as this book will show. Werfel used a very powerful motif that was easily and quickly understood by any somewhat-informed reader and most certainly, as this book will show, by any German who had been alive ten years earlier and who had been old enough to read or follow the news. The Armenian Genocide was well remembered when Werfel published his *Forty Days* in late 1933.

• • •

To humans in future centuries learning about the twentieth century, the story of this century must seem unbelievable if not implausible. One devastating war after the other, hot and cold, and mostly global. And genocide, and lots of it. Millions of children, elderly people, women, and men killed for no apparent reason. The organized eradication of whole peoples solely on the pretext of their alleged otherness, again and again. These were humanity's darkest hours, these were the times when we needed to invent and reinvent words to describe the unspeakable, the unimaginable: Holocaust, Shoah, genocide, and "ethnic cleansing." To the readers, history students, and historians in the future—and the further into our future, the more so— it must also appear incredible and implausible to assume that one major genocide was not in some way connected to the next. These genocides were something new in the known history of humanity, and certainly new in their own time. And indeed the Armenian Genocide and the Holocaust were connected—particularly, as this book will show, through actual individuals and bodies of people (nations, networks, intellectuals, politicians, readers, and so on).

Questions of guilt have long since distracted from the larger picture— either Germans wanting to deflect guilt or coresponsibility for the events of 1915/1916 or, in this context more prevalent and at the time of writing still much more pressing, and pressing onto historical scholarship, that of Turkish guilt. Will the deflections of guilt regarding whether or not this really was genocide matter in the long run? Will there be sympathy in a hopefully more enlightened future for those who were denied the legitimacy of feeling as victims of persecution, of injustice, of slaughter? Does it matter how many children's heads were split by axes, how many women were raped before they were killed, how many fathers and mothers saw their sons, wives, daughters, parents, and neighbors killed after being humiliated?

• • •

This is a German story; this is a Jewish story. It is only on a secondary level a "Turkish" or an Armenian story. It is much less about what actually happened between Armenians and Turks (and other Muslim inhabitants of the Ottoman Empire) during World War I and before. It is about what all this meant for Germany, a society that in just under twenty years would give birth to a regime that would carry out the largest genocide in (known) human history.

This is not a book that sets out to put Turkey on trial. This is a book about Germany and its road toward the Holocaust. The core argument of this book is simple: the Armenian Genocide was and is of towering importance for German history, even though its role there has so far been largely ignored. It was influential in Germany's turn to immense "ethnic engineering" later. The deep connection to Turkey explored in the following pages, however, in no way should suggest that Germany "copied" Turkey or that this Turkish connection reduces German guilt; quite the contrary. If anything, it increases German guilt, as this book will show that Germany was in an extraordinary position to have been lengthily and thoroughly exposed to the details and "repercussions" of genocide. Like perhaps no other country in Europe and the world, before 1933, and before 1939, it could have learned something "positive" from this. But it did not. This is why the core of this book is Part III, which sketches the great German genocide debate of the early 1920s. Part I serves as a background and an introduction to German policies toward and discussions about the Ottoman Armenians, while Part II deals with the genocide itself, though mostly with the German reactions and knowledge of genocide in progress. The last part of the book examines the way all this impacted the Nazis.

I am painfully aware how offensive this book might be to some of my Turkish and Armenian readers—for the former, the remainder of the book; for the latter, perhaps the following lines. The Armenian Genocide, as a historical event, has been caught in a hostage situation between pro-Turkish and pro-Armenian sides for one hundred years now. This hostage situation has made it almost impossible to properly integrate whatever happened in the Ottoman Empire in 1915/1916 into world and twentieth-century history. Yet, as this book will show, it had and has great meaning and relevance far beyond the confines of the Ottoman Empire. It needs to be freed from this hostage situation for the broader historical field, also because whatever happened in the Ottoman Empire during World War I was perceived and needed to be understood by contemporaries across the world; it had an impact on the world at the time and is part of our common history. And regardless of whether one believes the events in question constituted a "genocide," these events and how they were understood had a great impact on contemporary societies. The world around the Turks and the Armenians had to come to terms with whatever had happened, too—and, as this book will show, this did not necessarily lead to the expected results.

The Armenian Genocide is not "owned" by Turks and Armenians; rather, it is part of our world history and heritage, a dark part, indeed, but one that we, as humans, have to accept and integrate into our understanding of ourselves. And it is not just any part of our dark history: the Armenian Genocide is perhaps the original sin of the twentieth century; indeed a double original sin: first, killing or letting a state's own citizens die, almost to the extinction of an ethnic group (their citizenship perhaps distinguishes this from previous colonial crimes); second, failing to punish the perpetrators in the aftermath. It is thus not only the sin of the perpetrators but that of the bystanders, beginning with Germany and Austria-Hungary as the Ottomans' allies, but extending to the Entente, as those who did not punish the perpetrators for what they had done (except for the war crimes tribunal in Constantinople after the war). One has to think about what Martin Rade wrote in the 1890s about how the German public had stood by and had even justified the deaths of Armenians during the Armenian Horrors of the 1890s: "It is impossible to appreciate what kind of impression the fashion in which society and the press are discussing the Armenian Horrors will make on the generation of men growing up [today]. They are learning to worship an idol of opportunism and realpolitik which, if it becomes dominant, will cleanse away all noble dispositions."[1] What would it have meant for the generations of the early twentieth century to learn that the world stood idly by and permitted genocide?

· · ·

This is the story of humanity's darkest hours. What happened is almost inconceivable and almost impossible to describe. Not having either murdered or been murdered, it is almost impossible for us to understand what happened. Even people who were actually there as bystanders were not able to make much sense of it. Take, for example, the account of two German nurses, working with the Red Cross in Anatolia, who described in a detailed report what they had witnessed in 1915 during the Armenian Genocide. After recounting how men were killed, women abused, and children's skulls bashed in, they quoted an Armenian woman passing them by: "We want to become Muslims. We want to become Germans, whatever you want, just save us, now they are bringing us to Kemnagh and will cut our throats."[2] The nurses' reaction to this plea for life was to characterize the woman as "clinically insane." It was, in fact, probably a very sane reaction for somebody destined for slaughter, but the circumstances, events, and reactions—in short, the reality of it—were apparently difficult to comprehend.

The Ottoman Empire and its Muslim populations, too, had their share of victimhood in the late nineteenth and early twentieth centuries—subject to massacres, "ethnic cleansing," pogroms, forced migration, and abandonment by international politics and law. Yet, the continued attempts to use "Turkish" victims (in truth also Pomak, Bosnian, Kurdish, Circassian, Laz, Arab, Tatar, and so on) against "Armenian" or other Christian victims are only sacrilege against all of them. While there was suffering on both sides, which indeed needs to be acknowledged, what happened to the Ottoman Armenians was different and certainly exceptional. The Ottoman Armenians were citizens of the Ottoman Empire, which was, at the very least, responsible for their protection and their physical well-being, too. Exposing them, as a whole, to murder, rape, the elements, and starvation had to amount to genocide, and their lament against the Ottoman state that has terribly failed them has to be accepted. And, indeed, as contemporary Armenians in Turkey claim, the Turkish recognition of the genocide is a basic necessity also for the Turkish majority population; it, too, needs to heal and also to move on.[3] It is because of this, and the genocide's importance for German history and broader genocide studies, that this book will not be sidetracked by the still ongoing and very heated debate about whether what had happened in Anatolia during World War I was a genocide or not.[4]

This book is an attempt to understand the events from within their times and for those times; it is less concerned with our debates about them today. I leave the battles about establishing the factuality of all the events of 1915/1916 in Anatolia to others.[5] My battles here are with German history rather than Turkish historiography and politics. In order to bring the events across to my readers, I will discuss them as they were portrayed in the German consular reports and in the press at the time. This book is more about the discourses and the realities these discourses created than about the realities on the ground. This book is about trying to understand how a society—German society—could possibly engage in a multiyear debate about genocide—and, indeed, about the nature of genocide, full of details, horrors, and personal testimonies—only for that very society (or at least a part of it) to commit another, even more unimaginable genocide merely a few years later.

I find it of utmost importance that this book is part of an open, respectful, and continued dialogue with all the interested Turkish readers it may attract. It is one of the most deplorable aspects of some books on the topic that they, from the start, offend and alienate their Turkish readers. However, there is one term that cannot be circumvented in this book: genocide. Even if I were not convinced that the events of 1915/1916 could be accurately described as genocide (and I am convinced that they must be labeled genocide), I still could not write this book without using the term frequently. It is not a book about whether it was or was not a genocide. This is a book about the German reactions to what had happened. They by themselves warrant the label genocide because, for most of the people discussed in this book, it was, in effect, a genocide. Even at the time the events in question took place, German diplomats in Turkey, for example, recognized what was happening as "the total annihilation of a people." That is what we would now describe as a "genocide." To take as a basic definition the one the United Nations has enshrined in the 1948 Genocide Convention, "acts committed with intent to destroy in whole or in part, a national, ethnical, racial or religious group."[6]

Is it anachronistic to use the term "genocide" for 1915/1916? It is not. We are not using it to refer to the crime as defined by the UN in 1948 but rather to the crime it has constituted from time immemorial. It would be strange to assume that to murder an entire people could not be understood as just that before the term was coined; such an argument, by the sheer timeline, would then disqualify the Holocaust from the label "genocide" as well.[7] One of the reasons for using the term in the following is also that German diplomats of the 1910s and German newspapermen of the 1920s did not need the actual term "genocide" (in German, *Genozid*), coined in the 1940s by Raphael Lemkin, to understand what they termed a "murder of a nation," "annihilation of a people," or "extermination of the Armenians." Indeed, the German language before the 1940s had ample alternative expressions that convey the same concept, and in German these are still used alongside *Genozid* today: for example, the term "Völkermord," which translates as "genocide," or "Ausrottung/Vernichtung eines Volkes," which translates as "annihilation/extermination of a people." In their German versions, all these terms (like "genocide" itself) leave no doubt about intent. (Note that, for example, American World War I coverage used similarly clear and unambiguous vocabulary—such as "systematic" or "organized" "campaign of extermination" or "race extermination".)[8] Furthermore, when it comes to

Figure I.1 The debate about whether the term "genocide" is applicable to the events of 1915/1916 and whether its use is anachronistic, as reflected in a cartoon by Chappatte. (2015; "Armenian Tragedy" © Chappatte in *The International New York Times*/Globe Cartoon)

sensitive treatment of the language of the time, we should not fall into the discursive trap laid by such people as Julius Streicher, the virulent anti-Semite and editor of the vicious *Der Stürmer*. During his interrogations by the Allies in preparation for the Nuremberg Trials, he disputed at length that the term "extermination" (of the Jews), as used in his journal and speeches, actually meant murder. Without success, he tried to convince his interrogators that it meant merely relocation and/or removal from power. These are the echoes of denialism from the Armenian case. Extermination did mean murder in the instances quoted in this book, and the relevant authors were quite clear on that.[9]

The second reason for using the term "genocide" here stems from the very German diplomatic reports, after all by the Ottomans' German ally, that I mentioned before. There is still no sensible refutation of their credibility regarding the events of 1915/1916.[10] Often, indeed, the existence of the German sources is simply ignored.[11] While some have gone to great lengths to "prove" that similar American reports are not credible, especially the memoirs of American ambassador Henry Morgenthau Sr., and allege that, of course, the Entente countries produced only war propaganda, nothing of the sort can be said about the German sources.[12] In any case, why would these German diplomats, including the ambassador and almost every regional consul, send home reports of genocide if there was no genocide? What possible reason could they have had to invent a genocide? After all, they were already afraid of the very negative repercussions these events would have for Germany during and after the war. What reason could they possibly have had to forge such potentially self-incriminating reports, almost on a daily basis, for months? This point is perhaps clearest for the earliest such reports, from the consulates closest to the unfolding events; at that time even the consuls' superiors did not care much for these reports, and often they did not square with the anti-Armenian, anti-Semitic, and antiminority outlook of the diplomats themselves. Until somebody can offer a convincing explanation of why German consuls and ambassadors would forge potentially self-incriminating documents, the use of the term "genocide" in this book seems well warranted. Until these reports are refuted, they stand—and it is unlikely, if not inconceivable, that they ever will be refuted in their totality. I beg those readers who reject the term "genocide" for the events of 1915/1916 to bear with me and to evaluate my use of the term after reading this book to the end.

This is no comprehensive history of the Armenian Genocide; it is not even a comprehensive history of Germany and the Armenian Genocide— it is the history of Germany's understanding of the Armenian Genocide (in a broad context, beginning with the role of the Armenians in German history since Bismarck). It is the first extensive study of the role the Armenian Genocide played for Germany and German history.[13] Yet, it is built upon a strong foundation of previous research by many scholars to whom I am deeply indebted. This book seeks to pioneer the field and kick-start the debate: the role the Armenians played in Germany's political history deserves more debate and more research, as this book will show. This is a history of Germany and the Armenians focused on public and published opinion (it would, of course, also be interesting to investigate more closely the political discourse within the government and the Foreign Office, but this cannot be done here extensively). The overviews of the German discourses on the Armenians, at large and in the press, attempted in this book can only be approximate, as the societies we are dealing with (the German Empire—in peacetime and at war—the Weimar Republic, and the Third

Reich) had vast and vastly divergent press landscapes. These are approximations, but through its use of important national papers, cross-paper checks, and various press-clipping collections, the research presented here offers an overview of the main currents at various times. Only some articles can be cited as examples here, and even fewer can be discussed at length.

The first chapters of the book are somewhat biased, as their purpose is mainly to contextualize what will be called here "the great German genocide debate," which took place in the aftermath of World War I, until roughly about 1923 (the year of both the founding of the Republic of Turkey and the failed Hitler Putsch). The book might also appear biased because it will pay more attention to those espousing anti-Armenian discourses, opinions, and language than to pro-Armenian voices. Germany, as will become clear, was a battleground for those "for" and "against" the Ottoman Armenians. Those "for" the Armenians are, of course, of some importance for the debates, tendencies, and discourses excavated here. Others have reconstructed and discussed their activism and discourses. Yet in the greater scheme of things, unfortunately, the German pro-Armenian voices were not as important as the reactions they provoked. They simply never reached a broader base or became of great significance for German society or politics.[14] In any case, this book is not about doing them justice. It is rather about explaining how, in the great German genocide debate, those arguing against the Armenians could come to defend genocide and ultimately argue for genocide as a political tool. It is thus also a history of German anti-Armenianism. Of course, other European countries, too, had their own versions of anti-Armenianism, but none of these can rival Germany's in significance.[15] Not only was Germany an ally of those committing genocide, but German anti-Armenianism would become part of the "legitimizing" background for those who would later commit their own, even grander genocide.

Two terms are of key significance in this book: *denialism* and *justificationalism*. Denialism here denotes an approach that rejects the charge of genocide (against the Young Turks), mostly by denying intent and minimizing the extent of the atrocities.[16] Denialism is of course a familiar term in contemporary discussions of the Armenian Genocide. The other term, "justificationalism," has been coined by me for this book. It was necessary to do so because no existing term fittingly describes the "intellectual" effort and coherent and sustained theoretical attempt to "justify" genocide (any genocide). Justificationalism denotes a view in which one accepts (explicitly or tacitly) that there was a genocide in Turkey at the relevant time, but holds and argues publicly that those who brought it about were justified in doing so, that is, that it can be justifiable to kill an entire or large part of an ethnic, religious, or otherwise defined group. True, there were many justifying and excusing the violence against the Armenians before 1914. But in order to delineate the quality of what was being denied, the term will only be applied to those using it for the genocide after they and, in our case, society and published opinion by and large acknowledged it as such. One of the core results of the research upon which this book is built can be stated as follows: genocide justificationalism and denialism never really coexisted in Germany (at least not in a situation where there were significant numbers of both camps present at the same time). At one point in the early 1920s, the charge of genocide (against the Young Turks) was accepted across the board. Those who formerly had denied the charge of genocide evolved into genocide justificationalists. This makes the German-Armenian connection special, as such broad justificationalist argument and sentiment are absent from most other genocides in the twentieth century. However, it must be stressed that the line between denialism and justificationalism is a thin one and is often blurred. Denialist approaches often prominently feature justificationalist arguments, as will become clear in this book. (Other terms used here are "culturalism," denoting an attempt to understand violence against the Armenians as part of "Asian" or "Turkish" culture, or the "lack of civilization"; and "racialism," which describes the classification of races and, here especially, the understanding of the Armenians as a race rather than a nation or as Christian coreligionists.)

• • •

Peter Balakian's 2004 book *The Burning Tigris,* as well as Jay Winter's 2003 book *America and the Armenian Genocide,* dealing with the Armenian Genocide and the American response to it, argued that the genocide, and the late nineteenth-century massacres that preceded it, gave birth to the "first international human rights movement in American history."[17] Balakian even argues that the genocide and the American responses to it were crucial in molding America's international role and served as a template for future human rights activism.[18] This might be an overestimation of the Armenian impact; a similar argument, albeit one of a much darker character, will be made here in relation to Germany. Although German church and missionary circles also intervened repeatedly, for decades, in favor of the Armenians, and although there was also some heroism on the part of the Germans in the Ottoman Empire in order to save at least some Armenians, the "German template" worked in a different fashion. Violence against the Ottoman Armenians from the 1890s onward, and how it was understood, served as a major case in redefining Germany's policy along the conviction that the killing of certain peoples under certain circumstances could be considered "acceptable." The Armenian Genocide resulted not only in the first (real) genocide debate in Germany, and perhaps the most important one in history to that date, but also in the development of arguments *for* genocide, which were to be reactivated, fused, and transformed into arguments for the "final solution" of the "Jewish question."

Hitler and his colleagues are more important in these pages, even if they feature only toward the end, than, for example, Abdul Hamid II, Enver Pasha, or Talât Pasha, who will feature almost from the beginning. However—yet another disclaimer—what will unfold in the following pages is in no way meant to suggest that the Holocaust happened because of how 1915/1916 was perceived and understood in Germany. If our story begins many decades before the Holocaust, and indeed before the highpoint of the Armenian topic in Germany, this should in no automatic fashion suggest that already in the nineteenth century the path was set to the specific "appreciation" of the Armenian Genocide in the early 1920s and thus toward Hitler and the Third Reich. No tradition, no background, none of the new insights presented here can do away with the very specifics that enabled the rise of Nazism, and no foreign "role model" can deflect guilt from Hitler, the Nazis, and Germany. If, as this book will argue, the German public already understood by the early 1920s what genocide really meant, then, in combination with the whole context and background to this understanding that will be established here, this also means that they were in a position to know much better than is often assumed what Hitler and a Nazi state might mean. If anything, the genocide debate in the early 1920s, as well as the overall special historical connection between the Armenians and German society, doubles German guilt for the Holocaust, rather than deflecting it. To copy the crime you saw your neighbor commit, but in a more brutal and more extensive fashion, does not mean your neighbor is guilty of your crime; you are guilty all the more. The search for the origins of the "final solution," and our distressed and desperate quest to make sense of what happened, cannot be solved by pointing fingers at other, previous genocides. This is not my aim in this book.

In any case, the mass murder of populations is not exclusively a twentieth-century phenomenon. What is, however, new in the twentieth century is the sheer fact that genocide was both immensely possible, given the abilities of the modern state to kill millions, and, all of a sudden, immensely desirable to some, given the projected "benefits" of ethnically pure states. What this book then shows is not so much how an idea was implanted into the German or the Nazi mind, but rather how the idea was debated and acquired the semblance of reasonability and justifiability, especially in the 1920s. It was so widely debated that it became part of Weimar Germany's political normality, discourse, and conscience.

This book covers the time from the 1870s to the Holocaust, and thus touches on many very different political and societal backgrounds, actors, relationships, and facts. The reader may take comfort in the fact that through these changing times there are four "protagonists" that will accompany us throughout our story, four men who, in different ways, and for different reasons, became passionate warriors against genocide: Johannes Lepsius, Max Erwin Scheubner-Richter, Armin T. Wegner, and Franz Werfel. They are a strange group of people, to say the least, as they are very dissimilar historical figures. Who they are will become clear in what follows. One thing, though, unites them: their quest to raise the alarm in Germany about genocide.

PART I

Armenian Blood Money

CHAPTER 1

Beginnings
under Bismarck

The year 1878 was a watershed year for the Ottomans and for German-Ottoman relations. It was also a seminal year for the Ottoman Armenians. It began with what appeared, for a moment, as an imminent catastrophe for the Ottomans, of epic and almost terminal proportions.

From Tsargrad to Berlin

Early 1878: The Russian army was just about to enter Constantinople, at the climax of the Russo-Turkish War that had started the year before. Count Richard von Pfeil, a Prussian soldier in the service of the Russian army, later wrote a popular book about the campaign. It would reach its fourth edition in Germany within a year and was rapidly translated into English. Pfeil wrote there,

> After waiting for hours . . . we began our advance and soon, on reaching a height, we saw Constantinople with its numberless minarets and its golden cupolas and half-moons glittering in the bright sunshine before us. The impression which this made upon the troops was indescribable, and can only be explained by the tradition which has always been handed down among the Russian people that one day "Tsargrad" will belong to the Russian Empire, and that Russian worship will be celebrated in Hagia Sophia. All crossed themselves, some of them fell upon their knees, and others embraced and kissed their comrades, so that one was reminded of the history of the crusades when the pilgrims for the first time came in sight of Jerusalem.[1]

It was not to be. British warships made a show of force along the shore, menaced the Russians, and thus stopped the Russian advance on Constantinople. As a result, Russia and the Ottoman Empire negotiated the Treaty of San Stefano on the outskirts of not-to-be Tsargrad. This treaty was supposed to create a Greater Bulgaria stretching from the Mediterranean to the Black Sea, as well as to grant territorial gains to Montenegro, and full independence to Montenegro, Serbia, and the Romanian Principalities. But even this was not to be. The Great Powers were alarmed by the expansion of Bulgaria, viewed as a Russian proxy, and thus by the expansion of Russia at the expense of the Ottoman Empire. Calls for compensation started being made by other powers, great and small. This was more than just a way to cheaply gain territory (that is, without actually fighting for it); it was also an expression of fear for the balance of power and a means to reestablish it. In order to prevent a great European war over the Ottoman spoils, a congress was convened at Berlin in the summer of 1878. This must have seemed an acceptably friendly setting for Russia: it had had the kaiser's blessing in its war against the Ottomans, during which the German embassy had represented Russian subjects in the Ottoman Empire; and when the Russians had reached Constantinople, they had even been greeted by German congratulations and medals.[2] And even though Otto von Bismarck, Germany's "Iron Chancellor," was to say later that he felt like a Russian delegate at the congress, the 1877–1878 episode still resulted in heightened suspicions and frustrations among all the powers.

• • •

It was not a good start for the young Ottoman sultan, Abdul Hamid II, who had come to power only two years before, in 1876.[3] The year 1876 had seen one sultan deposed by a military coup (Abdul Aziz), and another leave the throne after merely three months due to severe mental health problems (Murad V). In every aspect, these were not good times to be the Ottoman sultan. Abdul Hamid II found himself in a position of little real power. His grand vizier, Midhat Pasha, and his entourage actually wielded all the power and expected the inexperienced, thirty-three-year-old sultan to acquiesce in their decisions, tactics, and goals. The rule of the Ottomans was threatened by nationalist revolts, and the European powers, especially Russia, were eager to cut themselves a slice of the Ottoman cake. The empire had lost Greece in the 1820s, and the loss of Serbia, Montenegro, Walachia, and Moldova was all but official by the 1870s. The old system of alliances had shifted and both empire and sultan saw themselves left alone, with no reliable ally, facing the ever-growing Russian threat as well as that of Christian nationalists everywhere—especially in the Balkans, but, as we shall see, also in Anatolia. And, to make things worse, the empire had just acquired both a constitution and a parliament (promulgated by Abdul Hamid in late 1876 and suspended by him already in early 1878).

And then, of course, there was the Russo-Turkish War, and the Treaty of San Stefano—"an unmitigated disaster for the Ottomans," in Erik J. Zürcher's words.[4] Finally, adding insult to injury, there was the Congress of Berlin. For the Ottomans and Abdul Hamid this was a disastrous congress. "The assembled diplomats," as historian Donald Quataert has summed it up, "parceled out Ottoman lands as if they were door prizes at some gigantic raffle."[5] The empire had to cede territories to Russia, and even to Persia; it had to accept the occupation of Bosnia and Herzegovina by Austria, and of Tunis by France; and it had to grant full independence to Serbia, Montenegro, and Romania, as well as grant such wide-reaching autonomy to Eastern Rumelia that its actual loss was visible on the horizon. In many ways the heavy territorial losses of the empire in Europe marked the end of the Ottoman Empire as a major European power. It also transformed the overall ethnic composition of the empire, only now it had clear Muslim majority.

The young Sultan must have been shaken and shocked by his own and his empire's powerlessness. The leading Ottoman representative, Alexander Karatheodori Pasha, found he had to negotiate much harder with the powers that were supposedly the empire's allies, England and France, than with the immediate and warring opposite, the Russian Empire.[6] It is not too far-fetched to claim that the experiences of these first years of government must have amounted to a trauma that, together with the continuous attempt to overcome it, put its slightly paranoid stamp on the following decades of Abdul Hamid's reign. Of course, later Armenian plots to assassinate him did not help either. Abdul Hamid saw the congress as proof of a conspiracy of the powers against the empire—but, crucially, one not involving Germany. Bismarck's heavy-handed and rather rude dealing with the Ottoman delegation had constituted a new low point of relations, but afterward, a rapid German-Ottoman rapprochement began, initiated by Abdul Hamid.[7] And though Bismarck did not reciprocate to the extent the sultan had wished, it had begun in earnest. It was to really take off under Wilhelm II in the 1890s. The only way out of the Ottoman foreign policy conundrum was, it seemed, Germany—the only power without direct territorial interests in his empire.

After his return from the Berlin Congress, the former Armenian patriarch Mkrtich Khrimyan was scolded for his poor diplomatic abilities and his lack of knowledge of foreign languages by his fellow Armenians. He retorted by saying that he had not been given the proper mandate and that, in any case, he spoke the only language that counted for anything in these matters, that of pain and suffering—apparently he had, literally, cried in front of the Great Power delegates in Berlin.[8] These tears, however, did not impress much. The former patriarch knew this now, and contrasted the thus far peaceful pleas of the Armenians with the more successful violent tactics of Balkan nationalists.[9] The Armenians had hoped to gain provisions similar to those received by the Bulgarians in Eastern Rumelia—such as, for example, autonomous rule under a Christian governor. In the end, all they were left with were vague promises of reform, to be enforced by all the signatories instead of only by Russia—in the San Stefano Treaty, Russia would have had the right to occupy Eastern Anatolia if far-reaching reforms were not instituted. Upon meeting Armenian delegates in the preliminary negotiations for the Treaty of San Stefano, the Russian archduke Nicholas Nikolayevich had even pompously called himself the liberator of both the Bulgarians and the Armenians. And with article 16 of the San Stefano Treaty, the Armenian question had, indeed, officially entered the world diplomatic arena.[10] While the Armenian delegation at Berlin was able to present its petition, it was excluded from the sessions deciding their fate. If Bismarck had been able to do so, he would have even excluded the Ottoman delegation as well. Bismarck thought they would only be cumbersome.[11] In any case, the resulting article 61 of the Berlin Treaty was rather vague, promising improvements, reforms, and security, but neither concrete steps for nor mechanisms of enforcing any reforms.[12] Russia had suggested making its withdrawal of troops from the Eastern Anatolian provinces conditional on the implementation of the reforms of article 61, but Britain objected—it had gained Cyprus from the Ottoman Empire on the understanding that it would defend the sultan's Anatolian provinces and support the empire at the congress.[13] Instead of a conditional occupation of the Eastern Provinces based on the promise of Armenian reforms, Russia now simply received the three provinces of Ardahan, Kars, and Batumi. Not surprisingly, for Bismarck, article 61 was little more than an "ornament" to the protocols—a judgment shared by many historians later: it was "suffi-ciently diluted to render it inoperative."[14]

The Lightning Rod of Europe

On the other side of the political fence were Bismarck and his Germany. Formed in war against France in 1870/1871, Germany was a latecomer to the Great Power game in Europe and in the world. Formed in war against France, Germany was, for the time to come, to be afraid of, if not obsessed with, both French vengeance and any combination of powers against Germany involving France. Formed in war, and not, for example, in the 1848 revolutions, the modern German state began its life with a serious deficit in democratic legitimacy and democratic culture.[15]

Modern Germany's architect and chancellor for the first two decades was Otto von Bismarck. His prime foreign policy goals were to safeguard the new German Empire, to protect it from French vengeance, and to prevent an encirclement of alliances. Bismarck's system of alliances across the continent has since become famous. He managed to bind and include all, except for France—and except for the Ottoman Empire. The Ottomans were a special case for Bismarck. In 1876, he had said in the Reichstag, the German parliament, that the Oriental question was not worth the "healthy bones" of even "one Pomeranian musketeer."[16] This well-known quote—which Bismarck himself later described as having been "ridden to death"—has long been taken at face value and therefore misunderstood. It has been taken to convey a genuine and total lack of interest on the part of Bismarck in the Ottoman Empire. In denying that the empire was worth the loss of any German "bones," what Bismarck meant to do, first, was to publicly distance Germany from the nature of the other Great Powers' interests in the Ottoman Empire.[17] Unlike other powers, Bismarck's Germany did not covet territorial gains there. Second, he meant to signal a lack of interest in the internal situation of the Ottoman Empire—something that would evolve into a very cynical policy vis-à-vis the Armenians. Third, he meant to assure his German audience that Germany would either stand at the sidelines or, on the other hand, try its best to prevent a European war from breaking out over the Ottoman Empire. In the end, Bismarck's statement was meant for public consumption; he and his Germany were indeed very much interested in the Ottoman Empire—just differently from how one might expect.

Bismarck was to claim later that he had acted as an honest broker at the Congress of Berlin, yet in the end he managed to anger both the Russians and the Ottomans. Brokerage here meant mainly keeping Europe from going to war. Bismarck wanted to use the Ottoman Empire as a kind of lightning rod for European tensions. And, as was to become increasingly clear in the following years, he was willing to give away Ottoman territory—even if it was not really his to give—in order to achieve peace in Europe. But there were boundaries to his willingness. First, he wanted stability, which also meant keeping the Ottoman Empire alive. A disintegration would have led to a war for dominion over the various territories, with Russia, Austria-Hungary, France, and England all involved and at each others' throats. Second, if the whole lightning rod construct was to work, there had to be clear checks as to what each Great Power could acquire, and also what they could ask for in the first place. And third, Bismarck did not want a comprehensive agreement over what to do with the Ottoman Empire. The "Oriental ulcer," as Bismarck dubbed the Eastern question, was to be kept open, so that there would not be too much agreement among the European powers, giving Germany a chance to consolidate its own position in Europe.[18] While Bismarck was, for example, willing to support British claims in Egypt, at some point and within the bounds of "reason," he was not prepared to support the whole British rhetoric of Armenian reform, which had been a major factor in the wake of the Congress of Berlin. For Bismarck, as for Sultan Abdul Hamid, these calls for reform were mainly crowbars intended to open up the Ottoman Empire for further British penetration and for the subsequent seizure of territories.

For Bismarck's idea of a balance of power in Europe, a stable Ottoman Empire was a basic necessity and, as historian Norbert Saupp summarized, a precondition for this was Germany's noninterference in Turkish internal affairs.[19] The Ottoman Empire was a pivotal piece of the Bismarckian puzzle—it was the magic cake that could be had and eaten at the same time, and that could be offered to everybody. At various times, various promises were made: to Russia, for example, Bulgaria and the Straits were promised, as was support for Italy's colonial ambitions in Northern Africa (Tripoli) and in Albania. The Ottoman Empire was the place where everybody could seek compensation. Yet, at the same time, Bismarck was guided by the belief that any conflict over Ottoman territories could lead to a European war. Bismarck's Ottoman juggling act was a difficult one.

What becomes clear very quickly when looking at Bismarck's policies vis-à-vis the Ottoman Empire is that he honestly did not care about the peoples inside the Ottoman Empire, whether Christian or non-Christian. In this respect, the Pomeranian musketeer quote hit the nail on the head. Before the Armenian question came to the fore, a rebellion of Christians in Ottoman Bosnia had broken out in 1875. Bismarck remarked that it was of no consequence for Germany if the Christians there, "after having let themselves be mistreated by the Turks for so long, were [or were not mistreated] longer."[20] In mid-October 1876, two years before the Congress of Berlin, Bismarck expressed his position about the role of the Ottoman Empire in German foreign policy clearly:

> The more difficult the situation gets, the clearer we need to see and express in our diplomatic activities that our main interest is not this or that kind of shaping of the [internal] relations/situation in the Turkish Empire, but rather the position in which friendly powers are put in relation to us and to each other. The question whether we will get into a lasting disgruntlement with England, more so with Austria, but mostly with Russia over Oriental troubles is infinitely more important for the future of Germany than all the relations of Turkey with her subjects and with the European powers.[21]

His Machiavellian cynicism went even further in another pronouncement a few days later, on 20 October 1876: "The whole of Turkey, including [its] various tribes, as a political institution is not worth so much that the civilized peoples of Europe should ruin themselves in great wars over it."[22] Nobody should thus wage war just to save either Turkey or its constituent "tribes." One of these tribes was the Armenians. Similarly, in a statement to Emperor Wilhelm I in 1883 about the Armenians, Bismarck stressed that he could not follow a policy that "would sacrifice . . . practical goals for a passing philanthropic nimbus."[23]

Already during the Montenegrin crisis of 1880, the evolving German pro-Turkish position paid off for the Ottomans. The Egyptian question proved more difficult for the evolving alliance. Still, Bismarck became an important power broker over Egypt: Britain looked to him to help defuse tension and to make sure other countries didn't intervene, while the Ottomans looked to him for help as well. In 1882, the British intervention came, and there was not much the Ottomans could do about it, except for a note of protest. Bismarck was not willing to lobby against Britain's designs and even signaled that Britain would not "meet with opposition from the side of Germany" if it chose to annex Egypt. As always, almost everything else was more important than the fate of the territories and the peoples of the Ottoman Empire. Or in Bismarck's words, "The solid and lasting friendship of the British Empire is much more important for us than the fate of Egypt." In line with his plan of relocating European problems to the periphery, he was able to make use of the Egyptian question for Germany's own gain and prevent a war. However, the Egyptian crisis also offered the first real collaboration between the Ottomans and Germany, with the latter helping the Ottomans save face.[24]

Throughout the 1880s, there were many more occasions when the sultan could be happy about Germany. During the Bulgarian Crisis in 1885, the Germans supported the Ottomans dutifully. When a crisis erupted over Greece and Greek ambitions concerning Turkey, Abdul Hamid was very happy about Germany joining the blockade of Greece and about Bismarck telling him that he could envisage giving one or two provinces back to the Ottomans as a punishment for Greek actions.[25] However, on no other issue could Abdul Hamid be as happy about Germany's support as on the Armenian question.

Armenian Questions

In June 1880, the ambassadors of the signatory powers of the Berlin Treaty (Britain, France, Russia, Italy, Austria-Hungary, and Germany) presented the Ottoman government with identical notes asking about the progress regarding article 61.[26] The Porte (the Ottoman government) responded by stressing that it was indeed preparing reforms, but for all the provinces of the empire. This turned out to be one of the last common notes on the Armenian question of the Berlin signatories. Already by the next year there was no more backing among the Great Powers for Armenian reforms, except on the part of Britain, where the violently anti-Ottoman William E. Gladstone had come to power. Gladstone was again putting pressure on the empire for Armenian reforms.[27] An intervention by Britain increasingly seemed imminent. It became clear to the sultan that he needed the protection of one of the powers lest he lose more of the empire. His predecessors had relied upon Britain, which now, in the eyes of Abdul Hamid, had become the main threat. The only European power left was Germany. So, duly, in late 1881 he sent a high-ranking delegation to Berlin. The delegation was ceremoniously received by the kaiser and by Bismarck. It had two goals: to ask for German military advisers, and to prepare the ground for a German-Ottoman alliance. Bismarck agreed to the first request. He put off the second, insisting that the Ottoman Empire needed first come to an understanding with Austria-Hungary. Apart from this, Bismarck also offered Abdul Hamid moral support and advice that was no doubt welcome. He expressed sympathy for Abdul Hamid's dissolution of the Ottoman parliament three years before, taking the view that such a parliament was unsuited to the empire's multiethnic character. And in relation to the pressure from Britain for Armenian reforms, Bismarck advised the Ottomans to treat such reforms in a "dilatory fashion," only instituting such minimal reforms as were strictly necessary for the preservation of the empire. Bismarck also advised the Ottomans to target a few British newspapers and get them to convey the Ottomans' version of the truth about Armenia.[28]

For Abdul Hamid this Berlin mission was a success; he had hoped to be able to hold off Russian and English Armenian pressure with the help of the Germans. And, indeed, from now on the sultan firmly expected German support in the Armenian question.[29] While he would not always get as much as he might have hoped in terms of a real alliance, he indeed could count on Germany in the coming years to help ward off pro-Armenian pressure. Repeatedly the Foreign Office and Bismarck instructed the Germany embassy in Constantinople and the diplomatic service in general to follow their own dilatory policy: to support English proposals only "with moderation" and to preserve Germany's standing with the sultan "in the interest of European peace."[30] In 1883, Bismarck made similar remarks to visiting Ottoman dignitaries. He repeated that if he were in their shoes, he would treat the issue in a dilatory fashion and would not yield one inch. The Porte should not be ready to give up authority in the affected regions by even a bit.[31]

For the first few years after the congress there was still something of a humanitarian exception in place.[32] Yet, already the German signature under the above-mentioned 1880 note of protest was to be one of the last humanitarian exceptions, and it was mainly to save face on the international stage.[33] But even this humanitarian exception had its limits: when, also in 1880, the German ambassador intervened with Berlin for starving Armenians, Bismarck wrote next to the report, "We have enough poor people in distress at home."[34] Especially from 1882 onward, it became

German policy to support the Ottomans against English and Armenian demands. From 1883 onward, Bismarck sharply slapped away questions from his ambassadors about joining the other powers in Armenian matters against the Ottoman Empire.[35]

In these early steps of rapprochement, the sultan did not end up getting as much from Germany as he had expected. It took quite some time for the first German military advisers to actually reach the Ottoman Empire, and a (formal) alliance continued to be denied. The one thing, however, that Bismarck was ready to give was his understanding in the Armenian matter; it was "cheap" to give. Indeed, as some historians stress, it was primarily, if not exclusively, the Armenian topic that brought Germany and the Ottoman Empire together. It was possibly even Germany's understanding and approval that further radicalized Abdul Hamid's stance toward the Armenians.[36] By the end of Bismarck's rule, in 1890, German-Ottoman rapprochement at the price of the Armenians was solidly in place.

Something else was starting to rear its ugly head as well, something that would become more prominent in decades to come but that also had its origin in the Bismarck era: German anti-Armenianism and Armenian-related paranoia. In 1888, the British government accepted a petition from an Armenian committee. With this the Armenian question was back once more—to the great annoyance of Bismarck.[37] As he wrote to Paul von Hatzfeldt, the German ambassador to London, "Given your excellent knowledge of the Oriental circumstances, you will agree with me that an Armenian never does hardly anything without pecuniary gain, and if the Armenians living in London . . . warm up to the fate and the situation of their compatriots that have stayed at home, it was probably the Russian ruble that was the decisive factor."[38] Theories abounded, especially that a French-Russian axis was operating behind the Armenian appeal to the British. As Friedrich Scherer has noted, this was the beginning of German paranoia about the Armenians, and the suspicion grew that a British, French, Russian, or even Franco-Russian plot lurked behind every stew that brewed in the Oriental cauldron.[39]

• • •

As a specialist on Bismarck and the Ottoman Empire has emphasized, "The restraint in the Oriental question that he had propagated for Prussia and Germany throughout his life stands in contrast to the great effort expended by him constantly [on this question]."[40] This contrast comes from the fact that restraint did not mean lack of interest; rather, it arose from the opposite, a pressing interest. For Bismarck, the Ottoman Empire was a land of political opportunity—it could be the lightning rod of Europe, keeping tensions away from Germany; it could be used to satisfy European ambitions away from the center of the continent, thereby making a European war unnecessary; and it could be used diplomatically to enhance Germany's standing without any immediate cost to Germany itself. Still, in 1896, after he was no longer chancellor, Bismarck followed his own course in the matter and wrote a private letter to Abdul Hamid. This letter, amid the "Armenian Horrors" discussed in Chapter 2, advised the sultan to be strong and to "not be intimidated" in the matter of Armenian reforms by England and to make use of Russia in this matter.[41]

Bismarck never allowed Germany to ally with the other powers in the Armenian question, except when it was inevitable and cost him nothing. In all other cases, Germany simply refrained from action—from these affairs "that do not concern us," as Bismarck put it.[42] Bismarck advised the sultan to only enact reforms that benefited all his subjects, thereby enhancing their loyalty. In all other cases of English pressure he advised the sultan to respond with symbolic gestures. In general, Germany also advised the sultan to refrain from anything that could invite Great Power intervention in Turkey. This was, by and large, Germany's course under and also after Bismarck.[43] One should always be wary of books with a direct narrative line from Bismarck to Hitler. German history faced many potential paths between the two, and 1933 was not predetermined by 1870/1871. However, in the narrow confines of Germany's Armenian policies, there exists indeed a rather straight line from Bismarck up to World War I. Bismarck came to see the Ottoman Empire as potentially the lightning rod of Europe and a "compensational object" for the Great Powers. The goals vis-à-vis the Ottoman Empire were to change in the coming decades, but, as in Bismarck's time, the Armenians continued to be used to endear Germany to the Ottoman Empire. The aspirations of the Armenians were on the one hand a cumbersome nuisance to Bismarck and later to Wilhelm II as well, but, on the other hand, they also offered opportunities. Neither one of the two was willing to care for the plight of the Armenians beyond the point at which doing so would negatively affect their designs for Germany's relations with the Ottoman Empire. On the contrary, the Armenian question was constantly used by Germany as a pawn in its game to endear itself to the Ottomans: it was a pawn in Germany's quest for a place in the colonial sun as well as for its new place in the game of the Great Powers in Europe. Germany's silence on the Armenians was something like blood money that Bismarck, Wilhelm, the Foreign Office, and other political leaders were willing and even thought it necessary to pay. This constant and decades-long cynical use of the life and liberty of a people—and a Christian people—accustomed the German political elite and public to anti-Armenian views and discourses, to a "pragmatic" approach to the Armenian question, and, most crucially in the long run, to a "pragmatic" approach to *human* rights, life, and liberty more generally.

CHAPTER 2

Germany and the Armenian Horrors of the 1890s

n 1888, Wilhelm II became emperor of Germany, and by 1890 Bismarck was no longer chancellor. Many things were to change, but one Bismarckian road remained to be traveled, now faster and much further—the one paved by Bismarck on the backs of the Armenians to Germany's "place in the sun." Despite the rapidly changing and evolving policy toward the Ottoman Empire, continuity is key to understanding Germany's official policy vis-à-vis the Armenians over the course of the German Empire. In Wilhelm II's time the potential scope of German Oriental politics expanded rapidly. As time went on, Germany's appetite toward the Ottoman Empire grew. It was no longer solely a lightning rod and a compensatory object for others in Germany's quest to prevent a European war. From "soft" economic penetration to full-blown colonization and land-grabbing schemes, Wilhelmian Germany knew few limits in its "dreams of the German Orient."[1] In the end, German policy toward the Ottoman Empire was a compromise of sorts between more radical colonialist designs and the continued officially proclaimed disinterest. At the center of this policy stood enhanced economic, cultural, and military relations. The planned and partially built Baghdad Railway, connecting Berlin to the Persian Gulf, was to become a key tool for German ambitions as well as a sphere of imperial-colonial projections. Despite semicolonial German ambitions and actions, the Ottoman Empire remained a partner, one whose stability and existence were to be upheld, at almost any cost, it seemed.[2] And while one could argue that already in Bismarck's time both empires were in a state of quasi-alliance, a formal alliance was only concluded right before the Ottomans entered World War I.

What is important for our story is that the evolution of Germany's Oriental dreams did not turn out to make much of a difference to Germany's official policy on the Armenians. The transition from Bismarckian policies to the Wilhelmian era was in fact seamless in relation to the Armenian question. Right before his dismissal, Bismarck had his ambassador tell the sultan that Germany had no interest in the Armenian question whatsoever, and that for Germany this was indisputably an internal Ottoman matter. And already, right after Wilhelm's ascension to the throne, German ambassador Joseph Maria von Radowitz had reassured the sultan, "that with us there is not the least interest in the Armenian circumstances [and] that we view this question as one concerning the domestic relationship between the sultan and his subjects and do not share the urge to cause the sultan any problems by emphasizing article 61 of the Berlin Treaty."[3]

The Armenians continued to be the sacrificial lamb on the altar of intensifying German-Ottoman relations and German imperial policies. Up until World War I, Germany's varied Oriental dreams managed to coexist with a continued commitment to the existence and stability of the Ottoman Empire. One school of thought simply believed Germany could fulfill its dreams best as a partner of the Ottomans; another held that distinct German spheres of interest and thus recognizable territorial claims were not yet clearly discernable, and so Germany had to wait and support the existence and stability of the empire until they were. So, for different reasons, German policymakers continued to support the empire, and concurrently continued *not* to support the aspirations of the Armenians. While official Germany's still often-repeated claims to have no interest in the territories of the empire became less and less credible, official Germany's lack of interest in the fate of the Armenians remained as pronounced and convenient as ever.

For the Wilhelmian years, the entrenched anti-Armenian stance of the political leadership and the Foreign Office is well documented. When, for example, in 1893 a British newspaper speculated about a conference for the Armenians at the alleged suggestion of Germany, the reaction in Germany was instant and harsh. The *Kölnische Zeitung*, a quasi-official newspaper, commented on the absurdity of the idea, especially since "here" nobody had ever cared for Armenian matters anyway. For Chancellor Leo von Caprivi, the suggestion of a conference *for* the Armenians in Germany was nothing less than a "malicious invention."[4] German diplomats, politicians, and the kaiser knew that Armenian aspirations and complaints were not entirely illegitimate, but German political goals and needs were so overriding that there were no scruples about "selling out" the Armenians, in perpetuity.[5] As historian Norbert Saupp stresses, the opinion that the survival of the Ottoman Empire and reforms for the Armenians were mutually exclusive dominated the German Foreign Office.[6] And the sultan was all too aware of the German position, and made use of it whenever he tried to employ Germany as his shield against the advances of the "Armenian Triple Entente," that is, Great Britain, France, and Russia. Then came the horrors of the mid-1890s, which did little to change political Germany's position on the Armenians. Quite the opposite: they gave Germany another chance to cement its role as Abdul Hamid's ally by selling out the Armenians.

What happened in the mid-1890s to the Armenians was not only—as some historians assert—an Ottoman trial run for 1915/1916. The 1890s horrors were also, in a way, a dress rehearsal for how Germany would deal with further Armenian "sacrifices" on the altar of its imperial policy.[7] We will discuss this dress rehearsal in this chapter by examining the reactions to the Armenian Horrors first by official Germany and then by the German press. The remarkable variance in circumstances between the 1890s and 1915/1916—for example, the fact that in the 1890s there was no wartime censorship and only an evolving German-Ottoman alliance, not yet formalized—made no difference to the end result: acquiescence in massacre and even something of official approval, even if the kaiser voiced discontent behind closed doors.

The Armenian Horrors, 1894–1896

Many years later, in 1966, after all that is discussed in this and the following chapters had long passed, Armin T. Wegner, one of our warriors against genocide, published an autobiographical essay in a major German newspaper in which he recalled,

> In the year 1895, when I was nine years old, one Sunday morning I went to the parental breakfast table. I had slept long. [My] parents and [my] brother had left the room [already]. At my father's place a newspaper lay open and the letters set in bold attracted me. The paper reported of the massacre that the Turkish Sultan Abdul Hamid II had carried out through Kurdish militia in Asia Minor like in a slaughterhouse. Until then I had never heard of this nation whose name was so similar to my own first name.[8]

For many in Germany, the news of atrocities against Armenians was indeed the first time they had ever heard of this faraway Christian people. The events of 1894–1896 in Anatolia and Constantinople quickly became known in Europe as the Armenian Horrors. They were a string of massacres, prominently in Sason, Zeytun, and Constantinople, as well as more widespread massacres in the provinces.[9] In total, the alleged death toll was somewhere between 80,000 and over 200,000; in addition, there was a mass of displaced, dispossessed, and starving survivors.

The German embassy in Constantinople had been warning of imminent massacres since the spring of 1894. However, the German ambassador, Hugo von Radolin, believed that it would be the Armenians who would provoke a massacre and "sacrifice thousands of their compatriots" in order to force a Great Power intervention.[10] Two weeks later, Radolin expressed his fears again and went further, adding that the Ottomans would do well to alleviate Armenian despair in order to prevent such an intervention.[11] Thus, already by early 1894, a threatening "Armenian logic" was well in place: not-so-good conditions for the Armenians; the Armenians provoking the massacre of their own population; Great Power intervention; and then possibly the loss of sovereignty or territory.

Once the atrocities began, in August and September in Sason, it took the German ambassador quite some time—until October—to send his first reports to Berlin, based on very sparse information.[12] His previous theory of Armenian intervention-provoking tactics shone through again: "[The Armenians] goad the Turks and when they need to use force in order to reestablish order, the Armenians cry for help against the barbarity of their oppressors."[13] Two months later, however, after more details of Sason had become available, the German ambassador was shocked and found the massacres not justifiable on any grounds.[14] Still, Germany's position did not change and it did not intervene for the Armenians. And once the "official" Ottoman version of the Sason events was presented, Radolin shifted back to wild anti-Armenianism: "My sympathies, however, are completely on the side of the Turks, and the Armenians are scoundrels, the whole lot of them, who do not deserve anything else but to be treated harshly."[15] We should be aware of the fact that, here as well as in later chapters, "treated harshly" was a political-administrative euphemism for massacres and murder. Radolin also stressed that it was "quite a trial of patience" for the Ottoman government not to be able to properly suppress "the unquestionably existing revolution," because of British threats and pressure.

Abroad it was alleged that Kurdish irregular bands, supported by regular Ottoman troops, had attacked and devastated many Armenian villages. The Armenian casualties were estimated at between 900 and 16,000.[16] An official Ottoman commission was formed that, at the beginning, had also included delegates of the Great Powers, from the British, French, and Russian consulates. It met over a hundred times. However, its anti-Armenian bias had quickly alienated the Great Power delegates, who then left and traveled to the area of the massacres by themselves to carry out their own investigation. The Ottoman commission tried to squarely put the blame on "Armenian brigands," while the Great Power delegates found that there had indeed been massacres and that the innocence of the Armenians was established beyond doubt.[17] The Ottoman side even alleged that the Armenians had burned down their own villages at the slightest sign of army intervention.[18]

From the beginning the sultan disputed the facts—both the numbers of dead and the identity of the dead. He feared that this situation could escalate fast and asked the kaiser to influence the British queen to not take the side of this "so dangerous revolutionary element." The kaiser refused to do this, and on his part the sultan refused to change his policies. Abdul Hamid told the German ambassador he would rather die than institute far-reaching Armenian reforms. For the sultan, Sason was a classic example of Armenian treachery: Armenian agitators had deliberately provoked both the conflict and the Ottoman excesses that followed, so that they could then be laid at the Ottomans' feet in the court of world opinion. In due course the German ambassador Radolin warned the sultan about what was at stake—the existence of the empire. They had to get rid of the rebellion as well as of some of the root causes—for example, supposedly inept local administrators—lest the Russians invade.[19]

In response to the Sason massacre, in May 1895, the Great Powers presented the Porte with a memorandum concerning further reforms for the Armenians. Abdul Hamid was severely offended by this move, and it took his government months to respond. Finally, in October 1895, after a lot of haggling, the Porte answered the Great Powers that it had accepted the proposed reforms; the reform program was then published in the Constantinople press.[20] In the meantime, however, at the end of September, Armenians had organized a demonstration in Constantinople and formulated demands in a petition, including the implementation of article 61, but going beyond that to include a repeat of their demand for the sort of

Figure 2.1 The Faithful Warner. "John Bull thinks it appropriate to advise Turkey that it is stuck in Armenia" (while he is stuck "in Egypt"). *Kladderadatsch* December 1894

Figure 2.2 Gladstone's New Toy. The new toy reads "Armenia," the old one "Bulgaria." *Kladderadatsch* September 1895

autonomy established at the Berlin Congress for Eastern Bulgaria. The immediate reaction was the butchering and plundering of Armenians in the
city for many days—a citywide anti-Armenian pogrom permitted and even
encouraged by state authorities.[21] In his report, Ambassador Anton Saurma
von der Jeltsch, after having stressed how nonsensical he found both the
demonstration and the demands of the Armenians, drew particular attention to the role of the police force. He wrote that the police did not only
tolerate "that the population was massacring the Armenians but was
cheering them on and took part itself in the slaughtering of already heavily
wounded and tied-up Armenians." He also described how Armenians
were then even "raided and slaughtered" in their own homes.[22]

"Their blood is upon England's head," commented the kaiser. For him,
as often in the coming years, the guilt was Britain's, and Britain's alone.[23]
The kaiser repeated such claims often: "It is mainly the English press and
the public opinion that it controls, that are responsible for the whole useless scandal of the Armenian question."[24] This interpretation of the Armenian question was also reflected in the German press. Already in 1894, the
satirical paper the *Kladderadatsch* had also put all the blame on Britain
(Figure 2.1). In a cartoon on the Armenian topic, Britain is depicted as
wanting to cut off the sultan's coattail, labeled "Armenia," with which the
sultan gets stuck, while Britain itself is stuck with its own coattail, labeled
"Egypt." This was poking fun at British pro-Armenian propaganda, as
Britain was portrayed as wanting to grab yet more territory from the empire. Another cartoon from the *Kladderadatsch* illustrates what was to be
the reading of nationalist anti-Armenian parts of the press for years to
come: it was all just typical atrocity propaganda. The paper depicted
British prime minister Gladstone inflating his newest distraction, a balloon
labeled "Armenia," after the previous distraction, the balloon "Bulgaria,"
had lost all its air (Figure 2.2). More often, however, the satirical press
blamed the hypocrisy of both Britain and Russia.[25]

The Constantinople massacre was followed by a string of massacres
in the provinces, alleged by contemporaries and historians to have been
long planned by the authorities.[26] On 11 November 1895, the German ambassador Saurma reported that the butchering of Armenians in Asia Minor
was still not over. He reported from Erzurum, a major Armenian population center in Eastern Anatolia, "The surroundings of Erzurum are [now
nothing but a] desert and smoking rubble. In some cases the villages are
still burning today. In Erzurum the corpses that could not be buried fast

enough were given to the dogs for food." The ambassador concluded, unsympathetically, "How pitiful to see how the Armenians let themselves be killed off entirely without resistance like sheep in the corners and recesses of the streets."[27] Two days later the Catholic patriarch of the Armenians came to speak with the German ambassador, and warned him that "within a short period of time the Armenian people will be totally exterminated [and this], seems to be the wish of the Turks anyway."[28] Thus already in the 1890s, we have the first usage of "genocidal terms" for what was happening to the Armenians—the intent to destroy and "exterminate" all the Armenians.

Especially important for the dynamics of this period was the three-month-long conflict between beleaguered Armenians and the Ottoman military at Zeytun (October 1895 until January 1896)—which would only be broken by European diplomatic intervention.[29] At this point, after there had already been so much conflict, there was little patience left in Europe for more bloodshed between Ottomans and Armenians—even in Germany. The kaiser's notes next to the reports on Zeytun from Constantinople illustrate this clearly: "Artillery fire into Yildiz [Palace, that is, the sultan's palace] is the only thing that will have any effect now."[30] The German ambassador was authorized to intervene in the name of "humanitarian interest" and was apparently instrumental in convincing the Porte to have European diplomats broker a truce and thus save about 30,000 Armenians.[31] Yet, Zeytun was to be the exception of German intervention to the rule of Germany's marked and loudly pronounced political disinterest. Afterward, the German Empire rapidly switched back to the wholesale support of Abdul Hamid and the integrity of the Ottoman Empire.[32] Nonetheless, the events of the years 1894–1896 effected a momentary cooling of German affection for Turkey and led to some distance.[33] It was feared that siding too closely with the sultan would leave Germany isolated in Europe.

With all the information reaching Germany, the German government clearly knew what was going on and, throughout most of the horrors, was willing to sacrifice the Armenians as the price of preserving Ottoman goodwill toward Germany. In reaction to the news of the massacres at Trebizond on 8 October 1895, the kaiser stressed, "This surpasses everything before, this is indeed a true St. Bartholomew's massacre! It is necessary to speak in a different tone with the Porte! Because these are Christians! And after all it is also against the other white Christians."[34] It is not clear here if, for the kaiser, the Armenians were not "white Christians," or if he wanted to exclude other Christian groups from his lament (such as other Oriental Christians). However, his reference to the wholesale slaughter of the Huguenot leadership in the St. Bartholomew's Day massacre in Paris in the sixteenth century makes clear that he, too, understood what was happening.

A month later the kaiser exclaimed, "And now as a Christian and a European, one has to watch quietly and even hand out good words to the sultan! Shame [*Pfui*]! On all of us!"[35] Two months later, in December 1895, now again in relation to Zeytun, he remarked, "This is totally bloodcurdling! Can nothing be done? Just once cannot [Ambassador] Saurma threaten on occasion, with all his contempt, this stupid dog of a sultan, if this situation does not abate soon?"[36] And finally, in reaction to the note of the Great Powers, he acknowledged that the urge for vigorous measures was understandable, "but the fact that England expects it from others, rather than [doing it] herself, is downright funny. After all the whole shenanigan was hatched by England [in the first place]."[37] This was to remain his verdict of the episode: that the whole thing was a result of British intrigues.[38] For Chancellor Chlodwig zu Hohenlohe-Schillingsfürst, as he admitted in private, it did not matter at all how many more thousands of Armenians would be exterminated by the Turks; what mattered was whether this could somehow lead to an accord between Britain and Russia.[39] This was one of many clear echoes of Bismarck's politics vis-à-vis the Ottomans.

German diplomats were not only reactive in their interpretations though. In July 1896, thus in the middle of the turbulent 1890s, and before the next round of massacres in the capital, German ambassador Saurma wrote about how the Armenians were viewed among the Ottoman leadership: "In the highest positions here there exists . . . the preconceived opinion that the Armenians constitute a part of the population that is spreading the seeds of rebellion against the authority of the state . . . and therefore must be rendered harmless for eternity." That this meant genocide or at least betrayed genocidal intent was not lost on the readers of this report. One of these readers was Wilhelm II, who commented, "This means that all Christians are to be beaten to death!" The kaiser continued by asking, ironically, whether the Christian powers must stand by quietly while this happened, and perhaps even support the Ottomans while they did it. "Shame on all of us!" he concluded once more.[40] Yet, his Christian Germany, more than the other powers, was to do exactly that. Despite all the kaiser's private outrage, for Germany it was not an option to intervene any further on behalf of the Armenians. In any case, already by early 1896 Germany had decided to end the temporary coolness with the Ottoman Empire and return to its former stance of unconditional support. It had become clear that Abdul Hamid would not change his course and, in any case, as the rifts inside the "Armenian Triple Entente" began to deepen, the risk of Great Power intervention in favor of the Armenians had started to recede.[41]

A key event in the radicalization of German public (printed) opinion, with fewer and fewer papers speaking out for the Armenians, was the occupation of the Ottoman Bank *(Dette Publique)* on 26 August 1896 in Constantinople. This incident was eagerly seized on by the Ottoman government as evidence in favor of its anti-Armenian measures; it was also an unexpected source of support for German anti-Armenianists.[42] Even the internal Protestant Church journals, like the *Allgemeine Evangelisch-Lutherische Kirchenzeitung,* now replicated anti-Armenian racial stereotypes—such as, for example, the Armenians being usurers.[43]

Rumors that the Ottoman government had been planning a pogrom against the Armenians in Constantinople had circulated for some time before. In a prescient article in the *Frankfurter Zeitung* three days before the bank occupation and the Constantinople pogroms, the paper reported the arrival of three regiments of mounted Hamidiye troops. The paper explained that these troops were Kurdish irregular troops organized by Abdul Hamid and already infamous for their role in the Armenian massacres, and they must have made a disconcerting impression among the non-Muslim population of the city given the past atrocities carried out by them.[44]

The Dashnakzutiun, an Armenian revolutionary party, decided preemptive action was necessary, and occupied the Ottoman Bank on 26 August 1896.[45] The Ottoman Bank was no ordinary bank, but a joint institution set up by the Ottoman government together with British and French investors. In the final decades of the empire it served as something of a medium of foreign intervention in Ottoman state affairs, mainly to secure the management of the Ottoman public debt. The Armenian attackers that had taken control of the building were armed with explosives, threatening to blow up the building with almost one hundred hostages if their demands were not met. Apparently the occupation was but the centerpiece of a whole series of terrorist attacks planned for that day in Constantinople—almost all of which were not executed, leaving the occupiers isolated in the bank. Among their demands were calls for a European commissar for the Armenian provinces, the submission of the police and paramilitary forces under European leadership, the reform of the judiciary, and an amnesty for Armenian political prisoners. These demands were not made to the Ottoman government but rather to the European powers—whose building and instrument of control over the Ottoman state they had occupied. The situation was resolved with the help of European diplomats, and the Armenian attackers were shipped off to France. The situation for the rest of the Armenian population in the capital was less safe.[46] Almost exactly at the time the bank occupation began, massacres commenced in Constantinople—the diplomatic reports were sure that these must have been long prepared.[47] The *Berliner Tageblatt* reprinted an eyewitness account of a raid in Constantinople in which Armenians were killed in the streets and in their homes "right under the eyes of the ambassadors."[48] Many thousands of Armenians died. Most of the killing was carried out by people from outside the city (Kurds and Lazes, it was alleged) who were guided by people who knew the city well. This proceeded in a somewhat "orderly" fashion. After such gangs had left a quarter, the municipality's garbage cart came and cleaned away the corpses, as the German embassy's dragoman, Count Eberhard von Mülinen, reported.[49]

The day after the bank occupation, the (other) Great Powers presented a note of protest regarding the citywide anti-Armenian pogroms.[50] The kaiser's reaction to the note of protest was in a mix of German and his mother tongue of English: "Too late—die armen Kerls sind tot" (the poor chaps are dead). He added that this had been exactly what Abdul Hamid had wanted. The sultan simply had to be removed, the kaiser exclaimed.[51] And still he would do nothing, either for the Armenians or against Abdul Hamid.

The German Press and the 1890s Massacres

Political Germany was characterized by a strange mix between (outward) apathy, (private) outrage, and (overall) pro-Turkish sentiments. Public Germany, or at least printed discourse, was little different, except perhaps that it added justifications for Turkish actions to the list. The massacre at Sason in August 1894 had very little resonance in Europe, and especially little in Germany.[52] It was only in late 1895 that most German papers began to react, and it was only in 1896 that a full-blown debate developed on the Armenian Horrors.[53] Throughout, however, the German press, by and large, was dominated by decidedly pro-Turkish views. Johannes Lepsius, a German

Protestant pastor who became Germany's leading pro-Armenian advocate and perhaps the most important German warrior against genocide in the twentieth century, summarized in 1897,

> It is necessary that the truth about Armenia finally comes to light. For three-quarters of a year, the German press has been swamped by news items from a source [official Ottoman statements] that is not only clouded through one-sidedness of judgment, but has, as we shall prove, through outrageous falsifications attempted to mislead Europe. It is therefore no surprise that until now almost no facts about the origin, the course, and the consequences of the mass butcheries, pillaging, and forced conversions have become known in Germany. At the same time much care has been taken to make the guilt of the "rebellious" Armenians, as instigators of all evil, shine in the brightest Bengal light.[54]

A major exception to the pro-Ottoman stance of the rest of the press that Lepsius described was the *Frankfurter Zeitung*, which had established itself as one of the leading liberal papers in Germany. It was founded in the 1850s by Leopold Sonnemann and Heinrich Bernhard Rosenthal, both German Jews—a fact that created a convenient pretext for much anti-Semitic slander by the nationalist press for decades to come. One of the *Frankfurter Zeitung*'s more prominent topics in the last decades of the nineteenth century was the Armenian question, which it had begun to cover occasionally as early as the Congress of Berlin. Starting in the autumn of 1895, it covered the topic almost daily. This did not make it unique per se; other papers, such as the quasi-official *Kölnische Zeitung*, covered the topic frequently as well.[55] But unlike them, it was pronouncedly pro-Armenian, so much so that it gained the distinction of being banned in the Ottoman Empire by the sultan.[56]

On 15 November, for example, the *Frankfurter Zeitung* recounted the scenes of horror of Erzurum via the *Daily News:*

> The disruptions of the peace began on 30 October and the soldiers took part in the plundering. In the Armenian quarter 204 corpses, mostly horribly mutilated, were collected that day. 31 October was quiet, but on 1 November it started again and on this day 306 corpses were collected. Young women have also been cut down attempting to defend their honor; many are missing. The number of victims is estimated at 1,000 in total. The wounded were cared for in the Catholic and Armenian churches. . . .

The slaughter began at the same time across the whole of the city, as soldiers were following a trumpet signal. A soldier declared to the confidante of the English paper that the order for the slaughter came from the Porte.[57]

The *Frankfurter Zeitung* also heavily criticized the Great Powers, including Germany, for having failed to enforce the guarantees for Armenian reforms in the Berlin Treaty. On 8 November it wrote, "the concerned powers have not been able to gain even the slightest guarantees so that even an attempt at the promised reforms could be made."[58] It had also criticized the Ottoman discourse in which "the Armenians are made out to be the attacker."[59]

From early on, the *Frankfurter Zeitung* also engaged in cross-paper debate. On 9 November it criticized the quasi-official *Norddeutsche Allgemeine Zeitung* for its pro-Turkish stance in an article that had ascribed all fault to the Armenians. The *Norddeutsche Allgemeine Zeitung* had claimed that "nobody would have laid a finger on the Armenians, had they not provoked this disaster with their own behavior." For the *Norddeutsche Allgemeine Zeitung*, it was clear that the Ottoman government was trying everything it could to "pacify" the region and that, ultimately, it had been American missionaries who bore the guilt for what had happened.[60]

The *Frankfurter Zeitung* and its critique of anti-Armenian reporting were an exception to the rule. While, for example, the quasi-official *Kölnische Zeitung*, as we have already seen, also exhibited a great interest in the topic and covered it almost daily, it restricted itself mostly to reprinting official Ottoman statements. In contrast to the *Frankfurter Zeitung*, it clearly blamed the Armenians for what had happened and dismissed any estimate of the number of Armenian victims as British propaganda.[61] One of its earliest larger exposés on the topic was penned at the request of Abdul Hamid by Colmar von der Goltz Pasha—the head of the German military mission in the Ottoman Empire. In his article about the "alleged" massacres, Goltz Pasha stressed that the horrors reports must be exaggerated, and that any knowledge of the Turkish people's character would make that clear to anyone. Even that a massacre of any significant magnitude had taken place at all was highly improbable, according to Goltz Pasha. It was the same mythmaking that was always afoot in such instances, he claimed. Whatever might have happened, it did not warrant the great attention it had received. While Goltz's was, rhetorically, not a very convincing rebuttal, it came from a very trusted mouth.[62]

On the other hand, the *Kölnische Zeitung* also printed eyewitness accounts that, far from claiming that the horrors had been exaggerated, described them in excruciating detail. On 26 October 1895, for example, it printed the report of "a fellow man from Cologne" on the massacre in Trebizond earlier that same month. He described how the streets were

> filled with corpses, the shops of the Armenians are closed or plundered, the women are shouting, the children cry for their provider, whole families are annihilated. . . . Two days later I entered the city, my feet were drenched with Christian blood, because the puddles of blood in the streets were still so many that it was impossible to circumvent them. . . . Of the Turks not even five men died, a sign for the fact that the Armenians had been unarmed and that the attack found them unprepared.[63]

Other papers, such as the *National-Zeitung,* even printed spreadsheets of the massacres that had taken place between 1 October and 30 November 1895 in the various parts of Anatolia, listing the time, place, and extent of all the massacres and devastations.[64] Even such details of massacres were, however, not enough to convince most of the nationalist press to condemn them. The *Kölnische Zeitung* argued in 1896 that proof had been found of preparations and plans for the rebellion at Zeytun on the part of Armenian secret committees and that this in turn authorized the Ottoman government to use full force against its mutinous subjects—now of course meaning all Armenians, not just suspected plotters.[65]

Especially vocal on the Armenian topic were parts of the Christian press, though mostly internal newsletters and publications. At the forefront was Martin Rade's biweekly journal *Christliche Welt,* which in 1896, for example, devoted almost 10 percent of its pages to the Armenian topic. Rade believed the German public was misled not only by the quasi-governmental press, but also by the pro-Turkish reporting of the press in general. One of the reasons the German press did not come out more in favor of the Armenians, Rade insisted, was the problematic nature of guilt. Given the dearth of reliable reporting from the affected Ottoman provinces, many journalists, he argued, were reluctant to side with the Armenians as long as there was a chance it would turn out that they had started the conflict that eventually caused their own massacring. And, in any case, much of the information that came from Britain was rejected in a knee-jerk fashion as British propaganda and thus had little further impact.[66]

Interestingly, for the Social Democrat *Vorwärts,* it was less Britain than Russia that was responsible for the atrocities, propaganda, and Armenian suffering. For the flagship of the Social Democratic press, an anti-Russian reflex in dealing with the Armenian topic had been in place even before the massacres began, as early as 1893.[67] Once the massacres started, however, the paper went even further, claiming that the Russians had invented "horrors" whenever and however it suited them—not only the Armenian Horrors, but also, earlier, Greek, Macedonian, and Bulgarian horrors as well. According to Russian propaganda, the *Vorwärts* scoffed, ten times more Greeks than had actually lived in Greece were killed in atrocities committed by the Ottomans. And now, according to the paper, it was the Armenians' turn to be the subject of similarly wild Russian fictions.[68]

As we saw in the examples from the *Kölnische Zeitung,* the 1890s massacres also saw a new kind of "atrocity pornography." Rade's *Christliche Welt* also regularly featured such vivid descriptions. Take, for example, a horrors tale originally published by E. J. Dillon in English: "In Erzurum a man went into the street as he heard a noise and feared for the safety of his children playing in the street in order to find and save them. He was pulled to the ground. . . . He had his clothes torn off and a piece of meat was cut out of his body and in fun offered for sale. 'Good, fresh meat, dead cheap!' called one of the mob." The tale continued with the mob pouring vinegar and other things into his wound. Then came his two little boys, one of them showing his crying and suffering father his own head wound from the massacre. He was then thrown onto his father and both were beaten to death, with the other boy, sitting in the blood of his brother and father, finally being killed by a stroke of a saber. The mob then turned its attention to other Armenians.[69]

Similarly, the *Frankfurter Zeitung* reprinted, among other atrocity accounts, a story told in gory detail of the torture of an Armenian by the police. It turned out he was innocent and was let go, but only when it was feared he was about to die, after having been starved for days, hung up and left hanging for days, beaten nearly to death, and buried alive, naked, in the snow.[70] Such portrayals were obviously difficult for the German public to read, due to their graphic descriptions of violence; but they were also difficult for the German public even to believe. One reason for this was that they conflicted with the popular image of the Turk as the only gentleman in the Orient, as Bismarck had influentially put it.[71] Another reason, as already stated, was simply that many of these reports had reached Germany via Britain, and were therefore discounted as propaganda.

As was to be the case during World War I and also in the 1920s, whenever pro-Armenian sentiment seemed to carry the day and was backed up by some kind of event exterior to the (German) debate, the anti-Armenian faction of the press relentlessly continued to put forward anti-Armenian article after article. However, the Christianity of the victims posed a problem for those wanting to justify Ottoman actions. On at least one occasion the *Norddeutsche Allgemeine Zeitung* tested another way around the Armenians' Christianity by claiming that the Armenian Horrors were God's punishment for the "foul and ossified" form of the Armenians' Christianity.[72] But this justification of mass murder was abandoned in favor of one that found wider and easier resonance.

Race started to be a central category in the debates, with a focus on supposedly unsavory characteristics of the Armenian "people." The *Post*, for example, reprinted characterizations of the Armenians that were meant to stifle any sympathies, taken from a popular travel book: "One can absolutely state that whenever one is being betrayed in Anatolia one is dealing with Armenians." The quoted author (Alfred Körte) continued: even a legal contract did not save one from Armenian deceit, as "every kind of treachery he [the Armenian] conducts as sport."[73] In another example, the anti-Armenian *Post,* in a dispute with the pro-Armenian *Reichsbote,* tried to show that this was not a persecution of Christians: "No Christian except for Armenians has been killed. They have been killed as members of a seditious people." In getting rid of the victims' Christianity, the papers not only shifted focus to their (alleged) national and racial qualities, but simultaneously began justifying the killing in a more global fashion, transcending immediate causes such as rebellion and sedition.[74]

The alleged appalling racial character of "the Armenian" was also used by the anti-Armenian/pro-Ottoman parts of the press to stifle sympathy for the Armenians in Germany. Rade quoted one such "northern paper" in his *Christliche Welt:* the Armenian, in contrast to the more acceptable Bulgarian, was "of disgusting ugliness and his outstanding characteristic was his deceitful cowardice; he does not dare the open fight for his freedom like the Bulgarians but works secretly with dynamite and runs away when he is chased. . . . Sympathy with them is thus totally inappropriate. . . . The Armenians are crooks and usurers who have sucked the very work-shy Turks to the blood [*sic*]."[75]

The pro-Armenian activists continued to speak out for the Armenians. When they were not rebuffed by racial interpretations, it was Bismarck and his Oriental policies that were channeled. In a reaction to a lecture evening organized by Johannes Lepsius, the pastor and pro-Armenian activist whom we met earlier, the *Kölnische Zeitung* developed an argument that would be repeated in the German press almost word for word over twenty years later: "Justice and injustice are on both sides entangled in such an inextricable fashion that there is hardly any reason in order to intervene in this unfortunate struggle from the outside. . . . Most certainly it will soon become obvious that the Armenians have to be left alone to their fate."[76] Lepsius's speech, in turn, was partially reprinted in the *Neue Preussische (Kreuz-)Zeitung.* He was quoted there: "I am saying with fullest consciousness nothing else but that the politics of the six Christian powers is the reason for the butchering of a Christian people."[77] The *Hannoverscher Courier* offered a very Bismarckian reading of the situation. It spoke against the trend of parts of the press and parts of the public to "mimic the sensitive one" in favor of the Armenians. The paper continued, saying that the Armenian question threatened to reopen the Oriental question, and thus threatened peace in Europe. And Europe had to think of itself first.[78]

"An Indictment of Europe"

Much more than the press, it was one person, Johannes Lepsius, who popularized knowledge of the 1890s massacres in Germany. In the period from the 1890s to the 1920s, five German books were pivotal for how violence against the Ottoman Armenians was understood in Germany. Three of these were either authored or edited by Lepsius. Lepsius had worked in the German community in Jerusalem as part of his education as a pastor in the mid-1880s.[79] In the mid-1890s, back in Germany, he was part of a group of Protestant pastors who had become pro-Armenian activists: a group that included Martin Rade, Ernst Lohmann, and Ewald Stier, as well as the theologian and imperialist thinker Paul Rohrbach. Gripped by accounts of the 1895 massacres, Lepsius decided to travel to the Ottoman Empire in order to learn what had really happened.[80] He reached Constantinople in April 1896 and made contact with the German embassy, which was well informed about the Armenian Horrors.[81] Lepsius also received information from the American embassy. While he was able to visit some places

Figure 2.3 1,001 Nights on the Golden Horn. "As reassurance our Scheherazade tells the sultan the fairy tale that in Germany assemblies have been dispersed in which the Armenian Horrors were discussed." This Scheherazade was German ambassador Saurma. *Kladderadatsch* November 1896

such as Kayseri, Mersin, Tarsus, Adana, and Urfa, he was not allowed to travel to other parts of Eastern Anatolia.

After his return, Lepsius traveled across Germany in a lecture tour and told packed halls about the Armenian Horrors in "hundreds of lectures," often with several thousand people in the audience.[82] In these unfolding activities of the German pro-Armenian activists, there were, however, many obstacles to overcome. Public lectures and assemblies on the Armenian topic were a favorite vehicle for raising awareness and funds. However, often these were actively hindered by the German state's representatives—for example, by preventing the renting of large venues, or even by censoring events while they were in progress. In some cases the police forbade Armenians to speak at events; in others they prohibited the collection of money.[83] The ironic cartoon in the satirical weekly, the *Kladderadatsch*, depicting German ambassador Saurma whispering into the sultan's ear that in Germany assemblies in favor of the Armenians had been disbanded by the police, was not entirely off the mark (Figure 2.3).

Another strategy used to raise awareness was Lepsius's large, sixteen-part series of articles published in the *Reichsbote* in August and September 1896 entitled "The Truth about Armenia."[84] Papers like the *Frankfurter Zeitung* discussed and summarized the series as well.[85] The reaction to the articles in Germany was "extraordinary"—among other reasons, because the Ottoman Bank incident and subsequent Constantinople massacres had broken out right in the middle of the publication of Lepsius's article series.[86] Lepsius used his articles and other materials as a basis for his book *Armenia and Europe,* which was published in the fall of 1896, and which by the next year had reached its seventh edition and 13,000 copies; it was quickly translated into English and French, and partially into Russian.[87] A colleague of Lepsius's remembered forty years later that, "In autumn 1896 one could see the yellow Lepsius book with its flaming red title in all German bookstores on display."[88]

In Lepsius's book one could read that, according to diplomatic reports, about 88,000 Armenians and 1,300 Muslims had died, almost 645 churches and monasteries had been destroyed, about 560 villages had converted to Islam, about 330 churches had been converted into mosques, and more than half a million destitute people had been left behind.[89] Lepsius's own estimate was that the death toll must have been at least 100,000. In his introduction he claimed that the Muslims in the countryside told him openly that the mullahs in the mosques had instructed them that the sheikh-ul Islam, the highest (Sunni) Muslim authority in the empire below the sultan-caliph, had given the order that all the Armenians should be killed. They were actually puzzled, Lepsius continued, about why this order had not been "properly" carried out—that is, why any Armenian survivors had been left to live at all. Again, this is a clear allusion to what we would understand as genocide. As a "solution" to this puzzle of genocide aborted, Lepsius reported, the myth had gained ground that the kaiser had intervened with the sultan, and convinced him to stop the massacres before they were "complete."[90]

Lepsius's *Armenia and Europe* was truly a book of horrors. Chapter 1 began with the massacre at Trebizond where, Lepsius claimed, the killing began and ended at the signal of a trumpet—a method used, he reported, in other places as well.[91] Lepsius proceeded to document massacre after massacre, for each province in turn, with all the major cities and killings, providing tactics, the identity of the killers, the number of killed Armenians, and so on. After this rather statistical chapter came a chapter entitled "Something for Steady Nerves." He prefaced this section by stressing that "numbers are dry" and they do not mean much to the reader, who glosses over them. What followed was an even more extreme example of the sort of "atrocity pornography" we have already seen in our discussion of press reports above. Lepsius described all the imaginable and unimaginable ways Armenians were allegedly killed in these "festive events"—"festive" because (according to Lepsius) there was music and merriment among the attackers. The book told of Armenians whose beards were set on fire, Armenians who were thrown onto piles of other Armenians being burned alive so they might choke, limbs being torn off, living people strung up on butcher's hooks, babies thrown onto bayonets, pregnant women cut open, churches burned into which people had fled, and finally all the gory details of how the corpses were mutilated and desecrated. Lepsius also did not shy away from discussing at length how Armenian women were degraded and raped by neighbors, soldiers, gendarmes, and others.[92]

After Lepsius had discussed various other aspects of the Armenian topic in another chapter, he devoted the whole second part of the book, thirty-five pages, to even more detailed descriptions of the 1895–1896 massacres, reprinting diplomatic reports, eyewitness accounts, and newspaper articles.[93] The third part was a German translation of an article by E. J. Dillon first published in the British *Contemporary Review* about Armenia before the massacres. Dillon, too, described what the Ottomans were doing in

Armenia as a "policy of annihilation."[94] Lepsius's erratic and rather repetitive book then included another long section, a list of "disgraceful deeds": further tales of horror for each province and locality.[95] Next the book featured an ambassadorial report from February 1896 that once more recounted the various massacres.

Lepsius was following the logic of the diplomatic reports, at least how he summarized and understood them, when he stressed that these massacres had been "administrative measures" *(administrative Maßregeln)*—a term that would not go away from the German debate and that is highly problematic in its own right. The German term "Maßregel" suggests some sort of an educational or pedagogical measure. It implies the image of father and child, or master and slave; the sultan is then simply "chastising" his unruly children.[96] This imagery, of the Armenians as unruly children, also had its own tradition in Germany (Figure 2.4). Lepsius also used the term "Vernichtungsmaßregel," meaning "annihilatory administrative measure"— which is, of course, an oxymoron because the education and annihilation of the same subject makes no sense.[97] Lepsius, in contrast to later uses, however, employed these terms to underline that these massacres were planned and coordinated by the government and that there was intent to commit genocide. Lepsius explained what all this actually meant: "What are the Armenian massacres? They are an administrative measure of the Sublime Porte, that had as its only motivation and purpose to finally [*endgültig*] render the reforms of the Great Powers nonexecutable through the annihilation of the Armenian people itself."[98]

Lepsius also discussed how the massacres were planned, organized, and executed—a feast of evil (a *"génie du mal"*) that required more planning than the mobilization of an army. This was a well-planned, covert "mass murder–robbery" *(Massen-Raubmord)*.[99] The method employed was, as he stressed, always the same: "To kill in the shortest time conceivable as many Armenians as possible and if possible to take all their property and destroy their estates."[100] It was precisely because of this coordinated execution of the massacres, Lepsius argued, that it was impossible to absolve the central authorities of guilt.[101] He took it as proof of not only the acquiescence in, but also the active organization of, the massacres by the local authorities. Lepsius further alleged that in many places, active preparations had been carried out in the ideological sphere with rumors and allegations against the Armenians—also in order to get the Armenians to make first steps. In his chapter "The Turkish Factory of Lies," Lepsius discussed how local

Figure 2.4 From the European Kids' Table. The assembled nations of Europe wait for their share of the "Ottoman cake," which is about to fall over while the "Armenian kid" is rocking the table. *Kladderadatsch* September 1896

leaders of the Armenian communities were forced to sign declarations assuming guilt and responsibility for the massacres themselves. And here Lepsius also discussed the macabre numbers game, offering the reader a table with the official Ottoman numbers of Armenians dead next to the numbers from the ambassadorial reports.

For Lepsius, the horrors were mainly the fault of the Great Powers—hence the subtitle of his book *Armenia and Europe: A Bill of Indictment*. He claimed, "Had the powers left Armenia to its own devices, then the Armenians would be still today, not a happy but not the most unhappy nation on earth."[102] For Lepsius there had been no reason at all that might have caused the hate of the Ottomans for the Armenians—except for that too-great interest of the powers in the Armenians. Thus, although Lepsius was the leading German pro-Armenian activist, he, too, implied that the Great Powers had stirred the Armenians into either rebellion or too much political activism. He also assigned a lot of blame to the Kurds, who were interested only in plunder, as he claimed, and who would in the future proceed to attack the Turks, once all the Armenians were gone.[103]

The reaction to Lepsius's book was divided and there was a strong anti-Armenian backlash. The *Hamburger Nachrichten*, for example, attacked the German "pastors" acting for those "Armenian terrorist murder gangs" who had to be dealt with not only by the state but as a state matter.[104] A journalist of the *Münchner Allgemeine Zeitung* even began privately denouncing pastors collecting donations for Armenians to their superiors.[105] Another reaction came from a botanist, Walter Siehe, who published an article series in the journal *Deutscher Soldatenhort* ("German Soldiers' Stronghold/Refuge"), apparently a widely read paper. He claimed to be an eyewitness, having traveled in Asia Minor during the massacres. One of his responses to Lepsius was that he had himself seen merely two Armenians being killed; another was that everywhere it had been the Armenians who had taken up arms first. And finally, he maintained, it was the Armenians' "moral unworthiness" that had pushed the otherwise incredibly tolerant Turks toward harsher measures.[106] Siehe's anti-Armenian and anti-Lepsius musings were readily reproduced in the major papers, for example in the *Neue Preussische (Kreuz-)Zeitung*.[107] Predictably, they provoked reactions from the pro-Armenian scene as well.[108] This controversy continued until 1897, when Siehe answered his critics in a two-part article series in *Die Post*. He stressed that the Armenian Horrors were a fairy tale of Christian persecutions that was being told to the German public, when in reality it was not the Armenians' Christianity but rather their racial character that was the cause for the Turkish measures.[109] Indeed, the alleged racial character of the Armenians was central to Siehe's argument, and to sway his readers he appealed to anti-Semitic sentiments: like the European Jews, the Armenians were hardworking and thrifty, but also ruthless merchants, usurers, thieves, fraudsters, and terrorists.[110] Somehow, Siehe and others using anti-Semitic and racial depictions of the Armenians apparently thought this by itself was justification for killing the Armenians in large numbers.

These were, however, only the first ripples of a major anti-Armenian backlash. It was to fully erupt in the wake of the kaiser's visit to the Ottoman Empire the next year, a subject to which we will turn in Chapter 3.

• • •

In the end, the 1890s massacres were but a "glitch" in German-Ottoman relations. In the midst of the horrors, in April 1895, when Ambassador Radolin visited the sultan one last time, as he had been recalled, he again assured him of German support and stressed that "the imperial government is sorry that he [the sultan] has troubles with some powers because of the Armenians. . . . As a representative of a befriended power that has nothing but his well-being in mind, I can express my conviction that the introduction of new reforms for the empire or some parts of it is quite unnecessary." In this audience he also made it clear that he thought that inept officials in the provinces, not the failure to bring about deeper reforms, had been responsible for the Armenian rebellion.[111] His successor, Saurma, was to express similar sentiments a year later, in the height of the massacres and of the propaganda battles. Saurma stressed that while he objected to the kind of measures the Ottomans had employed, at the same time he saw it was the sultan's "right and duty" to squash the rebellion: "If the Armenians let themselves be carried away to rebel against him, stern punishment was in order."[112] Again, it needs to be emphasized that here, "punishment" is a euphemism (and a justification) for massacre.

Once the dust had settled in Constantinople after the Ottoman Bank pogroms, the German policy vis-à-vis the Armenians was quickly back in place—indeed, in all actuality, and not in private expressions of outrage, it had never visibly changed.[113] Alfons Mumm von Schwarzenstein, a leading figure on the Middle East in the German Foreign Office, summarized this in November 1896 in a memorandum that was sanctioned and presented to the chancellor by the Foreign Office. Mumm stressed that all these events simply could not lead to support for a "tribe, that is of no interest for us by itself," for a "race that is in open rebellion against its sovereign." After all, Mumm maintained, "the characteristics of this race, their deviousness, as well as their rebellious machinations had to provoke the anger of the Turks and further that many things had occurred that could justify the Turks that they were acting in self-defense [*Notwehr*]." In Mumm's reasoning, the Armenians' "racial characteristics" were enough to anger the Turks. In addition, Christian compassion abroad had only provoked more Muslim anger, and Mumm strongly advised against any further shows of such compassion. In any case, he argued, a bloodier solution to the whole Turkish question was on the horizon, and in this light the massacres "were surely the lesser evil." Germany had to remain in a strictly observational role in all this, he advised, as some papers had also advised in the months before.[114]

In light of the future debates about the Armenians and about genocide, the German reception of the 1890s massacres is remarkable in a number of ways. First, the 1896 debates saw the first mention of the direct German equivalent of the term "genocide," that is, *Völkermord* (murder of a people or of nations), in the Christian journals. In his *Deutsch-evangelische Blätter,* Willibald Beyschlag wrote in early 1896, "However much one wants to subtract and doubt, it is not possible anymore to deny that for some years now the Turkish government and population have undertaken a bloody endeavor that at least comes close to the attempt at genocide [*Völkermord*]."[115] While this was not the first documented use of the word in the German language as such, it was the first time it was used in a political debate in Germany. This was well over forty years before Raphael Lemkin would coin the English and international version of the word.

Other actors, too, made use of "genocide language"—that is, language pertaining to a criminal act that goes beyond the death of members of a group in pogrom-like settings, toward the eradication of an entire group of humans, with full intent. Martin Rade wrote of the "fanatical system of extermination."[116] We have already mentioned the kaiser and his acknowledgment that the Ottoman apparently intended to annihilate all the Armenians. There was also Ambassador Saurma, who cabled to Berlin in late July 1896 that people in the highest places were welcoming a "total annihilation" of the Armenian people.[117] Another example is Otto Umfrid, Protestant theologian and later an opponent of Hitler's racism, who deliberated in a speech in 1896 that the annihilation of the Armenian people was being carried out according to a long-standing plan.[118] A notable "genocide" discussion led to a resolution of a Protestant assembly in Essen in 1896 that spoke of the "annihilation of a whole Christian people by the Turks."[119] And finally, the *Frankfurter Zeitung* claimed that the massacres had illustrated that the Porte was decided upon the "extinction of the entire Armenian nation."[120] And the list goes on.[121] That means that for some of the authors and activists at least, talking about the Armenians and the 1890s massacres also meant talking about what we label today as genocide.

Another important aspect, in light of later events, was the way the press had reacted in general to the news of massacres "far away in Turkey." While there was (a part of) the "liberal" section of the press (*Vossische Zeitung, Frankfurter Zeitung*) that advocated action for the Armenians, most conservative papers, like the *Neue Preussische (Kreuz-)Zeitung,* the *Post,* or the *Tägliche Rundschau,* printed pro-Turkish articles and described the Armenians, globally, as usurers and revolutionaries. The quasi-governmental and conservative press, like the *Norddeutsche Allgemeine Zeitung* and the *Kölnische Zeitung,* advised against actions on behalf of the Armenians for rather different reasons: they might goad the Turks into more massacres and would thus only harm the Armenians.[122] The anti-Armenian discussion in the *Kölnische Zeitung* went so far as to justify outright the destruction of peoples as a "gruesome necessity that arises out of justified governmental egotism."[123] Paul Rohrbach was to complain later about how sad it had been that the German press had followed the official press so willingly, and in what "repulsive, untruthful, despicably raw fashion" the German press as a whole had covered the Armenian Horrors.[124] Again prefiguring future trends, it was loudly denied in the German press that the German government was coresponsible for the massacres in any way.[125]

The anti-Armenian and anti-pro-Armenian propaganda in the German press, especially in papers close to the government, such as the *Norddeutsche Allgemeine Zeitung* and the *Kölnische Zeitung,* was to some extent carried out at the behest of the Foreign Office, which was worried that pro-Armenian activities in Germany would jeopardize its pro-Turkish policies.[126] The German Foreign Office also directly reacted to negative articles on the Ottoman Empire and the sultan, and used its overwhelming influence to launch counterpropaganda and to force retractions.[127] Apparently, Abdul Hamid spent money on various German papers and their correspondents in Constantinople in order to secure favorable reporting from them.[128]

Another remarkable feature was how quickly the discussion became about race rather than religion: even in Christian circles there was considerable debate about whether this really was a persecution of Christians or rather a "racial persecution." The latter claim was used by some in Christian circles as an argument against extending help and charity to the Armenians.[129] In a back-and-forth between Johannes Lepsius and Pastor Eugen Baumann, a high-ranking official in the German Protestant Church, the latter advanced the usual anti-Armenian racism: "Because the Armenians are not only a race hated by everyone because of their deviousness, but lately have become subject to the sharpest Turkish surveillance as politicians and martyrs for their patriotic hopes and aspirations, and because they are just a race and not a state or an organized people, these political aspirations cannot count on any kind of success or political support."[130] It was the same argument that was used by the majority of the German press against the Protestant attempts to collect money for the Armenians.[131]

Things became ugly fast. In their frustration, even Protestant circles resorted to anti-Semitism, for example in 1897, the *Deutsche Evangelische Kirchenzeitung*, as an explanation for the lack of compassion for the Armenians in the German press, claimed that most of the papers that opposed helping the Armenians were in fact "under Jewish influence" and thus had no interest in the fate of a Christian people.[132] Yet, being "under Jewish influence" was also the attack cry of anti-Armenian nationalist papers against the *Frankfurter Zeitung*'s pro-Armenian coverage. And indeed, even though Protestant circles around Rade and Lepsius had created awareness for the Armenians and begun charitable work for the Armenians by raising money, setting up orphanages, a carpet factory, and so on, the majority of the Protestant Church chose nationalism and alignment with official imperial policy over Christian compassion. After his book had come out and after the team of pro-Armenian activists had organized meetings and lectures, Lepsius applied for leave from his post as parish pastor in order to travel again to Turkey to oversee the implementation of his charitable projects for the Armenians there. He had even offered to hire a substitute pastor at his own cost, yet his church superiors denied him leave. This was a clear signal that not all of the Protestant Church stood behind Lepsius. He felt forced to resign his post and thus also to renounce his pension in order to continue his work for the Armenians.[133] In a way, the Protestant Church's refusal inadvertently pushed Lepsius into the life of a professional pro-Armenian activist.

The frustration over lacking sympathy as well as over the omnipresence of anti-Armenian justifications also led influential historian Hans Delbrück to write about Armenia. In the *Preussische Jahrbücher* he characterized the reaction of the German press to sympathy for Armenian suffering: "the whole of Armenia was for Germany not worth the bones of one Pomeranian musketeer."[134] Germany had sold itself out, he decried. "The worship of Mammon" had triumphed over morality.[135]

What is illustrative of the first large Armenian debate in Germany is the way the anti-Armenian faction—the majority of the press, the political leadership, and the Foreign Office—tried to stifle all criticism of Turkey.[136] Not only did it attempt to justify what had happened—through racial qualifications, appeals to German state interest, and warnings of a European war—but it launched an all-out war against any pro-Armenian sentiments. Not even charity was deemed permissible until there was no longer any charity needed within Germany—thus, in all probability, never.[137] The kaiser and the leaders of German politics knew what they were doing, whom they were backing, and what moral price they were in fact paying—despite all the whitewashing by the domestic press.

It has to be remembered that the other Great Powers had not intervened in favor of the Armenians in any significant fashion either, even if in some of these countries pro-Armenian movements were much stronger. The title of Lepsius's book was, after all, *Armenia and Europe: A Bill of Indictment,* and it was an indictment of Europe, not just of Germany.[138] That all these were dangerous precedents for the future was not lost on observers at the time, and this led Martin Rade to make his rather prophetic statement about the future generation of male Germans: "It is impossible to appreciate what kind of impression the fashion in which society and the press are discussing the Armenian Horrors will make on the generation of men growing up [today]. They are learning to worship an idol of opportunism and realpolitik which, if it becomes dominant, will cleanse away all noble dispositions."[139]

CHAPTER 3

The Triumph of German Anti-Armenianism

n 1898, the kaiser went on his second trip to the Ottoman Empire (the first had been in 1889). He traveled to Constantinople, Jerusalem, and Damascus. His trip was organized by the British travel agency Thomas Cook. This 1898 trip increased the need to come to terms with what had happened to the Armenians in the years before, as well as with Germany's tacit acquiescence in their death. The victory of the Ottoman army over the Greeks in 1897 also heightened the interest in Germany's quasi-ally. The kaiser's trip and the following discussion were a turning point in how the Armenians were understood in Germany. Until the trip, a racial reading of the Armenians had existed parallel to a religious and a geopolitical one, though the first had always been by far the most influential, both in public discourse and in official circles. The racial reading helped justify not intervening for an otherwise fellow Christian people. It helped ease the German conscience. But as dangerous as the racial prisms were by themselves, another danger loomed large in the German perception of the Armenian Horrors. Would these racial and imperialist justifications (for German acquiescence) also be extended to justify the killing of the Armenians in the first place?

In and following 1898, the racial prism was elaborated further, and ultimately it almost completely displaced the others. It followed a certain logic of necessity—the necessity to understand how Germany could align itself with the murderous sultan, and sit on its hands while a Christian people was being slaughtered. And even more: Germany and the Ottomans drew ever closer in these years. One outcome of the massacres had been a change in the landscape of foreign investment in the Ottoman Empire: due to the loss of Armenian lives, among them many intermediaries of European companies, as well as due to Germany's acquiescence to Abdul Hamid's bloody policies, Germany became something of a privileged economic partner. In the coming years, Germany was to enlarge its economic activities in the Ottoman Empire considerably. The concession to build the Bagdad Railway was among the rewards.[1]

Historian Hans-Walter Schmuhl goes so far as to claim that the new racial discourse replaced or rather "updated" all the old Orientalist stereotypes and refocused them, in their most extreme negative forms, on the Armenians. Schmuhl is right to conclude that this new racial discourse "massively fostered the dehumanization" of the Armenians, thereby justifying and excusing all kinds of violence against them.[2] However, this discourse had little similarity to German Orientalism. The German racialist anti-Armenianism, as we saw in Chapter 2 and as will become clear in this chapter, almost exclusively fed on and replicated the discursive building blocks of late nineteenth-century modern Central European anti-Semitism (while the rest of the "Orient" was understood in different terms). In the late nineteenth century, Central European anti-Semitism had undergone a transformation, and had become partially accepted in the public sphere in a new "modern" form that no longer relied primarily on religious otherness, but defined the "Jewish other" predominantly in racial terms. The dominant version of anti-Semitism was now essentialist and racialist.[3] And so was German anti-Armenianism, which was both a duplicate and an extension of modern German anti-Semitism.

The racial interpretation was necessary for another reason. Increasingly, parts of politically active Germany—pro-Ottoman, "peaceful imperialist," otherwise liberal politicians and thinkers, and German nationalists— began identifying with the Turks. As historian Malte Fuhrmann has emphasized, the relationship between Germany and the Ottoman Empire is not aptly described as "semicolonial." For (many on) the German side, the Turks rather became "an atavistic self." Thus they were viewed as being in a position similar to that of the Germans decades earlier—oppressed by foreign powers and held back in their national development. Many of the prisms and interpretations employed in the 1890s debates as well as for the time afterward, as discussed in this chapter, seem to affirm this strong identification with the Turks. And identifying with the Turks also meant siding with them against their enemies and devising interpretations that fit both emanations of the self—the atavistic Turkish one and, at least to some extent, the original German one.[4]

Another, but by far less prevalent, interpretation was the geopolitical reading, by which I mean understanding the Armenians as a dispersed nation like the Poles, split between the domains of different empires. While the "Polish parallel" was only rarely present in the German discourse on the Armenians, it cannot be denied that it had resonance in Germany, which was also having to deal with Polish aspirations. Yet, the Polish parallel and the associated geopolitical reading of the Armenians never came even close to the racial reading in importance, and there are only few documented usages of it.[5]

The kaiser's 1898 trip and the surrounding debates proved to be the catalyst for the clear predominance of an anti-Semitic-inspired reading of the Armenians. It was less what the kaiser himself did or said. Though of course, the mere fact that Wilhelm II traveled to Constantinople to see the sultan was sensational: it somewhat rehabilitated the blood-stained sultan, just two years after the massacres, but it also stained the kaiser with that very same Armenian blood.[6] In any case, the kaiser himself did not directly come into contact with the Armenian topic much on his trip. He told the sultan that for him the Armenian question was simply "outdated."[7] It was rather the backlash to the previous debate about the massacres that crystallized around the kaiser's trip. A wave of enthusiasm and even hysteria in Germany accompanied the trip (though there was also considerable criticism of Wilhelm's "Cook-organized crusade"). Today, the kaiser's assertion, in a toast at a Damascus dinner, that he was the friend and protector of all the world's Muslims draws more academic attention than the debate about the Armenians in Germany in the wake of the trip.[8] This focus is understandable, given both the contemporary importance of Islam in world politics, and the significance of the claim in light of the German-Ottoman jihad during World War I. At the time, however, the Armenian question was arguably of much more importance. To get a sense of the mood, this is how the leading Protestant biweekly, the *Christliche Welt*, began its reporting on the trip (the passage reprinted part of an article from the *Mesveret*, a paper published by dissident Turks exiled in Paris): "What shall those that have survived the bloody [Armenian] horrors, the parents and the children of the unfortunate victims, think when they see the German kaiser giving the man that has murdered thousands of human

Figure 3.1 On the Trip to Palestine. "Look there, my Sirs, over there is Crete, where the Christians are being massacred by the Turks, who are our friends." *Kladderadatsch* October 1898

beings the hand and a brotherly kiss?"[9] Even Ernst von Dryander, the kaiser's court chaplain, found it difficult during the trip to meet, greet, or even pray for the sultan as the latter requested, "because still the whole city was smelling of the freshly spilled blood of the murdered Armenians."[10]

Naumann's *Asia*

The kaiser was followed by groups of German travelers, among them the godfather of twentieth-century German liberalism (if there is such a thing) and rebooted imperialism in ethical guise, the pastor Friedrich Naumann. A cartoon in the satirical paper the *Kladderadatsch*, about Naumann and other German pastors traveling toward the Holy Land, trailing the kaiser, illustrates the urgency to explain and rationalize the overall German pro-Ottoman stance (though not in this case specifically relating to the Armenians) (Figure 3.1). It shows a group of German clerics on the deck of their ship, while their "tour guide," the personified *Kladderadatsch*, points to the island of Crete: "Look there my Sirs, over there is Crete where the Christians are being massacred by the Turks who are our friends."[11]

Until the trip, Naumann had, apparently, espoused rather pro-Armenian views himself in articles in his journal *Die Hilfe*, though the journal had featured both pro- and anti-Armenian articles.[12] In the *Hilfe*, Naumann chronicled his trip in a series of articles, which shortly afterward he turned into a book, *Asia* (named after the ship they traveled on). *Asia* became one of the most-read books of its time, the first edition selling out within eight days, the second edition appearing within a year, and its seventh appearing by 1913.[13] The book contained a lot of opinions and ideas that gave it the potential to become highly controversial. It began its narrative, following the trip chronologically, with disparaging comments about the "neo-Greeks," reflecting the disenchantment of Hellenic Germany with modern Greek "reality"—the Greeks of the modern age just did not live up to their ancient ancestors.[14] But it was also a book describing a pilgrimage of a Protestant pastor to the Holy Land. His harsh and disillusioned remarks about the Holy Land and his stated problem of how to now square this experience with his religion also could have been most controversial. And then there were some rather anti-Semitic remarks as well.[15] Yet, it was his ideas about the Armenians and their role in German policy that ultimately made the book so controversial (and perhaps also so successful).

Before the book had even come out, Naumann had been engulfed in a fierce controversy over a quotation in one of his newspaper articles on the trip. The quotation later also appeared in the book, in which Naumann then also discussed the reactions it had provoked in the press. The person quoted was a German living in Constantinople, a potter to the sultan's court, and the comment was about the alleged racial character of the Armenians:

> I am a Christian and hold "Love thy neighbor" as the first command-ment, and I say that the Turks did the right thing when they beat the Armenians to death. There is no other way for the Turk to protect himself from the Armenian. . . . The Armenian is the worst type in the world. He sells his wife, his still underaged daughter, he steals from his brother. The whole of Constantinople is being morally poisoned by the Armenians. It is not the Turks who have attacked, but the Armenians. . . . That the Armenians in Asia Minor are better [than those of Constantinople], is an English lie. I have been in the villages and know the situation. There as well it is the Armenian who is practicing all the usury. That the German Christians educate Armenian children, does not help at all. They are going to be just as wicked as the others. An orderly means of protecting oneself against the Armenians does not exist. The Turk is acting in self-defense.[16]

This "potter's quote" became a key quote of German anti-Armenianism.[17] In his book, Naumann added that the potter's German colleagues in Con-stantinople had agreed with that statement and that on the trip, "We have not heard a voice that has expressed itself differently. Sometimes the fury about the Armenians was a burning one. The Armenian is a revolutionary used by the English to overthrow the sultan."[18]

In a large part of what was a postscript to the core travel report of *Asia,* Naumann responded to the public controversy about the potter's quote in the German press. Most of the German papers, Naumann claimed, had fea-tured the quote. While the "semiofficial" press had done so approvingly and used the potter's views to justify their defense of the massacres, the "Christian papers" attacked both the potter and Naumann himself. Or, as he put it, "I am put on trial for having hurt the Christian conscience and feelings in the Armenian question." He acknowledged that the potter's sentiment was "somewhat related to anti-Semitism [in Germany], but even then it is part of the overall picture of the Armenian question." He went on to discuss the merits of the potter's statement and concluded with these thoughts: "even if [the Armenians] were the best of all the Oriental Christian peoples, this would change little regarding the following chain of thought."[19] And this chain of thought went like this: Naumann conceded that the massacring of 80,000 or even 100,000 Armenians was something that, "looked at by itself," left one no choice but to condemn it in the harshest terms; it went beyond all historical precedents, and the accounts that Lepsius had published in his *Report* had gone beyond all human suffering ever known. Yet, there was one thing that hindered the Germans from criticizing the sultan and from demanding his overthrow: "[It is] the fact that the Turk answers: I am fighting for my life as well—and the fact that we believe him." This "barbarity" was the "last bloody attempt" of an old great empire to save itself, of an empire that did not want to be killed off.[20]

Naumann then developed his historical view of the Ottoman state. The Armenians were somewhat comparable to the Greeks, Bulgarians, Serbs, and Romanians—all former subject nations of the Ottoman Empire that had gained independence in the course of the nineteenth century. However, if now the Armenians, too, were to leave the empire, this would mean, "as a glance at the map of the Turkish Empire will show everybody easily, the end, death."[21] In any case, the various national questions were nothing but crowbars to open up and destroy the empire, Naumann stressed. All the great powers, except for Germany, had used this method against the Ottomans before: "The process is as follows: one demands human rights, humaneness, civilization, or political freedom for the subordinate peoples, in short, something that puts them on equal footing with the Turks." And this, he argued, automatically leads to "revolutionary turmoil." Naumann then placed the Ottomans in a long line of empires, beginning with ancient Rome, to show that their reaction against such methods was nothing short of normal and understandable.[22] Again he emphasized that the empire would have simply died over the Armenian question, and stated the reaction was "a barbarian, Asian stroke of violence: They decimated the Armenians so much that they cannot act politically [anymore] in the coming time." While he conceded that this had been a horrible act, he stressed that it was one of political desperation and "a piece of political history in the Asian fashion."[23]

If his term "Asian fashion" sounded like a culturalist excuse, Naumann immediately labored to insert what had happened into mainstream European history. Naumann focused on the (alleged) historical stage of development of the Ottoman Empire as a justification for the massacres. For him, the empire was merely passing through a phase that Germany and the rest of Europe had already completed. He talked about the European wars of religion, and compared the "Roman Empire of Ottoman rule" to the Roman Empire of the German Nation (that is, the Holy Roman Empire). What the Germans had done in the Slav lands under their rule was, for Naumann, the same as what the Ottomans were doing to their subdued peoples and territories. He also compared the nationalities problems of Austria-Hungary and in "Poland" with those of the Ottomans today. He furthermore likened the Germanification of Eastern Prussia to the Islamification of Syria. "Now that we have forgotten our past it is an easy thing to be filled with indignation about the Turk when he is simply living by the old tenet of German state law in the fashion of the Habsburgs and the Wittelbachs: cuius regiu eius religio: or the ruler determines the faith."[24]

After having reduced violence against the Armenians to an inevitable European stage in nation- and empire-building, Naumann turned to justifying political Germany's silence. He started by postulating that the world was served best by a strong Germany, not by having Christian compassion become part of official policies. Germany had to look out for itself in the current "struggle of the peoples" *(Völkerringen)*. Naumann then presented a clear national choice that Germans had to make for themselves: "He who is international, that is who 'thinks English' [that is, who is a traitor to Germany], shall go with the Armenians, [and he] who is national, he who does not want to sacrifice the German future to Englishdom, has to stay on Bismarck's track in foreign policy, even it is difficult for one's soul."[25]

Naumann further underlined that the creation of Germany had changed the geopolitical situation in Europe and also necessitated new alliances: "We have to protect the Ottoman Empire because we triumphed at Sedan." (Sedan was a decisive battle in the Franco-Prussian war, 1870/1871, and a symbol of the unification of Germany in the battlefield.)[26] Naumann's book then turned more and more into an anti-British pamphlet, which included such outcries as "No fraternization with England! National politics!" He also rationalized: "Here one finds the moral reason for why we have to be politically indifferent to the suffering of the Christian peoples in the Ottoman Empire, however difficult this might be for our feelings. England knows that it will benefit from the disintegration of Turkey in any scenario."[27] Accordingly, Naumann advocated the following strategy: "We have to wait, grow, and to delay the catastrophe [that is, the breakup of the Ottoman Empire]."[28] Similarly Naumann excused the kaiser's relationship with the sultan: "He is a friend of the padishah because he believes in an independent greater Germany."[29] Indeed, in Naumann's analysis, Wilhelm II had no real choice: if he didn't support the sultan, he would betray Germany.

Naumann's statements—in combination with his criticism of German pro-Armenian activities that he held responsible as "the indirect cause of death" for the Armenians, as well as his advice to be "politically uninterested" in the Armenians—provoked anger among German Christians and reactions not only in the German, but also in the French press.[30] One of his critics was another German theologian and political thinker, Paul Rohrbach. He was in fact Naumann's friend, but then, Martin Rade—next to Lepsius the most prominent pro-Armenian activist at the time—was Naumann's brother-in-law and Naumann had attacked him and his camp directly and publicly as well. In his response to Naumann, Rohrbach stressed that pro-Armenian activities did not in themselves harm German interests. Rather, one had to understand that when the final dissolution of the Ottoman Empire came, the Armenians would become the carriers of German Oriental politics. Rohrbach also made the strong accusation that the chances and venues for Germany's Orient policies had been bought with Armenian blood:

> Did our government really have a choice between indirectly aiding the slaughtering of 200,000 or for all I care even only 100,000 human beings [on the one hand] and to forego gaining political benefits from Turkey [on the other]? If this is the case and we have indeed consciously made such a choice, then the seed of economic benefits awaiting us in the near future in the Orient is fertilized with the blood of these in the most part innocent people, then we have not the slightest reason any more to ponder about even the most horrible brutalities that other nations have ever committed.

And he even went further: "every ton of goods" exported to the Ottoman Empire was "paid for by one or a few corpses of Armenians."[31] It has to be remembered that Rohrbach was an imperialist thinker, an advocate of empire, himself. This was thus also a more general conflict over the role of morality and ethics in German imperial foreign policy.

Others also attacked Naumann for justifying atrocities and for his willingness to sacrifice the Armenians, even in atrocities yet to come, for the sake of German Oriental politics.[32] Also within his own party, the National-Social Association, he was criticized harshly. In one response to such attacks, Naumann again overtly justified massacres, in terms similar to those used in his book. He called the massacres "legitimate self-defense" *(Notwehr)* of "an old large empire lying in agony." For it, the detachment of Armenia would have meant its death. He even went as far as to repeat, in one of the very papers that had most strongly championed the Armenians (Rade's *Christliche Welt*), his claim that displays of sympathy for the Armenians had been, indirectly, the cause of their deaths.[33] In another response to his critics, Naumann further developed, and echoed, Bismarckian logic: "the unfaltering existence of Germandom in the world" was "tremendously more important than the entire Armenian question." Thus Armenian liberty, rights, and lives just had to be sacrificed, according to Naumann; there was no way around it. Again, he reiterated that German pro-Armenian activism constituted real and dangerous support, even if unwittingly so, for British world conquest.[34]

Indeed, what Naumann was doing, also on a more general level, was to justify the separation of morality from power politics by redefining the latter: he claimed that through its moral qualities, Germandom would one day heal the world—and that this would justify all the moral and ethical sacrifices made along the way. As already mentioned, this was no marginal debate and Naumann's was no marginal contribution. The book was a bestseller and Naumann an important national and imperialist figure. And, after all, he was a Protestant pastor, too. Here he was now justifying the killing of fellow Christians in nationalist and quasi-religious terms. Still thirty years later, a book identified Naumann and his justifications and redefinitions of German foreign policy as responsible for what had happened to the Armenians during World War I. The author was German pacifist Heinrich Vierbücher, who had served in the Ottoman Empire during World War I and who had been a witness to genocide himself:

> To fulfill the will of God, that means according to this man of God [Naumann] to think as follows: Hundreds of thousands are being slaughtered—about this you have to be dutifully outraged . . . after all, one is also an upright Christian—but: it is according to the special wish of God that the Deutsche Bank finances the Bagdad Railway. . . . The only conclusion that can be drawn from all this is that Turkey cannot be allowed to break apart today, but has to fall to the Germans tomorrow. And if until then a few hundred thousand humans [more] will be murdered, what a shame, but after all it must be God's will.

Vierbücher concluded his thoughts on Naumann in 1930 with the sentence, "Metaphysics, you have become the whore of violence."[35]

The Cure That Kills

Next to his understanding of German power politics and his anti-Armenianism, Naumann was building his arguments on a well-established theme in German discourse about the Ottoman Empire: a broad anti-reform stance. This further helped him to delegitimize the Armenians' claims, and to legitimize Germany's cold shoulder to those claims and to rally support for Abdul Hamid instead. Furthermore, it also complemented racialist anti-Armenianism. This antireform stance is "neatly" expressed in Naumann's *Asia:*

> In the Turkish Empire there is a word that has a dangerous sound, a word like powder and explosive fuse. . . . Whenever the sick man calls for a doctor, the latter prescribes "reforms." The sick man senses that he cannot stomach this medicine. He says, "Yes, doctor!," but then pours the Occidental drops into the Bosporus.[36]

This was not a new position, but one that had been forcefully expressed in the press and in political and diplomatic discourse, and had established itself as an important prism for understanding the Ottoman Empire in the 1890s, especially since the Armenian Horrors.[37] For the populist journalist Hans Barth, whose pamphlet we will discuss in the following section, four-fifths of all that was not so good in and about the Ottoman Empire was a result of Western reforms or pressure for reform.[38] The image of the sympathetic "sick man" who was being fooled, denigrated, and dismembered alive by the other European powers by the means of "reforms" became iconic, for example in the pages of the weekly satirical paper, the *Kladderadatsch.* One of these antireform cartoons shows the Great Powers demanding from the "sick man" that he reimburse them for his coffin(s), to which he replies, "But, my Sirs, I am not dead yet, after all" (Figure 3.2). What was supposed to cure him was in fact killing him, as various cartoons illustrated (Figure 3.3, Figure 3.4, and Figure 3.5). It has to be noted that the *Kladderadatsch* was featuring these and other antireform cartoons in the midst of the 1890s Armenian Horrors.

The view that "reforms" would mean the death of Turkey permeated all of Germany, from Chancellor Bernhard von Bülow, for example, to

Figure 3.2
An Abundance of Coffins. The Great Powers demanding from the "sick man" that he reimburse them for his coffin(s), to which he replies, "But, my Sirs, I am not dead yet, after all." *Kladderadatsch* November 1895

the Foreign Office and parts of the press.[39] Accordingly, Ambassador Adolf Marschall von Bieberstein formulated the following maxim in 1898: "The preservation of Turkey remains the political basic law."[40] It was simply a matter of life and death. A year later he wrote, "Turkey will be autocratic, or it will not be at all." Marschall argued, "The conglomerate of nationalities, tribes, religions, and denominations, with their diverging interests and centrifugal tendencies, often nourished from abroad . . . can only be held together with an iron hand. Every loosening of the reins, every concession to modern liberalism in the sense of participation of the people in governance would threaten the entire state with atomization."[41] A few years later his successor, Hans Wangenheim, would also be

Figure 3.3
Help in Destitute Times.
The sultan's chemist,
French president Félix
Faure, asks him, "Are
you already out of
danger?" to which the
sultan, his arm in a
sling labeled "Crete,"
answers, "Not yet. The
doctor wants to make a
visit." In the background
of the cartoon, one sees
Britain, John Bull,
approaching with a
large saw labeled
"concessions."
Kladderadatsch
August 1896

infected by the antireform bug. For him the word had taken on a "homicidal quality."[42]

This strand of anti-Armenian discourse, perhaps in a more immediate fashion than the others, illustrates the antidemocratic mindset that was at work in Germany at the time and that was being reinforced through the Armenian-Ottoman topic. Aversion to reforms was integrally linked to a very limited understanding of freedom and human and civil rights. It was American "poison," as one article in the *Berliner Tageblatt* labeled it. The antireform discourse clearly illustrates that a ruler- or leader-based discourse was favored over one based on rights and liberties. We saw this in Chapter 2, when, at the time of the horrors, Ambassador Radolin advocated better administrators rather than deeper reforms as the appropriate solution to the Armenian rebellion. More generally, in official circles and the

Figure 3.4 International Doctors' Congress. The collected Great Powers in front of John Bull, who advises that the sick limbs of the "sick man" have to be amputated. "Turkey," in the back, agrees—as he is not the only sick man in the room: John Bull's sick leg is labeled "India," Italy's is marked "Eritrea," Spain's are "Cuba" and "Philippines." *Kladderadatsch* August 1897

Die kranke Kuh.

Figure 3.5 The Armenian Cow. The Ottoman comes to milk his "Armenian cow" and finds the Great Powers about to "treat" it with their "cures" (that is, "reforms"). *Kladderadatsch* October 1895

popular press since the time of Bismarck, when German observers attempted to diagnose the "sickness" of the "sick man," they always predictably ended up pointing either to the machinations of the Great Powers, or to a lack of adept administrators—but rarely to a lack of law and liberty.

The "Jews of the Orient"

In 1913, German ambassador Wangenheim, discussing how Germany had perceived the Armenians in relation to the past massacres, described these massacres as a "natural reaction to the parasitic system of the Armenian business class. The Armenians are known as the Jews of the Orient."[43] Two years earlier, his predecessor Marschall had made a similar point about the racial qualities of the Armenians and the Greeks. This, in his view, explained the fact that anti-Semitism did not gain traction in the Ottoman Empire: "The economic activity, which elsewhere the Jews perform, namely the exploitation of the poorer, popular classes through usury and similar manipulations, is here performed exclusively by the Armenians and Greeks. The Spanish Jews who settled here cannot make any headway against them."[44] Of all the perceptions of the Armenians floating around in German discourses in the last three decades of the Kaiserreich, that of them as the "Jews of the Orient" was the most forceful and prominent one (compared to the antireform discourse, a geopolitical or "Polish" reading, or a more Christian perspective).[45]

It had not been uncommon to compare the Armenians to the Jews, even before the Armenian question entered international relations at the time of the Berlin Congress. Alternatively, Johann Gottfried von Herder and Voltaire, for example, were credited with saying that "the Jews" were just like "the Armenians" (and similar groups)—always to be found anywhere where there was money.[46] What emerged, however, in the 1890s debates was the perception of the Armenians as the "true Jews of the Orient."[47] "True," that is, in a double sense: because, for one, there were many Armenians in the Orient but few actual Jews; and because, for another, the Armenians were understood to possess the same racial qualities as the Jews in the anti-Semitic worldview, but in a more pronounced fashion. Indeed, they were often portrayed as something of "über-Jews." Over the coming decades, leading anti-Semites, including Adolf Hitler himself, would insist, like Ambassador Marschall before him, that the Jews would always lose out, in business and deceit, if pitted against the Armenians, because the latter possessed more of those qualities that had made the Jews so successful in business and usury elsewhere.[48] This image of Armenians as über-Jews was a result of decades of anti-Armenian discourse in Germany sustained by a whole plethora of characterizations, images, and proverbs copied from modern anti-Semitism. (And, as we shall see in Chapter 13, it also found fertile ground in anti-Semitic literature and racial [anthropological] thought.) Most descriptions of the Armenians focused on their sense for business, which, for most authors, made them seem like the Jews.[49] Only rarely, but mirroring similar phenomena in philo-Semitism, were these characteristics seen positively.[50]

Judging the German anti-Armenian literature, Uwe Feigel, a specialist for German Christian pro-Armenian activist history, concludes that these texts made no mention of the fact that the Armenians—unlike, obviously, the Jews—were Christian. Indeed, a total disregard for the Armenians' religion became a central aspect of German anti-Armenianism over the coming decades, as will become increasingly clear in this book.[51] In early 1899, even a Protestant newsletter insisted that the massacres had not been persecutions of Christians qua Christians at all, but instead were persecutions of members of a race whose essential characteristics in effect excused this persecution (a line of argument that would be made many times in the coming years and decades).[52] The *Neue Preussische (Kreuz-)Zeitung,* too, made a parallel argument: "If the Armenian butcheries had been pure persecutions of Christians, then the comportment of the kaiser would have been clearly contemptible. However, as every child knows, they were nothing of the sort. The Turk has not staged a hunt on the Christian, but a hunt on Armenians. He only wanted to deal a blow to the hated Armenian people, [a blow] from which they would not recuperate soon."[53]

The Jewish-Armenian parallel, if not equivalence, was continuously reaffirmed in the German press up to World War I. "Like the Jews everywhere in the world, the Armenians . . ." began many a characterization in the German (and other German-language) press. Typically, characterizations such as the next would then follow: "The accusations advanced here against the Jews one hears everywhere also against the Armenians; as merchants they are seen as unscrupulous, they seek to suck the host people dry."[54] The anti-Armenian–anti-Semitic parallel permeated all the politically relevant German spheres. As already seen, Ambassador Marschall also took part in this: "In Turkey the Armenians are the moving element in trade and business, for the poorer Turkish population, however, namely in the countryside, [they are] a true scourge. In this perspective their business practice is far more pernicious than that of which Jews in Germany are commonly accused. Here the Jew cannot succeed against the Greek let alone against the cunning and unscrupulous Armenian."[55] In the prewar period, one difference was occasionally noted, and credited to the Armenians' advantage, even in anti-Armenianist discourses: unlike the Jews, it was claimed, many Armenians were still living as farmers, not just as traders and usurers.[56] Over the decades, pro-Armenianists would frequently seize on this supposed advantage to further their arguments and to oppose the all-out equation of Armenians with Jews. Remarkably, though, the farming claim would be almost absent in post–World War I debates—a sign that anti-Semitic-inspired anti-Armenianism had carried the day and had radicalized.

Anti-Armenianism also found its way into fiction—and not just any fiction, but the work of one of the most successful German novelists of the time, Karl May, whose books were still widely read in the German-speaking lands throughout the twentieth century. Among May's best-known works were the novels of his "Oriental cycle," viewed by the author himself as his most important work, and some of which were turned into movies as early as the 1920s.[57]

May's usual protagonist was called Kara Ben Nemsi ("Karl, Son of the Germans," in May's invented language) when he traveled in Karl May's Orient, or Old Shatterhand when he and his horse had crossed the ocean and were on adventures in the American Wild West. In May's *In the Empire of the Silver Lion* (1898), Kara Ben Nemsi also commented on the massacres of the Armenians in the mid-1890s and in fact "plagiarized" Naumann's infamous potter quote about the Armenians word for word. Beginning with "I am a Christian," Kara Ben Nemsi/Old Shatterhand—this hero held so dearly still in post–World War II Germany and portrayed by Lex Barker in the German 1960s movies—then justified killing the Armenians on racial grounds and continued to express all the anti-Armenian stereotypes (see above).[58] Karl May thus significantly contributed to the further dissemination of Naumann's potter quote. Another comment on the Armenians, taken from another of May's texts, also illustrates how the Armenians, although Christians themselves, were excluded from Christianity in May's world:

A Jew dupes ten Christians, a Yankee tricks 50 Jews, but an Armenian even dupes a hundred Yankees. . . . Wherever some malice, some treason is planned, certainly the hawk's nose of the Armenian is implicated. When even the unconscionable Greek refuses to commit some villainy, there will no doubt be an Armenian who wants to earn the wages of sin.[59]

Anti-Armenian clichés and stereotypes permeated Karl May's novels of the Oriental cycle, and time and again one meets May's despicable Armenian with his crooked nose and the overall physical appearance of a vulture. And, moreover, in May's books it was basically the Greeks' and the Armenians' fault that the Ottoman Empire was sick.[60] Karl May was of course not alone in his peddling of anti-Armenianism; a host of German nationalist and imperialist publications on the Ottoman Empire espoused similar views. But May was by far the most successful author of the lot and his books were the most widely read books of the late Kaiserreich.[61] One historian views Karl May's as "a typical example of anti-Armenianism that had been schooled by a latent anti-Semitism."[62]

Naumann had exposed a very broad audience to justifications for killing Armenians and had made Germany's ears deaf to the Armenian plight as well as anti-Armenianism "morally" and politically more acceptable; Karl May disseminated the usual anti-Armenian images in his novels, again to a very broad audience and starting around the same time. And then there was the journalist Hans Barth, a correspondent for the *Berliner Tageblatt* in Rome, who first published an anti-Armenian article in the journal *Zukunft* and then shortly afterward the book *Turk Defend Yourself* (1898). Both were motivated by what he understood as "anti-Turkish agitation" in the German press. His book went through many editions (and a recent Turkish version dates from 2003).[63] Herein this "Dr." Barth justified massacres of the Armenians, peddled anti-Semitic stereotypes, attacked the Christian religion, and exhibited essentialist racism (including such claims as that Africans can never be Christians).[64] At first glance Barth's may appear to have been a fringe discourse, with its coarsely yelled hate, but its racialist arguments and even much of its style would become part of the mainstream and be faithfully replicated in public (newspaper) discourse for three decades to come.[65]

Already the very first sentence of Barth's book contained its whole theme: the Armenians and Greeks had been incited against the "noble and tolerant" Turks, who had then reacted, which in turn had, in Europe, led to calls for a crusade.[66] In many variations and from many sources Barth printed one disparaging remark and anti-Armenian claim after the other: that the

Christians of the Ottoman Empire were culturally inferior to the non-Christians, that everyone who had contact with the Armenians learned to hate them, that they sucked the life out of the Turks, that they held all the main property and capital, and that they were merchants and traders of the most superior abilities—and, as he insinuated throughout the book, that they were even worse than the Jews.[67] Not surprisingly, Barth also reproduced, more than once, (now familiar) anti-Armenian clichés: "A Greek betrays two Jews, an Armenian two Greeks." Like the *Post* newspaper at the time of the horrors (as we saw in Chapter 2), he approvingly reproduced passages on the Armenians from Alfred Körte's popular travel book: the Armenians were so devious that not even a contract with them helped; every kind of fraud was a sport to them; and Armenian merchants were "leeches," who filled up on the blood of their victims and then moved on to the next town.[68]

Barth was mainly writing against Lepsius and his *Armenia and Europe,* which he called a "Lepsiade," "part missionary tractate, part pulp fiction."[69] To this "absurd concoction" Barth had mainly one thing to say: "Requiescat in pace" (Latin, rest in peace).[70] There was nothing, he wrote, more "unjust, stupid, and disgusting" in modern history than the sympathy in Europe for the Armenians—a sentiment later expressed by Hitler in similar words.[71] Not surprisingly, for Barth the massacres of 1894–1896 were simply unjustified rebellions that had been justly suppressed. And of course it was all the fault of the other Great Powers—including the Americans (this was still rather a novelty in German anti-Armenian discourse, which had thus far largely ignored America's role in the Middle East).[72] Barth also quoted what Ambassador Saurma had supposedly told the Constantinople correspondent of the *Berliner Tageblatt,* a colleague of Barth's: that the Turks were within their rights to act as they did in 1894–1896; that the idea of Armenian reforms was neither justified nor executable; and, moreover, that the Armenians "had literally plundered Turkey for centuries" with "their ruthless and unashamed manner of acquisition." They were, according to Saurma, "usurers and dishonest."[73] Claims that, Barth implied, made killing them justifiable.

Throughout the book Barth spoke against the impossible and "stupid" idea of wanting a state for the spread-out and small Armenian minority.[74] "They would have done better to be content to fleece the poor, thoroughly honest, and diligent Turkish farmer and to settle as parasites in the fur of the pashas, as it has been from time immemorial."[75] And in the now clearly established anti-Semitic images, for Barth, such a nonsensical Armenian state would be "an Eden populated only by usurers, brokers, bankers, and grocers."[76] The Armenian uprising of 1894–1896, he claimed, was as ludicrous as if the "Frankfurt Jewry had, with the help of bombs, tried to carry out a putsch, transform the cathedral into a synagogue, and then crown Mr. Rothschild as King of New Jerusalem" in the Frankfurt town hall.[77] How could Armenian bankers have ever fallen for such schemes? Barth asked. In his vision they had become so rich, spoiled, and carefree that it seemed like a good way to pamper their own vanity. In another telling analogy, he dismissed the idea of an Armenian state as just as absurd as the idea of "Israel wanting to raise the walls of Zion again."[78]

As we already saw in our discussion of the German antireform discourse, for Barth (and for some of the texts he cites, often the *Berliner Tageblatt*), any notions of liberty and (human) rights were dismissed as "the poison of freedom" when applied to the Armenians.[79] Here, the generally antidemocratic—as well as anti-American—tendencies of German nationalism at the time came to the fore. Robert College in Constantinople, the American college that was the precursor of today's prestigious Bosporus University, was presented as a school for terrorists, a "bomb institute."[80]

Pro-Armenian writers were distraught that Barth's theses found a ready ear in the German press and were widely and often quoted and reprinted.[81] Even fifteen years later, in 1913, Barth's book was still the subject of debate between him and the German pro-Armenian scene—along with a new article by him justifying the 1890s massacres, this time in the official weekly of the military, the *Militärwochenblatt*.[82] This fact alone—that the official weekly of the German army would print Barth's justifications—was not a good omen for the coming war.

• • •

In 1902, Eduard Bernstein, a Jewish-German Social Democrat intellectual, organized an assembly in Berlin about the Armenians and Germany. This assembly passed a resolution condemning the "stoic indifference" in German political circles to Armenian suffering, and urging the German government to push for an implementation of article 61 of the Berlin Treaty.[83] At the assembly, Bernstein argued that the 1890s massacres had not been exceptional events, but rather part of a plan on the part of the Ottoman state for the systematic annihilation of the Armenians.[84] His targets were such authors as Barth, and, more generally, the trend in German public discussion to paint the Armenians in the most anti-Semitic colors.[85] But his and similar pleas fell on deaf ears. German anti-Armenianism was not only an expression of a "popular" sentiment, and sincerely felt by the authors expressing it; it was also presented to be based on and justified as a "political necessity." Even Naumann's critic, the otherwise pro-Armenian Rohrbach, argued for accepting this "necessity" in 1899: "In the time of the first stirring in relation to the [1894–1896] massacres naturally harsh words were uttered against the Turks, but all the insightful circles have since become reasonable enough to understand the Turk-friendly attitude of Germany as a political necessity."[86] And indeed, in 1899, when the Armenian patriarch begged the German ambassador to ask the kaiser to employ his influence with the sultan on behalf of the Armenians, the kaiser scribbled on the report his firm reply, "None of my business!"[87] In 1902, the chancellor expressed the same view in different words: "the Armenian movement has nothing to expect from the German government."[88]

The perceived parallel or near-equivalence of the Armenians and the Jews had widespread currency in the late Kaiserreich, and it was not only exercised through the transfer of anti-Semitic stereotypes onto the Armenians. Protestant cleric Martin Rade, next to Lepsius one of the most important and outspoken pro-Armenian activists, spoke out against the anti-Jewish pogroms in Russia as well. He compared the reasoning used to justify the anti-Jewish pogroms to that previously used against the Armenians—in the Russian case, that the revolution in Russia had been led mainly by Jews. This produced an immediate reply and the *Deutsche Zeitung* cynically titled it "It Is Anti-Pogroming Again" *(Es anti-pogromelt wieder)*.[89] Already by 1906, it appears, nationalist Germans were tired of hearing about the horrible fates of other peoples in other empires.[90] Or, alternatively, they were getting used to the idea that certain other "races"—such as Armenians and Jews—just had to be sacrificed on the altar of national and Great Power politics. They were now accepting, in other words, the very case that Friedrich Naumann had forcefully made in the Armenian context.

· · ·

The German perceptions of the Armenians—in all their variations—are illustrative of a broader development that occurred in Germany in the hundred years leading up to World War I. A transformation took place in how Germans perceived the world: a shift from a religious prism to a racial one. Germany's perception of the Ottoman Empire and "its constituent tribes," as Bismarck put it, serves as a case in point here—not the least because Germany's contact with the Ottoman Empire and its peoples was rather intense, compared to other regions of the world, and because here it had to deal with and understand a host of other Christian peoples. In the Ottoman case, this change from a religious to a racial understanding had begun in the wake of the successful Greek independence movement of the 1820s. In Germany there had been widespread enthusiasm and support for the Greeks, but the experience had turned sour afterward when real nineteenth-century Greeks did not conform to neoclassicist images of the heroic Greeks of antiquity. Naumann's disparaging remarks on the "neo-Greeks" at the beginning of his book *Asia*—or rather the fact that he felt compelled to discuss the Greeks in such an extensive, utterly negative, and disappointed fashion at all—illustrates this lasting disillusion well. Following the Greek enthusiasm debacle, the Near Eastern Christians were increasingly understood through alleged national and racial characteristics, rather than through the Christian faith they shared with most of Europe. It is no coincidence that the Greeks often featured on a par with the Armenians when the latter's racial qualities were discussed. The same is true for the catchall category of the "Levantines," which subsumed various Christian Middle Easterners and characterized them with the same stereotypes as the Armenians and the Jews.

As we will see in the following chapters, the German reactions to the 1890s massacres do not only constitute the historical background to the debates that would follow in the wake of the Armenian Genocide. In fact, and strangely enough, even the overall course of the public and diplomatic reactions was similar, to the extent that one could go so far as to claim that they were replicated in almost every respect in the genocide debate of the 1920s. First, there was doubt about the extent and even the reality of the violence against the Armenians. In both cases, a book by Lepsius helped to dispel doubts and established factuality. Aided by other voices, sources, and discussions, sympathy was expressed and even charity organized. Then, in a second step—owing to some external stimulus, in the 1890s the kaiser's trip, and in the 1920s the assassinations of Young Turks in Berlin as well as the victory of the Kemalist troops—some notion of national self-interest carried the day with sweeping anti-Armenian allegations that centered on their racial character and copied from as well as extended anti-Semitism itself.

CHAPTER 4

From Revolution to Abyss

E xcept for the anti-Armenian polemical debates and justifications of German "disinterest," the newspaper public had lost
interest in the Armenians in the years after the kaiser's trip to
the Ottoman Empire. Then came the Young Turk revolution of 1908. Now,
for a time, the Ottoman Empire was worthy of frequent news and even a
daily, often twice-daily, news section in many papers. Despite a strong sense
of apprehension and unease—about the very idea of revolution, the emergence of possibly a more democratic regime, and the alleged anti-German
sentiments of the Young Turks (as emphasized by British and Russian
papers)—the German maxim of upholding the status quo of Ottoman
power and internal affairs weathered the Young Turk revolution as well.[1]

The Young Turks and a return to constitutionalism seemed to promise
a new era. Many Armenians had collaborated with the Young Turks before
the revolution in the hope that the end of Abdul Hamid and the return of
constitutionalism and parliament would bring peace, security, and reform.
The new state of affairs in the Ottoman Empire appeared all too democratic
and pan-ethnic to be true. The German missionary Ernst Christoffel reported that, in Malatia, Muslims and Christians went together to the graves
of the victims of the 1890s massacres and swore their eternal loyalty to
each other.[2] The revolution was greeted by scenes of fraternization between
Young Turks and Armenians everywhere. Armenian revolutionary fighters
returning from the mountains were even greeted by official marching
bands and festivities.[3] For a moment, it appeared as if the Armenian question had found its resolution in the Young Turk revolution. Yet, it only
appeared so. Within a year the massacres were back. In 1909, the "Old
Turks" around Abdul Hamid tried to stage a coup and to get rid of the Young

Turks. The massacres that broke out in the Adana province, it is often claimed, were the result of orders from the Old Turks in an attempt to provoke confusion, to get the Great Powers to intervene and then depose the Young Turks.[4] There is, however, little evidence for this, and it appears more likely that local Old and Young Turks were responsible.[5]

Various German authors mentioned around 20,000 victims for the April 1909 massacres focused on the Adana province.[6] The Great Powers had ships nearby and threatened to intervene, but this did not stop the pogrom immediately. The German leadership wanted to send a ship, too, but mostly in order to protect its economic interests in the region. These had become suddenly more intertwined than usual with the Armenian issue, when Armenians took refuge in a German cotton plantation. Surprisingly, the German chancellor attempted to persuade the kaiser of the necessity of sending a ship by employing pro-Armenian arguments, to which, not surprisingly, the kaiser reacted angrily: "Why warships? The Armenians do not concern us at all!"[7]

For the kaiser, the Adana massacre was a nuisance, threatening developing German–Young Turk relations.[8] The Foreign Office and the political leadership also maintained their anti-Armenian stance. The Foreign Office even did its best to discredit its own consul in the region who had reported in detail on the massacres. It accused him of having fallen victim to Armenian lies and reminded him that the Armenians were "the most mendacious nationality" of them all and that they were just trying to cover up their own guilt.[9] But there were other German witnesses, such as the commander of the German ship *Hamburg*—a ship had been sent, after all, to protect German property. He had cabled home, "Horrors inhumane; misery indescribable; in the bloodshed yesterday about 2,000 died. Armenians from Mersin are fleeing to Cyprus. Turkish officers say that no Armenian is to be left alive."[10] This time, however, the Ottoman government instituted a commission to investigate the massacre and found that the Armenians bore no guilt for the massacre, though the commission's findings were never published.[11] The grand vizier and the justice minister later that year made statements exonerating the Armenians.[12]

The German press hardly took notice of the Adana massacre. The usual suspects reacted in the expected manner.[13] The *Frankfurter Zeitung*, for example, reprinted many agency reports and thus documented meticulously what was going on. And the *Kölnische Zeitung*, also in line with its own tradition, blamed the Armenians themselves for the atrocities—by reacquiring arms, the paper argued, they had provoked the Turks. Apparently, this time around, the fear of jeopardizing the newly reconstructed special relationship with the Young Turks hindered broader discussions from the start.[14] Yet, the Adana massacre did change some people's views. Walter Siehe, ten years earlier one of the most vocal opponents of German pro-Armenian sentiment, was an eyewitness to the massacres and printed his report in the *Reichspost*. While Siehe again assigned some guilt to the Armenians, he also felt he had to acknowledge that "it is clear that what we have here is a well-organized common reactionary Turkish conspiracy against the hated Armenians. All Muslims carried badges during the massacres." He, too, put the number of Armenian victims at beyond 15,000.[15]

The Armenian quarter of Adana was destroyed with the help of Ottoman troops. One of the most influential proponents of a German-Ottoman alliance, Ernst Jäckh, journalist and schemer, wrote about the Adana massacre in his influential book on the Ottoman Empire, *The Rising Crescent* (1911). He had visited Adana shortly after the massacres, in the early summer of 1909, while traveling with his friends Paul Rohrbach (the imperialist thinker and pro-Armenian activist) and Hjalmar Schacht, the future minister of the economy of the Third Reich.[16] Jäckh described the quarter as in ruins, quiet as death, and smelling of corpses: "like hecatombs [that is, ancient sacrifices of hundreds of animals], high heaps of corpses lie in the streets that have been consumed by fire and in large quantities the discharge from the hastily collected cadavers flows into the sea below, the waves of which carry the victims of Kurdish bloodlust as far as Cyprus."[17] Like many witnesses of the 1890s horrors, in his section on the Armenian massacres, he indulged in what I have called "atrocity pornography," that is, retelling the most incredible atrocities with the most graphic descriptions and details. Jäckh, otherwise known as the "Turk Jäckh," later a close friend of Enver Pasha—one of the triumvirate of pashas ruling the empire during World War I—was the main proponent of the German-Ottoman alliance, and now even he put the number of Armenians killed in the 1890s massacres at 200,000. He stressed that next to these horrors those of ancient human history looked like child's play.[18] Jäckh further argued that these massacres had nothing to do with religion but were rather racially and nationalistically motivated—something he claimed they shared with both the massacres of Jews and Armenians in Russia and the persecution of Jews in the Middle Ages in Germany. He wrote, "the old Christian Germany had in its persecutions of Jews wanted and done the same as the old Turkey did to the Armenians."[19]

Jäckh's book *The Rising Crescent* received mixed reviews, and the Armenian topic was an important part of this. Albrecht Wirth, also an "expert" on the Ottoman Empire, criticized Jäckh for distinguishing between honorable Armenian farmers and less honorable Armenian city dwellers; Wirth claimed he had traveled Armenia far and wide and "had found the [Armenian] farmers not any more loveable." Wirth also regurgitated anti-Semitic stereotypes when he claimed that the Armenians dominated the press, apparently both in the empire and in Europe.[20] In one of Wirth's next books he explicitly called the Armenians "bloodsuckers."[21] After World War I, he would find his way to the Nazis, writing for Dietrich Eckart's anti-Semitic *Auf gut Deutsch* as well as Hitler's flagship paper, the *Völkischer Beobachter.*

• • •

For the Young Turks who had (indirectly) taken power in 1908 (and again in 1909), it must have hardly felt that the Crescent was rising, as the title of Jäckh's book claimed; rather, they must have had a strange sense of Hamidian déjà vu. (Abdul Hamid II himself had been forced into abdication and early retirement in Thessaloniki after the countercoup of 1909 had failed.) The Young Turk era, like the Hamidian era, had started with a heightened sense of powerlessness. Like Abdul Hamid on his accession, the Young Turks were traumatized by their and their empire's weakness in 1908/1909. They came to power and promptly had to accept the loss of territory. From the Congress of Berlin to the eve of World War I, the Ottoman Empire had been shrinking considerably and at an increasing speed. The "sick man" was no longer sick or dying; he was being eaten alive. All of North Africa had been annexed by other European powers: the last loss of territory had occurred in the war over Tripolitania (modern Libya; 1911–1912), which had also led to the loss of the Dodecanese Islands to Italy. Most importantly, Egypt was firmly lost, too. In the course of the Young Turk revolution, the loss of Bosnia and Herzegovina had been formalized and, by the end of the two Balkan Wars (1912–1913), the Ottomans had all but been kicked out of Europe. Before, the empire had rested on the two regions of Rumeli (the European part of the Ottoman Empire) and Anatolia. Now Rumeli had been reduced to the small hinterland of Constantinople. What was left was Anatolia—which was now the last refuge for Muslim resettlers and the last core territory of the empire. And it was threatened, too, at least in the eyes of the elites, as it was inhabited by sizeable non-Muslim and also non-Turkish Muslim groups (Armenians, Greeks, Kurds, and many other smaller groups). And further south, the Ottomans were losing their grip over their remaining Arab lands as well. Kuwait was de facto British, Mecca insubordinate, and a new Arab nationalism had awakened, deeply hostile to the Turkish overlords. Alarmingly for the Ottomans, the last time they had actually won a war, against Greece in 1897, they had been denied the spoils of war by the Great Powers.

In this period, from the last decades of the nineteenth century until Mustafa Kemal Atatürk's War of Independence in the early 1920s, the empire experienced an increasing feeling of ethnic claustrophobia. The empire was shrinking and had to act as the last refuge for ever-growing numbers of Turks and Muslims from the Balkans (especially Bulgaria) and from Crete, as well as from the Caucasus and all the other places where once the Ottoman sultan had ruled. From the late eighteenth century to 1913, between five million and seven million Muslims had immigrated to the empire, more than half of them from the Russian Empire.[22] At least 400,000 had arrived as a result of the Balkan Wars alone.[23] By 1923, when Atatürk ended his struggle for the territory roughly of today's Turkey, it is estimated that one-fifth of all Muslims in Anatolia were either themselves refugees, or were the descendants of refugees—and that estimate is possibly too low.[24] In the late nineteenth and early twentieth centuries, these refugees—of Turkish, Circassian, Pomak, Romany, Bosnian, Laz, Tatar, and other ethnic backgrounds—had to compete for land and resources in Anatolia with other Muslims, unruly Kurdish tribes in the east, seminomadic populations elsewhere, and various Christian communities. Adding to the potentially explosive brew was the fact that many of these refugees, or their forefathers, had suffered violence and expulsion at the hands of Christians in their former homes. The Circassians from Russia, for example—the largest ethnic group among the Muslim resettlers—had been subject to deportation and massacres by the Russians in which tens of thousands had perished. Their memories, and those of the many refugees with similar histories, were not likely to be helpful in maintaining the precarious intercommunal peace in Anatolia.[25]

The last decades before World War I must also have taught the Ottomans that atrocities were a powerful tool as much of war as of propaganda. Because, as an almost empirical point and as a learning experience, in the end the civilian lives lost in all the alleged atrocities actually made little difference to the outcome of a war. The only things that mattered were the aims and relative might of the warring or threatening powers. So far, Muslim victims had mattered precious little to the European powers carving up the empire. During the Bulgarian Horrors in 1876, "the European press focused on the Christian suffering but ignored that of Muslims." The same is true for other conflicts up to and including the Balkan Wars. And on the other hand, the Armenian Horrors in the 1890s had not provoked a military intervention by the Great Powers either.[26]

• • •

By 1914, many things had changed in the Ottoman Empire. But in a way, the more things had changed, the more they had stayed the same. After yet once more almost losing power, the Young Turks were now so thoroughly in power, indeed, that some even spoke of the Young Turk regime as the first modern military dictatorship and the first one-party dictatorship. Enver Pasha, who had been in Berlin as military attaché, was now minister of war—appointed at age thirty-three, the same age at which Abdul Hamid had been made sultan—and the empire was, or at least felt, as threatened as ever. Just two years before World War I, in the Balkan Wars, the Bulgarian army had reached the outskirts of Constantinople.[27] This was a Young Turk replay of one of the most traumatic Hamidian experiences forty years earlier. The importance of Constantinople for the empire, both real and symbolic, cannot be underestimated, and neither can the trauma of almost losing it yet again.

It was in this atmosphere that the Armenian topic came back. If it had become a bit quieter about the Armenians in the international media in the years preceding World War I, that does not mean that the Armenian question had ever gone away. Now, indeed, it became the most salient of all the national questions in the Ottoman Empire. In a strange twist of fate, a willing Johannes Lepsius and a reluctant Germany acted as intermediaries to an Armenian reform plan that actually was, also very reluctantly, accepted by the Ottoman government in early 1914.[28] The plan envisaged reconstituting two "Armenian" provinces in Eastern Anatolia and granting them limited autonomy under the supervision of two independent European inspectors general. The adoption of this plan was only possible because, for a short period of time, the powers were in agreement, this time even with Germany on board.

How could this have happened? It is not entirely clear why, but apparently Germany's change of heart had mainly to do with the fact that it perceived the Armenian question to be so dangerous for the continued existence of the Ottoman Empire, as well as for its own designs there, that it felt it had to be somehow resolved and removed from the table of international diplomacy once and for all.[29] The specter of Ottoman reforms had continued to haunt Germany until 1914. As the kaiser noted in 1913 next to a report from Constantinople, "We barely rid ourselves of the damned Macedonian reforms [and now] the Armenian [reforms] come up."[30] Macedonia had been another orphan of the Berlin Congress and another "testing ground for Turkish defiance of treaty obligations."[31]

Even the otherwise rather anti-Armenian German ambassador Wangenheim—who as we will see was to deny the reality of genocide for months in 1915—acknowledged the need for Armenian reforms in 1913. He urged his superiors to change Germany's approach to the Armenian question and to act as the Armenians' protector. This would likely require, he acknowledged, a radical shift in the way the German press discussed the Armenians. He received an official rejection of all his proposals two months later from Berlin.[32] Nevertheless, his interventions in favor of Armenian reforms might have had some impact on the German leadership, which, after all, just a few months later instructed him to support the Russian reform proposal of June 1913. It foresaw the creation of a greater Armenian province in Eastern Anatolia governed from Erzurum.[33]

There are two aspects of the topic that might reconcile this temporarily pro-Armenian Wangenheim with the other Wangenheim, whom we will meet in Chapter 6: first, the Armenian topic had proven to be a constant threat to the stability of the empire; and, second, following the ideas of people like Rohrbach, some had perhaps begun perceiving the Armenians as possible carriers of German politics, German penetration, and finally German overlordship of territories in the Ottoman Empire, especially along the Bagdad Railway.[34] The suspicion that the Russians would incite intercommunal violence in Eastern Anatolia, which would then cause the massacre of the Armenians and give pretext for a Russian intervention, was still alive, and not entirely without justification, as Russian internal communications show.[35]

Furthermore, in late 1913, the opinion was gaining ground that the Young Turks might be predisposed to an even bloodier solution to the Armenian question than Abdul Hamid. The German ambassador warned his chancellor that the new "military dictatorship" of the Young Turks was well established and in full force and that any previous inhibitions about harming the empire's Christians were finally gone. Germany was expecting bad things for the Christians of the empire under this new regime.[36] However, in sum, it is still not entirely clear what brought about Germany's temporary willingness to change its decades-old anti-Armenian policy. It also is not clear what this meant for the overall course of German policy toward the Ottomans. In any case, it appears the main motivation for Germany to temporarily align itself with an Armenian reform plan was to secure the stability of the Ottoman Empire: as one Foreign Office memorandum warned, there were yet no clearly delineated territorial zones of German influence, and a premature breakup of the empire would likely rob Germany of its investments in the region.[37]

In the end, Germany was a rather unwilling participant in the reform plan and did not really do its best to speed up its implementation.[38] Even the most minimal implementation of the reform plan was dragged on, and then World War I began. One major reason for the delay was the discord between Germany and Russia about the appointment of Liman von Sanders as the top German military adviser with command powers over Constantinople troops.[39] In any case, this latest episode of the Armenian question only illustrated what the Young Turks must have feared: the empire was being chewed up from all sides. It also reaffirmed the image of Armenians as traitors: The Ottomans had just lost about 70 percent of their European population and more than 80 percent of their European territories—and now they were to accept the first steps leading to the loss of "Armenia"? It was in this intense atmosphere of national mourning over the Balkan losses that the 1913 Armenian reforms were pushed through, after the Armenians had appealed to foreign powers.[40] Talât Pasha, one of the leading Young Turks, openly conveyed his anger over this betrayal of his former Armenian colleagues, who had worked with him in the Young Turk political organization, the Committee of Union and Progress. Talât implied that revenge was afoot.[41]

PART II

Under German Noses

CHAPTER 5

Notions of
Total War

hortly before his suicide in 1919, the former governor of Diyarbakir mused, "The Armenians will either sweep the Turks aside
or will be swept aside by the Turks."[1] This reflects what many
important actors felt during World War I as well as during World War II—
an understanding of the war as existentialist and total. It would be about
all or nothing, Great Power status or demise. In Germany, statements by
the army leadership, as well as by the press, made this war out to be a struggle
of life and death for Germany—and for the Ottoman Empire.[2] Even from
early on (in November 1914), the German papers outlined a horror scenario of a peace treaty for the Ottoman Empire dictated by the Entente. It
foresaw the Ottomans losing the Arab provinces, Armenia, and Syria; further concessions and interference; and possibly even the loss of Constantinople.[3] It was thus no surprise that one of the articles in the German press
discussing the declaration of jihad was titled "Victory or Demise."[4] For
the Ottomans, who had similar fears, the struggle significantly involved
one more enemy to fight than those they shared with Germany: the enemy
within.

Though, perhaps not everybody was in thrall to specters of a life-and-
death struggle. Most people in Europe and in the Ottoman Empire did not
and could not really know what to expect of the war that broke out in 1914;
few would have expected it to become a "total war."[5] But since the last major
wars, a lot had changed that would influence the course of this and the next
world war. There had been many processes of radicalization both in warfare and in national politics: in Germany, in the Ottoman Empire, but also
in the other combatant countries. It is impossible even to sketch all of
these here. However, some of these aspects of radicalization do need to be

considered, before we can begin our examination of the Armenian Genocide and the reaction to it in and by Germany.

This chapter serves as an introduction to the second part of the book,
and explores some of the backgrounds of the Armenian Genocide. This and
the following chapters deal with the Armenian Genocide during World War
I and how Germany, both official and "public," reacted to it. Indeed, the following three chapters all investigate aspects of the same question: What
could Germany have known? This question might sound strange, but one has
to bear in mind that after the war it was often claimed that, due to censorship,
the German public knew nothing, a claim we will investigate in Chapters 7
and 8. As will become clear in Chapter 6, official Germany knew, in fact, everything, yet it did not intervene—thus, lack of knowledge cannot be a defense of German inaction. We will thus look at the sphere of diplomacy—
what did Germany's diplomats know?—as well as the wartime press, the
German parliament, and the activities of German pro-Armenian activists.
But first, this chapter will cast some spotlights on various processes of radi-
calizations that had taken place in the years leading up to the genocide.

The entanglement of Germany and the Ottoman Empire was so extensive during this period that it is impossible to do this topic exhaustive justice here. To grasp the challenge, one just has to recall that up to 25,000
troops, many hundreds among them officers, served in the Ottoman Empire by the end of the war; that the education of Ottoman officers had been
reformed by German military advisers, most prominently by Colmar von
der Goltz in the 1890s; and that during the war the various echelons of the
Ottoman High Command were all staffed with German officers.[6] But, of
course, it does not stop there.

•   •   •

From the founding of modern Germany until World War I, things had been
rather quiet in Central and Western Europe. Germany had avoided any
wars on the continent and had only been involved in colonial wars. But of
course these colonial wars had included the genocide of the Herero and
Nama people in German Southwest Africa and mass atrocities in German
East Africa, as well as those during the Boxer Rebellion in China. As historian Isabel Hull has shown, this, in combination with the lessons of the
1870/1871 Franco-German War, had left its imprint on German military
culture. Germany's war experiences had led, among other things, to a military culture in which the border between civilians and combatants had di-

minished to a gruesome extent. The fact that during the Franco-German War German troops had to occupy a large swathe of France, and that the civilians did not behave as foreseen and began resisting the military occupation, was an especially irksome experience. The myth of ubiquitous *francs-tireurs* (free shooters) was born: civilian enemy populations who would shoot at German soldiers, from behind the lines, thereby "stabbing" them in the back. The army decided that, as these people were not enemy soldiers, they could accordingly be treated even more harshly, including by "collective punishment."[7] Another worrisome experience in modern Germany's foundational war was the fact that the Polish population of Prussia— in other words, not civilians of an enemy state but "enemy civilians" within—had behaved in an openly pro-French manner during the war and that the military command even thought it necessary to keep troops in the Polish regions in case unrest broke out.[8]

The *franc-tireur* myth came back with full force in 1914 when Belgium was invaded and occupied; it became the iconic term for enemy civilian populations in wartime Germany.[9] From the beginning of the war, the German military and government were "obsessed" with "the notion of mass civilian resistance."[10] This spiraled into paranoia and then into violence toward the civilian population of Belgium, which was, for the German army, "a reservoir of potential guerrilla fighters."[11] German papers peddled stories of "Belgian atrocities" committed by civilians against German troops.[12]

Equally disturbing was another aspect of German military culture: a belief that in wartime, "military necessity" dictated the complete subordination of every other part of society to the military, whether in conquered territories or at home. Military necessity was to trump all other considerations—the welfare of civilians, whether enemy or German, international conventions and treaties, domestic politics, and so on. As Hull notes, most of the German army's guide- and rulebooks made little or no reference to how to treat civilians.[13] Colmar von der Goltz's famous treatise, *A Nation in Arms* (1883), similarly made no reference to how to treat enemy civilians or how to administer conquered territories.[14] This was a book, incidentally, that would heavily influence future Turkish leaders such as Enver Pasha and Mustafa Kemal Pasha, who would have read it as part of their studies at the War Academy in Constantinople—an academy that Goltz himself had reformed in his time as adviser there in the 1880s and 1890s.[15]

Hull argues that, given the nature of the prevalent army handbooks used in training, German recruits after the turn of the century would have been under the impression that "killing civilians guilty of harming the German war effort"—in other words, who had committed "wartime treason" *(Kriegsverrat)*—was "legal and proper."[16] This kind of latitude toward civilian populations, by a military that saw itself as supreme in wartime over all other aspects of society, permitted a host of "acceptable practices," such as destruction of property, starving prisoners of war, killing civilians and suspected saboteurs or spies, and, in the colonies, even starving native populations "en masse to win a guerilla war."[17] The army regulations of 1900 even stated explicitly that, in relation to civilians, "mildness and leniency in the wrong place can become harshness toward one's own troops."[18] "Wartime treason" became a key term and reflected the hysterical fear of civilian populations that had developed in the German army.

In occupied Belgium, more than 100,000 civilians were found guilty of wartime treason from late 1915 to late 1916.[19] Furthermore, only weeks into the war, the German army was already deporting civilians from Belgium.[20] And the Ottomans knew what was going on in Belgium. It is documented that during the war Talât Pasha brought up the killing of suspected Belgian *francs-tireurs* when German diplomats protested the Armenian deportations. Talât claimed that the Germans had killed 40,000 Belgians.[21] One wartime consul in the Ottoman Empire also alleged that local Muslims thought that Germany was behind the Armenian deportations because of what they had heard of German measures in occupied Belgium.[22] It may also be worth stressing here that the two highest-ranking German military men in the Ottoman Empire during World War I had both been stationed in German-occupied Belgium before being dispatched there. One of them, Colmar von der Goltz, had even served as governor-general in Belgium.[23]

Another idea that permeated German military culture was that of victory as "annihilation." As Hull convincingly argues, victory could not be imagined in any other way than total destruction of the enemy.[24] This kind of logic and warfare had led to the genocide of the Herero and the Nama people in German Southwest Africa (1904–1907). Hull identifies another reason for the German army's excesses vis-à-vis the civilian population: the extreme expectations of order in its dealing with civilians.[25] Given the predominance of military ideals among the Young Turk leaders and their training by German military advisers, it is not unreasonable to think that such ideas existed there as well.

Given the limited sources we have at our disposal, it is difficult to say just how much information, influence, and military culture was transferred from Germany to the Ottoman Empire. Yet, given that Goltz and others had reformed and transformed the Ottoman military academy and had taught people like Enver Pasha, and, furthermore, that military advisers and other German military personnel had been part of the Ottoman army for quite some time, we have to assume that German tactics, recent military history including "traumatic experiences," and military culture were well known and had been absorbed by part of the Ottoman army leadership.

• • •

One of Germany's key strategies in relation to its Ottoman ally in World War I was to have the sultan declare holy war, a jihad, in his function as caliph, as (somewhat self-styled) head of the Muslim world. Much has been written in recent years about the role that the "kaiser's jihad" did, or rather did not, play in the course of the war. Especially its intellectual fathers, such as Max von Oppenheim and Ernst Jäckh, have attracted much, perhaps too much, attention.[26] Yet, the role that the Ottoman Empire and the jihad played for the German home front has so far been almost completely neglected. A closer look at the German wartime press shows that the kaiser's jihad was not only some wild behind-doors fantasy, but rather an important theme in wartime reporting and domestic German propaganda. Already in the weeks before the Ottoman Empire actually entered the war on Germany's side, numerous newspaper articles developed, expanded, and expounded the German jihadi dream. The global jihad was only declared on 11 November 1914, but already in October, the *Neue Preussische (Kreuz-)Zeitung,* for example, claimed in one of its headlines that "Islam Has Awakened from Its Sleep."[27] In the first months of the war, if one believed the German press, the outbreak of an unprecedented global (Muslim) revolt against the Entente in its colonies was daily imminent or, in fact, had already begun. In the winter of 1914, the press reported daily that Egypt was just about to revolt; that Afghanistan had already mobilized for a jihadi liberation of India; that Persia was on the brink, as well as tribes in Libya, Tunis, and Algeria; and that, in short, the jihadi fight was about to begin any minute now.[28] Numerous essays pointed to the German-Ottoman jihad as being perhaps the key to winning this war.

The idea that Islam would be Germany's secret weapon in a coming war had struck the kaiser a long time before World War I began. In 1905, for example, he noted that, given that all the powers in Europe were allying against Germany, "Islam and the Muslim world is our last trump."[29] When this jihad was proclaimed, it was, on the one hand, the first jihad with global ambitions, yet, on the other hand, it was one with many exceptions—excluding the other Central Powers and their nationals. From the beginning, it was clear to those involved, as Enver Pasha admitted to his friend Hans Humann, that the fury unleashed by the jihad fatwa would be suffered mainly by the Ottoman Empire's own Christian populations.[30] The call for jihad, in this "modern form," transcended borders—including, crucially, the borders between combatant soldiers and civilians, at home in the Ottoman Empire and abroad.

The jihadi euphoria in the German press was accompanied by a view propagated in the first months of the war that the Ottoman Empire—not unlike its German partner—was victorious on all fronts. For months, according to the German press, the Ottoman army was conducting a successful and swift campaign, whereas in fact it was for the most part suffering checks and agonizing defeats.[31] Ottoman military failures—like German military setbacks—were never discussed in the German press. Thus the disaster at Sarikamish (discussed below) was never even mentioned. The alleged Ottoman conquest of the Caucasus simply faded away. Similarly, many alleged Ottoman attacks on Egypt were announced in the German press, but then simply faded from mention.

The jihadi enthusiasm in the press helped normalize in the German public a view of civilians—already, as we have seen, deeply ingrained in the military—as potential combatants and legitimate targets even within their own states. It envisaged and reported on "tribes" rising and being annihilated in retaliation. One could even argue that the way the German press and propaganda understood the jihad, it was *primarily* civilian rather than military in nature. For example, when examining the situation in Persia in December 1914, the *Neue Preussische (Kreuz-)Zeitung* discussed two tribes that did not participate in the kaiser's jihad, because they were pro-Russian, but stressed with great satisfaction that they "had been totally annihilated" (apparently by Persian-Turkish jihadis).[32] Similarly, it observed how Christian Nestorians had "participated in the campaign of Russian revenge by attacking Muslim villages, plundering the unprotected inhabitants, and killing them."[33] Papers reported gleefully how Russia saw itself forced to take "disciplinary measures" against its own Muslim populations, and also made much of the alleged fact that Russian Muslims were deserting en masse to the advancing Ottoman army.[34] These stories created an image of minority groups as a potential fifth column within a country, working with its enemies. Specifically, the flip side of the jihad logic was that Christian minorities within the Ottoman Empire could be expected to side with and work for the Entente. So the reasoning was clear, when applied to the Armenians: shouldn't we (contemporary Germans) just expect them to desert to Entente armies, or support them in other ways?

The prematurely announced Ottoman successes did not in fact come. There was only one significant and lasting Ottoman victory, at Gallipoli, where the Ottomans beat back an Entente landing force after months of fighting and trench warfare. (The victory at Kut el Amara was reversed after a few months.) In the German press, the theme of the jihad and the Ottomans as Germany's secret weapon quietly petered out, as if it had never existed. Similarly, there was little coverage, let alone debate, of Ottoman defeats and their underlying causes. As the war went on, the Ottomans became a silent partner, at least in the pages of the German press, and were almost forgotten. This combination of grandiose expectation and unexplained failure, in the pages of the press, prepared the ground perfectly for the sort of theory that sprang up in Germany after the war about the German and the Ottoman defeats: the theory that there must have been treachery, that some group must have "stabbed the nation in the back." And in the Ottoman case, of course, that group would be the Armenians. Other than "Armenian treachery," little else was ever discussed in the pages of the German press that might have explained the Ottoman military failure in the war.

• • •

World War I was to be also a war of atrocity propaganda from all sides.[35] As John Horne and Alan Kramer conclude, "atrocity accusations were central to the 'war cultures' which emerged in 1914–15 in all the belligerent societies."[36] Helmut von Gerlach, a German politician who, coincidently, had been an eyewitness to the 1890s massacres in Constantinople, and was a colleague of Naumann, summarized German atrocity propaganda like this: "The Russians were accused above all of cutting the arms and legs off the men, the breasts off the women. The French and Belgians were accused of gouging out eyes. There were variations and combinations. But the leitmotiv remained always the same: in the east, hacking and cutting, and in the west, gouging."[37] Of course, the Entente powers also engaged in atrocity propaganda against Germany—indeed, as historian David Welch points out, even more.[38]

The German response to allegations by the Entente of German atrocities was, on the one hand, to counter with claims of Entente atrocities, and, on the other, to vehemently deny that Germany ever did or could commit such crimes.[39] This propaganda reflex was also extended to the Ottomans in the German press and propaganda. Defending the Ottomans from atrocity allegations was a continuation of the by now traditional "protective German shield" when it came to Ottoman treatment of the Armenians, but now it included a much more uniform denialist press response, often already including sweeping justifications for whatever the Ottomans were doing. Indeed, as will also become clear in Chapter 8, the Ottomans' own propaganda war was being replayed in the German press. Already long before the Armenian Genocide had (in earnest) begun, the German press was waging an atrocity allegations war against the Russians in relation to the Oriental theater of war by reproducing Ottoman allegations. Such allegations covered the whole range of imaginable transgressions of the rules of war, such as bombarding Greek Orthodox churches, open cities, and hospitals as well as torturing Ottoman diplomats, deporting Ottoman civilians "under outrageous cruelties," bayoneting civilians, burning down villages, killing wounded soldiers and civilians, and so on.[40] These allegations continued well into the months when the Armenian massacres had become part of Entente propaganda.[41] It was also in the Russo-Ottoman context that the term "disciplinary measures" *(Maßregeln)*, later so central in the debates about the Armenian Genocide, made an early appearance, though at first as a term describing Russian atrocities and violations of the international law.[42]

And in due course the papers would also report on atrocities carried out by "Russian and Armenian gangs" on Ottoman territory, as, for example, on 21 March 1916 in the *Neue Preussische (Kreuz-)Zeitung*. The paper detailed the destruction of towns and mosques, the plundering of animals and foodstuff, and the butchering of the local population—"enormous cruelties" among the population, "sparing neither children nor old people." Young girls—at least fifty of them—were carried off. All the male population aged between sixteen and fifty-six was deported to Russia. The situation in the province was so horrible that it "defies any description."[43]

Furthermore, the Armenians were not the only ones "deported" during the war. Between half a million and a full million Russian Jews were deported as well, as were large numbers of Lithuanians, Latvians, Poles, and other groups, though under different, yet still often horrible, conditions.[44] The Russian Jews, too, were depicted as and believed to be traitors, now, in turn, by the Entente propaganda.[45] As part of the counterallegations against the Entente, the German papers focused especially extensively on the atrocities allegedly committed by Russia against its own Jewish populations.[46]

One of the central allegations of atrocities against Germany was the Belgian case. A British parliamentary commission on Germany's Belgian atrocities was chaired by Lord Bryce, and its concluding report was thus referred to as the *Bryce Report* (officially it was called *Report of the Committee on Alleged German Outrages*), made public in May 1915. Though the *Bryce Report*'s findings were not to be substantiated until after the war, its effects were damaging, especially so in neutral America.[47] This was a major blow to Germany's reputation and propaganda war.[48] Lord Bryce was to also feature prominently in the debate about Armenian massacres, thus further cementing the link between German and Ottoman atrocities; this nexus alone sank further any notion of truth in the swamp of wartime propaganda.

As an extension of the Ottoman propaganda machine, the German press also tried to refute allegations of anti-Greek and anti-Jewish measures and massacres carried out by the Ottomans. Such Entente allegations were dismissed in the same way that allegations against Germany itself would be: as all lies.[49] Furthermore, the papers also discussed the military worth of the Christian minorities, in a universal fashion, and duly suggested that they were both cowards and traitors. An essay in May 1915 lauded the fact that the Ottomans put the Christians in labor battalions and that they were now working for the Ottomans "like in ancient Egypt"—the reference to slave labor and the pyramids was not meant as criticism; rather, this was openly praised.[50] As we will see in Chapter 8, it was into this euphoric, confused, and crowded propaganda battle of atrocity allegations—of "Greek fairy tales," "English horror fraud," and Russian atrocities—that reports of the Armenian Genocide were to arrive in Germany in 1915.[51]

• • •

Douglas McKale has called Germany's and the Ottoman's war in the Middle East "war by revolution."[52] There is some truth to this, even beyond the kaiser's wonder weapon, the jihad. In late August 1914, the revolutionary

Armenian Dashnak Party held its congress in Erzurum. A Young Turk delegation asked the Armenians to galvanize the Armenians in Russia into acts of sabotage and revolt. The Armenians refused.[53] Having been revolutionaries themselves, the Young Turks saw the Armenians as "usable" across borders—a bad omen for the coming war.[54] Furthermore, the German Foreign Office not only developed and pursued the kaiser's jihad, in which Muslims were to be mobilized against the Entente powers "from within," but also produced an internal paper on a parallel mobilization of the Russian Jewry, in which Jews were to carry out acts of sabotage and in the end topple the tsar, the "greatest enemy of Jewry."[55]

It certainly did not help the overall situation inside the Ottoman Empire that Enver Pasha had launched a suicidal attack against Russia at Sarikamish in the winter of 1914. Ill prepared, Enver threw the Ottoman Third Army against the Russians. In a stroke of Enverian "genius," the Ottoman minister of war thought he could have the Ottoman army trek over the ill-guarded mountain passes and sneak up on the Russian army on the other side where nobody would expect them. Many of Enver's "barefoot soldiers" died of the cold and of illness rather than in combat. The numbers are still in dispute, but of an army of over 100,000 men, only around 50,000 retreated back to Erzurum.[56] Afterward, the Ottoman propaganda began its war against Armenian treachery.[57] The Entente's landing at Gallipoli in April 1915, just down the Straits from the Ottoman capital and the ensuing trench warfare, which was to last eight months, also did not help to ease the tensions and anxieties inside the empire.

These are but a few contexts that factored into the events during the war in Anatolia and its reception in Germany. But there are many more: there was an urgent agrarian question, a Kurdish question, and questions regarding aspects of taxation and centralization, as well as many shades of national and religious questions.[58] Also, there can be no doubt that the revolutionary tactics employed by some of the Armenian parties and revolutionaries in the aftermath of the Congress of Berlin aided the rise of the conviction among anxious Ottoman leaderships that the Armenians were no longer a "loyal nation" and were a real danger to the integrity of the empire.[59] This includes resistance, countermassacres in wartime, and contacts with enemy armies—for example with Russia during World War I. Also, as Donald Bloxham stressed in relation to the Armenians of Anatolia, "the distinction between acts of self-defense and acts of revolt was and remains blurred." But this does not mean that what unfolded in the Ottoman

Empire during World War I was, as many Turkish historians claim, a civil war situation.[60] Even if one freely acknowledges and discusses Armenian revolutionary activities and armed conflict between the two groups during World War I, this cannot excuse genocide. The end of empire, ethnic claustrophobia, military culture, atrocity propaganda and propaganda culture, and so on are explanations but not excuses. One should not follow in the footsteps of the justificationalists and denialists (of today and of the 1920s) in their "abuse of context."[61]

In matters of atrocities and genocide nobody really needed to learn the unimaginable from others. Yet, there are instances where cross-national influences were obvious and documented. The Boer War, with the first major use of "concentration camps" for the mass internment of enemy civilian populations, was also widely received and discussed.[62] There are more precedents that could be discussed, but let us just mention one more: Abdul Hamid himself had "learned," as he told a German officer, from French colonial practices in Northern Africa how to extend control—in his perspective: first, provoke rebellion, then crush and annihilate the rebellious populace.[63] Furthermore, one could make an argument that in World War I not only was the border between military and civilians blurred, but so was perhaps that between "normal" military warfare and atrocities. The use of poison gas claimed half a million Russian soldiers' lives alone.[64] And the death count of World War I, upward of fifteen million soldiers and civilians, also puts the Armenian Genocide into the perspective of a new, brutalized world.

• • •

With the 1913 reform plan, the Armenian question had gained a lethal urgency it had never possessed before. Some go as far as to claim that this newest Armenian threat, in the form of soon-to-be relatively autonomous provinces, could only ever be removed by the Ottomans under cover of war. From the beginning, the Armenian question, as well as the threat of foreign intervention, had been connected to demographics and statistics. Throughout the aftermath of the Congress of Berlin there had been a macabre numbers game between the Ottomans and the Great Powers.[65] Again and again, the Ottomans submitted statistics to show that the Armenians were but a small minority in the eastern provinces.[66] There was also extensive redistricting in order to overcome any Armenian preponderances.[67] The numbers game continued during the 1894–1896 massacres, with Abdul

Hamid claiming that the Armenians nowhere numbered more than 3–4 percent.[68]

Newer research has shown that the Armenian Genocide was but one piece in the greater puzzle of Young Turk "ethnic engineering." Taner Akçam shows that there were plans and measures targeting the Kurdish and other non-Turkish Muslim populations during the war, as well as in the years to come afterward. Akçam has shown how the "5–10 percent rule"— that is, that nowhere should there be more Armenians than that, even in the areas to which Armenians were being deported during World War I— became a keystone of Young Turk demographic policy and implied annihilation.[69] The fact that Muslim resettlers *(muhadjirs)* were at the ready to take over freshly vacated homes and properties right after Armenian deportation treks had left further underlines that what was at work here was a larger scheme of ethnic engineering.

The numbers game still continues today. It is not quite clear how many Armenians died in the Armenian Genocide. One of the reasons for this is the unreliability of the statistical data from before the war, a result of the decade-old numbers game itself. Estimates put the pregenocide population of Armenians in Anatolia at around 1.5 million, but numbers range from 1.2 to 2.1 million; similarly the number killed is highly disputed and estimates range from 800,000 to 1.5 million.[70] But even the German admiral Wilhelm Souchon, stationed at Constantinople during the war and a rabid anti-Armenianist, someone who saw the Armenians as "subversive bloodsuckers" and their end as the salvation of Turkey, wrote in his diary in August 1915 that three-quarters of all of the Ottoman Empire's Armenians had died.[71]

CHAPTER 6

Dispatches from
Erzurum

A rmin T. Wegner (whom we last met in Chapter 3) was not
only a witness to genocide; he was also an observer of how, in
turn, German soldiers on the ground witnessed genocide. On
his way to Baghdad, he wrote, "we often, when we made camp for the night,
passed by the camps, the death camps, in which the Armenians, helplessly
expelled into the desert, were facing their eventual demise. The Turks
avoided and denied these camps. The Germans did not go there and
behaved as if they did not see them."[1] But not all Germans chose to look
away; almost all of the German consuls in Anatolia, as we will see in this
chapter, extensively chronicled the ongoing genocide and voiced their protest.[2] Yet, what Wegner described for the German soldiers is a parable for
Germany as a whole—it knew, it could see everything, it was "right there,"
yet it did not want to see.

What is called the Armenian Genocide or, perhaps more correctly, "the
genocide of the Armenians," took place mainly in the years 1915 and
1916. Its conservatively estimated death toll ranges somewhere between
800,000 and 1.2 million people. While there is an overwhelming amount
of evidence in the archives of many countries, many of its details are still
in dispute—though mostly disputed only by those historians denying the
existence of genocide in the Armenian case from the start. Our access to
Ottoman sources is limited, as certainly are, both in numbers and in
scope, the sources that survived. This is why the diplomatic reports of the
countries represented in the Ottoman Empire as well as any other foreign
eyewitness accounts are of such importance in the history of this genocide today. It is important to note that there were not too many foreign
diplomats able to report on what was happening in Eastern Anatolia. Most

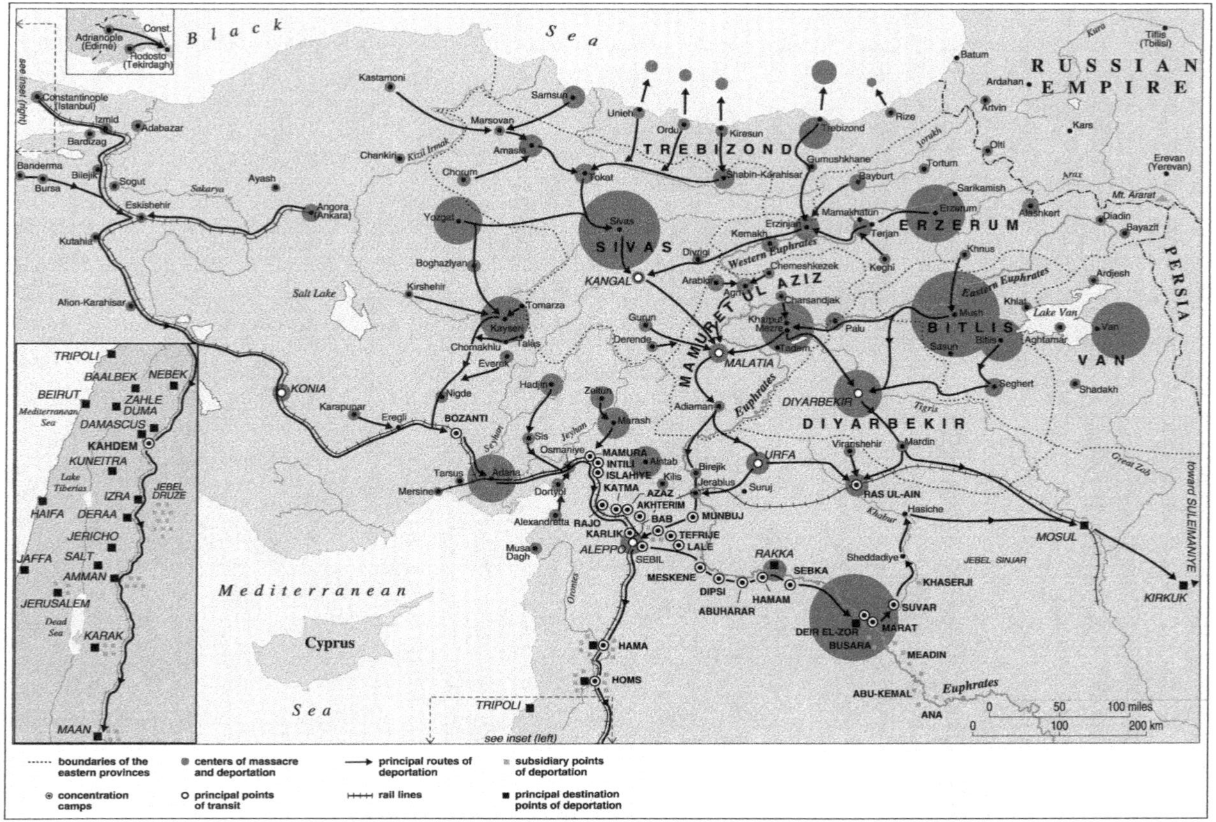

Map 1 The geography of the Armenian Genocide (according to the Armenian National Institute, English edition © 1998 ANI)

Legend:
- ······· boundaries of the eastern provinces
- ⊛ centers of massacre and deportation
- ⊕ concentration camps
- ⊙ principal points of transit
- → principal routes of deportation
- → subsidiary points of deportation
- ┼┼┼ rail lines
- ■ principal destination points of deportation

see inset (right)

Black Sea

Mediterranean Sea

Cyprus

RUSSIAN EMPIRE

PERSIA

TREBIZOND

SIVAS

MAMURET-UL-AZIZ

ERZERUM

DIYARBEKIR

BITLIS

VAN

0   50   100 miles
0   100   200 km

countries had to withdraw their diplomatic personnel because they were at war with the Ottoman Empire. Austria-Hungary had few consulates in the region anyway, and the Americans burned many of their documents after war broke out, while the originals had often been intercepted by the Ottomans.[3] Germany was present in many regions, yet the surviving documentation also only partially reflects what German diplomats actually knew. As becomes clear in one such surviving document, an agreement was in place between the German embassy and the Young Turks about the Armenian topic that "there was to be no written record of such conversations."[4] Historian Wolfgang Gust has also pointed out that it is rather strange, if not suspicious, that there are no direct pieces of commentary on the topic of the genocide by Kaiser Wilhelm II, who otherwise commented on everything.[5] It is reasonable to suspect that there was a strong sense of conspiracy. We know, for example, of one case in which a German officer with the Bagdad Railway countersigned a deportation order by mistake. The Foreign Office, panic stricken, immediately tried to destroy all copies of the document (but in the end it failed).[6] Furthermore, it is also not unreasonable to assume that there was a second round of document cleansing after the end of World War I, perhaps at the time when Lepsius was given access to official records (see Chapter 9).

The Armenian Genocide had many roads and expressways leading up to and feeding it. This is true both figuratively speaking and in relation to its geography. There was something both contemporaries and researchers have labeled "concentration camps," and there was a final destination point for (most of) the deportations—the desert around Deir Zor in today's Syria (at the time of writing, mid-2015). However, the killing took place at the starting points and on the way, as well as at the terminus. It was thus relatively delocalized, as becomes apparent when one searches for an "Ottoman Auschwitz"—but then again, the Holocaust was also far more delocalized than the often almost singular focus on the iconic Auschwitz would suggest. The "Ottoman Auschwitz," speaking rather too figuratively, was a mobile one (Map 1). And this is why documenting the Armenian Genocide takes one to many places across the Ottoman Empire, and involves the painstaking tracking of individual deportation treks to their destinations as well as of the actions taken before deportations in the places of origin.

The province and the city of Erzurum in Northeastern Anatolia was important for the genocide and for later efforts to reconstruct its course, for a number of reasons: it had a large Armenian population, the largest after Sivas; it was one of the geographical and chronological starting points of the deportation, as it bordered on Russia; it was a thoroughfare for deportation treks from the surrounding regions; it was here that a major Russian offensive was expected; and it was also a major news hub both for the Caucasus front and for Armenian matters.[7] And, finally, it is a very well-documented place, because the German vice-consul there wrote extensive reports and also tried to follow up on what had later happened to Armenian deportees from his district. Of all the German consuls he was, in fact, the one who lobbied for and helped the Armenians most actively.[8]

Even long before the war had begun, Erzurum had been one of the places from which dispatches reached Berlin about the future drama. As Ambassador Hans Wangenheim told his chancellor in November 1913, the consulate in Erzurum had informed him of ominous conversations that had taken place across the Ottoman-Russian border, in Tiflis, about the Armenian question.[9] And only two months later, in January 1914, Berlin received more detailed news from Erzurum by a circuitous route involving a series of Russian sources: meetings had taken place there "in which there is open talk of massacres. At the order of the Mullahs, the population has put on white turbans. Everything has been prepared for massacres, which are to begin at a sign from Constantinople."[10] This was still months before the beginning of World War I and the Ottoman entry into the war. The German government was thus well aware of how volatile the Armenian situation was in Eastern Anatolia. And it took it just as seriously as the Russians. The German consul at Erzurum received orders to instantly write a detailed report on the Armenian question. The Russian report had also noted that the Young Turks were blaming "those powers who want to interfere in the reforms [in Eastern Anatolia]" for any eventual massacres.[11]

When the war started, the Armenians were fearful—not only of the Young Turks, but of the Germans as well. A German consular report from late December 1914 related that the Armenians, in some regions at least, feared that if the Germans won the war, the "existence of the Armenian nation on Turkish soil would be destroyed." They believed so, the report stressed, because the Germans had in the past always supported and motivated the Ottoman government in its persecution of the Armenians.[12] These fears were not far off the mark—not at all.

Beginnings

There were many German witnesses to genocide in Eastern and Southeastern Anatolia. They and their reports cannot all be discussed here; the

German archives hold a vast amount of such reports. Here we will focus on one vice-consul and his reports as an exemplary case. One reason for choosing him is that he not only reported extensively and was present at the center of the earlier deportations, but he continually petitioned his embassy in Constantinople to intervene on behalf of the Armenians, and he even personally attempted to save individual Armenians. From the beginning, his reports are thoroughly detailed, and among his colleagues he was the most vocal opponent of the measures against the Armenian population. Through his reports, we can not only partially reconstruct the early phase of the genocide; even more important for us here, in combination with the answers he received from his superiors in Constantinople, this diplomatic correspondence sheds light on what the German embassy and the Foreign Office knew, and what they did (and did not do) with this information.[13]

Max Erwin von Scheubner-Richter was born in 1884 in Riga, and spent much of his prewar life in the Russian Empire. A Baltic ethnic German from the Russian Empire, Scheubner joined the German army as a volunteer in 1914. He became consul at Erzurum quite by accident, and it was likely the last thing he had expected upon enlisting. He had been on his way to the Caucasus front, as part of a German contingent destined for special missions in Persia and the Caucasus, when the consul at Erzurum died. Scheubner was appointed interim or "caretaker" consul, and stayed on for many months. It was at this time that the Armenian Genocide began.

The Armenian topic became prominent in Scheubner's reports from March 1915 onward.[14] It was also in March that he spoke to the governor of Kharput, who had told him that the Armenians had to be exterminated. Scheubner was outraged.[15] Scheubner's first reports to his superiors on the Armenian question were very succinct and dealt with the alleged Armenian uprising in Van in Eastern Anatolia, not far from his post. Still today, this alleged uprising in Van holds a central place in the denialist and justificationalist arguments.[16] It also served as a pretext and a justification for anti-Armenian measures at the time, not just in Van itself, but in general. It epitomized and once more "proved" the alleged treacherousness of the Ottoman Armenians—it became, as Vahakn Dadrian put it, "the alpha and omega of the plea of 'military necessity.'"[17] On 24 April, Scheubner reported that about 400 Armenians had been killed in Van and that the uprising had been quashed. These numbers were duly passed on to the German Foreign Office and to the German chancellor by the German ambassador Wangenheim in Constantinople.[18] An internal note by Johannes Mordtmann, the embassy official responsible for Armenian issues, also referred to the fact that on 24 April an Armenian dignitary had been killed in the streets of Erzurum. In his discussion of what the embassy had heard from Eastern Anatolia, it becomes clear that Mordtmann and others knew far too much to believe Ottoman propaganda and to believe that the Armenians were indeed planning a general uprising or had been shooting at their fellow Turkish soldiers. It also becomes clear from Mordtmann's notes that many, including the Armenian patriarchate in Istanbul, thought that large-scale massacres were imminent.[19]

On 26 April, Scheubner forwarded a request from the local Armenian bishop that the embassy inform his patriarch about the events in Van. Mordtmann wrote in his notes that he did, and stressed that it was important to do so as the patriarch had no news sources of his own.[20] In another telegram on the same day, Scheubner reported that several prominent local Armenians had been killed while in police custody in Van. He closed his telegram by stressing that the Armenian population of Erzurum was fearing a massacre and that the bishop was pleading with the consulate for protection.[21]

His ambassador's answer two days later, on 28 April, already shines a light on the stark difference of opinion between the two: While Scheubner had been reporting that the Armenians of Erzurum were keeping quiet and there was no uprising to be feared there, the ambassador saw them as guilty, too—guilty by association before they had yet done anything. And when the consul was relaying pleas for protection, his ambassador answered, "You should apply yourself only to hindering rioting by the mob [against the Armenians] and to getting a proper trial for the politically suspect [Armenians]." He added that there should be no outward semblance of official German protection for the Armenians. He also added, for Scheubner's personal information, as he stressed, that hundreds of Armenian notables had been arrested by the Ottomans because there had been "signs of a revolutionary movement."[22] This "personal information" alludes to the budding conflict between them: the ambassador thought he needed to educate his vice-consul about the Armenian topic because Scheubner was, apparently, too favorably disposed toward them. That, indeed, Ambassador Wangenheim himself was not overburdened by pro-Armenian sentiment will become obvious in what follows; but it is also clear enough already in the telegram he sent to the German chancellor another two days later. In Wangenheim's text, the "notables" that had been killed in Van had now become "bandit chiefs," and the Armenians as a whole were now armed to the teeth as well as clearly "and beyond a doubt" in cahoots with the

Russians. Wangenheim, it is clear, readily accepted the official Ottoman line: no massacres had been carried out and the whole Van affair was rather an Armenian uprising that had resulted in just as many Turkish casualties as Armenian ones.[23]

Scheubner's reports in the following days were all about whether a massacre could take place in Erzurum. On 4 May, he was still optimistic and thought it could be prevented. And then, on 15 May, his extensive reporting on the Armenian issue began. With his lengthy report that day, Scheubner began not merely to extensively relay information, but to offer interpretations of the situation, of political decisions taken, as well as of the prehistory and the ramifications of it all. Scheubner reported that the initial reason for the outbreak of unrest in Van had been the killing of Armenian notables. He further mentioned that the mood among the Armenians in the region had been uneasy. He admitted that they had been collecting weapons, speculating that at first this had been as a means of protection in the event of further massacres, and then, later, for an armed uprising. He then stated that the Turks had made many mistakes in dealing with the Armenian question, and that the Russians had been inciting the Armenians to rebellion even before the war, especially in Van. After the war had brought about first positive results for the Central Powers and after Germans had been stationed in the region, he claimed, Armenian sentiments toward Germany became more positive. "This shift of mood was especially noticeable when the local Armenians became convinced . . . that the outbreak of a massacre was prevented only by the presence and activity of the [German] consulate here. The Armenian bishop thanked both General Posseldt and myself a number of times for protecting the Armenians."[24] The German officer Posseldt had commanded the fortress at Erzurum, but because of his collaboration with Scheubner and his stark rejection of the discourse of "military necessity," he was soon replaced by a Turkish commander.[25]

Scheubner did not believe there was much chance of the Armenians of Erzurum rising in revolt, even though, as he stressed, the Turkish military presence was minimal. In his mid-May report he was still optimistic—it had not come to a massacre; "just" a few notables had been murdered. Furthermore, the Ottoman government appeared to have stepped in to prevent greater violence. The searches of Armenian houses had not revealed anything incriminating. The only scenario in which he could imagine a massacre, he concluded, was if "a fiasco at the front forced Turkish troops to retreat to Erzurum." He then reassured his ambassador that, following his instructions, he had not intervened on behalf of the Armenians in any direct manner, and had rejected all Armenian pleas and petitions. On the other hand, he had advised the local authorities against any ideas of "settling accounts" with the Armenians, and had pointed out the detrimental effects such "domestic disturbances" would have at such a time. His final conclusion again repeated his hope that the presence of the German consulate did much to foster "calm conduct" among the Turks and the Armenians of Erzurum and the region.[26]

However, another telegram later the same day reveals that his optimism was premature: "[The] Armenian population of the surrounding villages is being deported and sent to the troops in the field (?) [sic]. Population very anxious because of this."[27] And the next day, on 16 May 1915, he wrote,

> The measures of deporting the entire Armenian population to Mamak-hatoun, etc., are carried out following the orders of the High Command of the Army and are being justified as military necessities. Since the male Armenians had been drafted into labor battalions already, it is mainly women and children who are being expelled, leaving behind all of their belongings. Because an uprising of the Armenians here is not to be expected, the measure of cruel deportation [grausame Aussiedlung] [is] without reason [unbegründet] and evokes bitterness. Civil authorities are not involved and do not accept responsibility for the consequences.[28]

His telegram on 17 May again drew attention to the opposition of the civil authorities. Now he speculated that perhaps the purpose of the deportations had been to ruin the Armenians economically.[29] He also asked the embassy to inform the Armenian patriarch in Constantinople about the events in Erzurum. Mordtmann recorded that he informed the patriarch and had advised him to direct his pleas to the War Ministry, that is, to Enver Pasha. Meanwhile, the ambassador in turn informed his chancellor, citing the consulate in Erzurum (and thus allegedly Scheubner) as his source, about the Russian conquest of Van, and about massacres the Armenians had supposedly carried out against the Muslim population there. The contrast between what was reported "from the ground" and what was relayed to Berlin could not have been greater.

The Embarrassment of It All

The very next day, 18 May, Scheubner cabled to Constantinople, "The misery of the deported Armenians is appalling. Women and children are camped in the thousands around the city without food. Pointless [word highlighted in the report] measure of deportation evokes the greatest bitterness." He then asked if he could intervene with the commanding officers.[30] He received an answer the next day, on 19 May, allowing him to intervene and furthermore authorizing him, in case the deportation orders could not be withdrawn because of "military considerations," to at least insist that the Armenians be treated more humanely. He was urged to do so not in an official manner, but rather "within the borders of friendly counsel."[31]

In the meantime, other consuls had written and reported extensively about what was happening, especially Consul Walter Rössler at Aleppo. Scheubner and others had related that there had been no instances of Armenian violence apart from those in Van, nor had there been anything found in the searches of Armenian houses in various locations that warranted the perception or treatment of them collectively as traitors preparing a general Armenian uprising. None of this had led the embassy to do anything for the Armenians, however. And so, on 20 May, Scheubner wrote his ambassador about new developments, namely that now the Armenians in a plain north of the city were being deported and that the Ottoman governor of Erzurum did not agree with the measure but was not able to do anything about it. Again, Scheubner stressed how pointless and unjustified these measures were. In contrast to those of Van, he claimed, the Erzurum Armenians were neither organized nor armed. The entire male population between the ages of seventeen and forty-eight had been drafted into the army anyway. Furthermore, all those sympathizing with Russia had long crossed the border already. Again Scheubner stressed how futile (zwecklos) the deportation was and how mindlessly (unsinnig) it was carried out. He detailed how the deportation was hurting the local economy in many ways and how it was opposed by many Turks, especially those owning larger farming estates. He then described riding out to see how deportees camping around the city were doing:

> The misery, desperation, and bitterness are great. The women threw themselves and their children in front of my horse and asked for help. The sight of these crying poor [souls] was pitiful and embarrassing [peinlich]—even more embarrassing was for me the feeling of not being able to help. The Armenian population considers the representative of the German Empire to be its only protection at present and expects help from him.[32]

"Peinlich," which could be translated as embarrassing or awkward, became a key term in Scheubner's reports in the coming weeks. His use of the term was by no means coincidental, but rather appears to have been central to his strategy to convince his ambassador to let him do something for the Armenians or to have the embassy intervene. After his ride through the Armenian encampment, he had asked the bishop and locals of Erzurum to collect bread for the deportees. And because the local Armenians were not allowed to leave the city, he had ordered his consulate employees to deliver the bread every day with the car of the consulate. He further stated that he was fighting rumors in the city that the deportation of the Armenians was the result of German advice. Scheubner also warned that these measures would lead to the economic ruin and partial annihilation of the Armenians—perhaps, he speculated, they were intended to do so. This in turn could result in a desperate act by the Armenians, and then in another massacre of the latter. He closed, "Should [this] not happen, then the local Armenians would prove that they are the most submissive and peaceful subjects of the Turks."[33]

This letter, as a source and an artifact, illustrates much more than just Scheubner's attitude and the situation in Erzurum. It was read by Friedrich Bronsart von Schellendorff, chief of the General Staff of the Ottoman Army. Before coming to the Ottoman Empire, he had been closely involved in the incipient massacres in German-occupied Belgium. He had actually buttressed the *franc-tireur* myth, seeing shooting civilians where others had seen none, and had ordered that an example be made of one such *franc-tireur* town, where around 130 civilians were killed by the German army in August 1914.[34] Now, in the Ottoman Empire, only Enver Pasha—as minister of war—and, at least nominally, the sultan were above Schellendorff. Of his anti-Armenian persuasion there can be no doubt: he was to go on record later, in 1919, as saying that "the Armenian is, like the Jew, a parasite outside his homeland, who sponges off the wealth of another country where he has established his domicile. Annually, Armenians move in droves into Kurdish territories, like Polish Jews emigrating to Germany, to dominate and subjugate Kurdish villages. Hence, the hate that discharges itself in medieval style through the murder of the Armenians."[35] Now, in May 1915, Schellendorff commented on Scheubner's letter, making short marginal notes. Where Scheubner wrote how embarrassed he felt at not being able to help the Armenian deportees outside Erzurum, Schellendorff added, "Even more embarrassing is the murder of over 4,000 Turks by Armenians near Van." Where Scheubner stressed that the Armenian population viewed the German Empire as their only protector, Schellendorff remarked, "After all, we cannot help a people that is in the middle of a dangerous rebellion against the Turkish government." And finally, where Scheubner mentioned that he was distributing bread daily among the deportees, Schellendorff's note exclaimed, "The consul would do better to send the bread to the Turkish poor [instead]!"[36] Schellendorff was later to complain—quite likely with Scheubner in mind—about "whining German consuls who understood nothing about the military necessity for the resettlement."[37]

Scheubner's comprehensive reports on the Armenians resumed two days later, on 22 May. Now he detailed how the houses of the deported Armenians were given to *muhadjirs*, Muslim immigrants. He pondered whether this had not been the whole point of the deportation in the first place, that is, to make room for these immigrants. He observed that the Ottoman soldiers could not possibly treat enemy foreign nationals any more harshly than they were treating the Armenians, who were Ottoman citizens after all. To his report, he attached a letter from the bishop of Erzurum again detailing the latest gruesome developments and asking for help.

The ambassador answered by diligently repeating the official Ottoman discourse that the Armenians had planned and carried out seditious acts and rebellions. And, apparently in his own words, Wangenheim added, "These and other developments, such as the discovery of bombs and arms with the Armenians in Everek (close to Kayseri), Diyarbakir, Engin and in other places, justify the harsh measures of the authorities against the Armenians, especially in Erzurum, and excuse occasional excesses of the Muslim civilian population." He then also pointed out that two Armenian parliamentarians had been arrested under suspicion of being connected to the "revolt in Van." All this, he concluded, should show him, Scheubner, "that the conduct of the Armenians makes it more and more impossible for us to intervene on their behalf, despite our interest in them and despite our compassion for those among them who are suffering innocently."[38] With this somewhat patronizing answer, the German ambassador in Constantinople sought to put his morally zealous consul in his place and justify his own lack of action. A few days later Wangenheim would urge the German chancellor not to have anything on the Armenian topic published in the German press, and he tried to justify this by claiming that it would endanger the Armenians themselves—an argument directly taken from the 1890s debates.[39] And, toward the end of May 1915, the ambassador cabled his consul in Erzurum that the Armenians in Erzurum had been very much incriminated by the discovery of bombs and written material and by the fact that they had planned to start an uprising in the event that the Russians advanced—even though Scheubner had told him earlier that these allegations were not true. Wangenheim added that the deportations "were also in the interest of the deported, that is to save them from massacres."[40]

Rapidly the ambassador's stance on the Armenians had hardened. On 21 May, the German consul in Adana, who just like Scheubner had wanted to intervene on behalf of the Armenians in his province, received a negative answer by Wangenheim. The ambassador now explained, "As regrettable and, in many respects, detrimental to our interests as the persecution of the Armenian population is, the most recent events in the border provinces—such as the uprising in Van, and other activities in the country's interior—do in fact justify the severe measures [*harte Maßregeln*] taken by the authorities. The Imperial embassy is, therefore, not in a position to prevent these measures for the time being."[41] However, a few days later, the embassy did consent to take one small step to help: they agreed to relay a message from American missionaries in Erzurum, made through Scheubner, to a Mr. Peet of the Bible Society in Constantinople, requesting funds to help the deported Armenians. With the embassy's aid the funds were sent, and perhaps the hardships of a few deportees were thereby eased temporarily.[42]

This was not enough for Scheubner, who tried his luck again, now with a different strategy. He sent the embassy a letter by the local bishop, to be forwarded to the Armenian patriarch in Constantinople. The letter repeated the points previously made by Scheubner. Among them was the exclamation that "this emigration means total annihilation." The bishop then pleaded with tears in his eyes, as he put it, that the patriarch in turn appeal to the "highest places," including the sultan and kaiser, to stop this "violent emigration." The text appears very much as if it was written by Scheubner and the bishop together, possibly on the initiative of Scheubner after his failure to get the ambassador to intervene. Indeed, it seems to have been addressed as much to the ambassador as to the stated addressee, the patriarch. It ended with the request to thank the German ambassador "for the invaluable humanitarian help of the local consul Mr. Scheubner"— something the ambassador was probably not very happy to read.[43]

Unmoved, Wangenheim answered Scheubner the very same day that he could not pass the letter on to the patriarch, and that Scheubner should "politely refuse" to accept such letters in the future. As an excuse, Wangenheim claimed that the diplomatic cipher could not be used for such matters. He passed on, again for Scheubner's "personal information," the news that a former Ottoman parliamentarian, an Armenian, had been among the Russian occupying force in Van. This was enough "evidence" for Wangenheim to again make his point that "the Armenians are themselves responsible if now innocents had to suffer under the measures the Turkish government was forced to take against insurgent elements, which are threatening the safety of the state." He then asked Scheubner to spread the word in "local Armenian circles when the opportunity presents itself" that "the common principles of the law" prevented Germany from interfering on their behalf. However, he added that he would try to convey the contents of the telegram to the Armenian patriarch without saying where they came from.[44]

Scheubner did not give up. On 2 June, he bombarded the ambassador with a series of cables containing updates on events, and repeating his request that the embassy intervene with the Ottoman Porte. It was clear now, he wrote, that *all* the Armenians of Erzurum and surrounding regions were to be deported immediately. He warned,

> This deportation of such magnitude equals massacres, because of the lack of means of transport not even half of them will reach their destination, and this will mean the ruin of the Armenians and of the [whole] country. [These] measures cannot be justified on military grounds, because there is no reason to expect an uprising by the local Armenians, and the deportees are old men, women, and children.[45]

He elaborated on his last point in a further telegram, insisting that "in Erzurum and its surroundings no bombs or the like have been found, which the governor can confirm."[46] This openly contradicted his ambassador's charge from a few weeks before. In another telegram Scheubner pleaded, "the Armenian population sees in me, as the only representative of a Christian power, their natural protector. [The] situation [is] difficult and embarrassing [*peinlich*]. I ask your Excellency to, please, support me by intervening with the Ottoman government accordingly."[47]

Scheubner's telegraphic bombardment was without success. Wangenheim answered that he could not intervene, as he had told him already in previous telegrams, and also insisted, as he had done before, that the consul not intervene with the local military authorities. This, however, Scheubner had already done by the time the reply arrived.[48] Four days later, he disobeyed another of his ambassador's instructions, relaying to the embassy yet another plea for help from a local bishop—this time from the Catholic bishop asking the German and Austrian emperors for protection.[49] A few days later, Scheubner had grim news to report: his worst fears of the deportation turning into massacre had been realized. The deportation from Erzurum and its surroundings was now well under way, and on the road to Kharput a trek had been attacked, with most of the men and children killed and most of the women kidnapped. Scheubner wrote that the Ottoman government would not and did not want to do anything for the deportees' protection, and asked his ambassador for instructions about what to do to prevent such butcheries in the future.[50] Wangenheim replied that Scheubner should tell the governor that such incidents would harm the image of the Ottoman government abroad and at home. It would also invite further foreign interventions and would have an unfavorable impact on the peace talks later. And then he added that even though the German government could not object to the deportation of the Armenians as far as the war situation warranted it, the butchering of defenseless people should cease and he appealed to the local authorities to protect the Armenians. Wangenheim clearly did not understand or did not want to understand the true nature of what was going on.[51]

This was to finally change, abruptly, sometime around mid-June. Indirectly, it was the fault of Johannes Lepsius. He had been bothering the German Foreign Office with letters, expressing his fears for the Armenians and preparing a trip to the Ottoman Empire to conduct talks with Armenian and Ottoman leaders to find a more peaceful and amicable solution. In the coming weeks Wangenheim would advise against such a trip. But, in these very days in which the Lepsius trip was being discussed, the embassy's man at the Armenian desk, Mordtmann, talked with Talât Pasha, the minister of the interior, who told him frankly of the government's intentions. According to Mordtmann, Talât "expressed himself without reservation about the intentions of the government which was using the World War to make a clean sweep of its internal enemies—the indigenous Christians of all confessions—without being hindered in doing so by diplomatic intervention from other countries."[52] Mordtmann understood that this meant that Talât Pasha was intending to "annihilate the Armenians," as he noted a few weeks later.[53] Talât's blunt declaration changed Wangenheim's perspective. Now the German ambassador warned in his reports to the German chancellor that this was no wartime necessity operation, but one bent on exterminating the Armenians. Though he still decided to advise the Foreign Office to refuse to allow the Lepsius mission, a few weeks later, he wrote to his chancellor that the current extension of the deportations to other regions "and the manner in which the deportation is being carried out shows that, indeed, the government is pursuing the purpose of annihilating the Armenian race in the Turkish Empire."[54]

Toward the end of June, Scheubner, who had been keeping his embassy up to date on each new trek leaving the area, as well as on the unwillingness of the military authorities to provide any protection for the treks, reported that now all the remaining Armenians had been ordered to evacuate. He wrote, "This order which has no military basis can only be attributed to racial hatred."[55] Two days later he reported that the owner of the consulate building, a very pro-German Armenian professor, had been arrested on the street under "baseless accusations." Scheubner called this episode a "cheeky violation" of consular rights and matters by the Turks, and he asked for protection and instructions from his ambassador.[56] He had to cable again the same day, as the consulate's translator, of many years' standing, was about to be deported as well, again on a flimsy pretext. Scheubner offered an interpretation of these actions: they were meant, first, to show the Germans that the capitulations (that is, the special rights regime for foreigners) did not exist anymore; and second, to cut all connections between the consulate and the Armenians.[57] When the embassy finally answered on 3 July, it claimed it was not able to do anything for these people as they did not belong to the category of "privileged clerks."[58]

Scheubner continued to try to save the translator, along with two other Armenian employees of the consulate.[59] His strategy was now, in early July, to point out that the manner in which they were arrested was hurting the image of the German consulate in the city. He tried to convince his embassy that this was an insult against Germany, and that only if the three were allowed to remain in Erzurum, and in the employ of the German embassy, could the honor of the German embassy be restored. And indeed he convinced Mordtmann to intervene with Talât Pasha. On 6 July, it even appeared that Mordtmann had been successful.[60] Scheubner sent a long report to the embassy on 8 July, with his letters to the local authorities attached. He received the answer that the German embassy could not do anything for these Armenians. The embassy also repeated the claim that a continued German intervention on their behalf might even make matters worse.[61] On 14 July, the embassy confirmed to Scheubner in a telegram that Mordtmann's efforts had been in vain, and that the Ottoman government would not allow these three to remain in Erzurum.[62]

"Final Goal": "Extermination"

After this, for almost two weeks, Scheubner sent no further telegrams or letters on the Armenian topic to his ambassador. It seems he had resigned himself, at least temporarily, to not being able to make a difference. At the end of July, he resumed his reports with more bad news: more treks of deportees from Trebizond and Erzindjan had now been massacred, like those from the Erzurum area, and again all the men were dead and the women in a "dismal condition."[63] The next day, in a more extensive report, he wrote that the parallel government that the Young Turks had established in the region, circumventing the local authorities, was "admitting without hesitation" that the "final goal [*Endziel*] of their approach vis-à-vis the Armenians" was "the wholesome extermination of the latter in Turkey." He quoted an "influential figure" saying that after the war there would be "no more Armenians in Turkey." Scheubner continued,

> As far as this goal is not attainable through various massacres, it is hoped that the hardship of the long marches to Mesopotamia, and the unfamiliar climate there, will do the rest. This solution of the Armenian Question appears to be an ideal one, from the point of view of hardliners, to which group almost all military and government officials belong.[64]

On 5 August, Scheubner sent a long letter to Constantinople to mark a significant milestone: there were now no more Armenians left in the whole province.[65] He offered an overview of the previous months' events. Until April, he wrote, everything had been more or less fine, except for the fact that the Armenians had feared that massacres would come; the murder of an Armenian bank director had helped to fuel such fears. Then in May, the "known events in Van" led the government and military authorities to harsh disciplinary measures *(scharfe Massregeln)* against all Armenians. At first all Armenians in the army were transferred to labor battalions. Then the Armenian inhabitants of the Erzurum and Passin plain—now that only women, children, and old men were left—were expelled from their villages and were, supposedly, deported to Mesopotamia. "These measures, justified as necessary for military reasons, were executed in an unnecessarily brutal fashion." On the road to Mesopotamia, the treks of deportees were assaulted by Kurds and Turkish irregulars at various places. "The number of dead probably amounts to between ten and twenty thousand." A similar fate, he reported, came to other Armenians who happened to live along the path of the trek.

Scheubner continued his overview with reports on the fate of various other groups of deportees—including a group of 500 notable Armenians from the city of Erzurum, the first group to be deported from the city in June, almost all of whom he understood to have died on the road. He also detailed what happened to the subsequent groups of deportees. He then turned to an overview of his own actions in the matter. He had been constrained, he said, by the instructions of his ambassador, which had prevented him from protecting even innocent Armenians. Accordingly, all he had been able to do was to intervene for a "humane deportation," and to keep his interventions within the sphere of "friendly advice." But, because the local governor was also not much in favor of the deportation orders, his "friendly advice" had been partly heeded, and he had been able to alleviate the Armenians' suffering a bit, by such means as getting them more time, securing some protection for them, and organizing means of transport.

Scheubner added an insight into local, non-Armenian opinion. Those in "reasonably thinking Turkish circles," he said, were opposed to this "policy of annihilation." There was even a widespread view that the Germans had originated the policy, not the Ottomans: often, he claimed, he had been asked by Turks to explain why the German government had prompted such policies. Scheubner concluded his lengthy letter with a summary of his own perspective, which is interesting enough to quote in full:

It would go too far here to delve into the origins of the persecutions of the Armenians and to analyze whether they could have been avoided

with [more] appropriate measures [*zweckmäßige Massregeln*] and nego-
tiation by the government [with the Armenians]. As much as I know
nothing has happened in such matters on time. Furthermore, it is self-
evident that where the Armenian revolutionary committees and Russian
emissaries have provoked rebellions, the full force of the law is being
brought down upon the guilty parties. I would even have expected and
wished for much harsher preventative disciplinary measures [*Vorbeu-
gungsmassregeln*] by the government and the military authorities, but
not—as it happened in most cases—[such] ex post facto retributionary
measures. There is, as far as I know, no evidence (at all) for a planned
and prepared general uprising of the Armenians.

Thus for example in the province of Erzurum neither arms nor incriminating pamphlets have been found. If a rebellion had been planned
here, then the most promising opportunity was in January, when the Russians were just 35 km from Erzurum, and the garrison of Erzurum consisted of merely a few hundred men of the gendarmerie, while there were
some 3–4.000 Armenians in the army workers' battalions.[66]

After writing this long report, Scheubner still did not give up, though there
was little left for him to do in Erzurum, as all the Armenians were gone.
On 7 August, just two days later, he wrote to German chancellor Theobald
von Bethmann-Hollweg directly. He described how he had done everything he could to alleviate the Armenians' suffering, and also recounted
his efforts to safeguard now-abandoned Armenian property, with a
view to protecting any German investments and outstanding payments
to German companies and the Deutsche Bank. He wrote a further, longer
letter directly to the chancellor on 10 August—in fact, he submitted what
he called a "small memorandum" on the Armenian issue, on the pretext of
needing the chancellor's opinion on how to proceed with possible strategic
alliances with any Armenian groups that he might encounter when he continued with his original mission beyond the Ottoman border in the Caucasus. His mission to the Caucasus here clearly emerges as the reason
and motivation for authoring his two "final" large memoranda on the
Armenian issue in 1915, first to his embassy and then, circumventing the
former, directly addressed to the imperial chancellor.

His memorandum to the chancellor discussed the big picture of the Armenian question. And while he did not use the term "final solution," this is
obviously what he was talking about:

The Armenian question, which has been occupying the diplomats of Europe for many decades, is supposed to be solved in the present war. The Turkish government has used the state of war, and the opportunity provided by the Armenian uprisings in Van, Mush, Karahissar, and other places, to forcibly expel the Armenians of Anatolia to Mesopotamia. By the repression of Armenian schools, prohibition of correspondence in the Armenian language, and similar measures, it hopes to finally suppress the political and cultural ambitions of the Armenians. Perhaps it also hopes to damage the Armenians economically, so that in the future it will no longer be possible for them to lead an independent cultural life. At this stage I will disregard the fact that these measures by the government were carried out in such a way that they meant the absolute extermination of the Armenians. Indeed, though, I do not believe it would be possible in any way other [than extermination] to destroy a culture that is older and much higher than that of the Turks. Also, the Armenians seem to me to be very resilient as a race, just like the Jews. Because of their education, their commercial capabilities, which usually verge into unscrupulousness, and their adaptability, they should be able to succeed in regaining their economic strength even under the most unfavorable circumstances. Only a policy of violent extermination, a forcible annihilation of a whole people, could lead the Turkish government in this way to its longed-for goal, to a "solution" of the Armenian question. But whether a solution of this kind to this question is advantageous either to Turkey or to us, I greatly doubt.[67]

It is striking that only in his memorandum to the imperial chancellor did he employ the strong and by then well-established anti-Armenianist parallel between the Jews and the Armenians. He had refrained from using such stereotypical descriptions and judgments in his letters to his embassy. Perhaps he thought this was somehow a necessary frame of reference. Now he offered the following description of Anatolia:

The inhabitants of Anatolia are mainly made up of Turks, Armenians, and Kurds. The Kurds are the lowest as far as culture is concerned, the Armenians the highest. From a moral point of view, the Turks must be judged as coming out on top. . . . In the towns the Armenians also dominate the economic sector: almost the whole trade is in their hands. Because of their extremely distinctive keenness for gain and their greed, they do not make a pleasant impression.[68]

However, it also becomes clear here that not only Scheubner's strategy had changed, but also his goals:

> I am therefore of the opinion that it would be useful for us, not only for ethical reasons but also for practical reasons, to stand up for the principle that the Armenians who have survived expulsion, and are loyal, should be allowed to return to their former homes after the war. . . . The Armenians scattered throughout the whole of the East, thanks to their naturally inborn mercantile capabilities, would be in a position to monopolize the whole economic life and, just like the Jews, would play an often useful, but not always desirable role in it.[69]

He also cast doubt on the finality of the "solution":

> Furthermore, I do not believe that the Armenian question will have found a solution in a political respect in the enforced expulsion to Mesopotamia. The Armenians who have settled there and those who have fled to Russia will want to come back and, together with the Armenians in the United States, will ask for the support of the European powers. The mass deportation, in combination with the atrocities carried out on the part of Turkey, would therefore only provide a reason for a renewed intervention in the internal affairs of Turkey.[70]

These were Scheubner's final words from Erzurum on the Armenian matter. He left for Northern Persia on his original mission to wage guerilla warfare against the Russians. His post was handed over to another interim consul, now, in fact, an interim for the interim, Count Friedrich-Werner von der Schulenburg, later Hitler's ambassador to Moscow. Scheubner continued to report to the embassy, from the road. His next report on the Armenians was submitted by the embassy to the imperial chancellor, in excerpts, on 9 November. Here Scheubner described what he had witnessed along the way from Erzurum to Mosul:

> On the journey from Erzurum to Mosul via Khinis, Mush, Bitlis, and Sairt, all the villages and homes I came across, all of which used to be inhabited by Armenians, were found to be totally empty and destroyed. I did not see any living male Armenian. It is said that a number of them fled into the mountains. Around 500 Armenian women and children find themselves in deplorable conditions in the Armenian church in Bitlis. Armenian women are thought to be held captive in Turkish households.

On the entire journey, I and the German gentlemen who were accompanying me saw the corpses of Armenian men, women, and children: most displayed signs of multiple bayonet wounds. This was seen despite the route having been cleared of corpses by gendarmes at the instruction of the government. According to statements given by Kurds, all Armenians in the area around here had been murdered. According to my information a revolution or an uprising prepared by Armenians had taken place only in Van, in other places it was self-defense. The Turks, among them officers, have spread the news and in many cases actually believe it themselves, that the German government arranged for the extermination of the Armenians.[71]

Scheubner did not give up. One year later, on 4 December 1916, when he was already back in Munich, he authored yet another lengthy memorandum to the chancellor, still using his now absolutely defunct former title, "caretaker at Erzurum." His ostensible reason for writing was to answer a letter from the chancellor from a year before; but his real reason, it seems, was once again to air at length his views on the Armenian Genocide. He described a relevant episode from his travels, when he, in command of a company of German and Turkish soldiers, was traversing the empire on the way to Persia. Near Hesak, they were given the order to storm a rebellious Armenian village. However, Scheubner was reluctant to follow this order, especially after finding out that these supposedly "rebellious" Armenians had been afraid of massacres and were ready to hand over their weapons if assurances were made. Scheubner said he escaped this "compromising" situation by handing over command of his Turkish soldiers to the ranking Turkish officer, while he himself and his German colleagues withdrew from the area. Scheubner speculated that the whole point of the order had been to implicate him and Germany in general in the Armenian matter. He further stressed that despite his difficult situation, during the whole expedition in Northern Persia, he made sure that no massacres among the resident Armenians were committed by the Turkish troops in the area.

Scheubner went on to give another grand résumé on the Armenian Genocide:

The fear I spoke of in my report from Erzurum, namely that the evacuation of the Armenians would be tantamount to their annihilation and that this was the purpose behind it, has unfortunately turned out to be true. The evacuees of this tribe who are still alive in Mesopotamia are in a desolate condition. It would not be saying too much if I tell you that the Turkish Armenians, with the exception of several hundred thousand living in Constantinople and other cities, have been practically wiped out. . . .

I feel obliged to direct Your Excellency's attention to the following: a number of discussions with leading Turkish personalities left me with the following impressions: A large part of the Young Turk Committee is of the opinion that the Ottoman Empire should only be built upon a purely Mohammedan, pan-Turkish foundation. Those inhabitants who are neither Mohammedan nor Turkish should be made to become so by force or, if that is not possible, annihilated.

For these gentlemen, the present time seems to be the most suitable for putting this plan into effect.

The first item on their program was finishing off the Armenians.

A supposed revolution prepared by the [revolutionary Armenian] Dashnak Party was put forward as a pretext to satisfy those powers that are allied with Turkey. Furthermore, local unrest and self-protection measures on the part of the Armenians were exaggerated and taken as an excuse to justify the evacuation of the Armenians from endangered border districts. At the instigation of the [Young Turk] Committee, the Armenians were murdered along the way by Kurdish and Turkish gangs, in some places also by gendarmes.

[Secondly, at] about the same time, the Nestorians [actually Assyrians, another ancient Christian people] in Eastern Kurdistan, after brave resistance, were turned out of their homes by the governor of Mosul, Haidar Bey, and partially annihilated. Their fields and homes were ravaged. . . .

[Thirdly,] Halil Bey's campaign in northern Persia resulted in the massacre of his Armenian and Syrian battalions and the expulsion of the Armenian, Syrian, and Persian populations from northern Persia. It left behind a great bitterness towards the Turks.

[Fourthly,] a settling of scores with the Arabs is also being considered, but the presently unfavorable military situation made it apparent that this was not yet the right moment. In the meantime, a suitable substitute was attempted by heavily recruiting Arabs and dispatching Arab troops with the most inadequate equipment in climatically unfavorable areas (winter campaign 1914 Erzurum, 1915 northern Persia). . . .

I have finally come to the conclusion that our restraint in the Armenian question has caused visible damage to our reputation in Turkey and Persia because many considered it to be a sign of weakness. More decisive action against the rigorous attempts of the Young Turk Committee would be of help to our reputation, and not only among the non-Mohammedans and the Arabs, but also the Old Turks and the present minority of the Young Turks would like us much more. . . .

"If we, the Turks, bleed to death in this battle for the existence of the Ottoman Empire, then there shall exist no other nations within it anymore either." This remark by a Young Turk politician characterizes best the point of view held by the circles of the Young Turk Committee. And the logical consequence of the weakening of pure Turkishness (the Anatolians), more and more appearing mainly because of a lack of organization and foresight, is the violent annihilation of the other nations living in Turkey.

It appears to me to be in our political and economic interest to turn our attention to this process of annihilation and to counteract it wherever possible.[72]

State Secretary Arthur Zimmermann passed Scheubner's report on to the embassy in Constantinople with the words, "The opinion that too great a restraint in the Armenian Question would damage our reputation with the Young Turk rulers as well, cannot be denied."[73] This note by Zimmermann suggests that the mood, and perhaps even the official stance, had changed. Scheubner would have found more receptive ears in Wangenheim's replacement Count Paul Wolff-Metternich, who took over the ambassadorship in the late summer of 1915, just after Scheubner's own departure. And indeed, under the new ambassador, Germany had intervened for the Armenians, albeit very timidly, in some limited circumstances. Metternich had even advised the German chancellor to put pressure on the Turks and to use the German press to express disgust at the "Armenian persecutions." There was no need to be so afraid of offending the Turks, he urged: they would not be able just to switch sides and make peace, anyway.[74] The chancellor seems to have become rather angry at this suggestion. To publicly criticize an ally during a war in this way had never happened in history so far, he wrote. "Our only goal is to hold Turkey at our side until the end of the war, regardless of whether the Armenians perish over that or not. If the war carries on for a while we will need the Turks very much."[75]

Apparently, the Turks called Metternich "the Armenian ambassador." He had told the Turks that the persecution and maltreatment of hundreds of thousands of innocents was not legitimate state self-defense.[76] Metternich was dismissed as early as 1916 because, as Edgar Vincent, Viscount d'Abernon, put it, "he could not be cured of the pernicious habit of protesting against Armenian massacres."[77] His successors again turned to a more silent stance in the matter.

The Beginning of Whitewashing

Back to the summer of 1915. By July, even Ambassador Wangenheim could no longer deny, block, or ignore the charge of genocide. In a report on the Armenian question to his chancellor in July 1915, he noted that Armenians in areas not at all relevant to the war were now being deported as well: "This situation, and the way in which the relocation is being carried out, shows that the government is indeed pursuing its purpose of exterminating the Armenian race from the Turkish Empire."[78] However, this acknowledgment of genocide in progress did not lead to moral condemnation, but only to a strategic reaction: "The Porte," he wrote, "does not realize the effect that these and other enforced measures, such as the mass executions here and in the country's interior, are having on public opinion abroad and the further consequences for the treatment of the Armenian Question in future peace talks." And even this was mostly a pretext. Wangenheim's main concern in relation to this genocide in progress was Germany itself:

> In order to effectively counteract any possible later invective on the part of our enemies such as being jointly to blame for the rigorous Turkish actions, I have considered it my duty to point out to the Porte that we can only approve of the deportation of the Armenian people if it is carried out as a result of military considerations and serves as a security against revolts, but that in carrying out these measures one should provide protection for the deportees against plundering and butchery. In order to lend the necessary weight to these objections, I have summarized them in the form of a memorandum which I have personally handed to the Grand Vizier. . . . I later sent copies of this memorandum to the Foreign Ministry and the Ministry of the Interior.[79]

By that time, the German ambassador had received more and more reports from his consuls that did away with any further doubt about the scope of the Ottoman government's "disciplinary measures." The embassy and the Foreign Office also received a host of reports from other sources. Thus, for example, in June 1915, Consul Rössler had attached letters from the Swiss deacon Jakob Künzler in Urfa. Künzler, for example, had written, "When I look at the situation of the Armenian people and then remember the words of the famous Turkish major, Nafiz Bey, who said that after this war we must eliminate the Armenian people or force them to emigrate, then I fear that the duration of this war will be used for the purpose of decimating this people, as much as possible."[80] In July 1915 there was a report from Major Dagobert von Mikusch, who had traveled back from Mosul and "personally saw 200 bodies. The militia and gendarmes have at least tolerated the massacre and have probably taken part in it."[81] But the Foreign Office also received lengthy reports from correspondents of the *Kölnische Zeitung* and the *Tägliche Rundschau* detailing their knowledge of the Armenian Genocide.[82] Ernst Jäckh, for example, also reported to the Foreign Office in October 1915 after having talked with Talât Pasha: "Talât certainly made no secret of the fact that he welcomed the annihilation of the Armenian people as a political relief."[83]

The German embassy knew that what had happened had been wrong, and that its own role, not just that of the Ottomans, would be under scrutiny and attack in the future. In August 1915, State Secretary Zimmermann advised gathering material for a future white book that was supposed to show, on the one hand, that the Armenians had threatened the very existence of the Ottoman State and had to be suppressed, and, on the other hand, that the German consuls had done their best to alleviate the suffering of the Armenians.[84] Thus, from 1915 onward, Germany prepared this double strategy: on the one hand, blaming the Armenians to justify whatever had happened to them; and, on the other hand, defending itself by claiming it had helped the Armenians. By November 1915, the embassy had already organized itself well to defend itself against allegations of guilt and conspiracy, as can be seen in a memorandum it sent in answer to a request by Goltz Pasha. At the time Goltz was the highest ranking German Ottoman military pasha, but not integrated into the Ottoman General Staff. He had been posted to the empire in late 1914, after which he was first military adviser to the sultan and then in command of the Ottoman Sixth Army. He had asked the embassy for the relevant materials on the Armenian question. In return, the responsible chargé d'affaires, Konstantin von Neurath, Hitler's future foreign minister (for much of the 1930s), composed a short memorandum on the embassy's official position on the matter. Neurath renarrated the decisions that had been taken in relation to the news from the ground that the consulates had supplied, as well as to the requests from these consulates, especially the ones in Erzurum and Adana, to intervene on behalf of the Armenians.

The memorandum began,

I. Instructions from the Imperial Embassy to the Imperial Consulates concerning the handling of the Armenian question:

On 31 May, the consulates in Erzurum, Mosul, Adana, Aleppo, and Bagdad were informed that in order to curb Armenian espionage and to prevent Armenian mass uprisings, the [Ottoman] Ministry of War had decided, among other measures (such as closing the Armenian schools, suppressing Armenian newspapers, etc.), to resettle in Mesopotamia all not quite impeccable [*nicht ganz einwandfreien*] families from the insurgent centers. . . . [The consulates were also informed that] Enver Pasha had urgently requested that we not hinder him from doing so. A remark had been added to this information that, out of consideration for Turkey's political and military situation, we should moderate the government's measures in their form of implementation, but not basically hinder them.

Previously, on 19 and 21 May, special decisions had been made to this purpose in response to inquiries made by the consulates in Erzurum [by Scheubner] and Adana [by Rössler]. In this connection, the consulate in Erzurum was informed that it should keep its intervention on behalf of the Armenians within the limits of friendly advice to avoid giving it the character of an official representation. On 21 June, the same consulate was instructed to intercede firmly with the governor against the slaughtering of the deportees, because such incidents damaged the reputation of the Turkish government both in neutral foreign countries and among its own friends, and undermined the authority of its public officials. This instruction also states:

"Reprisals and acts of vengeance on the part of the Russians and the Armenians in the areas occupied by them are inevitable. Also, this provides fresh grounds for foreign intervention in Armenian matters and will make Turkey's position unnecessarily difficult in future peace negotiations. Even if we cannot raise any objections to the deportation of the Armenians, as far as this is justified by the state of war, we must be all the more forcible in insisting, also in our own interest, that a stop be put to the massacring of defenseless people. It is the duty of the local authorities to prevent such occurrences with all means available if they are not willing to burden themselves with such a serious responsibility."

On 25 June and 9 September, the consul in Trebizond was instructed to recommend protection for the deportees to the governor.

He, as well as the consuls in Aleppo, Erzurum, Mosul, and Samsun, repeatedly interceded in the aforementioned way with the provincial authorities. . . .

II. Our point of view in the Armenian Question was that the Turkish government, in the interests of the military and of the country's inner security, had the right to resort to extraordinary means which could be described as acts of self-defense, such as, for example, the compulsory deportation of the Armenian population from the areas threatened by the Russian invasion and by the actions of the French and the British fleets.

On the other hand, the German Foreign Office and the Imperial Embassy disapproved of all the different kinds of excesses which set in as a result of these compulsory measures: the murder of individual persons, the mass executions that took place, particularly in Diyarbekir and Kayseri, the attacks on the deportee transport, the systematically organized slaughter of thousands of defenseless men and women in individual towns (in Mush, Erzerum, Erzindjan, Trebizond, Diyarbekir, Angora, Malatia), the extension of the slaughters to Christians of other denominations who have no common political interests with the actual (so-called Gregorian) Armenians and, in part, are enemies of theirs; also, the merciless treatment of the evacuees who, robbed of all means of subsistence, were abandoned to hunger and misery, did not seem to be justifiable.

From a military point of view there was just little justification for the evacuation of the Armenian population from those parts of the country far distant from the theatre of war.

The economic damage, which this measure caused, affects the country's trade, agriculture, and industry in the same measure. German interests have already been severely affected.

In the common interest of the allies, the Imperial Embassy has repeatedly pointed out the political and commercial effects of the persecution of the Armenians to the Sublime Porte and urged that the worst abuses be brought to an end; in doing so, it deliberately did not place an emphasis on the humanitarian point of view and also avoided the impression that it wished to involve itself in an internal political matter.

In numerous cases in which German interests have been affected, the Embassy interceded in an official and semi-official form for individual Armenians. The Embassy also repeatedly instructed individual consulates to intercede in the appropriate form against atrocities, which had occurred and for a humane treatment of the Armenians. Finally, through us, the Sublime Porte became aware of individual, particularly grave excesses. The Imperial Embassy is all the more embarrassed by the opinion of large circles in the interior of the country, particularly in Anatolia, that the German government supposedly provoked the Turkish government's offences against the Armenians, and that the consuls in the provinces supported and encouraged the local authorities in their persecution of the Armenians. This opinion is held not only by the Armenians, but also by the Turks and, as the news repeatedly shows, is being spread deliberately by Turkish public officials and military of both higher and lower rank. Germany, on its part, must protest strongly against these statements, and the Imperial Government reserves the right to take forceful measures against this in public at the opportune moment.[85]

Thus, by the end of 1915, while the embassy and its consulates had internally acknowledged the extent and intent of the genocide as genocide, time and again, it had also prepared a line of defense, of interpretation and argumentation, for the "outside." In this line, what had happened was a mix of justified military measures and "excesses." And the consuls, who in fact had done what they could to help the Armenians *in spite of* a reluctant and anti-Armenian embassy, were now presented as merely implementing official policy. This very much was Germany's official line for the rest of the war and the postwar years.

•   •   •

It is important to stress that, even apart from consuls like Scheubner who did what they could, it would not be fair to say that Germany, and German officials, did not intervene at all on the side of the Armenians.[86] As we have already seen, the advent of Wolff-Metternich as ambassador after mid-1915 did result in the occasional though timid protest against anti-Armenian measures—though it appears these were mainly meant to save face and to control the political, reputational, and diplomatic damage the genocide might cause. Another motivation for Germany's timid protests may have been the fact that the Young Turks seem to have been deliberately spreading rumors that the genocide was carried out at the behest of Germany.[87] There were also some military "heroes." Goltz—the addressee of the memorandum above—together with Liman von Sanders in another region, came to hold a special distinction among German military officials: they both used their military powers to actually prevent deportations of Armenians and Greeks where they were operating, even going so far as to threaten the use of the troops under their command to do so.[88] Meanwhile Kress von Kressenstein, another high-ranking German in the Ottoman army, convinced Djemal Pasha to refrain from deporting the Christian and Jewish populations of Jerusalem.[89] And Erich von Falkenhayn, at the time chief of staff of the Ottoman Army, intervened with Enver Pasha to protect Bagdad Railway employees. Falkenhayn actually believed his protest telegram alone would absolve Germany of any guilt of association with the Armenian Genocide.[90] In any case, it has to be noted that most of these interventions came after the deportations had by and large been finished, and thus after most of the genocidal project had been carried out already. Falkenhayn's intervention, for example, was in November 1916—thus well over a year after the last treks had left Erzurum. In the crucial period of the Armenian Genocide—when Scheubner was bombarding the embassy with his reports and pleas—the German embassy had chosen to close its eyes and regurgitate Ottoman propaganda, most importantly vis-à-vis its superiors in Berlin, thereby also severely limiting political Germany's options of interpretation and reaction to the genocide.

Besides Scheubner at Erzurum, there were other German consuls just as motivated to document what was happening and to urge their government to intervene. One of them was Consul Rössler in Aleppo. Among his first pro-Armenian actions was an attempt to travel to Zeytun, where an Armenian resistance against Ottoman troops had begun. The German consul in Damascus, Wilhelm Padel, had been informed of this by Eberhard Count Wolfskeel von Reichenberg, another German military man serving with the Ottoman army.[91] Padel in turn tattled on Rössler in a telegram to the ambassador: "The military authority considers this journey to be extremely questionable and requests that he refrain from undertaking it." The ambassador agreed and ordered Rössler not to travel to Zeytun.[92] Wolfskeel, who had intervened with Padel to get the embassy to stop Rössler, was personally involved in the whole matter and much more so than most Germans serving with the Ottoman army at the time. He was one of the very few German officers (if not the only one) who had actually taken part in the Ottoman actions against the Armenians: at Zeytun, for example, he had shelled an Armenian monastery. Later he was even dispatched with Ottoman forces to fight against the very same Armenians resisting at Musa Dagh who were immortalized by Franz Werfel in his novel, *The Forty Days of Musa Dagh*.[93]

In response to allegations by Armenian researchers, most prominently Vahakn Dadrian, about Germany's guilt in the Armenian Genocide, historian Donald Bloxham speaks of "a case of mistaken identity" for Germany.[94] Bloxham might be right to respond in such a fashion to assumptions of Germany's guilt as an alleged coperpetrator. Dadrian's case is not yet convincing. The claim that the Armenian Genocide was a result of joint German-Ottoman decision making cannot yet be proven.[95] However, this does not mean that Germany was not guilty in another way: guilty in failing to stop the Young Turks. As in the decades before, from Bismarck to Wilhelm II, and as neatly legitimized by Naumann, parts of the German political elite saw the Armenians as expendable. In other words, Germany knew what was going on and chose to accept the death of the Armenians as part of the cost of doing business or war. It is true, as Bloxham has also rightly pointed out, that the prevalence of anti-Armenian views among the Germans in the Ottoman Empire does not in itself prove that they played an active role in the Armenian Genocide. But these perceptions helped them close their eyes to the plight of the Armenians and buy into Ottoman propaganda.[96]

The reasons for not intervening on behalf of the Armenians, and thus for not stopping genocide, that were advanced during and after the war followed a simple logic: The Ottoman Empire is our ally, we need this ally in this struggle for the life and death of the German nation, and we cannot alienate or lose this ally. Intervening in any fashion for the Armenians would be meddling in the internal affairs of this vital ally, and thus unacceptable. It could lead to the alliance splitting up. Indeed, Undersecretary Zimmermann, a man close to the kaiser's entourage and probably instrumental in pushing his policies in and through the Foreign Office, believed that the German-Turkish alliance rested almost exclusively on the leading Young Turks. Alienating them, for the sake of the Armenians, would mean breaking up the alliance, he argued.[97] While, unfortunately, this argument may sound logical to many readers—given that we humans rarely care enough about other humans far outside our kin group (family, village, nation) to jeopardize our own well-being—it is flawed. Yes, the price would have been high, perhaps very high, but nevertheless Germany had a choice not to intervene. There was no democratic discussion about what the German government or nation was allowing to happen under the cover of war; thus responsibility rests with those leading the nation and the war, and those controlling censorship matters. It is futile to play the game of historical what-ifs, but would an intervention with the Ottoman leadership—which was deeply Germanophile—really have led to the end of the alliance? Did the Ottoman Empire have so many options? Did the war really seem so life-and-death in early to mid-1915? It probably appeared so to many contemporaries. But a fundamental choice to intervene or not to intervene existed nevertheless.

The German embassy and the German government chose not to act on what they knew, consciously and deliberately so. They continued to support the Ottoman ally, and continued to finance their war and their government with huge levels of loans and subsidies.[98] Bloxham stresses that the other powers would not have reacted much differently had the Ottoman Empire been their ally during the war.[99] And Austria-Hungary, for example, followed Germany's line, too. Ulrich Trumpener argues that never in modern history has a belligerent country given up an ally for "humanitarian considerations."[100] Yet, all this still does not mean that Germany was not guilty of something. Similarly, Bloxham infers that the protests of Metternich about the Armenians led to a considerable deterioration of German-Ottoman relations, yet there is no evidence that the Armenian topic was really the cause for this deterioration in the latter phase of the war.[101] In fact we really do not know, and have no way of actually knowing, what the price of a harsher and more substantial German intervention at the right point would have been.

The role of German officers and military advisers in the Armenian Genocide is still not clear. Given the loss of much of the relevant German source material and the lack of accessibility to Ottoman sources, this question will perhaps never be conclusively resolved. Historian Christoph Dinkel has made an extensive study of the German military's role. But even he cannot make a convincing argument for direct German involvement in the planning and execution of the genocide; it remains highly speculative. However, Dinkel is right to point out that many of the ranking German officers

in the empire had been bitten by the anti-Armenian bug. Grigoris Balakian, an Armenian deportee, recalled that almost all German officers he
had been in contact with were "as Armenophobic as the Turks" and called
the Armenians "Christian Jews"—though he himself was saved by German
soldiers and engineers (see Chapter 11).[102]

Next to Bronsart, one of the most important anti-Armenianist Germans
was Hans Humann. Humann served as naval attaché, a position he seems
to have reached due to his family's good relations with the Tirpitz family—
Admiral Alfred von Tirpitz was one of the towering German military, or
rather navy, figures. In any case, Humann's role went much beyond that
of naval attaché. His father was the famous German archeologist Carl
Humann, who had excavated the Pergamon altar, and Hans seems to have
known Enver Pasha for many years already before World War I. This friendship enabled Humann to establish a direct line to Enver, and Humann,
with Otto von Lossow, served as the intermediaries between the Young Turk
leadership and Germany, totally circumventing the ambassador. It is also
alleged that he had a direct connection to the kaiser's entourage. Many have
since called him the "most influential German" in Constantinople during
the war.[103] Humann was a very unfortunate choice as prime go-between
between Germany and the Young Turk leadership. An anti-Semite and
expansionist-imperialist, he went on record as saying that "the Armenians
are being more or less exterminated—as a result of their conspiracy with
the Russians! This is harsh but useful."[104] Humann and his colleague and
friend, Lossow, the military attaché, were also the prime movers behind the
dismissal of the pro-Armenian ambassador Wolff-Metternich.[105]

But how much can we actually make of such people and their anti-
Armenian views? Perhaps not too much, because it still does not answer
the question of direct initiation or complicity. However, given the fact that
the German and Ottoman military structures were deeply intertwined,
given that much of the Ottoman military High Command was saturated
with German officers, and given that German advisers had been training
the Ottoman military, one can be sure that Germans were closely involved.
It is still not at all clear how far German military influence and control over
the Ottoman Empire really extended during the war. But what is clear is
that Germany would have had an interest in obscuring the extent of this
influence, during as well as after the war. The number of German military
personnel in the Ottoman army was never higher than 10,000 until 1916,
but it had reached 25,000 by the end of the war.[106] One case of direct in-

volvement in genocide is documented by personal admission. Otto von Feldmann, head of operations at Ottoman headquarters during the war, wrote, "Even German officers—I myself among them—were forced to advise freeing the rear of the army from Armenians in certain areas at certain times. The duty of self-preservation of the Turkish army did not permit leaving strong forces behind to guard rear lines. Without that, however, no operation was possible, no reverse at the front could be sustained, so long as Armenians lived in the rear."[107] It would be surprising if Feldmann had been the only one "advising" the Young Turks in this respect. But probably we will never know the full extent.

• • •

When it comes to Germany's traditional role vis-à-vis the Armenians as a silent bystander, a protective shield, and an "enabler" for the Ottomans, once more, events had unfolded in a familiar pattern. We in fact see this pattern, in slight variations, repeated three times in our story: first in the 1890s, then during the war, and finally in the immediate postwar years. First, Germany

Figure 6.1 The kaiser (left) with Enver Pasha in Constantinople in 1917 (German First World War Official Exchange Collection, Imperial War Museum. © IWM, Q 69989)

exhibited official silence and a blind eye. Then, as before, there was an intervention by Lepsius, though in this case a very indirect one, aided this time by unexpected bluntness from Talât. Next, there was widespread though mostly unavailing sympathy; even Wangenheim changed his stance and came to accept that genocide was in progress, and his successor was now openly very sympathetic toward the Armenians, though official policy did not change much. Back home in Germany, as we will see in Chapter 7, even parliamentarians—thanks in part to Lepsius's further publication and campaigning—now began siding with the Armenians and acknowledged that a genocide had occurred. Finally, there was a backlash. When, in early 1918, a German parliamentarian sent his report on his trip to the Ottoman Empire to the Foreign Office, it was answered in a statement that assigned the blame to the Armenians and denied the extent of the violence against them.[108] And is it a surprise that Kaiser Wilhelm II—who over the years had displayed an uncanny skill for doing the wrong thing at the wrong time—should choose 1917 to honor the Ottomans with another state visit? (Figure 6.1)

CHAPTER 7

"Interlude of the Gods"

While official Germany did not want to intervene for the Armenians, parts of Protestant pro-Armenian Germany did, again in the person of Johannes Lepsius. He traveled to Constantinople in the late summer of 1915, when, unfortunately, not only had the fate of the Armenians been long decided, but much of the genocide had already been carried out. It had been a struggle for Lepsius to get official permission to travel there, and to meet Enver Pasha. Ambassador Wangenheim had intervened with his superiors on 2 July 1915 to prevent Lepsius from coming to Constantinople. The ambassador wrote that Lepsius's trip and his potential intervention on behalf of the Armenians "could cause us a great deal of inconvenience ... and harm our other, more important interests."[1] This "inconvenience" was also felt in Berlin: State Secretary Zimmermann noted in his report that he had tried to stop Lepsius but did not succeed.[2] Thus Lepsius traveled to Constantinople.

His meeting with Enver Pasha has been immortalized by Franz Werfel in his novel *The Forty Days of Musa Dagh* (see Prologue). Indeed, at the very time Lepsius was talking with Enver, the Armenians who had taken refuge on top of Musa Dagh were making their last stand. It was in fact his chapter about the meeting—"The Interlude of the Gods," the chapter in which Lepsius tries to convince Enver Pasha to stop the Armenian Genocide—that Werfel had been reading out loud to an audience on his lecture tour in late 1932, warning Germany of Hitler, when he saw the future Führer in the Breslau hotel lobby.

Strangely enough, Lepsius's meeting with Enver Pasha had been set up by Hans Humann, that close friend of Enver and arch-anti-Armenianist whom we met in Chapter 6. Humann, as we saw, thought the genocide "harsh but useful"; he appears only briefly and in a more benign form in Werfel's account, as the "amiable Corvette-Captain." Perhaps Humann took the trouble to arrange the meeting because he—or his superiors in Berlin— thought such a meeting would appease pro-Armenian activists in Germany. It would not—not at all.

•   •   •

In the "Interlude of the Gods," Werfel follows Lepsius's own account of the meeting when it comes to the main dialogue, though of course many details are imaginatively fleshed out. Here I will follow Werfel's account, also because it gives us an idea of how Werfel used this meeting in his 1933 novel to warn Germany of Hitler. Thus, much of what follows is Werfel's fictionalized version of an event for which we will probably never know what was said exactly.[3]

The meeting had been canceled a few times, and when Lepsius arrived ten minutes late, according to Werfel, Enver was furious and asked, "What do I care about the Armenians?" In Werfel's portrayal, Enver Pasha, "the Ottoman God of War," is an ice-cold gambler. Werfel's chapter title makes one wonder who the other gods are. Lepsius is an unlikely candidate. At the end of the scene, Enver talks to Talât Pasha, and it becomes clear that they are the gods, deciding the fate of men, while Lepsius is a mere mortal calling out to the gods, though in vain. Werfel's use of Lepsius's being ten minutes late, of course, alludes to the fact that he was too late with his intervention anyway, by many months.

Lepsius spoke with Enver Pasha in German, which the latter apparently spoke very well. Enver said, "The war is very difficult. But our people know what they need to do." "Is it quite the same in the interior, Excellency?" Lepsius asked, drawing attention to the internal dimension of the war, that is, to the Armenians. Werfel writes in his novel, "Enver glanced with delight into the farthest corner of the room. 'Certainly. Great things are happening in the interior.'" "Excellency," Lepsius answered, "these great things are well known to me." When Enver referred to the war in the Caucasus, Lepsius interceded, "But by interior I mean the peaceful provinces, not the war zone." Enver replied that, during war, "all the regions are war zones, more or less." Lepsius then went on to press his case:

> His Excellency is aware, perhaps, that I am not here as a private individual, but as representative of the German Oriental Society, who

require my report about certain developments. . . . Our Foreign Office, indeed our Chancellor, is in active sympathy with my mission. On my return, I am to deliver a lecture in the Reichstag on the Armenian Question, for the information of the members of parliament and the German press. . . . I come to you in my distress, Excellency, because I am convinced that a commander of your rank, a hero, will not do anything that might besmirch his name in the [pages of] history.

Enver replied,

Ever since my friends and I have been in control of the government, we've always striven to grant the Armenian nation every form of support and unconditional justice. There was an old understanding. Your Armenian friends acclaimed our revolution most cordially; they swore all kinds of oaths of fidelity to us. These pledges were broken over night. We shut our eyes as long as possible, as long as the Turkish nation, the ruling people, was not in danger. We are, after all, living in Turkey, are we not? But when, after war was declared, cases of high treason, betrayal, and subversive tendencies kept increasing, when desertion got out of hand, when it came to open revolt—I am only thinking of the great revolt in Zeytun—then we were forced to take opposing disciplinary measures or lose the right to be the people's government and to wage war [at all].

Werfel's account continues:

Lepsius nodded, as though he were well on the way to becoming convinced. "In what, Excellency, did these legally proved cases of high treason and betrayal consist?" A broad gesture from Enver. This plenitude of crimes could never be fully listed. "Conspiracy with Russia. Sasonov's speech praising the Armenians in the Petersburg Duma [already] was clear enough. Furthermore conspiracy with France and England. Machinations, espionage—everything you can think of."

Lepsius then asked if these cases were indeed being investigated by proper courts. An argument ensued, in which Lepsius insisted that people had been executed, people who had been arrested before they could have done anything. Enver replied that, viewed from here in Constantinople, so close to the Gallipoli front, the empire just could not allow people to remain in place who were only "potentially high treasonous." Then they argued about Zeytun, which Enver called "one of the largest and most infamous revolts in the history of the Turkish Empire." Lepsius disagreed, saying that his reports on Zeytun seemed to have differed considerably. Enver asked him about his sources, and when Lepsius mentioned the American ambassador, Henry Morgenthau, Enver replied, "Mr. Morgenthau is a Jew. And the Jews are always and fanatically on the side of the minorities."[4]

The discussion continued, and Enver and Lepsius battled over the term "warzone." Lepsius denied that there were any military considerations at work here. Enver then replied,

> Dr. Lepsius, may I show you the other side? Germany, luckily, has no or few internal enemies. But let's suppose that, in other circumstances, she found herself with traitors in her midst—Alsace-Lorrainers, shall we say, or Poles, or Social-Democrats, or Jews—and in far greater numbers than at present. Would you, Mr. Lepsius, not endorse any and every means of freeing your country, which is fighting for its life against a whole world of enemies without, from those within? Would you consider it so cruel if, for the sake of victory, all dangerous elements in the population were simply herded together and deported into distant, uninhabited territory?

Lepsius did not accept this line of argument: "It isn't a question of protecting yourselves against an enemy in your midst, but of the planned extermination of another nation." The argument progressed and again Lepsius pleaded for a peaceful solution. Werfel's account continues: "Here for the first time Enver Pasha laid bare his deepest truth. His smile had no longer any reserve in it, a cold stare had come into his eyes, his lips retreated from a strong and dangerous set of teeth: 'There can be no peace . . . between human beings and plague germs.'"

As the argument went on, Lepsius realized that he could not win. "The pastor sank down into his chair. Lost. All over. Words were superfluous. If only the man were malicious, if he were Satan! But he had no malice, he was not Satan; this quietly implacable mass-murderer was boyishly charming." The mix of positive and negative attributes used for Enver in Werfel's novel certainly echoes Werfel's shock of seeing Hitler in person in the Breslau hotel lobby and realizing that he did not appear as the devil incarnate. To warn against Hitler, Werfel knew he must not only make him (or Enver, his "stand-in Hitler") out to be the devil; he also had to appear human.

Lepsius's final plea was answered by Enver in the usual fashion. Werfel writes, "Again the boyish Mars bared a row of smiling teeth, 'You may be sure, Mr. Lepsius, that our government will avoid all unnecessary harshness.'" After the meeting was over, in Werfel's account at least, Enver walked to Talât Pasha's office. "Yes, the German! He tried to threaten a little, with the Reichstag." Talât answered, "These Germans are only afraid of the odium of being made partly responsible. But they may have to come begging to us for more important things than Armenians."

Thus ended Werfel's (fictionalized) account. Whatever was said in reality and in detail between Lepsius and Enver, Lepsius had failed. He had tried to convince Enver to stop genocide in progress, arguing and reasoning about the motivations, pretexts, and consequences (for the Turks). In his own report, Lepsius especially emphasized the economic consequences of genocide. Not having been able to convince Enver, he then tried to get the Ottoman leader to allow him to set up a relief organization in the Ottoman Empire for the Armenians still alive. After another rebuff from Enver, Lepsius tried to at least save one of his Armenian friends. He failed on all counts.

• • •

Back in Germany, Lepsius reported to the Foreign Office and the chancellor about the genocide.[5] But he also took steps to spread the word publicly. On 5 October 1915, Lepsius gave a lecture in the German Reichstag, apparently mainly for the press, in which he went so far as to call the German government "slaves of the Ottoman government."[6] It appears this conference, and what Lepsius detailed about the Armenian Genocide there, unnerved the German newspapermen considerably.[7] At the same conference, Paul Rohrbach stated that "these events made it impossible for us to continue to carry coresponsibility for the Turkish alliance. Military censorship has prevented us from speaking in public. But we can and must tell our government that we can no longer recognize the alliance as one entered into between two equal states."[8] The next day, Lepsius was reprimanded by the German Foreign Office, which, in the voice of State Secretary Zimmermann, argued that the Armenians were "insurgents" and that, regarding the Ottoman ally, "realpolitik" had to prevail: "We did not and do not believe that a break with Turkey over the Armenian question would be right."[9]

But Lepsius did not stop there. In the following months he wrote and published a book, his *Report on the State of the Armenian People in Turkey* (1916) and distributed it widely.[10] Around 20,000 copies were printed: 500 were meant for German parliamentarians, a few more for the major newspapers, and all the others for missionary circles as well as all of the

German Protestant parishes in Germany. To get around the censorship regime, he prefaced the report with the disclaimer that it was "top secret" and that it was not meant to undermine official censorship on the matter. He sent out most copies of the report by regular mail. And this seems, perhaps surprisingly, to have worked: while a small number were confiscated, most copies of the report seem to have reached their destinations.[11] One of these was Scheubner, who received his copy just weeks before he sent his 1916 memorandum on the Armenian Genocide to the chancellor (as discussed in Chapter 6).[12] At least, as Lepsius himself claimed in late 1918, every German Protestant pastor should have received a copy.[13] If true, this would have meant that every such pastor, if he had taken the trouble, could have read about the Armenian Genocide and told his parishioners about it.

The 1916 Lepsius report was similar to his 1896 report. Again it chronicled the massacres and fate of Armenians for each district. In style it differed slightly, being more subdued in tone and avoiding the full panoply of atrocity pornography that had marked the previous report. Yet, it, too, must have seemed shocking: the details of the atrocities were still many, vivid, and quite infernal. What made it even more shocking was that this time, unlike the last time, as Lepsius showed in his discussion, behind the atrocities lay a definite intention to "systematically exterminate" the whole Armenian nation. Already the opening lines painted a stark picture: by now, they claimed, "six-sevenths" of the whole Armenian nation were either deported or dead.[14] Especially in connection with the logistics of the deportations, Lepsius made a forceful argument for establishing intent. If this really was intended as a resettlement scheme, Lepsius argued, and not an "extermination through deportation," then the Ottoman government would have at least made some effort to provide means of transport, food and drink, and security along the way, and would also have needed to make wide-ranging preparations at the terminus of the deportation. All of which, Lepsius stressed, had not been done.[15] He also forcefully rejected the interpretation that what had happened were spontaneous atrocities carried out by a population that had been exploited by the Armenians. Instead, he stressed that these were systematically executed measures that included the careful expropriation of property.[16]

In his report, Lepsius reprinted American consular reports and cited German consuls extensively. It is obvious that he had had access to the materials of both embassies in Constantinople. Besides detailing the horrors of the genocide, Lepsius also did his best to refute various myths about the Armenians in wartime Germany, for example the "myth" of the uprising at Van, and the German perception of the Armenians as quasi-Jews (Lepsius's emphasis on the fact that most of the Armenians had been farmers was aimed at the latter view).[17] The widespread currency of these myths he blamed in large part on the German press and its portrayal of the Armenians, which came in for particular criticism in many sections of his report.

Lepsius was not alone in lobbying for the Armenians at this time. Armin T. Wegner was also determined to speak out. Wegner, whom we have already met (Chapter 2 and Chapter 6), was a novelist who served as a field medic in the Ottoman Empire, where he witnessed the Armenian Genocide. He got this post, in Goltz's Mesopotamian expedition, due to his mother's friendship with the Tirpitz family—not unlike Humann. Wegner saw service not only in Mesopotamia, but also at Gallipoli, where he had witnessed the horrors of trench warfare, and, before that, at the battle of Tannenberg in Eastern Prussia, which was to become one of the main legendary German victories of World War I.[18] Wegner claimed later that his activities for the Armenians as well as his letters home from Turkey led to his being sent back to Germany permanently.[19] On his return from the Ottoman Empire in late 1915, Wegner was eager to meet with politicians and journalists in order to spread the word about the Armenians. He contacted such famous journalists as Maximilian Harden and Helmut von Gerlach, as well as other famous personalities such as Count Harry Kessler and the politician and later Weimar foreign minister Walther Rathenau. Perhaps due to censorship and the desire not to offend the Turkish ally, all Wegner's efforts were without success, at least for now.[20] One of the people he wanted to meet was Theodor Wolff, the famous German-Jewish liberal journalist who was to found the liberal German Democratic Party with Friedrich Naumann in 1919 and who was the editor in chief of the *Berliner Tageblatt*. Wolff, however, refused to meet him.[21] Later, in 1919, Wolff would publish Wegner's open letter to President Woodrow Wilson (see Chapter 9); but in 1915, Wolff was following the general press trend in Germany—not to see and not to hear. Wegner went on to contact Lepsius, Paul Rohrbach, and Martin Rade, the core of the Protestant pro-Armenian activists.[22]

• • •

Upon learning of the Armenian massacres, Paul Rohrbach—pro-Armenian activist and preeminent imperialist thinker—had written to Ernst Jäckh, the leading Turkophile imperialist and schemer, and announced that he had to quit the German Turkish Association. Rohrbach stressed, "Of course, I will and I must remain quiet for the course of the war in public, but I will confidentially disseminate Niepage's letter [discussed below] and as soon as we are again allowed to discuss the Armenian question in public, I will give a description of the events as truthfully as I can." He also later promised Jäckh that he and his colleagues would abandon their propaganda in favor of the Armenians for the duration of the war, and would try to persuade Lepsius to do so as well.[23] This alludes to Rohrbach's convictions and moral qualms—how to be pro-Armenian, pro-Ottoman, and utterly a German imperialist at the same time, and all during a world war. It also alludes to a pact between pro-Armenian circles and the German government as well as to the existence of other clandestine reports such as Niepage's letter to the Reichstag parliamentarians.

Martin Niepage was a teacher at a German school in Aleppo (in today's Syria), where he witnessed the Armenian Genocide in 1915. Aleppo was a major thoroughfare and Niepage was exposed to the horrors of the starved, violated, and half-dead deportees. In 1916, he sent a letter to the German parliament describing what he had seen. As a result he was sentenced to death by the Ottoman authorities, though this sentence was not carried out. The fact that Rohrbach distributed Niepage's letter suggests that he believed its contents. Niepage's letter included endorsements pertaining to the truthfulness of his claims by the principal of his school, the Aleppo German Technical High School, and other colleagues there.[24] Niepage, right in the first sentences, made it clear that what he had witnessed was "a new phase of Armenian massacres . . . which aimed at exterminating, root and branch, the intelligent, industrious, and progressive Armenian nation, and at transferring its property to Turkish hands."[25] Niepage also immediately ridiculed the notion of "military necessities." And he poured scorn on the idea that the Ottomans had done nothing more than mete out justified, proportionate punishment for genuine crimes of treason and sedition—on the contrary, he claimed: for one guilty person, 10,000 innocents were slaughtered. It was through slaughter and starvation that the government intended to "exterminate the whole nation"—a charge he repeated throughout his report.[26]

Niepage detailed the various horrors he had seen and heard of and contrasted this with his job—to educate and to spread German culture and knowledge—and with Germany's historical standing in the region. Now Germany was not only silently standing by but was largely held responsible for these crimes by (civilian) "Turks and Arabs" alike.[27] After all, such people would say, Germany was "Turkey's schoolmaster in everything." Niepage had talked to German consuls in the area, and the consul of Aleppo promised to forward Niepage's report to his superiors and even wanted to affix pictures he had himself taken. Niepage claimed that he had followed the reports of the consuls in the area when estimating the death toll, so far at one million.[28] But it was not only secondhand knowledge that was passed on here. Niepage stressed that he saw the horrors in the streets of Aleppo and that his very own students "were driven out to die of starvation in the desert."[29] He rejected the notion that Germany could not use its influence to stop the genocide, even at this late stage, and appealed to the members of the Reichstag to, at the very least, make available funds to save the remnants of the Armenian nation.[30]

Rohrbach had mentioned the Niepage report in his letter to Jäckh in order to protest the Armenian Genocide and Germany's acquiescence, as well as to announce his resignation from the German Turkish Association. It was extremely odd that he mentioned Niepage's letter to the Reichstag parliamentarians in his letter to Jäckh; indeed, it is hard not to suspect that he intended the consequences that followed, since they were quite predictable. After all, Jäckh was working at the censorship office, and he immediately passed Rohrbach's letter on to the relevant people in the office, with the result that Niepage's letter and the printed pamphlet versions were seized.[31] However, it is documented that, for example, Philipp Scheidemann, head of the Social Democrat parliamentary group, knew the contents of Niepage's report.[32] Niepage's report was discussed in early 1917 in the French press and then also in the quasi-official *Kölnische Zeitung*, which used the occasion not only to discredit Niepage and his report, but also to further attack the Armenians. It approvingly quoted an Englishman who had written that the Armenians "had brought their own extermination upon themselves."[33]

Another personal account of the genocide had been written by the former correspondent of the *Kölnische Zeitung* in Constantinople, Harry Stürmer. He had left the Ottoman Empire and fled to Switzerland, where he published his *Two War Years in Constantinople* (1917), which focused mostly on the Armenian topic.[34] His book began with a criticism of German warfare in general, in part by relating a story by a former comrade who had served in Belgium and who had placed illegal weapons in Belgian houses as pretexts for requisitions.[35] The main part of the book was devoted to the "great Armenian persecutions" and the Young Turks' "racial-chauvinistic bestiality."[36] Like Lepsius before him, Stürmer spoke of "extermination measures" *(Ausrottungsmassregeln).*[37] He detailed various massacres and described how the Armenians were systematically starved to death on deportation marches as well as in "concentration camps."[38] But he focused especially on what he saw as an overall plan to annihilate the Armenians. An important part of this plan, he argued, were the various accusations of conspiracy made against the Armenians—for example, that they were in league with the Russian enemy. These, he said, were a "cynical forgery" necessary for the Ottoman government to "execute its well-thought-out system to exterminate the entire Armenian race."[39] He believed this system originated personally with Talât Pasha, but he also believed the Germany government shared responsibility, "for the disgraceful deeds that they allowed the Turks to commit."[40] He also attacked both the press at home, and German officers serving in the empire, for the prevalence of anti-Armenian propaganda and beliefs.[41]

· · ·

It is not clear who had access to and who actually read Niepage's and Stürmer's reports. Both were in the end published abroad, Stürmer's in German in Switzerland, and Niepage's in English and Danish in London and in French and German in Switzerland.[42] Without a doubt, Lepsius's report had the widest reach within Germany. However, not unlike the dynamics of the 1890s in Germany, now again, it was not so much Lepsius's report that was to influence how the matter was discussed, mainly, but probably not exclusively, due to censorship. It was rather, again, a violently anti-Armenian pamphlet in the style of Hans Barth's 1898 pamphlet that won the contest of pamphlets on the Armenian topic. This time it was authored by C. A. Bratter and it was widely quoted and plagiarized in anti-Armenian articles in the press, both during the war as well as in the debates in the 1920s. It only differed from Barth's *Turk Defend Yourself* insofar as it acknowledged that there existed some "peaceful" Armenians as well, living as farmers.[43] Its main argument was that the Armenians were revolutionaries and had been utilized by Britain. As a consequence, the Ottomans had been acting perfectly understandably, and within their rights, to suppress them. Bratter, too, recapitulated the already well-established logic of Armenian atrocities: "The revolutionary Armenians are incited by England or Russia to uprisings, outrages, and treason." And then the exploited and bitter

Turks take their dreadful revenge.[44] What was taking place was yet another well-organized "atrocities" campaign by the Entente, Bratter stressed. It is not necessary to once more reproduce all the aspects of German anti-Armenianism, but it is worth stressing that for Bratter, too, all the current atrocities—which thus for him did exist, at least to some extent—were the Armenians' own fault and were somewhat well-deserved; it was Turkish self-defense.

And in Parliament . . .

Before turning to the German wartime press and how it discussed what was happening to the Armenians, our focus needs to be, briefly, on the Reichstag, German parliament. Although parliament was not a particularly powerful player in wartime politics, and its debates were held pretty much behind closed doors due to censorship, it is still important to see what happened with the topic there. It is not entirely clear what German parliamentarians knew about the Armenian Genocide at what point, and what their sources were. But as will be seen in the various 1918 sessions in which the Armenian topic was discussed, its members knew too much to believe wartime propaganda. Indeed, this was probably the case even as early as 1916. Among their sources was, of course, Lepsius's lecture in late 1915, as well as his clandestine report, which had probably reached many parliamentarians. And then there were also reports from a special rapporteur of the Reichstag and a trip by a parliamentarian delegation consisting of a few dozen members to Constantinople. Also, Matthias Erzberger (in the Weimar Republic, vice-chancellor and finance minister), as special emissary of the chancellor, and Gustav Stresemann (also a future chancellor) had traveled there in early 1916.[45] The list of people who journeyed to wartime Constantinople also included leading industrialists like Walther Rathenau, Hugo Stinnes, and August Thyssen.[46]

Very likely as a direct result of the activities of Lepsius, Christian Germany (both Protestant and Catholic) had submitted a petition to the chancellor on the Armenian question.[47] The German press reprinted the chancellor's answer in full: "The Imperial government, as it has done in the past and will continue to do in the future, regards it as one of its most noble duties to use its influence to ensure that Christian peoples are not persecuted because of their religion. German Christians may trust that I will do everything in my power to take into account the concerns and wishes thus presented to me."[48] The chancellor had done two things with his answer: First, he had mentioned neither the Ottoman Empire nor the Armenians directly. Second, he had restricted his promise to cases of persecution on the basis of religion—which, if one were to believe the Ottoman and German discourses, did not apply in the case of the Armenians anyway. Indeed, it had been almost two decades since any significant portion of the German press had thought the Armenians were being persecuted because they were Christian—and they definitely did not in 1915.

The chancellor's answer did not satisfy everybody. The famous Socialist leader Karl Liebknecht was obviously not so naive as to fail to understand that the chancellor had, in fact, rejected the petition in no uncertain terms. Liebknecht had apparently also spoken with Lepsius after the latter's return from Constantinople.[49] He too submitted a question to the chancellor in writing on 18 December 1915:

> Is the honorable Imperial Chancellor aware of the fact that many months ago the Armenian population in the Turkish Empire, our ally, were expelled from their places of residence and were butchered in the hundred thousands?
>
> What measures has the honorable Imperial Chancellor taken with respect to the allied Turkish government, in order to get it to atone for these events, to ameliorate the situation of the remainder of the Armenian population in Turkey and to prevent a repetition of similar horrors?[50]

In the scarce German literature on the topic, Liebknecht's question has often been mentioned, but the reaction to it has rarely been discussed. In fact, it resulted in the first "debate" about the genocide in the German parliament, though not a very propitious or edifying one. Yet, what was Liebknecht to expect from Chancellor Bethmann-Hollweg, who just the day before had noted (as discussed in Chapter 6), "The proposed public reprimand of an ally during an ongoing war would be a measure the like of which has never been seen in history. Our only goal is to keep Turkey on our side until the end of the war, regardless of whether Armenians perish because of it, or not."[51]

Almost a month later, on 11 January 1916, Liebknecht's question was read aloud in the plenum of parliament, and Ferdinand von Stumm, director of the political section of the Foreign Office, delivered the chancellor's answer:

The honorable Imperial Chancellor is aware of the fact that the Porte has been forced, due to the seditious machinations of our enemies, to transfer the Armenian population of certain areas, and to assign them new places of residence. Because of certain repercussions of this measure, an exchange of opinions between the German and the Turkish government is taking place. Further details cannot be disclosed.[52]

Then Liebknecht spoke, wanting to "supplement" his question. The reaction in parliament, as the official record reads, was "amusement" (Heiterkeit). Nonetheless, Liebknecht was allowed to speak, or at least to begin a sentence: "Is the honorable Imperial Chancellor aware of the fact that Professor Lepsius unequivocally speaks of an extermination of the Armenians..." What happened next is not clear. The record only reads, "Ringing of the President's bell—The speaker tries to continue to talk—Shouts: quiet! quiet! quiet!" It is not clear whether the bell was rung in response to the reaction of the other parliamentarians, or in response to what Liebknecht had said himself. In any case, the president of the Reichstag told Liebknecht that this constituted a new question, which he could not allow at this point. To this, Liebknecht wanted to raise a point of procedure: "Until the honorable president has listened to the question in its entirety, he will not be able to determine if it is a new question or not." Again he was interrupted by "amusement." Liebknecht continued, "Furthermore, I would like to stress that the honorable president did not come to [this conclusion] on his own"—interruptions "oho!"—"but rather that the house had to shout it to him." The president answered that he had no choice but "to refuse to tolerate" this critique of the way he conducted the business of the house, and moved on to the next inquiry (which was also one of Liebknecht's). This was greeted by the house with a "lively bravo." And this was all the Armenian Genocide got in the Reichstag in early 1916: laughter and an official "we do not care."[53]

Later in 1916, in September, the issue was raised again in the Reichstag's budget committee—the only place, at that time, where parliamentarians could have a real debate and, potentially, a slight impact on the government. A debate took place in which State Secretary Zimmermann claimed that Germany had done everything it could to help the Armenians, short of breaking the alliance; and this would be unthinkable as "more important than the Armenians . . . are our sons and brothers" dying on all fronts and dependent on the support of the Ottomans.[54] This response provoked the head of the Social Democrats (SPD) in parliament, Philipp Scheidemann, to write to the chancellor to complain about the lack of "satisfactory explanations" from the government. He asked the chancellor if they had, or would, press the Ottoman government to stop the slaughter. Again he received an evasive answer.[55]

Apart from these cases of direct attention, the (new) Armenian Horrors also occasionally received more glancing mention in parliament, showing that it was not taboo to speak of them. For example, Oskar Cohn, member for Nordhausen of the newly founded USPD, the Independent Social Democrats, submitted a question in May 1917 about the deportation of Jewish residents in Palestine because of "military necessities." He asked the chancellor if he was aware of this situation and if he would use his influence with the Ottoman government "so that a repetition in Palestine of the Armenian Horrors is excluded with certainty."[56]

It was only in 1918, when parliament discussed the Treaty of Brest-Litovsk, ending the war with newly established Soviet Russia, that the Armenians were on the agenda again. And it was again up to the Socialists; everyone else refused to take up the matter. Friedrich Naumann, in the Reichstag as a member of the Progressive People's Party, was one of them. The pastor and pro-Armenian activist Ewald Stier had urged him to use his influence in parliament and with the government to lobby the Ottomans to allow the creation of an independent Armenian state. Naumann's response was very much in line with the spirit of what he had written and said during the debate surrounding his book *Asia* twenty years earlier (see Chapter 3), though he now added new details in the form of a rather boldly callous argument. The pro-Armenianists, he contended, wanted us to believe that the Armenians had been wiped out. Now, suddenly, they were claiming that there were enough Armenians left to build a state. He was thus arguing that if there had indeed been something we today would understand as genocide, then obviously there was no point in a new state. But if there had not been a genocide, then the only scenario in which a new state would make sense would be if the Armenians were now in a majority in Eastern Anatolia; and if they were, then that would suggest that the Turks and Kurds who had settled there had been wiped out, presumably by the Armenians. So, in that case, the Armenians did not deserve a new state. Either way, then, there was no good case for an independent Armenia. In this rather flashy argument, Naumann was in fact overlooking the fact that there might be survivors deserving of some kind of protection. In any case, Naumann continued, it was naive to ask Germany to lobby the Ottomans to do something that was so obviously not in German interests: an autonomous Armenia would automatically lead to the loss of the Ottomans' Arab provinces, and thus to the end of empire for the Ottomans and the profound weakening of a crucial German ally. Humanitarian considerations—as he had also argued twenty years earlier—should never be allowed to trump Germany's political interests. Naumann flatly refused to help.[57] In the end, and not surprisingly, Naumann even chose to defend the Turks in the Reichstag.[58]

So, once more, it was left to the Socialists to introduce the topic of the Armenians into the debate on the Brest-Litovsk Treaty. The person who did so was Georg Ledebour of the USPD, in a long speech in the plenum on 19 March 1918. He observed that none of the delegates to the Brest-Litovsk Treaty negotiations had represented or considered the Armenians, and that this showed in the resulting treaty. In particular, Ledebour objected to a provision ceding the provinces of Ardahan, Kars, and Batumi back to the Ottoman Empire. He argued that there were no significant Turkish populations in these districts, but rather a mix of Georgians, Laz, and Armenians. Thus the Turks had no demographic claim to these provinces, only a historical one, which he, in the name of his party, utterly rejected. To cries of "very true!" by his fellow USPD members, he warned that "the Armenian and Georgian population of these areas were facing the danger of extermination if the Turks marched in."[59] He continued, "And this is not baseless conjecture—the Turks have now, in the war, virtually exterminated the Armenian population in the provinces [that had been] populated mostly by Armenians." His party reacted to this with a "Hear! Hear!" He continued, "The numbers on this vary. The exterminated Armenians are estimated from 500,000 to more than one million—exterminated by Turkish troops, by the ally of Germany!"

Two sessions later, on 22 March, it was the USPD member from Königsberg, Hugo Haase, who brought up the Armenians. Like Ledebour, he warned that territories with Armenian populations must not be handed over to Turkey. He also mentioned the testimony of the German teacher Niepage (discussed earlier in this chapter). He then recalled to the members of the Reichstag the testimony of Lepsius (which he implied that they were familiar with), which had included the claim that at the least a third of the deportees had died. He quoted Lepsius: "At the beginning of the deportation, the men were systematically separated from their families and battered to death on the way; the boys were either Muslimized or killed. Girls and women have had to suffer dreadful things." Here he was interrupted by a "Hear! Hear!" from the Independent Social Democrats. He continued to quote from Lepsius: "Mass butchering, kidnapping, forced Islamicization, plus hunger, superhuman exertion, and other deprivation transformed the megacaravans into a miserable heap of half-naked, sick, [and] dying women, children, and old people, who, when they reached their destination, could not find anything with which to sustain themselves any longer." This now was greeted by "outraged shouts" from the Independent Social Democrats. He then stressed that "even a Turk," Kemal Midhat Bey—grandson of the famous reformer Midhat Pasha—had issued a proclamation deploring this and calling for the abolishment of the current government. Again, there were calls of "Hear! Hear!" from the Independents. In short, Haase concluded, it was unthinkable that Germany should accept the responsibility of giving the Turks yet more Armenian territories.[60]

Most of these interventions in favor of the Armenians went unanswered in German parliament. Haase, however, received an immediate reply by fellow parliamentarian Gustav Stresemann of the National Liberal Party, future German chancellor and Nobel Peace Laureate. Stresemann began by claiming that the German government had always influenced the Ottoman government in a humanitarian direction: it was wholly without guilt in this respect and there was not much more that could have been done. "And furthermore," he implored Haase, "if you were giving an objective overview of the situation, you would have to acknowledge in what an extraordinarily difficult position militarily Turkey found itself because of the behavior of the Armenians in the border regions in the first months of the world war . . ." Here Stresemann was interrupted and the stenographic report noted, "Lively approval—dissent among the Independent Social Democrats—laughter among the National Liberals." He continued unfazed: ". . . and that it is because of these circumstances that it [Turkey] came into this situation—that is, took these measures—that later led to complaints."[61]

The reaction of the Independent Socialists and perhaps also the laughter among his own party suggest that by 1918 parliamentarians did not buy the official German and Ottoman propaganda anymore. Haase spoke once more that day, and challenged Stresemann's attempt to defend the Turks by quoting again from Kemal Midhat, this time at length. Midhat accused the Young Turk government of inventing accounts of Armenian revolutionary activity—in "more than one" pamphlet, he noted wryly—"because, after all this murdering of women and children, it was necessary to invent all kinds of indictments against the unfortunate Armenian people." But even if there had been some revolutionaries among them, Midhat continued, the government's job would have been to find them and prosecute them according to the law. "However, to kill or deport, to plunder, and then to butcher more than a million peaceful inhabitants and fellow citizens, who were convinced of their [own] innocence, is a deed that cannot be described by words and which we liberal and patriotic Turks condemn from the depths of our soul, [and] which the Islamic religion condemns in the harshest terms." Haase continued with his own commentary: "Thus writes a Turkish liberal, and it is telling that here in the German Reichstag, a German National Liberal is standing before us trying to excuse the Turks who have been charged with these crimes."[62]

A few months later, on 25 June, Stresemann spoke once more on the Armenian topic in the Reichstag. On the previous day the Reichstag's special rapporteur, Prince von Schoenaich-Carolath (of Stresemann's National Liberal Party), had also addressed the Armenian question in the plenum, on the one hand urging the Turks to show leniency, but on the other hand observing that perhaps the Armenians were not free of guilt as well.[63] Stresemann's tone, in responding to the prince the next day, was notably different from before. He now seemed to acknowledge, indirectly, the scale of what had occurred, by observing that "the relations between Armenia and Turkey are always, wherever they live together, tending toward reciprocal extinction." For him this seemed to be more a matter of "natural law"— unfortunate, but impossible to change—than a matter in which moral outrage would be appropriate. Still, he said, the tales from both sides made one question humanity. He acknowledged that the security of the villages in the treaty districts had to be ensured. Other than that, he made no concessions to his critics.[64]

Haase seems to have been responding to Stresemann's remarks when he spoke at the same session. Haase stressed that the Caucasian question was of the utmost importance, because "how it is answered will determine whether the Armenians shall be entirely abandoned to extermination." "Nobody who has heard them will probably be ever able to forget the shocking cries for help of the Armenians." He noted the Ottomans had massacred about 800,000 Armenians: "Here, in this house, members of various parties, including the rapporteur . . . Prince von

Schoenaich-Carolath, have depicted the inhumane fate this tribe has had to suffer and have denounced the brutal fashion with which this extermination has been carried out." He went on to narrate how the populations of various localities had been subject to pogroms and systematic massacres in the newly conquered Caucasian provinces.[65]

Only the USPD voted against the Brest-Litovsk Treaty; the SPD, though, abstained (though the Armenian topic was but one of many reasons). It is interesting to note that, although in parliament requests for the protection of the Armenians in the Caucasus were harshly rebuked by the representatives of the government, which in any case mostly let the parliamentarians speak among themselves on the topic, behind closed doors the mood was different. By the summer of 1918, even the German ambassador in Constantinople seems to have been firmly on the side of the Independent Socialists in parliament. He, too, suggested that German troops be sent as a buffer between the advancing Turks and the Armenians in the Caucasus, to protect the latter.[66]

· · ·

The tapestry of the German-Armenian nexus was woven with strange threads. Interestingly, Harry Stürmer had taken part as a volunteer in Germany's genocidal colonial war in Southwest Africa (1904–1907) against the Herero and the Nama people. Paul Rohrbach had also been there and had written extensively about it.[67] Stürmer explicitly blamed "Rohrbachian world politics" for Germany's imperialist interest in and blind support of the Ottoman Empire.[68] Interestingly also, one of the motivations for Niepage's report to the German Reichstag was the fact that the construction of a German-Turkish "palace of friendship," as Stürmer called it, had begun in Constantinople while, under the cover of war and by Germany's side, the Young Turks were "exterminating the Armenian nation." It is a dark coincidence that Friedrich Naumann, the author of *Asia* and thus the great justifier of Germany's blind eye, or rather of Germany's Armenian "blood money," gave a speech at the groundbreaking of the German-Turkish Friendship House in Constantinople in 1917, praising the greatness of the Young Turks.[69]

CHAPTER 8

What Germany
Could Have
Known

When we look at official, governmental Germany, the question of what Germany knew about the Armenian Genocide is easy to answer: it knew almost everything. In fact, it is safe to assume that no other government was as well informed about the genocide in progress as the German government, except, of course, for the Ottoman government itself. And the rest of German society? This is a more difficult question to answer. As we saw in Chapter 7, Johannes Lepsius had tried to educate Germany about the Armenian Genocide. His lecture at the Reichstag was addressed mainly to journalists, but parliamentarians probably also listened to it. His report had been sent out to journalists, parliamentarians, and all German Protestant pastors. Thus, by early 1916, much of "elite" Germany, too, was in a position to know quite a lot. What about the general public? This is another exceedingly difficult question, for one, because we can never be sure about who read what and how. For another, there was heavy censorship. And, indeed, current historiography claims that because of wartime censorship the German public did not know anything.[1] This myth has its origins in the claims of German journalists in the immediate postwar years (see Chapter 9). At that point, they tried to justify what they described as inaction and silence. Others, like Helmut von Gerlach, also exclaimed later that they were forced to be silent, but he meant something different. Gerlach had met with Armin Wegner after the latter's return from the Ottoman Empire, had wanted to speak out *for* the Armenians, and had not been able to do so. However, most of the German press, as we will see, was not so much silent as rather aggressively agitating against the Armenians—they "outdid each other in [their] enmity toward the Armenians."[2] This self-serving myth of forced silence—exonerating not only the German press but also German society—was accepted by many of the researchers working on the topic. It needs to be demolished here and simply cannot be upheld, as this chapter will show.

Given that the following answer—to the question of what the German public could have known—not only touches upon the broader question of German guilt and coresponsibility but also directly pertains to the discourses on the Armenian Genocide after the war, it is necessary and fruitful to sketch the press coverage in some detail here. This chapter discusses many of the highlights of the debate on the Armenians in the German wartime press and examines some articles in detail, as representative examples. If somewhat repetitive, the following exposition shows that there was indeed knowledge, awareness, and discussion—much more so than has thus far been acknowledged.

Maximilian Harden, an influential German journalist and writer, claimed after the war that he had overheard a "minion of the kaiser" tell the director of the war press office that he was transmitting the wishes of both General Headquarters and the kaiser when he said that nothing of the Armenian topic must reach the press.[3] For some reason, this was not to be the line of the censorship office. Perhaps it was just too unrealistic and too dangerous not to discuss the topic at all—in the end, it was a major topic of Entente propaganda, and Germany could not be hermetically sealed off from foreign news and newspapers. One of the censorship guidelines thus read, "The Armenian question must not be treated in a manner that is detrimental to Turkey. Publications on the topic are only permissible with the express consent of the High Censorship Office."[4]

The Russian Threat

The Armenian issue became prominent in German papers around the same time as the Ottoman Empire entered the war on the German-Austrian-Hungarian side, in late October 1914. As we saw in Chapter 5, even before that there had been general, intensive coverage of all things Ottoman and Muslim, as hopes ran high that Muslims everywhere would rise and join the "jihad made in Germany."[5] And "Armenia" would be central in the Ottoman Empire's struggle against Russia, the papers claimed. At first, this was meant in a rather literal geographical fashion.[6] The maps and the people at the time understood Armenia as the larger border region between the Ottomans and the Russians in the Caucasus.[7] Erzurum would be the focal point of Russian attacks—as was stressed from the early weeks of the war.[8]

The actual Armenians entered the German wartime press in the context of what the papers called "the latest Russian propaganda move." On 31 October 1914, it was reported that the Russian governor in the Caucasus had addressed an appeal to the Ottoman Armenians, promising that if they "did their 'duty' toward Russia, and if they united with their brethren under Russian suzerainty, their 'national aspirations would be fulfilled.'" The German papers condemned this as unwarranted meddling in Ottoman internal affairs, and approvingly quoted the Ottoman paper *Tanin*: "In one sole point we agree with the Russian decree for the Armenians. Indeed, it won't take long until the hour will come which will free the peoples from their yoke, living under the most miserable despot regime." It was, of course, Russian despotism that the Ottoman paper was talking about, which chimed nicely with German wartime propaganda against Russia, which also portrayed it as a cruel despotic regime.[9]

On 4 November 1914, it was Paul Rohrbach's turn, in the *Kölnische Zeitung*, to warn that Armenia and the Caucasus would now become a theater of war: "[The Armenian] provinces . . . used to be the gateway through which all the anti-Turkish influence crawled; disturbances arose partially through English pounds, partially through the rolling Russian ruble. The poor Armenians were the tool of the enemies of the Turks."[10] This situation appeared to have ended some years ago, Rohrbach explained, when Russia's relations with its own Armenian population soured; for a time there had been no more talk of a united Greater Armenia under Russian protection. Instead, Macedonia became the gateway for all pressure on Turkey. But today, he argued, Macedonia was no longer an apt tool for Russia and Britain against Turkey. His implicit suggestion was clear: the "gateway" was about to move back to Ottoman Armenia, and Armenians were about to become Russian and British "tools" again. And thus Rohrbach, otherwise a pro-Armenian activist, has the questionable honor of being the first author in a major paper during the war to portray the Armenians as potential traitors and Entente tools.

It is worth noting that Rohrbach was not, by far, the only one peddling images and fear of Armenian treachery in these early weeks of the war. One of the more lengthy treatments of the Armenian question during this period appeared in the Social Democrat *Vorwärts* in late November 1914.

Because the paper argued that the most important battles would be fought in "Armenia," as it had "been an object of conflict between Russia and Turkey for generations," it offered an expansive reading of the Armenian question.[11] In its rather reductive view, problems in Ottoman Armenia had their roots in the Russo-Turkish War (1877/1878), and specifically in the fact that invading Russians had been led by Armenian generals. This, the *Vorwärts* claimed, had inspired Sultan Abdul Hamid to commit acts of revenge against Ottoman Armenians, ushering in an "era of Armenian persecutions" that had grown in the 1890s into an "annihilatory campaign against a whole people." The resulting "butcheries" had gone on, the paper noted wryly, "without awakening any considerable echo in 'Christian' Europe." Also in the 1890s, the paper continued, Armenian land had been taken and given to Kurds, leading to the impoverishment of the Armenians, 85 percent of whom were farmers. And while the Young Turk revolution ended the era of butchery, it did not change the agrarian situation. This led to the disappointment of the Armenians, who had previously supported the Young Turk revolution. And this, in turn, the paper suggested, created an opening for the Russians, who, with the consent and approval of Britain, were aiming to advance their imperial goals by gaining territory throughout Armenia and Asia Minor. They would, as quotes from Russian politicians were thought to prove, now pursue "a total and radical solution of the Armenian question"—what this could mean, the paper did not spell out. Though the Russians had oppressed the Armenians living within their own borders, they now presented themselves as the "liberators" (scare quotes in original) of the Ottoman Armenians. In a sense, the Social Democrat paper tried to have it both ways: on the one hand, it acknowledged the terrible suffering of the Ottoman Armenians in the past, and offered a quasi-Marxist analysis of their economic conditions; yet, on the other, it stressed that the Armenians were making common cause with the Russians and that Armenia was one of the war aims of the Russians at this very point.

In its treatment of the Russians, the paper also offered a preview of what would be a common charge: that no Entente power really cared about the Armenians, and that any profession of such concern was just self-serving propaganda. Like other papers in these months, it recalled the Armenian massacres of the 1890s merely to point out either Entente hypocrisy, Russian intrigue, or potential Armenian treachery.[12]

Already by the end of 1914, then, the German press had introduced many of the themes that would come to dominate its wartime Armenian coverage. It added another worrisome topic in early 1915: population movement or "ethnic cleansing." In early January 1915, the papers reported on a lecture given by Professor Sachan, director of the Oriental Institute in Berlin. He had discussed the various ethnic groups in Anatolia, describing both the Armenians and the Kurds as mainly "diligent farmers" (thereby implicitly rejecting a central tenet of anti-Semitism-inspired anti-Armenianism, that all or most Armenians were parasitic city dwellers). However, he argued, ethnic cohabitation as it existed in the Ottoman Empire was a recipe for disaster: "The final and most important task [in the reform of the Ottoman Empire] is to remedy the misfortune of mixed settlement that today makes the various tribes tear each other to pieces. The only solution is the resettlement of the [non-Turkish] farmer population—the execution of which is both possible and necessary here, and for which legislative measures should be taken as soon as possible."[13] What was to happen to the city population of Armenians and other non-Turkish groups, he did not say. Yet, he clearly implied that now, during war, was a good time for such schemes of ethnic engineering.

The main context, though, in which the Armenians were mentioned in the war coverage of early 1915 was still that of the Russian threat. Now, a few months into the war, the picture of Russia's designs on Ottoman territory became ever more specific: they always featured "Greater Armenia" as the main prize, in case Constantinople itself could not be awarded to Russia, and they always were seen as threatening the very existence of the Ottoman Empire. A lengthy essay on the war in general, in the *Neue Preussische (Kreuz-)Zeitung* on 3 March 1915, predicted that the next major stage in the war would be fought in Ottoman and Russian Armenia, and then speculated about what Russia stood to gain there, taking the details, it said, from what Russian newspapers had been discussing for weeks. "It is good to know of even such farfetched ideas now," the paper wrote.[14] One of the plans—needless to say, opposed by the paper—was for a Greater Armenia that would include Cilicia as well as the Gulf of Alexandretta, thus cutting right through the Ottoman Empire down to the Mediterranean Sea. The paper also reported that some Ottoman Armenians were already fighting as volunteers on the Russian side—and that the British public were arranging collections for them. Some Ottoman Armenians, in other words, were not only potential traitors, but actual ones: they were already colluding not just in the defeat, but in the total dismemberment of the empire.

The Armenian "Stab in the Back"

It was in the context of this propaganda war that German readers got their first intimation, in May 1915, that many Armenians were now being killed in the Ottoman Empire.[15] By this time, atrocity propaganda had become a major aspect of the wartime press, with the German press especially battling against allegations of "Belgian atrocities" carried out by the German army (see Chapter 5). And, as we saw in Chapter 6, this was about two months after Scheubner had started to report to his embassy on events in Van and Erzurum. The German newspaper-reading public, however, was introduced to the topic of Armenians dying by a remarkable source: Talât Pasha, the Ottoman minister of the interior himself, in an interview conducted by Wilhelm Feldmann, printed in early May 1915 in the *Berliner Tageblatt*.[16] In the introduction to the interview, Feldmann alluded to recent reports of Ottoman atrocities in the Entente press, reminding readers that such reports were little more than enemy propaganda. As a corrective, Feldmann wrote, it would be good to hear from Talât about the attitudes of the various peoples of the Ottoman Empire since the beginning of the war. The first to be discussed were the Greeks, who, Talât stressed, were nothing but loyal. (Greece had not yet entered the war and was still being wooed by the Central Powers.) The Armenians, however, were a different story. According to Talât, they "pursued a goal that could only be realized through the disintegration of Turkey." There was even, he claimed, an Armenian master plan: "At the outbreak of war the Ottoman and Russian Armenians held a meeting and decided that the Caucasian Armenians would fight with the Russians against Turkey. The Ottoman Armenians, on the other hand, were to wait for a Russian advance." This went considerably further than the other accounts we have seen: the Armenians, according to Talât, were not merely potential tools, but, as a *whole,* were active and organized agents. This had left the Ottomans no choice, Talât claimed. The "removal" of the Armenians from the Eastern provinces, near the Russian frontier, had become a "military necessity." Further, the Entente landings at Gallipoli made the removal of Armenians from Western Anatolia necessary as well. And in both areas, that necessity had been further reinforced when searches of Armenian houses had "everywhere" revealed "rifles, ammunition, and bombs." Now came the remarkable revelations: Talât admitted that "during the transfer to Mesopotamia the Armenians were raided by Kurds and partially killed." Talât claimed that the Ottomans had tried and convicted some Kurdish leaders responsible for the atrocities. Besides blaming "some Kurds," Talât also admitted, "Unfortunately, in the execution of this disciplinary measure severe excesses took place because of inadequate officials."

Talât, feigning distress, continued,

> We are no savages. The reports of the sad events have kept me up many a night. The guilty officials have received the punishment they deserved. We have been blamed for not making a distinction between guilty and innocent Armenians. [To do so] was impossible. Because of the nature of things, one who was still innocent today could be guilty tomorrow. The concern for the safety of Turkey simply had to silence all other concerns. Our actions were determined by national and historical necessity.

It is worth noting that this is the same man who a few weeks later, as we saw in Chapter 6, would privately tell Mordtmann of the German embassy that the Young Turks intended to use the cover of the war to make a clean sweep of their internal enemies and, in particular, to annihilate all the Armenians. Not surprisingly, the gulf between what he was willing to say publicly and what he would admit privately was rather wide. Still, he did acknowledge publicly that Armenians had been slaughtered during the deportations; and he also made the remarkable claim that all Armenians were guilty because they could, potentially, be guilty. This interview itself was a strong indicator that something brutal and of broader scope was happening to the Ottoman Armenians.

While we cannot do a case-by-case comparison of what actually happened in Anatolia, what the consuls reported, and what the press decided to print, the German press coverage of early June 1915 astonishingly illustrates the gap between the reality in Anatolia and what was being described by the press in Germany. During this period, according to the press, the Armenians were rising up in many places across Anatolia, including in Erzurum; and yet, as we saw in Chapter 6, this was when Scheubner was reporting from Erzurum that the Armenians had kept quiet and then were being deported from the city en masse.[17]

In early June, German readers got their next exposure to the possibility that what was happening to the Armenians in Turkey might be more than just deportations accompanied by "accidental" atrocities, as Talât had suggested, but rather something more widespread, sinister, and intended or at least approved by the Ottomans. This time, though, it came from a source that, as we have seen, readers had been thoroughly schooled, or at least were expected, to distrust: an official statement from the Entente powers. German papers were allowed to reprint enemy proclamations and war reports, but, strangely enough, only in full.[18] And on 7 June 1915, many reprinted the following joint statement from the governments of France, Great Britain, and Russia:

> For approximately one month now the Turkish and Kurdish population of Armenia has been carrying out mass murders among the Armenians with the acquiescence and often with the support of the Ottoman authorities. In the middle of April such instances of mass murder took place in Erzurum, Terdshan, Eguin, Bitlis, Mush, Samsun, Zeytun and in all of Cilicia. The inhabitants of about one hundred villages in the vicinity of Van have been all murdered and the Armenian quarter [of Van] has been besieged by the Kurds. At the same time the Ottoman government went on a rampage against the defenseless Armenian population of Constantinople. In view of this new crime against humanity and civilization, the Allied governments are publicly announcing to the Sublime Porte that they will personally hold responsible all members of the Turkish government, as well as of its subsidiaries, who are taking part in such mass murders.[19]

Not surprisingly, the papers did not print this statement without accompanying comment. Even the headlines chosen were telling: in the *Neue Preussische (Kreuz-)Zeitung,* for example, the headline was "An Armenian Conspiracy," while in the *Berliner Tageblatt* it was "An Armenian Revolution." More importantly, though, in every case the statement was followed by the official Ottoman reply—sometimes identified as such (as in the *Berliner Tageblatt,* where the subheadline was "Official Turkish Declaration"), but in other cases not, so that it looked as though what followed was the paper's own commentary (as was the case in the *Neue Preussische [Kreuz-] Zeitung*). Either way, the substance of the reply was a fierce denial of the mass murder accusation:

> It is entirely wrong that murders or even mass murders of Armenians have taken place in Turkey. The Armenians of Erzurum, Terdshan,

Eguin, Bitlis, Mush, Samsun, Zeytun and of Cilicia have not even committed any acts that would have disrupted the public order or the public peace and that would have necessitated disciplinary measures from the government.

Strikingly, this denial seemed to backtrack on Talât's statement a few weeks earlier by denying that there had even been any murders at all. It did seem to imply, though, that "mass murders" would be among the legitimate "disciplinary measures" at the government's disposal: it was just that there hadn't (in those locations) been any call for them. In their comments, the German papers instantly started to blame the Armenians and to justify not-even-existent Turkish measures. So, for example, the *Neue Preussische (Kreuz-)Zeitung* argued,

> Anyone who is familiar with the circumstances knows sufficiently well that it is the agents of the Triple Entente, especially those of Russia and England, who are using any opportunity to stir up the Armenians to rebellion against the imperial government. These incessant machinations have intensified since the outbreak of hostilities between the Ottoman Empire and the abovementioned governments. . . . In light of these facts, it was the duty of the imperial government to use all the means in its legal powers to suppress the revolution. The imperial government thus saw itself forced to seek the military suppression on the one hand, and on the other to arrest revolutionary Armenians.[20]

From here on, the papers gave further details of the "Armenian revolution." They claimed that documents had been found proving that the Armenian revolutionary committees were supported by the Entente, and also that bombs and Russian rifles were found in searches in the provinces.[21] The *Berliner Tageblatt* stopped there, but the *Neue Preussische (Kreuz-)Zeitung* added further details: it described instances of Armenian treason and atrocities, whole villages massacred by Armenian volunteer bands, the derailing of trains, and open rebellion in various locations (Adana, Dörtyol, Jungurtalik, Alexandretta, and Zeytun—mentioning the last location directly contradicted the official Ottoman claim that nothing had happened there). It also accused Armenians of deserting the Ottoman army and attacking gendarmes, and added that a revolutionary Armenian congress had convened in Romania and had decided that the Armenians were to act as soon as the moment was opportune. And, finally, the paper also relayed a promise from the Ottoman government to make publicly available all the documents proving all these allegations—a frequent claim in the coming years.[22] The overall message was simple: though the mass murder charge was incorrect, and all the areas mentioned in the Entente statement had been (coincidentally) quiet, elsewhere in the country the Armenians were in open revolt, which would make any (vaguely specified) "disciplinary measures" imposed there by the Turks fully justified.

Two days later, on 9 June 1915, the "measures" were specified in the quasi-official *Norddeutsche Allgemeine Zeitung,* which reproduced a statement issued by the Ottoman government that the deportations were solely "temporary measures of relocation." Consul Rössler at Aleppo wrote the German chancellor that he could not believe his eyes when he read this and saw how much the German press was being manipulated by the Ottomans to spread their lies and propaganda.[23]

As for the Entente statement, readers of the German press continued to be reminded of it—and reminded to disbelieve it—for the rest of the month. On 17 June, it was the turn of the *Magdeburger Zeitung,* which ran a long front-page article on the Armenian question under the byline of a "Dr. Baron von Mackay." He dismissed the Entente note of protest as "the newest product of the well-known lie hatchery operated by our Entente friends."[24] But his focus was not so much to make claims about events within Turkey that might contradict the "lies" as it was to expose the real motives of the Entente powers in spreading them. He looked to history to pour scorn on the possibility that Russia and Britain might really care about the fate of the Armenians. During Abdul Hamid's reign, he claimed, Russia had actually intervened in Ottoman Armenia to encourage violence against Armenians: as he put it, the Russians "systematically fanned the embers of violence [against Armenians] that was commonplace under Abdul Hamid." This was because Russia, he claimed, wanted "Armenia, but without Armenians." Meanwhile, Britain in the same period had pretended to stick up for the Armenians while secretly doing its best to use the Armenians to weaken and ultimately break up the empire. Now, he claimed, what was behind the Entente note wasn't genuine concern either, but, as always, a desire to stir up trouble. The rejuvenation of the Ottoman Empire under the Young Turks and their military successes were motivating the Entente to "again fan the embers at the Armenian fire pit to attack Turkey from behind its back"—especially now that the Entente had suffered such blows as the Gallipoli disaster. Mackay repeated the familiar claim that the very existence of the Ottoman Empire was at stake: while taking Constantinople would mean a blow to the "head of Turkey," taking the Armenian provinces would be a deadly stab to the Turkish heart.

On 23 June 1915, it was the turn of the *Münchner Neueste Nachrichten* to respond to the Entente note of protest, in this case with an article headlined "The Armenian Revolts," by Franz Carl Endres, a German officer with the Ottoman General Staff. Like Mackay in the *Magdeburger Zeitung*, Endres questioned the motives behind the Entente statement, in his case focusing specifically on the role of the British. He claimed that since the Dardanelles (Gallipoli) campaign was not going well, the Entente wanted to open up wounds in the interior of the country: "I think that all of this is a typically English idea. England has for decades brought the Armenians into uproar whenever it needed some sort of concession from Turkey, and the Armenians actually fell for this English bluff in the years from 1889–1896."[25] Endres summed up: "It is the old tune, the tune of English intrigue in the Orient."

Unlike Mackay, however, Endres also considered the substance of the Entente accusations, adding detail to the original Ottoman response that, as we have seen, denied mass murder but justified "harsh measures." Mass murder of Armenians was unthinkable in the new Turkey of the Young Turks, Endres claimed. Though cruel butchery of Armenians had occurred in the past, today the " 'Committee of Union and Progress' [the Young Turks] speaks the decisive word, mass murder of the Armenians is simply an impossibility." And: "Everybody who knows Talât Bey and Enver Pasha personally has to laugh at this swindle by *Havas*." (The *Agence Havas* was a major French news agency.) Endres had personally seen, he claimed, how hard the Turkish government worked to appease and include (into the nation) the other ethnic groups. But with the Armenians, he wrote, these efforts were not always rewarded: for while there were some Armenians who sought to integrate into the Ottoman Empire and participate fully, there was another group that was either just fanatically Armenian or bought by British gold, opposing the empire and committing treason. This was in spite of the fact, he argued, that anyone, even an Armenian, with any geographical knowledge knew that the revolutionaries' goal, a unified, autonomous Armenia, was "a wholly impossible desire," the reason being that the Armenians were divided into three parts, one Turkish, one Russian, and one Persian. (The fact that this situation was similar to that of the Poles he did not mention.) Moreover, even in Turkey, Armenians were not concentrated in one area: "Armenians—especially the intelligentsia and the rich—live dispersed in the whole empire, as the Jews do in Europe, and so would gain nothing from autonomy for Armenia." Endres emphasized that there were some Armenians who sought to integrate into the Ottoman Empire and participate fully. Yet, a group of Armenians persisted in rebelling against the empire; and, faced with this, the Ottomans were justified in replying with "harsh measures": "if the Turkish government has now taken harsh measures, nobody can reproach it." (As in earlier articles, the nature of these "measures" remained vague.) Endres claimed that he had witnessed the spy activities of Cilician Armenians firsthand, and had been surprised by how lenient the Ottomans were "with these traitors." He asked, "If under these circumstances a Turkish patriot—[and] this has not [yet] been proven—got hold of an Armenian traitor and killed him without ado, what would it matter?"

In the meantime, other papers as well were ramping up their charges against the Armenians. A new theme entered the coverage: that the Armenians themselves were mass murderers—of their Muslim fellow citizens. According to the *Neue Stuttgarter Tageblatt* and the *Leipziger Tageblatt*, the Armenians had massacred 150,000 Muslims at Van.[26] There were similar, though less specific, claims in the *Berliner Tageblatt*, which on 14 July published the response of the official Ottoman news agency, *Agence Milli*, to an article in the Swiss *Gazette de Lausanne*, which had claimed that the "Ottoman government was giving its protection to riots against the Armenians living in Turkey, and that these riots often amounted to slaughters."[27] The response of the *Agence Milli* was that "those who are in the pay of our enemies always employ the same wretched means. We think it useless to refute such absurdities."[28] The *Agence Milli* then continued by asking "these papers" what they would do if their conationals rose up against their fatherland, deserted to the enemy and then fought their brothers who were still fighting for the fatherland. "This is the case with these Armenians who are being celebrated as heroes and martyrs, while they themselves are the cause and means of gruesome outrages that have been committed by them and their coreligionists against the Muslim population of our Eastern provinces." In a lengthy article on the "Turkish Awakening" also published on 14 July, the *Rheinisch-Westfälische Zeitung* described, among other things, that after an initial thaw in ethnic relations after the Young Turk revolution, "the Ottomans of the Christian tribe [here meaning the Armenians] went back into their mountains, grabbed their rifles once more, and [began] as usual to kill their Muslim fellow citizens."[29] This was recounted in a matter-of-fact and incidental fashion, as if it were common knowledge that Armenians often, if not usually, kill Muslims.

Over the summer and into September 1915, though coverage slowed down somewhat, the papers continued to provide a platform for the official Ottoman position. In July, the German papers, the *Neue Preussische (Kreuz-)Zeitung* and the *Deutsche Tageszeitung* among them, felt they had to print "The Truth about the Armenian Rebels." What followed sounded like an official Ottoman declaration:

> The imperial government some time ago announced the measures regarding the removal of the Armenians from their homes where their presence was thought to be detrimental and dangerous for internal security and peace and for national defense. Our enemies have found in this yet another pretext by which to influence public opinion against us. Their papers, as well as those of the neutral countries they have been able to win over, are trying to cover up the truth, and claim that the Armenian element is utterly innocent, and that its elementary, natural, and holy rights have been violated.[30]

The reality, the statement continued, was very different: the Ottoman government had been forced to such a harsh stance against "the revolutionary Armenians." Daily, it claimed, the military authorities were finding new proof that the Armenians were joining the fight on Russia's side, and were doing so according to a long-standing, detailed plan. This "illegal and revolutionary break-away movement," formerly restricted to the front and adjacent locations, was now spreading to the rear of the front. The report then recounted various atrocities committed by rebel Armenians, and noted that the military had been forced to divert troops from battle with the enemy in order to suppress the internal rebellion. This all led to a situation in which

> the imperial government had to take certain preventative and restrictive measures. As a consequence of the execution of these measures these Armenians have been removed from the border areas and from the rear of the front. In this fashion they have been removed from the more or less effective influence of the Russians and thus they have been rendered incapable of damaging the higher interests of the country's defense and domestic security.

And thus, without comment from either of the two papers, this identically reprinted article closed.

The theme of the Armenian stab in the back was reinforced with a series of articles. One came in the form of an op-ed by an Ottoman diplomat based in Germany, Halil Halid Bey, on 2 September. In an article with the sardonic title "On the Wrong Horse" in the *Berliner Tageblatt,* he explained how it had come that the Armenians had bet "on the wrong horse"—the "horse" in question was the Entente, whose Gallipoli campaign had become stuck in trenches for months:

> The policy of protecting this or that Christian community in Turkey had been mainly a Russian strategy. . . . More than twenty years ago England began to copy Russian policy, by beginning to sustain and promote the Armenian revolutionary movement in Turkey. A worldwide agitation in favor of the Armenians was initiated and British diplomacy worked to stage a crusade against Turkey.[31]

All the while, Britain's and Russia's goal was to "lay hands" on Egypt and other Muslim lands, and break up the empire. As so many other articles had insisted, Halid exclaimed the empire faced a threat to its very existence—and inciting Armenian revolution, allegedly, was just as much a part of British and Russian military strategy as the Gallipoli and Caucasus campaigns.

The "Horrors Razzmatazz"

In early October 1915, the Armenian issue burst into prominence again in the German press, and by now the interpretation of the Armenians stabbing the Turks in the back had strongly taken root. On 4 and 5 October, the papers discussed a report from the French *Agence Havas* that President Wilson had made a formal request to Germany, through its ambassador, that it get Turkey to stop the "massacres of the Armenians." According to the report, President Wilson had already tried several times, through the American ambassador in Constantinople, to appeal to the Ottoman government directly; and he was now drawing the attention of Germany "as well as all other nations" to "the conditions in Armenia." According to the report, his government was also about to initiate an aid program, run through its embassy, by which "the fleeing Armenians" would be able to travel to America.

The *Neue Preussische (Kreuz-)Zeitung* took a well-worn line of response, not addressing the substance of the charges, but instead accusing the Americans of hypocrisy. America, it said, "had [ample] opportunities much closer to home to show its sense of humanitarianism. While it installs the Monroe Doctrine [proscribing intervention by European powers in the Americas], it still feels well entitled to meddle in the interior matters of other states."[32] The *Deutsche Tageszeitung* offered a more elaborate reply that verged on the hysterical. It sarcastically posed a question in its headline—"For the Armenians?"—and answered with an implicit but nonetheless resounding "of course not!"[33] It saw the news about the request to Germany (and the implicit assumption of the Armenians being in need of protection) as another Entente lie, "because, for the time being, such a request hardly seems credible." Much more credible, according to the paper, was that the British were again using "any (and every) measure [taken] by the Turks against Armenian unrest" as part of their propaganda war against the Ottoman Empire, "by using tried and trusted methods."

> For many years now the "Armenian Horrors" have been a stock piece of inventory of British and Russian politics, used to meddle in the internal affairs of Turkey and to weaken it. What has typically happened is that Russian and English emissaries, equipped with the necessary cash, have approached the Armenians and incited them to riot against Turkish rule; if the Turkish government has then stepped in, the British-Russian "cultural world" has shouted: Armenian "horrors!" . . . England and Russia have always used this device of humanitarian sentimentalism with characteristic consistency and skill, and only a few years have passed since German women, deeply moved, took a strong and helpful interest in the Armenians—men, women, and children.

But not only was "humanitarian concern" a tool of selfish British and Russian ends, according to the paper, the Armenians did not even *deserve* humanitarian concern anyway. Launching into an extraordinary racist rant, the paper raged,

> The Armenian is known in the Orient as a cunning exploiter, and a leech on the Ottoman population. The Ottoman, on the other hand, is unsuspecting and good-natured, thereby making an exceedingly convenient object of exploitation—up to a certain point and degree. Then despair overtakes him and he rises up violently against his tormentors. However

regrettable such lawless self-help might be by itself from the point of view of civilization, it is obvious that precisely the Armenians [of all the ethnic groups] are the least worthy of the compassion and emotional uproar of the civilized world. This is true even in peacetime, let alone under the current circumstances.

The *Deutsche Tageszeitung* concluded by printing the following part of its commentary in bold:

> It is of course out of the question for the German Empire to meddle in the domestic affairs of our Turkish ally at the request of a third power. If the ruling authorities in Turkey think it is time to take action against the unreliable, bloodsucking, and rebellious Armenian element, then it is not only the right, but the duty of the Turkish government to do so. Especially in wartime, it would be folly to treat such elements with kid gloves. In any case, Turkey can rest assured that the public opinion of the German Empire agrees: this matter concerns only the Turkish Empire.

But the *Deutsche Tageszeitung* was only warming up, and the next occasion to attack the Armenians and justify violence against them was just five days away. In the meantime, the press had, however, received new instructions from the censorship office. On 5 October, Johannes Lepsius had spoken in the Reichstag, in front of the press (see Chapter 7), on the Armenian Genocide. The censorship office reacted swiftly and issued the following order topic only two days later, on 7 October:

> About the Armenian Horrors the following is to be said: Our friendly relations with Turkey must not only not be endangered by these inner-Turkish administrative issues, but in the current, difficult situation not even be examined. This is why, for the time being, it is one's duty to be silent. Later on, if direct attacks in relation to "Germany's coresponsibility" are leveled from abroad, the topic will need to be handled with greatest care and restraint and it will be necessary to constantly stress that the Turks had been severely provoked by the Armenians.[34]

Those "attacks in relation to 'Germany's coresponsibility,'" which the censorship office expected "later on," supposedly in some distant future, were to come sooner than anticipated: indeed, they came that very day, 7 October 1915, in the form of a discussion in the British House of Lords. Overeagerly anti-Armenian papers like the *Neue Preussische (Kreuz-)Zeitung* saw and seized the censor's cue. The next day, on 8 October, the *Kreuzzeitung* began the discussion of the "Armenian Debate in the English Upper House." The debate there had been led by Lord Bryce. His name alone signaled that whatever would follow was typical British propaganda (at least for most readers): He was already well known to the German reading public as the author of the *Bryce Report* on German atrocities in Belgium *and* he had been active for the Armenians since the 1890s.[35] Lord Bryce had presented his information on the Armenian massacres. Before dismissing what was said in the House of Lords as lies and empty enemy propaganda, the German papers did give an overview of some of the claims by Bryce and others during the debate—so the German public would have been exposed, for example, to Bryce's estimate that 800,000 Armenians had died, and that in some districts the entire population of Armenians had been annihilated; they would also have been exposed to queries by other peers about whether these numbers could be believed (in particular, the skepticism of Evelyn Baring, the Earl of Cromer, was widely reported). And finally, they were exposed to the sort of accusations against Germany that the censorship office had anticipated just one day before: accusations that it must share responsibility. To all this, the *Neue Preussische (Kreuz-) Zeitung* responded with its favorite charge: "Again another piece of true English hypocrisy. The noble Lords forget to tell the world that the victims are the result of an uprising that the Armenians had started after Turkey's entry into the war. The English Lords had nothing to say about the innocent victims of the Russian devastation tactics [employed in the East]."[36] To the specific charge that German consular officers had instigated the Turkish population to commit these atrocities against the Armenians, the *Neue Preussische (Kreuz-)Zeitung*, now citing the *Kölnische Zeitung*, replied on the next day: "Similar [wretched] lies . . . circulate in the English press. It is obvious why there are efforts in England to shock the world right now with [tales of] new German atrocities. The fairy tales from Belgium are not effective enough anymore."[37] This echoed the critique of the satirical paper *Kladderadatsch* in the 1890s that the Armenian Horrors were just propaganda and were merely a replacement for the now ineffective Bulgarian Horrors (see Gladstone's Armenian balloon, Chapter 2).

The *Deutsche Tageszeitung* replied in the same near-hysterical vein it had exhibited in relation to the Wilson charges. It gave its story another of its sardonic headlines: "The Razzmatazz about the 'Armenian Horrors' Begins" *(Der "Armeniergreuel"-Rummel beginnt)* and elaborated in the article, "It appears that the curtain is rising on another large 'Armenian-Horrors razzmatazz,' with all the usual mechanisms."[38] Once again, in other words, Britain was trying to stir up worldwide frenzy about the fate of the Armenians for its own purposes. It reported that the United States was threatening to break off diplomatic relations with Turkey if the "Armenian 'murders'" did not stop. The paper expressed its hope that the Turks would not be intimidated—and continue with murdering Armenians? one might ask. Yes, the paper continued,

> If [the Turkish government] thinks it is necessary that Armenian uprisings and other machinations be suppressed by all available means so that a repetition can be prevented, then these are no "murders" and no "horrors" but rather are measures of a justified and necessary nature [rest of sentence in bold]—even more justified and more necessary as today the Turkish Empire stands in the most difficult struggle for existence it has ever faced and has [already] foreign enemies enough. To demand that it nurture an internal enemy in its bosom as well, just to please the English and the Americans, is a bit much to ask.

Too long, the paper argued, had the Ottomans suffered foreign meddling in their affairs. These times were now over: "and they will remain over, as long as the German Empire resolutely stands by the conviction that what it [the Turkish state] chooses to do with the rebellious and bloodsucking Armenians is an internal matter that concerns only its [Germany's] Turkish ally" (all set in bold). This was a blank check and was meant as such.

After this, the *Deutsche Tageszeitung* ventured into cross-paper debate. Its target was the *Frankfurter Zeitung*, which had printed long justifications of the anti-Armenian measures, and had also defended the conduct of the German consuls, insisting that rather than inciting violence (as had been claimed in the House of Lords), they had tried to alleviate the hardship of the Armenians. The *Deutsche Tageszeitung* answered, "We not only do not understand this attempt at justification [of Ottoman and German actions], but think it is politically wrongheaded." The paper claimed that even to offer explanations of Turkish state conduct (which it had just done itself) was to begin a conversation about a matter that was a domestic Turkish affair. To begin such a conversation was "tactless" and would only serve the Entente: it would drive a wedge between Germany and Turkey. And finally, on the claims about Germany sharing responsibility, "We should think there is nobody left in Germany today who cares if another couple of cartloads of 'horrors' are dumped onto our slate. It is indeed totally irrelevant." The last year had shown, the paper continued, how fast lies can travel (the Belgian atrocities being the implied example). The paper proclaimed, "The place of the German Empire, and of each and every German, is by the side of our Turkish ally, and without criticism at that" (all set in bold). It railed against the naive people who were falling prey to the Armenian propaganda, and singled out "professorial soul mates of the Armenians."

Three days later, on 12 October, the *Frankfurter Zeitung*, which, as we might remember, was formerly a strongly pro-Armenian paper, printed another long article on the Armenian topic; perhaps it saw itself as challenged by the *Deutsche Tageszeitung*'s critique. It echoed the charge in other papers that Britain was now trying to stir up concern for the Armenians for its own purposes, and had done so in the 1890s as well. Both cases, according to the paper, were in fact examples of a long-standing British strategy apparently applied all over the world, not just in Armenia:

> The recipe is simple enough. England has always been willing to make the fate of the oppressed her own cause—yes, in most cases it created such "oppressed" [peoples] with her agents in the first place, in order to then have the right, in the eyes of others, to meddle, and to gain the greatest advantage for herself. So it is in the Armenian question. It is nothing else but the little door through which England may freely enter Turkish [internal] politics—a door that England has zealously kept open. England even went so far as to tell the poor and unknowing Armenian people, through its agents, that the English army would come to its aid in zeppelins and destroy the might of the [sultan]—only . . . the Armenians had to begin the revolution first [on their own].[39]

It was a fact, the paper claimed, that during the war Armenians had undertaken a range of treasonous actions, all with Britain as paymaster: they had spied for the Russians in the province of Erzurum and the French at the Mediterranean coast, and had been involved in a plot in Constantinople destined to topple the Ottoman government. The paper then turned to the recent alleged massacres themselves, taking the line that if any deaths had occurred, they were the regrettable but understandable work of the mob, not the state. The Armenian, the paper asserted, "is the most hated man of all the Orient—thanks to his higher intellect and higher commercial abilities, he constantly takes advantage of the cumbersome Turk as merchant, tax farmer, banker, and agent, and becomes rich while the Turk is impoverished." As a result, it would be "totally understandable if the uneducated population in Anatolia, led by half-educated officials, fanatical clergymen, and unreflecting chauvinists, had fallen victim to such generalizations, and had beaten to death, guilty and innocents alike." The paper asked its readers—as other papers were doing at this time—to imagine what the French would do if there was a tribe living among them that openly sympathized with the Germans. And in the Ottoman Empire, with the army away at the front, the paper continued, it was impossible for the government to prevent such events in its interior. The paper described the situation as one of "lynch law": implying that something like law or retribution was at work. The paper did not speculate on the possible number of deaths, apart from dismissing the estimate of 800,000 as "impossible." As many papers had, it approvingly noted Lord Cromer's skepticism about this figure, and added,

> Nobody who is familiar with the situation in Turkey would believe such numbers [that is, 800,000]. With such a number more than 30 percent of all Armenians living in Turkey, including women and children, would have been killed. This is totally impossible.

Still, the paper went on, if even only a few innocents had been killed, Germans would be genuinely distressed; the real crime of the Entente was to suggest that German consuls had actually helped the mob with its atrocities.

As the *Deutsche Tageszeitung* had foreseen (in different terms), now indeed a broad Armenian debate ("razzmatazz") began, and even the provincial press participated. On 12 October, two regional papers, the *Pfälzer Volksbote* and the *Pfälzische Volkszeitung*, had also printed lengthy commentaries on the latest accusations from Britain. In the *Pfälzer Volksbote*, it was the charges against Germany in particular that had touched a nerve. The debate had already progressed, and this resulted in an angry opening sentence in the *Pfälzer Volksbote* about the fact that the House of Lords had dared to claim that German consular officials had encouraged atrocities against the Armenians and that the enemy press had asserted that Armenians had been slaughtered by the hundreds of thousands "in the name of the kaiser." The *Pfälzer Volksbote* angrily dismissed these both as enemy lies: they were just the latest in a string of such lies, invented, as other papers had also claimed, now that charges of atrocities in Belgium and France were losing their effectiveness. As others frequently did in these months, the paper sniffed that refuting "these ridiculous claims" would be "beneath our dignity."[40] The *Pfälzer Volksbote* went on to claim that Armenian community leaders had urged the Armenians to be loyal Ottomans: "But English and French gold turned out to be stronger." The familiar accusations that the Armenians themselves were mass murderers reappeared again here in even more sensational form: the paper claimed that, "according to reliable reports," the Armenians had murdered more than 1.5 million Turks, in the rear of the Turkish army fighting the Russians. In this "time of such an existential struggle," the Armenians had proven themselves to be the worst enemies of the Ottoman Empire. And while "retributionary measures" *(Vergeltungsmaßregeln)* were always horrible, this was "avenging justice" that just could not be held accountable to notions of "sentimental humanitarianism." "The blood that has flowed in Armenia is a gruesome indictment against those [that is, the Entente] who have driven this unlucky people to riots and high treason." The paper continued that a year ago, in Belgium, the Germans had seen how firmly an army had to act in order to protect itself when the enemy civilians decided to turn against it; and that then, Germany had been the target of the same accusations as the Ottomans were facing now. "Like today, there was then not a word of reproach against the perfidious and murderous population [that is, the Belgians] which, like the Armenians now, were instead celebrated as heroes [by the Entente press]." Then, switching tack, it recounted all the horrors that had befallen the German soldiers and population at the hands of all "the wild peoples" that the Entente had chosen as their allies—Belgian *francs-tireurs* as well as Russian and "African hordes" were singled out especially. It asked if these "soft-hearted" Entente humanitarians really believed that Germany's civilian population would have fared any better than the Armenians, had the "African and Asian hordes" been let at them.

On the same day, an even longer article on the same topic ran in the *Pfälzische Volkszeitung,* the *Pfälzer Volksbote*'s regional companion. After glancing briefly at the recent charges against Germany—which, the *Pfälzische Volkszeitung* approvingly noted, the *Norddeutsche Allgemeine Zeitung* had already shown to be "ordinary lies"—the paper turned to the main charge against the Turks. So, the paper asked, had no Armenian murders taken place at all? Had they sprung purely from the realm of fantasy? "Certainly not," the paper answered, "but what happened in Armenia was nothing more than a well-earned castigation, that had been necessary to protect state interests."[41] The paper explained this conclusion by making the familiar point about the Armenian stab in the back: encouraged by "countless" British and Russian spies and agitators roaming the country, the Armenians had revolted at the very moment when Turkey was engaged in a struggle for its existence, and had directly caused significant military reverses. At the time, the Turks had been advancing on the Suez Canal, in the Caucasus, and in Persia; but they had been forced to withdraw a considerable proportion of their troops to quash the Armenian rebellion and restore order. Thus, what the Armenians had committed was "one of the most nefarious acts one could think of"; it was an act of high and state treason *(Hoch- und Landesverrat)*. In light of this, anything that happened to them afterward could not be considered a crime, the paper claimed. Again, another blanket justification for the murder of civilians, given that a group as a whole was considered guilty.

But let's return to the national press, where the flurry of articles provoked by the recent accusations from abroad still showed no sign of slowing down. On 14 October, just five days after its last article on the subject, the *Neue Preussische (Kreuz-)Zeitung* yet again discussed the "Armenian Lies of the English Press." This article was a response to an article in the London *Times* by its Cairo correspondent about the "so-called Armenian Horrors." In the *Times* article, the massacres were painted in the most terrifying colors and, again, the German consuls were identified as the instigators and leaders of these massacres. The *Kreuzzeitung* declined to discuss the *Times'* main claims, but focused on one detail: according to the *Times,* the former Ottoman minister of public works, an Armenian, had been deported and killed. The *Kreuzzeitung* wrote, "Well, there's a mishap for the poor *Times.*"[42] The former minister, the paper claimed, was in Berlin studying the German taxation system: "We want to give the *Times* some advice: they should limit their future atrocity reports to more general descriptions and, as compensation to their readers, make them a bit more gory. But they should be much more careful about stating facts, especially names."

A day later, on 15 October, several national papers, including the *Vossische Zeitung* and the *Neue Preussische (Kreuz-)Zeitung* (the latter copying from the former), printed another article on "The Conspiracy of the Armenians." These articles reported on an interview the "leader of the Young Egyptians," Dr. Rifaat, had given to the Danish *Extrabladet*.[43] He claimed the Turks had been forced to take "reprisals" in Armenia: "The massacres were not being pursued because of a reckless lust for the annihilation of the Armenian nation, but because England had incited a wide-reaching conspiracy, including roughly speaking all the Armenians living in Turkey, in order to begin a great uprising as soon as the Allied fleet entered the Straits."[44] Thus Rifaat actually acknowledged that there had been "massacres," though he claimed they were justified, and even spoke of the alleged "annihilation of the Armenian nation." Talât Pasha, Rifaat claimed, was the "best friend and protector of the Armenians." He would not have taken such measures, if they had not been necessary: "The English had prepared the insurrection very carefully. The Armenians were equipped with weapons and ammunition in [great] quantities, even with police uniforms for the provisionary government to be set up by the Armenians." Unfortunately, for the Armenians, the revolt had begun too early and had been betrayed to the authorities. Furthermore, Rifaat alleged, there were numerous documents in the hands of the Ottomans proving that it had been the British who had organized this "greatest known uprising in the history of Turkey." This conspiracy also involved, Rifaat claimed, various Arab sheikhs. He reiterated that "Turkey was solely acting in self-defense." This was no "local conspiracy," but one threatening the very existence of the empire, with the goal, among others, of delivering Constantinople to the Entente. "The cries of woe about the cruelties in Armenia, ringing out in England, are being sounded just for political reasons; this Armenian blood is on the hands of the English." The papers seem to have agreed with him, which is suggested by the fact they let his words speak for themselves, without adding further commentary.

The debate continued. On 18 October, it was the turn of the *Kölnische Volkszeitung* to respond to Entente allegations about the Central Powers being "the carriers of Barbarism." It did not, in stark contrast to the other papers, attack the Armenians specifically, but rather condemned "the Christian peoples of Turkey" in a global fashion, this despite being the paper of German political Catholicism. It wrote, "It must not be forgotten here that it was specifically the Christian peoples of Turkey who had been used by England, France, and Russia as their advance force in pursuing their selfish plans, and as a humanitarian pretext for the dismemberment of Turkey" (all in bold).[45] While in the next sentence the paper was willing to admit that the situation of the Christians there was not "enviable," it again stressed that it was the fault of the Entente and that any problems in the relations between the Turkish government and the Christians there were "an internal affair of Turkey." This article also featured the slogan, "What weakens Turkey, weakens us too, and vice versa." The *Kölnische Volkszeitung* also agreed with Naumann (see Chapter 3) that foreign policy ought to be free of Christian and moral considerations. Yet, the paper of the German Catholics went even further: it hinted that most Armenians were not "real" Christians anyway, because they were not Catholic. Writing about the number of Christians in the Ottoman Empire, it said it was "either big or small," depending on how one wanted to look at it; there were about 700,000 Catholics in the empire, plus an even greater number of "schismatic Christians" (the category that included most of the Armenians). Only if the schismatics were counted was the number "big." Thus the paper implied that the Armenians' status as Christians was borderline; strictly speaking, they were not really Christian at all. The implication was clear: Why should "we" care what happened to them anyway?

Before addressing the Armenian issue again directly, the *Neue Preussische (Kreuz-)Zeitung* and other papers printed many articles presenting lists of accusations of violations of international law against the Turks by the Entente.[46] On 28 October, the *Kreuzzeitung* addressed "The True Purpose of the Armenian Disturbances," as announced by the headline.[47] Quoting the Turkish embassy, it reported that the Armenians had staged another insurgency (in mid-September). In Urfa, the paper claimed, Armenian insurgents had attacked gendarmerie units, taken control of the city, plundered "foreign" property, and, finally, started to massacre local Muslims. The Ottoman government had to withdraw troops from the front to suppress this insurgency. The paper developed a twisted logic in which the purpose was to kill some Entente foreigners, damage property, and then get the Turks blamed for all this. Another purpose, of course, was to get troops to withdraw from the front and to keep them there—again, to undermine the country's military success with a "stab in the back."

Around the same time, the *Berliner Tageblatt* featured an interview with Halil Bey, the president of the Ottoman parliament, conducted by the famous writer Emil Ludwig. In his introduction to the interview, Ludwig boasted that he had not avoided asking tough questions, but instead had gone straight to the "Armenian question," "the black ice of Turkey."[48] Halil Bey answered very candidly—so candidly that Ludwig regretted, "for the Turks' sake," not to be able to make much of it public. Expectedly, Halil Bey spoke about the treacherousness of the Armenians before the war, their conspiracies "day and night" with the Russian embassy, their desertion to the Russians when they occupied Van, and so on. Halil Bey explained,

Now, these are traitors and we have to deal with them. You are thinking about certain riots and blunders? Believe me, the government is not guilty in these cases and deplores these things very much. But, as you know, we don't have gendarmes in the interior of the country anymore, everybody is in arms and a soldier [now]. And so it happens that we cannot put a check on the anger of the Muslims against these traitors [*Landesverräter*] everywhere. The government only wants to get these Armenians far away from the radius of action [of the armies] so that they cannot conspire with the enemy anymore.

The "Armenian Horrors razzmatazz" found a domestic highpoint and an endpoint in November, when the papers reported on the petition that Christian Germany (both Protestant and Catholic) had submitted to the chancellor on the Armenian question—very likely a direct result of the activities of Lepsius (see Chapter 7).[49] The papers had reprinted the chancellor's (clearly evasive) answer in full. In its article on the chancellor's reply, the *Neue Preussische (Kreuz-)Zeitung* quoted the *Kölnische Volkszeitung*—as we have seen, the paper of Catholic Germany—which expressed satisfaction at the chancellor's answer. The *Kreuzzeitung* once more reaffirmed the claim that "the Entente had seduced Christian subjects of the Ottoman Empire into insubordination" and with this also made clear that it understood that the Armenians were not being "punished" for their Christianity.[50]

After the chancellor's answer, it took two months for the Armenian topic to be of interest to the papers again. Only the *Deutsche Tageszeitung* felt it had to comment again on the topic, by presenting Bratter's pamphlet (see Chapter 7) and by praising it as a reference work so that the Germans would finally understand the nature of the "Armenian Horrors razzmatazz" (as simple atrocity propaganda).[51] On 29 January 1916, the *Berliner Volkszeitung* weighed in with its own analysis of the Armenian Horrors.[52] It echoed other papers in claiming that the British, realizing they could not take Constantinople via sea or Salonika, were now trying a different strategy, that of "slander." It then quoted at length the *Koloniale Rundschau*, which in turn had quoted the *Economist*. The *Koloniale Rundschau* had claimed that charges of Armenian atrocities were "analogous" to the tales of the Belgian Horrors, and were designed to incite (neutral) America against the Turks. The *Berliner Volkszeitung* scoffed at how quickly estimates of the number of dead had risen: from "as high as 100,000" at the beginning, to 800,000. Then it also cited an Italian consular report about the Armenian population of Trebizond (it is a different locality in the other papers), which had been wiped out completely. The *Economist* had also quoted Lord Bryce, who feared that the entire Armenian population might have been butchered. The *Berliner Volkszeitung* apparently quoted this to show that such claims (of genocidal atrocities) were totally and utterly unrealistic, simply because, apparently, such crimes were unthinkable.

The *Berliner Volkszeitung*, without having so far actually refuted anything directly, went on to stress, "For Germany these events in Armenia are of no consequence for our stance toward Turkey. These are purely internal events of an ally, in which we are no more allowed to interfere than England is allowed to meddle in Russia's treatment of the Jews. After all, England has outlawed Jewish papers that covered the misery of the Russian Jews during the war." But then, after proclaiming this principle of noninterference in Turkey's internal affairs, it launched, as so many other papers had done, into an attack on the Armenians as a justification for Turkish actions: "In any case, it is established by impeccable sources that the Armenians have attacked the Turks at many points and abused them, and that many Turkish villagers have been killed. That the Turks would then vigorously defend themselves was not only their right, but was necessary for military reasons."

In February 1916, the papers used "the occasion of the fall of Erzurum" to the Russians to discuss the Armenian question once more. The *Neue Preussische (Kreuz-)Zeitung* began by declaring that "a review of the history of the last decades will show how things really are."[53] Mocking the humanitarian concerns of the British and the Americans, it wrote, "The English-American complaints about 'Armenian massacres' are, as is well known, of older date." And then, echoing directly, almost verbatim, what Rohrbach had written in late 1914, it stated that

The five Turkish provinces, which are mostly populated by Armenians, used to serve as the gateway through which anti-Turkish influence wound its way into the country. And the response to this turmoil, created partially through English pounds, partially through Russian rubles, was the slaughter of the seditious Armenians: the bloodbath of Trebizond, the bloody clashes in Van, and finally the horrible events of August in the year 1896 when thousands of Armenians were beaten to death in the alleys of Constantinople and when the English and the Americans were literally calling for a crusade against the sultan. And yet the patience with which the Turks have endured the Armenian intrigues throughout time is plainly admirable, because the Armenians were a constant threat to existence of the Turkish Empire even if their numbers are comparably small. They have been the natural allies of the enemies of the house of Osman and have dragged it into the most severe conflicts with foreign countries. If the Armenian plotters were still, time and again, able to find vocal advocates in European diplomacy, then the nakedness of egotism shone through the shabby coat of humanitarianism all too clearly. One and only one political trick was used again and again: to bring Turkey into an embarrassing situation—if it wasn't Russia [who did this], it was England, and vice versa. . . .

Thus it has remained until today and naturally now that Turkey is at war, the Armenians and their foreign friends are doubling their efforts to harm the empire of the sultan. This is the whole point of this exercise, and this time as well, the shabby coat of teary-eyed compassion cannot hide the nakedness of the egotism.

• • •

Things became quieter on the topic in most of 1916 and 1917.[54] This was probably also a result of the deal brokered between pro-Armenian circles and the German Foreign Office: the pro-Armenian activists would remain quiet about the fate of the Armenians and the German government would rein in anti-Armenian propaganda in Germany.[55] Despite this promise, the occasional article highlighting (continuous) Armenian treachery found its way to the readers.[56] One article in the *Kölnische Zeitung* of early 1917 deserves to be mentioned: In it, the paper approvingly quoted an Englishman who had written that the Armenians "had brought their own extermination upon themselves."[57] Thus, remarkably, by focusing on justifications for the Ottoman wartime measures, the paper had given away that these amounted to an "extermination." Later in 1917 there were, for example, also reports on the yearly congress of the Young Turk party at which Talât Pasha regurgitated all the usual accusations against the Armenians (desertion, rebellion, and so on), but also admitted that the deportations had not been carried out in an orderly fashion, thus implicitly admitting that there was some truth to the allegations of the Entente.[58]

By 1918, the deal between the government and the pro-Armenian activists seems to have been unilaterally dissolved: the Armenians were discussed again more extensively. In February 1918, the papers once more reported on "Armenian cruelties," that is, on cruelties committed by "native

Armenians" and Russian deserters who were persecuting "inhabitants of Ottoman origin" in Anatolia. Citing Ottoman press reports, it was claimed that Armenians had been plundering villages, "raping the women," and even butchering entire villages, for a month already. There was also the example of a village where the mosque and the town hall were blown up. One such article ended with the claim that "these barbarities are but a few of the many that are now coming to light."[59]

And, in April 1918, there was again a whole host of articles on the Armenian topic. For example, the *Internationale Korrespondenz* reacted to the reports that now "Armenian bands" were carrying out massacres against Turks.[60] The *Tägliche Rundschau* printed an interview with the vice president of the Ottoman parliament, Hüssein Djavid Bey.[61] The introduction observed that the current fights in the Caucasus again warranted a reexamination of Armenian-Turkish relations, especially since the Entente was again peddling its usual propaganda. Hüssein Djavid stressed that until the Berlin Treaty (1878), the relation between Turks and Armenians had been fine and even very warm: "After the Berlin Treaty, the [great] intrigue imported from abroad began, and, in fact, it mainly came from Russia." Russia now found one chance and reason after another to weaken and to discredit the Ottoman Empire. Hüssein Djavid then described the folly of those who wanted an independent Armenia. He asked, "Where should such an Armenian state exist, what should be its borders, who would populate it?" This last question was shockingly cynical, given that, indeed, the year was 1918 and a large part of the Ottoman Armenians were dead. Such a state, he continued, simply was impossible, given that Armenians were nowhere in a majority but lived everywhere with Kurds and Turks. But, as he stressed, these "hotheads" were immune to reason. "Interesting here is the role of England who was posing as the champion of this [Armenian state] and who was speaking up for the so-called political rights of the Armenians in a storm flood of brochures. In truth, however, the English government does not care in the least for the Armenians." He then recounted the developments in Eastern Anatolia during the war, stressing the treacherous behavior of the Armenians over and over again: "About the revolt of the Armenians in Eastern Anatolia behind our fronts, I believe I do not have to add anything"—after having said almost nothing on the subject himself. Hüssein Djavid regretted that certain things had occurred but blamed it on the fact that the "common hatred" against the Armenians had become so powerful that it just could not be stopped. A former Armenian parliamentarian had stood at the top of an invading Russian force—and these Russian-Armenian bands had "plundered, scorched and raped" everywhere. What had followed, that is, the deportation, had been absolutely necessary in order to reestablish order and was anyway just a temporary measure; after the war they would be allowed to return. He closed by stressing that the victories of the German and Austrian armies, especially against Britain, would put an end to the chimera of Greater Armenia.

Throughout the last year of the war, many papers continued to repeat anti-Armenian stereotypes and justifications in their articles on the topic.[62] Finally, in July 1918, the Turkish and German advances into the Caucasus kicked off another debate about the relationship between the Caucasus, its peoples, and the Ottoman Empire. This served for both Turks and Germans as a welcome occasion to repeat anti-Armenian assumptions, rationalizations, and stereotypes.[63]

All this is probably just a snippet of the coverage of the Armenian topic in the wartime German press; it is all that could be reconstructed with the newspaper resources at hand.[64] But this discussion of some of the major articles and debates already makes one thing very clear: the Armenian topic was not absent; it was discussed, and all the allegations of massacres and of the "annihilation of the Armenian nation" were treated in the very same fashion in which the 1890s massacres had been discussed, denying the full extent of violence and justifying violent measures against Armenians, including the killing of civilians. Though it is true that the full extent of what was happening in Anatolia was not conveyed in the press, even the most naive reader must have realized that something of note had happened to the Armenians of the Ottoman Empire, something that went beyond pogroms and mob violence. The German press and the Ottoman government had protested too much. The myriad justifications and denials must have made it clear that the Entente allegations were serious indeed. And, at the same time, the German readers had again been exposed to a plethora of justifications for violence and murder against civilians, centering especially on racial aspects and the alleged collective wartime treason, the Armenian stab in the back.

• • •

From the beginning, the Armenians were deeply intertwined with the notion of Entente propaganda in German wartime discourse. This was not only true for the press and parliament, but is evidenced in other spheres of discourse as well. In his 1915 booklet, entitled *The World War in the Light of Judaism,* Rabbi Joseph Wohlgemuth, later a teacher at the Hildesheimer Rabbinical Seminary in Berlin, made this connection before much was known about the 1915 massacres. The chapter "War and Morality" contrasted the Entente outrage over the destruction of the cathedral in Reims by the Germans with the suffering of humanity over the past decades and in the war itself. "But in the case of the butchering of the Armenians [he was perhaps referring to the 1890s], the pogroms, [and] all the gruesome side effects of the Balkan Wars, this selection of humanity [that is, the Entente public] did not think it appropriate to raise blazing protests."[65] Note that this German-Jewish author mentioned the plight of the Armenians before that of his coreligionists in the East. What he also did, however, was not only make a familiar point, and attack the hypocrisy of anti-German propaganda, but also condemn the genuine horrors of war. And, in a strangely apologetic and too optimistic fashion, he claimed in his chapter on the "Profanation of the Divine Name" that "it cannot be repeated often enough how lucky the German nation and her allies—now also including Turkey—are, that in this world war we are the ones attacked [and thus] are acting in self-defense, that we are fighting for our sheer existence."[66] Self-defense and the struggle for one's existence were ubiquitous excuses for the genocide, and the crucial context in which the Armenian Genocide was portrayed in the German press, in government justifications, and even in interdiplomatic correspondence.

It is a difficult question just how much the average German, or German newspaper reader, actually knew. But knowledge about the newest "Armenian butcheries" did float around, even if it was somewhat lacking in detail. A book published in 1916 by Felix Theilhaber, a prominent German Zionist, titled *The Jews in the World War,* for example, mentioned the "Armenian butcheries" and their role in British propaganda, and asserted that most Germans knew about them.[67] The Poale Zion (a major Marxist-Zionist Organization) published a German-language booklet in 1917 about the Jews in the war in The Hague. It warned of what could happen to the Jews in Turkey. Its reference to the Armenian Genocide was cryptic, but it was clear nonetheless; it was no coincidence that the paragraph warning of the annihilation of the Jews in Palestine by the Turks and Muslims ended with a single word followed by an ellipsis: "Armenia . . ."[68]

As we have seen, censorship and its results were, expectedly, uneven: pro-Armenian views were hit hard; anti-Armenian views were even encouraged.[69] Books were censored, too—for example, a mention of the uprising at Van and subsequent deportations was deleted from Hugo Grothe's 1916 book on Turkey.[70] Other books published on Turkey were rather open and blunt, as, for example, the already-discussed pamphlet by Bratter, but also the widely fêted books by Ewald Banse, *Turkey* (1916) and *The Turks and Us* (1917), in which he congratulated the Turks for getting rid of these troublemakers.[71] Thus, the censor's gates were open for anti-Armenian views—which would, of course, have substantial repercussions on the course of the debate about the topic after the war. As we will see in the following chapters, Germany would have to grapple with a resurgence of the vilest anti-Armenian stereotypes. On the other hand, there was a pronounced silence in the public German discourse on the Armenians' suffering itself.

Even silence can be macabre, and the "German silence" on the Armenian Genocide often was much more than that. Often, the press suggested that Germany was actually beneficial to the regions in which the Armenians were living. So perhaps also in the page-large drawing in the satirical weekly the *Kladderadatsch* in May 1916, titled "German Spring along the Bagdad Railway," showing a dancing woman, the personified Germany, throwing flowers along the railroad (Figure 8.1).[72] Given what the German newspaper men knew about the Armenian Genocide by that point, at least behind closed doors, this was a very macabre cartoon, and its intention is not entirely clear; in fact it would not have made much sense to the general reading public. Perhaps it was a cloaked reminder to those "in the know" that still nothing had been done for the Armenians.

After the war, when in shock about losing the war, the so-called stab-in-the-back myth was advanced by various nationalist and military players in Germany. It claimed that Jews, Socialists, and, in a wider sense, "Democrats" had sabotaged the German war effort to such an extent that it amounted to a stab in the back of the otherwise victorious German armies, and thus forced a defeat through the stroke of a pen. This motif was to gain powerful currency in the Weimar years and was to no small extent influential on Hitler's and the Nazis' eliminatory anti-Semitism. A stab in the back as a motif of deadly treason is no original image, and it has something very "natural" about it. The direct origins of the specific German stab-in-the-back myth are traceable to such figures as Erich Ludendorff, who had been, together with Paul Hindenburg, military supreme ruler of Germany during the war. The myth can be dated toward the end of

Figure 8.1 German Spring along the Bagdad Railway. *Kladderadatsch* May 1916

the war (but well before the war in effect ended).[73] However, before this German (re-)invention, appropriation, and usage of the image to explain Germany's defeat, the image was, as we have seen, widely circulating in the German press in relation to the Armenians as part of German propaganda. Given that Armenians had long been equated with Jews in

Germany and that the Ottoman Empire, too, was portrayed as both victorious and struggling for its existence, an assumption of an influence of the Armenian topic on the genesis of this so quintessentially German motif is not far-fetched. It has to be remembered that, as a result of the early jihadi euphoria of the German press and the absence of any discussions or mentions of Ottoman military failures, all the reading public was ever offered as an explanation of Ottoman military failure was the Armenian stab in the back. Propaganda or not, for the German reader of the papers the only really visible case of a "stab in the back" for the duration of World War I was the Armenian case.

The virulent anti-Armenian bias of the German press was not a result of total ignorance of the actual events in Anatolia. At one point, as Helmut von Gerlach, the editor of the *Welt am Montag,* reports, an article in the *Deutsche Tageszeitung* had been published that was so virulently anti-Armenian that a German Foreign Office representative told the assembled German press at a censorship conference that he was sorry for such a mockery of the truth. "We all knew after all," the censor told the newspapermen, "that many things are happening in Turkey which are not nice." Gerlach continues, "We were not supposed to provoke the whole world by accusing the victims."[74] Furthermore, Karl Otten, a former censor, affirmed in 1919 that not only diplomats but also the press had been well aware of the suffering of Armenia.[75] There is also evidence that ordinary German soldiers knew much about the Armenian Genocide as well. Otten, who was employed as a letter censor during the war, later wrote, "I remind [you] of Armenia whose suffering was known to our press and our diplomats as much as they were to me, who held news about them in my hands and was supposed to confiscate it."[76]

It has to be stressed that the interested reader, in the major cities at least, would have been able to buy Swiss German-language papers such as, for example, the *Neue Zürcher Zeitung.* Some claimed after the war that these papers were quite popular during the war.[77] The *Neue Zürcher Zeitung* had discussed the Armenian Genocide quite in detail and had condemned both the Turks and the Germans for it.[78] Also, French, British, and Russian papers could be bought in the major cities.[79]

Censorship or not, old patterns of perceptions had forcefully reemerged in the German wartime press and reached new heights in the justifications for murdering (parts of) domestic civilian populations.

PART III

Debating Genocide

CHAPTER 9

War Crimes, War Guilt, and Whitewashing

When World War I ended, Germany was surprised and shocked that it had lost the war, especially since German wartime propaganda had suggested that all was going splendidly on all fronts. The kaiser was gone, so was the empire, and democracy was declared. Revolutions and attempted coup d'états had to be suppressed in the first years of the Weimar Republic, and a harsh victors' peace was expected. Whatever had happened in the Ottoman Empire during the war certainly was no priority for Germany's press after the war. But, as we shall see, it would become one quickly. In this chapter we will look at how the Armenian Genocide was discussed in the first two years after the war. What characterizes these years is the interplay between information and whitewashing, accepting the charges of genocide and denying or justifying what had happened.

As we saw in Chapter 8, there had not been total silence on the Armenian Genocide during World War I in Germany, as is all too often claimed and repeated in the literature on the topic.[1] As we saw, this can be established simply by looking at wartime coverage; but if we needed more evidence, even a cursory glance at the national newspapers immediately after the war would provide it. The *Neue Preussische (Kreuz-)Zeitung*, for example, began its very own postwar coverage of the Armenian topic with a series of exceedingly short news items reporting on the arrests of people responsible for the massacres during the war. No background information was given, so that no reader could have possibly understood what the *Kreuzzeitung* was talking about, had the general public not known about the massacres beforehand. Thus the reporting on the Armenian Genocide during World War I must have been "successful," at least insofar as it established the topic to such a degree that it could be casually referenced now, after the war and after censorship was lifted.

The Pro-Armenian Activists

For German pro-Armenian activists, a "casual" treatment of the topic was not enough. In December 1918, in a six-page report in his own periodical, *From the Work of Dr. Lepsius,* Johannes Lepsius was the first to answer the question, What has been done to the Armenians? He set out to address one of the three charges being hurled at Germany at the time: the Belgian atrocities, submarine warfare, and the Armenian topic. And while he mainly labored to exonerate Germany from any direct guilt in relation to the Armenian Genocide, in the course of doing so he described in depth what had happened in Anatolia. A secondary purpose in this drawn-out discourse on the Armenian Genocide was to rally support and collect money for Armenian survivors, now reduced to "a nation of beggars." Only in this context did he stress that there might be some guilt on the part of Germany (in case it did help the survivors now). Lepsius put the following accusation firmly into the mouth of Entente propaganda, but his readers should have felt it was indeed aimed at them: "through acquiescence and coward inaction [they/Germany] became an accessory in the demise of a Christian nation."[2] Lepsius further provided an estimate of the victims of the genocide: out of a previous population of about one million and three-quarters, he estimated one million to be dead, a quarter million forcibly converted or forced into harems, as well as another quarter million now left as refugees in the Caucasus. He wrote of the "systematic starvation" and "butchering" of the deportees. While he also used terms such as "mass murder," his strongest condemnation was contained in the term of "systematic annihilation."[3]

As Lepsius's article illustrates, pro-Armenians from church and missionary circles played a strange role in these early months of the debate. Their attempts to inform about the Armenian Genocide were deeply entwined with the overall goal of exonerating Germany. Take for example the open letter to the *Frankfurter Zeitung* by the pastor Ewald Stier published on 21 January 1919.[4] Stier's article follows the text, at least the beginning, of a letter he had sent to the German Foreign Office in October 1918 as a board member of the German-Armenian Society.[5] (Stier had been active in pro-Armenian work since the mid-1890s.) He began his article by criticizing the German press, charging that "many German papers outdid [the Ottoman official reports] with accusations against the Armenians, allegedly on the Entente's payroll."[6] He claimed that anyone "who has followed the German press in recent years . . . could hardly come to a different judgment than that Germany shared the Turkish point of view and condoned Turkish actions." In a similar vein, and this seems to have been even more important to Stier, wartime censorship had prevented the world from being told about German relief efforts for the Armenians, which he claimed had been considerable. Stier's text was a report of the Lepsius faction of the pro-Armenian missionary landscape, and it emphasized just how much that group, and especially Lepsius himself, had done for the Armenians and thus for Germany's honor and reputation as well.

The exceedingly long essay by Julius Richter published in the *Allgemeine Missionszeitschrift* a mere two weeks after Stier's letter can be viewed as a reply from the other side of the pro-Armenian missionary spectrum.[7] While mentioning the massacres and the desired "eradication of the Armenian people" by the Ottomans, Richter, too, mainly tried to combat allegations of German guilt. Richter claimed that the Entente propaganda regarding Armenia and German guilt had been even more successful than that of the "alleged Belgian Horrors." Nevertheless, he claimed that German officers had advised the Turks to relocate the Armenians, but claimed that they had not been aware of the lack of necessary means to protect them on the way. Because of this charge against German officers, Richter's piece was followed by angry rebuttals, even from his own circles.[8]

In any case, these texts and reports were the first in the postwar weeks to use fully fledged "genocide language": both Richter and Stier had frequently used such terms as "extermination" and "annihilation of the Armenian people." Yet their message was mixed: Richter, for example, acknowledged that it had been German officers who had advised "translocation" of the Armenians in the borderlands, but it had been the Turks who had failed to care for the deportees and had even used this as a chance for the annihilation of the group. Surprisingly perhaps, he tried to lay blame at Lepsius's feet: Richter claimed that with all his work for the Armenians, Lepsius not only overstretched the German Orient Mission (the missionary organization for, among others, the Armenians), but with his work angered Turkish government circles, "which [only] worsened the fate of the Armenians further."[9] In contrast, he claimed, the pleas to Djemal Pasha when he had visited Berlin (pleas presumably issuing from Richter's own circle) had actually alleviated the lot of some Armenians for a while. Despite the fact that (the leadership of) the pro-Armenian circles were exceedingly small and were now in a unique position to educate the German public about what had happened, what they did was point fingers at each other, to try to absolve Germany of any guilt, and even to trot out standard anti-Armenian stereotypes and accusations. Thus Richter had not only recounted the anti-Semitic parallel, but also mentioned the massacres carried out by Armenians, and hinted strongly at "Armenian disloyalty." But Richter also criticized German anti-Armenianism by stressing that German journalists had helped Turkey by "throwing stones at the Armenians," and that, while censorship had banned all critical articles, it had allowed articles that inflated alleged massacres carried out by Armenians.

These first embers of what was to become a fiery debate were enough to make the German Foreign Office nervous, especially concerning the question of German guilt. It tasked Karl Axenfeld, the German missionary and chair of the Foreign Office Orient and Islam committee, to inquire with Bronsart von Schellendorff, the former chief of staff of the Ottoman Army, about the involvement and guilt of German officers in the genocide. Similarly, Otto Göppert, former diplomat with the German embassy in Constantinople, wrote to Otto von Feldmann, who had served with the Ottoman General Staff on the same question.[10] And, in a next step, the German Foreign Office initiated further rebuttals to the claims of guilt.[11] Alluding to the expected German debate, Göppert had written in his letter, "the Armenian question can ignite any day now."[12]

"Save the Honor of Europe, President Wilson"

One of the many starting points of the unfolding great genocide debate was an open letter that Armin T. Wegner wrote to President Wilson that was published on 23 February 1919 in the *Berliner Tageblatt*.[13] As we saw in Chapter 7, Wegner was an author and soldier who had witnessed the genocide himself; as we also saw, he had tried to spread the word when he got back in 1915 but had been rebuffed by most of the people he had contacted—including, in fact, the editor of the very same *Berliner Tageblatt*, Theodor Wolff.[14] In his open letter, Wegner asked President Wilson to make true on the promises embodied in his Fourteen Points. Wegner stressed that the armistice negotiations had treated the Armenian issue as secondary or even tertiary, and that this should not and could not happen again at the peace negotiations in Paris. He underlined his plea by emphasizing his impartial role in the matter as a German, belonging to a nation that was closely allied to the Ottoman Empire. "It is," he claimed, "the voice of a thousand dead who speak through me." He claimed that all they had done was to be helpless, speak another tongue, and be born as children of a different creed. He also emphasized that all the accusations leveled against them were nothing but defamations invented "to cover [the perpetrators'] frantic and brutal violence."

More emphatically, he stressed that he had witnessed the Armenians' "awful extinction," from the beginning until the "extermination of their wretched remainders on the banks of the Euphrates River [and] in the rocky wastelands of the Mesopotamian desert." "No nation on earth," Wegner declaimed, "has ever suffered such injustice as the Armenian [nation]." He not only frequently used terms such as "exterminate" (vernichten) and "annihilate" (ausrotten), but also gave a quasi-pornographic description of the suffering inflicted and the methods used to butcher the Armenians—methods, he stressed, that could only be compared to those of an insane criminal. Such a litany of pain and suffering was the first of the postwar period on this topic, but it was reminiscent of the 1890s and for the first time revealed the truly inconceivable "reality" of genocide:

The [majority] of their men were slaughtered en masse; they were bound together with chains and ropes, thrown into the river, or rolled down the mountain with fettered limbs; they sold their women and children in the public markets; [they] drove old men and boys with deadly thrashings onto the streets for forced labor. And if this weren't enough, having [already] stained their criminal hands for all eternity, [they] chased the people, having deprived them of their leaders and spokesmen, out of the towns, at all hours of the day and night, half-naked, straight out of their beds; plundered their houses; burned the villages; destroyed the churches or turned them into mosques; stole their cattle; took their mules and their carriages; snatched the bread out of their hands, the clothes from off their backs, the gold from their hair and mouths. Officials, military officers, soldiers, [and] shepherds competed with one another in their wild delirium of blood, dragging the delicate figures of orphan girls out of the schools for their bestial pleasures; beating with clubs heavily pregnant women or [already] dying people, who did not drag themselves any further, so that the woman gave birth on the country road and expired, and the dust beneath her transformed into bloody mud. . . .

Here they died, slain by Kurds, robbed by gendarmes, shot, hanged, poisoned, stabbed, strangled, mown down by epidemics, drowned, froze, died of thirst and starvation, decomposed and nibbled on by jackals. Children cried themselves to death; men smashed themselves to pieces against the rocks; mothers threw their little ones in the wells; pregnant women threw themselves singing into the Euphrates. All the deaths of this earth, all the deaths of the ages, they died them all.

And Wegner went on and on, relentlessly. This seems to have been far too much and far too early for a German public who was by and large still unfamiliar with the extent of what had happened in Anatolia during the war. His plea closed with the call upon the American president to "save the honor of Europe." Yet, his open letter, though thoroughly passionate, fell on deaf ears—both abroad and in Germany. No real debate ensued, though the letter was apparently reprinted in other papers.[15] One reason for the lack of an immediate debate was that the German press and public were distracted by the chaos in Munich and Bavaria in the aftermath of the assassination of Kurt Eisner by Count Anton Arco-Valley (21 February), which would lead to the establishment of the short-lived Bavarian Soviet Republic. But this does not mean that the letter was futile or that it did not receive any attention. Later on in the debate, it was referenced quite often.[16] For Wegner, however, this seemingly unsuccessful exercise appears to have convinced him to become more active yet. Already a month later, we find the German newspapers—most of the larger ones, at least—reporting on his public lecture at the Berlin popular lecture theater, the Urania, organized by the German-Armenian Society. This lecture was of interest to the papers and the public at large, not only because it showed the gruesome reality of the Armenian Genocide in pictures, but also because it provoked a clash between Armenian and Turkish audience members, some of which had to be escorted out of the lecture theater to be arrested by Berlin police. The report in the *Berliner Zeitung am Mittag* (which was also reprinted in the *Vossische Zeitung* in its evening edition) is worth quoting here:

Yesterday, tumultuous scenes took place at the otherwise so peaceful lecture hall of the Urania. Dr. Armin T. Wegner, a thorough authority on Armenia, gave a slide lecture about the expulsion of the Armenian people into the desert. A Turk, sitting in one of the first rows, disrupted the deliberations of the lecturer continually with [his] heckling. He was removed from the lecture hall by force and for a short while there was calm. Yet soon, with another picture, there were emotional screams. Some Turks shouted [that] the picture was falsified and they entered into bitter altercations with the Armenians present. One . . . visitor shouted into the hall: "The Turkish community will not put up with these defamations and will [officially] comment." Downstairs a veritable brawl erupted between the two nationalities. Only with the greatest difficulty was it possible to remove the rowdies and to finish the lecture. The scuffle, however, started anew in the cloakroom. The squabblers were kicked out of the building by attendants of the theater. But even on the street, their fighting continued. One Armenian, brandishing a gun, was handed over to the police and then escorted away.[17]

The *Berliner Abendzeitung* reported Wegner's claim that the German government must have been lied to by the Turkish rulers, otherwise they too would be guilty of the actions that had condemned one and a half million Armenians to death.[18] The German Foreign Office also anxiously followed Wegner's activities. A few days later, an internal memorandum of the German Foreign Office recapitulating Wegner's lecture was authored by Walter Rössler, formerly the German consul at Aleppo, who had, like Scheubner, intervened repeatedly for the Armenians. Having attended the lecture, Rössler stressed that it had been basically a repetition of the open letter to Wilson. Again Wegner had claimed that Germany had made itself guilty by association with the Turks.[19]

The tumultuous scenes provoked by the lecture were perhaps not surprising, given the shocking content of Wegner's lecture and the accompanying photos, which revealed details of the genocide in gruesome detail. After a few pictures exhibiting the past and the "culture-creating" potential of the Armenians, Wegner recounted horrifying details of murder: victims had been rolled down mountains, limbs bound together, with "Kurdish women waiting for them at the foot of the mountain with their knives to stab into the bound [victims] until they died in their own blood."[20] He showed relentless pictures of Armenian victims, of corpses strewn in the city and countryside alike. One photograph, for example, showed an Armenian child sitting on the curb, a second, apparently dead or exhausted child next to him, while two meters away the corpse of a third child, naked

Figure 9.1 Wegner's Slideshow. Starving and starved Armenian children. (Armin T. Wegner, *Die Austreibung des Armenischen Volkes in die Wüste: Ein Lichtbildvortrag*, 33, ed. Andreas Meier. © Wallenstein Verlag, Göttingen 2011)

and dead, lies in the (literal) gutter (Figure 9.1). And even if a photo in itself appeared more tranquil, Wegner's accompanying narrative surely was not. There was, for instance, a picture of a young Armenian woman in her Sunday dress shyly averting her eyes from the camera (Figure 9.2). Reaching this picture in his lecture, Wegner explained that

> the Armenian women and girls are generally very beautiful. Looking at you is the dark [and] beautiful face of Babesheea who was robbed by Kurds, raped, and freed only after ten days; like a wild beast the Turkish soldiers, officers, soldiers, and gendarmes swept down on this welcome prey. All the crimes that had ever been committed against women, were committed here. They cut off their breasts, mutilated their limbs, and their corpses lay naked, defiled, or blackened by the heat on the fields.[21]

Similarly, the next picture showed Armenian orphan girls on their way to church, in a dark picture in which the clad-in-white girls appear like

Figure 9.2 Wegner's Slideshow. "Babesheea." (Armin T. Wegner, *Die Austreibung des Armenischen Volkes in die Wüste: Ein Lichtbildvortrag*, 37, ed. Andreas Meier. © Wallenstein Verlag, Göttingen 2011)

ghosts (Figure 9.3). In his accompanying text Wegner discussed their fate, how the most beautiful among them were destined for Turkish harems, and how some would find a cruel fate with gendarmes "sitting on their head and legs . . . beating them until they [finally] became quiet."[22]

What Wegner's pictures and his lecture set out to show was what had also been the theme of his open letter: that the Armenians "had died all the deaths of the ages." His relentless slideshow showed all the ways the Armenian people were made to suffer and die, of sickness, typhus, dysentery, rape, murder, hunger, and so on. In his Urania lecture, he spoke of the "completely successful destruction of the Armenian people."[23] The horrifying pictures of naked child corpses must have been more than a bit upsetting to his audience. While he was criticized for using pictures from different contexts—such as one of a foot caning, which was actually from Persia and not from Anatolia—and while he did indeed make extensive use of pictures taken by others, it was less his "liberal" use of photographic material than the gruesome narrative that unfolded in his lectures that was shocking, new, and too much for Germany at the time.

Figure 9.3 Wegner's Slideshow. "Armenian orphan girls on their way to church." (Armin T. Wegner, *Die Austreibung des Armenischen Volkes in die Wüste: Ein Lichtbildvortrag*, 38, ed. Andreas Meier. © Wallenstein Verlag, Göttingen 2011)

Many of Wegner's pictures have since become iconic images of the Armenian Genocide, especially perhaps the one of the woman carrying her child (Figure 9.4). Wegner also told his audience that it had been forbidden to take any pictures of the deportees and of the genocide and that

Figure 9.4 Wegner's Slideshow. "Refugees at the Taurus Pass." (Armin T. Wegner, *Die Austreibung des Armenischen Volkes in die Wüste: Ein Lichtbildvortrag*, 51, ed. Andreas Meier. © Wallenstein Verlag, Göttingen 2011)

he had to hide his diaries and picture plates on his body to smuggle them out of the country. He also mentioned that on his return from Mesopotamia to Constantinople in December 1916, he was told to leave the Ottoman Empire. He was then arrested by soldiers of the German military mission and detained on a German ship, he claimed. He later found out that he had been deported back to Germany at the wish of the Ottoman government, because of his sympathies for the Armenians.[24]

Wegner was to go on tour across Germany with his slideshow lecture. The next stop after the Urania was Breslau, on 22 April 1919.[25] His commitment to Armenia also led the Armenian community of Berlin to give him a scholarship of 10,000 reichsmarks in 1921 in order to complete his novel about the Armenians, which, however, he never did. Only a novella *(Sturm auf das Frauenbad)* and a short story ("Der Knabe Atam") about the Armenians were ever published in his lifetime. In late 1922 and early 1923, Wegner published another open letter, now addressed to all the victorious powers, in a number of journals, among them the pacifist *Die*

Weltbühne, to press them to fulfill their duties with respect to the Armenians.[26] In any case, even if he was not successful in kicking off a debate in Germany or in getting Wilson to remember the Armenians, Wegner's role and his passion for the Armenians was to be eulogized in 1923 already by Stefan Zweig, the famous Austrian-Jewish novelist, in the *Berliner Tageblatt.* Zweig not only referred to Wegner's open letter but also to his other texts: "His first words after the war were not of enthusiasm . . . but of accusation, [in his] gruesome depictions of the Armenian Horrors, which clueless Germany had been first made aware of by his words and which have never been depicted with a similar degree of passion and holy manly embitterment [*sic*]."[27]

Wegner was not alone in his lecture activities in 1919. Two weeks before his lecture at the Urania, the *Weimarsche Zeitung* reported on a lecture on the Armenians at the Weimar local group of the German Officer's League by a Dr. Kahrstedt. The difference in style and content seems to have been striking: Kahrstedt gave a rather dry ethnographic lecture for the most part, with a few comments that did not suggest particular sympathy for Armenian suffering. He had warned his audiences of the "racial chaos" that threatened to drown the "old Mongolian Turkish blood." Commenting on the "extermination of the Armenians," the orator stressed that "the Armenian population took upon itself great guilt through [its] treasonous machinations."[28] As in the decades before, accusation and justification stood sharply opposed.

War-Crimes Questions

Germany was not yet receptive to Wegner's pleas. One of the reasons was that it was preoccupied with the unfolding postwar settlement and the questions of war guilt and war crimes. Before the war, Liman von Sanders—or rather his appointment as top military adviser to the Ottomans with far-reaching powers—had been the focal point of a minor international crisis involving Germany, Russia, and the Ottoman Empire. Indeed, it came to be called the "Liman von Sanders Crisis," and is to be counted among the many steps leading to World War I.[29] Thus Liman von Sanders had already become a household name in Germany before the war; and after the Great War, his name again became emblematic of the latest German–Turkish–Great Powers crisis. The German papers disproportionately focused on the Sanders case to show just how unfairly and vindictively the Entente was treating Germany. The first articles about him and alleged war crimes in the Ottoman Empire started appearing in the German press in February 1919. One such article, in the *Vossische Zeitung*, just one day before Wegner's open letter was published, spoke of him being accused of having given orders to murder Armenians and "Syrians."[30] Earlier, some papers had already mentioned that Enver Pasha and Djemal Pasha had been "demoted," yet had not discussed the reason for that.[31] A week before, some papers had mentioned that the former governor of Diyarbakir had committed suicide upon his arrest for "participation in the Armenian massacres."[32]

At the end of February, many papers commented on the Entente charges against Liman von Sanders; many tried to exonerate him of the charge that he had taken part in the "Armenian massacres," and stressed that he had in fact tried to stop them wherever he was stationed and whenever he could.[33] In March, the papers reported that Sanders had been arrested by the British and sent to Malta to await trial in Constantinople.[34] Later that month, it was reported that he would not be tried in Constantinople after all, but that his case would be discussed by the Allies in Paris as part of the peace negotiations.[35] Meanwhile, the Entente press was discussing the notion that the Germans had ordered the annihilation of the Armenians. In an article in *Le Figaro*, the famous French novelist Pierre Loti claimed that it was well known that Liman von Sanders had ordered the massacres of the Armenians.[36]

Only a few weeks after the Armenian topic had begun making a slow comeback with the activists' activities as well as with the emerging war-crimes question, most larger papers featured a small report on 14 April about the hanging of Tokat Kiamil Mahmud Pasha on the charge of "coresponsibility for the Armenian massacres."[37] The next day, the Social Democrat *Vorwärts* also discussed it and concluded that, "with this, the reckoning for the monstrous annihilations of the Armenians [*Armeniervernichtungen*] has begun in Turkey. The Turkish government is well advised to prosecute those guilty with relentless rigor."[38] This condemnation of the Armenian Genocide provoked a very fierce reaction from the Communist *Rote Fahne* two days later, on 17 April:

Thanks to the war politics carried out and endorsed by the *Vorwärts* and its fellow travelers [meaning the SPD] the German reader has learned very little [in the past] about the Armenian Horrors [during World War I]. He does not know anything about how this people was removed from its places of residence due to "military considerations" and was brought to foreign cities and to internment camps; on a grand scale and with oriental brutality, meaning even greater than what . . . [Germany] inflicted on Northern France and Poland.

The German reader then also does not know that—just as tens of thousands of Northern Frenchmen and Poles died—of the Armenians hundreds of thousands died. . . . Many thousands collapsed on their route due to hunger and exhaustion and died miserably.

Almost an entire, great, and gifted people was annihilated in this fashion.

All this, the *Vorwärts* and its peers have concealed from the German reader.

And it has also kept secret that German eyewitnesses of these horrors begged the German government in the interest of humanity to at least lift a finger to make the "high ally" stop these shameful acts.

It has also kept secret not only that the German government refused to [lift a finger], but that it was precisely the German military men in Turkey who had encouraged the Turks in their executioner's work.

The *Vorwärts* now is also silent about [the fact] that back then Karl Liebknecht posed a "small question" to the government in order to appeal to its conscience and that the people who speak through the *Vorwärts* today are exactly the same who shouted him down and who suppressed the voice of humanity.

Those who did this are just as guilty of the murder of the Armenians as Kiamil Pasha.

Kiamil Pasha was hanged; this gives the *Vorwärts* satisfaction.

What does the *Vorwärts* plan to do with Kiamil Pasha's German helpers?[39]

Perhaps in reaction to the *Vorwärts–Rote Fahne* discussion, Liman von Sanders published an article himself later in the same month. It appeared in the journal *20th Century (20. Jahrhundert)* and was discussed in the daily press as well. The *Berliner Lokal-Anzeiger,* for example, dedicated a rather long article to it on 24 April under the title "Germany and the Armenians."[40] The paper summarized Sanders's main points in a very sympathetic fashion, indeed conveying them as if they were the paper's own views. Sanders claimed that the relationship with the Armenians was a domestic affair "into which [the Turks] never let any German officers look." Of course, this was a bit of a stretch for the very simple reason that much of the Ottoman military had been commanded by Germans. Sanders claimed that no Germans had taken part, either in the measures themselves or in the deliberations leading to them. The Entente claim that the government had wanted the consent of "the Turkish General Staff [which] consisted of German officers" was fabricated, Sanders claimed. Rather, German officers "had intervened, according to their duties, on behalf of the Armenians whenever possible." Sanders repeated similar claims and justifications in his memoirs published in 1920 under the title *Five Years in Turkey.*[41] And while little more was reported on the Sanders case, the Entente decision to return him to Germany in August 1919 made it onto the front pages of even the smaller provincial papers.[42]

On 29 April 1919, five days after the article on Sanders's justifications, came another reaction to the international claims of German complicity, this time in the regional press. This article helps demonstrate how deep knowledge of the genocide had already spread. The author "H. Pfisterer," writing in the *Schwäbischer Merkur,* opened his very lengthy article on the topic with the claim that "one of the most severe accusations leveled against Germany during the war was that it is liable for the demise of the Armenian people."[43] He claimed further that during the war the Entente had used this charge as a propaganda tool, fomenting anger against Germany, garnering the support of the neutral countries, and, most importantly, swaying public opinion in the United States so much that it had pushed that country into the war. And now again, Pfisterer continued, "[this accusation] plays a vicious role"—alluding to its potential use against Germany at the Paris peace negotiations. In his historical overview, Pfisterer claimed that the Armenians' siding with Russia had, in a quasi-automatic fashion, led to the massacres of the 1890s. The Balkan Wars again sowed further discontent between the Ottoman and the Armenians. Then, when World War I began, the author claimed, on the one hand the Entente powers had armed and agitated the Armenians and, on the other hand, the Ottomans saw that their only chance of creating an "Islamic Great Power on nationally Turkish grounds required the annihilation of all alien peoples, especially the elimination of the Armenian people." Pfisterer continued, opposing the central arguments of those denying the extent of what had happened by stating that "this political reform idea, if it may be called such, and not only the locally relevant military necessities, was the reason for the annihilating deportation of the Armenian people . . . in early 1915." He continued,

The timing was convenient for the Turks: at this very time they were rendering such a crucial service to Germany with their defense of the Straits [at Gallipoli] that our government was unable, from the beginning, to lodge any meaningful protest against this insane endeavor, even from an economic perspective. The deportation of the defenseless population . . . took place under such horrid conditions that, according to moderate German estimates, about one million Armenians perished.

When he came to discussing who bore the guilt for what had happened, he put the blame squarely on the Entente: "Their egotistical Orient politics have done everything possible to make the Armenians seem worthy of suspicion in the eyes of the Turks and have pushed the latter toward the desperate and inhumane way out pursued by them." Then, predictably, he plunged into a long exoneration of Germany, which, he claimed, had done everything it could to save the Armenians. But Pfisterer also criticized the German press: it had followed the official Ottoman line too much and had justified some of the measures ex post facto. He concluded that no other power had intervened on behalf of the Armenians as much as Germany. His final sentences were a bit strange and shocking: "The accusation of Armenian murder [*Armeniermord*] has to vanish from [the peace] negotiations with political as well as with Christian Germany and this then might serve for the spiritual resurrection of our people."

It might have been motivated by a desire on the part of official Germany to impress the Entente and to dust off the remnants of guilt, but on 14 May 1919, a large remembrance service for the victims of the Armenian Genocide was held in the middle of Berlin, at the Hedwig's Church. The German government as well as most of the embassies took part in it.[44] In the following weeks, the first articles justifying what the Ottomans had done appeared in the press.[45]

Lepsius—Advocacy and Whitewashing

These were but the first convulsions of a larger debate to come. And again, as in the 1890s, it was unleashed by Johannes Lepsius. During the war, as discussed in the previous chapters, he had printed his "clandestine" report on the Armenian Genocide and done his best to circulate it in spite of censorship laws. After the war, he was to gain more dubious fame by helping the German government, or more precisely, the German Foreign Office, in their efforts to whitewash and bury German involvement in and responsibility for the Armenian Genocide. The result of his allegedly "open access" to Foreign Office documents was his 1919 *Germany and Armenia*, a collection of German diplomatic documents.[46] The origins of this book go back to the midst of the war and the height of the genocide itself. As discussed in Chapter 6, on instructions from Berlin, Ambassador Wangenheim had asked his consuls to collect all information about anything they had done to help the Armenians, in order for it to be published as a white paper after the war "in the hope of impressing Entente and German public opinion," as Frank Weber has put it.[47] The Foreign Office knew from the beginning that this would be necessary—and, significantly, not only to answer to the Entente, but in order to dampen the apparently inevitable domestic wrath as well. And who better to publish such a white paper than the most famous German pro-Armenian activist?

At the last minute, the German Foreign Office had tried to persuade Lepsius to hold off on the publication a bit longer, as it did not want it to be in the hands of the Entente prosecutors "at a time when the question of the responsibility for the Armenian murders will be solved in a judicial fashion" at the tribunals for war criminals in Constantinople.[48] When Lepsius asked for further reports, especially those by Rössler—who had been especially active in trying to save Armenians—to round off the documentation, the German Foreign Office replied that it did not want any further documents that incriminated the Turks in the public eye, especially if these documents did nothing to further exonerate Germany. For the German Foreign Office, this was wholly and exclusively an exercise in German exculpation.[49]

In any case, the resulting whitewashed volume succeeded in its primary purpose: for most Germans discussing the subject in 1919 and 1920, it would now be an established fact that Germany was "innocent" of any involvement in the Armenian massacres, precisely because of the Lepsius volume. As a whitewash, then, the book was a success; but its other effect—and perhaps this was Lepsius's main motivation—was to spark public interest in and a debate on the Armenian Genocide itself for many months to come.

The debate on the Lepsius documents began with an article in the SPD *Vorwärts* on 11 June 1919, and was to continue well into 1920 in both the national and the provincial press.[50] That first article, "The Documents on the Armenian Question," opened with the statement that in 1915, "horrible things had happened on Turkish territory. Great parts of the Armenian

people, including women and children, were—under the pretext of war necessities and as punishment for the deeds of a few individual Armenians—
deported and killed en masse or exposed to hunger and exhaustion in
a deadly fashion."[51] The article immediately continued with the claim—
which, as we saw in Chapter 8, was disingenuous to say the least—that the
German press had been forced to stay silent on this matter during the war
because of censorship. This "forced silence," the *Vorwärts* believed, had
been construed in Entente propaganda as proof of the coresponsibility of
Germany. And while the article then continued, saying that "for the annihilation of the greatest part of the Armenian people there is no sugar-coating,"
it quickly proceeded to point out that it had not been the fault of the Turkish
people either. The "chief culprits" were, according to the Social Democrat
paper, the two grand viziers Said Halim and Talât Pasha, Minister of War
Enver Pasha, and Minister of the Navy Djemal Pasha.

Then the paper sketched the genocide itself:

> The formal course of events was, as a rule, the following: under the
> pretext of the endangerment of the military security of Turkey, first the
> notables were arrested, and largely silenced forever. Next, the disarma-
> ment of the male population was carried out and then the weaponless
> population deported toward Mesopotamia. In many cases, the men were
> taken aside and killed right at the beginning of the deportations. Younger
> women were raped and sold into Turkish harems. The children, as far as
> they had not been killed or starved to death already, were often carried
> off into Muslim orphanages in order to be Islamized. . . . The caravans
> that reached the Mesopotamian plains were mostly only miserable dev-
> astated remainders of the previously expelled . . . Armenians. It is esti-
> mated that more than two-thirds of the Turkish Armenians had had to
> die in these years of horror.

The *Vorwärts,* in what was the first article on this collection of Foreign
Office documents, encapsulated the dual role of Lepsius's book in one
(convoluted) sentence: it not only offered a great survey of the sum of hide-
osities, but showed that the German government did everything it could
have done to protect the Armenians. The dual approach of the Lepsius
volume, to document but also to exonerate Germany, tripped up many a
journalist and politician in these years, including the *Vorwärts,* which
featured the fairly cynical sentence, "those Armenians for whose salvation

the German strength did not suffice could take delight in the almost touching care of the German consuls in Inner Asia Minor."

And thus began a whole series of articles on the Lepsius volume. Many of those discussing it in the next four weeks did so in a similar fashion—on the one hand stressing that Germany was wholly innocent and on the other hand condemning the crimes, which in their totality many recognized as "genocide." However, it took a bit of time after the *Vorwärts* article for the debate to take off. One reason was simply that the press review copies had only just been sent out; the *Vorwärts* obviously did a quick, eagerly motivated overnight job.[52] This timing alone suggests that the main paper of the Social Democrats, who had supported the government during the war—a stance that in turn had led to a part seceding from the party to found the USPD—rushed to distance itself from the possible stigma associated with the Armenian Genocide and possible German coresponsibility.

Over a month passed before the book was discussed, on 28 July 1919, in the *Berliner Tageblatt,* a national paper with one of the largest circulations. This was probably the longest and most vehemently outraged article on the matter to date—it was also, at least at this point, the most influential one, its central tenets being reproduced in other articles across the German press.[53] It was also influential abroad, as, for example, is documented for the Netherlands.[54] It prominently took up most of the front and second page in the daily lead commentary, and was written by Theodor Wolff, the famous editor in chief of the paper. It is worth quoting at length as it encapsulated and prefigured much of the debate of the coming months and years. Wolff embedded the Lepsius volume in the broader developments of coming to terms with the world war: "It seems as if we are standing at the beginning of a period of disclosure."[55] Lepsius's publication of the Foreign Office documents was only the beginning, Wolff expected, but it was one of "extraordinary historical and moral significance," as Lepsius was, in "over five hundred pages, submitting [these documents] to the judgment of the civilized world." Wolff also mentioned Lepsius's wartime report and how it had been suppressed by censorship in order to preserve "the pure image of the war." He wrote that reading the documents in the Lepsius volume, "one could plead to the cruel god, three times," but he emphasized that "there is a degree of misery and nefariousness that makes the big words small. . . . There is that kind of horror that does not allow for pathos."

Wolff discussed how the Young Turks took the decision to realize their nationalist ideas and to "secure for the Turkish race and pure Islam the sole sovereignty and thus as a first step to 'assimilate' or annihilate the Armenians." Based on the Lepsius volume, Wolff recounted how the whole undertaking began with the arrest and eventual murder of the Armenian intelligentsia in Constantinople "so that every loud cry of protest was made impossible." He went on to criticize the legend of the Van uprising, which, he claimed, was not an uprising at all but a "heroic act of self-defense motivated by the murders committed by the provincial governor Djevdet Bey, a brother-in-law of Enver Pasha, as well as by the fact that the authorities were openly planning further murders." He continued that "after the Enver gang had gained the pretext for 'security measures,' on the grounds of supposed military necessity, by provoking these conflicts, began the 'deportation,' began the butchering and then the strangling angel [of death; *Würgeengel*] pushed the unlucky nation from all sides, under beastly agonies, into its grave." He then recounted how everybody, "men, women, children," were "beaten to" the border of the desert, to the "concentration camps" (*Konzentrationslager;* Wolff put the euphemistic term—that is what it was, after all—in quotation marks). He related how the men were murdered first and some of the women and girls sold into harems "and Kurdish villages."

Wolff quoted "the director of the German consulate in Erzurum" (this was Max Erwin Scheubner-Richter, though he was not mentioned by name here), in his telegram to the ambassador: "Annihilation of the expelled Armenians on the way to Harput via Erzindjan." Wolff went on to recount some of the horrors and some of the numbers of killed men and women in parts of the deportation campaign. Those who were able to reach the concentration camps "died of hunger cramps," he wrote. Wolff quoted more details of the horrors and finally concluded, "If you want more of the sort, the five hundred pages [of the Lepsius volume] are filled with such. On Turkish soil, according to the existing estimates, approximately one million human beings were thus annihilated, in unspeakable atrociousness, and, in addition, [a] hundred thousand in the Caucasus."

Responding to the Entente claim that Germany and German officials had favored if not instigated this "extermination of the Armenians," Wolff was convinced that the documents exonerated Germany. He concluded that Talât, Halil, and Enver were lying as much as they could—a rather shocking claim to make in particular of Enver and Talât, who were still held in high esteem by the German public (published opinion). In his discussion of whether Germany could have done anything, Wolff claimed that the Turks took the stance that "if you don't like it, then go!"

Wolff also criticized the German press: "The polemicists of the Entente were given an easy job when they were asked to proclaim that Germany was sanctioning the strangling of the Armenians, since from Germany there was not one indignant peep. Only after . . . the supreme command and the war press censorship office were gone were we able to reprint here a report by Armin T. Wegner that told of the events in a shocking fashion." Wolff was, of course, referring to Wegner's open letter. But it is worth recalling that, as we saw in Chapter 7, when Wegner first returned from the Ottoman Empire during the war and wanted to tell Germany about what he had seen, Wolff was one of those who refused even to meet him.

Wolff now also related that, as the Lepsius volume documented, one day Talât Pasha had told the German ambassador who was protesting the butchering of the Armenians, "Germany would, in a similar case, act just the same as Turkey." Wolff attempted to refute this with a culturalist remark, at least partially. He emphasized that what the "hungry wolves of the [Young Turk] committee"—a quote from Ambassador Metternich—"had done to the Armenians is without precedent, full of Asian blood rabidity [Bluttollheit], and in its frightfulness had no match anywhere. But we, who do not live in Asia, want to have the Belgian disgrace and similar things atoned for as well and that is why we are not only hoping for a white book on this topic but for an indictment [of those responsible] at the state court."

The following day, a similar article appeared in the Braunschweiger Landeszeitung using the very same image of the "strangling angel of death" pushing the Armenians into their grave. It, too, used the term "concentration camps" (also in quotation marks), gave the number of victims as one million, and it, too, featured many details of the killing and suffering. It stressed—in contrast to Wolff, who had used the term—that "animalistic" or "bestial" was not the right term for the brutalization that had taken place in Turkey simply because it was an affront against animals. It also featured a discussion of the criminal behavior of the "Enver gang."[56] Another day later, the Vossische Zeitung responded to Wolff's article in its "The Extermination of the Turkish Armenians" and agreed with him by repeating most of his statements and arguments. It, too, like Wolff's Berliner Tageblatt, pulled out and repeated in bold letters the line, "a million

Armenians were exterminated." The *Vossische Zeitung* even indented it like a separate headline, all for dramatic effect.[57]

Three days later, the *Kölnische Volkszeitung* published its article on the volume and was sure that what had happened to the Armenians was "the greatest crime in human history."[58] It stressed, just as the previous articles on the matter had done, that Germany's innocence was proven by the volume, but also renarrated many gory details of the crimes as well as the key facts that were put forward in most of these articles (concentration camps, one million victims, no Van rebellion, intent for genocide, and so on). For the paper, "the murder of the Armenian people" *(Hinmordung des armenischen Volkes)* "was one of the gravest indictments against the barbarity that has horribly manifested itself in this war." The acknowledgment of what we would call "genocide" established itself among the major papers.[59]

Another few days later, on 7 August, the *Vossische Zeitung* printed a reply to its article on the Lepsius volume. In it, Hubert Urban, a German who was formerly "an assistant of the military attaché of the Turkish embassy," stressed that the Armenians were not "innocent lambs," as they were depicted in the press.[60] Indeed, he claimed they had exploited Turkey in such a flagrant manner, as usurers, that how the Turkish government treated them in return was surely a domestic matter, not an international one—another of the first justificationalist arguments, while not denying the charge of genocide, it justified what had happened through racial stereotypical assertions. At this point, however, the *Vossische Zeitung* no longer endorsed such views and so did not allow Urban's claims to pass without comment. Instead, it noted sarcastically that one did not need to have worked at the Turkish embassy to know that most Turks were honorable people. Yet, the paper went on, it was also obvious that an exception should be made for Enver Pasha and company, "who let about one million Armenians, among them several hundred thousand women and children, be choked to death by Circassians or starved to death on the edge of the desert." The *Vossische Zeitung* concluded that "the notion that the bestial annihilation of a whole people, even if motivated by 'revenge,' has 'no international significance,' is an inventive one."

German newspaper readers were soon to hear a more prominent figure defend the Ottoman government's actions: none other than one of the Three Pashas: Djemal Pasha. His op-ed was published in the *Frankfurter Zeitung* on 3 September 1919.[61] The paper justified printing Djemal's "justificational essay" by pointing out that the Entente papers were leveling such grave accusations against Djemal that it was its duty to allow him space to reply. The fact that, by now, German papers across the board were also charging the Ottoman government with "genocide" (that is, the intentional murder of an entire people) was ignored by the *Frankfurter Zeitung*. Djemal indeed mainly replied to the verdict of the Constantinople special court that had sentenced him, Talât, and Enver Pasha as well as others to death—all three pashas being in hiding outside the country at this point.[62] It appears as though he was not yet aware of the fact that German public opinion was beginning to turn against them.

Djemal attributed the death sentences given to him and other Ottoman leaders to the fact that they had declared war on the Entente, as well as the fact that they had been "unable to prevent the Armenian massacres." He made it sound as if those "massacres" had not happened at the instigation of the Ottoman government and claimed that the Constantinople court had no real evidence and thus no concrete proof. He then stated that once his colleagues were able to publish their accounts and sources, the whole world would see that Enver and Talât had "personally no guilt" whatsoever. Djemal then defended himself by stressing that he never had allowed any atrocities against the Armenians whatsoever. On the contrary, he claimed, he did everything to "mitigate the fate of the deportees"—giving out food, intervening against marauders, setting up orphanages and workhouses, and so on. Finally, he also cited more than a dozen documents from the Lepsius volume, by concrete citation, that he asserted supported his claims of having helped the Armenians. While he noted that he found some contestable documents in there as well, he obviously felt he could use this by now well-known book to prove his innocence. And indeed, by using the Lepsius volume for his defense, Djemal thus clearly and very publicly endorsed it and affirmed its basic veracity. The interesting thing about Djemal Pasha's defense is that he did not directly deny the alleged extent of the atrocities and the dying at all—he "only" denied intent. Djemal Pasha's arguments, or rather his self-serving justifications, were also discussed in other papers in the coming weeks—for example in the *Neue Preussische (Kreuz-)Zeitung* and the *Deutsche Allgemeine Zeitung*.[63] Djemal Pasha was to come back to Germany with this line of argumentation three years later, in 1922, when his memoirs were published and Germany was still debating the Armenian Genocide.[64]

The Lepsius volume did not convince everybody and the debate did not come to an end, even months after the publication of *Germany and*

Armenia. In mid-September, the *Deutsche Orient-Korrespondenz* again discussed the question of German guilt, now prompted by allegations in the London *Times* that the Lepsius publication "proved" Germany's guilt—an absurd claim, the paper asserted, as even in the *Times* article it became clear that Germany had done everything it could have.[65] The German press continued to pour out articles based on the Lepsius volume, well into 1920. A further impetus for discussion came in the winter of 1919, when Lepsius's clandestine wartime report was republished. The *Essener Volkszeitung* published an essay on 2 February 1920 with the title "Death March of the Armenian People—Germany's Guilt?" that incorporated the new title of Lepsius's report (as its main title).[66] It began by stating that wartime censorship had been disastrous, as it had prevented the truth about the Armenians from becoming known.

As was so often the case in this early phase of the debate, it was all about Germany: "Now, that the files are available and we, [here] at home, are seeing things that make our hair stand on end, only now are we able to grasp the disaster that has come over us [*sic*]; though it is a consolation to the friend of mankind that the complete innocence of the German authorities has been proven."[67] Thus without any apparent irony the *Essener Volkszeitung* understood the Armenian Genocide mainly as a disaster for the Germans—probably in the sense of today's "PR disaster." The article ended with a call to the German press to use both Lepsius publications in order to speak out *for* the Armenians. And while the paper insisted on German innocence, it also conceded that there was a strong prima facie case to be made for Germany's guilt: "All this happened while Turkey was allied with Germany and German officers commanded in Turkey. Who wouldn't be surprised if this circumstance was widely used to make Germany accountable for these outrageous mass murders?"

However, then the *Essener Volkszeitung* continued to give its account of the genocide with all the horrible details already presented in the previous articles, including the estimate of over one million dead. The paper also established clear intent and dismissed the alleged "rebellion of Van" as Ottoman propaganda and a pretext for genocide. It also identified the motives and the culprits: the Young Turk Committee, "whose spiritual masters were Talât Bey, the minister of the interior, and Enver Pasha, minister of war and commander in chief." According to the paper,

> in order to inflame [the passions] of national fanaticism and to make it
> subservient to their goals, [they had] proclaimed the exclusive rule of

the Turkish race as their goal. It is obvious that such an exclusive rule can only be erected upon the grave of the non-Turkish peoples, and it is only once one understands this that one can see what Talât Pasha really meant when he told a member of the German embassy that the Ottoman government would use the world war to thoroughly clean its house of the "internal enemies," without being troubled by the intervention of foreign powers. These "internal enemies" were the Christian peoples in the Turkish Empire, most prominent among them the Armenians.

The *Essener Volkszeitung* further claimed that Enver and Talât Pasha had enriched themselves without any shame. The paper was especially analytical when it came to genocide: the deportations—even as deportations—were meant to kill all Armenians, "because the Turks did not take the least precautions for the feeding of the masses on the trail of suffering. They were supposed to die. . . . Of [1.4 million] people only a third were left after this caravan of death. And this [third] then became victims of systematic starvation. Those left afterward had to undergo forced conversion to Islam."

This is but a cursory survey of the reaction to the Lepsius volume. His collection of documents had single-handedly pushed a large part of the German press into acknowledging the charge, extent, and intent of genocide (in the terms of the time).[68] In sum, the Lepsius volume "succeeded" on two accounts: first, it provoked debate and created an awareness of the genocide; second, it "proved" beyond doubt to almost all of the German press and also the public (it appears, at least) that Germany was not guilty of coconspiracy and coexecution of the genocide. It is quite remarkable how ready the German public was to accept that otherwise-mighty Germany could not have done anything to save the Armenians.

Abroad, the reception of both the volume and the German reaction to it was not as forgiving. It is worth quoting the *New York Tribune*'s article "Germany and the Armenians" from 14 August 1919 at length to see how the book and the debate were understood there:

What did Germany do to save the Armenian people from extinction? We have at last the final German answer to this question and from a source no less competent than Dr. Johannes Lepsius. . . . He is the German publicist [that is, writer or journalist] who, when the German press was working overtime to clear the Turkish government from the charges of Armenian Horrors, issued, on the basis of first hand intelligence, his "Report on the Condition of the Armenian People in Turkey," containing the most sweeping indictment so far at hand of the methods and purposes of the Young Turkish government and endorsing in full the reports of American witnesses and the findings of the Bryce committee....

A curious feature of this book was the omission of references to the share of the German government in the responsibility for the extermination of Armenians. Dr. Lepsius dismissed this phase with a perfunctory remark to the effect that Germany has vainly protested against the horrors. The inference was obvious that his failure to attempt a defense implied an admission of Germany's guilt.

The correctness of this surmise is now proved beyond the possibility of doubt by the appearance in Berlin of another book of Dr. Lepsius's, entitled "Germany and Armenia" and purporting to be based on the "entire material in the archives of the German Foreign Office." The Berlin newspapers are playing up this book as a complete vindication of Germany's course, and ridicule the charges raised by the Entente press, to which, they say, Dr. Lepsius has now dealt a mortal blow.

Unfortunately for this argument, the German papers also print extracts from Dr. Lepsius's new book, and the passages quoted do not seem to bear out the accompanying editorial exultation. Yet it may be assumed that the extracts were chosen with a view to making out the strongest possible case for Germany's innocence.

Well, we are told that on July 4, 1915, the German Ambassador at Constantinople submitted a memorandum to the Grand Vizier which "repeated, in the most solemn form, the representations, made as early as June, against 'such shameful occurrences'" as the massacre of a few hundred thousand Armenian Christians. Strange to say, the memorandum, in spite of its "most solemn form," did not make much of an impression, as twelve days later Ambassador Wangenheim wrote to the Imperial Chancellor: "The Porte continues to deport and annihilate the Armenians.... We cannot prevent the Turkish government from doing so, but must assign to her all responsibility for the political and economic consequences of the measures."

Nor did the heroism of the German Ambassador stop here. In 1916, we learn, Secretary of State Zimmermann declared in a Reichstag committee that "the Turkish Minister of Interior had said the Ambassador was making a bore of himself" with his complaints about Armenia. Finally, on March 19, 1918, the Secretary of State said: "The German government went to the limit in exerting pressure on Turkey. No German government could have assumed the responsibility for a break with Turkey, with the consequent exposure of our southeastern front."

In other words, Germany said naughty, naughty, Turkey did not care, and Germany shrugged her shoulders. This is what the "complete vindication" actually amounts to. It leaves the matter standing just where it stood before. The one significant fact is that this sort of stuff, even today, eight months after the so-called revolution [in Germany], still is swallowed by German public opinion.[69]

More, similar articles appeared abroad. They did not find the Lepsius volume to be the vindication of the German government that it was accepted to be at home, but rather to be proof of what had been widely assumed abroad before, that the German government had not done anything beyond "academic protests," as the London *Times* called it.[70] Such articles—in particular the *Times* article and its echo in countries like the Netherlands and Denmark—led the German Foreign Office to caution its legations abroad to make more circumspect use of the Lepsius volume. So this exercise in German whitewashing did not go quite as the Foreign Office had planned: it had not managed to substantially change opinion abroad; it mainly succeeded in convincing the public at home of Germany's innocence, but in doing so had begun a genocide debate.[71]

The Backlash Year

Very much as in the 1890s, a broad momentum of "acceptance" (of the allegations of violence carried out against the Ottoman Armenians) was followed by a backlash. The second year of the German genocide debate was characterized by the predominance of denialism. Denialism here denotes an approach that rejects the charge of genocide (against the Young Turks), mainly by denying intent and minimizing the extent of the atrocities. As we have seen, in the first year many papers had already accepted that what had happened was something we today would describe as genocide. The second year saw the development of a pronounced faction of "genocide deniers"—a faction of papers resisting the charge of genocide by minimizing the extent of the atrocities (often through comparisons to less extensive crimes) and either justifying them or denying intent. Toward the end of this German genocide debate, as we shall see, it was this faction—though now in its "evolved," justificationalist form—that would carry the day.

This denialist backlash could take place mainly because those who had accepted the charge of genocide seem to have been content with the fact that Germany's innocence had been "proven" and did not much discuss the matter further. Thus the topic was "resolved" for them and they handed over the public arena to those who still felt it necessary to talk about it more. And those papers that came to constitute the core of the denialist camp—such as, for example, the *Neue Preussische (Kreuz-)Zeitung* and the *Deutsche Allgemeine Zeitung*—had the urge to talk quite a lot more. This was to be the long year of the denialists, beginning in early January 1920 with an article in the *Kreuzzeitung* and ending in mid-March 1921 with the assassination of Talât Pasha. Though the year of the denialists was not entirely without opponents: some papers printed eyewitness accounts of German soldiers who had served with the Ottomans.[72] But remarkably, the denialists were the most vocal and now offered the most extensive coverage of what had happened to the Armenians.

While some had already earlier tried to either deny (the extent) or justify what had happened, most anti-Armenian papers had remained uncharacteristically quiet in the first year of the unfolding genocide debate. Some had, however, repeated the usual pejorative and racially charged negative statements about the Armenians, and had justified the massacres as military or even "racial self-defense," but these voices had been largely drowned out. In 1920, however, they started to gain strength and prominence, and this began with the *Neue Preussische (Kreuz-)Zeitung* on 2 January. Here the *Kreuzzeitung* vented the general air, or rather stench, of the times: it stressed that still now, that is, in the unfolding Turkish War of Independence, the Armenians were still acting as the "tools of the Entente," and not even only in the Armenian provinces, "but everywhere."[73]

Its article on the "Armenian Question" opened with the claim that "whoever has dealt with Armenian history before will know" that "the Armenians in their centuries-old history have proven that they, like certain other peoples, are not fit to construct their own states after all." With "certain other peoples" the paper was clearly referring to "the Jews," and the notion of not being "state-building nations" prefigures the later Nazi notion of "culture-creating peoples" that was to become an integral building block in Nazi anti-Semitism and its Aryan/non-Aryan distinction. The Armenians, according to the *Neue Preussische (Kreuz-)Zeitung,* had always had a rather "ambiguous role" vis-à-vis those states under whose suzerainty they happened to live. This, the paper alleged, could be traced back to Babylonian times—again equating, or rather confusing, the Armenians with the Jews. This "ambiguous role"—an obvious code here for treacherousness, disloyalty, and backstabbing—was enough for the *Kreuzzeitung* to claim that one just could not blame Turkey for the Armenian Horrors (the term now being applied in the debate to the genocide as well as to the 1890s massacres). While, the paper went on, it would not be necessary here to expand upon the insurgencies of the Armenians in the last decades—as if everybody knew about them—it was the Entente dimension that deserved further exploration. The *Kreuzzeitung* explained:

> During the war not only on the Mediterranean front, but also on the Caucasus front against the Russians, the Armenians committed wartime treason [*Kriegsverrat*]. These are facts which cannot easily be disregarded, and it would be good if we Germans asked ourselves what we would have set in motion if a foreign people with a certain strength had acted this way in our country during the war.

Although the paper then made a reference to the "Oriental circumstances," the call for Germans to reflect upon what they would have done was, of course, telling and refuted any budding "culturalist" interpretation: the *Kreuzzeitung* in no ambiguous fashion was endorsing large-scale "ethnic engineering" (or at least ethnic punishment) as a solution for certain problems, especially so in times of war. Given that the extent of annihilation had already been known for over half a year and that it was already part of the public discourse, the *Kreuzzeitung*'s call for a "normalized," if not pragmatic, view and a translation of the events into a German context was highly dangerous. Using the term "wartime treason" was an intended allusion to the stab-in-the-back myth, and the paper's readers must have thought of "the Jews" when they read the passage quoted above, in which the paper was talking about a hypothetical German situation. Given the nationalist discourse in these months, the only thing hypothetical—in this parallel scenario—was that "the Jews" did not possess the same strength in numbers as the Armenians did (a "problem" that Nazi discourse would overcome by focusing on, or rather obsessing over, Jewish power and world conspiracy).[74]

A few weeks later, Ernst Paraquin, who had served as a high-ranking officer in the Ottoman Empire and who had been replaced by a Turk after speaking out on behalf of the Armenians, published a two-part op-ed in the *Berliner Tageblatt*. Paraquin especially attacked Turkish denialism: "With hypocritical indignation the Turkish government denies all barbarous conduct against the Armenians." He unequivocally affirmed that "the Armenian question was solved by annihilating the Armenians."[75] Such a clear condemnation and acknowledgment of genocide by a former high-ranking "German Ottoman" should have made an impact, were it not for the fact that this was drowned in a sea of denialist voices.

The next major denialist exposition was the article by "Serman" in the *Berliner Lokal-Anzeiger* on 5 February 1920.[76] This author, probably a member of the Turkish exile community in Berlin, focused on three points: first, the massacres had merely been a wartime measure that had been absolutely necessary; second, Talât Pasha was a good man; and, finally, that these were the same kind of "crimes" as had been committed elsewhere during the war and even afterward. The latter point was underlined by a reference to Ireland and the fact that "nowhere were harsher measures taken than there." But his main focus was on the war and the character of the Armenians: "Whoever was a little acquainted with the situation in Turkey during the war, knew that there was treason and espionage lurking everywhere, be it on the part of the Greeks, the Arabs, or the Armenians; he will not be surprised [to know] that draconian measures had to be taken in order to be able to wage war at all."

The heated conflict over the extradition of "war criminals"—which most of the German press continued to put in quotation marks—from the Central Powers to the Entente continued to influence the German Armenian debate in this year. This made the connection to all other "imperialist" or war crimes all the more "obvious" and "necessary" for the German nationalist denialist camp. On 12 February, German papers published the "extradition list" of the Entente on their first page. In the *Neue Preussische (Kreuz-)Zeitung,* for example, it took up almost the whole title page.[77] In its Turkish section, the second entry was "for the Armenian massacres," naming Enver, Talât, and Djemal Pasha as well as others.

Two weeks later, an article in the same paper showed just how much denialist expositions were incorporating relativist reasoning. Under the title "Armenia and Amritsar," the *Kreuzzeitung* began its discussion with reference to the press debate about the "alleged mass murder of the Armenian people"—the paper was now backpedaling a bit, as previously it had not called the factuality of mass murder into question.[78] Oddly, it claimed that this was a recent debate—"in the last few days"—even though the debate and indeed the paper's own participation in it had been ongoing for many months. It stressed that "certain sects," "which are especially strongly represented in England," were highly motivated in this struggle—another clear reference to the Jews. It then recounted various propaganda victories of this "sect" and of the Entente, only to then claim that "apparently nobody stops to think about Ireland where the shooting and the murdering continues. It appears as purest irony that the report of the official inquest into the case of Amritsar just arrived from India." The paper thus equated the Ireland conflict as well as the massacres carried out by British troops at the temple at Amritsar (in April 1919) to the Armenian massacres. In total relativism and in total disregard for the human misery involved in all these cases, the paper made fun of all the dead by asking, "What now if the Indians were able to send an extradition list to the English government!?" Nevertheless the paper closed by acknowledging that one had the right to be angry about the "bloodbath [carried out] among the Armenians," and pointed out that even at this very moment "Armenian massacres" were taking place in Anatolia. This was an unexpected concession, one that the paper would not feel it needed to make again in the coming year.

Around the same time, other papers also reported that Armenians were once again being massacred (by Kemalist troops in the Turkish War of Independence).[79] Now, with the Paris peace negotiations still ongoing—the Treaty of Sèvres was only signed in August 1920, over a year after the Treaty of Versailles—news about the Armenian question at the negotiations was also used as a running commentary about the unfair treatment of Turkey and, in extension, of Germany by the Entente.[80] Especially vocal was one article in late April 1920 in the *Deutsche Tageszeitung* about how "Turkey was being robbed of even the last semblance of independence under the guise of the 'protection of religious minorities.' "[81]

In these months, the Armenians continued to be painted in the worst colors. On 28 April, under the headline "Armenians against the French," the *Neue Preussische (Kreuz-)Zeitung* rather happily reported that the French were withdrawing their troops from Urfa in Southeastern Anatolia because the Armenians had come to an understanding with the Kemalists: "It is remarkable that the French justify their withdrawal with the defection of the allegedly through and through Entente-friendly [previous five words in bold in original] Armenians." While the report called into question the prevalent idea of pro-Entente Armenians, it determinedly sustained and underlined the belief that the Armenians could not be trusted, not even by their "friends."[82] What had happened there, and the *Kreuzzeitung* was delighted to report this, was something of a "double wartime treason." An article in the *Deutsche Zeitung* on 4 July 1920 again stressed the use of Armenian militia and gendarmerie units in the French occupying forces against the Turks. Here, and in other papers such as the *Deutsche Allgemeine Zeitung,* the Armenians during these months were portrayed as the eternal fifth column.[83]

The allegations of genocide and of German complicity were answered once more in June 1920 in a lengthy opinion piece in the *Deutsche Zeitung.*[84] It began by reminding its readers that already during the war and afterward so much had been written about the "Armenian Horrors" that there would indeed be no need to speak about them anymore, were it not for the fact that the Entente propaganda machine was so successful at continually reviving the issue. The rebuttal that the paper offered allegedly illustrated just how bloodthirsty and cruel the Armenians themselves had been under cover of the Russian occupation of parts of Eastern Anatolia during the war. The main thrust of the article was not only to show just how cruel the Armenians—as a race—really were, but also to stress that there were claims about "horrors" on both sides and that it would probably remain an unclear chapter of the war forever; it was simply not resolvable, the *Deutsche Zeitung* declared. But

> it can be assumed as [a matter of] fact that both sides waged a war of annihilation with all its consequences. They will quibble in vain about the question of who has committed the most horrible acts and who started. . . . One thing is however clear: the emissaries and the gold of the Entente have constantly stirred up the Armenians in order to stab Turkey in the back when it was critically struggling over its existence [last part in bold].

The year of the denialists was strongly interwoven with the events surrounding the fate of the contemporary Armenians. The haggling over and ultimately the rejection of a US mandate for Armenia by Congress was of special interest for the anti-Armenian faction, almost in a manner suggesting that this had entertainment value for them. This just showed, the nationalist papers agreed in unison, that Armenia was merely a propaganda tool and that not even the oh-so-noble United States really cared so much as to help the Armenians. The question of a mandate for Armenia was to be discussed until the end of the year.[85] November and December 1920 were especially busy months for the Armenian topic, as it was also discussed at the League of Nations.[86] The *Neue Preussische (Kreuz-)Zeitung* summed up the discussion on the "Armenian mandate" in mid-December by stressing that mandate was just another word for "colony" anyway.[87] It purported to read the whole Armenian question solely through the prism of "Entente morality": it was merely used to subdue Turkey; "it was the sorrowful child of the Oriental question." The *Kreuzzeitung* gleefully concluded, "So this is now the liberation of Armenia from the Turkish yoke—the country is further away from peace than ever in its history." And the *Kreuzzeitung* blamed not only the Entente for that; again, it mainly blamed the Armenians themselves. It asserted again that the Armenians were just not a state-building people, and lacked even the potential for home rule. Not so the Turks: "They are just a great historical people that cannot be wiped off the map." With such a conclusion the paper suggested that genocide and massacres—to wipe off and to be wiped off the map—were tests of historical greatness and of racial character and worth.

A similar approach was implicit in Liman von Sanders's article of January 1921, in which the famous German Ottoman claimed that "the state of the Armenians, which was established through a line of a pen on the map, only exists on paper."[88] He made fun of the Treaty of Sèvres and the so-called Armenian government, and stressed that almost nowhere in the projected districts was there an Armenian majority—which, as he should have known, was the result of the Armenian Genocide. It is quite remarkable that this was one of the last lengthy treatments of the Armenian topic in the German press before Talât Pasha was assassinated. It appears as if in January 1921, one could already openly make fun of the Armenians and the genocide. This was to change again with the assassination in Berlin.

CHAPTER 10

Assassination in Berlin, 1921

As Chapter 9 showed, a genocide debate had begun in 1919 and 1920 in Germany. In the first two years it had mainly focused on the question of German guilt. But it had also led to the acceptance of the charge of genocide (leveled against the Young Turks), including the full extent of what could be known and the intent to commit genocide (in the terms of the times) by many papers. This had been followed by the now quasi-traditional backlash in the form of a drive to deny the extent of the massacres by a rather large, if not overwhelmingly large, part of the press, with any remnants of the press that had accepted and condemned genocide quieted. All this was to change in 1921, and it began with a shot fired on the Hardenbergstraße, just around the corner from Berlin's famous and mundane shopping street, the Kurfürstendamm.

• • •

Although this might seem too much of a cliché, 15 March 1921 probably was indeed a rainy spring morning in Berlin. The street just around the corner from the Kurfürstendamm and Zoo Station was crowded with people. A young man walked up to an older, neatly dressed man from behind. He stood very close as he drew his revolver. The bullet entered the back of the head and exited through the victim's left eye. The victim fell over and died immediately. Bystanders did not let the assassin escape, and started beating him. He screamed something along the lines of "It's ok. I am a foreigner and he is a foreigner!" A few moments later he told the police that he was not the murderer but that, in fact, the victim was "the murderer"—the murderer of a nation.[1]

The victim was none other than *the* Talât Pasha—as the *Berliner Tage-blatt* had written even in 1917, he was so well known in Germany "that a description seems superfluous."[2] His assassin was Soghomon Tehlirian, an Armenian student who carried out the death sentence to which various Armenian organizations had condemned Talât Pasha as the prime author of the genocide. Tehlirian was a member of Nemesis, an Armenian organization devoted to executing all of those held responsible for the genocide—but at this point nobody yet knew about this organization, and it would not be until 1957, when Tehlirian published his memoirs in Cairo in Armenian, that he revealed his real story "to the world," or at least that part of the world that took any notice of it.[3]

Obviously, the assassination of the former Ottoman grand vizier was a sensational story for the German media. A few months later, Bronsart von Schellendorff would claim that this assassination had resonated all across Germany, even in the smallest village.[4] Furthermore, Talât Pasha's death finally confirmed that he had indeed been hiding in Berlin since the war, though many newspapers had been sure that he was in Berlin all along. When the nationalist-conservative Kapp Putsch failed in 1920, Talât had been seen and heard at the press conference in Berlin that followed it, criticizing the dilettantism of the attempted coup d'état.[5]

The way the German press reacted to the assassination allows us to see where they stood after the first two years of the German genocide debate. On the day of the assassination, 15 March, some of the evening editions of the major papers already took note of it, most of these on the front page.[6] Most papers were not yet sure who had been murdered though.[7] Others knew that it had been Talât Pasha and some, like the *Deutsche Allgemeine Zeitung,* already printed a first obituary of this pro-German Turkish leader.[8] The immediate mood was one of outrage and sympathy for the victim. None of the papers mentioned or knew the motives of the assassin. Only a few, like the *Neue Preussische (Kreuz-)Zeitung,* speculated about possible and probable political reasons behind it, but failed to mention the Armenian Horrors of World War I, or any Armenian connection for that matter.[9] Others even mentioned (romantic) "jealousy" as the motive.[10] As so often, the *Kreuzzeitung* set the mood for many in the nationalist fold: it gushed about what a wonderful person and great statesman Talât Pasha had been, the poster-boy patriot and devoted friend of Germany who had been forced to leave his country precisely because he had been too pro-German.[11]

The next day, all national papers, as well as most of the provincial ones, covered Talât Pasha's assassination, printing obituaries as well as, in some cases, comment pieces. The *Vossische Zeitung* devoted the longest front-page article in its morning edition to the assassination.[12] It encapsulated many of the themes and interpretations that were to abound in the German press in the coming months. It began by mentioning that Talât Pasha and Enver Pasha had been included in the infamous extradition lists of the Entente, two years before, because they, together with other members of the government, had been responsible for the "butchering of the Armenians." It portrayed the assassination as an act of "blood revenge" carried out by a single Armenian in the name of his entire nation. The *Vossische Zeitung* also commented that during the war "the Turkish nation had evidently set itself the goal to use this opportunity to end the age-old feud . . . preferably by exterminating all reachable members of the [Armenian] tribe." However, while accepting both the extent and intent of genocide, the paper also advanced a whole battalion of *justifications for* genocide: for example, the Armenians had been "widely distributed, of high intellect, and difficult to handle," "during the war they sided openly with the enemy," and, anyway, the Armenian massacres had been an integral part of enemy propaganda during the war.

In the *Vossische Zeitung*'s evening edition, yet another article on Talât Pasha appeared, penned by Erwin Barth.[13] Here the "rare statesmanlike qualities" of Talât Pasha were praised, and it was observed that it was only under pressure from the Entente that he had been sentenced to death. And while Barth acknowledged repeatedly what had happened, though only cryptically, he also found many excuses and claimed that Talât was the wrong target for Armenian revenge—a sentiment shared by other papers at the time.[14] Thus, on the one hand, he wrote that "certainly there was not one human who would deny the great suffering of the Armenian people in the last war and would excuse its authors." On the other, he pleaded, in a typical culturalist fashion, that from the "civilization and additionally from the great distance of Western Europe," one could not pass judgment on the Armenian Horrors. Especially so since they "have been exploited by Entente propaganda together with the supposed German horrors committed in Belgium." Barth continued with his culturalism: "It is the primitive level of the Oriental people that makes understandable the cruel harshness of [their] national and religious struggle." And while he was ready to condemn the excessive severity of the measures, he also stressed that guilt was certainly not found on one side alone.

Some still tried to ignore or downplay the Armenian connection. The *Neue Preussische (Kreuz-)Zeitung* wrote in its morning edition, "The motives still lie in the dark, but it cannot be excluded that this might have been an act of revenge for the Armenian murders [*Armeniermorde*] allegedly instigated by Talât Pasha."[15] In its evening edition, it featured another two articles, one on Talât Pasha, and another about the first interrogation of the assassin.[16] It saw the assassination as the "deed of an Armenian fanatic" and claimed that while there might have been political motivations, it had mainly been an act of personal revenge, a deed that had shattered "these beautiful days of March, in which in all Turkish hearts a new spring of life is awakening."[17] This was a reference to the Turkish War of Independence and its message of national redemption as perceived by the German nationalist media at the time (see Chapter 14).[18] Others claimed that behind the deed was not so much revenge but rather the (eternal) Armenian desire to further weaken Turkey to the point of breaking it up and "realizing their national dreams."[19]

On the first day of what was to become the "Talât Pasha media event," it was the *Deutsche Allgemeine Zeitung* that established itself as the clear avant-garde of the nationalist-denialist camp.[20] The paper was in fact the renamed *Norddeutsche Allgemeine Zeitung,* formerly the mouthpiece of the imperial government.[21] It had been handed over by its owner, Hugo Stinnes, to Hans Humann, who now controlled it not only as editor in chief but with all the powers of an owner. We met Humann last during our discussion of World War I in Constantinople, where he was one of the most influential Germans, a friend of Enver's, and a major Armenian-hater. Humann had almost incriminated himself in nationalist circles as he had been assigned to the German delegation for the peace negotiations in Paris. Had he stayed on, he surely would have been held responsible for the "slave treaty," the Treaty of Versailles, by his fellow nationalists later. In the end, the Armenian topic saved him. American ambassador Henry Morgenthau's book had just appeared and had indicted Humann for his part in the Armenian Genocide. Thus he was kicked off the delegation at the last minute, about which he was very happy.[22] Now, with his paper, in Margaret Lavinia Anderson's words, he "continued the war against the Armenians by other means."[23]

Humann's *Deutsche Allgemeine Zeitung* poured praise over Talât Pasha in numerous articles on 16 March; it covered the assassination in no fewer than four articles on that day.[24] In an especially spiteful piece about "The Armenian Murderer," it expressed satisfaction that finally, the (allegedly) sentimental, pro-Armenian German public were being presented with an "Armenian murderer," and not only the "Armenian martyr," which was all they had seen or wanted to see up to now.[25] (The implication, of course, was that the former image better expressed the Armenians' true nature.) The *Deutsche Allgemeine Zeitung* then maintained that during the Great War, the Armenians had not only "conspired constantly with the English" but had been responsible for major Turkish defeats. While the paper acknowledged that the deportations had not been the nicest things—"all this is not pretty"—it stressed that this was, in essence, a racial question and that there was guilt on both sides, "at the very least." It further stressed that the souls of all the Armenians were filled with a fanatical hatred for the Turks, inconceivable for the Germans, and that, at that very moment, political crimes were committed by Armenians against Turks in Constantinople on a daily basis. The paper further claimed that "it has transpired [in the past] that they have married off their women to Turks only so that they would kill [their Turkish husbands later]. Nice 'martyrs.'" And if all that was not enough, the paper was also the first to offer a full postwar exposition of anti-Armenian clichés, prominent among which was the following characterization: "The cunning of ten Jews equals that of a Greek and ten Greeks are not as cunning as one Armenian. In every petty bazaar, even the European is overcome by disgust at the Armenian." It also stressed that "the Armenian" was "sucking the Turks dry. He undermines their country. The Turks cannot defend themselves against this. They [then] do that with the fist, according to old traditions. They avenge themselves. Avenging themselves until blood flows." It continued, "The Armenian question is not about 'Christian martyrs.' Whoever knows the Orient, knows how tolerant the Muslim is. It is thus a question of race and of blood vengeance. And, at the very least, there is guilt on both sides. [Oh,] how the Armenians have damaged Turkey and us during the war! It did not end with [their] rebellions and raids."

The *Deutsche Allgemeine Zeitung* was also the first paper to start a cross-paper debate on the topic, and indeed it did so on this very first day after the assassination. It attacked unnamed papers that, it said, were acting in a wholly irresponsible fashion by protecting the "cowardly murderer"

Tehlirian by pointing out that he had been motivated by the suffering of the Armenian people.[26] It had to be made clear, the paper countered, that the Armenians—with very few exceptions—had made common cause with the enemy. It mentioned the incredible number of 120,000 Armenian volunteers who had fought in the armies of the Entente. (This was probably a misleading reference to the number of Russian Armenians serving in the Tsarist armies.) The paper made the familiar points that the "purportedly so very democratic English government was on the rampage in Ireland right now," and that the situation in Turkey had not been comparable to European conditions anyway. The paper then homed in on the stab-in-the-back image: Tehlirian had killed Talât Pasha from behind. Not surprisingly, the article's concluding sentence read, "This is the true Armenian manner!"[27]

Similarly, the *Deutsche Zeitung,* another nationalist paper, called the assassination an act of vengeance by an "Armenian criminal" against Talât Pasha, who, "as was known, had taken rigorous measures when nothing else had worked." It continued with the hope and the prediction that "perhaps now [all] the shouting about the 'Turkish horrors in Armenia' will [finally] fall silent."[28]

Another extreme reaction was that of the Communist *Freiheit*— "extreme," however, only in the sense that it was characteristic of only very few papers at the time. It was one of the few papers that was sympathetic to Tehlirian and called Talât Pasha a "war criminal." It also mentioned more than one million victims of Talât Pasha's "Armenian butcheries."[29] The *Freiheit,* just as the *Deutsche Allgemeine Zeitung* had done, but with a different target, also began a cross-paper debate. It attacked the Social Democratic *Vorwärts* as an "agent of the reaction," especially because it had only good words for the "butcher of the Armenians" *(Armenierschlächter)*—once again the Armenian topic was inserted into the inner-Left conflict. The *Vorwärts* extensively cited Theodor Wolff of the *Berliner Tageblatt,* who, among others, had written after the assassination that Talât Pasha had no sense of guilt and that he had been part of this "effacement of a people" *(Austilgung eines Volkes).* Wolff was further quoted saying that "Talât Pasha was a politician who wanted to secure political unity through the annihilation of foreign religionists and foreign races."[30]

An interesting feature of the first day after the assassination was the lack of a moral compass that Christian Germany exhibited, as shown in the coverage of the paper of political Catholicism, the *Germania.* While acknowledging the horrific nature of the Armenian butcheries *(Armenier-metzeleien)*, the paper put the victims at "merely tens of thousands," where most others spoke of more than a million. Its explanation for what had happened was simple culturalism: "The Turkey of the 20th century is no civilized European country."[31] And, finally, another feature of the first day was the timid emergence of a new kind of argumentation that floated in what was otherwise the denialist camp—one that accepted and justified genocide at the same time. The *Berliner Lokal-Anzeiger* offered a lot of the by now usual details of the horrors of the deportations and the genocide. But at the same time, it claimed that at the time of the Young Turk revolution of 1908, "it was only [Talât Pasha's] brutal course of action against the Armenians that led the [Young Turk] uprising to its goal."[32] In other words, the Armenians had somehow already endangered the 1908 revolution, and the (1909) Adana massacre then had been necessary for the revolution's success. Together with the tale of genocide in the same article, it timidly suggested that a "brutal course of action," like genocide, might be necessary to achieve one's political goals. In its evening edition, the same paper stressed that there had been Armenian conspiracies behind the assassination, which had been carried out just "for the money," and stressed how valuable Talât Pasha would have been for the future of Turkey.[33] The reporting of the *Berliner Morgenpost* and the *Hamburger Nachrichten,* for example, was in a similar vein, acknowledging the "murder of the Armenians" *(Armenier-mord)* committed during the war, but also claiming that there was guilt "everywhere" and speaking of the "Turkish-Armenian blood feud" that had been "raging for decades in the Turkish Empire."[34] A few papers, however, like the *Königsberger Hartungsche Zeitung,* used the occasion to reexamine the Armenian Genocide. It tried to establish the "blood guilt of Talât Pasha that cannot be washed away" for having decided at the beginning of the war to "exterminate the Armenians." The paper did so by once more discussing the evidence provided by the Lepsius Foreign Office volume at length.[35]

Talât Pasha was laid to rest in Berlin and many important dignitaries of political Germany attended the ceremony, including an emissary of the exiled kaiser and two former foreign ministers. It was organized by Ernst Jäckh (whom we have met in previous chapters). The ribbon on the wreath of the German Foreign Office read, "To a great statesman and a faithful friend." The final speech at the coffin was by a fellow Young Turk, Behaeddin Shakir.[36] With the reports on the burial ceremony for Talât Pasha on 19 and 20 March, the first, intensive part of the Talât Pasha assassination news cycle ended. In the days before, on 17 and 18 March, some papers had speculated about possible conspiracies behind the assassination.[37] Most papers used the burial to restate and reformulate their points of view, in their discussion of the eulogies delivered at the grave.[38] The *Neue Preussische (Kreuz) Zeitung,* for example, again justified whatever had happened in Anatolia as an "imperative dictate of self-preservation" for the Turkish leadership and painted the Armenians as a dangerous fifth column.[39] The *Deutsche Allgemeine Zeitung* again bombarded its readers with a series of articles on 20 March: one on "The True Talât," another on his burial, and a third on the British responsibility for the assassination.[40] Again the paper attacked other nationalist papers for painting Talât Pasha in the wrong light. Now its target was Friedrich Hussong, a journalist and nationalist agitator, often characterized later as Goebbels's teacher.[41] He had—but all in good faith, the paper conceded—described Talât Pasha as a "revolutionary" in an article in the *Berliner Lokal-Anzeiger.* But the *Deutsche Allgemeine Zeitung* could not accept this idea of the "revolutionary Talât," and, apparently, it had to nip it in the bud, perhaps because a true revolutionary would be willing to give his life for the cause and because "revolutionary" just carried too negative an undertone in the anxious atmosphere of the 1920s, so soon after Germany's own democratic revolution. In any case, and as it had made clear many times before, for the paper, Talât Pasha was a genuine and honorable statesman, full stop.

• • •

In the lengthy and influential essay discussing the Lepsius documents in 1919, which we discussed in Chapter 9, Theodor Wolff had argued that the leading Young Turks, especially Enver's family, had done what they had done to the Armenians out of greed. He had estimated that the confiscated property of the Armenians amounted to the equivalent of one billion reichsmarks. Wolff had emphasized that—as reported in the German press in the weeks and months surrounding the publication of his article—"Talât, Enver, and their accomplices" had been sentenced to death by a Constantinople court: "Should fate or a gendarme reach them one day then there would be no reason to view this day as one of mourning."[42] Yet that was exactly what most papers did in March 1921. In a swift reversal of published opinion, from the first year of the genocide debate to the beginning of the third year, the murder of a nation did not outweigh the execution of Talât Pasha by a "survivor." Denialism had been successful. But this was to change yet again with the trial of Soghomon Tehlirian.

CHAPTER 11

Trial in Berlin

For two months after Talât Pasha's burial, April and May 1921, things became quiet on the Armenian topic. Only the *Deutsche Allgemeine Zeitung* continued to lobby the German public with the occasional, aggressively anti-Armenian article.[1] There had not been much sympathy for the assassin, this "Armenian fanatic," as the otherwise heavily pro-Armenian *Kölnische Volkszeitung* put it.[2] With the trial of Talât Pasha's assassin, in early June, the topic not only came back, but immediately regained its character as a media event, and with good reason. Now, for one week, all the major papers covered and commented on the spectacular trial, which itself lasted only one and a half days. And then, after the trial, the German papers continued to offer comments on the spectacular verdict of the trial for many months to come.

The verdict, it appears, had just puzzled the German public and media, and they needed a long period of digestion. The final résumé of the *Deutsche Allgemeine Zeitung,* for example, came only in late July—even though the paper had already featured many long essays on the topic. And even in November, some papers, such as the *Germania,* published a lengthy two-part feature on the verdict, Talât Pasha, and the Armenian question. The *Christliche Welt,* a Christian journal with more than a thirty-year history of pro-Armenian coverage and activism, published its final résumé only in March of the following year. The title of this belated résumé encapsulated the fact that a debate had erupted in postwar Germany that just would not come to an end: "A People That Just Cannot Die."[3] And even in 1926, Alfred Rosenberg, later Hitler's chief ideologue, as some characterize him, felt the urge to comment on the verdict in an article.[4]

• • •

By any account, this trial was one of the most spectacular trials of the twentieth century: a court drama that featured a multiple and constant reversal of roles—judge, state prosecution, and defense, as well as victim and defendant, would all see their roles mixed up. Indeed, the matter was so completely turned around that in the end it was the Ottoman Empire and the victim, Talât Pasha, who were on trial. As the *Vorwärts* put it, "In reality it was the blood-stained shadow of Talât Pasha who was sitting on the defendant's bench; and the true charge was the ghastly Armenian Horrors, not his execution by one of the few victims left alive."[5] And then, though Tehlirian repeatedly admitted that he had indeed killed Talât, he was acquitted and set free. He was not even convicted of a lesser crime such as manslaughter or charged with public endangerment.

A look at how the trial progressed, right from the very first hour, reveals why the question of genocide became so very central and why the trial was turned around against Talât Pasha and, by extension, against the Ottoman Empire. Although the German government, especially the Foreign Office, and also the prosecution had professed the wish not to have it turn into a political trial, already the first minutes of the trial made that impossible. The list of people who were responsible for the direction taken features at the top, of course, Tehlirian, who stated right after the charges had been read out that he was not guilty, though he acknowledged that he had killed Talât Pasha. But a very close second was the presiding judge Lemberg himself. Third on the list would be, again surprisingly, the state prosecutor, and only fourth would be the three-man defense team for Tehlirian itself.

The trial began with a discussion about the order in which witnesses were to be heard. Already at this point the debate turned to the Armenian Genocide—and the state prosecutor hastily protested that the deed had been committed here and not in "Armenia." The judge then began by asking Tehlirian about personal details—date of birth, parents, and so on. By the sixth question, they had already arrived at 1915—the ominous border in time, before and after the commencement of genocide. In a strangely interventionist fashion, Judge Lemberg steered the questioning and thus the trial toward the Armenian Horrors. By the fifteenth question, he was asking directly about the massacres of 1915—the preceding questions had been rather factual, merely quick exchanges of short sentences. The judge pressed on about what had happened to Tehlirian and his family in 1915: "Did the massacres in Erzindjan come as a complete surprise or were there [warning] signs of them?" Tehlirian answered, "We were of the opinion that massacres would take place, because there was news circulating the whole time that people had been killed." Then the judge asked, "Were there any opinions about these massacres? What did they say about them? Why did they take place?" Tehlirian responded by drawing attention to the 1890s massacres. The judge continued to ask many questions about the genocide, such as, for example, if the defendant knew from his own research or talks at home about the reasons for and origins of these massacres. When Tehlirian answered that at home there had been talk about the "new Turkish government," that is, the Young Turks, "taking measures," Judge Lemberg asked, "Might this Turkish government have used the reasoning . . . that it was because of military necessities?" The presiding judge not only knew about the genocide but, obviously, also knew about the German and Turkish discourses surrounding it.[6]

Tehlirian stated that, at the time, he had been told there were "religious and political reasons" for the massacres. The judge was apparently still not satisfied and responded, "It would probably now be advisable to discuss the prehistory of the deed in connection to the personal circumstances of the defendant." The state prosecutor interjected and pleaded that now finally the charges should be read out, but Judge Lemberg responded, "We wish to be thoroughly informed by the defendant about how the massacres came to be and what his family has experienced. The defendant shall recount bit by bit and his story will then be translated." This was, as we shall see, exactly what the defense needed: it reflected their core strategy.

> *Tehlirian began:* After the war started in 1914 and the Armenian soldiers had been drafted came the news, in May 1915, that the schools had to be closed and that the respectable people in the city and the teachers were supposed to be sent off to camps.
>
> *Judge:* Did they take them into certain camps, concentration camps [*Konzentrationslager*]?
>
> *Tehlirian:* I don't know; they had to assemble and were taken away. . . . When these columns of people were led away there were these rumors that those deported earlier had been already killed. And then we learned by telegram that of those deported from Erzindjan only one man was still alive. . . . In early June, the order was given that the

population should prepare itself to leave the city. We were also told that all valuables could be left for safekeeping with the [local] authorities. Three days later the population was deported early in the morning.

The judge then asked about the logistics of the deportation, how much they were allowed to take with them and, of course, where they were destined.

Tehlirian: South . . .

Judge: Who escorted the caravan?

Tehlirian: Gendarmes and mounted soldiers as well as other soldiers.

Judge: In great numbers?

Tehlirian: From both sides of the road.

Judge: From behind and in front?

Tehlirian: From both sides.

Judge: In order to prohibit anyone from leaving?

Tehlirian: Yes.

Judge: How did your parents and your siblings die?

Tehlirian: As soon as the convoy had put some distance between itself and the town, we were told to stop. The gendarmes started plundering and tried to get [all the] money and the valuables of the convoy.

Judge: The guards looted the deportees?

Tehlirian: Yes.

Judge: Now, how were your parents killed?

Tehlirian: During the looting we were shot upon from the front of the convoy. One of the gendarmes carried off my sister. . . . I cannot remember this day anymore. I do not want to be reminded of this day. I would rather die now than to speak about this dark day again.

Upon which the judge stressed: Yet, I have to point out that it is of the utmost importance to this court to hear about these things especially from you, because [after all] you are the only one who can say anything about them. Perhaps you could get a hold of yourself and give it a try.

Tehlirian then continued and exclaimed: They took away everything and [started] beating me. Then I saw how my brother's head was split in two with an axe.

Judge: Your sister was carried off. Did she return?

Tehlirian: Yes, my sister was carried off and raped.

Judge: She did not come back?

Tehlirian: No.

The judge pressed Tehlirian for all possible details: Who split your brother's
head in two?

Tehlirian: When the massacre was started by the soldiers and the
gendarmes, the rabble joined in. Then my brother's head was split.
My mother fell.

Judge: From what?

Tehlirian: I don't know. From a bullet or something else.

Judge: Where was your father?

Tehlirian: I did not see my father. He was farther ahead where there was
fighting too.

Judge: What did you do?

Tehlirian: I felt a blow on my head and then fell down. What happened
afterward, I do not know.

Judge: Did you remain at the site of the massacre?

Tehlirian: I do not know how long I was lying down there. Perhaps two
days. When I woke up, I saw a lot of corpses around me, because the
whole convoy had died that day. I saw stretched-out heaps of dead
bodies. But at first I was not able to make out anything clearly, because
it was a bit dark. In the first moment, I did not know where I was, then
I saw the truth—that they are all dead bodies.

Judge: Did you also find out that among the corpses were your parents and
siblings?

Tehlirian: I saw the body of my mother lying on her face and that the
corpse of my brother was laying on top of myself. More than that I was
not able to find out.

The judge pressed Tehlirian for the details: You said then that the rabble
came to join. What did you mean by that?

Tehlirian: I only know that when the gendarmes began killing, the city
people arrived.

Tehlirian, under the constant guidance of the judge's questions, recounted his story. When he arrived at his wanderings in the mountains,
fleeing from further violence, and recalled how an old woman in a village
in the mountains took him in, the judge asked, "Were these compatriots
[*Landsleute*] that took you in?" "Kurds," Tehlirian answered abruptly,
thereby calling into question the stereotype already prevailing in the
German papers at the time about the Kurds as the main executioners of
genocide. Tehlirian further stated that he spent months in hiding with var-

ious Kurds before he went on to Persia, on foot, with other survivors. He then continued with his story of ceaseless wandering in various countries.

The judge asked Tehlirian whether he or his family and friends had any idea about who had been the instigator of the massacres. This was when one of his three defense attorneys, Adolf von Gordon, made one of his first interventions, asking whether Tehlirian had heard that Talât Pasha had been sentenced to death by a Constantinople court. Next, the defense asked the defendant about details of the massacre—how many Armenians had lived in Erzindjan and what kind of instructions they had received for their march. Then, for the first time, the state prosecutor intervened, after having been silent since the very first minutes of the trial, and asked who had given the order for the deportation, the provincial or the military governor?

The charges against Tehlirian were only read after further details of the prehistory, such as the 1909 Adana massacre, had been discussed as well. At this point, the judge emphasized that the translator should stress in his translation that Tehlirian was charged with premeditated murder. When asked if guilty, Tehlirian replied, "No." The judge commented that previously he had acknowledged his guilt. Tehlirian replied, "I don't consider myself guilty, because my conscience is clear." Asked why, he said, "I have killed a man, but a murderer I was not [sic]." When asked whether he had had a plan to kill Talât Pasha, he stated he had not had a plan, but then, contradicting himself, recounted how the idea was born: "Approximately two weeks before the deed, I was feeling bad and the images from the massacre came in front of my eyes again and again. I saw the corpse of my mother. This corpse stood up and came up to me and said: You saw that Talât is here and you are totally indifferent? You are no longer my son!" The judge, losing what was left of his impartiality, repeated to the jury once more what Tehlirian had just said, and asked him to state what he did next. Tehlirian answered, "I suddenly woke up and decided to kill that man."

The court debated for a bit longer whether or not there had been a plan to kill Talât. Again the judge intervened openly in favor of the defendant: when defense attorney Gordon asked him whether he had decided to kill Talât Pasha or whether the doubts about being able to kill a person had made him drop the idea, Judge Lemberg pointed out that "there had been changes in his resolve."

Another interesting exchange took place over whether Tehlirian had been satisfied with his deed. Upon reaching the point in the narrative where

Tehlirian was brought to the police station, the judge asked, "What did you now think about the deed?"

> *Tehlirian:* I felt a contentedness of the heart.
> *Judge:* And how is it today?
> *Tehlirian:* Still today, I am very content with the deed.

The judge then, perhaps inadvertently, gave a bit of a hint about how he saw the situation: "But you surely know that nobody, under normal circumstances, can be his own judge, no matter how much happened to him?" While he wanted to probe Tehlirian's conscience, he did hint at the fact that these were perhaps not "normal circumstances" after all. Tehlirian alluded again to his dream of the command from his mother, and stressed that Talât had been responsible for the massacres. Judge Lemberg asked, "But you must know that our law forbids murder, outlaws killing a man?" Tehlirian replied, "I do not know this law."

And then, while the question of premeditation was still being discussed, the state prosecutor finally intervened again after a long absence from the proceedings. However, he, too, supported the defense's strategy by drawing the discussion away from premeditation to, once more, the question of the massacres. He stressed that while Tehlirian might have known about the Constantinople court ruling sentencing Talât Pasha to death, this verdict had taken place under the guns of British warships and under a totally different kind of government (in the German nationalist term of the early 1920s, a "fulfillment government," selling out the nation to the Entente). He implied that he did not really believe in the validity of this verdict, but saw it instead as victor's justice, and hoped that the court would agree with him. He then addressed the defendant directly and asked if he, after waking up after the massacre of his family, buried the corpse of his brother—a question that, surely, did not support his own strategy much. Tehlirian answered in the negative, and Judge Lemberg intervened quickly: "But, [you know,] the defendant had to flee, after all he was in grave danger."

After further discussion about how the deportations were announced to the Armenians, the judge finally proceeded to taking evidence. After hearing a few eyewitnesses to the assassination and its immediate aftermath (including police officers, the coroner, and so on), the court proceeded to the questioning of the two landladies with whom Tehlirian had resided, successively, in Berlin. Here, the discussion came to focus on his suspected "epilepsy." This was followed by a series of Armenian witnesses. For example, a twenty-two-year-old Armenian living in Berlin, whose family had been in Erzurum when the massacres began. His parents had been killed and only some of his other relatives, who had managed to leave the town, had survived. Another witness, heard in the afternoon, Tehlirian's translator, also was asked if he had lost relatives in the massacres. He replied in the affirmative, but now referred to the massacres in 1896, where he lost his father, mother, grandfather, a brother, and an uncle. Another witness, an Armenian tobacconist in Berlin, also brought up these "old, evil stories," as the judge called them. He reported that all his acquaintances and all his relatives at home, in Erzurum, had been killed during the 1915 massacres. But much more emblematic of the way the whole trial went was the beginning of the cross-examination of the tobacconist's wife, twenty-six-year-old Christine Tersibashian:

Judge: Of the [assassination] you know nothing?

Tersibashian: No.

Defense (Gordon): I ask to interview the witness about the horrors. Especially if she was in her home country during the war and where she lived.

Tersibashian: I was in Erzurum.

Judge: Is this where you are from?

Thus Judge Lemberg began the cross-examination with a "leading" question. He knew that this would contribute nothing to the direct details of the Talât Pasha assassination, even though the witness was an acquaintance of the assassin. Then the questioning proceeded, again, toward the massacres of 1915, for which, after all, Mrs. Tersibashian was an eyewitness. She related her experiences in Erzurum, setting the scene perfectly for one of the "expert witnesses" scheduled for the next day by the defense, the former German vice-consul of Erzurum, Max Erwin Scheubner-Richter (Chapter 6). Under the guiding questioning by the judge, Tersibashian recounted how the deportation out of Erzurum had been carried out.

Judge: Tell us how many people were guarded, how it happened, how far you traveled, and what happened [then].

Tersibashian: Our family consisted of twenty-one people. Only three survived.

Judge: How large was the whole contingent?

Tersibashian: Five hundred families.

Judge: How did your relatives die?

Tersibashian: . . . We had rented three oxcarts and took with us what we could fit, food and money. We thought we would be taken to Erzindjan. My father and my mother were with us [as well], three brothers, the oldest thirty years old, three boys and the little one of six months, the married sister with her husband, six children, the oldest twenty-two years old. With my own eyes I saw the waste of them all, only three remained and were saved.

Judge: In what fashion?

Tersibashian: When we had left the city and were in front of the fortress of Erzurum the gendarmes came and searched [us] for weapons. Knives, umbrellas, etc. were taken away from us. When we passed this city we saw heaps of dead bodies and I had to walk over corpses [myself] so that my feet became stained with blood.

She then recounted the beginning of the massacre:

Tersibashian: When we continued [after Erzindjan] the guards picked out five hundred young people. Also one of my brothers. But he was able to flee and to come to me. I dressed him up like a girl so that he could stay with me. The other young people were herded together.

Judge: What happened to the selected ones?

Tersibashian: They tied them all together and threw them into the water.

Judge: How do you know this?

Tersibashian: I saw it with my own eyes.

Judge: That they were thrown into the river?

Tersibashian: Yes, that they were thrown into the river and that the current was so powerful that all who had been thrown into the water were ripped away. . . .

Judge: What further happened to your relatives?

Tersibashian: We then arrived in Malatia with whatever we were able to carry on our backs. There they took us up the mountain and separated the men from the women. The women were approximately ten meters away from the men and were able to see with their own eyes what happened to the men. . . . They killed them with axes and threw them into the water. . . . When it became a bit darker, the gendarmes came and picked out the most beautiful women and girls and took them as women for themselves. A gendarme also came to me and wanted to take me as his woman. Those who did not want to comply, who did not want to give in, were impaled with bayonets and their legs were ripped apart. Even pregnant women's ribs were cut open and their babies taken out and thrown away. [*Great commotion in the courtroom; the witness raises her hand.*] I swear that this is true.

Judge: How were you saved?

Tersibashian: My brother also had his head cut off. When my mother saw this, she fell over and was instantly dead. Then a Turk came to me as well and wanted to make me his wife and because I did not agree, he took my child and threw it away.

After hearing more horrible details of what had happened to this convoy, such as that her brother had to leave his wife behind because she was too pregnant, Judge Lemberg asked the witness if all this was really true. Mrs. Tersibashian then stated that "what I have told you is even less than the reality; it was much more horrible." The judge again wanted to know whom the people held responsible for what had happened. She answered, "It happened on Enver Pasha's orders and the soldiers forced the deportees to kneel and shout: 'Long live the pasha!' because the pasha had allowed them to live." This was again followed by commotion in the courtroom—perhaps because Enver Pasha in this period remained a rather admired figure in Germany, still relatively untainted by the Armenian Genocide. The second attorney of the defense, Theodor Niemeyer, added that even though these stories must appear unbelievable, there existed "thousands of such reports." In his closing statement for the defense the next day, Gordon also mentioned the reports of the two German nurses who were in Erzindjan at the same time, which we discussed in the introduction to this book. He stressed that their testimony as well as that of Mrs. Tersibashian—who had traveled through the region with her convoy from Erzurum—showed that Tehlirian's story was "true to the core, and no 'pathetic narrative.'"

In order to further underline the credibility of Mrs. Tersibashian's statements, the defense called upon two expert witnesses, Johannes Lepsius and Liman von Sanders. The state prosecutor concurred. And thus Lepsius took the stage, this giant of German pro-Armenianism whose appearance at this trial was immortalized in the 1991 French movie *Mayrig* (Armenian for "mother"; starring, among others, Omar Sharif). Lepsius was advised by the judge not to go too far in his elaborations, but to focus on whether the stories told by the witness were credible. Lepsius began:

> The general deportation was decided upon by the Young Turk Com-
> mittee, Talât Pasha as minister of the interior as well as probably also
> Enver Pasha as minister of war, and with the help of the organization of
> the Young Turk Committee it was carried out. This deportation . . . ,
> which had probably already been decided upon by April 1915, affected
> the whole of the Armenian population of Turkey with minor exceptions
> which I will mention later. Before the war the population of Turkey had
> included 1,850,000 Armenians. . . . On official order the whole of the
> Armenian population of Anatolia was deported to the Northern and
> Eastern border of the Mesopotamian desert, to Der-es Zor, Rakka,
> Meskene, Ras-el-Ain, and as far as Mosul. Approximately 1,400,000
> Armenians were deported. [Now] what did this dispatch mean? In one
> decree signed by Talât there was the phrase: "The destination of the
> deportations is nothingness" [*Das Verschickungsziel ist das Nichts*].
> Following the spirit of this order, care was taken that of the whole popu-
> lation deported from the East Anatolian provinces . . . only about ten
> percent reached the destination of the deportations. The other ninety
> percent were murdered on the way or—except for the cases in which
> women or girls were sold off by the gendarmes and carried off by Turks
> and Kurds—died of hunger and exhaustion. The Armenians—deported
> from Western Anatolia, Cilicia, and Northern Syria, a considerable
> number of humans flooded together in the concentration camps—were
> to the greatest extent annihilated by systematic starvation and period-
> ical massacres. Thus, whenever the concentration camps were filled up
> by new convoys and there was no more room for the masses of people,
> they were led to the desert in groups and butchered. Turks have de-
> clared that the example that the English provided with the Boers in
> South Africa gave them the idea of the concentration camps. While of-
> ficially it was claimed that the deportations were but preventative mea-
> sures [*Vorbeugungsmaßregeln*], authoritative figures openly admitted in
> private that this was about the annihilation of the Armenian people.

"What I am telling you," Lepsius continued, "emerges from the documents that I have [edited and] published from the records of the imperial embassy and those of the Foreign Office. These are mainly reports of the German consuls in the interior [of Turkey] and of the German ambassadors in Constantinople." He then observed that, similar to the two testimonies heard by the court of personal experiences during the deportations—those by Tehlirian and Mrs. Tersibashian—hundreds more existed, mainly in German, but also in American and English publications. "The facts themselves cannot be denied," he claimed. The "methods of execution" of the orders had been the same everywhere, "otherwise one would have to ask oneself: How could it have been possible to kill one million people in such a short time? This was only possible with the most brutal methods." Lepsius also pointed out that the military court in Constantinople had identified Talât Pasha, Enver Pasha, and Nazim Bey as the main authors of the genocide and had sentenced them to death.

Lepsius went on to emphasize that those of the local authorities who refused to carry out the deportation orders were either replaced or even murdered by their colleagues. He also discussed why those who were not deported had been excluded from the general order, stressing especially and beyond measure the roles of the German consuls, the military representatives, and the ambassador. (It is interesting that he made mention of Consul Rössler, but not of Scheubner-Richter or the conflict we saw in Chapter 6 between him and the embassy; perhaps he deliberately omitted anything that did not fit the story he had been consistently telling since the end of the war: that Germany had done everything it could for the Armenians.)

Lepsius also addressed the anti-Armenian claim that the Armenians had "exploited the Turks," and that the Turks had risen spontaneously against the Armenians. He stressed that both the massacres of 1895/1896 as well as the recent ones had been "administrative measures" (meaning not spontaneous acts of violence). He then addressed the question of how one could understand this from a historical point of view.

The Armenian question is no native plant; it is a creation of European diplomacy. The Armenian people became the victim of the political interests of Russia and England. . . . The humanitarian reasons, the "protection of Christians," were [but] pretexts [for interfering in the affairs of the Ottoman Empire]. When, in 1895, Abdul Hamid signed the Reform Plan that England, Russia, and France had forced upon him, and responded with a whole series of Armenian massacres, Lord Salisbury declared that [now] the Armenian question was settled for England. Count Lobanow made the sultan understand that he should not be worried since Russia would not insist on the execution of the Reform Plan. The sultan drew the [relevant] consequences. The massacre of Sason, 1894, which had then initiated the Reform Plan, claimed one thousand Armenians and the massacres of 1895/96, following the Reform Plan, cost the lives of 100,000 Armenians. The massacre of 1915/1918, which was preceded by the Reform Plan of 1913, reached the number of one million victims. This scale from 1894, 1895, up to 1915: 1,000, 100,000, 1,000,000 represents a fever curve which has hardly any rival in the history of global massacres. And in the meantime, in the year 1909, there was the Cilician massacre which claimed 25,000 victims.

Lepsius continued to explain how the Armenians had been but pawns in the great diplomatic game of the powers, and he also quoted Talât Pasha saying about himself that he was "continuing the work of Abdul Hamid." Lepsius concluded by summarizing how he had shown how both Abdul Hamid and then the Young Turks had come to the conclusion that "nothing better could be done with the Armenians than to annihilate them."

When asked whether this was not a case of centuries-old religious hatred, Lepsius stressed that it was a rather new phenomenon. He explained further: the whole idea of creating a pan-Turkic, pan-Islamic empire was, according to Lepsius, that of the Young Turk Committee and Enver Pasha. Lepsius affirmed defense attorney Niemeyer's clarification that "just as when one says 'pan-German' or 'pan-Russian' or 'pan-Turkish,' one wanted to annihilate everything that was not purely Turkish."

Next up was Liman von Sanders, who began his testimony by stating that he wanted to "supplement" what Lepsius had said from "the military point of view." He stated that, in his opinion, what had happened in Armenia and was usually subsumed under one label, "the Armenian massacres," should in fact be divided into two parts:

> The first [part] is . . . the order of the Young Turk government for the deportations of the Armenians. For this one can accordingly hold the Young Turk government responsible, for the order as such, [but] for the consequences only partly. [And] the other part is the battles that took place in Armenia [for two reasons]: firstly, because the Armenians tried to save themselves [and] did not want to comply with the disarmament order by the Turkish government; and, secondly—and this has been proven beyond doubt—because they made common cause with the Russians against the Turks. This has naturally led to battles and, as

usual, to the slaughter of the defeated party. I believe, these are [two] things one has to differentiate.

He went on to claim that the Ottoman government had only reacted to reports from the country's highest military and civil authorities, and concluded that such deportations were a military necessity. Sanders neglected to mention that the "highest military authorities" were mainly leading German military men. He also neglected to acknowledge that Enver Pasha had been *the* leading military authority and Talât *the* leading civil authority for most of the war. He then, as was perhaps to be expected, claimed that the commanding officers in the relevant areas were all Turkish, with not one German among them. Next he discussed those who had carried out the deportations, namely the gendarmes whose numbers had been swelled up by "not quite the best elements," partly by thieves, partly by "unemployed people." But then he offered a whole salvo of excuses, for example, that the enlargement of the gendarmes corps had been necessary because the Turkish front had been in such dire conditions that many Turks, "not only Armenians," had died; and finally, all of this was also a result of the "lack of organization of the Turkish Empire." He further claimed that perhaps many of the lower ranks among the guards of the convoys had misunderstood the jihad and had thought it "meritorious" to massacre Armenians.

He further tried to explain what he did—as if he himself were on trial, too—whenever he received orders to deport Armenians and Jews from his district. He referenced the instances in which he saved these groups by saying, "Also in the book by Dr. Lepsius this instance is mentioned." Sanders thus had read Lepsius's book; he, too, was showing that he was part of the German discourse and debate that had been going on for years already. Before he concluded his testimony, he made a general attack on the foreign press (representatives of whom were of course also in the courtroom), for what he called their defamations of German officers, and again claimed that the officers had done everything they could, indeed their "duty," to save the Armenians wherever they could. He asserted that he did not know whether Talât had been the author of the genocide, but mentioned that the main order for the deportation had been "the one of 20 May 1915," as if everybody knew which one that was.

All in all, Liman von Sanders spoke only briefly. His testimony takes up a mere two pages in the 130-page-long court transcript published later. Neither the defense, the prosecution, nor the interventionist Judge Lemberg asked him any questions or interrupted him at any point—whether it was lack of interest, respect for the renowned German pasha, or that each believed his statement to perfectly fit their case as it was.

Sanders was followed by the Armenian bishop Grigoris Balakian, who had traveled from Manchester to speak at the trial.[7] Balakian spoke in "broken German," and no translator was needed, the court record noted. He recounted how, when the war had begun, he had traveled back to the Ottoman Empire from Berlin, where he had stayed before. Balakian was one of the leaders of Constantinople's Armenian community who had been deported in late April 1915—the date of their deportation, which marked the beginning of the genocide, is remembered today as the Armenian Genocide Memorial Day on 24 April every year in Armenia and the diaspora. Balakian described how his convoy had been broken up, and how most of the deportees had been beaten to death in Ankara. The surviving sixteen were deported farther, together with Armenians from other places: "The official name was 'deportation,' but in reality it was a systematic policy of annihilation."

Balakian explained,

> When we reached Yozgat, which was the most bloody place, we saw in a valley not far away, [a] four-hour [walk] away, a couple of hundred of [detached] heads with long hair, the heads of women and girls. With us was a captain of the gendarmes by the name of Shükrü, who led us. I asked the captain [to explain, as] I had heard that they were beating to death the Armenian men, but not the women and girls. Well, he said, if we only killed the men and not also the women and girls, then in fifty years there would again be a couple of million Armenians. Thus we also have to kill the women and the girls so that there will never again be inner or outer unrest [affecting our country].

The Turkish captain had told him further, "We killed them all, though not in the cities. That was forbidden, because in 1895/96 Abdul Hamid had given the order to beat them all to death in the city. Then the European peoples, the whole civilized world found out and would not allow it. [Now,] no one was supposed to be left so that no witness would ever reach any court." In front of this Berlin court, Balakian now continued, "The captain told me: 'I can tell you, no problem, because, after all, you will end up in the desert and will die there of starvation and will have no chance to bring this truth to light." As Balakian told the court, the captain had continued his tale of massacres and even boasted that he himself had ordered the clubbing to death of about 40,000 Armenians. He had told Balakian that another reason for deporting them out of the cities first, and only then to kill them, was also to give the Turks the chance to find all the Armenians' valuables, otherwise hidden and buried. Given that the deportees had been "allowed" to take precious belongings with them on the trip, they had been an easy and bountiful prey.

When Balakian was in the middle of another tale of the captain's gruesome adventures, he was interrupted by defense attorney Gordon who, perhaps surprisingly given his role, objected that they had heard too many of these stories by that point. This was now the story of a convoy of about 4,600 women and girls, against whom around 13,000 villagers "with wooden axes and also iron utensils" had been mobilized. This large mob had been authorized to kill everybody except for the "most pretty girls," whom they were allowed to take home with them. However, while Gordon pressed on about a telegram by Talât Pasha, Balakian was eager to officially bear witness, in front of the world—after all, there were reporters in the room not only from German, but also from major British and American newspapers. Balakian continued with his story, which, apparently, was even too gruesome for the defense attorneys. The captain had told Balakian how all the women and girls of their convoy had been beaten and hacked to death, "everything, women, children, everything." The young bishop told the court that, after hearing this story, he had asked the captain if he had no quarrels with his conscience "before God, before humanity, before civilization?" The captain had answered, "I am not responsible, I received the order from Constantinople. . . . If a soldier kills somebody in war, he is not guilty."[8]

The Talât telegram that Gordon had asked about had been shown to Balakian by the former vice-governor of Osmaniye in Cilicia, Asaf Bey, and read, "Please telegraph us promptly how many of the Armenians are already dead and how many still alive. Minister of the Interior, Talât." The bishop added that at the time he had not understood the meaning of this: "to exterminate a whole people through massacres, something like that has never happened in history before." Asaf Bey explained to Balakian and another Armenian present that it translated to, "What are you waiting for? Begin the massacres [immediately]!" This was now one of the few times that a member of the jury interceded and asked whose signature was below the telegram. Balakian repeated that it was Talât's and swore that he had seen it with his own eyes.

The defense then directed their questions toward how the young bishop had been saved, and by whom. This was a story destined to invoke the sympathies of the audience as it was perhaps the only "feel-good moment" in the trial, which otherwise provided an overwhelming refrain of despair and murder—for Balakian, it emerged, had been saved by Germans: first by engineers working on the Bagdad Railway, and then with the help of German soldiers, who had dressed him up as one of them, taught him to salute like a German, and so made it possible for him to travel and escape to Constantinople.

Balakian was then asked by the defense about Liman von Sanders's statement that it had not been so much Talât Pasha's fault as that of the lower, executing authorities. Balakian responded that the Armenians were convinced that Talât Pasha was personally responsible: "this is not only the general opinion, but also the truth." The bishop stated that as a member of the Armenian patriarchate in Constantinople, he had known Talât Pasha personally. "He had the fullest influence. He did everything with full awareness." He also quoted a Turkish major, coming from Erzurum, who had told him with great pride that "what all our earlier sultans had not achieved, we have done: we have murdered a historical people in [merely] two months."

The defense then addressed Liman von Sanders again on the question of who had really been responsible for the cruelties committed, and also wanted to submit and read out various orders and telegrams by Talât Pasha. One of these was intended to prove that Talât had ordered the local authorities to include Armenian orphans in the deportations and have them exterminated as well, "because, after all, only elements harmful to Turkey could emerge out of these children." Now, however, and for the first time, the state prosecutor intervened in order to get the trial back on track, away from the victim and back to his assassin. He objected to any further submission of evidence in support of Talât Pasha's guilt for the Armenian Genocide, stating that there was no doubt in his mind that for Tehlirian, Talât had been responsible for the genocide. This would then fully explain motive. This court, the state prosecutor argued, could not resolve the question of Talât's guilt, "Because then a historic verdict would have to be reached [here] for which totally different material would be necessary than what we have." Again, the state attorney had adopted a line of argument that was potentially vulnerable and open to challenge; one could have argued that this Berlin court was saturated with enough evidence to at least establish a very reasonable presumption as to Talât Pasha's responsibility. And indeed that is how the defense team now replied, with Niemeyer objecting, "Yet, I want to point out that Talât was the responsible highest government official, namely the grand vizier. He signed [everything]. Talât was responsible for everything, one [just] cannot think differently." And while his colleague, Gordon, withdrew his motion for having further orders read out, the state attorney had obviously already lost the sympathy of part of the jury. Juror Otto Ewald, a "house owner" from Berlin-Charlottenburg, intervened with a question for Balakian about the order he had mentioned. Balakian once more affirmed that he had seen it with his own eyes. Thus the jury was still focusing on the question of Talât Pasha's guilt, rather than Tehlirian's.

Judge Lemberg then ended the inquiry into Talât's role with the claim that "the jurors believe you [that is, Tehlirian] that, in execution of the deed, you were of the conviction that Talât Pasha was the one who had to pay for the massacres." With this, the hearing of witnesses ended, and what was left for the first day of the trial were the reports of the medical experts.

There were five of these, and the testimony of all of them related to the question of accountability: that is, whether Tehlirian was an "epileptic," and, if so, whether this could have made him unaccountable during the deed. But if those in the courtroom expected to be given a break from stories of massacres and human misery, and to hear dry medical analyses instead, they were mistaken: what followed was another renarration of the massacre that Tehlirian had lived through, and the horrible psychological wounds it had inflicted upon him. Reading the testimony of these experts from today's perspective, it seems clear that none of the five had anything but a very vague understanding of Tehlirian's condition, which they diagnosed as "epilepsy" and even as "psychopathy." Though there were signs of epileptic seizures, their explanations went rather in the direction of what today we would recognize as post-traumatic stress disorder (PTSD). And while the experiences of World War I would indeed eventually lead to our modern concept and understanding of PTSD, things were still less clear in 1921.

The first medical expert was Dr. Robert Stoermer. He did not believe that Tehlirian's affliction had induced him to kill Talât Pasha that morning, but rather that it had been a long-planned deed. The images of the mother, who had appeared in a dream during the night before the assassination, were important for establishing the psychological background of the deed. Tehlirian now related that the images of the murdered Armenians had appeared before him that morning as if they had been real. The judge then asked him whether he was now claiming that he did not act consciously that day. Tehlirian answered by referring to his mother and what she had told him during the night. Oddly, it was now one of Tehlirian's defense attorneys, Gordon, who pressed him for a clarification, sounding more like a prosecutor when he asked, "Does the defendant deny that he acted with forethought?" To which now, with another and even stranger reversal of roles, not Tehlirian but the judge replied, "Yes." And then the judge asked the interpreter to advise Tehlirian that the medical expert had just claimed that Tehlirian was fully responsible for the deed.

The next expert, Dr. Hugo Liepmann, was of the opinion that Tehlirian was clearly a "psychopath"—a condition caused by the events of 1915— and that, therefore, there existed mitigating circumstances. Next was Dr. Richard Cassirer, who agreed with Dr. Liepmann in using the term "psychopath," and indeed said he was a severe case, but also agreed with Dr. Stoermer that Tehlirian's was a case of "affect epilepsy," which had changed his personality completely—again as a result of his experiences during the massacres. Next up was Dr. Edmund Forster, who revealed a bit of what appears to have been a consensus within the medical profession at the time. He claimed that the experiences of the world war had not resulted in a statistically significant rise of mental disorders. And in any case, the war had only brought out in some cases what had already been there in "psychopathological personalities." For him, not surprisingly, Tehlirian was such a personality. It is interesting to note just how callous and arrogant the underlying assumption was: regardless of how traumatic and brutal your war experiences, if they affected you, it meant only that you had already been damaged goods before the war. It seems not to have crossed his mind that perhaps the not-so-significant rise in the statistics resulted from the inability of the medical profession to see and name what was happening to the traumatized soldiers. Forster was chief resident doctor of the renowned Psychiatric Hospital in Berlin at the time (and had treated Adolf Hitler three years earlier, during World War I, at the military hospital Pasewalk, after the future Führer had temporarily lost his eyesight—"hysterical blindness," as Forster had called it).[9]

In any case, Forster was also of the opinion that Tehlirian was not accountable for his actions that day in March. And then followed yet another specialist, Dr. Bruno Haake, who equally diagnosed "affect epilepsy," and affirmed and even topped the previous experts by stating categorically that in his opinion a free formation of will was, in Tehlirian's case, impossible and had to be ruled out. And thus ended what one of the defense attorneys would call the following day "the struggle of the expert witnesses over [the term of] epilepsy."

And thus also ended the first day of the trial.

• • •

The second day of the trial was short. There were no more witnesses or experts to be heard and all that was left were the closing arguments of both sides, as well as, of course, the decision of the jury. This was, thus, a rather swift and short trial, just as the Foreign Office had wanted (though, of course, with an entirely different course and outcome). Judge Lemberg addressed his court and the jury at a quarter past nine on the morning of the final day with three questions: "[First, is] the defendant, Soghomon Tehlirian, guilty of having killed, with premeditation, another human being, Talât Pasha, on 15 March 1921, in [Berlin-]Charlottenburg? . . . Secondly, did the defendant carry out this killing with reflection? . . . Thirdly, are there any mitigating circumstances?"

After some back-and-forth about a juror's comment regarding what an "Indian" in the audience had said about the religious origins of the whole matter, the concluding arguments commenced with that of the state prosecutor: "Dear jurors! It is not the judicial aspect of this criminal deed which has given it special attention, and given it this tremendous concern that has directed the eyes at home and abroad upon this courtroom." He deliberated how the "psychological background" reached as far back as the world war, how "a hand reached up out of the masses of the unnamed [and] unknown and felled down a man . . . who had led the fate of the fatherland in a time of the greatest struggle of the peoples and who, as a faithful friend of Germany, had walked along the heights of history." The prosecutor then took great care to focus exclusively on the assassination itself and to stress that it had been carried out with full intent. However, then he came to discuss motive and again got caught in the web of genocide that the defense, together with the judge, had been weaving since the beginning of the trial. Yes, it was a political deed, he admitted, and yes, it was "political revenge." He stressed that ghastly things had happened, to the Armenian people as well as to the defendant and his family—and that fate had stricken the heart "when all his relatives were delivered to death and he had to witness this." Again, the prosecutor appears to have been slightly unsure about his role at this trial. And then he messed up even further. He recounted how the examination of evidence had centered so much on Talât Pasha's role as originator of the genocide. He admittedly tried to save Talât Pasha's "honor." By urging the jury to look at the person of Talât Pasha, and at the evidence presented at the trial, he probably gave away the jury and indeed the verdict. Because, had he not been sleeping the previous day, he would have been aware of the fact that no evidence had been presented in that Berlin courtroom that could have saved Talât Pasha's honor at all (not even by Sanders). If one had listened to what had been said in the courtroom, as no doubt the jury had, then one must have had the impression that Talât had indeed been the instigator, and indeed had even openly boasted about his project and indeed about the success of mass extermination. One should not forget that the court had heard Lepsius as *the* prime expert on the Armenian Genocide; we will return to the importance of his testimony again.

The state prosecutor then admitted that the Armenians, perhaps, saw Talât Pasha as the man responsible. He added that he had spoken to many Germans who had served in Turkey, who denied the intent to annihilate and rather saw it all as something necessary out of "national and military considerations." This is not only reminiscent of the discourse of the *Deutsche Allgemeine Zeitung,* but we in fact know that its editor in chief, Hans Humann, had personally lobbied the state prosecutor's office intensely before the trial. Thus one of the Germans who had served in the Ottoman Empire with whom the prosecutor had spoken had definitely been Enver Pasha's close friend Humann. The state prosecutor was interrupted at this point by Judge Lemberg, who told him that he could not now go back to what had been said during the examination of evidence by presenting mere hearsay. The irritated prosecutor retorted that he must be allowed to stress the discrepancies between Lepsius's and Sanders's testimonies. He tried to discredit what Lepsius had said by claiming that "the deliberations of Professor Lepsius, as interesting and as thorough as they were, did have the one flaw that they, in my opinion, interpreted too much of intent and systematicity into these events: a systematicity that shows that it was not the result of personal experiences on the ground at the time but rather is drawn from later reports." Here, by focusing on Lepsius, he was also trying to discredit the Armenian survivors who had told the court of the very same "systematics." This was to become the most misquoted and plagiarized sentence of the trial, as we will see later.

The state prosecutor then claimed that he was right to trust the testimony and experiences of Liman von Sanders more than those of Lepsius. It is worth noting, though, that Sanders had not really contradicted Lepsius's testimony at the most crucial points (at least for this trial)—and that Lepsius, after all, had just two years before edited and published the documents of the Foreign Office on the topic and had thus had access to the German diplomatic service's evidence. Lepsius stood in front of the court quasianointed by the Foreign Office's authority on the matter (whether the Foreign Office liked it or not). It was difficult not to accept his authority on the Armenian topic; as we have seen, the German press, including anti-Armenian papers, had not dared to do so (Chapter 9). Sanders had only questioned Lepsius's testimony insofar as he thought fault or guilt was to be sought *more* in the executing bodies of the deportations; he did not claim that Talât Pasha was innocent. Yet, at the same time, Sanders, too, had accepted and reinforced Lepsius's overall authority by citing documents published in the Lepsius volume in order to exonerate himself (though he was not on trial). And, furthermore, by attacking Lepsius's credibility, given that in court, reference was made mainly, if not exclusively, to his *Germany and Armenia,* the prosecution was trying to discredit a book sanctioned and, in fact, prepared by the German government, that is, the Foreign Office, as well as the wartime reports of German ambassadors and consuls. The prosecutor offered the jury the option of either believing the German government, a whole plethora of German diplomats, and a pastor of international reputation as an expert on the topic for almost three decades, or believing one single military officer, whose testimony was slightly misrepresented by the prosecutor, as Sanders had not even tried to refute the central points of Lepsius's statements and was obviously mainly interested in saving his own skin and clearing his own name with the help of Lepsius. The prosecution's strategy was, obviously, not without serious flaws.

State prosecutor Gollnick then emphasized that a "dislocation" *(Dislokation)* had been ordered by the Constantinople government because reports of (future) Armenian treason existed, "that [the Armenians] conspired with the Entente and were determined, as soon as the war situation allowed, to stab the Turks in the back and to achieve their independence." As this plea shows, the prosecutor was not even able to get the stab-in-the-back myth right. This was an attempt to reach out to subconscious German feelings of betrayal and despair by alluding to the images of treachery and dishonesty encapsulated in the budding German stab-in-the-back myth.

Yet, by connecting this so directly to the rather noble and understandably normal desire for national independence, he unwittingly refuted his own plea and turned its logic upside down. After all, "true national independence" was what many German nationalists, in their own words, sought and fought for desperately in these years, dominated by discourses of Entente "slave treaties," fulfillment politics, and the nation being "raped" by the victors.

And it went only further downhill from here; and quite quickly so. Gollnick then maintained that the decision—taken for "reasons of saving the state [and] . . . the military situation"—had to be distinguished from its execution. A weak argument, given that the jurors had become convinced, and obviously so, in light of their questions to the witnesses, that Talât Pasha was the originator of a deliberate plan to annihilate the Armenians. The state prosecutor went on, "One has to recognize that the soil of Asia Minor is not the soil on which such relations between cultured peoples exist as they do here—[well,] I want to express myself correctly: relations to which we were used before the war." Again, the prosecutor undermined his own argument; he wanted to make the culturalist argument, but then admitted—something that in these years only the Communists, the pacifists, and the Nazis would do—that the Armenian Genocide was in fact part of a new brutalization of mankind and of war in general. But then again, he tried to advance the culturalist case in the next sentence: "The traditions of Asia Minor are wild and bloody, and the expert witness has drawn attention to the fact that a 'holy war' had been declared." He then described how the mere fact that the Armenians were being concentrated and convoyed off had been the signal to the population "to lunge at the Armenians."

The state prosecutor then returned to the actual deed under review at the trial, and in reference to the motive, revenge for the massacres, stated, "My sirs, [this is] without a doubt a noble motive if we take into account the gravity of the crimes [that is, the Armenian massacres] that have been committed." In the next sentence, he again expressed his sympathy for the crime and the defendant. This, for some reason, he thought was an apt introduction to deal with the question of intent and he tried to establish that the plan to kill Talât Pasha had been made approximately fourteen days before the actual deed. He then went on to plead that this was a cold-blooded deed for which there were no mitigating circumstances. He also tried to discredit the notion that there were psychological factors by exaggerating the differences in the medical experts' reports. And at the end of his closing statement, Gollnick again returned to the victim, Talât Pasha, emphasizing what an honorable and patriotic man he had been.

And if we need to further substantiate that the prosecutor's strategy was deeply flawed and that he was either incompetent or unmotivated, then we could mention that the concluding statements of the three defense attorneys were so lengthy that they, together, take up thirty-five pages in the published protocol, whereas the state prosecutor's barely fills six pages. He did not even use the time available to him: he spoke for less than a fifth of the time the opposing team would use to address the jury. It appears, from this fact alone, that he already had given up by the end of the first day of the trial when he went home to prepare this statement.

Defense attorney Gordon went straight for the jugular: "I was very happy to find in the first state prosecutor a fellow colleague in some ways, a [fellow] defense attorney. However, not a defense attorney for Tehlirian, but a defense attorney for Talât Pasha—however, only basing [his defense] on data that various gentlemen have reported and told him. . . . I have here an arsenal of telegrams, I have examined a witness who sat there and said 'These telegrams are authentic because I have received them myself!'" He then stressed that it was enough for this case to understand that for Tehlirian, "together with the entirety of his people," Talât was the author of the horrors and that "you [that is, the jury] have indicated that you believe him." Gordon then repeated the cable Balakian had quoted, in which Talât Pasha had asked how many had been killed already. "We all understand what that meant." He further stressed that when it came to Talât's being the architect of the Armenian Horrors of World War I, "What is enough is the fact that here, in merely a few months, one million four hundred thousand people of a total of 1.8 million were deported and of these 1 million people were killed; that from different parts [of the country] the treks of the unlucky were sent to the very same centers without making sure that there was protection [for them] anywhere. Please, think about it yourselves: Can this happen without any systematic management from above? Was the Turkish government really so weak that it was not able to do anything about that? Do you want to believe this? Then affirm this! I am not affirming this!"

Defense attorney Gordon made the argument for establishing genocidal intent in the case of the Ottoman Armenians as still today it can hardly be made better, by connecting the vast concerted logistical and administrative efforts involved in the deportations with the crucial lack of care (protection, nourishment, shelter, transport) provided by the government for the deportees—who were, after all, its own citizens and civilians. And of course the tally of those killed, by itself, also impresses upon the observer the feeling that this was, indeed, impossible without intent.

After dismissing Tehlirian's contradictory statements about his own intent, Gordon quickly resumed retelling the assassin's biography, with, of course, a special focus on his experiences during the deportation and the massacres. He brought before the jurors' minds, again, the powerful image of Tehlirian lying unconscious "in the middle of thousands of dead bodies." Gordon also addressed the propaganda and discourses outside the courtroom, by prefacing this with, "This horrible massacre is after all so incredible that we had the feeling at first: Who knows if the jurors will believe him." He then continued with Tehlirian's biography and his wanderings after surviving the massacre, as well as his psychological state during these years and later in Berlin.

Gordon, too, turned to Talât Pasha, but focused on and rejected the culturalist argument that it was a "mitigating" circumstance for Talât that he operated in Asia, where life is supposedly cheap. "I am far from pronouncing a final verdict on the man Talât . . . but he, like some of his colleagues, strove for the annihilation of the Armenian people, [and] while he employed means for this that appear insufferable to us Europeans, it would be unjust to say that such horrors find understanding in Asia—[to say] that there a life is worth less [than here]." In fact, he argued, "in Asia, a life was worth just the same, if not more." He moved on to make a point about the world war in general: "What two French geniuses have said of the horrible events of the world war is true for [Talât Pasha] as well: 'Behind the individual acting men stand geniuses, stand demons who lead them, they are but the tools of justified and unjustified thoughts and mass suggestions which humans push in front of them like chess pieces [and] who believe . . . they are in truth acting under constraint.' What horrible things may have happened in this case, we do not want to be so petty as to lay the blame on one unfortunate human being. Just as horrible a fate has come over us." Thus, Gordon connected the matters of the trial to Germany and to the horrible and still very much traumatic experience of World War I. In trying to reign in those jurors who were perhaps sympathetic to Talât because of patriotic sentiments of a bond between the two nations in arms, the defense now tried to turn the issue into one of humanity, war, and a kind of justice above national laws.

This line was also followed and indeed emphasized by the next defense attorney to deliver concluding arguments, Johannes Werthauer. He told the jury just how immensely important this verdict was going to be, for everybody involved: "The eyes of the world are upon us, and your verdict will, perhaps, be valid as law for thousands of years." Though this may have sounded unduly dramatic at this point in the trial, after some deliberations, Werthauer homed in on it and delivered. First, however, he dismissed the claim that the death sentence pronounced in Constantinople was invalid, because it was reached under the pressure of "English naval artillery": English justice had always been exemplary, he said, and there was no need to doubt that particular trial and verdict. He pointed out that one of those found guilty alongside Talât was indeed executed and that while he himself abhorred the death penalty, this must have given the Armenians the idea that Talât did indeed deserve to die.

Werthauer then developed a notion of "self-defense." He talked about how it had been believed that Enver Pasha and Talât Pasha had lived in Germany as Germany's "guests"—though he emphatically denied that their stay really had this character. He then claimed that Enver Pasha, "as the newspapers are reporting," was now sitting in Russia with the Bolsheviks, plotting new plans to wage war against the Armenians and to annihilate them. "If Talât, as he had surely wanted, had followed Enver now, then new horrors against the Armenians could have taken place within eight to fourteen days." This, he argued, was not only true—which it was not—but it also meant that Tehlirian had, in fact, acted in self-defense for his people and had little choice, once he had stumbled upon Talât in Berlin, but to eliminate the threat in the way he did. This was not far off from what the German newspapers had been speculating about for some time before. In 1919, some German papers had reported that Talât was watching closely what was going on in Turkey from Berlin and speculated that he would surely return to Turkey soon, to a position of high influence.[10]

Next, Werthauer came to the nub of his defense, that this would be a verdict for the ages:

Talât Pasha might personally have been an upright man, but he was part of a government of militarists and a militarist stands in opposition to justice. Somebody can be an officer or a soldier, wear a uniform the whole long day and deal with weapons all the time, and he still does not have to be a militarist; he can retain the principles of law and justice within himself and carry out his job dutifully. On the other side, there is the enormous mass—and I believe it is almost all of them—of militarists who have never worn a uniform, who sit behind an inkpot, write articles, and bloodthirstily rally to the flag of violence. In opposition to the man of justice, the militarist is as a man of violence. Justice is the highest thing in the world for the man of justice. . . . If he is religious, then justice comes right after God, and only then comes man. If he is not religious, man[kind] is the holiest of all. The militarist is different. He is a man of violence: for him the law applies only as far as it can be brought into "harmony" with "military necessities," as the common phrase goes.

Werthauer went on to stress that one could find people like these anywhere in the world. Now, at that very moment, Germany was suffering at the hands of militarists "across the River Rhine," he emphatically exclaimed, referring to the French occupation of the Ruhr. The Germans had sent such "men of violence" to Turkey to train their armies, "which was none of our business to begin with." He also included the Bolsheviks in his list of militarists, and concluded this line of thought by stressing that it was not the Turkish nation who had wanted to annihilate the Armenians, but such men of violence. "They want war, want violence."

Werthauer also touched on the issue previously taken up by Liman von Sanders, that the gendarmes' corps was of the lowest quality. If this were the case, then the Young Turk leaders "should not have given the order for deportation" in the first place, Werthauer argued. He further stressed that, yes, these gendarmes carried a lot of guilt, but not as much as the people in Constantinople who had delivered the Armenians into their hands. And he went further and further with his full humanist condemnation of every aspect of both the actual genocide and the alleged justifications for it. For him, prisoners of war were "holy," because they had wanted to fight for their homes and their home country and only by misfortune ended up as prisoners. "Whoever shouts 'bastard' at a prisoner or raises his hand against [such] a prisoner, is in my view forever excluded from the company of decent men." These were arguments calling for a noble kind of warfare, and for a deeper concern for all humans.

And, never tiring of attacking all and any anti-Armenian discourse, Werthauer also indirectly addressed the anti-Semitic–anti-Armenian confluence: he explicitly called the Armenians "this people of craftsmen and farmers," in contrast to the image of usurers and traders that anti-Armenianists made them out to be. He also tried to make it clear to the jury that what they were dealing with here was "the murder of a people." Werthauer then compared Tehlirian to William Tell: "Which jury in the whole world would have convicted William Tell who shot down the provincial governor?" Just sentences before, he had described this provincial governor as being "of the blood of the pan-Turks, of the men of violence." He continued: "I ask [you], is there anything more human than what we have been told here? The avenger of a million murdered, the avenger of a whole people faces the person responsible, the author of all the suffering. He comes as the representative of his father, who had been fifty-five years old, and of his mother, who had been fifty-two years old . . . , of his sister, of his brother-in-law, and of his brothers, and finally also as the representative of his sister's two-and-a-half-year-old child! The Armenian nation, one thousand years old, stands behind him." He closed with the emphatic plea not to forget that the "eyes of humanity" were upon the jury and its verdict.

Next up was Niemeyer, who, like his colleagues before him, attacked the German anti-Armenian discourse head-on. "[I] cannot help it but have to say a word for the Armenians: a few malign sayings, which are traveling from hand to hand like a miserable 50-cent-bill, have given the Armenians a bad name." He then listed some of the typical anti-Armenian sayings in the fashion of "A Greek sells off three Jews, an Armenian three Greeks" (see Chapters 2 and 3).

Niemeyer then connected himself personally to the Armenian issue by recounting that he had been to Constantinople twice in 1899, where eyewitnesses had told him of the 1890s massacres. Niemeyer was followed by Gordon again, who once more called what had happened "the systematic extermination of the Armenians." Then came Werthauer again, who stressed that this was no court of victors' justice; it was not about the fact that Enver, Talât, and company had declared war, "but rather because they undertook deportations, because they committed one of the most vicious crimes that history has ever known on the Armenian population." He again emphasized that the verdict in this case would probably still be important in a thousand years and that politics had to be left out of it. "In this empire of malice all politics basically comes to an end and I cannot understand how one can speak even one word in favor of the deportation orders." The defense finally closed with the plea for a nonguilty verdict in order to end all these lies and set the record straight, for the Armenians and also for Germany.

With this, the very lengthy concluding arguments of the defense, which probably lasted several hours, ended. It was now time for Judge Lemberg to finally instruct the jury about their duties and the possible repercussions. And after just one hour of deliberation, the jury gave their verdict, which was limited to a single-word answer to the question of whether Tehlirian was guilty of intentionally killing Talât Pasha. Their answer was "No."

Then Tehlirian was officially proclaimed to have been found not guilty, and was set free. According to the court transcript, he was "congratulated by his defense attorneys, his countrymen, as well as the audience."

Contrary to the speculations in subsequent press and academic discourse, the jury did not necessarily find Tehlirian innocent because of "temporary insanity."[11] While it is true that intent had been discussed at the trial often in reference to his "epilepsy of the soul" and his psychological state in general, the jury did not deliver its reasoning, just a simple "no." Thus all we can do is speculate about its motives. From an empirical point of view, it has to be noted that the state prosecutor's strategy had been non-existent, or at least flawed to such an extent that it seems improbable that he could have won his case without other factors helping him. Another point to be noted is that the defense for Tehlirian did not make much use of the medical reports and these potentially mitigating circumstances at all in their final pleas, but concentrated rather on the political aspects of the deed, the genocide, and the verdict.

Thus this spectacular trial, which had hardly lasted two days, had ended. Many witnesses and experts who had been invited had not even been heard. Among them were Bronsart von Schellendorff, former chief of the General Staff of the Ottoman Army; the military men Ernst Paraquin and Franz Carl Endres; and Armin T. Wegner, as well as the former vice-consul of Erzurum, Scheubner-Richter.[12] The former consul of Aleppo, Walter Rössler, was still in the diplomatic service at the time and did not, or rather was not allowed to, accept his invitation from the defense. The defense had written him in late May 1921. It had stated that Rössler would be an important expert witness. He had been in contact with Lepsius in the previous weeks and had acknowledged that the Talât telegrams bore the "character of authenticity." Rössler answered defense attorney Gordon that he could indeed come, but had to check with his superiors first.[13] In the sketch of his letter to the Foreign Office that survives, it becomes clear why this could have been a problem. If he were allowed to testify, he wrote his superiors, he would need to be able to break official secrecy. And then "there would be no way around for me to express my conviction that Talât Pasha was indeed one of these Turkish statesmen who wanted and systematically carried out the annihilation of the Armenians." He further stressed that in the very probable case that certain documents containing "orders by Talât Pasha in the matter of the deportation and extermination of the Armenians" would be shown to him in court, he would have to attest to their probable authenticity. "I further would have to acknowledge a statement as true that was made to me by the deportations commissar sent from Constantinople to Aleppo: 'You don't understand what we want, we want an Armenia without Armenians.'" This was perhaps too much for the German Foreign Office, and while it could not rein in any of the other expert witnesses, because they were no longer in their employ, Rössler was barred from appearing.[14] Rössler, just like Scheubner-Richter, had protested to his superiors much during the war and had helped feed Armenian deportees through American funds. After the war, in June 1919, he had published an article in the *Preussische Jahrbücher* under a pseudonym explaining the difficult position of the Turks. Yet, in a letter to Lepsius during the preparation of the Talât Pasha trial, he had underlined what he had stressed during the war as well—that for three years "the extermination," "the systematic annihilation" of the Armenians was "the consciously pursued policy" of the Ottoman government.[15]

And though it does not matter for our topic—the German discussions about the Armenian Genocide—it is perhaps interesting to note that Tehlirian's story was in truth different from what he had told the court. He was, in fact, a member of these "Armenian murder organizations" and had traveled to Berlin with the sole purpose of assassinating Talât Pasha as retribution for the genocide. He had not been with his family when they were killed during the genocide but had, in fact, been fighting as a volunteer in Russian units against the Ottoman army. He had been coached in his story of his family's imagined slaughter as presented to the Berlin court—though his family had been murdered during the genocide nonetheless.[16] While his story was not completely accurate as his own, it was an accurate story of a survivor. In any case, Tehlirian came to personify the Armenian Genocide at this point in the German debate.

Turning Points: The Media Coverage of the Talât Pasha Trial

It was perhaps no surprise that the Talât Pasha trial quickly turned into a big media event. The trial was not only an important event in itself for Armenian, Ottoman, and world history; it was also a media event in and of early Weimar Germany. Though it took some time for the trial to reach the provincial dailies, it was indeed discussed there as well, and often on the front page.[17] The courtroom had been crowded with all sorts of spectators; "there was a tremendous rush to the courtroom, which was tightly packed long before the trial began," as one paper wrote.[18] Among the spectators were many journalists of domestic and international newspapers. The dossier of the trial shows that international papers such as the London *Daily Telegraph,* the *Chicago Daily News,* and the *Philadelphia Public Ledger,* to name but a few, had asked for tickets long in advance, as had German papers such as the *Deutsche Allgemeine Zeitung,* the *BZ am Mittag,* the *Berliner Morgenpost,* the *Freiheit,* and the *Vorwärts.*[19]

The trial both baffled and severely split the German press landscape. How the trial was covered by a given paper directly illustrates what its editors and journalists thought about the Armenians and the genocide. The Talât Pasha trial makes for an ideal case study of the so-called gatekeeper effect. This effect describes the power of the media to set the agenda of public discourse, that is, to select the topics that the public then thinks and talks about, and of course also what they do not think and talk about. While this, of course, never works perfectly, there is an important truth here reflected in a key assumption about propaganda: propaganda is never really successful in directing what the people think about a topic, but rather which topic the people should think about—something the Nazis would also take very seriously and apply ceaselessly. As seen in our discussion of the trial itself, there was a whole plethora of possible things to report. While it had lasted only two days, it was filled with a whole series of spectacular claims and pieces of information. Which of these would each newspaper choose to cover?

The coverage of this "political trial" *(Neue Preussische [Kreuz-]Zeitung)* or "international congress" *(Berliner Lokal-Anzeiger)* really took off only on 3 June, the day after the first day of court proceedings. However, all major papers had already run reports on the first day, in some cases lengthy ones.[20] The Berlin papers, in their evening editions, were among the few on the first day (2 June) to print Tehlirian's testimony, in lengthy articles. They recounted how Tehlirian had survived the massacres, in what fashion his brother had been killed, and mentioned the fact that Talât Pasha had already been found guilty by a Constantinople court.[21] Similarly, the *Deutsche Allgemeine Zeitung,* in a very lengthy article, recounted Tehlirian's testimony, but it chose to designate the massacre merely as a "clash," and used a very skeptical style throughout. But it did give its readers a full report of almost everything that had been said until the charges had been read out. It concluded with Tehlirian speaking about his mother's ghost and its command to kill Talât. However, in the long list of the various witnesses the *Deutsche Allgemeine Zeitung* featured, it failed to mention Lepsius, as well as the three Armenian witnesses.[22] The *Deutsche Zeitung*, on the other hand, tried to obfuscate with its indirect speech and its confusing narrative, for example telling of the massacres of his family and then discussing that he had still not found his parents, as if they were still alive.[23] In any case, in the reports about the first day of the trial, most German readers could read all about the shocking details of Tehlirian's experiences in 1915, about how Tehlirian's family was murdered, how his brother's head was split into two by an axe, and how Tehlirian had lain unconscious under his brother's corpse for two days. Some also quoted the testimony of Mrs. Tersibashian and her story of massacre and survival.[24]

Tehlirian's testimony was central not only to the trial itself but also became crucial for the press coverage and the direction it would take. This was especially obvious on the second day of coverage, 3 June, when all major papers featured very extensive articles on the previous day's session. Most of them focused extensively on Tehlirian's testimony. The *Berliner Börsenzeitung*, which had already covered his testimony in the evening edition at length, now repeated parts of it and expanded on it in an article filling up more than half a page.[25] In retelling Tehlirian's story, it switched to the first person for many paragraphs in a row so that it was at some point no longer entirely clear that it was, in fact, quoting somebody. It also featured Mrs. Tersibashian's account of the massacres and further quoted at length from Lepsius. Here, as in most papers on this day, one could read the quotation from Talât's decree that "the destination of the deportations is nothingness," as well as about the estimated one million dead and Lepsius's sentence about how, when the "concentration camps" were filled, Armenians were led to the desert and then slaughtered.[26] Some papers, like the *Berliner Börsenzeitung* and the *Berliner Morgenpost*, focused extensively on Lepsius's testimony. They also featured his conclusion that what had happened in the Ottoman Empire was not a relocation but that there had been intent to "annihilate a whole people." These papers typically also featured the testimony of Bishop Balakian.[27]

The tale of horrors and massacres mesmerized the newspapers. Before the trial, the *Berliner Morgenpost*, for example, had been rather undecided, sometimes acknowledging, sometimes doubting the events of 1915.[28] Now this abruptly changed: "What comes to light in the cross-examination of the defendant and in the evidentiary hearing by far eclipses anything that has ever been heard, even in this place. Such a haunting description of the Armenian Horrors has hardly ever been given so far. Not only among the audience, but also among the jurors a spiritual shock was clearly visible."[29] Similarly so in the *Deutsche Zeitung,* otherwise firmly in the denialist camp, but in these days obviously shocked and somewhat undecided.[30] While it saw the whole Armenian question as a result of the "opposition of Russian and English diplomacy," it did mention Lepsius's testimony, the estimated one million victims, the concentration camps, and so on. Yet, it focused disproportionately on the question of German guilt and on Liman von Sanders's testimony. Still, it summarized Balakian's testimony and, as with most papers on this day, was rather uninterested in what the medical experts had had to say at the trial.

Many papers now realized the full extent of the events of 1915 and expressed this in such terms as "unparalleled horrors," or "a distressing image of Armenian Horrors." One paper stressed that it all was simply beyond the human imagination.[31] Most German newspapers had also printed Lepsius's conclusion that "this was not a resettlement but the open intent to exterminate a whole people. Only with the most brutal methods could one million people have been exterminated in such a short amount of time."[32] And then there were papers like the *Germania* and the *Vossische Zeitung,* which conveyed their opinion and approval by setting the following sound bites from their courtroom coverage in bold print: "thousands of such reports [that is, documenting the genocide] are available," "the destination of the deportation was nothingness," and also that "one million Armenian men, women, and children died." Furthermore, the *Germania* highlighted that there had been a clear intent "to annihilate a whole people."[33]

On the other side of the media-scape were the firmly denialist papers, which tried to minimize what was said in front of the court. The *Neue Preussische (Kreuz-)Zeitung,* for example, renarrated only bits and pieces of Tehlirian's testimony.[34] Lepsius was also only mentioned in passing and in a single, nondescript sentence: "Prof. Dr. Lepsius talked as expert witness about the Armenian question." Nothing of his testimony was reprinted there. Instead, the denialist papers chose to concentrate on Liman von Sanders. The part of his testimony portraying the Armenians as a fifth column in Turkey received particular attention, as did his claim that Germany was not involved in the massacres.

The same anti-Armenian bias was to be felt when it came to the coverage of the concluding arguments of the prosecution and defense. The *Neue Preussische (Kreuz-)Zeitung* and the *Deutsche Tageszeitung,* for example, selectively quoted from the state prosecutor's closing arguments, at quite some length, but only summarized the defense's closing arguments in two sentences. They emphasized the part in which the prosecutor had maintained that claims about the intent of the Constantinople government to annihilate the Armenians were baseless. The papers then wrongly quoted him further that "the elaborations of Professor Lepsius," which the papers had not summarized or described at all, "have the fault of too great a systematicity and that they are drawn from later reports." Thus the papers chose to misquote the prosecutor's remark in order to discredit all of Lepsius's testimony and work. As we have seen, the prosecutor had, in fact, used the word "systematicity" not as a slur on Lepsius's work but as a criticism of one aspect of it: that he attributed too much systematicity to the massacres and therefore saw them as deliberately planned from the top when in fact (according to the prosecutor) they were not. Here, it was (mis)used to describe the entirety of Lepsius's work, however.[35]

While the reports of the medical experts at the trial received some attention, they were not nearly as prominent as they probably should have been.[36] Also, in the end, their reports were much less clear than some newspapers made them out to be. The *Vorwärts* was sure that it had not been the medical expertise and the alleged epilepsy that had motivated the jurors to acquit Tehlirian, but rather "they [had] followed the same moral law based on which Friedrich Schiller acquits the murderer William Tell. Tehlirian, too, can justify himself with the Tell saying 'avenged have I the holy nature.'"[37]

No matter where the papers stood on the topic, the outcome of the trial, this spectacular verdict, left most of them in shock.[38] After very extensive trial coverage, the *Berliner Börsenzeitung,* for example, concluded its multicolumn article simply with the heading "The Verdict," under which it laconically wrote, "The defendant was acquitted," and then ended abruptly—without a single further word.[39] The paper had yet to find words for what had happened here. As one of the very few exceptions, the *Berliner Lokal-Anzeiger* felt instantly ready to comment, but then rather uncharacteristically babbled: "The Armenian who killed the Turk was acquitted. The jurors are nothing more or less than human; they have let their heart do the talking. . . . Free of guilt. Not guilty. Innocent. And still a murderer."[40] Many of these essays written "too soon" after the verdict betray the confusion of their authors with all the new realities of the Armenian topic, the postwar world, and the trial itself. Emil Ludwig, for example, otherwise famous for his clear prose, also got caught up in conflicting lines of thought while writing on the verdict in the pacifist *Die Weltbühne*. He, however, concluded with the hope that in the future some kind of an international organization (a "Union of Peoples") would make it impossible that "a Turkish pasha" could, just by mere order, annihilate a whole people.[41]

Others, like the *Berliner Volkszeitung*, joined the feelings of "millions" who applauded the verdict, as it claimed. From the beginning, it wrote, this trial had not been about the death of Talât Pasha, but about "the murder of an entire people," "condemned to annihilation" by Talât. It approvingly quoted the title of Franz Werfel's novel *Not the Murderer, but the Murdered Is Guilty* (a novel which had no connection to the Armenians, though).[42]

• • •

When Talât Pasha was murdered in early 1921, nobody could have expected what was to come just a few weeks later. By March 1921, the German postwar debate about the Armenian Genocide seemed to be over. So it is perhaps not surprising—but does attest to the rather immoral opportunism of one of Weimar Germany's greatest politicians—that Gustav Stresemann submitted an application to the German-Turkish Association in late April 1921, thus a month after the burial had taken place, to stage another ceremony honoring Talât Pasha. Stresemann was at the time leader of the German People's Party, later foreign minister and chancellor of Germany, as well as a Nobel Peace Laureate in 1926. In a recent book, Sabine Mangold-Will suggests that Stresemann wanted to arrange such a ceremony in order to sharpen his public profile and to gain public exposure.[43] Luckily for Stresemann and his further career, the German-Turkish Association declined. In retrospect, after the trial, such a ceremony would have seemed more than a little macabre and distasteful to the majority of German newspapers and the German public. It surely would have hurt Stresemann's public image much more than it could have possibly benefited him. In any case, this does not shed a good light on Stresemann, who had traveled to Constantinople during World War I and, after meeting Enver Pasha, had scribbled in his diary, "diminution of Armenians: 1–1,5 million."[44] Stresemann had known about the Armenian Genocide, more than most German politicians at the time, and still he was willing to use Talât Pasha, the widely acknowledged author of the genocide, to further his career. The next time Talât Pasha was to be honored publicly in Germany was by the Third Reich in 1943, when his remains were transferred to Turkey.[45]

CHAPTER 12

The Victory of Justificationalism

W ithin the larger German genocide debate of the early Weimar years, 2 and 3 June 1921, the days the Talât Pasha trial was covered in the press, marked a high point and a turning point. Before examining this crucial point in the debate, it is necessary to briefly recap what we have discussed so far. In Chapters 1, 2, and 3, we have seen how the German public and the political elites got used to using the Armenians to endear themselves to the Ottomans, how parts of these groups understood the violence against the Armenians as partially or wholly justified, and how already, long before World War I, a main feature of anti-Armenianism had been a racialist perspective—part and parcel of excusing the violence against the Armenians was a racialist view of them as quasi- or über-Jews. Throughout World War I, but more poignantly in the postwar years, this anti-Semitic prism was used and "reaffirmed"— also by the portrayal of the Armenians as backstabbers. During World War I there had already been knowledge of widespread and intentional violence, indeed murder, of the Armenians despite censorship. And as part of the propaganda efforts of the press, but also continuing previous anti-Armenian trends, this renewed violence against the Armenians was again excused, justified, and even portrayed as necessary—military necessity and administrative or disciplinary measures became key terms here. After the war—despite the widespread knowledge among the political elites and the press—the topic was off to a rocky start. Only with Lepsius's renewed activities and mainly with his volume of Foreign Office documents did parts of the press acknowledge the charge of genocide (against the Young Turks). Then again a backlash had occurred, with parts of the press denying the extent of what had happened to the Armenians during the war, while others had begun justifying whatever had happened. Again, it has to be stressed that most of the main actors in this debate certainly knew of the full extent of the genocide. For example, Hans Humann, who, with his *Deutsche Allgemeine Zeitung,* was leading the anti-Armenian charge against acceptance of the genocide as fact, was Enver's close friend and had been one of the most important people at the German embassy during the war. Bronsart von Schellendorff, whom we are about to meet again, was chief of the Ottoman General Staff during the war; there must have been little that he did not know—and some historians claim today that he must have been a chief instigator of the genocide in the first place (see Chapter 6).

What changed in the immediate aftermath of the Talât Pasha trial was that many more papers became committed to a pre-Lemkin definition of genocide, which means that while previously most of the papers had used the still rather nondescript formula of "Armenian Horrors" or "Armenian massacres" to refer to the events of 1915, now the terminology became equivalent to that which we would commonly describe with the term genocide. Many papers had done so already in the wake of the publication of the Lepsius volume. When the papers now wrote about the "annihilation of a people" (in multiple papers as *Ausrottung eines Volkes* or *Ausrottung des armenischen Volkes*), the "near-complete extermination of his nation" *(nahezu völligen Vernichtung seines Volkes),* "an annihilated people [that] had risen from the grave" to march past the jury at the trial, "the barbarian extermination of the Armenian people" *(barbarische Vernichtung des armenischen Volkes),* or "its total extermination" *(seine völlige Vernichtung),* then there can be little doubt that they were describing what we, post-Lemkin, describe as genocide.[1] Some papers, like the *Berliner Volkszeitung,* were even cautioning Germany directly—what happened to the Armenians was that very same "theory of annihilation" that had been "floating around in the heads of German strategists" during the war come to full fruition.[2] And while, for example, the *Neue Preussische (Kreuz-)Zeitung* still disputed "intent," on 3 June, it did not dispute that the Armenians had been "exterminated" *(ausrotten).*[3]

The Talât Pasha trial had shocked the German public and press mainly in two ways: the horrors of genocide and the surprising acquittal of a confessed assassin.[4] It took most of the press a few days after the verdict to be able to offer their own commentary on what had happened, beyond just reporting the events of the trial; apparently they needed time to gather their wits and to decide what to make of it all. But once it started, essayistic debate raged on at full intensity for over a month. And, as already mentioned, the ripples of the trial and the subsequent debate could still be felt a year after the assassination. Until the end of the Weimar Republic, there were still publications occasionally discussing the trial and the "Armenian William Tell."[5]

While the other papers were still digesting what had happened, the *Deutsche Allgemeine Zeitung* was, as always in this matter, ahead of the pack and ready to shoot. At a time when the coverage of most other papers was restricted to summaries and quotes from the courtroom testimonies, the *Deutsche Allgemeine Zeitung* launched a full-blown campaign against Tehlirian, the Armenians, and pro-Armenian Germany. Hans Humann had been much better prepared than the others for such a "political trial." Already in the weeks leading up to the trial, he had lobbied the prosecution to do everything it could in order for it not to turn into a political trial. This clearly did not pan out, not at all. One might even go as far as to speculate that prosecutor Gollnick's messy, uninspired, and apparently lackadaisical performance was perhaps, in turn, motivated by his disgust at Humann's lobbying. Perhaps he indeed did not want Tehlirian to be convicted and secretly sided with the Armenian cause. That would have made his performance actually rather clever; if he did want Tehlirian to be convicted, on the other hand, it would just have been an abysmal performance, nothing more. Perhaps that is all that it was, because it appears that Gollnick was indeed rewarded by Humann, whom he served in the coming months as a member of his editorial board at the *Deutsche Allgemeine Zeitung.*[6]

During the trial itself, it was only the *Deutsche Allgemeine Zeitung* that was ready to offer its opinion and to feature lengthy opinion pieces on the whole matter. In the following days, weeks, and months, Germany saw the relative predominance (in the press) of a new and radicalized kind of anti-Armenian argumentation that had repercussions for far more than just Germany's understanding of what happened in Anatolia. This was the justificationalist argumentation, which accepted all the horrors and, indeed, even the full intent of genocide, but at the same time strove to justify what had happened—thus *justifying genocide.* There had been justificationalist articles in the previous years already, most prominently in the *Neue Preussische (Kreuz-)Zeitung.* But at that point, one could argue as a point of distinction, these papers had not yet acknowledged the full extent of what we would call "genocide." What happened in 1921 was a transformation of the denialist bloc and argument—to a point where it no longer denied much of anything. It must be counted as the "achievement" of the *Deutsche Allgemeine Zeitung* to have spearheaded and guided this transformation, given its immense lobbying activities—now in the form of a constant stream of anti-Armenian essays. At the end, one could find justificationalist articles in such papers as, for example, the *Deutsche Zeitung,* the *Deutsche Tageszeitung,* the *Neue Preussische (Kreuz-)Zeitung,* the *Weser Zeitung,* and also, surprisingly, the *Berliner Lokal-Anzeiger,* which had previously fully acknowledged and condemned the genocide, as well as the *Frankfurter Zeitung,* which had been a champion of the Armenians in the 1890s (Chapter 2).

The Rise of Justificationalism

The *Deutsche Allgemeine Zeitung* had already begun on 3 June to reiterate its denialist discourse. It would hold out the longest to deny genocide—until the middle of the month—but even if the other papers of the (formerly) denialist camp had begun acknowledging genocide before, the damage and the transformation of the discursive field by *Deutsche Allgemeine Zeitung* was done. Its argument on 3 June, thus still during the trial, would become the justificationalist argument par excellence for the whole bloc: stressing the treacherous behavior of the Armenians during the war and the hundreds of thousands of (Muslim) victims of their wartime treason. The Turks, the paper maintained, had no other choice, and the real culprits for the tragedy were the Entente powers.[7]

On June 4, another lengthy essay in the *Deutsche Allgemeine Zeitung* reiterated the very same points in slightly different language. Now special emphasis was put on the argument that the Turkish nation had been involved in "a struggle for its very existence" when the Armenians rose against them, "in their back"—"back" *(Rücken)* becoming a key term and obviously also playing into contemporary feelings evoked by the German stab-in-the-back myth.[8] The *Deutsche Allgemeine Zeitung*'s style of argumentation very much prefigured and mirrored today's denialist approach with its emphasis on victims and suffering on both sides, wartime necessities, a lack of intent, and the alleged treason of the Armenians.[9] On the same day, the *Deutsche Zeitung* printed an article in a similar vein, also emphasizing the absolute necessity of the measure from the point of view of the Ottoman government and blaming mainly the Entente for what happened, because they had made the Armenians rise against the Turks.[10] Similarly, the

Deutsche Tageszeitung stressed that, while there was an "entanglement of guilt and guilt," the "original guilt" was definitely the Armenians', who had led a "guerrilla war" against the Turks, claiming 100,000 Turkish victims. The *Deutsche Tageszeitung,* like the *Deutsche Allgemeine Zeitung,* at this point still denied the charges of genocide, even of large-scale massacres.[11]

It was around 6 and 7 June that the nationalist camp's discourse changed insofar as it now acknowledged genocide, but again tried to justify it by blaming the Armenians for what had happened to them. The first such salvo against the Armenians came on 6 June, when the *Vossische Zeitung* printed an open letter by Şefik Arslan.[12] Another telling example was the *Frankfurter Zeitung* and its exceptionally conflicted essay on the topic on 7 June.[13] The paper tried to do all things at once: to find Tehlirian guilty of "treacherous murder," to find Talât Pasha and the Ottoman Empire guilty—with full knowledge and full intent—of genocide ("the barbarian annihilation of the Armenian people"), and to blame the Armenians themselves for their fate. Reading this article, it becomes clear very fast that its author was overwhelmed by and could not cope with all the new realities the Talât Pasha trial had brought about. The article maintained that Talât Pasha had to have known how the deportation order would be carried out in practice and what it would mean for the deportees. And still the paper pointed out that "the Armenians were not of the angel-pure innocence" the pro-Armenian papers made them out to be. While it conceded that the Armenian uprising did not entirely justify what happened later, it asked its readers in its final sentence not to condemn the Turks too quickly.

On the same and the following day, the *Berliner Lokal-Anzeiger* published a lengthy, two-part, front-page opinion piece by a certain "Professor Moritz."[14] This Professor Moritz acknowledged the fact that the Ottoman government at first used military necessity as a justification for the deportations, but then "in the second half of 1915 as well as in the following year it was openly admitted by members of the [Ottoman] government that their goal was not solely the relocation of the [Armenian] nation, but that it was nothing less than its total annihilation"—an objective that was largely fulfilled, the author acknowledged. "Of the 1.5 million Armenians which were subject to this disciplinary measure almost a million had perished, a quarter of a million were saved by the mostly compulsory conversion to Islam, and only the last quarter of a million were successful in hiding or fleeing." But then the author asked if, while the guilt of the Young Turk Committee was established "beyond any doubt," the other side was really "totally innocent in this catastrophe." And then this Professor Moritz claimed that the Germans so far had not had any chance to really get to know the Armenians. Apparently, he thought it was up to him to "introduce" the real Armenians, which he did by discussing their (alleged) racial character. In its second part, published the following day, Moritz's essay proceeded in a pseudoscientific manner to expose the alleged vileness and treacherousness of the Armenian character. It did so by presenting a potpourri of anti-Armenian quotes from various authors, among them Mark Sykes (the British politician and adviser on the Middle East), and then exploring the various pro-Armenian strategies of the Entente. In the end, then, what the essay did was to excuse genocide, mainly on racial grounds. This line of argumentation—to acknowledge genocide and to justify it, or at least excuse it, at the same time—was now the norm in the nationalist bloc and continued to be put forward in the coming months.[15]

In the meantime the *Neue Preussische (Kreuz-)Zeitung* also continued its anti-Armenian campaign.[16] Its lengthy, front-page article, "The Armenian Horrors: An Attempt to Save Talât Pasha's Honor," happily accepted the premise of Professor Moritz's *Lokal-Anzeiger* article, which it also referenced at great length.[17] It, too, tried to have it both ways, that is, to accept that genocide, in all its horror, had taken place and at the same time to justify it. It acknowledged right away that Tehlirian had wanted to avenge the demise of his nation and that "during the war the Armenian people had to suffer infinitely," which, the paper stressed, was a fact that could not be denied. The *Kreuzzeitung* accepted the estimate that about one million Armenians had died, and acknowledged that there was an extensive documentary record, provided in part by Lepsius's books. But then the article began its principal argument, that the Armenians were not "the innocent lambs" that their German friends made them out to be. It began by citing the two-part opinion piece by Moritz in the *Lokal-Anzeiger* as quasi-proof, only to continue: "They are seen to be greedy and shifty and that is why they are held in the same esteem in the Orient as the Jews are in the Occident."

Next the article examined the topic of the allegedly treacherous behavior of the Armenians during the war as puppets of the Russians—something, the paper stressed, one could not just "argue away" as Lepsius had done. The Armenians' stabbing in the back of the Turks had endangered military operations and indeed the very existence of the nation. The *Kreuzzeitung* claimed that the Ottoman government then had had "recourse" to measures that might appear in their radicalism unusual to the European observer, but were after all understandable for an "Oriental state struggling for its existence." The measure in question was, in the words of the *Kreuzzeitung*, the eradication of "the evil at its roots." Then the paper at first again spoke of "only" deportation orders, but then conceded that under the given conditions the people in power knew of and very probably welcomed the consequences of their orders, that is, genocide. It then also conceded that the Young Turk leaders had had no other choice but to deny all this. And then, swiftly changing the tone again, the paper stressed just how bloodily the Armenians had avenged this catastrophe in the Russian-occupied Anatolian territories during the world war. Yet again, the *Kreuzzeitung* spoke of the "extermination of the Armenian people" and argued that none of that could diminish the responsibility of the government, whose guilt would stand in front of the tribunal of world history. And, in yet another swift change of perspective, it claimed that, if the Turks were guilty, then so were the Entente powers who had used the Armenians against the Turks—once more suggesting that the Armenian stab in the back had somewhat automatically triggered this genocide, thereby again offering a justification for genocide in general.

The *Deutsche Allgemeine Zeitung* also continued its campaign with more essays on the topic. One justificationalist opinion piece, published on 8 June, probably written by Humann himself, reaffirmed once more that the Armenians had stabbed the Turks in the back. Another by Felix Guse, also a former "German Ottoman," on 28 June 1921, stressed that the Armenians had revolted wholly unprovoked and that "it must be emphasized that the Armenians must assume the blame for all that followed," that is, the genocide.[18] Two days later, yet another large front-page essay justifying genocide was printed.[19] This one was penned by Lieutenant Colonel Otto von Feldmann.[20] One of the German Ottomans, a friend of Humann's and Enver's as well as one of Enver's "barefoot soldiers" at Sarikamish (rather, an officer of the General Staff; still, his feet froze solid there and he had to have half of his right foot amputated later), Feldmann had served with the Ottoman General Staff and would later be chairman of the hypernationalist German National People's Party (DNVP) in northern Germany and Hindenburg's campaign manager. He would also be part of the Nazi parliamentary group from 1933 until 1938. Feldmann had been at the Talât Pasha trial as a witness (for the prosecution), but had not been called upon. His essay was also reprinted, verbatim, in other papers, such as, for example, the Bremen-based *Weser Zeitung* five days later. Feldmann, not unlike the others, also launched a tirade against the Armenians, full of hate for their alleged greed and the way they had sucked the Turks dry. His central argument was that the Ottomans would not have been able to wage war on the front with Russia if the Armenians had been allowed to remain in their areas of settlement, it having been a clearly established fact that the Armenians felt themselves to be Russian rather than Ottoman subjects. The "duty of self-preservation of the front," as he called it, simply made the deportations a necessity—a necessity that also forced him and other German officers to advise the Turks to "clear certain areas in the rear of the army of the Armenians." As we discussed earlier (Chapter 6), Feldmann was the only one of the German officers serving with the Ottomans who admitted that he and others had advised the Young Turks in their Armenian deportations. And it was precisely this article that contained this admission.

This was followed twenty days later by yet another "expert account" in the *Deutsche Allgemeine Zeitung,* penned by Bronsart von Schellendorff under the title "A Testimonial for Talât Pasha."[21] Schellendorff had been a close colleague of Feldmann's who had worked together with him and Enver Pasha on all military matters. Though he had come to the Ottoman Empire at the same time as Liman von Sanders, and had in fact served under him, the two men had come to be in a state of conflict and even animosity. The historian Vahakn Dadrian believes Schellendorff to have been one of the original instigators of the genocide.[22] And Schellendorff's very extensive essay on 24 July 1921 does everything to support such a claim, though it does not conclusively establish it.

Schellendorff began his lengthy "testimonial"—which cannot be summarized here in full—by claiming that witnesses "who had seen the truth" had not been allowed to address the court during the Talât Pasha trial. He thus implicitly claimed that Sanders was either lying or did not know what he was talking about, and the superior witness he had in mind was, of course, himself. Schellendorff had been in the courtroom as well, but had not been called upon, just as Feldmann had not. Now, he stated, after having studied the matter further, he was ready to finally bear witness. He then dove "deep" into history:

> The Armenian Horrors are age-old. They took place again and again, ever since Armenians and Kurds lived close to one another in the border regions of Russia, Persia, and Turkey.

> The Kurd is a nomad and a cattle-owner; the Armenian a crop farmer, craftsman, and merchant. The Kurd has no school education, does not understand or know the value of money and knows that to charge interest is forbidden by the Koran. The Armenian, as a merchant, exploits this inexperience without scruple and fleeces him. The Kurd feels cheated and revenges himself against the usurer and—there you have it: "Armenian Horrors!"

Thus, the first thing that has to be noted about Schellendorff's unfolding argument is that he suggested that the Kurds were the ones to blame for the massacres, but he implied that, at the same time, their motivations were "understandable." Furthermore, he suggested that a population like the Armenians with such immovable racial characteristics must come into such a sharp conflict with other populations that revenge and thus murder would be unavoidable. Schellendorff echoed the arguments of the 1890s justifying violence against the Armenians.

He went on to claim that during the war, the "dangerous uprising" of the Armenians in the border provinces began, and that there had been no reason or justification for such a rebellion. According to Schellendorff, everything was just fabulous in the 1915 Ottoman Empire: the Armenians had the same rights as everybody else and thus no reason to rebel or even complain; fears of massacres do not even compute in his logic. He claimed that this rebellion had been planned long beforehand; an associated "Armenian plot against government officials and officers" in Constantinople had been uncovered in time.

In Schellendorff's reading it was not the Turks but the Armenians who had done the massacring, which "was easy for the Armenians," given that all Muslim men fit for military service were in the army at the time. (He thus implied both that Armenians were disloyal and that they did not serve, when in fact the men had been drafted just the same.) Regarding the massacres carried out by the Armenians, Schellendorff swore that he, as an eyewitness, could attest that they had been worse than what happened to the Armenians later.

According to Schellendorff, after all the former Ottoman chief of General Staff of the army, this general Armenian rebellion was so immense that it endangered all the Ottoman military operations in the East against Russia. He spoke of an exodus of the Muslim population in these regions out of fear of Armenian massacres, and the need for the Turks to act fast. He then stated that the cabinet declared the Armenians, all of them, enemies of the state and gave the order for deportation. He went as far as to assert, fantastically, that the Armenians were to be deported to these Northern Mesopotamian sparsely populated areas for their own safety, that is, far away from the war and the Kurds, and also for their own benefit, in that they would be able to colonize this "promising land." Schellendorff went on to claim that the deaths of the deportees were just unlucky side effects of the war, that is, the difficult logistics and the lack of food, medicine, and so on. He concluded,

> This then raises the question of whether one should have foreseen such circumstances and so should have refrained from the resettlement. . . . The state necessity of the Armenian emigration from the rebellious regions has to be affirmed. The consequences had to be borne.
>
> Just take our current state of affairs in Germany. Suppose there were a ministry with the power to order: "All Polish insurgents will be removed from Upper Silesia and put into prison camps!"—or: "All violent Communists will be put on boats and dropped off at the shores of Soviet Russia!"—Would there not be a storm of applause across Germany?

It becomes clear that for Schellendorff—as for many of the justificationalists—genocide was a "reasonable," "justifiable," if not unavoidable cost of doing political and military business in the twentieth century. He differed from the justificationalist camp as he did not explicitly accept the charge of genocide—though it has to be remembered that it is not unreasonable to suspect that he himself had been involved in the decisions for genocide. In an atmosphere in which almost all of the papers accepted the charge of genocide—the *Deutsche Allgemeine Zeitung,* in which he was writing, included—his argument of "accidental genocide" still has to be counted as part of the broader justificationalist spectrum.

Schellendorff's use of the German analogy shows that he indeed believed this to be a universal phenomenon; he obviously also believed that just because there were people who hated Poles and Communists, it would be right to fulfill their darkest fantasies. Schellendorff, in this part of his essay, also answered defense attorney Werthauer who, during the Talât Pasha trial, had stated that given the circumstances on the ground, the deportation should never have been ordered in the first place. Schellendorff, readily accepting the premise that the deportations had been merely intended as "deportations," responded tersely: "The consequences had to

be borne." Thus it was acceptable if a people perished, as long as it was because of "military necessities."

The topic just saw no end in this turbulent year. On 12 September, some
papers picked up a journal publication by Lepsius. He had published some
decrees signed by Talât himself in the periodical *Der Orient*. The *Welt am
Montag* took this opportunity, in its article "The Butcher of Armenians,"
to attack all those who had showered Talât with "venerating obituaries":
"And yet, there is nothing more depressing for every decent German than
the fact that this mass murderer had been the protégé of the German government throughout the war."[23] Those who wanted to know who Talât really had been should consult the decrees now published by Lepsius. The
paper then also reprinted one of Talât's telegrams, addressed to the local
authorities in Aleppo, in which it was affirmed that the Young Turks had
decided upon the "extermination" of all the Armenians living in Turkey. It
also stated that all were to be included in this order, including women, children, and the sick. It included the warning that all those who refused to
carry out this order were to lose their citizenship; it was signed by Talât as
minister of the interior.

On the other side of the divide, the *Deutsche Zeitung* also continued to
speak out for the Turks and, in this context, this meant *for genocide*. In its
mid-September article, "A Word for Turkey," for example, it emphasized
again that the Armenians had been a fifth column and that they had stabbed
the Turks in the back while the Turks had been fighting for their lives during
the war. It made fun of "these poor Christian Armenians," who had committed the worst imaginable massacres against the Turks. Again, as in other
papers and as before, it was claimed the Armenians had brought upon
themselves what had happened, and the paper made it appear, in an abstract
fashion, as if in such a context there was little else to do.[24]

Later in 1921, the court transcript of the Talât Pasha trial was published
as a book. The preface was written by the pro-Armenian author and
activist Armin T. Wegner, who claimed that this had been a "tribunal of
humanity" and its verdict was of "world historical significance."[25] Wegner
also frontally attacked the German justificationalist discourse: "And all
these fierce accusations which are being leveled against the Armenian
people in order to find the guilty reasons [*schuldige Ursache*] for these horrors in their own behavior cannot excuse what has been committed against
them."[26] Against the (Armenian) stab-in-the-back myth, he wrote that it
was all too understandable that some Armenian soldiers might have

crossed over to the Russian enemy, given what they had had to endure at the hands of the "master race" *(Herrenvolk)* for decades.[27] Then, like others we have seen, he drew an analogy with Germany: "Similar things [that is, fighting for the enemy] have happened with the Central Powers in their Polish and Czech regiments, and still nobody among us thought about punishing innocents for this, for example by pouring the whole Polish population of Germany into the Baltic Sea or letting the Czech population of Austria die of cold on the passes of the high mountains or on the glaciers of Tirol."[28] While Wegner was perhaps right for the time of the war, later, as we will see in the following chapters, the Nazis did indeed speculate about "pouring" the Jews onto the shores of the Baltic in scenarios modeled on the Armenian case. Schellendorff had already suggested a few weeks earlier that similar "measures" could be extremely popular in Germany.

The publication of the court transcript gave the newspaper debate a new impetus, and led to another new treatment of the whole topic, in which Tehlirian's story and that of the Armenian people were told yet once more. This was perhaps not surprising given the heated and still ongoing debate anyway; but it may also have had to do with Wegner's direct attacks on the justificationalist discourse. Wegner had singled out the discourse of "militarily necessary measures" for special criticism.[29] The *Westdeutsche Zeitung* commented on the publication that, while it was not necessary to start again with this difficult topic, the telegraphic orders by Talât, which were published in the appendix of the book and had not been part of the trial, were very interesting. They illuminated Talât's role in an "unambiguous" fashion as thoroughly worthy of condemnation.[30]

Another reaction was a lengthy opinion piece by Willy Meyer, "Captain, retired," which appeared in the *Germania* on 11 November, spread in two parts over the morning and the evening editions, in each case on the front page.[31] Meyer was one of a group of "pacifist officers," as Wolfram Wette and Helmut Donat have labeled them.[32] He began with an unattributed quote, probably from Talât Pasha: "The best way to get rid of the Armenian question is to get rid of the Armenians" (in the German version, "aus der Welt schaffen" already hints at genocide). After mentioning the trial and its newly published transcript, Meyer recounted Tehlirian's story for the German public one more time: how Tehlirian's family had been massacred; how he had been wounded, had survived, and had been sheltered by an elderly Kurdish woman; and, finally, how he had reached Berlin, where he then had stumbled upon Talât. Next Meyer turned to Ottoman history,

recounting how one after another all of the empire's Christian peoples—
"the Greeks, the Egyptians [*sic*], the Bulgarians, Romanians, Serbs, Mon-
tenegrins, and the Albanians"—had sought and achieved independence,
creating a fear that the Armenians would be next. So the Turks "for this
reason used the war in order to annihilate this people. So-called 'military
necessities,' which also in other places brought so much misery, were used
as a pretext" for "the extermination of the Armenians." Meyer then went
on to describe how the "methodical butchering of the Armenian people"
had been carried out. It was "organized in an excellent fashion," he said, and
the supreme authority in the matter had rested with Talât, "who exercised
his cruel craft in a very efficient fashion." Meyer then listed the various
stages of this annihilatory craft: First, the men fit to bear arms were drafted
into the army, where they were shot. Second, the other Armenians were
disarmed. Third, the leaders of the community in Constantinople were
deported and almost all of them killed. Fourth, Armenian newspapers
were closed down and the Armenians were denied access to the postal
system. Fifth, the Turks were forbidden, under draconic penalties—"death
penalty, burning down of their houses"—to help the Armenians. Sixth, the
deportation order came overnight, so that no time was given to pack much
or to sell property or belongings. Seventh, all were deported, with no exceptions made for the sick, children, or the elderly. Eighth, after the deportations had begun, the men were massacred, while some of the women and
girls were carried off into harems and Turkish families. The rest were left
to die of hunger and exhaustion.

In the second part of his opinion piece, Meyer called this the "greatest
persecution of Christians of all the centuries"—this was a remarkable
comeback of the Armenians as Christians in German discourse, perhaps a
strategy to reject the otherwise dominant racialist discourse about them.
He not only put the number of victims at one million, "exterminated without
any remnants," but also repeated the by now iconic Talât Pasha quotation
(from Lepsius), that "the destination of the deportation is nothingness."
Meyer also attacked the prevalent anti-Armenian stereotype of the town-
dwelling merchant and usurer by observing that "80 percent of the Armenian people were crop farmers"—though he conceded that the rest were
also tradesmen and controlled pretty much all of Ottoman internal
trade. Before he closed his two-part piece, he also made mention of Lepsius's report as well as other publications. And indeed, it was clear that
military officer Meyer, though ostensibly reviewing the trial transcript, had

drawn on many other sources as well in his detailed analysis. By late 1921, however, an article condemning the Turks so unreservedly was the exception to the now prevalent justificationalist rule.

Probably as a reaction to Meyer, and right before Christmas, the *Deutsche Allgemeine Zeitung* attempted another version of genocide justificationalism, in an article on 22 December 1921 on "The Christians in the Orient."[33] It began by acknowledging many thousands, if not hundreds of thousands, of victims, but almost exclusively held the Kurds responsible. These had "always used any chance to annihilate Christian villages." Moreover, Humann's paper again asserted that foreign powers had tried to organize "the Christians" militarily—thus alluding to the stab in the back. And finally, it came full circle from its acknowledgment of Christian victims in the opening paragraphs to claim that it basically was all "enemy propaganda," especially the claims that German officers had had anything to do with all this.

The 1922 Assassinations

The Talât Pasha assassination simply would not go away: even a year later, the papers were still discussing it. On 12 February and 9 March 1922, for example, the *Deutsche Allgemeine Zeitung* featured long commentaries on Talât Pasha's memoirs, published in German at the time.[34] A week later the *Deutsche Tageszeitung* printed its own article on the memoirs, and a month later the *Neue Preussische (Kreuz-)Zeitung* did as well.[35] The prosecution at the Talât Pasha trial had had access to Talât Pasha's memoirs, or at least excerpts from them, but had chosen not to use them.[36] In the meantime, the Armenian topic had also been discussed internationally, prompting the *Kreuzzeitung* to report on the debate about an "Armenian home" in terms of a "colony" for the Armenians—thereby echoing similar debates on the proliferation of "mandates" as well as on a Jewish home in Palestine.[37]

On 5 April 1922, the *Deutsche Allgemeine Zeitung* again offered a lengthy attack on the Armenians, and again justified genocide, the occasion for the article this time being a response to an earlier article in the *Berliner Börsenzeitung*.[38] This again shows how the issue had really taken on a life of its own in the press, with discussion—and, occasionally, real interpaper debate—continuing even without obvious external stimuli. The *Deutsche Allgemeine Zeitung*, as always, underlined the treacherous nature of the Armenians, whom Russia, France, and Britain had pushed to commit "high treason" against the Turks, "which had led to the widely discussed countermeasures of the Turks." The paper thus suggested, as it had often done before, that it was legitimate to react to treacherous acts committed by a small part of the population with the mass murder of the entire population; it even implied that this was something quasi-automatic and "natural," as the word "countermeasures" suggests.

Just as the debate was starting to cool off at the end of April, it happened again: two former leading Young Turks were assassinated in a Berlin café, Cemal Azmi, the "butcher of Trabzon," and Behaeddin Shakir, "the chief technician of the Armenian Genocide" or the Young Turk equivalent of Himmler, as some would put it much later.[39] Shakir had coordinated the execution of the genocide from Erzurum—he had been the "parallel Young Turk government" in the province that Scheubner had talked about in his reports (Chapter 6). Shakir had also delivered the closing eulogy at Talât Pasha's grave one year earlier.

This time, however, there would be no spectacular trial since the assassins were able to escape. This time, there also was no fundamental turn in public opinion. Most papers, from the beginning, reported in a markedly hostile and anti-Armenian fashion. This time, the papers were sure from the start that the deed had been politically motivated, that is, was retribution for the Armenian Genocide. The *Vossische Zeitung* stressed that "the murderers are without a doubt to be sought in the midst of the many Armenians living [in Berlin]. The Armenians dispersed all over the world are members of the Armenian secret organization, which has its headquarters in America and whose goal it is to do away with the leading persons of the Turkish war party."[40] The *Vossische Zeitung* suggested here that *all* the Armenians in the world were organized in one single secret organization, stressing the subversive character of "all Armenians." Yet, a few sentences later, when it wanted to make a point about Germany and specifically about Berlin, it claimed that the Armenians there formed "numerous secret organizations." Thus, what mattered rather than consistency was that Armenian conspiracy abounded and that this was now a German problem too.

Interestingly, the Catholic *Germania* also immediately attributed the assassinations to "the execution of Armenian blood revenge." It, too, repeated the claim that all Armenians were part of the same single "secret organization."[41] As was to be expected, the firmly anti-Armenian *Deutsche Zeitung* also made much of the fact that the "former members of the central council" of the Young Turks were being "systematically" murdered by "the Armenian secret organization," and recounted all the various assassinations of the last year. This article was tellingly titled "The Armenian Murderer Organization."[42] This was subsequently picked up by other papers almost in a verbatim fashion.[43] Unlike the previous year, there no longer was any appreciation in the German press that the horrors of genocide made revenge, or rather, the execution of the death sentence of the Constantinople court, an understandable wish in the eyes of the survivors.

On the second day after the assassinations, the verbal attacks on the Armenians were stepped up and extended to another group: the Jews. The *Neue Preussische (Kreuz-)Zeitung* featured a very lengthy essay on the assassinations and their meaning for Germany.[44] It opened with the claim that of all the Armenians questioned in Berlin, none were showing any remorse for the assassinations—an odd observation, suggesting that even if they were not assassins themselves, they should still feel remorse for what other people did by a mere logic of racial belonging—not unlike suggestions made in relation to all Muslims in reaction to terror attacks in recent years.[45] Next, for the umpteenth time, the by now classic claim that the Armenians had stabbed the Turks in the back during the war was repeated, as was the new theme of the (one and only) "secret Armenian organization." But then the *Kreuzzeitung* ventured into a new direction: a sweeping interpretation of Berlin, and especially of Western Berlin: "There are more of them staying here than one would believe." In the Talât Pasha trial itself, the judge and a witness had estimated that the Armenian community in Berlin numbered about a hundred people. But now these numbers were vaguely inflated; perhaps "them" merely referred to the kind of shady people described further in the article. Discussing what the paper painted as something of an Armenian pandemic, it claimed that "they" resided under false names and with French passports—in itself a highly unsympathetic detail, given that not only was France one of the victorious Entente powers, but the French occupation of the Ruhr region had made France, of all the Entente powers, especially unpopular in nationalist circles. But there was more for the *Kreuzzeitung*: "The foreigner question is becoming urgent." The assassinations should finally wake up the government. With "300,000 foreigners" in Berlin, the paper claimed, the capital had become "an El Dorado for foreign criminal elements" and it especially pointed at the "Eastern Jews" *(Ostjuden)*, these "foreign currency traffickers." The "Eastern Jews had wandered with [their] greasy bags" into the western part of Berlin. Berlin had lost its "German character," the paper ascertained.

The paper then brought both themes of the article together: "What a wonderful supplementation the immigrated Eastern Jewry has received in the form of the Armenians, who in their character do not differ much." Both groups, the paper claimed, gave rightful asylum titleholders a bad name, especially now, after the assassinations. In its quest to blur the border between the identities of the two groups, the *Kreuzzeitung* ended with the following plea: "We demand sharp, radical measures, and are expecting this time, if the murderers are actually caught, a different punishment [in bold] than the acquittal of Talât Pasha's murderer. That verdict could not have but encouraged further deeds of blood. Now it is time to think of state interests and to finally cleanse Berlin of these elements which do not belong here." The interesting thing here is, of course, that the paper, when demanding a cleansing, was no longer speaking of assassins or "merely" of all the Armenians, but of the Eastern Jews as well. Given how the article tried to connect the two groups before coming to this final plea, there was nothing ambiguous or coincidentally vague about the confusion of groups here. And in fact it was not something completely new: even in the articles about Tehlirian's acquittal one year earlier, other papers, including, not surprisingly, the *Deutsche Allgemeine Zeitung*, had highlighted that now Tehlirian would probably become "the hero of Western Berlin"—with "Western Berlin" standing as code for the alleged shady milieu of Eastern Jews, illegal aliens, and Armenians.[46]

The *Deutsche Zeitung* published a very similar article the same day.[47] Here, too, the assassinations were seen as the work of one single (global) "Armenian vengeance association." What was being "avenged," the genocide, was merely referred to euphemistically as the "deportation" and "its consequences." And, exactly as in the *Kreuzzeitung*, the paper stressed that "the Armenians interrogated in Berlin may have nothing to do with the crime, but they did not regret it." It then came back to the genocide:

> The conduct of the Armenians who, as the Young Turks understood, were stabbing them in the back while they were fighting for the survival and unity of Turkey, gave cause for the deportation.
>
> The same mood is apparently prevalent among the Armenians in Berlin. There are more of them staying here than one would believe.

This last sentence, coincidentally or not, was the very same sentence as had appeared in the *Kreuzzeitung*; and the *Deutsche Zeitung* now launched into a similar tirade against "them" with their assumed names and their

French passports in the "new West of Berlin." For this paper, too, the Tehlirian verdict was responsible for a whole series of murders. It concluded with the claim that the Armenians had done everything they could to make it difficult for Turkey to hang on in the war and that they were now pushing sharply anti-German politics in the Entente countries. The Catholic *Germania* followed suit with a similar article.[48]

In the coming days, a whole range of articles continued to speculate about the assassins. At one point suspects were arrested in Leipzig, at another point thirty Armenians were allegedly arrested in Berlin. Then there was the often-featured widow of Talât Pasha, who, coincidentally, had been a witness to these assassinations as well and was asked to help with the investigation.[49] The connection of the Armenian topic with the "foreigner question" was widespread: The *Berliner Lokal-Anzeiger*—after reporting on the assassination itself in a similar manner as the *Deutsche Zeitung,* and very extensively—featured another article below its assassination coverage about the "Foreigners in Berlin." This article began with a reference to the assassination and then discussed how this could have happened. The answer: the city was swarming with foreigners.[50]

Just a couple of days later the *Berliner Lokal-Anzeiger,* also lacking any sympathy for the Armenian avengers, cited documents from the Lepsius volume in order to exonerate the two assassinated Young Turks.[51] In a similar vein, the article on the funeral two days later discussed the far-reaching security measures taken by the police because "one has come to expect the improbable from the Armenians."[52] On the same day, the *Deutsche Zeitung* again tried to tackle the "foreigner question" in combination with the Armenians, "Berlin West," and the Jews.[53] The theme was the parable of the sick national body and the assertion that every doctor had to identify the illness in order to find a cure. The *Deutsche Zeitung* identified the disease as "the Jews," especially those in Moscow (that is, those allegedly steering the Bolsheviks), but also the Jews in Germany. It then asked who benefited from the disunity of Germany. Its answer was the cryptic "Berlin West," which was, for this paper, too, synonymous with "the Eastern Jews," Armenians, and criminal foreigners. The following final conclusions of the *Deutsche Zeitung* are worth quoting in full:

Just now we have read how certain newspapers justify the murder of German-friendly Turks in Berlin, solely because the cowardly criminals were Semitic cousins. These papers take the same approach in all matters concerning Jewish issues, and in the end the destruction of all things venerated by the Germans serves the same purpose. . . . The German sickness can be cured neither with constitutional remedies or socialization pills, but solely and exclusively with the sharp knife of the ethnic surgeon.

The putrefaction-spreading pathogen has to be removed!

Otherwise Germany will die of the un-German essence [*am un-deutschen Wesen*].

The Jewish-Armenian confluence ("Semitic cousins") will be further discussed in the following chapters, but its implications are dangerously obvious: the Armenian question was solved by the Young Turk "ethnic surgeon"—now something similar had to be done to resolve the Jewish question.

·   ·   ·

In July 1922, the second of the Three Pashas, Djemal Pasha, was assassinated, this time outside Germany, in Tbilisi. This likewise motivated the justificationalist camp to attack the Armenians. So, for example, for the *Neue Preussische (Kreuz-)Zeitung*—for which it was another "wicked murderous deed" of the Armenians—the event confirmed the Armenians' alleged racial character, and gave it another chance to haul out the old stereotypes.[54] This topic continued to draw some attention until mid-August, when, for example, the *Kreuzzeitung* reported that no fewer than 199 Armenians had been arrested in Tbilisi—again evoking notions of collective guilt.[55] One day later, on 18 August 1922, the first reports were published on the death of the last of the Three Pashas: Enver Pasha.[56] However, until these were verified, Djemal Pasha's death continued to draw attention with articles in the coming days drawing again upon established anti-Armenian images.[57] The Armenian topic continued to be regularly discussed in the German press. One example is a violently pro-Turkish op-ed published in the *Berliner Tageblatt* in October 1922, in which the former Italian prime minister Francesco S. Nitti justified and minimized the extent of the Armenian Genocide.[58] In December 1922, Djemal Pasha's assassination was discussed in Count Ernst zu Reventlow's *Der Reichswart*—Reventlow being an early supporter of the Nazis. Reventlow honored Djemal Pasha and discussed his "last years." Here again the Armenians figured as the bad guys; no possible motivations for the assassinations were mentioned.[59]

The Treaty of Lausanne and the Armenians

In late 1922 and the first half of 1923, the Kemalists and the Entente were negotiating a new peace treaty in Lausanne. The Turkish War of Independence between, on the one side, the Turkish nationalists (the Kemalists), and, on the other, the Entente (as well as the Ottoman state and the Armenians)—this conflict that excited and mesmerized nationalists in Germany (Chapter 14)—was about to come to an end. The resulting Lausanne Treaty replaced the "Turkish Versailles" (that is, the Treaty of Sèvres). This was the first and only revision of a Paris peace treaty before Hitler.

Remarkably, despite the earlier outrage over the genocide, no paper spoke up for the Armenians now. The lasting effect of the great German genocide debate was the clear preponderance of a justificationalist and anti-Semitic style of argumentation in the press and the public sphere. Most of the time the Armenian topic was merely implicit in the German discussions of the Lausanne negotiations and the discussion of the Kemalist successes there. Often, however, developments in the negotiations led to sudden anti-Armenian outbursts in the press. An early example is a mid-December 1922 article in the Catholic *Germania*. Under the suggestive title "Summary 'Solutions,'" the paper reacted to a papal note to the Lausanne negotiations.[60] The papal note had drawn attention to the situation in Constantinople and the fear among the Christian population of Turkish reprisals and massacres when the Kemalists would take possession of the city. The Armenians in particular were endangered and had nowhere to go. The Holy See referred to the previous genocide and warned that the Kemalists or irregular troops would now "finish the job."[61] Never mind that the *Germania* was the paper of German political Catholicism, it felt it needed to defend the Turks against a Christian onslaught:

> In general the Turk is tolerant; every connoisseur or occasional visitor of the Orient also knows that the average Turk, heir to old soldiers' and farmers' virtues, stands out from other national factions of the Orient as a humanly pleasant type. Perhaps the saying: "The Turk is cheated by the Jew, the Jew by the Greek, and all of them by the

Armenian" is a true survey of the economic life of the Orient in which the Turk, despite all his loss of force still seemingly aristocratic, always draws the short straw.[62]

And then, while it professed to deplore the Armenian Horrors (of World War I), it concluded its article by counseling Germany to examine the developments in minority history in Turkey in case something similar—meaning the loss of control over economic life and national independence—should ever happen to Germany. Thus, just like, for example, the *Neue Preussische (Kreuz-)Zeitung* three years earlier, when it had suggested (as we saw in Chapter 9) that there might be lessons for contemporary Germany in how the Young Turks had handled the presence of a backstabbing minority in its midst, the *Germania,* too, called upon Germany to "learn" from the genocide. It even suggested that a similar background situation could arise in Germany, too, and that then Germany should act as the Turks had—thus presenting genocide as a possible political tool of the future.

Two weeks later the *Deutsche Allgemeine Zeitung*—with a title also including the ominous word "solution"—cheered on the Turks in Lausanne by shouting from its pages, "The Turks are totally right when they say that minorities in Lausanne mean simply Christian propaganda." The paper was, of course, referring to the mention of the Armenians at the treaty negotiations. In any case, the paper suggested, the Armenians would never return to Anatolia.[63] The next day, the *Deutsche Tageszeitung* sounded a similar horn by declaring that Western propaganda had always exploited minority concerns to weaken Turkey and that any "Armenian homeland" would be a threat to Turkish sovereignty.[64] It continued by minimizing the genocide by discussing "concentration camps" and how they had been used by France as well as, especially, the British in the Boer War before. It also stressed that Turkey could not allow itself to now declare an amnesty for the Armenian and Greek traitors—suggesting that each group as a whole was treacherous. Britain, the paper continued, only ever intervened on behalf of the Christians in the Orient when it suited its needs; the real reasons were rather such things as oil or strategic locations of influence—thus again trivializing any (pro-)Armenian positions from the start.

As the Lausanne negotiations went on, the Armenian topic continued to be raised occasionally: there was further speculation, for example, about the number of victims of the genocide, and further consideration of the topic of an Armenian homeland.[65] There were various proposals: an American suggestion of an "Armenian state" in the sanjak of Alexandretta, a rather ironic Turkish counterproposal to erect an Armenian homeland on American soil, and an offer to set up an Armenian home on Ukrainian territory.[66] And then there also was a rather chilling remark from Atatürk's former first commander and now leader of the Turkish delegation at Lausanne, İsmet (İnönü) Pasha, who "assigned all the blame to the Great Powers, who kept bringing up the Armenian question, while for Turkey, it was solved."[67]

In May 1923, the continuing extensive Lausanne coverage in the German papers found a catchier Armenian story, in the form of a reported assassination plot against İsmet Pasha, which had been prevented, but behind which, of course, again, the "treacherous Armenians" lurked.[68] When the Armenians featured in the coverage of Lausanne next, it was also as "traitors": On 18 July 1923, shortly before the signing of the Treaty of Lausanne, İsmet Pasha was quoted by the German press as saying that all those Armenians who were not guilty of treacherous acts were free to return to Turkey. This, of course, implied that most of the Armenians *were* indeed guilty of treason.[69] Thus, parts of the German press were able, in their Lausanne coverage, to cement further their image of the Armenians as eternal traitors and eternal terrorists; they had done so in their general coverage of the Turkish War of Independence as well.[70]

Even more significant for our discussion, the end of the Lausanne negotiations led the press to draw some highly ominous conclusions about the ideal ethnic makeup of the successful state of the future—and how a nation might get there. The *Neue Preussische (Kreuz-)Zeitung* offered its reading of the Treaty of Lausanne on 25 July 1923:

> With the term Kemalism . . . one describes the whole system of government which has now a free rein. Now it is possible to implement the program of the [Young Turks] . . . so that the state will be strong and nationalist down to the last detail. [This was] a program that could not have been implemented in the Turkey [that existed until] 1918, with its mishmash of peoples. . . . Now, however, an almost purely Ottoman [meaning Turkish] Turkey can be implemented . . . within which a great power resides today.[71]

The *Kreuzzeitung* not only appreciated but, in fact, advocated the merits of the ethnically pure state—because, to nationalist German newspaper readers, what had unfolded in front of their eyes in the last few years during the Turkish War of Independence and then again during the Lausanne negotiations was nothing less than a nationalist miracle—a miracle that had to be understood somehow, and the ethnic reading was one welcome by many: including the Nazis, as we will see in the following chapters. The *Kreuzzeitung* even wondered whether, perhaps, it would have been better for the New Turkey to have rid itself of Constantinople as well, now that it was reconstituting itself. For the German nationalists, Constantinople was the embodiment of multiethnic mishmash, sickness, and perversion—like Vienna was for Hitler (as we will see in Chapter 14). After stressing that Turkey had managed to overcome the negative consequences of the war and that Germany, by contrast, was still in the dust, the paper speculated that now, after the Greeks and Armenians had gone, the Jews would take their place. Turkey now needed, the paper urged, "national protectionism" in order to continue the success that had led to Lausanne. It concluded that the Armenians, as so often, had been totally neglected by the Great Powers, but did not care enough to elaborate any further.

The *Deutsche Allgemeine Zeitung* also offered another late reading of the Turkish success in October 1923—just weeks before the Hitler Putsch—under the telling headline "Turkish Possibilities."[72] Here it stressed again that the whole Armenian topic had to be understood as nothing but Entente propaganda lies. "The praised American 'mandate over Armenia' turned into a vicious 'campaign of vengeance' of the lowest Armenian rabble. . . . Those who had been deported by the Turks, with good reason, to Northern Mesopotamia came back in French uniforms . . . and devastated Cilicia and Northern Syria." Thus not only did the *Deutsche Allgemeine Zeitung* openly state that the deportations had been ordered "with good reason" and that there was no motive for vengeance for the Armenians anyway (alas, with scare quotes around vengeance), it also painted the Armenians again as the worst of the worst, their goal only bloodshed, and their grievances nothing but propaganda.

The almost unanimous reaction to the signing of the Treaty of Lausanne in the Right and Far Right papers was to stress that now, with not only the Armenians gone but the Greeks as well, the Turks were stronger than ever before, "rejuvenated," and could peacefully rebuild their country.[73] In their reading, the Turkish victory at Lausanne meant that Turkey was not only externally but also internally free. The nationalist papers also stressed that the Armenians had always been a threat to Turkish freedom, during the

Ottoman Empire as well as the War of Independence.[74] We will come back to these conclusions regarding the "utility" of genocide in our discussion of the Nazis in the following chapters.

• • •

In the post-Lemkin world, "intent" has become a key aspect of the definition of genocide and the identification of a case as such. And it is one of the interesting aspects of the German genocide debate that "intent" to annihilate *all* Armenians was regularly accepted and was perceived as established beyond doubt, even by many of those who defended the actions of wartime Young Turk leaders. The Talât Pasha trial had established *genocide as fact* for the German newspapers all across the spectrum. Now, the camp of those who accepted the full extent of the Armenian Genocide as established fact had grown so considerably that they formed a clear majority. Indeed, so established was the "genocide" now that even the most pro-Turkish and anti-Armenian nationalist papers had to accept it. This has, of course, immense ramifications—both for the history of genocide in the twentieth century and for German history. But what happened next on the nationalist end of the spectrum is perhaps even more important: while the mood and the overwhelming evidence were such that genocide could no longer be denied, many nationalist papers now both accepted the charge of genocide against the Turks and justified it at the very same time.

Hans Humann and his *Deutsche Allgemeine Zeitung* had "won" the debate. They had established their brand of genocide justificationalism across the board (at least so among the former denialist, pro-Turkish papers). This justificationalism solidly rested on the alleged racial characteristics of the Armenians, directly taken from modern anti-Semitism, and identified them as "something" that needed to be eliminated. While the Talât Pasha trial had first led to the acceptance of the charge of genocide across the board, it and the trial's outcome had also led to the justificationalist backlash. The three-step progression—denial, acceptance, and justificationalism—of the events of the 1920s resembles closely the progression—denial/relativism, acceptance, and anti-Armenianist justifications—of the events of the 1890s in Germany and those that occurred during the world war in relation to political and diplomatic Germany. The difference from the 1890s was that this development now took place in relation to genocide and in a supposedly democratic society. The 1922 assassinations had reinforced the justificationalist bloc's self-confidence, and there was no longer (much of) any show of pro-Armenian sentiment or sympathy, even in the rest of the press. Now, the core justificationalist bloc even felt ready to extend its wrath to the "foreigner" and the "Jewish question" in Germany. The inclusion of Jews as legitimate targets in these discourses only reflects the logic of the by now traditional confluence of Armenians and Jews in the nationalist mindset.

But Humann and his campaign in the *Deutsche Allgemeine Zeitung* were not the only reasons for the justificationalist victory. By the 1920s, Germany had become accustomed to the "Armenian Horrors razzmatazz." It had also become somewhat used to justifying violence against the Armenians on racial grounds. Furthermore, German anti-Armenianism already had a tradition of several decades and it underscored and expanded modern anti-Semitism. It used the same vocabulary and imagery of modern anti-Semitism, and "reaffirmed" some of its central tenets in an allegedly similar or equivalent case. An additional key factor in the victory of justificationalism was another topic related to Turkey in the first years of the Weimar Republic: the Turkish War of Independence. The struggle of the Kemalists against the Entente partition plan for the Ottoman Empire had captured the imagination of depressed nationalist Germany. Countless articles on the "Ankara Turks" had featured expositions of "Turkish lessons" for Germany (see Chapter 14). The role-model Turkey that was developed in the German nationalist press in these years—from the center to the Far Right—no doubt also influenced the way the Armenian topic was discussed. The marked shift away from a mass of pro-Armenian voices in 1921, in the coverage of the Talât Pasha trial, to a marked absence of such voices already a year later coincided with the turning of tides in the Greco-Turkish War in favor of the Kemalists.

Besides the shocking logic of genocide justificationalism, there is another interesting feature of this first German genocide debate that deserves our attention. There were some papers, as might have become clear from the passages quoted above, that tried to understand this genocide through a culturalist interpretation, as something that could have happened only in an Asian or Oriental setting, something that could never happen in "civilized" Europe. This culturalist or Orientalist reading suggested that, while regrettable, the German reader could find comfort in the fact that such an event would only ever be possible in "uncivilization," that is, in a non-European or non-Western region of the world. It is in this context enlightening that only the extreme ends of the political spectrum, that is, the Socialist and the (proto-)Nazi papers, rejected this culturalist view from the beginning and either implied or emphasized that the opposite was true. As Count Reventlow—later a Nazi politician—stressed in his *Der Reichswart,* Talât Pasha had no choice but to "neutralize" the Armenian revolutionary potential. It was well known, Reventlow claimed, that "Oriental combat" was not a lenient matter, but then, on the other hand, he pointed out, neither was European warfare.[75] The Nazis saw things the same way (as the following chapters will show). Similarly, albeit with a totally different moral point of view, the Socialist *Freiheit* wrote (time and again) that while these deeds were in a way exceptional, there was enough in the history of Europe that showed that non-Orientals were capable of the same and also that it had grown out of the same hypernationalism that had given birth to many other recent war crimes (such as the German atrocities in Belgium).[76] It is one of these strange, paradoxical, and disturbing instances of foreboding that only the extreme ends of the political spectrum of the Weimar Republic saw what was going on and what could happen—but not the more moderate commentators at the center. Of course, all this is only true for the time up until the Talât Pasha trial and the rise of justificationalism, as we have seen. From that point onward (and with a few exceptions already noted earlier), some papers implied that "Turkish solutions" might also be applicable to Germany at some point in the future. The whole justificationalist logic as put forward since the summer of 1921 did not rely on culturalism but rather on military, national, and racial considerations—all of which were also "transferable."

Furthermore, as another rather condemning empirical observation, it has to be noted that it was only the Socialist *Freiheit* that offered a comprehensive critique of German anti-Armenianism and thus of anti-Armenian racism. In an assessment of the nationalist press, under the headline "Glorification of the Armenian Horrors," it attacked the German nationalist papers as a bloc and then highlighted especially the *Deutsche Tageszeitung,* which had "glorified" the "butcher of the Armenians, Talât Pasha" and was "verbally abusing" the Armenians in the most cruel fashion.[77] The *Freiheit* was the only major paper to take issue in such a fashion with the racist anti-Armenianism prevalent in the press at the time.

We could go one step further and ask how much the 1919, and then later the 1921, charge of genocide against the Young Turks was actually accepted among the newspaper-reading public. We will never know, but perhaps the two backlashes (denialism and then justificationalism) were more in tune with popular sentiment than what pro-Armenian parts of the press were writing. Alfred Rosenberg, Hitler's ideologue, wrote in 1926 that it had been only the "Jew press" *(Judenpresse)* who had welcomed the outcome of the Talât Pasha trial. A reader in a letter to the *Vossische Zeitung* a few days after the trial expressed his lack of understanding for the verdict. The author had apparently served as an officer in the Ottoman Empire during the war. He repeated the military necessity justification and claimed that because of the lacking infrastructure, many Armenians just had to die. "Talât cannot be held responsible for that!"[78]

Two things have become apparent: first, the constant and reaffirmed transferal of anti-Semitic stereotypes and discourse onto the Armenians; second, how much all this was focused on race. When the charges were read out at the Talât Pasha trial, a small detail about Tehlirian was mentioned that never achieved any significance at all: he was a Protestant Christian. This was a trial of a Christian, who was a member of the Protestant Church, being tried in the heart of Protestant Germany. However, the fact that Tehlirian was a Christian and even a Protestant was never really mentioned in the public debate, and if it was, it never mattered. The same can be said about the Armenians at large—that a *Christian* population, one of the oldest in the world in fact, was nearly wiped out by a *Muslim* state rarely featured in the discussion. This was about nations, and more accurately it was about race. Almost no Christian solidarity can be felt reading the articles of the German debate, whether they stem from the pro-Armenian or anti-Armenian side, not even in those papers with an otherwise Christian outlook (for example, the *Germania*). The Armenians were never really perceived (with few exceptions) as fellow Christians, but—again a parallel to the prevalent anti-Semitic discourse—as a different race. This then also reinforced the racial notions of prevalent anti-Semitism, which used the very same vocabulary. While we should be careful not to overinterpret, we should not assume that the use of the same vocabulary and the absence of the Christian aspect escaped the contemporary newspaper reader.

It is sometimes alleged in the research literature that one of the problems surrounding the topic at the time (at Lausanne, Paris, or in the debates in Germany) was that the term "genocide" did not yet exist. But such a claim is totally beside the point and only attests to the lack of historical imagination and empiricism of the authors in question.[79] The people talking about what had happened in 1915/1916 were not clumsily prevented from grasping what had happened just because a word had not been coined yet. The significance of Lemkin's term stems from its connection to a UN definition of a crime against humanity and the relevant convention. But to imagine, comprehend, and describe what it meant to deliberately annihilate a whole people was exactly what the people at the time, and especially so in Germany, did with a plethora of words: destruction, demise, extermination, annihilation, murder, and so on. German society and German public and political discourse did not need Lemkin's term—the German language provided such terms in the form of noun constructions for the annihilation, murder, or extinction of a people. These had been used already in public discourse in the debates of the 1890s massacres. In 1915 and 1916, people also readily used such words when describing such events—though mostly in diplomatic and political settings as well as in Church publications and Lepsius's report. By the end of the genocide debate in 1923, these genocidal terms had the strongest imaginable connection to the Armenian topic in the German language. No other topic had seen the use of such language and to such an extent until that date, probably until the 1930s and even the onset of the Holocaust—except perhaps the alleged threatened extermination of the German people by world Jewry as imagined in Nazi discourses and propaganda.[80]

The large debate ended in 1923, more or less with the signing of the Lausanne Treaty. But the topic would not go away so easily. Until 1933, when the Nazis came to power, German pro-Armenian voices also continued to speak out about the Armenian Genocide, though mainly in book publications.[81] For example, in 1930, Heinrich Vierbücher, whom we last met in our discussion of Naumann (Chapter 3) and who had served as a translator with Liman von Sanders, published his book *Armenia 1915: What the Imperial Government Concealed from the Germans*.[82] And the following year, Martin Niepage, the German teacher who had worked in the German school in Aleppo and who had addressed a pamphlet to the German parliament during the war (Chapter 7), gave a lecture in Hamburg about the relationship between the "Armenian massacres" and pacifism to an overcrowded lecture hall.[83]

However, the press, or at least the overwhelming majority of the press, continued with its anti-Armenian discourse.[84] The justificationalist discourse was to be put forward in the press for the remainder of the Weimar years: in 1925, in another discussion of the past and contemporary misery of the Armenians, the *Berliner Tageblatt* exclaimed, "This is the price for treason!"—the "price" in question, it has to be remembered, was genocide.[85]

The nationalist newspapers were to continue, throughout the Weimar years, to repeat that the Armenians had always been a threat to Turkey's independence, a fifth column, and that only now—after their annihilation and expulsion—could true freedom and independence have been achieved.[86] And it did not stop with newspapers; these interpretations can be found in general histories of Turkey published in these years as well as German history textbooks used during the Weimar years in German schools.[87] And an academic text from 1929 on Turkey generalized so much as to call the First World War a (general) "racial war" and a "war of annihilation" *(Vernichtungskrieg)*.[88]

People like Humann, and thus the *Deutsche Allgemeine Zeitung,* also probably continued to reaffirm their version of justificationalism in the occasional article in the later years of the Weimar Republic. Felix Guse placed another of his justificationalist essays in the military journal *Wissen und Wehr* in 1925. Later, in 1940, in the midst of Hitler's war of annihilation, Guse published his book about the Caucasian front during World War I in which he repeated his version of events—of Armenian treason and of justified genocide.[89] Humann went on to become adviser to Franz von Papen in his campaign for the chancellorship as well as after Papen's election in 1932. In early 1933, Papen would be instrumental in making Hitler chancellor.

Though there was debate about the fate of the Armenians in other countries, too, especially during the war, and notably in the United States, the German debate was the broadest and most significant genocide debate up to that point. Not only so because of its breadth—for years in the center of the public discourse and in the most important dailies—but also because of its depth: this was a debate about the nature of genocide. It had included horrifying details of its execution, discussions of intent, and even possible justifications. It is rather unfortunate for German history that the latter had dominated the debate in its last two years and that justificationalism had carried the day.

Some historians have claimed that there was no "coming to terms" with the Armenian Genocide in interwar Germany, and that this lack of coming to terms made the Holocaust possible.[90] But as we have seen, it is simply not true that Germany did not come to terms with the Armenian Genocide. Rather, Germany came to terms in a manner that we would perhaps not expect and cannot morally condone. That this indeed had a bearing on Germany's road to Auschwitz will become clear in the following chapters.

PART IV

The Nazis and the Armenian Genocide

CHAPTER 13

Racial Discourse
and the Armenians

We have seen that the Armenians and the Armenian Genocide were not far removed from German society, neither in
time nor in space. As the previous chapters show, this is true
for the time up until the 1920s and the early 1930s. But what about the time
after? What about the Nazis and the Third Reich? In the reconstruction of
how the Armenian Genocide impacted the Nazis, the Armenian-Jewish
conflation—that is, how the Armenians were understood as quasi- and even
über-Jews in German discourse—is key. In the decade and a half before the
Nazi takeover, the Armenian Genocide had not only been widely discussed
in Germany, it also involved a group that was typically understood through
the prism of contemporary anti-Semitism. The Armenian Genocide was
understood through another group that lived in Germany and throughout
Europe and that was also perceived as "problematic" by nationalists, indeed one that was understood by anti-Semites to pose another "question," that is, the "Jewish question." This chapter will examine more closely
this Jewish-Armenian conflation as it expressed itself in anti-Semitic and
racial texts from the late nineteenth century up to and during the Third
Reich. Chapter 14 will look at the appraisal of the "results" of genocide,
that is, the role that Mustafa Kemal's "New Turkey" played as a postgenocidal country in Third Reich discourses on the new *völkisch* modernity and
völkisch states (*völkisch* refers to a mixed category between racial and national). The last chapter of this section, Chapter 15, will investigate further
connections and will serve as a conclusion.

The turn to the Jews in the Armenian Genocide debate, especially in
1922, but also regularly before, was no coincidence. We have already seen
that "the Jews," or more precisely modern Central European anti-Semitism,

were the lens through which the Armenians and the Armenian question were perceived by a large portion of politicians, journalists, and commentators in Germany. Before discussing the Nazis themselves, it is important to examine a strand of political and (pseudo)scientific thought that had constantly reaffirmed the Jewish-Armenian conflation: racial anthropology and racialist literature. If what the present book does can be understood as tracing and reconstructing an aspect of the dark intellectual history of genocide, then it has to be recognized that a key building block of the Nazi worldview was anti-Semitism, as well as the idea that all and everything was about race and nation (or the *Volk,* which has both national and racial connotations, especially so in the Nazi usage).[1] And while they did not play a pivotal role in the discourses, at least not explicitly, the Armenians had made an appearance in many of the central texts of German anti-Semitism and racialist worldviews for decades. This includes such key texts of Nazi racialism and anti-Semitism as Hans Günther's various "racial handbooks," Theodor Fritsch's famous handbook, and also, for example, Houston Chamberlain's *Foundations of the Nineteenth Century* or Henry Ford's *The International Jew.*

As we have seen, the perception of Jews and Armenians as similar, equal, or even identical had a long tradition by the time World War I had ended. This Armenian-Jewish conflation was not only conveyed and reaffirmed in the press and other publications on Turkey, but also in racial anthropology and popular racialist texts. Racial anthropology, in its popularized, *völkisch* form, enjoyed great success in the 1920s and 1930s, and among the Nazis as well. "Racial guides" *(Rassenkunden)* were published in ever-increasing editions—Fritsch's books reached double-digit editions in the Third Reich.[2] It has to be noted that scientific racial anthropology, to which we will turn first, was not the same as the crude, populist racism and anti-Semitism of these racial handbooks.[3] But it informed and misinformed its populist offspring and therefore needs to be examined here as well and first. In the following, our discussion will move in concentric circles from racial anthropology to anti-Semitic texts and only then to the Nazis themselves.

Felix von Luschan and the Armenians

One of the fathers of modern racial anthropology was the Austrian Felix von Luschan, who held a professorship in Berlin from 1900 until 1922.[4] He may also serve as a case in point both for the potential dangers of this "science" as well as for some of the participants' reluctance to reach or accept anti-Semitic and racist conclusions. Many of the popular and populist racialist handbooks cited and misappropriated Luschan extensively. His observations on alleged physical similarities between Jews and Armenians, especially the so-called bent nose, proliferated widely in the racial texts of the time. Luschan himself had summarized his position on the relationship between Jews and Armenians in the Huxley Memorial Lecture in 1911 in London: "When I first upheld in 1902, in my paper on the anthropological position of the Jews, the homogeneous character of these groups, I called them 'Armenoids.' But there can be no doubt that they are all descended from tribes belonging to the great Hittite Empire."[5] According to Luschan and others, "Armenoid" described a larger racial background group whose influence could be seen in many (Near Eastern) peoples. But, confusingly, the term was also often used synonymously with "Armenians," and consciously so (as the indexes of books on race from the period show). Furthermore, the Armenoid race was presented as the source of all the racially negative traits that the racist and anti-Semitic discourses identified in the Jews.

Luschan rejected the blossoming simplistic, racial, and annihilatory discourse of many books on race, which (thought they) were inspired by him and quoted him extensively. His very harsh and derisive review in the *American Anthropologist,* in 1915, of a book proposing the wholesale deportation of African Americans "whence they came," or "the desert in Sudan," illustrates this neatly.[6] But, as the same review also shows, Luschan was no stranger to the more radical ideas of social engineering. He wrote there, "Certainly there are criminals and persons with inferior morality and inferior intellect in every human group, white and colored; but we shall sooner or later learn to eliminate them." He did not say what he meant by "elimination" here, but in view of the further course of history, such statements carry the odor of criminal negligence, uttered as they were by a leading specialist on "race." At the same time, Luschan was anticolonialist— he called the white man the only beast in Africa. Luschan also rejected the whole opposition of Aryans and Jews in racial terms as well as the "Aryan theory," which saw "race" where most scientists saw only a shared linguistic background as it imagined a common race based on and parallel to the Indo-European language family, as well as a common racial ancestry relating to the origins of that language family.[7] Luschan made his rejection of this theory clear in his 1922 book *Peoples, Races, Languages*—and he did so in reference to the Armenians: while acknowledging that the Jews spoke a Semitic language, Luschan asserted that their closest racial relatives were the Armenians, who spoke an "Aryan" language, thus turning the Aryan theory on its head.[8] This reasoning was often cited in other works on the topic. It is illustrative to look at how Luschan's reasoning was quoted, for example, in Carl Helm's book *Aryans, Savages, and Jews* (1923):

> [Just as it is wrong to speak of an Indo-Germanic language,] it is utterly wrong to speak of an Indo-Germanic tribe; there is no such thing and never has been. In the same fashion the term "Aryan race" is to be absolutely rejected; it is even problematic to speak of "Aryan" languages as this term is ambiguous, and used by some only to refer to today's Persian, Armenian, and their closest relatives, while others use the term more broadly.
>
> Especially misguided, finally, is the use of the word "Aryan" in opposition to "Jewish" as it has come into fashion in recent years. From a somatic point of view most of the Jews belong to the old Near Eastern people, rather than to the Semites, and are thus the closest relatives of the Armenians—and are thus, of all things, close relatives of a people who [as we have just seen] speak an "Aryan" language, even in the narrowest sense of the word.[9]

In his book, Helm explicitly tried to refute the ideas held by the " 'racially aware Aryan' who had the swastika in his brain and on his breast"—however successful such an endeavor could hope to be.[10] Helm also affirmed and repeated Luschan's conclusions, chief of which were "1. The whole of humanity consists only of one species: *Homo sapiens*. 2. There are no 'savage peoples,' only peoples with a culture different than ours, but there are some singular white 'savages,' raw and uneducated Europeans suffering from tropical frenzy.... 4. There are no inferior races."[11] And this list goes on.

Back to Luschan himself, who also emphasized in his 1922 book that "just as there is no Indo-Germanic or 'Aryan' race, there is no Jewish [race]; neither is there a Jewish type, but merely a general Oriental [one], in which not only the Jews but also the Greeks and Armenians, and in a smaller part many other Near Easterners, take part."[12] In opposition to notions of racial purity or racial unity, now also writing against Jewish authors postulating the racial unity of all Jews, he reasserted that "nowhere in the world did any culture come into being except through the mixing of races and through mutual exchange of all kinds of spiritual and other achievements, that is through trade and commerce."[13]

Luschan's and Helm's attempts to rebut Aryan theories make one thing clear: the Armenians were part and parcel of the debates on race in general, on the "Aryan race" specifically, as well as on the Jews. They were often pivotal in the attempt to refute claims about the Jews. Given the fact that in other spheres of society the Armenian-Jewish conflation was and had been practiced and reaffirmed since the 1890s, such as in the press, books, and pamphlets, the rebuttal's use of the Armenians was perhaps not a rhetorically strong case. However, already the debates about the Aryan theory make it clear that any Nazi worth his salt would have known about the Armenians. Indeed, the easiest way to hold on to the Aryan theory was to turn the Armenians themselves fully into Jews, even über-Jews, which, again, was not far off from what public discourse in Germany had been doing since the 1890s.

Racial "Handbooks"

The most prolific and popular German writer of "race handbooks" (*Rassenkunden;* also "race studies") in the interwar period was Hans F. R. Günther, who published many such guides from the early 1920s until late into World War II.[14] They were very influential on the broader anti-Semitic spectrum—they were also approvingly quoted by publications of the Führer SS and the Hauptamt SS.[15] Already before Hitler's ascent to power, in 1930, Günther was appointed to a professorship at Jena University by Wilhelm Frick of the Nazi Party, which was part of a coalition government in the state of Thuringia at the time.[16] His publisher had advertised him as the "founder of German racial thought."[17] Günther's major publication was his *Racial Handbook of the German People*.[18] It had first appeared in the 1880s as the *Catechism of the Anti-Semites* (1887) and was republished in the early 1920s in a much-expanded version. The "Günther," as the book was called, was available in softcover, hardcover, and in a "nice," "decorative" half-leather edition for the style-conscious anti-Semite. The "Günther" seems to have been very successful throughout the interwar period, with a new edition every year, on average. And for the anti-Semite who did not want to read the more-than-500-page "Günther," there was the "People's Günther" *(Volks-Günther),* a smaller and "exceedingly cheap" version of the book (as the publisher marketed it).[19]

For Günther, the "Armenoid race" was equivalent to the "Near Eastern race." And this race was pivotal, because Günther explained the "spiritual" characteristics of the Jews exclusively in reference to the alleged "Armenoid race," equating Jews, Armenians, and Greeks: "The peoples of mainly Armenoid racial stock such as Armenians, Greeks, [and] Jews distinguish themselves through special commercial abilities in trade and business in which they benefit, in addition to [their] high degree of intelligence, mainly from the ability to empathize with the souls of other people."[20] The "Günther" called upon the reader to learn more about the "racial soul" of the "Near Eastern race" in Günther's *Racial Handbook of the Jewish Race.* There he made further claims about the Armenians who were dispersed all over the Middle East and Europe, "even to China and India their greed has brought them."[21] In his *Small Racial Guidebook to the German People,* first published in 1929, but subsequently republished many times in the Third Reich, he made the following statement—which, given the importance of the Jews to the whole Nazi racial worldview, was neither accidental nor peripheral: "The Jewish people carries a strong Near Eastern influence. The most essentially Near Eastern people is probably the Armenian people."[22] This was a paragraph on its own, and the book's index also betrays the fact that for the author the Armenians (and Armenoids) were synonymous with the Near Eastern race.

In his *Racial Handbook of Europe,* Günther again reaffirmed the almost-equality of Jews and Armenians as well as the classification "strongly Near Eastern."[23] Here, Günther elaborated further on these claims, noting not only the "enterprising mercantile initiative" of the "cunning" Armenians, but "their inclination for fraud" as well as "the cold cruelty [with which] they often exploit their victims."[24] He further claimed that "it appears also that these commercial abilities are more prominent within the races with Near Eastern characteristics, the stronger the influence of the Near Eastern race is on them." Given that, for him, the Armenians were the most typically or essentially Near Eastern of the Near Eastern peoples, this would suggest that they were the most "crafty" of them all. Günther also insisted on the Armenians' lack of ability to either rule or be ruled (which some researchers have found to be a veiled justification of the Armenian Genocide).[25]

Theodor Fritsch, one of the chief anti-Semitic writers in interwar Germany, acknowledged Günther's books as his main source in his discussion of the races in his *Handbook on the Jew Question: The Most Important Facts for Judging the Jewish People.*[26] In 1933, Fritsch's publisher featured a blurb by Adolf Hitler in advertisements for the book in which Hitler said, "I hope that the 'Handbook' will eventually find its way into every German family."[27] By 1944, it was in its forty-ninth, much-expanded edition. Fritsch, too, reaffirmed the Armenian-Jewish conflation. In the chapter "The Racial Science of Judaism," Fritsch described the two "basic races" that for him constituted the parent races of the Jewish race. One of these was the "Near Eastern race," which according to him was also called "the Armenoid race," and the other was the "Oriental race." The Ashkenazi Jews, in this view, were mostly of the Near Eastern race.[28] His discussion of the physical and social traits of this "race" is essential to understanding the conflation of Jews and Armenians:

> The Near Eastern race is of medium height, stocky, short-headed with a steep back of the head and medium broad face. The nose jumps out strongly and appears bulky; the cartilage part of it is bent downward and the end is fleshy. The lips are strong, the lower lip bulges against the upper lip. The mouth is wide, the chin lower and receding. The ears are rather large and fleshy. Hair and skin are essentially dark. The growth of body and beard hair is strong. The eyes are brown.[29]

He then approvingly quoted Günther at length:

> Various images of devils and fiends, of "Mephistophelian" figures, indicate that the occidental peoples must have connected the traits of the Near Eastern race with the "devilish" features of spiritual properties . . . and partially still do so today. . . .
>
> The spiritual properties of the Near Eastern race can be most clearly researched in those peoples on whom this race had the strongest impact, such as, for example, the Neo-Greeks, Turks, Jews, Syrians, Armenians and Neo-Persians. The Near Eastern race is known for its special trader's spirit, a special ability for trade and commerce. . . . This is made evident by the fact that in the Near Orient, in cities inhabited by Greeks and Armenians, the Jews barely or never gain a foothold. Popular humor expresses this in a drastic fashion by saying that a Greek is worth seven Jews and an Armenian [in turn is worth] seven Greeks. . . . The results of their special trader's spirit are being cultivated by a smooth wit, by imaginative oratorical skills, by a pronounced gift, even a zeal, for empathy with the strange life of the soul, for the calculation of people and circumstances, and a gift for the interpretation and reframing of foreign spiritual properties.[30]

In Fritsch's *Handbook* one also finds an idea about history and states so characteristic of Nazi racial discourse, here in relation to the Near Eastern parent race: "Abilities for state-building and for state-conservation seem to be lacking, in their place there is an inclination and ability to form communities of faith."[31]

Houston Chamberlain

Perhaps the bible for anti-Semites and those swimming in the *völkisch* currents that would later give birth to the Nazis was Houston Chamberlain's *Foundations of the Nineteenth Century*, published in 1899 (first in German, not in English). This "swastika Brit," as the pacifist weekly *Die Weltbühne* called him in 1921, also made mention of the Armenians in this, his main book.[32] Chamberlain wrote there, "As these lines are being penned [that is, probably around 1898], the whole civilized world is raging against the Turks; the European powers are being forced by the voice of public opinion to intervene for the protection of the Armenians and the Cretans."[33] He claimed that had the Turk not been so tolerant in the past, now there would be idyllic peace in the Ottoman Empire. "It is the Christian who throws in the yeast of conflict," until the otherwise so peaceful Muslim reacts "with the brutality of . . . a force of nature and exterminates the troublemaker."[34] All this was very much in line with Barth's *Turk Defend Yourself*, which had been published the year before, and there is even the whiff of plagiarism in Chamberlain's text (see this text, Chapter 3). Later in the book, Chamberlain also addressed the question of whether the Armenians were Aryans and made it clear that they were not. On the contrary, he claimed, the Syrians, the Jews, and the Armenians "are virtually indistinguishable today." This was so because their original common race was "every day asserting itself more and more." He further stressed that the Armenians

> show the same passionate penchant for usury as the Jews, only to a much higher degree, so that in the Levant they say: one Armenian is worth three Jews. Interesting recent information about the character of the Armenians is provided by David Hogarth's *A Wandering Scholar in the Levant* . . . , particularly about their genius for intrigues and sedition.[35]

This quote is illustrative of two things: First, for Chamberlain, too, the Armenians were even worse than the Jews. Second, his reference to contemporary English-language texts illustrates that the Armenian-Jewish conflation was not exclusively a German phenomenon.

Chamberlain's description of the Armenians had provoked a discussion between him and Albrecht Wirth, an imperialist and *völkisch* writer whom we last met in Chapter 4 who would later find his way to the Nazis. In the early 1920s, for example, Wirth regularly wrote articles, also on Turkey, for the weekly of the Nazis and the SA, the *Heimatland,* but also for the *Neue Preussische (Kreuz-)Zeitung* as well as the Nazi Party daily, the *Völkischer Beobachter.* In Munich, where he taught at university, he would also befriend Nazi Party cofounder Dietrich Eckart and, through him, made Hitler's and Rudolf Hess's acquaintances, too. Two decades earlier, in his book *Race and World Power in History* (1901), Wirth had written that Chamberlain was right about the common racial origins of the Armenians and the Jews, which led to the "Jew-like" physiognomy of the Armenians, but that Chamberlain had been wrong to find so little Aryan influence in them.[36] But, in any case, for Wirth in 1901, too, the Armenians were a "lower race" *(Unterrasse)* and were very similar in their racial character to the Jews: "The [geographical] dispersion of the Jews is not without analogy. Fairly similar is the dispersal of the Armenians over the whole world and their commercial adaption to the circumstances created by Europeans and Muslims."[37] Chamberlain reacted to Wirth's criticism about the Aryan influences on the Armenians, and the two continued their debate on the Armenians in the subsequent editions of their books.[38] As time progressed, Wirth would call the Armenians "Indo-Germanic" (1914) and also "half-Aryan" (1917).[39]

Wirth was also a connoisseur of Turkey and Turkish history. In his books he forcefully advocated the future German-Turkish alliance (in 1911) and approved of and even concretely foresaw the German-Austrian-Turkish alliance (1912).[40] In his *History of the Turks* (1912), he wrote that "Germandom is especially tightly intertwined with Turkdom, for better or for worse."[41] He also made mention of the 1890s massacres, but prefaced it with the sentence, "whenever life was too good for the anyway unruly subjects of the padishah—Christians, Kurds, or Albanians—then they started a rebellion."[42] Yet, then he stressed that the Armenian butcheries were unjustifiable, for "if perhaps 30,000 were guilty, then 300,000 were punished for that." Still, he was not really objecting to the idea of collective guilt, as 30,000 was still a wholly abstract and exceedingly high number—and guilty of what? He did not say; he only rationalized: "On the other hand one cannot pretend that the Armenians did not openly advocate revolution and anarchy, mostly following English or American teachings."[43] The person of

Wirth is another example of just how intertwined racialist debates and the broader political discourse on the Ottoman Empire and the Armenians were in Germany and even in the early history of Nazism.

Jewish Rebuttals and the Armenians

Anti-Semitic and mainstream racialist authors were, however, not the only ones stressing and reaffirming the Armenian-Jewish conflation. German Jewish authors did so as well, but, obviously, with a different goal. One German-Jewish author who spoke out against the Jewish and Aryan race theories in the strongest fashion by using the racial Jewish-Armenian conflation was Constantin Brunner. His book *Jew-Hatred and the Jews* was written during World War I, when the German Jews were again subject to anti-Semitic slurs and even humiliation by the authorities (such as head-counts of Jewish soldiers in order to check whether and how many Jews had avoided the draft). In this book, which was aimed against contemporary anti-Semitism and racialist theories, Brunner wrote jokingly that now it was "proven" that the "Jewish nose" came from the Armenians—he was following Luschan in his discussion of the "nosification" *(Nasification)* of the Jews by the Hittites. For Brunner it followed that one had to ask, "Now, where might the Jews keep their original noses?"[44] Similarly, S. Weissberg in his book *The South Russian Jews* (1895) had already emphasized (like Luschan) that "the Jewish nose" would be better called the "Armenian nose" in the future.[45] However, such a playful rebuttal of anti-Semitic race theories, apparently, failed to impress *völkisch* nationalists and anti-Semites.

In a similar vein, Arthur Ruppin, the famous Zionist and German Jewish sociologist, also acknowledged the Jewish-Armenian conflation. For him, just as for Luschan, it was significant because it cast doubt on the "Semitic theory."[46] In his *The Jews in the Present Age* (1920), he repeated the saying that three Greeks were worth one Armenian, and three Jews one Greek when it came to trade. He mused that the superiority of such peoples—Jews, Armenians, Greeks, Indians, and Chinese—was due to their ancient civilizations and their ancient roots.[47] In a slightly confusing argument he claimed that even if for science the Jews were clearly recognizable as a race, the same could never be true for lawmaking since, among other reasons, the Armenians and the Syrians exhibited the exact same racial physiognomy.[48] He went as far as to claim that the Jews and the Armenians looked so similar that "the most experienced anthropologist would try in vain to find the one or the other out of a group of Jews and Armenians."[49]

Fritz Kahn published his *The Jews as a Race and a People of Culture* in 1922.[50] Kahn was active in Jewish organizations, also in Palestine, and his books were later burned and very expressly banned by the Nazis. He, too, was in dialogue with Chamberlain, and not only about the Jews, but also about the Armenians. For Kahn, likewise, the Armenians were not only closely related, but, indeed, constituted the racial origin of the "pure" Jewish traits. For him, the Armenians were, despite the fact that some thought of them as "Aryans" because of their language, the race "most closely related to the Jews." The Armenian was, for Kahn, "more Jewish than the Jew" in his physiognomy, and it was from him that the Jew received all his typical physical traits.[51]

Many more usages and affirmations of the Jewish-Armenian conflation by German Jewish authors could be cited here. Also take, for example, the book by Alexander Schüler on the *Racial Nobility of the Jews* published in 1912 by the Jüdischer Verlag (Jewish Publishing House) in Berlin, founded by such prominent Jewish figures as Martin Buber and Chaim Weizmann. It also stressed the similarity between the Jews and the Armenians who had "kept themselves pure" over the centuries and had thus cultivated their "ability for culture" *(Kulturfähigkeit)*.[52] The use of the latter term was a rebuttal of *völkisch* theories denying that either people had such an ability. Friedrich Hertz, Austrian Jewish sociologist and father of the pioneer peace movement, in his 1915 book aimed at racial theories and especially against Chamberlain, compared the Armenians to the Jews and other similar peoples; the Armenians had become the "most cunning merchants" of the entire Near East, according to him.[53] In his (German-language) book on the *Racial Characteristics of the Jews,* Jewish American physical anthropologist Maurice Fishberg pointed out that the similarity between Jews and Armenians was not only a matter of physiognomy, but also a matter of destiny, as both had been mistreated by majority populations; discussing the so-called Jewish "Ghetto Face," he wrote, "The Armenians ... whose fate has not been better than that of the Jews, are in their facial features virtually indistinguishable from the Jews."[54] The same author also stressed that "the fact that the Armenians are often taken for Jews is a well-known matter [*eine alte Sache*]. The Jewish physiognomy is to be found as often among them as among European Jews."[55] However, Fishberg used the similarity in physiognomy of Armenians and Jews, as well as of other peoples and the Jews, to contend that the idea of a homogenous Jewish race was nonsense. And so his book concluded, "Judaism was and is a religion but never a race."[56]

What all these discourses did, whether in the form of anthropologist or racialist and populist texts or even, inadvertently perhaps, in the form of Jewish rebuttals, was to constantly affirm and reaffirm that both peoples were the same. Especially for popular racialist texts, the Armenians were often even "worse" and took on qualities of "über-Jews" or the "original Jews."[57] The handbooks of the racial anthropologist pseudoscientific variant were highly popular books throughout the interwar years. Their literal depiction of the Armenians is reflected in their actual illustrations. Books like that by Siegfried Passarge, which featured many pictures of "Jews," contained also many in which the racial type of the Jews in question was identified as "Armenoid," thus also reaffirming the alleged similarity of the two groups (Figures 13.1 and 13.2).[58]

Nazi Racial Texts

Thus, perhaps not surprisingly, for top Nazis such as Hitler and Alfred Rosenberg, the Armenians were equal to or even worse than the Jews. Not only racialist authors, but also the fathers of modern anti-Semitism such as Chamberlain and Henry Ford had reaffirmed the Jewish-Armenian nexus as well as the status of the Armenians as something of proto- or über-Jews. In his famous anti-Semitic pamphlet *The International Jew*, the German translation of which was extremely popular among German anti-Semites, Ford had counted the Armenians among the "cunning sputum of humanity."[59] And while this was a mere list-mention of the Armenians, it was not an unimportant one as the Nazis revered Ford and his anti-Semitism.[60]

When describing the victory of the Asian type of Russians after the Russian Revolution, that is, the Bolsheviks, in his *Myth of the 20th Century* (1930) Rosenberg mentioned Armenians and Jews in one breath as those taking over power.[61] Hermann Esser, Hitler's former deputy, in his *The Jewish World Pestilence*, first published in 1933 and republished by the main Nazi publishing house in 1939, had approvingly (mis)quoted Johann Gottfried von Herder on how the Jews were just like the Armenians, Bantians, and Gypsies, always to be found anywhere where there was money. In Fritsch's famous handbook, the quote was attributed to Voltaire, but, for the Nazis, a German thinker was just more authoritative than a French one. What mattered, apparently, was the sentiment.[62]

ift auch in Spanien und Süditalien erkennbar. In Spanien und Süd=
italien, befonders in Sizilien, zeigen fich leichte **Einfchläge orien=
talifcher Raffe.** Diefe beiden Raffen find in der Blutmifchung

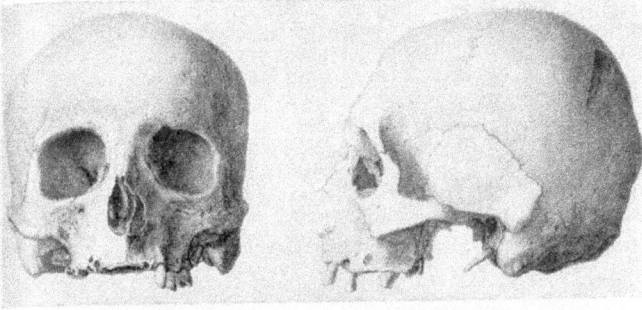

Abb. 236. Schädelbruchftück (Ralvarium) aus Kleinafien. Vorderafiatifche Raffe.
(Aus Quatrefages und Zamr, Crania ethnica)

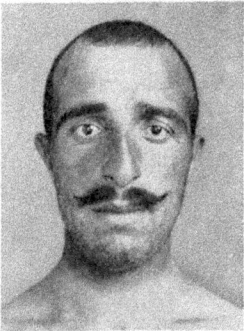 

Abb. 237. Imeretiner aus Rutais.   Abb. 238. Armenier aus Aintaab (Syrien)
(Aufn.: Anthrop. Inft., Wien)   (Aufn.: Prof. v. Lufchan, Berlin)

Vorderafiatifche Raffe

des Judentums ftark vertreten. Auch bei den Zigeunern zeigen fich Ein=
fchläge diefer beiden Raffen.

Die Zigeuner brachten die Raffenbeftandteile ihrer nordindifchen Heimat,
und zwar am ehesten der unteren Schichten der dortigen Bevölkerung mit
fich. Sie fcheinen um 300 v. Chr. von Nordindien ausgewandert zu fein,
hatten in ihrer Hauptmaffe um 200 n. Chr. Perfien erreicht, um 1000 Süd=
ofteuropa, um 1400 Mitteleuropa, um 1500 England, im 19. Jahrhundert
Amerika. Sie haben auf ihren Wanderungen immer wieder Blut der um=
gebenden Bevölkerungen, in den Balkanländern und in Ungarn wohl vor

Figure 13.1 "Near Eastern Race." Examples of the "Near Eastern Race," as
depicted in Günther's *Racial Handbook of Europe* (1929). Right: "Armenian from
Aintab," a picture by Felix von Luschan. Left: "Imeretin from Rutais."

Abb. 63. Grusinischer Jude (Georgien)
Armenoid, mit großer gerader Nase

bräunlichen Ton des Mediterraniers — auf Abb. 66 kommt die helle Haut unter dem Tarbusch zum Vorschein — und des hellen Armenoiden gibt es schwarzbraune Hamiten in allen möglichen Mischformen. Der Zustrom südarabischen Blutes im Beginn des Islams und dauerndes Einsickern seit ältesten Zeiten dürfte sich hier bemerkbar machen. So zeigt Abb. 65 einen hellbraunen, ganz „jemenitisch" aussehenden Knaben mit typischer südarabischer Ramsnase und Mundpartie.

Abb. 67 stellt einen schwarzbraunen persischen Juden vor, dessen Kopfform unter dem Turban nicht erkennbar ist, dessen Hakennase und langes Gesicht aber deutlich das armenoide Erbgut verraten. Der weiße Bart ver

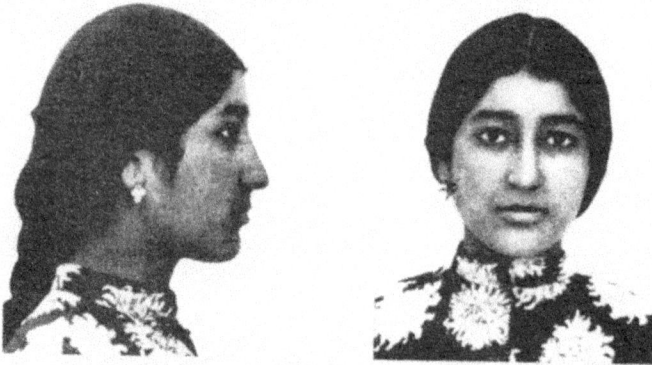

Abb. 64. Jüdin aus Bochara
Schädel armenoid, Gesicht vielleicht auf indogermanische Völker hinweisend

Figure 13.2 "The Anthropology of the Jews." Two examples of Jews of "Armenoid background" in Otto Karl Siegfried Passarge's *Das Judenthum als Landschaftskundlich-Ethnologisches Problem* (München: J. F. Lehmanns Verlag, 1929). Top: "Grusinian Jew (Georgia), Armenoid, with large, straight nose." Bottom: "Jewess from Buchara, cranium Armenoid, face perhaps indicative of Indo-Germanic peoples."

Time and again, various Nazi propaganda materials and pseudoscientific texts on the Jews affirmed the conflation of Jews and Armenians, if only in passing. Examples include Martin Staemmler and his *Racial Care in the Völkisch State* (1933), Karl Georg Kuhn's *The Jews as a World-Historical Problem* (1939), and Karl Baumböck's *Jews Make World Politics* (1942). Staemmler reasoned that, "After all, it cannot be a coincidence that the Armenians are also part of the eternally 'tormented' [*gequälten*] peoples like the Jews. After all, it cannot be a coincidence that in the Balkans they say: 'one Armenian is worth seven Jews,' in order to express that certain Jewish characteristics emerge stronger in the Armenian." Staemmler's regurgitation of anti-Armenian clichés was in turn also reprinted in the daily press.[63] The list could go on.[64]

Prominently, this list also includes the pamphlet *The Demand of the Hour: Out with the Jews* (first published in 1928, republished again in 1933 and 1934). Its author was Johann von Leers, also the author of *the* authoritative Third Reich biography of Hitler. Leers became a university professor under the Nazis, and was a propagandist for Goebbels as well as his "advisor on Jewish affairs."[65] Leers was, as Robert S. Wistrich characterized him, "one of the most prolific and vicious literary Jew-baiters in Nazi Germany" (after the end of the Third Reich, he became an adviser to Egypt's Gamal Abdel Nasser on anti-Semitism).[66] Leers's introductory chapter, "Historical Survey," began with a section on the "biological foundations" in which the Armenians featured prominently, right in the opening sentence: "In ancient history we find in Asia Minor a racial type almost singularly dominating [the racial landscape]; today we find it represented in very strong fashion in the Armenian people, as well as constituting, in general, the [racial] foundation of the population in vast parts of Asia Minor. We call this clearly discernible racial type the Near Eastern race."[67] He then quoted Fritsch's *Handbook of the Jew Question* on the "Near Eastern race" or "Armenoid" race. In Leers's text, the key quote from Fritsch's handbook, which in turn incorporated quotations from Günther, neatly illustrates how these theories and texts build on each other:

The spiritual characteristics of the Near Eastern race can today be researched best in these peoples on whom it had a strong [racial] impact (so for example the Neo-Greeks, the Jews, Syriacs, Armenians and the Neo-Persians). The Near Eastern race has been attributed special abilities in trade and commerce. . . . This already becomes clear from the fact that in the whole Orient in cities predominantly populated by Greeks and

Armenians the Jews can only with difficulty or not at all gain a foothold. Popular humor expresses this in a drastic fashion by saying that seven Jews are worth only one Greek and seven Greeks only one Armenian . . . [ellipsis in original][68]

Leers went on to quote further passages from Fritsch, also familiar to us, about the Near Eastern race's cunning intellect, the ability to speak in an imaginative language, empathy, and so on. Leers then stressed that this race had mixed with the "Oriental race," which had given it many of its physical features. Concluding his section on the biological-racial characteristics, he stressed again that the Jews' "gift for trade" came from the Near Eastern race.[69] After a lengthy discussion of the plight of the Germans at the hands of the Jews, Leers's pamphlet concluded with the question, "What should we do?" and then reprinted in very bold letters the answers that the party program of the Nazi Party had given to this question, among others the exclusion of the Jews from the nation and from citizenship.[70] It ended with the words, in even bolder letters, "Every German who loves his people will therefore approve the demand of this hour. Therefore with Adolf Hitler, with the National Socialist German Workers Party for a free, clean Germany."[71] What "clean" meant in this context was clear. And even though the Nazi Party program, as quoted by Leers, spoke only of the expulsion of the Eastern Jews and the stripping of citizenship of the German Jews, we must assume that the cipher of the Armenians must have inspired some more extreme thoughts in Nazi readers. There was no direct discussion of the Armenian Genocide, as the book had focused on the alleged rise of the Jews to power in Germany, but, after all, the pamphlet had opened with a discussion of the similarity of the Armenians and the Jews, and it had closed with calls (albeit somewhat veiled) for "cleansing." In another book on the races, Leers also stressed, as Günther had, that the Armenians lacked the ability for ruling and being ruled.[72] It may be worth mentioning here that Leers's biography of Hitler—the authoritative Nazi biography of the Führer throughout the Third Reich—had also opened with a reference to Turkey, Atatürk, and the similarities between Nazism and Kemalism. It was all very suggestive.[73]

Hitler and the Armenians

The similarity, if not the sameness, of the Jews and the Armenians was affirmed and reiterated in racial anthropology and racialist discourse, in the core texts of Nazi anti-Semitism, in other racial and anti-Semitic texts of the time, and also in the many texts on the New Turkey in the Third Reich (see Chapter 14).[74] It is thus not surprising that the Ministry of Propaganda felt it needed to issue a directive to the press in 1936 highlighting that the Armenians were not, in fact, Jews.[75] But, then again, the Führer himself had affirmed this conflation in the past. Hitler had used the Armenians frequently in his speeches before 1933 as an example of a "lesser race" similar to, if not worse than, the Jews. At a general party meeting in Munich in the summer of 1927, he had examined how the Jews did business and how they were able to dominate the economy. He concluded,

> It is impossible that a non-Jew would be able in the long run to compete with the Jews in a Jewish area [of business]. At least for the Aryan it is impossible. There are peoples who are able to do so, like the Greeks and the Armenians. Indeed, these peoples have come so far that they are able to economically defeat even the Jew. However, by doing this they have become Jews themselves. They have these specific, disgraceful characteristics we condemn in the Jews.[76]

In an article in September 1929 in the *Illustrierter Beobachter*, Hitler ranted on about the Jews and then asked what the Jews should ever do in Palestine, a region where there were already two other peoples with the same qualities as the Jews, "the Armenians and the Greeks."[77] This echoed closely the (recycled) claim of a contemporary anti-Semitic book, *The Enigma of Jewish Success*, that Jews would never be able to economically compete with Armenians.[78]

In an article in October 1929, by way of underlining the need for a political change, Hitler painted a bleak picture of the German nation sinking down to the state of a slave nation, and he used the Armenians as the example for such a process. After recounting the various dictates that the German nation and its politicians had wrongly accepted since the armistice at Spa, he asked his readers if it was a surprise that the Entente now expected the Germans to accept further concessions:

> No, this is all a very consistent development. Once one has given up honor and freedom, one will gradually get used to being a slave. A sense of [what constitutes] national shame slowly gets lost and if the enemy is also sitting inside such a nation, is working against it, and obliterates all national traditions, even a healthy sense of national culture, then one should not be surprised if, within a couple of decades, a formerly heroic

nation descends to the level of a wretched Armenian. Swine, corrupt, sordid, without conscience, like beggars, submissive, even dog-like.[79]

Similarly, in his 1928 Nuremberg speech he had warned the Germans of a bleak *völkisch* future, if nothing was done for their liberation and for a higher population growth; if not, "we will slowly become a nation of Armenians."[80] This now was not a reference to racial characteristics as such, but to annihilation and genocide. A similar statement by Hitler is documented for the early 1920s.[81] Fifteen years later, he made a similar remark, though behind closed doors, about the miserable existence of the Armenian population postgenocide.[82]

In an article in the *Illustrierter Beobachter* in May 1930, Hitler protested the Germans' proclivity for identifying with the fate of lesser peoples not worthy of the Germans' admiration, and, next to the "misguided" German sympathy for the (modern) Greeks, he especially singled out the German sympathy for the plight of the Armenians, which had been produced with "drawn out depictions of 'Armenian Horrors.'"[83] But despite Hitler's mild obsession with the Armenians in the time from 1927 until 1930, the Armenians did not very often pop up explicitly during the Third Reich, though Hitler did continue to use the Armenians as an example of a lesser race on a par with the Jews. Thus, for example, at his famous table talks, he explained the race laws and the fact that they were not only meant to protect against the Jews: "In the education of the German people about its race laws it has to be emphasized time and again that these race laws are also meant to protect against the contamination of German blood by Armenian or otherwise un-Aryan blood."[84]

. . .

Taken by themselves all these utterances and quotations mean very little when it comes to the prehistory of the Holocaust. However, there was a very concrete context to them—the Armenian Genocide and the previous massacres as they had been perceived and understood in Germany. Indeed, it was not just that the genocide had been noticed in Germany, but that it had led to wide discussions worthy of being called a "great genocide debate." Racial anthropological and racist texts and their use and reaffirmation of the Jewish-Armenian conflation do not directly show that the Nazis were inspired by the Armenian Genocide. They do, however, offer further substantiation to the claim that modern German anti-Semitism, with all its stereotypical building blocks, was the main prism through which many nationalists, including the Nazis, perceived both the Armenians and, by extension, the Armenian Genocide. (They also, partially, explain why German pro-Armenian circles were fixated in the first years of the Third Reich on proving that the Armenians were in fact not Jews.)[85]

And furthermore, even if the Armenians were often rather peripheral to the overall arguments of these texts, the way they featured in them placed them right at the heart of anti-Semitic discourse: First, the "Armenoid race," used synonymously with "the Armenians," was seen as the major parent race of, and thus responsible for, the negative characteristics found in the Jews; second, the Armenians were perceived as the same as or worse than the Jews, as depicted in modern anti-Semitic discourse (also in the cases in which the "Near Eastern race" was perceived as the parent race); third, they played a central role in the debate about the "Aryan theory," that is, the existence of an alleged "Aryan race" in opposition to the "Semitic race." Thus not only had racial anthropology and (popular) racial handbooks put the Armenians on the mental map of anti-Semites and Nazis, these texts also reaffirmed the core ingredient of the justificationalist argument: the Armenians' (alleged) racial characteristics.[86] The Nazis further affirmed and reiterated the Jewish-Armenian conflation.

As we will see in Chapter 14, the Ottoman Empire and later the New Turkey were portrayed as a "parallel case" to Germany in contemporary media, propaganda, and other publications. Clearly the fact that in such an imagined parallel case, with a racial group equivalent to the Jews posing a problem equal to the one allegedly facing Germany, this racial group had been done away with was in and by itself a strong suggestion of violent solutions to the Jewish question.

CHAPTER 14

The Nazis' New Turkey

There can be no doubt that the Armenian Genocide held a crucial position in the broader Nazi worldview. However, it did not exert its power on the Nazis and within the Third Reich so much through direct discussions of the Armenians and their fate during World War I as through a discussion of what came next: the New Turkey. The depiction and appraisal of the state created by Mustafa Kemal Atatürk during and in the aftermath of the Turkish War of Independence (1919–1923), the New Turkey, by Nazis and German nationalists must also be viewed as a discussion and an appraisal of a "postgenocide" country, as it was exactly in this fashion that it was understood. In the Nazi vision of the New Turkey, this meant a state that had, on a grand scale, "solved" its minority question, in a "final" manner. And in these discourses the New Turkey, the resulting new national body, emerges as a kind of "postgenocidal wonderland." This chapter will thus explore the role the New Turkey and its leader Atatürk played in Nazi discourse. In doing so it builds on my work in a previous book: it will repeat some of that book's central claims in compressed form, but add a stronger focus on the ethnic dimension.[1] Chapter 15 will bring this together with what has been discussed in the previous chapters.

The Turkish War of Independence and the Nazis

The first years of the Weimar Republic have been of crucial importance for us here, and they are once more. First, as we have seen, these were the years in which what I have called the great German genocide debate took place. Second, these were also the years in which the German media obsessively discussed Mustafa Kemal's national resistance to the Entente dictates. And third, concurrent to both, the Nazi movement was born and lived through its "adolescence." In these years, the German press from the center to the Far Right was ecstatic about the Turks defying the dictated peace of the Entente and fighting against them on the battlefield, heads held high. Viewed from a desolate, traumatized, and shocked nationalist Germany, this was a nationalist dream come true.

We have not looked at how the Turkish War of Independence was discussed in the early 1920s in the previous chapters for good reason: the Turkish War of Independence and the Armenian Genocide are two distinct topics and, surprisingly perhaps, they were indeed discussed separately in the German press of the early 1920s, reflecting the difference in regimes involved—the Young Turks had committed the Armenian Genocide (1915–1918), while it was the Kemalists who were fighting the postwar settlement (1919–1923). However, for many of those fascinated with the rise of the New Turkey under Mustafa Kemal (the later Atatürk), the previous "ethnic cleansing" of Anatolia of Armenians (and others) was often part and parcel, if not a fundamental precondition for, the unfolding Kemalist success, especially so for the Nazis.[2] Once more, as with the culturalist explanation and the question of whether such a genocide could occur in "cultured Europe," only the two extreme political fringes differed markedly in their assessment from the rest of the press landscape (see Chapter 12). In that context, both Nazis and Communists had agreed that something similar could indeed happen in Europe and was no "Asian deed." In relation to the distinction between the topics of the Armenian Genocide and the Turkish War of Independence, again both the Communists and the Nazis differed from the majority of published opinion, as they saw them as one large but single topic. The Communists (and Socialists), far from making a hero of Kemal, labeled him "the butcher" and viewed him as just another extreme nationalist-militarist strongman, like Enver or Talât Pasha.[3] And for the Nazis, distinctively and qualitatively more so than for the rest of nationalist and hypernationalist Germany, the Armenian Genocide was a precondition for the successful Kemalist national revolution and resistance. For the Nazis it was in many respects even *the* precondition. In their view, the war against the "Turkish Versailles" was the logical next step on the road to true national independence, within and without—one that could only be fought successfully once the minorities had been "neutralized."

In any case, for the center to Far Right Weimar press, the Turkish War of Independence was a major topic, an ongoing nationalist spectacle, a media event. From 1919 until 1923, it followed the war with an amazingly high frequency; for example, the *Neue Preussische (Kreuz-)Zeitung,* one of the leading nationalist papers, published no fewer than 2,200 articles and reports on Turkey in this time. For the center to Far Right German press, the Turkish War of Independence was important news, often daily, often on the front page, and mostly integrated with German topics by terminology, overall discourse, and layout. Most importantly, perhaps, Turkey was presented as a "parallel Germany": everything was similar or even the same, except for the fact that now things were going the way they were supposed to in Turkey, while Germany, in their vision, was stuck under the thumb of the Entente and with politicians who behaved like Entente puppets.[4]

Shock and amazement at the Turkish victories over the Greeks, the Armenians (an Armenian state had been set up on former Russian territory), the Ottoman army, and the Entente powers were quickly followed by the enthusiastic propagation of Turkey as a role model for Germany in its own postwar struggles. Turkey was used as a battle cry in the newspapers against the weak and "internationalist" new Weimar democracy and its "fulfillment politicians," against the Versailles Peace Treaty, against continued Entente "violations" of Germany, and even against democracy as such. The Nazis were at the forefront of those propagating "Turkish lessons" for Germany. As I have shown elsewhere, the Hitler Putsch of 1923 was as much influenced by the role model of Atatürk and his alternative government in Ankara from where he had "liberated" the country as it was by the example of Mussolini and his "March on Rome" (perhaps even more so). In his speech at the trial of the putschists, Adolf Hitler had cited Atatürk's model in his defense. He had also referred to the political acumen of Enver Pasha.[5]

The *Völkischer Beobachter,* the mouthpiece of the Nazi Party, had from early on championed Turkish lessons. In early 1921, right in the weeks after the paper had been acquired by the party, it had featured headlines such as "Heroic Turkey" and "Turkey—The Role Model." The paper had also proclaimed, "Today the Turks are the most youthful nation. The German nation will one day have no other choice but to resort to Turkish methods as well."[6] In another article, in February 1921, the Nazi paper had also written, "Turkey, a healthy nation of farmers, which had unfairly been given the name of the sick man, is making the only possible kind of politics—that of a healthy egotism with weapon in hand!"[7] A few weeks later the *Völkischer Beobachter* repeated that at one point in the future Germany would "not be spared" the "practical application" of the Turkish case.[8] The paper, at this point, only alluded to, but did not flesh out, what these "practical applications" would be.

It was the weekly *Heimatland,* the paper of the SA (the radical paramilitary wing of the Nazi party) and other organizations close to or part of the Nazi movement, that formulated the Turkish lessons most clearly and extensively. In June 1921, a two-part essay in the paper admiringly discussed the "National Self-Help of the 'Sick Man'" and also repeated the well-established allegations of treachery, of a "stab in the back," by the Greeks and the Armenians.[9] In the *Heimatland,* the Kemalist successes were repeatedly advanced as proof of the value of truly national politics and as criticism of fulfillment politics at home.[10] In the weeks leading up to the Hitler Putsch (1923), a six-part series of articles in the paper discussed the Turkish example and elaborated on the Turkish lessons for Germany and the Nazis in detail—this was by far the most extensive series on Turkey at the time and, in fact, in the whole interwar period in any newspaper. Its author was Hans Tröbst, who had served with the Kemalists, the only German soldier to do so. In this series he not only renarrated the history of the Turkish War of Independence, but also offered an analysis of the key lessons of the Kemalist success. The first of three points on his list was the "creation of a domestic united front" and here, too, violence ("terror") was key:

> Such a united front can be confined, in the first instance, to a certain part of the country. But there it needs to be established by all available means. The leaders who want to create such a front need to be aware that they are playing with their lives. An awareness of this will give them the ability to destroy anybody working against them ruthlessly and forever. . . . This destruction must take a shape that is final and visible to everyone. This way the movement is preceded by terror, and only terror in its most blatant form today has an impact on unnerved and tired mankind. In this respect the Turks are exemplary teachers.[11]

The next point was "national purification":

> Hand in hand with the establishment of a united front must be national purification. In this respect the circumstances were the same in Asia

Minor as here. The bloodsuckers and parasites on the Turkish national body were Greeks and Armenians. They had to be [in bold print] eradicated and rendered harmless; otherwise the whole struggle for freedom would have been put in jeopardy. Gentle measures—as history has always shown—will not do in such cases. And consideration for the so-called "long-established" or "decent" elements, or whatever catchwords are used, would be fundamentally wrong, because the result would be compromise, and compromise is the beginning of the end.... Almost all of those with foreign roots in the area of combat had to die; 500,000 [victims] is a low estimate.[12]

Tröbst then explained why such a "national purification" had been "absolutely justified and necessary," pointing to the racial characteristics of the minority groups: "The Armenians and the Greeks multiplied very fast in comparison with the Turks, commerce and development were solely theirs and they understood in the most perfidious way how to exhaust the ever more powerless [Turkish] population which was totally at their mercy." An additional reason was the treason committed by the minorities who had enjoyed the "hospitality" of the Turks and who had exploited the working population, the Turks, without shame. The term "stab in the back" was used for what the Christian minorities had allegedly done, just as it was in the other papers of the time. For Tröbst it was all too clear what kind of conclusions the Turks had to draw from this: "Healthy common sense had already forced the Turks, now that they were cleaning their house out anyway, to do this as well, so that they would not need to do the same again after a generation."[13] Tröbst also described how the property of the minorities was given to new Turkish settlers from abroad whose resettlement would further strengthen the nation.

Furthermore, Tröbst enthusiastically applauded the exchange of populations between Greece and Turkey decided upon at Lausanne (1922–1923), which he, however, depicted as a one-sided expulsion of Greeks by the Turks. He concluded his discussion of national purification with the following sentences: "The Turks have provided the proof that the purification of a nation of its foreign elements on a grand scale is possible. It would not [really] be a nation if it were unable to deal with the momentary economic difficulties resulting from this mass expulsion!"[14]

Tröbst's third point concerned how the Turks had managed to create an army out of nothing and how an industrialized country such as Germany should have no problem doing something similar. His final conclusions were as follows:

> A united front, national purification and a true army of volunteers, these are today the essentials for a national rebirth of a nation.
> This is, in a few words, the great lesson we can take away from the Turkish struggle for freedom.
> When will the savior of our country come, he who will fulfill the demands of the hour? . . .
> And if we here all thought as "they [did] over there in Anatolia," then might would rise against might and we would all enjoy peace.[15]

It is not only with historical hindsight that this article series in a Nazi paper appears to be condoning genocide and radical ethnic cleansing. A contemporary, the German Jewish writer Siegfried Lichtenstaedter, commented on the Tröbst articles in his book *Antisemitica* (1926). He understood the lessons formulated in the articles to mean that the Jews of Germany and Austria should and had to be killed and their property be given to "Aryans."[16]

Two weeks after the end of Tröbst's series, the *Heimatland* issued a front-page call for an "Ankara solution" for Germany, and thus for an alternative government in Munich modeled on recent events in Turkey; another week later, more discussion of the Turkish role model; and then, a few days later, the Hitler Putsch took place. Thus the Turkish lessons as defined by Tröbst (and others) were certainly no marginalia in the history of Nazism. This is also evidenced by the fact that Hitler had invited Tröbst to speak in front of the assembled Nazi Party leadership in September 1923, because "what you have witnessed in Turkey is what we will have to do in the future as well, in order to liberate ourselves," as Hitler's secretary wrote, in Hitler's name, to Tröbst.[17]

One of the coconspirators in the Hitler Putsch, Otto von Lossow, had switched sides at the last minute and had thereby doomed the whole endeavor from the start. In 1923 he was commander of the German army in Bavaria, but during World War I he had been the military attaché of the German embassy in Constantinople. Together with Hans Humann, his friend and colleague, he had functioned as a go-between for Germany and the Young Turk leadership. At the Hitler trial, a few months after the failed coup d'état, an argument between him and Erich Ludendorff, German "war hero" and putschist coconspirator, broke out over the *Heimatland*'s "Ankara solution." Lossow tried to distance himself from the Ankara solution and thus from the Hitler Putsch by inflating minor differences of opinion about the article in which it was proposed. As a (one-off) commentary on the ongoing Hitler trial, Hans Tröbst answered Lossow's attempts to distance himself from the "Ankara in Munich" solution in a front-page article in the now-leading Nazi newspaper, the *Völkischer Kurier*. Again, he expanded on the "ethnic problem," which the Turks, he claimed, had solved "in a most exemplary fashion." He then mashed up the Armenian Genocide and the Turkish-Greek population exchange:

> The alien blood suckers were given one month to leave the country in order to create room for the national colleagues [*Volksgenossen*]. Who hinders us from doing the same? Just as the American Armenians immediately sent ships in aid of their brethren in Anatolia when they realized what the bell had tolled . . . , so will the coreligionists of the children of Israel in America and England organize the necessary ships when at some point in the future they will be "treading water" on the shores of the North Sea. And if [they do] not? What business of ours is it?[18]

Thus, ethnic cleansing in the form of mass expulsion, with the possibility of genocide, was already an option for at least some of the early Nazis.

The Nazis' New Turkey

Fandom of Mustafa Kemal and his New Turkey turned into a cult once the Nazis had come to power in 1933. In the first year of the Third Reich, Hitler gave out the official line on Atatürk in an interview with the Turkish daily *Milliyet*: Mustafa Kemal had been Hitler's "shining star" in the darkness of the 1920s. This quote was reprinted on the front page of the *Völkische Beobachter* and other papers. When Atatürk died in 1938, the Propaganda Ministry told the press that this was, indeed, the regime's official line on Turkey.[19] Nazi admiration and fandom of Atatürk and the New Turkey was reaffirmed many times, especially so in 1933, the first year of the Third Reich.

Take, for example, the tenth anniversary of the Turkish Republic, which was fêted with a special ceremony by the SA: On the morning of 30 October 1933, SA men marched to the Turkish embassy to hold a guard of honor for the Turkish Republic. They stood there the whole day. And it was no small band of SA men. As pictures show, there were many dozens of them, probably over a hundred. Later that day Ernst Röhm, leader of the

SA, and the rest of the core SA leadership came to congratulate the ambassador and to walk past the honor guard with him—many of this honor guard had served in the Ottoman Empire. The whole ceremony illustrated that this was not the Third Reich, but rather the Nazi movement paying its dues to its ideological heroes and role models (as the press also confirmed). Earlier in 1933, after the Nazis had come to power, Röhm had embarked on a "pilgrimage": he first traveled to see Benito Mussolini in Rome and then to see Mustafa Kemal Atatürk in Ankara.

The Nazi cult around Atatürk and the New Turkey found expression in hundreds of articles in the official press, statements of Third Reich officials, diplomatic protocol, and statements by Hitler himself, time and again. Hitler was to say later that Mustafa Kemal Atatürk had been the teacher and Mussolini and Hitler his students.[20] Hitler's close friend Heinrich Hoffmann related in his memoirs that Hitler adored Atatürk and had a bust of him that was one of his "most cherished possessions."[21] And finally, in the midst of his invasion of Poland, he told the Turkish ambassador that he was "copying Atatürk."[22] He was probably referring to Atatürk's revisionist war, but this was, after all, also the beginning of the eliminatory campaign in the East that would culminate in the Holocaust.

Popular biographies of Hitler but also of Atatürk—four Atatürk biographies were in print during the Third Reich—also further cemented the "Turkish Führer's" status as a role model for Hitler and the Nazis. These texts, commercially rather successful books, it appears, were full of adulation and identified Atatürk as *the* perfect Führer. The similarity between Hitler and Atatürk was constantly reaffirmed and discussed in detail, also, for example, in the most authoritative Nazi biography of Hitler, that by Johann von Leers. For him, Nazism and Kemalism, as well as Italian Fascism, were basically different expressions of the same phenomenon—"*völkisch* movements of rejuvenation," which "herald the coming of a new age." Leers began the narrative of his Hitler biography by listing these movements: "In Turkey the heroic representative of the old Turkish soldier spirit, the Ghazi Mustapha Kemal, drives off the foreign pest with the fire of improvised cannons manned by old men and children, in Italy Mussolini succeeds in the renewal of the Roman spirit." He then directly proceeded to his discussion of Germany and Hitler.[23] The Third Reich used Atatürk's life story extensively—in books, articles, and speeches—to prove the value of the Führer principle and to prepare the German nation for the coming sacrifices and hardships as well as the coming total war.[24]

A crucial aspect of the Nazi vision of Atatürk was the championing of the New Turkey as "the most modern state" in the Nazi press.[25] The various texts on Atatürk and Turkey stressed time and again that after the first miracle, the Turkish War of Independence, a second miracle had taken place in Anatolia: the incredible construction of the New Turkey. The Nazis' vision of Turkey was one of a hypermodern *völkisch* state—"völkisch" encapsulated the Nazi race-centered view of the national community. The presentation of the New Turkey in the Third Reich focused on such aspects as the construction of cities, factories, and infrastructure as well as the nationalist restructuring of all aspects of society (and it simply ignored all other aspects of Turkish reality that conflicted with the image of a vibrant and successful example of *völkisch* revival and reconstruction). So hypermodern was this *völkisch* success story that Third Reich functionaries openly "admitted" in their speeches at the tenth anniversary in late 1933 that Turkey was far ahead of Germany on the path of *völkisch* reconstruction, and it was promised that, in the coming years, Germany would do its best to catch up.[26] And they were, obviously, not talking about the construction of infrastructure.

The Armenians and what had happened to them were not forgotten by the Third Reich texts on Turkey.[27] They played a crucial role in all the deliberations about the New Turkey, because the question of race was central to the Nazi vision of Atatürk's success. The few direct comments about the Armenian Genocide by Hitler—and there are similar quotes by other leading Nazis—that are documented (see Chapter 13) pale in significance beside the role the Armenians (explicitly and implicitly) played in the overall discourse about the New Turkey in the Third Reich. There was nothing coincidental about the frequent attribute "*völkisch*" (ethnic/racial) for the New Turkey. Had the Turks not rid their territory of the Ottoman multiethnic character during World War I and in the Turkish War of Independence, it is hardly conceivable that the Nazis would have been quite so excited about the New Turkey.

"From the mishmash of peoples to *völkisch* purity and a vibrant and potent new state" could have been the byline to all the (hyper)nationalist and Nazi narratives of the New Turkey in the interwar period.[28] And pre-Kemalist Constantinople was the incarnation of everything that was wrong with the Ottoman Empire for such texts. It featured here as the archetypical multiethnic metropolis, which had never been a Turkish city at all and which continued to be a focus of anti-Kemalist and anti-*völkisch* politics, even after 1923.[29] Atatürk's pre-1919 Constantinople assumed a role in these narratives very similar to that of "Hitler's Vienna" for the German leader.[30] One of the Atatürk biographies in print in the Third Reich began its narrative with "the hoarse, excited yelling of the haggling Armenians, Levantines, Greeks and Jews" in Constantinople.[31] When a Turkish gendarme passed them by, their momentarily humble and submissive demeanor changed again into "a poisonous grimace." The text continued with the fictive direct speech, "when the English come to Constantinople, we will cut the throats of the Turks."[32] This, in combination with the behavior of the Entente and their "slave treaty" of Sèvres (the "Turkish Versailles"), is the setting of many narratives on Atatürk and his New Turkey; it described, at least in the minds of these German authors, what Atatürk was really up against when he began his struggle for "true" independence. The choice against the "cosmopolitan" Istanbul (the Armenian population of which had been largely excluded from the deportations during World War I) and for the "national" Ankara, broadly and frequently lauded by the Third Reich texts, thus conveyed a clear ethnic message.[33]

The Kemalist revolution, *völkisch* and Nazi texts had argued from the beginning, was so successful because it had rested upon the foundation of national purity.[34] Thus from the early 1920s onward, a key precondition for Atatürk's success as defined by Nazi, *völkisch*, and, later, Third Reich texts, had been "the destruction of the Armenians," as Dagobert von Mikusch reaffirmed in his Atatürk biography—a "compelling necessity" (this was the same Mikusch who had submitted a report on the Armenian Genocide to the German Foreign Office during World War I; see Chapter 6).[35] Perceiving the Armenians as an "inassimilable foreign body," Mikusch concluded, "If one disregards the human side [of it], then the expulsion of the Armenians from their body of state for the New Turkey was a no less compelling necessity than—granted there are certain differences in the preconditions—the annihilation of the Indians for the state of the Whites in America."[36] In his Atatürk biography, which appeared in the prestigious Men and Powers series that had also featured Leers's Hitler biography, Fritz Rössler underlined that what had happened to the Armenians had not been a persecution of Christians at all, but rather constituted the "neutralization [*Unschädlichmachung*] of life-threatening foreign bodies."[37] His book also included a chapter with the telling title "The Annoying Armenia Is Being Liquidated."[38] The Armenians, as long as they were there, various authors claimed, remained an eternal threat to the

Turks: "Every time the hearts and weapons of the Armenians found themselves on the side of the enemy."[39] The Armenians were also, again, identified as a major threat during the Turkish War of Independence in some
Third Reich narratives of the war—even as perpetrators of massacres
against Turks.[40] Needless to say, the various previous anti-Armenian stereotypes continued to be used and were reaffirmed in Third Reich publications on Turkey.[41]

But the "cleansing" of Anatolia of the Armenians was just the beginning
of the rise of the New Turkey, in the Nazi vision. Looking back on postwar
history, the *Hamburger Tageblatt* summarized in 1935 that before Turkey
could become a state that was "national and only national," it had to rid itself of the other group that had usually featured in almost as negative a
fashion as the Armenians (and who, in racial and anti-Semitic texts, had
been equated with both the Jews and the Armenians): the Greeks.[42] And it
did so in the exchange of populations, as agreed in the Lausanne Treaty.
While some nationalist papers had feared already in 1922 that the proposed
exchange of populations between Turkey and Greece might be a dangerous
precedent for the German minorities in Central Europe, some authors
lauded this mid-1920s exchange as a "totally new way of solving the minority problem."[43] When the exchange was first announced in early
December 1922—during the Lausanne negotiations—it was heralded as
something completely new and as a "new migration of the peoples in the
Balkans" in the German press. It was one to involve more than one million
people, and one that might have to involve brute force in its execution, as
the papers speculated in 1922.[44] The official press service, the *Nationalsozialistische Partei-Korrespondenz,* also appreciated this solution in 1933:
"Something truly unique was accomplished in the sphere of military
politics and population science: the resettlement of the nationals of foreign
background to their homelands and the return of Turkish nationals to
Anatolia."[45] This way, the paper continued, the potential seeds of future
conflict were destroyed and Turkey could live in peace with its neighbors
and rebuild. What was achieved through the population exchange between
Turkey and Greece was nothing less than a "harmonization" or "stan-
dardization" of their populations, the Nazi flagship paper, the *Völkischer
Beobachter,* claimed.[46] Some authors recognized that the Lausanne exchange was in fact only the official formalization of what had already
happened: "The minority problem in Anatolia was solved in a very simple
fashion; the fleeing Greek troops had taken the Christian population of

Anatolia with them! There was no more Armenian or Greek question in Asia Minor."[47] One of the first books detailing the reasons of the Kemalist success restated this point more than once: "Only through the annihilation of the Greek and the Armenian tribe in Anatolia was the creation of a Turkish national state and the formation of an unflawed Turkish body of society within one state possible."[48] A 1925 book on the New Turkey also lauded this "gigantic sweep of the broom" that "hurled the Greek element into the sea."[49] Third Reich authors and politicians reaffirmed that the double "ethnic cleansing" of Anatolia remained a precondition for the success of the New Turkey.[50]

And, as Joseph Schechtman pointed out in his 1946 study of population exchanges in Nazi Europe, the Lausanne Greco-Turkish population exchange agreement had attracted a great deal of attention in the world and also in Germany. It "was referred to expressly as the pattern for the German-Italian agreement [1939] on the transfer of the German minority from South Tyrol, which inaugurated the far-reaching transfer program of the Third Reich."[51] Its "model character" for Hitler himself is widely acknowledged.[52]

• • •

Thus recent Turkish history provided a whole plethora of recipes for or solutions to ethnic problems for the Nazis. The Greco-Turkish population exchange agreed upon in the Treaty of Lausanne was one of these. The policy of the New Turkey to open its doors for and to actively encourage ethnic return migration in the 1920s and the 1930s was also discussed in the German press; it was another ethnic solution. Finally, genocide was yet another and it was surely, in the logic of most texts, the most complete and foundational solution.

Through their enthusiastic discussion of Turkey as the *völkisch* success story of the contemporary (if not all of the modern) world, the Nazis were implicitly endorsing "final solutions" to the minority and racial questions. What had been largely a "military necessity" in the early stages of the genocide debate of the 1920s had been complemented by arguments of it as a national and racial necessity. For the Nazis it became almost exclusively a "*völkisch* necessity," as conveyed in the texts glorifying the achievements of the New Turkey as a model *völkisch* state. This was focused on the cleansing of the country of foreign groups, but, it has to be stressed, not all solutions amounted to genocide. But they were all "final" solutions in the sense that the minorities had been removed and expelled from the territory, and therefore from the national "body." This corresponds to what Christopher Browning has described for the evolution of the Holocaust—the expulsion and resettlement of the Jews were options pursued by the Nazis for some time before they turned to extermination.[53] However, the propagation of such a *völkisch* necessity, such a clear, obvious, and "tested" precondition for *völkisch* success, combined with the clear and present awareness of genocide, means that if necessary, genocide was an option that was "acceptable," or at least something that was being presented and discussed as acceptable.

CHAPTER 15

No Smoking Gun

O ne day in the winter of 1941, as he "walked through the streets of the Warsaw Ghetto," Hermann Wygoda, "Ghetto smuggler," tried to make sense of what was happening to him and the people around him: "I wondered whether God knew what was going on beneath Him on this troubled earth. The only analogy I could find in history was perhaps the pogrom of the Jews in Alexandria at the time of the Roman governor Flaccus, as reported by Philo Judaeus, or the massacre of the Armenians by the Turks during World War I."[1] He was not the only one seeing this parallel. The Social Democrats in exile (the SOPADE) reported continuously on the situation in Germany in their "Germany reports" *(Deutschlandberichte).* In February 1939 they warned, "At this moment in Germany the unstoppable extermination of a minority is taking place by way of the brutal means of murder, of torment to the degree of absurdity, of plunder, of assault, and of starvation. What happened to the Armenians during the [world war] in Turkey, is now being committed against the Jews, [but] slower and more systematically."[2] If an inmate of a Nazi ghetto used the example of the Armenian Genocide as a prism through which to understand what was happening to him and his fellow Jews, and if the German exiled Social Democrats, too, used this prism to understand what was going on in Germany, is there any reason why we should expect the perpetrators to have been any less aware of it, if not inspired by it?

There can be no doubt, from the evidence I have presented in the previous chapters, that the Nazis knew of and were (at least in part) inspired by the Armenian Genocide. However, anybody familiar with the intricacies of research on the Nazi "final solution," and the search for documents containing and thus dating the order for the Holocaust, would surely be shocked if I was able to present here *the* definite source or quote proving that the Nazis took direct inspiration in their decision for the Holocaust in the Armenian Genocide.[3] Precisely because the genocide debate in the early 1920s had been such an extensive and far-reaching one, and because it had established such an awareness of genocide, a document on a discussion of the Armenian Genocide as a model could potentially also solve any questions regarding the origins of the "final solution" and even put a clear time-stamp on it. Indeed, given the clear understanding of German society of the Armenian Genocide as "genocide," the search for an "Armenian smoking gun" simply replicates the search for the Nazi order for genocide. With the sources that we have today, it must remain equally futile. There is no such Armenian smoking gun.

What exists, however, is cumulative evidence—and a large heap of it—that, taken together, amounts to proof of a clear awareness and influential role of the Armenian Genocide on the Nazis. We have looked at the tradition of German anti-Armenianism, and at how Germany had traditionally understood violence against the Armenians from the 1890s until and beyond the Armenian Genocide itself. We saw how violence against this group, viewed as equivalent to the Jews, had been excused and even outright justified for decades in (large parts of) German discourse. We have reconstructed the great German genocide debate of the 1920s, and its progression from outrage to denial, to acceptance, and then to genocide justificationalism. Furthermore, the Armenians played a role in racial discourses and the definitions of "Aryans" and "Jews"—discourses that reaffirmed the Armenians' parallel status as either "Jews of the Orient" or even "über-Jews," "worse than the Jews," and as a parent race responsible for all the negative traits anti-Semites would identify in the Jews. The German genocide debate of the early 1920s had ended on a justificationalist note—the Armenians had to be destroyed because of their treacherous and parasite-like character; this had been presented as a military, state, national, and even racial necessity. In the Nazi discourses about the New Turkey, which in turn was portrayed as a model for a new, *völkisch* state, the annihilation of the Armenians also played a central role and was portrayed as a *völkisch* necessity.

This chapter serves as a conclusion, synthesis, and endpoint of the discussions in this book. It brings together notions explored in the previous chapters and analyzes how the Nazis made sense of the Armenians and the genocide, and how this affects our understanding of the Holocaust. Like Chapters 13 and 14, it further surveys some examples of how and where the Nazis—and people in the Third Reich for that matter—would have come across the Armenians and the Armenian Genocide. This chapter will begin with a person often (and mistakenly) viewed as the *only* direct connection between the Armenian Genocide and Hitler. In a final general discussion it will then review our evidence for the connection between the Armenian Genocide and the Holocaust.

A Web of Genocide

We are back in the summer of 1921, in the days of the Talât Pasha trial. In this summer in Berlin, for two days, a strange constellation in the history of humankind and genocide occurred. When *he* went to the courtroom in Berlin, in these days, *he* would find *himself* as an expert witness as part of the defense of Soghomon Tehlirian, who had assassinated Talât Pasha in broad daylight. Part of the prosecution's team was the man who had succeeded *him* as consul in Eastern Anatolia in 1916, Count Friedrich-Werner von der Schulenburg, later the Third Reich's ambassador to Moscow.[4] One witness for the prosecution, who in the end was not called to the stand, was Bronsart von Schellendorff, the war-era Ottoman chief of staff who some believe to have been the instigator of the Armenian Genocide, and who would officially lead Erich Ludendorff's hypernationalist Tannenbergbund in the late 1920s, an organization meant to organize part of the *völkisch* Far Right after the demise (and ban) of the Nazi Party–close organization, the Frontbann—and while in opposition to Hitler, it, too, ceaselessly preached the cleansing of Germany of aliens and "parasites." Another witness for the defense was the pro-Armenian activist Johannes Lepsius, who, as we have seen, had not only documented the Armenian Genocide but was a close friend and pro-Armenian colleague of Paul Rohrbach's. Rohrbach (who probably was also present), in turn, was an influential imperialist thinker and writer, who himself had witnessed and prominently written about the Herero Genocide in German Southwest Africa over fifteen years earlier.[5] Another person present at the trial, one who, like *him*, had been asked to appear as a witness for the defense but in the end was not called on, was Armin T. Wegner.[6] Wegner was a determined warrior against genocide and would, in 1933, address a letter of protest to Hitler, pleading that he rethink his violent anti-Semitism. In the audience was also the young

German Jewish law student, Robert Kempner, who would later become part of the American prosecutorial team at the Nuremberg trials.[7]

He, himself, Max Erwin von Scheubner-Richter, former consul at Erzurum (Chapter 6), had just said good-bye at his hotel to his friend, Adolf Hitler. They had traveled to Berlin together, and likely even shared a room at the hotel. While Scheubner was there to take part in the trial, Hitler had come to Berlin to lobby industrialists for money for their new party, the Nazi Party.[8] Though we have no record of this, we can even speculate that Hitler would have made his way to the courtroom as a spectator, if any tickets had been available; likely there were not, however, as they had been in hot demand for weeks.

With hindsight we can identify this "web of genocide" as it manifested itself in Berlin over the two days of the trial. It was, obviously, only partially recognizable at the time; but while Germans could not look twenty years into the future, they were at least already becoming familiar with the *idea* of what we now call "genocide"—that is, with the idea of a deliberate attempt to annihilate a whole people. The first four and a half years of the Weimar Republic were saturated with the Armenian Genocide. While Hitler was not directly part of the great German genocide debate of those years, he has to be thought of as always there, because, in fact, he was there: he was in Germany. And if he did not take part in the debate himself, he was in the audience, and we may assume that he was an especially attentive member of the audience—if only because we know he was an avid newspaper reader in these years, and was already fascinated by all (political) things Turkish.

The Armenian (and Turkish) topic and German politics in general were deeply intertwined, and especially so on the Far Right. This manifested itself, beyond discussion and debate, in intertwined threads in actual life stories. We have already met Hans Humann, who agitated against the Armenians in his paper, the *Deutsche Allgemeine Zeitung,* and who had transformed the previously denialist anti-Armenian camp into one of open genocide justifiers. He was not only a close friend of Enver Pasha, but had gone to school with Franz von Papen, with whom he was to remain friends later. Humann (and Scheubner) had taken part in the Kapp Putsch (1920)—a conservative attempt at a coup d'état.[9] Humann would be Papen's political adviser before and after the latter became chancellor in 1932. Papen was the last German chancellor before Hitler, and then vice-chancellor under Hitler. Humann died in late 1933, and in his eulogy

Papen called him a "spiritual fighter for the new Germany that we are . . . building now."[10]

Another example of this entanglement is Karl Helfferich, who had been director not only of the Anatolian Railway, but also of the Deutsche Bank and who, after the war, was one of the most high-profile opponents of Center Party politician Matthias Erzberger, and of the "fulfillment politics" associated with his name and government. Helfferich was an important ideologue of German economic imperialism and had become, by the end of World War I, an expert of sorts on Turkey, too. In 1921, he published a booklet called *The German Policy toward Turkey* in the series "In the New Germany—Essays on Basic Questions of German Politics." The booklet was an expanded version, he wrote in the preface, of a series of lectures he had given in 1920. This was also the year in which he had married the daughter of Georg von Siemens—of the industrialist Siemens family, and founder of the Deutsche Bank—and had been elected to the Reichstag, where he became leader of the right-wing opposition. There he soon managed to raise his public profile with an anti-Semitic publicity stunt, refusing to answer a question of fellow parliamentarian Oskar Cohn (whom we last met in Chapter 7), of the Socialist USPD, for the sole (and quite explicit) reason that Cohn was Jewish. When Walther Rathenau was assassinated two years later, in 1922, Helfferich was held responsible by many of the Left's parliamentarians, as he had prepared the ground for Rathenau's and Erzberger's assassinations with his vicious campaign against them. In his speech in the Reichstag honoring Rathenau, Chancellor Wirth quoted the famous line, "The enemy stands on the right," and pointed to the right, probably mainly at Helfferich.

In his 1921 book on Turkey, Helfferich said little about the Armenian topic. But as a specialist writing on Turkey as well as the world war in general, his relative silence is conspicuous. In the book—and thus in the lectures he had given in 1920—he only mentioned the Armenians when he stressed the close connection between the Armenian topic and British propaganda. Helfferich claimed that Britain's anti-Turkish policy had manifested itself "in all severity . . . on the occasion of the Armenian massacres of the year 1896"—thereby illustrating that "England's humanitarian stirrings always seem to be [somehow] in harmony with [its] political interests."[11] Thus, for an influential nationalist like Helfferich, too, even after the publication of the Lepsius documents (1919, see Chapter 9), massacres and genocide were nothing but British propaganda and imperialist pretext.

And there were many other figures whose life stories linked the Armenian Genocide to later events on the German road to the Holocaust. The future commander of Auschwitz, Rudolf Hoess, had served in the Ottoman Empire during World War I, where, according to his memoirs, which he wrote while awaiting execution, he killed and loved for the first time (though not at the same time). His memoirs, however, are silent on the fate of the Armenians, even though he had been present (at the right time) in the broader region in which the Armenian Genocide took place.[12] Another case was Hans-Heinrich Dieckhoff, a career diplomat and the brother-in-law of Joachim von Ribbentrop, Hitler's foreign minister from 1938 to 1945. Dieckhoff would later be Hitler's ambassador to Washington and Madrid, but during World War I he was still on his first diplomatic posting, at the Constantinople embassy. There, according to his biographer, he had his core formative experiences as a diplomat, arising specifically from the challenges for the embassy in dealing with the Armenian Genocide (which we have discussed in Chapter 6).[13] Are we, for example, to believe that Dieckhoff would not have spoken about his time in Constantinople, his professionally formative years, and the Armenian Genocide more specifically, with his brother-in-law, Hitler's foreign minister?

A Nazi Martyr and an Opponent of Genocide

And then there was, of course, Max Erwin von Scheubner-Richter. In many ways his story was not untypical of a member of the early Nazi movement. After the (official) end of the world war, he returned to his native Riga in the Baltics, and served as an administrator for the ethnic Germans there, hoping to organize the city and the region under German leadership against the coming Bolshevik threat. He was unsuccessful in holding off the Bolsheviks, which then heightened his hatred (and perhaps fear) of the Bolshevik threat. His subsequent retreat to Munich led him to German White Russian groups, where he became friends with Alfred Rosenberg, later an important Nazi ideologue, as well as Dietrich Eckart, who was a key person in early Nazism, and thus connected Scheubner to the Nazis. Among the early Nazis, Scheubner rose to be Hitler's "closest" adviser and friend.[14] The friendship grew to include Scheubner's wife, and the Scheubner family home became Hitler's "home away from home" in the time up to the 1923 Hitler Putsch.[15] With Turkey all the rage among German nationalists and the

Nazis, and with a genocide debate in full swing, would they not have discussed the Armenian topic over tea there?

Apart from becoming so close to Hitler, in two other crucial ways, however, Scheubner was not a "typical" Nazi at all. The first, of course, is that this is the same Scheubner who, as we saw in Chapter 6, was a witness and fierce opponent of genocide. And second, just two years after the Talât Pasha trial, Scheubner would become a Nazi martyr, dying in the Hitler Putsch of 1923. In the final minutes of the putsch, the future Führer marched at the head of the putschist procession, his arm linked with Scheubner's, to the Feldherrnhalle at the center of Munich. They were met by resistance from the Munich police, and Scheubner was hit by one of the bullets that stopped the putsch. As John Dornberg put it, "As he fell, he pulled Hitler down with him so hard that the *Führer* dislocated his shoulder and screamed in pain."[16] Unfortunately, Scheubner in his death probably kept Hitler out of the hail of bullets—"in his dying convulsions [Scheubner] had pinned [Hitler] down so that he could not get back up"—and thus saved his life.[17] Scheubner was thus one of the most important "blood heroes" of Nazism. Munich was later officially declared the "capital of the movement" by the Nazis, and during the Third Reich two temples, called "The Eternal Guard," were built at the Feldherrnhalle, holding the tombs of those who had fallen in the Hitler Putsch, Scheubner's among them. They became a central place of memory and political ritual for National Socialism: every year the Nazis staged a ceremony at these temples commemorating the Hitler Putsch. Visiting foreign diplomats and politicians would lay wreaths there (Figures 15.1 and 15.2).

The only book published on Scheubner, this blood martyr of Nazism, from his death to the end of the Nazi era, was a biography by his former adjutant Paul Leverkuehn, issued in 1938 under the title *Guard on Eternal Watch*. Before that, as the book itself pointed out in its opening sentence, "the only thing ever published about and by him [were] his consular telegrams from Erzurum which Johannes Lepsius has reprinted in his collection of documents about the German attitude on the Turkish-Armenian question." Scheubner had given Leverkuehn a signed and dedicated copy of Lepsius's book "in memory of common struggles."[18] This means that, before 1938, any Nazi wishing to learn more about this seminal Nazi martyr would have had to look at these reports on the Armenian Genocide. After 1938, he would also have had the option of reading Leverkuehn's

Figures 15.1 and 15.2 "Honor Temples 'Eternal Guard.'" The Königsplatz in Munich during the Third Reich was the central place for the remembrance of the failed Hitler Putsch of 1923. Above: The annual ceremony for the 8/9 November events, in 1936, with members of the SS and the SA. Right: The Turkish

biography of Scheubner; but the effect, perhaps surprisingly, would have been the same. This book was, as we shall see, nothing less than a grand monument to one man's heroic struggle against genocide in Eastern Anatolia. It must be one of the most bizarre details of Nazi history that Scheubner not only became a Nazi cult hero, but that the only biography published about him itself should turn out to be, in effect, an extended attack on genocide, with the erstwhile Nazi hero appearing as an antigenocide crusader. Given the timing and tone of the book, it does not seem unreasonable to assume that Leverkuehn's intentions were similar to Werfel's with *The Forty Days of Musa Dagh* five years earlier: that is, he used the story of the Armenian Genocide to warn of the possible fate of the Jews and to plead with Germany to stop before it was too late.[19]

ambassador to Germany, Mehmed Hamdi Arpag, and the secretary of state in the Turkish Foreign Ministry (and later foreign minister) Numan Menemencioğlu lay down wreaths at the tombs of the martyrs of the Hitler Putsch (Scheubner prominent among them) in 1938. (Hoffmann Bildarchiv, Bayerische Staatsbibliothek, München)

The bulk of Leverkuehn's book deals with Scheubner's time in the Ottoman Empire and on the Oriental front. The Armenians enter the story early, when the author speculates that it was Enver Pasha's disastrous campaign at Sarikamish that created "an urge for self-cleansing that looked for the causes of the catastrophe in others and naturally found it where national and religious passions encountered a foreign body in one's own country."[20] And before even introducing the Armenians properly, Leverkuehn questioned the allegations of treason against them by claiming that the only successful battles Enver Pasha had ever fought had included Armenian soldiers on his side. In his discussion of the disturbances at Van, Leverkuehn again challenged the received wartime and postwar version of events, according to which the Armenians had spontaneously risen up against the Turks to assist a Russian invasion. Instead, attributing his version of the episode to Scheubner, he blamed Enver's uncle, the governor there, who, he said, had started the violence himself in order to "solve the Armenian question."[21] If the Armenians had responded violently, he continued, this had been provoked by the arrest and murder of prominent Armenians in the town.[22] Leverkuehn's general account of the "racial character" of the Armenians was also fairly sympathetic, focusing on their role as farmers, as opposed to the traditional anti-Armenianist picture of urban traders and usurers.[23] Leverkuehn then recounted what we have already discussed in detail in Chapter 6, with a strong focus on Scheubner's activities in support of the Armenians. And while Leverkuehn emphasized that Scheubner had not been especially sympathetic to the Armenians on racial grounds, he quickly proceeded to show that what Scheubner saw as their main problem was their undying love for their home.[24]

Leverkuehn's version of the central events in Scheubner's story differs in interesting ways from what we discussed in Chapter 6 and what emerges from the diplomatic documents. In Leverkuehn's version, the German embassy in Constantinople is helpful, while the local Turkish governor became more or less Scheubner's adversary: here the governor simply embodies "the Turk." In Scheubner's own reports, by contrast, as we saw, the roles are basically reversed: the local governor was an ally for Scheubner in his efforts to help local Armenians, while the embassy was more obstructive than helpful, and sided with the Young Turk government. Throughout it all, however, the main figure is Scheubner himself, heroically lobbying the German and Turkish authorities to intervene on behalf of the Armenians, to save innocent and helpless Armenians from slaughter. In Leverkuehn's version, the Ottoman governor even threatens Scheubner: he tells him that if Scheubner does not change his stance toward the Armenians, his safety can no longer be guaranteed.[25] But Scheubner continues to fight against genocide, "treating personal danger to his life with indifference."[26] But of course, he does not succeed in stopping the deaths, even in his own area; and, by the end, Leverkuehn tells us, the "Armenian question in Turkey no longer exist[ed]. Indeed! In the ravine of Kemnagh, the first bottleneck of the Euphrates, most of the deportees found their end."[27] Scheubner and his colleagues had not been able to stop the "will of annihilation of the Turkish Porte." Leverkuehn estimated that "of 1.8 million [Armenians in Turkey], at the most four hundred thousand survived"—thus giving one of the highest death toll estimates in German accounts to that date, of at least 1.4 million.[28]

Leverkuehn did not go into great detail about the reasons for genocide, but he alluded in passing to several possible causes: the desire to find a scapegoat for the catastrophe of Sarikamish; the hatred the Armenians had attracted for their love of their nation and home and for their diligent work ethic; and a desire on the part of Turkey's leaders to do away with the Armenian question once and for all. Leverkuehn obviously thought that this was an "Asian thing"; he concluded his section on the genocide by characterizing it as happening "in an Asian manner, far away from European civilization." Was this a veiled warning, and criticism, directed at those toying with the idea of a European genocide?[29]

The book also described Scheubner's further adventures, once he left Erzurum, in the summer of 1915, as the senior German officer in a joint German-Ottoman military expedition bound for Northern Persia. Leverkuehn himself had been part of this expedition, serving as Scheubner's adjutant. Leverkuehn now also described how they encountered multiple treks of Armenian deportees: "the shadow of death hover[ed] over the beauty [of this] country."[30] On more than one occasion Leverkuehn detailed the devastation left behind by the Armenian deportations, even though the expedition's Turkish guides tried for the most part to lead it around such areas.[31] Indeed, in spite of such efforts, the Armenian Genocide did not let the group go. At a dinner with governors and military leaders in Eastern Anatolia, Scheubner was pejoratively called "a consul with feeling." Scheubner, in Leverkuehn's account, replied with a challenge to his Turkish hosts about their policy of genocide: "If they thought it militarily necessary to expel the male Armenian population from the war zone, what was the point now of continuing their war against women and children?"[32] If we are to believe Leverkuehn, Scheubner felt so threatened, even by the Turkish members of his own expedition, on account of his opposition to the genocide, that he advised Leverkuehn to do as he did himself: to always keep his revolver loaded and ready under his tunic.[33]

On the way to Persia, Scheubner and the rest of the expedition were asked by a local governor to help quash an Armenian rebellion. Scheubner was not convinced by the official story of yet another Armenian rebellion and decided that he and his German officers would not take part.[34] Later on, Scheubner and Leverkuehn heard from the local governor at Süleymaniye that a little earlier there had been an ambush during an inspection trip by Enver Pasha. According to Leverkuehn, the governor was quick to blame the Yazidis (another non-Muslim indigenous group). As Leverkuehn commented, "naturally the governor wanted to undertake a punitive expedition against them—in order to, again, annihilate a people that is not Muslim, but otherwise peaceful."[35]

It was only when Leverkuehn's book turned to the postwar years and Scheubner's activities in the Baltics that the latter's anti-Semitic and "social-national" persuasion was discussed—Scheubner seems to have told Leverkuehn that the ideas of Friedrich Naumann converted him to a version of National Socialism long before the advent of Nazism.[36] Scheubner also emerges as profoundly anti-Semitic, and his ideas about the Jews are quoted at length in the book. Despite his antigenocidal past, in 1923 Scheubner openly called for the "most ruthless struggle against everything foreign in the German national body." He also advocated the "ruthless cleansing of Germany" of all foreign and inimical elements. These and similar passages are very much in harmony with Nazi ideology and are not surprising for a Third Reich book.[37] But they must have produced some irritation on the part of the readers of this particular book because one of its major themes thus far had been Scheubner's resistance against and objection to the "cleansing" undertaken by the Ottomans. Scheubner was thus a paradoxical figure in Nazi history. No one else among the early Nazis was in a better position to know the consequences of racialist antiminority agitation and advocacy for the "cleansing" of a country. Furthermore, his story, as presented by his former adjutant, stood as a monument against genocide in the Third Reich.

It is remarkable that in 1938, one year before the onset of World War II, and the same year in which Leverkuehn's biography of Scheubner was published, another important book in connection to Germany and the Armenian Genocide was published in the Third Reich. This one was the memoirs of a man who had found himself on the other side of the Hitler Putsch of 1923 and who had commanded a Munich garrison: Friedrich Kress von Kressenstein. He had been one of the leading German Ottomans. In his memoirs *With the Turks to the Suez Canal*, he wrote about the shame he and other Germans had felt about German complicity in the Armenian Genocide (though he speaks of deportations only): "We Germans, all of us, soldiers and civilians, who had been condemned to witness this gruesome tragedy found it incomprehensible and were outraged about the fact that the German government and German public opinion . . . did not dissociate themselves from the Turks, but through their silence made us Germans virtually morally complicit."[38]

But back to Scheubner, who had died in 1923, during the Hitler Putsch, and who had left behind a widow. It seems the Nazi Party and especially Hitler wanted to look after her and so, in 1926, Hitler asked her to come and work at the party headquarters in Munich and to build a press archive for the party. She worked there for almost two years. In these years, the Nazi Party was still fairly small, and we can assume that the people working at the headquarters spent a good deal of time together. We may also assume that they talked to each other, about everything and anything, about "God and the world," as the German idiom goes. Across the hall from Mathilde von Scheubner-Richter's office was that of Heinrich Hoffmann, Hitler's photographer and close friend. She would likely have talked to him, and she would also probably have talked to the young man with whom she shared her office: Heinrich Himmler—at the time merely a regional party official, but later one of the leading Nazis and one of the chief authors and executors of the Holocaust.[39] To assume that in these years Himmler and Mrs. Scheubner, who sat in the same room day after day and who also were to remain on friendly terms later on, would not have spoken about the Armenian Genocide and her husband's experiences of it—perhaps the most important period in his short thirty-nine-year life—would be strange, to say the least.[40] Especially so given that Himmler, at this time, was also very interested in Turkey. In the early 1920s, he had even toyed with the idea of emigrating to Anatolia. He had a Turkish friend from his university times with whom he would probably also have talked about what had just happened a few years before in Turkey, especially because at the very time both of them were studying in Munich, in the early 1920s, the German papers were constantly talking about the Armenian Genocide, as we have seen (Chapters 9–12). In their surviving letters, they discussed "Turkish solutions" to Germany's problems as well (though not explicitly relating to the minorities). In 1923, Himmler's emigration to Turkey seemed so imminent that his friend asked in a letter if he had begun learning Turkish yet.[41]

Conspiracy for Genocide

What is striking about the relationship between the Armenian Genocide and the Third Reich is the absence of direct mentions of the genocide in most of the texts published during the Third Reich.[42] This is all the more striking given how much awareness existed of the Armenian Genocide in the years up to 1933 in Germany and how relevant it would have been to the Nazis, who otherwise raided all of recent and distant world history to make their points. However, if we understand the Holocaust as one of the greatest criminal conspiracies in history, then the omission of the Armenian Genocide in the documents of the Third Reich might have been part of this conspiracy. Yet, while logical, obvious, and in need of an explanation, there is no proof one way or the other for an official policy of not mentioning the Armenian Genocide in the Third Reich. But it seems a plausible explanation for this remarkable silence.

The change of rhetoric and strategy among the Nazis, especially Hitler, when it came to Turkey and the Armenians was striking. Until the end of the 1920s, Hitler would publicly speak of the Armenians as an extension of his anti-Semitism (see Chapter 13). On the other hand, he would, in the time from 1923 until 1933, refrain from championing Turkish solutions and from praising his role model Atatürk. After 1933, he would sanction and indeed take the lead in establishing a minor Nazi cult around Atatürk as his role model and "shining star," but he rarely mentioned, or at least left us few documented references to, the Armenians. His apparent silence on this topic—which was shared by other top Nazis during the Third Reich—is more than a little conspicuous. Leading Nazis made reference to all sorts of peoples and historical examples—and often these speeches and their hatred of the Jews knew no bounds. That no one would mention the Armenians is indeed so conspicuous that one is tempted to assume that some sort of agreement existed among the leadership not to publicly mention this precedent. Hitler, and with him most of the Third Reich, suddenly stopped talking about the Armenians, and also the genocide was not as openly referred to anymore as before. Except for books on the history of Turkey and Atatürk, as discussed in Chapter 14, other books only mentioned the genocide in coded or euphemistic references. Thus, for example, Max Biehl, in his violently anti-Semitic pamphlet *England—The Usurer Banker* (1940), only mentioned the "exit" or "excretion" of the Armenians from the Eastern Ottoman Provinces.[43] Similar treatment was to be found in the newspapers. Take, for example, the flagship of the Nazi press, the *Völkischer Beobachter*. It featured the occasional essayistic article on the German-Turkish alliance during World War I. All of these, however, fail to even mention the Armenians.[44]

The absence of the Armenians is very conspicuous in many contexts in the Third Reich, not only in Hitler's speeches, orders, "table talks," and so on. Take, for example, Hermann Wanderscheck's books on World War I propaganda. From 1939 onward, Wanderscheck was in Goebbels's employ at the Propaganda Ministry, but had "worked towards the Führer," as Ian Kershaw has put it, already before that. In Wanderscheck's 1936 book *World War and Propaganda,* he focused almost exclusively on British atrocity propaganda during World War I. Yet, the Armenians are only mentioned when the reader is introduced to Lord Bryce, author of a report on the Belgian atrocities (see Chapter 8). This was all the 270-page book had to say on that matter. Similarly, in his 1940 pamphlet *English Lies: Propaganda during the World War and Today,* in over seventy pages he mentioned Armenia only once, buried in a list including more than seventeen items, but offered neither a discussion nor a refutation of British propaganda in this case.[45] This is striking as there is no immediate reason that such anti-British (and anti-Entente) books should not mention the Armenian case. The only reasonable explanations are either that Wanderscheck simply assumed that British allegations of genocide in the Armenian case had been true, in contrast to the other British allegations he discussed such as those about the Belgian atrocities, or, and this seems more plausible, that there was some kind of understanding in place that the Armenian Genocide was not to be discussed during the Third Reich, except in publications dealing explicitly with the history of Turkey.

• • •

In early 1940, *Life* magazine featured an excerpt from Nevile Henderson's upcoming memoirs. *Life* heralded it as "this war's first great memoirs" and the excerpt included a very telling sentence by the former British ambassador to Germany: "Atatürk (Mustafa Kemal) built a new Turkey on the ruins of the old; and his expulsion of the Greeks, which perhaps suggested to Hitler that he should do the same in Germany with the Jews, has already been forgotten and forgiven."[46] This quote is in many ways reminiscent of an alleged Hitler quote from his speech to military leaders in August 1939. Before the beginning of operations against Poland, Hitler is thought to have sworn his army to the utmost brutality, and to have ended this part of his speech with the following words:

> Our war aim does not consist in reaching certain lines, but in the physical destruction of the enemy. Accordingly, I have placed my Death-Head formation [that is, the SS] in readiness—for the present only in the East—with orders to them to send to death mercilessly and without

compassion, men, women, and children of Polish derivation. Only thus shall we gain the living space which we need. Who, after all, speaks today of the annihilation of the Armenians?[47]

While the Henderson quotation has so far received no attention whatsoever, the latter quotation has been variously used as proof, or even disproof, that the Nazis were inspired by the Armenian Genocide.[48] Hitler's question was perhaps never posed. The document and its trail are sketchy, and the sentence in question is absent in other accounts of the meeting—though, of course, that may simply mean that others did not write down this remark concerning genocide, not necessarily that it was never actually uttered.[49] Armenian scholars, in their quest to finally get the Armenian Genocide the official recognition it deserves—today it is officially recognized as a genocide by neither Turkey nor Israel—have often used this alleged quotation from Hitler in order to prove that the Holocaust and the Armenian Genocide were connected and that the latter, indeed, really was a "genocide."[50] If Hitler saw it as such, then that should prove it, this rather strange argument suggests. In an equally strange argument, historian Heath Lowry attempts to move from the undeniably true proposition that we can't be sure the relevant sentence was ever uttered by Hitler, to the sweeping conclusion that there was therefore no Armenian inspiration for the Holocaust, and that in fact the Armenian Genocide never occurred at all.[51] The fact that the speech was not about the Jews but about the Poles, in this logic, only further supports the denialist conclusion.

There is another alleged quote from Hitler that is often used in this context, and the fact that its provenance is also questionable has done nothing to help the case for illustrating the connection between the two genocides. In an interview with the editor of the *Leipziger Neueste Nachrichten*, Richard Breiting, Hitler is claimed to have turned to the topic of "resettlement policies," to have mentioned that Greece resettled "a million men" in 1923, and then to have spoken the following significant words: "Think of the biblical deportations and the massacres of the Middle Ages and remember the extermination of the Armenians. One eventually reaches the conclusion that masses of men are mere biological plasticine."[52] This interview was edited and published by the historian and journalist Edouard Calic in 1968. However, the authenticity of the document has often been called into question—and this has been used as yet more "proof" of the absence of any connection, if not of the nonexistence of an Armenian Genocide.[53]

But this is entirely the wrong way to go about it. The burden of proof is actually not on showing that Hitler and the other Nazis did know of the Armenian Genocide; it is quite the reverse: there is no reason whatsoever to believe that the Germans had actually forgotten about the Armenian Genocide by 1939, as the famous Hitler quotation is often believed to have proven—and less even that the leading Nazis had not been somewhat inspired by it.[54] And furthermore, there is every reason to believe that what Hitler meant in that part of his speech—if he did in fact ever utter it—was similar to what the Nevile Henderson excerpt suggested (in reference to the Greeks): the Turks (as a whole) had never had to "pay" for the Armenian Genocide; they got away with it unscathed, without negative consequences. Indeed, quite the contrary, if we were to adopt the perspective of German (extreme) nationalists and Nazis in the 1920s and 1930s, the New Turkey was instead a hugely successful new state, built upon the solid foundation of wholesale "ethnic cleansing." The Nazis, as a political movement, had grown up with Turkey, that is, the Turkish War of Independence. Hitler was in such awe of Atatürk that he had even modeled his first attempt to take power, the Hitler Putsch, on Atatürk's rebellion. But this also means that Hitler "grew up," politically, as a Nazi, that is, with the debates about the Armenian Genocide. How could it and the debates we have discussed in the previous chapters not have impressed and inspired the future Führer?

Lessons of Genocide (in Lieu of a Conclusion)

There can be no doubt that the Nazis had incorporated the Armenian Genocide, its "lessons," tactics, and "benefits," into their own worldview and their view of the new racial order they were building. Werner Best, Nazi legal specialist and politician, wrote in a book compiled in honor of Heinrich Himmler and presented to him in 1942 that "history proves that the annihilation or expulsion of a foreign nationality is not contrary to biological law, if carried out totally" (this excerpt was also published in the journal *Zeitschrift für Politik*, in June 1942).[55] The contexts provided by the previous chapters should show that whenever such phrases were uttered in the Third Reich, we must assume there was some awareness of modern history's first great genocide debate, and thus of the Armenian Genocide itself, in the background. Any Nazi would quickly come across the Armenians if he delved into the racial anthropology of the Jews and discussion of the "Aryan thesis." No Nazi could avoid noticing the overall infatuation of his party and movement with the New Turkey, and would find out about the Armenians' role in this quickly. Any Nazi old enough to have been a newspaper reader in the early 1920s would know about the great German genocide debate.

Thus the Armenian Genocide was not forgotten by the early 1930s in Germany. Germany had its own very specific history of debating and perceiving the Armenians and the violence against them. One characteristic of Hitler is in itself enough to show that he simply must have known about the Armenian Genocide. He was an avid reader, not only of newspapers, but also of books. As I pointed out earlier, if he had been alive and reading newspapers in the early 1920s in Germany, as of course he was, he simply could not have missed the topic. But it is equally true that two of his favorite authors, whose books he devoured, would also have led him automatically to the Armenians. It is a well-documented biographical detail that during World War II, Hitler reread all of Karl May's novels—and here, as we saw in Chapter 3, he would have come across, for the second time in his life, May's regurgitation of anti-Armenian stereotypes and even his recycling of Naumann's "potter quote."[56] Another author Hitler adored was Sven Hedin, the famous Swedish explorer and travel writer who felt himself to be "German." Hedin had hitched his wagon to Germany's star long before Hitler came along, and in the 1930s he rehitched his wagon to that of the Nazis. Hedin had traveled to the Ottoman Empire during the Great War. Just as he had written two glowing books about the German fronts of World War I as exemplary exercises in wartime propaganda, so he wrote a book about the Ottomans in the Great War. His reluctance to scold the Ottoman ally for the Armenian Genocide had earned him criticism as early as 1917, for example in the form of the (English-language) book *Sven Hedin, Nobleman,* and had stained his reputation. The author of that book had thought Hedin partially responsible for the Armenian Genocide (or, as he put it, the "extermination of a Christian people") because he was so famous at the time that his opposition might have made a difference.[57] After becoming infatuated with the Nazis and Hitler as well as with the Jewish question, Hedin, too, began looking for "solutions." In the late 1930s, he thought about the possibility of sending world Jewry (by force, of course) to Mesopotamia. Hedin knew that this region had been the destination of the last genocidal project and, in the words of one of his biographers, Sarah Danielsson, "he thought the region was suitable, in principle, as a place to dump 'undesirable' elements." On his visits to the Third Reich, Hedin peddled his "Armenian solution" to the Jewish question to leading Nazis. Among them was Hermann Göring, a close acquaintance of Hedin's as well as a member of Hitler's inner circle. Hedin and his sister Alma pitched the idea to Göring while visiting him at his house in 1939.[58] As Danielsson points out, "according to Hedin's notes, Göring showed great interest in the issue and considered it quite practical. He even promised to support the plan, should it come up as an alternative."[59]

In his essay about Scheubner, German historian Karsten Brüggemann discusses the way Scheubner featured in Ernst Nolte's theories and thus in the famous *Historikerstreit* (the German "historians' quarrel" in the 1980s). In his critique of Nolte, Brüggemann claims that, in the early 1920s, Auschwitz was still inconceivable despite Hitler's rhetorics; thus Scheubner could not have been Hitler's expert on genocide, and to discuss him as such would be absurd and unprofessional.[60] However, while one has to oppose Nolte's claims and the whole relativist school of thought as it surfaced in the *Historikerstreit,* this does not mean we should not take Scheubner's role seriously.[61] One also has to disagree with the claim that Auschwitz was inconceivable in the early 1920s. Of course, the mass industrial killing of German and European Jews (and others) in the fashion that it happened may very well have been inconceivable at the time—but genocide, or even a genocide of German or European Jews, was not. As the previous chapters have shown, genocide was not only conceivable in Germany at the time, it was widely debated. And, furthermore, it was debated through the prism of viewing the Armenians as equal, similar to, or worse than the Jews. Thus the debate about the Armenian Genocide in the 1920s was, at least to some extent, also a debate about Jews.

On the other hand, the notion that Scheubner was "possibly the crucial personal link" between Hitler and the Armenian Genocide—as Mike Joseph proposes—is overstated.[62] While Scheubner was indeed an important link—it would be equally improbable to think that Hitler and Scheubner would not have talked about the Armenian Genocide—there were many others, and no doubt I have only uncovered a few here.[63] The awareness of the Armenian Genocide in interwar Germany was so great that, indeed, no single person or group of people was needed to transmit knowledge. In any case, many such people existed. Many of the top political figures around Hitler before and during the Third Reich had served in the

Ottoman Empire and many had direct contact there with the Armenian topic. It has to be remembered that the Nazi Party was a small, radical fringe group, mainly held together by a core of party activists in the early 1920s. Would they not have spoken about all sorts of things? Would they not have spoken with Scheubner about the Great War? I have shown (also in another book) that the Nazis were quite obsessed with the Kemalists and Atatürk in the early 1920s, and Hitler was well informed about them. Is it conceivable that they would have spoken about contemporary Turkey, but would have ignored what had happened there just a few years earlier—and, moreover, would they have done so at a time when the German press was still actively discussing those earlier events? Most certainly not. There cannot be the slightest doubt that the leading Nazis were well informed about the Armenian Genocide and that they knew of it as what we would now call a "genocide"—that is, as a deliberate attempt to exterminate an entire people. There can also be very little doubt that the Nazis knew the details of the execution of genocide in the Ottoman Empire.

One could argue that, apart from the German ambassadors in Constantinople and Consul Walter Rössler in Adana, the Germans in the Ottoman Empire who knew the most about the Armenian Genocide when it occurred were Scheubner, Humann, Schulenburg, and Konstantin Neurath (all of whom we have met in Chapter 6; the latter, for example, composed the large 1915 memorandum of the embassy on the Armenian topic). And this group is closely connected with National Socialism: Scheubner as a Nazi of the first hour; Schulenburg as Hitler's ambassador in Moscow; Neurath as foreign minister of the Third Reich from 1933 until 1938 and then as Hitler's reichsprotektor for occupied Bohemia and Slovakia, nominally Reinhard Heydrich's superior; and Hans Humann as a hypernationalist agitator in the 1920s and a close associate of Franz von Papen, Hitler's first vice-chancellor and future ambassador to Vienna and Ankara. Papen, too, had served with the embassy in Constantinople during World War I. He was, of course, also in the know. And to this group we must also add the already mentioned Dieckhoff, Ribbentrop's brother-in-law and Hitler's ambassador to Washington and Madrid. We have also already mentioned Rudolf Hoess, the commander of Auschwitz, and Otto Feldmann, the German officer who had admitted to having advised the Ottomans in their "ethnic relocation" scheme, who later was the chairman of the hypernationalist DNVP in northern Germany and Hindenburg's campaign manager, and who was then part of the Nazi Party's parliamentary group from 1933 until 1938.

Furthermore, even if Scheubner had never talked with Hitler about the Armenians, would Hitler not have read or at least have been presented with a summary of Leverkuehn's book on his old friend and savior? Hitler obviously also knew of Enver Pasha—he had mentioned him in his defense speech during the Hitler trial in 1924. In 1943, the publishing house Die Wehrmacht, of the German Army, published a book on Enver Pasha's exploits in Central Asia after World War I. And let us not forget Talât Pasha, whose remains were transferred from Berlin, twenty-two years after his assassination there, for a proper burial in Istanbul in 1943. Indeed, even without Scheubner, it would have been impossible for Hitler to shield himself not only from awareness, but from actually having very extensive knowledge of the details of the Armenian Genocide, including its execution on the ground, as well as the international and German reactions to it.

Of course, knowledge of the Armenian Genocide and inspiration drawn from it are two separate things, at least analytically speaking. As this book has shown, the way the Armenian Genocide inserted itself into German and Nazi history and discourse, there are two aspects of inspiration and motivation radiating from the Armenian Genocide. First, Hitler's alleged words at the Obersalzberg—about who "still talked" about the Armenians—might not come from a watertight source, but the statement still accurately sums up one of the major lessons the Armenian Genocide must have held for the Nazis: it must have taught them that such incredible crimes could go unpunished under the cover of war, even if one lost that war.[64] That one could "get away" with genocide must have been a great inspiration indeed. This included not only the international community but also potential domestic reactions.

Especially if the people (to be) murdered were of the "Jewish-Armenian" category, then who would intervene on their behalf? The Armenian Genocide had made genocide thinkable and, apparently, justifiable—this had been "tested" for quite some time by then. The lessons a bystander such as Hitler must have learned about the morality of Germany are even more shocking. Had the Christian churches, the German parties, and papers reacted with proper outrage, at any point from 1915 to 1923, to the fate of the Armenians in Turkey, Hitler might at least have been more afraid of the domestic repercussions of genocide. They had remained almost silent, especially the churches. There had not been true outrage, no moral media tsunami; a debate, yes, even a very long and drawn-out one. But the great German genocide debate of the early 1920s was marked by the relative and overall absence of strong moral, religious, philosophical, and humanist condemnations. Perhaps German society had been so dulled by the trauma of the war and of losing it, so permeated by military and militaristic thinking, and so much used to "acceptable" violence against the Armenians and to justifications of violence against this particular victim group that not much more had been available as a reaction. But the lack of a robust response by Christian Germany must have seemed especially significant to Hitler—for if this was its reaction to the extermination of Christian people, who would speak out against killing Jews? This does not take away the guilt of the Nazis, and of wider German society in 1933–1945, but it is a strong indictment of German society in 1915–1923. Especially early Weimar Germany had laid some first, solid foundations upon which genocide would be built twenty years later. And what happened then—that is, the lack of general outrage and open opposition to the Nazi genocide—only confirms that the lesson Hitler and others like him must have taken from the Armenian Genocide was indeed a correct one.

A second major lesson and inspiration was conveyed through the Nazis' understanding and portrayal of the New Turkey as a "postgenocidal paradise" of sorts. If the Nazis believed their own depiction of the New Turkey, what were the ethnic implications for Germany? If the New Turkey was such a *völkisch* success, such a vibrant country, such a seminal proof for what a truly liberated country could do, then what would that mean for countries (allegedly) plagued and menaced by internal (ethnic) enemies? The role the Nazis had assigned to the New Turkey in their beliefs, ideology, and propaganda—that of an "ethnic cleansing" success story, of a state that was now enjoying the benefits of past "cleansing"—must have constituted a perpetual reminder that Germany was not "cleansed," and a strong motivation to think about "cleaning house."

Another related lesson would have concerned timing. The Nazis must have seen that the Turks got away with genocide because a great war meant dealing with a whole series of important and difficult international and national questions, also in the aftermath. War, in other words, provided an opportunity structure for violent solutions in relative safety. The nexus between war, opportunity, and genocide had been noted time and again in the German discussion of the Armenian Genocide. We saw a particularly clear example in Chapter 9, when pro-Armenian activist Julius Richter, in condemning genocide and the Young Turks in 1919, had described the world war as a "propitious opportunity for annihilation" (*günstige Gelegenheit zur Vernichtung*).[65]

Another lesson—as it might have emerged from the German public reception of the genocide—might have been the rather astounding ability to find "willing executioners" among the population. The tales of horror had rarely if ever included many people resisting orders for massacre—even though many Turks, Kurds, and other Muslims had in fact helped Armenians—but had always depicted a wide variety of willing executioners: from people organized in various civil and military formations to different kinds of civilians, from both the dominant and the nondominant ethnicities, including former neighbors and also, prominently, civilian women.

Finally, the genocide debate in Germany itself, how genocide had been discussed, offered further potential lessons for the Nazis. First, it showed that there was no need to be afraid of such a genocide debate. Despite a years-long debate, except for justifications and denialism, there were no real consequences. Secondly, the debate as well as the wartime coverage showed that it was incredibly hard to convince the public that genocide was indeed taking place or had happened. This disbelief is a constant companion of genocide: As Raphael Lemkin, the father of the term "genocide," thought to himself during World War II, "genocide is so easy to commit because people don't want to believe it until after it happens." He found that the memory of the allegations of atrocities against both sides during World War I made it now, during World War II, difficult to convince people that Germany was committing genocide.[66] Alfred Hitchcock, too, when producing his documentary on German concentration camps, was wary of this disbelief. He ordered his assistant to avoid cuts in the materials lest it be perceived as atrocity propaganda. In the propaganda battle during World War I, a German paper tried to refute Lord Bryce's allegation that the Armenian massacres were the worst in human history since Tamerlane by citing the counterexample of the Bartholomew's Day Massacre; apparently it could not imagine that that could be easily topped by what was happening in Anatolia at the time.[67] During the German genocide debate of the 1920s, too, genocide was so unfathomable to most that an overdetermined amount of evidence needed to be produced—and in the German case, not even the documents of its own diplomats and embassy had been enough for a sustained recognition. Only the spectacular Talât Pasha trial had brought this about.

• • •

What does all this change? In many ways, not much. It depends on how we understand the human condition and on how unthinkable we may find genocide. Up until Hitler, the Armenian Genocide was the greatest modern murder of a people, and it was the only one for which intent to commit genocide was clearly established by international and German public opinion. (The genocide of the Herero and the Nama people in German Southwest Africa [1904–1907] was, arguably, different insofar as intent [and extent] had not been established and publicly acknowledged; there had not been a public debate about genocide as such, but rather about colonial violence.)[68] The Armenian Genocide and its presence in German discourse must have made the murder of a whole people more conceivable. The continuous dehumanization of one national or, in some minds, racial group, from the late nineteenth century until the 1920s in the center of German society and public discourse, of one of the oldest Christian peoples no less, to the point that their wholesale murder was deemed justified or justifiable by large segments of the nationalist press was an unfortunate test case and an unfortunate tradition for Germany. Furthermore, the fact that the Armenians were understood in Germany primarily through anti-Semitic lenses made the connection between the Armenian Genocide and what Hitler defined as Germany's "problem" blatantly and dangerously obvious.

Radical "ethnic engineering" was not something the Nazis had to copy from Turkey; it was, together with racialist pseudoscientific thought, all around them. However, it is undeniable that over its recent history, Turkey must have seemed to the Nazis, and Germans more generally, like one big ethnic population laboratory, not only during the most recent Kemalist years, and the Armenian Genocide a few years earlier, but stretching back at least to the Balkan Wars of the early twentieth century. Moreover, given Germany's infatuation with all things Turkish, it was a population laboratory about which the newspaper-reading public of the 1920s and 1930s—including, but not only, the Nazis—could easily have achieved something of an "expert status."

There are also many parallels between the two genocides (drawing here, again, mostly upon the perception of and debate about the Armenian

Genocide in Germany): killing under the cover of a major war, in fact, a world war in both cases; killing mainly away from major population centers and mainly after the target population had been physically removed from their former places of mixed residence; deportation itself as part of the extermination process; death by attrition; extermination as part of larger ethnic restructuring schemes, with "vacated properties" earmarked for and rapidly occupied by members of the dominant ethnic group; organized robbery of the group by structuring deportations so that most immovable and moveable goods stayed behind or were easily discoverable, all this in a rather "orderly" fashion; the preparation for physical violence in the form of an antiminority discourse that had branded the group not only as an "other," but as an "other" threatening the very survival of state and nation by its mere existence, and so on. Of course, there were differences, too. For example, in the Armenian case, many women and children were taken away to be "Turkified" instead of killed, though such a large number were also killed that it is clear that this was not a rule of sorts.[69] Often, conversion and taking women as additional wives served as a means to extend protection to them. It is difficult to make a case for a one-to-one transfer of genocidal tools and strategies from one case to another, mainly because in the German case the implementation of genocide underwent a gradual evolution and, it appears, did so very much in response to its own specific conditions and circumstances.[70] But this does not mean that those responsible for the evolution of the Nazi Holocaust did not know of, or were not thinking about, the Armenian Genocide when they underwent a process of radicalization toward genocide.

The argument that without the Armenian Genocide there would not have been a Nazi Holocaust is unnecessary and to some extent folly. For one, the two happened in direct sequence, a mere twenty-something years apart—that is a fact. Secondly, we cannot know what would have happened had the Armenian Genocide not occurred. It appears that the Nazi hatred of Jews and the propensity toward radical and violent "solutions" were so great that it would not have made a large difference. Perhaps its execution and evolution would have been different—perhaps more circumspect. In any case, one thing is clear: The two were not separated by any great distance in space and time. They were intimately and directly linked.

The Armenian Genocide, its reception, and the reactions to it, constituted an enormous "motivation"—on the one hand because of the "benefits," as identified by hypernationalist and Nazi discourses in their discussion of the

New Turkey in interwar Germany, and, on the other, because of the lack of a general deterrent, intervention against, and punishment of the perpetrators of genocide. And if the latter was indeed the case, as I would argue it was, then one has to ask oneself if, since World War II, the world has done enough to deter states from butchering civilian populations. What is our deterrent today?

Epilogue

Armenian Writings on the Wall

O f the four warriors against genocide that we have met in our story, only Franz Werfel and Armin T. Wegner lived long enough to see the Nazis come to power in 1933. Max Erwin von Scheubner-Richter, as we have seen, died in the arms of Hitler (or at least was fatally wounded while arm in arm with Hitler) at the failed Hitler Putsch in 1923. Johannes Lepsius died a few years later (he spent his last years editing a multivolume, officially sanctioned collection of German Foreign Office documents, spanning the time of the entire Kaiserreich, 1871–1918, on all aspects of foreign policy). That left only Wegner and Werfel to warn of the next catastrophe. It is remarkable that both of them, early on, drew parallels between the Young Turks and the Nazis, and that both decided to use their talents and influence as writers to warn Germany of what Hitler might do. We have already seen how Werfel did his best to finish *The Forty Days of Musa Dagh* in late 1932 and 1933. And just like Werfel, Wegner also rushed to finish his Armenian novel in these very months. He had already started many years before, but then got stuck (again) and never finished it. Perhaps he realized that it was too late anyway. It appears he knew about Werfel's project, and it also appears that his motives in resuming the novel at this time were the same as Werfel's: to warn of what the Nazis might mean for Germany and to warn of genocide.[1] One day before he was arrested by the Gestapo, in August 1933, Wegner wrote to his wife, who had fled to London (she was Jewish). In the letter he sketched the connection he saw between the events he was exploring in the novel and what was happening in Germany now:

Between the Young Turkish movement of 1908 and the National Socialist popular movement of 1933 there are so many parallels. Back then the

359

Young Turkish conspirators called themselves social patriots—is that expression not in itself very similar and strikingly fitting? . . . By comparing both movements, my insights into both become clearer; I am learning to understand both the National Socialists and the Young Turks and understand even, through the fateful blood urges of a people, the conduct of the Young Turks against the Armenians, which I had trouble comprehending before. . . . Here, as there, the awakening self-awareness of a people unjustly held back; here, as there, the rancorous animosity against an alien body within the nation (Armenians, Jews).[2]

In his novel, he told his wife, he would deliberately transfer many Nazi ideals and points of view onto the Young Turks. This would be a permissible technique, he claimed, because he was trying to depict what was happening in Germany in the guise of another nation. "I find no fault in that; never can one recognize oneself and one's nation better than in the foreign mirror, when all the close and small coincidences of the present fall away which only cloud the image all too easily."[3] But he was unable to get a grip on his story line, and never finished his Armenian novel. Perhaps a reason for his inability to finish was the daunting nature of the task: he was aware that the novel, if completed, "must figure among the cruelest which have ever been written about human misery."[4]

What he did however do in his role as a warrior against genocide—and this was one reason for his arrest by the Gestapo (Hitler's "secret police") later that year—was to write an "open letter" to Hitler—though, as a critic of Wegner's asserts, it was not really "open," as it was sent to Hitler directly and not published anywhere in the press.[5] (Wegner later wrote that it had been impossible to publish it in the press and that sending it directly to Hitler was the only way.)[6] It was, as we know from Chapter 9, not Wegner's first open letter—in 1919 he had written an open letter to President Wilson, urging him not to forget the plight of the Armenians in the lead-up to Versailles. Then, his letter had stood in striking contrast to the silence of almost everyone around him on the subject. The same was true now.[7]

In his letter, Wegner tried to present Hitler with a positive image of "the Jews" in Germany. He wrote in reaction to the first signs of violence against them, and the boycott of Jewish businesses, in early 1933. Not unlike Scheubner in his letters to the Constantinople embassy during World War I, Wegner appealed to Hitler with a rhetoric warning of the damage to the image of Germany, rather than speaking out against violence and for the German Jews as such. He assumed a position in which he, Wegner, needed to educate Hitler about the Jews—"Herr Reichskanzler, you don't know the Jews!"[8] Wegner went through a list of anti-Semitic claims and tried to refute each one. So, for example, he addressed Hitler: "You invoke the claim that the German people are acting in self-defense." Wegner explained to Hitler why the Jews had not actually threatened the German nation, but instead had been highly beneficial to it, something he supported with a host of examples. When he turned to anti-Jewish measures, his main argument against them was not that they were unjust, but that they "shamed" the country: indeed, he wrote of "embarrassing shame" (peinliche Scham). There was an echo here of Scheubner's strategy in writing to his ambassador in Constantinople during the war: then, as we saw in Chapter 6, Scheubner referred repeatedly to the "embarrassment" to Germany of failing to help the Armenians. Wegner concluded by appealing to Hitler to save the "dignity of Germany"—just as he had urged President Wilson to "save the honor of Europe" fourteen years before.

It is remarkable that Wegner composed the letter the way he did. It is less remarkable, perhaps, that he did not mention the Armenians, even though they were certainly one of his main inspirations in writing this letter. It seems not too outlandish to assume that Wegner fell victim to the same kind of culturalist reading of Germany under Hitler as many German Jews who did not leave in time because to them it was just unimaginable that a "civilized" nation like Germany could ever commit such a monstrous crime. Wegner appealed to Hitler as if the latter would be open to reason, as if he was just another regular statesman and politician. Wegner, too, seems to have underestimated the essentialist value that radical, eliminatory anti-Semitism held for Hitler. If one looks at Wegner's speeches and writings about the Armenian Genocide, there is open engagement with the culturalist line of interpretation, even if he found himself defending against culturalist allegations against him and stressing that there were good Turks, too. In this respect, Wegner just did not (yet) understand the nature of genocide; his letter to Hitler simply had to fail (of course also for other reasons).

It is still not entirely clear if Wegner was arrested solely for his open letter.[9] After his arrest, he was (he claimed) tortured by the Gestapo before being transferred to the Oranienburg concentration camp, close to Berlin, where he spent many months.[10] For his open letter alone, Wegner was thought to deserve commemoration, in 1967, as a "righteous among the nations" by Israel's central Holocaust memorial and institute, Yad Vashem.

Figure E.1 Armin T. Wegner at Yad Vashem. In 1967, Yad Vashem recognized Armin T. Wegner as "righteous among the nations." The picture shows Wegner at the tree-planting ceremony at Yad Vashem, Jerusalem. (Department of the Righteous, Yad Vashem, Jerusalem)

As Yad Vashem puts it on its website, "Of all that nation of thinkers and poets, of intellectuals, only Wegner had the guts to send such an open letter to the new Führer of the Reich."[11] By the time Wegner came to Israel in the 1960s, to be honored as a righteous among the nations at Yad Vashem, he was a broken man. He had lived in Italian exile since the 1930s.[12] He had not chosen to return to Germany after the war and became forgotten there, living in Rome until his death. The picture of Armin Wegner on this day at Yad Vashem shows an exceptionally sad man. He received recognition and high honors, yet he had not saved even a single Jew. He had known, he had seen something of Armenian proportions coming, but could not reach anyone. Wegner had failed, spectacularly so. The expression on his face at Yad Vashem illustrates his personal failure and sadness like no other source possibly could (Figure E.1).

Franz Werfel did not fare much better, at least when it comes to his main purpose. As a warning, his Armenian novel was almost noneffective. For the potential victim group, it was too late. The others did not want to listen. As a legacy it is, however, extraordinary. Before turning to the extraordinary life of the novel *The Forty Days of Musa Dagh,* we need to go back to the winter of 1932, the same winter Adolf Hitler had walked past Werfel in the Breslau hotel lobby. Werfel had been on tour, giving readings of the chapter "Interlude of the Gods" (see Chapter 7) from his unfinished manuscript, to warn Germany of Hitler and of the possibility of an Armenian fate for Germany's Jews. Werfel said later that the Armenians were his "stand-in Jews."[13] On this tour, Werfel was reading the chapter in which Johannes Lepsius meets Enver Pasha and pleads with him to stop the genocide. That Werfel was addressing the German nation through the mouth of genocide-warner Johannes Lepsius becomes clear not only through the text of the chapter itself, but also from the way he must have read it to the audience. One short review from the winter of 1932 of one of Werfel's evening lectures centered on the dramatic effect Werfel employed—it had seemed to the reviewer as though Lepsius were not talking to Enver Pasha, but to the audience, to Germany, instead.

The review criticized Werfel for being too emphatic and emotional in his treatment of his topic. The reviewer obviously had not missed the point of Werfel's chapter—to warn Germany of genocide and Hitler—but apparently preferred to evade that issue by focusing on technical criticism. We should perhaps not be surprised to hear that this unsympathetic review was published in the *Deutsche Allgemeine Zeitung,* the very paper that had successfully spearheaded genocide justificationalism in the great German genocide debate eleven years earlier. By the winter of 1932, Hans Humann—who, we might remember, also had been the person who had set up the meeting between his close friend Enver Pasha and Lepsius in the first place—had actually left the paper to work as political adviser to Franz von Papen. Papen had assumed the chancellorship the summer before, had now stepped down again, and would, seven weeks after the review was published, become vice-chancellor under the new chancellor of Germany, Adolf Hitler. Von Papen—and, indirectly, Humann—would therefore, just a few weeks later, significantly help Hitler come to power. Perhaps the fact that Humann was no longer in control of the paper explains why the review was so mild, and did not engage in a discussion of the warning or even dispute the charges against the Young Turks (and, for the future, against Hitler). Yet again, perhaps it was not so much a mild review, but rather a cautious attempt to neutralize Werfel's warning by attacking his abilities as a novelist.[14] An outright attack in the *Deutsche Allgemeine Zeitung* on Werfel, his claims about the Armenians, and his warning about Hitler's intentions might just have provoked a national debate, especially because of the paper's past prominence in relation to the Armenian topic, and also because of the timing—these were the weeks in which it was starting to look possible, and soon even likely, that Hitler could come to power. In any case, Werfel did not manage to spark much, or even any, debate with his reading tour. And then he failed to finish his novel in time—Hitler came to power just weeks after Werfel's tour. A few months later, Werfel's books were publicly burned along with other now "undesirable" authors. When, surprisingly, the *Forty Days* was published toward the end of 1933, only a few had the chance to buy the book before it was banned and the remaining copies were seized.[15] Werfel had failed to reach the Germans with his warning and his book.

And still Werfel's *Forty Days* became one of the most important "genocide novels" of the twentieth century. One reason is, not surprisingly perhaps, its importance for Armenians. It has become so ingrained in Armenian identity that it is still considered essential reading for Armenians worldwide—without the need for school curricula to prescribe it.[16] And it does not stop there: A recent oral history study carried out in Turkey documented that in families whose own members had survived on Musa Dagh, Werfel's book is used to tell the family story to the next generation.[17] A novel inspired by what the grandparents and great-grandparents had themselves actually experienced has become a medium through which new generations learn of their own family's history.

But the significance of *The Forty Days of Musa Dagh* goes far beyond the confines of the Armenian-Turkish conflict. Werfel's book has touched many lives. Arthur Miller read it "way back, when it first came out."[18] It was on Frank Sinatra's bookshelf in his Hollywood dressing room after World War II.[19] Edward Said read it growing up.[20] And Vaclav Havel, the future president of Czechoslovakia, read it while in prison as a dissident in 1979, and thought it "wonderful."[21] Ethnic Germans in Romania read it in their German schools in the Ceaușescu years. And these are but a few of those it reached. Just shortly after its publication in Germany, it was published in English in 1934 in the United States, where it sold 34,000 copies in the first two weeks, and soon reached bestseller status.[22] It also seems to have circulated clandestinely in the Third Reich. Karl H. Schlesier, who had been an adolescent in Germany during the Third Reich, recalls in his memoir

From Flakhelfer to Grenadier that for his seventeenth birthday he received Werfel's *Forty Days* as a present from his parents—his one and only present! It had been difficult to get, he knew, as Werfel's books had been burned and outlawed. His mother had obtained it from a librarian who had been told to remove Werfel's books from the shelves, but who had secretly kept them rather than destroying them.[23]

It appears that Werfel's warning was well understood at the time by those who actually had the chance to read the book, and that many of those tried to spread the warning further. Hungarian Jewish mathematician John von Neumann, writing and living in the United States at the time, referred in a letter to a colleague to a "recent speech by Hitler," in 1939, that mentioned the Armenians (it is not clear which speech he meant). Neumann thought that an "Armenian outcome" was a possibility for European Jewry. He was influenced in this belief, he said, by a book that had used Werfel's *Forty Days* in its narrative.[24] Thus, by 1939, the novel's warning had already begun to trickle through into secondary books.

Perhaps the most important contribution of *Forty Days* was, however, to Jewish life and identity in Europe and Palestine.[25] It rivals accounts of the Shoah itself—as, indeed, it was a narrative foreshadowing the Shoah. Israeli historian Yair Auron, who has worked extensively on the impact of the novel, points out that "the reader of this extraordinary novel will find it difficult to believe that the book was written before the Holocaust."[26] And, as Auron has shown, it was indeed a direct part of the history of the Shoah, as the Jews in the Nazi-imposed ghettos in Eastern Europe devoured this story of resistance, hope, and salvation.[27] Before the war began, the book had already been translated into Polish and Yiddish, and we have a whole series of testimonies from ghettos all over Nazi-occupied Eastern Europe showing how its distribution and influence only grew after the war began.

One such testimony comes from Marcel Reich-Ranicki, by far the most famous German literary critic of recent decades. He related of his time as an inmate of the Warsaw Ghetto that the book "enjoyed unexpected success in the ghetto, being passed from hand to hand."[28] More detailed testimony comes from William Mishell, who described life in the Kovno Ghetto, in Lithuania, in 1942:

> [We] were attending most of the concerts and reading books [in the ghetto]. One of the books was *The Forty Days of Musa Dagh*, by Franz Werfel, which made an indelible impression upon us. The bloody, ruthless

massacre of over a million Armenians by the Turks in 1915, in full view of an entire world, reminded us of our fate. The Armenians were starved to death, shot, drowned, tortured to exhaustion, and left in the desert to die of sunstroke and dehydration. We compared their fate with ours, the indifference of the world to their plight, and the complete abandonment of the poor people into the hands of a barbarous, tyrannical regime. Our analysis of the book indicated that if the world did not come to the rescue of the Armenians, who were Christian after all, how could we, Jews, expect help? No doubt Hitler knew all about these massacres and the criminal neglect by the free world, and was convinced that he could proceed with impunity against the helpless Jews. Our conclusion was that if we were ever able to survive this war, it would not be because somebody came to our rescue, but because Hitler ran out of time.[29]

In the Vilna Ghetto, also in Lithuania, the book had a similar impact, as remembered, fittingly, by two librarians of the ghetto library. One, Dina Abramowicz, wrote that it was one of the most popular books: "The idea of a total annihilation of a racial group, the method of destruction, the helplessness of the victims, and the futility of diplomatic rescue efforts—this presented such an astonishing similarity to our situation that we read the book with a shudder, perceiving it almost as a prophetic vision, revealing for us our inevitable fate."[30] But not all chose to understand Werfel's story in such pessimistic ways. For many Jews it was empowering. Abramowicz's colleague Rachel Margolis, later a partisan fighter, wrote,

> Working in the library was a supreme blessing for me. There were many readers, especially on Sundays, sometimes as many as seven hundred people a day. . . . For the most part people read the detective stories of Edgar Wallace, the primitive writings of Marczynski and Dolega-Mostowicz—anything they could fill their head with, distract themselves, not think about. Tired, hungry people, penned up together, sweltering, losing themselves in a book. Works in greatest demand were those describing something similar to our lives at the time, for instance, *The Forty Days of Musa Dagh*, by Franz Werfel about the persecution and the massacre of the Armenians in Turkey in 1915. People signed up on the waiting list for that book.[31]

We also have evidence of the book's impact in the Białystok Ghetto in Poland. Here, Haika Grossman recalls the activities of Hashomer Hatzair, the Zionist youth movement, which was active in the ghetto: "They educated themselves. . . . Their teachers were the movement and *belles lettres.* They read *Musa Dagh* and *Mademoiselle Fifi.*"[32] When the Jewish ghetto underground debated what to do, three options were considered: revolt, rescue, or escape to and resistance in the forests. Herschel Rosenthal pleaded: "Our fate is sealed. We are therefore left with only one possibility: organizing collective resistance in the ghetto at any price; to view the ghetto as our 'Musa Dagh,' and to add a chapter of honor to the history of Jewish Białystok and of our movement."[33] Mordechai Tenebaum, a commander of the Białystok underground, wrote in a letter on 23 May 1943, "*Musa Dagh* is all the rage with us. If you read it, you will remember it for the rest of your life."[34]

Elsewhere in German-occupied Poland, in the Sosnowiec Ghetto, the book was also "all the rage," and again had particular significance in the youth movement. Inka Wajbort recalls how the book was read by her and other adolescent members of the Hashomer Hatzair:

> The book passed from hand to hand. . . . It completely captivated me. For four full days I was engrossed in the book and could not tear myself away. . . . I myself was at Musa Dagh; I was under siege. I was one of the Armenians doomed to death. If I lifted my eyes from the book, it was only to hear the cry—Mama, how could this be? The world knew and kept silent. It could not be that children in other countries at the same time went to school, women adorned themselves, men went about their business, as if nothing had happened. . . . And there, a people was annihilated. . . . [Back t]hen I did not deal in comparisons. Then, in the summer of 1941, I did not yet sense that a new Musa Dagh was imminent. That happened later.[35]

At Sosnowiec, just as at Białystok, an uprising took place during the liquidation of the ghetto, but it failed and almost all of the former inmates died at Auschwitz.

Yair Auron has collected a whole set of similar testimonies about the novel's impact in Nazi ghettos across Eastern Europe. He and others also found that Werfel's *Forty Days* as well as Leo Tolstoy's *War and Peace* were the favorite books across the ghettos in Nazi-occupied Eastern Europe.[36] Auron tells of one ghetto resident, Yitzhak Katznelson, crying out in 1943 to his brother, "Who will write the Jewish *Musa Dagh*? When the Armenians were killed, they were mourned by a Jewish book but when the Jewish people is killed who will mourn for it? Who will weep for it?"[37] Auron also relates an anecdote about Yitzhak Zuckerman, one of the leaders of the Warsaw uprising, as told afterward by one of his colleagues: "When he wanted to enlighten us he said that it was impossible to understand the Warsaw Ghetto uprising without reading Franz Werfel's *The Forty Days of Musa Dagh*." And finally, Auron quotes the words of Arcadius Kahan, who gives a vivid description of how the book would actually have been read, in this case in the Warsaw Ghetto:

> A glance into the package convinces the woman that this is the real thing, [the] *Forty Days of Musa Dagh*, the novel by Franz Werfel about the Turkish massacres of the Armenians. This is the most popular novel among the adults in the ghetto. They'll read it aloud this evening, if there is electricity.
>
> There is light in the room and still time before the police hour. The father opens the book and begins to read aloud.... The neighbor girl pulls out a book of her own, and while the grown-ups listen to the gruesome details of the massacres, the girl plugs her ears with her fingers.[38]

The book apparently also circulated beyond Eastern Europe, in Nazi-occupied Western Europe as well. For example, it was read in the Dutch underground, members of which claimed, "It was a 'textbook' for us."[39]

It would unfold its power in Palestine too. As early as 1934, the book had been translated into Hebrew.[40] And already in 1933, Dov Kimchi wrote an extensive review of the forthcoming book, based on excerpts published abroad. He wrote, among other things, that "we Hebrew readers ... read into this book on the Armenians our very own tragedy."[41] A year later, in 1934, another review, by R. Seligmann in *The Young Worker (Ha-Poel Ha-Tzair)*, expressed similar sentiments, observing, "The book is very interesting for the educated reader in general, but the Jewish reader will find it of special interest. The fate of this Armenian tribe recalls, in several important details, the fate of the people of Israel, and not surprisingly the Jewish reader will discover several familiar motifs, so well known to him from the life and history of his people."[42] In 1936, Moshe Beilinson wrote a more critical review. He was irritated by the fact that a Jew would erect such a monument to the suffering of another people. But he, at least partially, understood Werfel's intentions: "This is no more than a shell, for in truth this is a Jewish book, not only because it was written by a Jew, but in a less abstract sense, simpler and more concrete, the author speaks of us, of our fate, of our struggle."[43]

Later, during World War II, the book took on an even more immediate resonance in Palestine. Erwin Rommel's famed Africa Corps seemed unstoppable, and the Yishuv (the Jewish settlement in Palestine) feared a possible Nazi invasion. One of the ideas discussed for Jewish resistance was to concentrate all Jewish forces in Palestine on Mount Carmel, and from there to fight and hold out against the armies of the Third Reich. The plan had many names: "Northern Program," "Carmel Plan," "Masada Plan"—and also "Musa Dagh Plan." As they planned to defend themselves on one mountain, the story of the Armenians holding out on another mountain not far away served as a direct inspiration. Auron relates how Meir Batz, one of the founders of the Jewish self-defense militias, Haganah and Palmach, was asked at this time if he had read *The Forty Days.* "When he replied that he had, he was told, 'We want to turn Mount Carmel into the Musa Dagh of the Palestinian Jewry.'" The same evening, on a patrol, Batz thought to himself, "I imagined to myself the Jewish Musa Dagh which was to ensure the future of the Yishuv, and guarantee its honor."[44]

After the war, the book still instilled a sense of urgency, heroism, and hope. Yossi Harel, the man who, with the ship *Exodus,* would bring over 20,000 Jewish Holocaust survivors through the British blockade of Palestine after World War II, was also captivated by Werfel's tale. As his biographer Yoram Kaniuk has put it, "As very young men, Yossi and his friends read *The Forty Days of Musa Dagh,* a book by Franz Werfel about the Armenian revolt in the mountains of Anatolia. They found in this book a moral code. Hidden within it, the book contained pain and bravery, loyalty and isolation, and it won the hearts of the young Palestine Jews."[45] Apparently, when he left on his trip to save and bring Holocaust survivors to Palestine, he packed only a few things to eat and "three items for 'ideological fortification'—a Bible, the poems of Hannah Senesh and Nathan Alterman, and Franz Werfel's *The Forty Days of Musa Dagh.*"[46] Sailing along the shore from Palestine, Harel would stand on deck and look out for Musa Dagh in the night, reflecting on his role in the saga of Jewish survival (Figure E.2).

• • •

The "success" of yet another warrior against genocide was to be much more visible and even more important. He was also a contemporary to our story

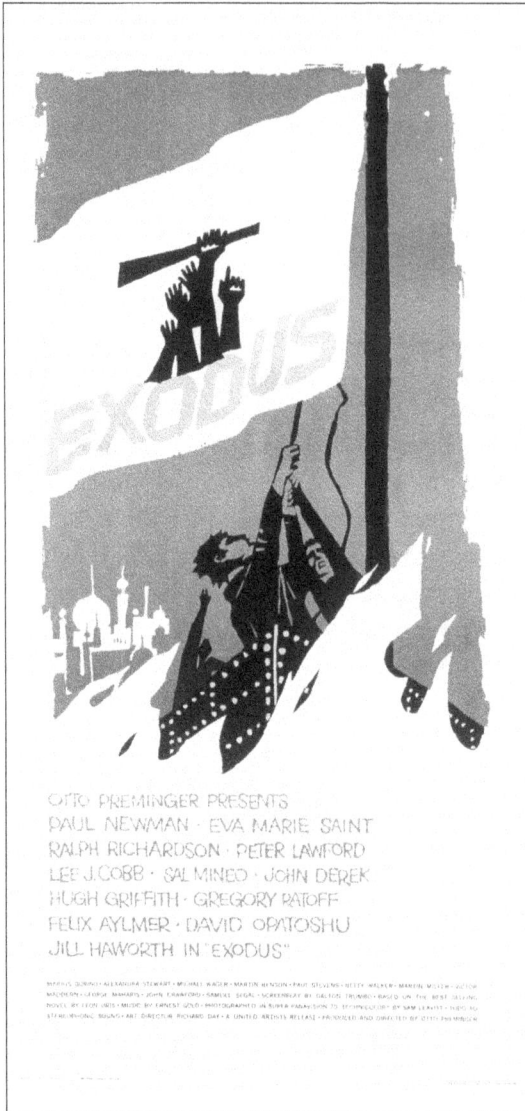

Figure E.2 *Exodus* (1960, US). Yossi Harel's story was later made famous by the Otto Preminger movie *Exodus,* based on the novel of the same name by Leon Uris. This is a fitting example of the power of stories in the modern world: the act of resistance inspired a novel, which in turn inspired a man to act, which again inspired a novel and a movie. ("EXODUS" © 1960 Metro-Goldwyn-Mayer Studios Inc. All rights reserved. Reproduced courtesy of MGM Media Licensing)

and he was influenced not only by the Armenian Genocide but also by the Talât Pasha trial: the Polish Jewish lawyer Raphael Lemkin, the future father of both the term "genocide" and the UN's 1948 Genocide Convention. A law student at the time of the Talât Pasha trial, he had followed the trial closely in the press, perhaps even in the German-language press (and even if not, the coverage in the Polish press was likely influenced by the German press coverage and debate). Later in life, he recalled asking his law professor in Cracow at the time why it would not have been possible to convict Talât Pasha of the crimes he had committed against the Armenians in a court of law, outside his home country. The professor answered with a parable "explaining" state sovereignty: "Consider the case of a farmer who owns a flock of chickens. He kills them, and this is his business. If you interfere, you are trespassing." "But the Armenians are not chickens," was Lemkin's shocked reaction.[47] In his memoirs, Lemkin wrote,

> Tehlirian acted as the self-appointed legal officer for the conscience of mankind. But can a man appoint himself to mete out justice? Will not passion sway such a type of justice and rather make a travesty of it? At that moment, my worries about the murder of the innocent became more meaningful to me. I didn't know all the answers, but I felt that a law against this type of murder must be accepted by the world. . . . Sovereignty, I argued, cannot be conceived as the right to kill millions of innocent people.[48]

Notes

Unless otherwise noted, all English translations are the author's own.

Prologue: Franz Werfel Meets Adolf Hitler

1. Alma Mahler-Werfel, *Mein Leben* (Frankfurt am Main: Fischer, 1985 [1960]), 199.
2. Peter Stephan Jungk, *Franz Werfel: Eine Lebensgeschichte* (Frankfurt am Main: S. Fischer, 1987), 206.
3. Rolf Hosfeld, *Operation Nemesis: Die Türkei, Deutschland und der Völkermord an den Armeniern* (Cologne: Kiepenheuer and Witsch, 2005), 241; Mahler-Werfel, *Mein Leben*, 175–178.
4. Jonathan Kreutner, "Die Reaktion der deutschen Juden auf die Verfolgung der Armenier von 1896 bis 1939," in Hans-Lukas Kieser and Elmar Plozza, eds., *Der Völkermord an den Armeniern, die Türkei und Europa*, 133–146 (Zurich: Chronos, 2006), 142.
5. Margaret Lavinia Anderson, "Who Still Talked about the Extermination of the Armenians?—German Talk and German Silences," in Ronald Grigor Suny, Fatma Müge Göcek, and Norman M. Naimark, eds., *A Question of Genocide: Armenians and Turks at the End of the Ottoman Empire*, 199–217 (Oxford: Oxford University Press, 2011), 217.
6. Robert Fisk, *The Great War for Civilization: The Conquest of the Middle East* (London: Harper Perennial, 2006), 406–407; Vahakn N. Dadrian, *The History of the Armenian Genocide* (New York: Berghahn, 2004 [1995]), 410.

Introduction: Questions of Genocide?

The title is obviously inspired by Ronald Grigor Suny, Fatma Müge Göcek, and Norman M. Naimark, eds., *A Question of Genocide: Armenians and Turks at the End of the Ottoman Empire* (Oxford: Oxford University Press, 2011).

1. As quoted in Axel Meissner, *Martin Rades "Christliche Welt" und Armenien: Bausteine für eine internationale Ethik des Protestantismus* (Berlin: LIT Verlag, 2010), 80.

2. Thora von Wedel-Jarlsberg and Eva Elvers, "Report on the Events at Erzindjan (28 June 1915), German Foreign Office R 14087," in Wolfgang Gust, ed., *Der Völkermord an den Armeniern 1915/1916: Dokumente aus dem Politischen Archiv des deutschen Auswärtigen Amts* (Springe, Germany: Zu Klampen, 2005), 258–263.
3. Ferda Balancar, ed., *The Sounds of Silence: Turkey's Armenians Speak* (Istanbul: International Hrant Dink Foundation Publications, 2012).
4. See a recent jurisprudential approach that does away with uncertainty: Geoffrey Robertson, *An Inconvenient Genocide—Who Now Remembers the Armenians?* (London: Biteback Publishing, 2014).
5. See some recent examples of scholarship: Raymond Kévorkian, *The Armenian Genocide: A Complete History* (London: IB Tauris, 2012 [2006]); Taner Akçam, *The Young Turks' Crime against Humanity: The Armenian Genocide and Ethnic Cleansing in the Ottoman Empire* (Princeton, NJ: Princeton University Press, 2012); Taner Akçam, *A Shameful Act: The Armenian Genocide and the Question of Turkish Responsibility* (London: Constable and Robinson, 2006); Uğur Ümit Üngör, *The Making of Modern Turkey: Nation and State in Eastern Anatolia, 1913-1950* (Oxford: Oxford University Press, 2011); Ronald Grigor Suny, Fatma Müge Göcek, and Norman M. Naimark, eds., *A Question of Genocide: Armenians and Turks at the End of the Ottoman Empire* (Oxford: Oxford University Press, 2011); Richard G. Hovannisian, ed., *Remembrance and Denial: The Case of the Armenian Genocide* (Detroit: Wayne State University Press, 1999); Hans-Lukas Kieser and Dominik J. Schaller, eds., *Der Völkermord an den Armeniern und die Shoah* (Zurich: Chronos, 2002); Hans-Lukas Kieser and Elmar Plozza, eds., *Der Völkermord an den Armeniern, die Türkei und Europa* (Zurich: Chronos, 2006); Vahakn N. Dadrian, *The History of the Armenian Genocide* (New York: Berghahn, 2004 [1995]).
6. On the shortcomings of this and other definitions, see Mark Levene, *The Meaning of Genocide* (London: IB Tauris, 2008 [2005]), 35–89.
7. See, for example, Robertson, *An Inconvenient Genocide,* 188–189.
8. As quoted in Peter Balakian, *The Burning Tigris: The Armenian Genocide and America's Response* (New York: Harper Perennial, 2004), 282.
9. Longerich also argues that terms such as "extermination" and "annihilation," as used by Nazis before 1941, did not necessarily mean mass murder. However, given the way these terms had been used in the debates about the Armenian Genocide in the Germany of the early 1920s, it appears that these terms were highly charged already before the onset of the Holocaust. Peter Longerich, *The Unwritten Order—Hitler's Role in the Final Solution* (Stroud, UK: Tempus, 2001), 16; Office of the United States Chief Counsel for Prosecution of Axis Criminality, *Nazi Conspiracy and Aggression—Supplement B* (Washington, DC: United States Printing Office, 1948), 1426–1436.
10. One recent attempt at doing this confused the changes in the Lepsius volume (see Chapter 9) with the overall content of the German Foreign Office

sources, which that author simply ignored. Cem Özgönül, *Der Mythos eines Völkermordes—Eine kritische Betrachtung der Lepsiusdokumente sowie der deutschen Rolle in Geschichte und Gegenwart der armenischen Frage* (Cologne: Önel-Verlag, 2006); see, on the other hand, a recent Turkish book working with, and publicizing extensively, the German Foreign Office documents: Serdar Dinçer, *Alman Belgelerinde Alman-Türk Silah Arkadaşlığı ve Ermeniler* (Istanbul: İletişim, 2011).

11. This is true even in McMeekin's book about German-Ottoman relations, where he claims that we know about the "Armenian massacres" mostly through American reports and then goes on to discredit these. Sean McMeekin, *The Berlin-Baghdad Express: The Ottoman Empire and Germany's Bid for World Power, 1898–1918* (London: Penguin, 2011), 133.

12. See, for example, Heath W. Lowry, *The Story behind Ambassador Morgenthau's Story* (Istanbul: Isis, 1990).

13. There are, of course, some works that have focused on different aspects of German-Armenian history and that have made this book possible, for example: Norbert Saupp, "Das Deutsche Reich und die Armenische Frage, 1878–1914" (PhD dissertation, University of Cologne, 1990); Friedrich Scherer, *Adler und Halbmond: Bismarck und der Orient, 1878–1890* (Paderborn, Germany: Ferdinand Schöningh, 2001); Mehmet Cebeci, *Die deutsch-türkischen Beziehungen in der Epoche Abdülhamids II. (1876–1908): Die Rolle Deutschlands in der türkischen Außenpolitik* (Marburg, Germany: Tectum, 2010); Vahakn N. Dadrian, *German Responsibility in the Armenian Genocide: A Review of the Historical Evidence of German Complicity* (Watertown, MA: Blue Crane Books, 1996); Rolf Hosfeld, *Operation Nemesis: Die Türkei, Deutschland und der Völkermord an den Armeniern* (Cologne: Kiepenheuer and Witsch, 2005); as well as the books by Wolfgang Gust, most importantly his source edition, Gust, *Der Völkermord*; Kieser and Dominik, *Der Völkermord an den Armeniern und die Shoah*; Kieser and Plozza, *Der Völkermord an den Armeniern, die Türkei und Europa.*

14. See an article from 1915 in *Die Hilfe* that claims that the Armenians could never count on much sympathy in Germany, neither in the 1890s nor during the 1909 Adana massacre, not even during World War I. Max Roloff, "Türken und Armenier," *Die Hilfe*, 9 September 1915.

15. See the examples cited in Margaret Lavinia Anderson, "'Down in Turkey, Far Away'—Human Rights, the Armenian Massacres, and Orientalism in Wilhelmine Germany," *Journal of Modern History* 1 (2007): 80–111.

16. See Hovannisian's discussion of denialism (as well as other chapters in the same volume): Richard G. Hovannisian, "Denial of the Genocide and the Holocaust," in Hovannisian, ed., *Remembrance and Denial*, 201–236; also see Henry C. Theriault, "Denial and Free Speech: The Case of the Armenian Genocide," in Richard G. Hovannisian, ed., *Looking Backward, Moving Forward: Confronting the Armenian Genocide* (New Brunswick, NJ: Transaction, 2003), 231–261.

17. Balakian, *The Burning Tigris*, xvii; Jay Winter, ed., *America and the Armenian Genocide* (Cambridge: Cambridge University Press, 2003).

18. Kieser makes similar claims about the impact of the Armenian Genocide on Christian America, especially the American missionary societies: Hans-Lukas Kieser, *Nearest East: American Millennialism and Mission to the Middle East* (Philadelphia: Temple University Press, 2010).

1. Beginnings under Bismarck

1. Richard Graf von Pfeil, *Experiences of a Prussian Officer in the Russian Service during the Turkish War of 1877–78* (London: Edward Stanford, 1893), 285–286.

2. Friedrich Scherer, *Adler und Halbmond: Bismarck und der Orient, 1878–1890* (Paderborn, Germany: Ferdinand Schöningh, 2001), 44.

3. My narrative of Abdul Hamid's situation is greatly influenced by Mehmet Cebeci in his book, *Die deutsch-türkischen Beziehungen in der Epoche Abdülhamids II. (1876–1908): Die Rolle Deutschlands in der türkischen Außenpolitik* (Marburg, Germany: Tectum, 2010).

4. Erik J. Zürcher, *Turkey: A Modern History* (London: IB Tauris, 1997), 79.

5. Donald Quataert, *The Ottoman Empire, 1700–1922,* 6th ed. (Cambridge: Cambridge University Press, 2010), 2, 59, 68; Donald Bloxham, *The Great Game of Genocide: Imperialism, Nationalism, and the Destruction of the Ottoman Armenians* (Oxford: Oxford University Press, 2005), 46.

6. Cebeci, *Die deutsch-türkischen Beziehungen,* 45–49.

7. Ibid., 48–50.

8. See ibid., 245.

9. Bloxham, *The Great Game,* 45.

10. Cebeci, *Die deutsch-türkischen Beziehungen,* 234–238.

11. Scherer, *Adler und Halbmond,* 46–47; Cebeci, *Die deutsch-türkischen Beziehungen,* 42–43.

12. Cebeci, *Die deutsch-türkischen Beziehungen,* 243–244.

13. Axel Meissner, *Martin Rades "Christliche Welt" und Armenien: Bausteine für eine internationale Ethik des Protestantismus* (Berlin: LIT Verlag, 2010), 21–22.

14. Bismarck to Münster, 17 May 1883; also, Bismarck to Wilhelm I, 18 May 1883, in Johannes Lepsius, Albrecht Mendelsohn Bartholdy, and Friedrich Thimme, eds., *Die große Politik der Europäischen Kabinette, 1871–1914,* vol. 5, *Neue Verwicklungen im Osten* (Berlin: Deutsche Verlagsgesellschaft für Politik und Geschichte, 1922), 200; Vahakn N. Dadrian, *The History of the Armenian Genocide* (New York: Berghahn, 2004 [1995]), 187.

15. See Götz Aly's recent discussion of this in connection with the Holocaust: Götz Aly, *Why the Germans? Why the Jews? Envy, Race Hatred, and the Prehistory of the Holocaust* (New York: Metropolitan Books, 2014 [2011]).

16. Scherer, *Adler und Halbmond,* 16.

17. Ibid., xiv.

18. Ibid., 58.

19. Saupp, "Das Deutsche Reich," 25.

20. Bülow to Münster, 4 January 1876, in Johannes Lepsius, Albrecht Mendelssohn Bartholdy, and Friedrich Thimme, eds., *Die große Politik der Europäischen Kabinette, 1871–1914,* vol. 2, *Der Berliner Kongress und seine Vorgeschichte* (Berlin: Deutsche Verlagsgesellschaft für Politik und Geschichte, 1922), 30.

21. Dictation of Bismarck, 14 October 1876, in Lepsius et al., *Die große Politik,* vol. 2, 64.

22. Bismarck also remarked that none of the powers had helped Germany with diplomatic pressure in its difficult hours over the last decade, so neither should Germany now do such things for other peoples. Dictation of Bismarck, 20 October 1876, in Lepsius et al., *Die große Politik,* vol. 2, 70, 71.

23. Bismarck to Wilhelm I, 18 May 1883, in Lepsius et al., *Die große Politik,* vol. 5, 200.

24. Cebeci, *Die deutsch-türkischen Beziehungen,* 45, 157, 187, 189, 193, 229, 729; Scherer, *Adler und Halbmond,* 74.

25. Cebeci, *Die deutsch-türkischen Beziehungen,* 122.

26. Ibid., 256–257. Lepsius dates it to September: Johannes Lepsius, *Armenien und Europa: Eine Anklageschrift,* 3rd ed. (Berlin: Verlag der Akademischen Buchhandlung W. Faber and Co., 1897), 76–77.

27. Cebeci, *Die deutsch-türkischen Beziehungen,* 63–65.

28. Ibid., 66–68, 266–267; Uwe Feigel, *Das evangelische Deutschland und Armenien: Die Armenierhilfe deutscher evangelischer Christen seit dem Ende des 19. Jahrhunderts im Kontext der deutsch-türkischen Beziehungen* (Göttingen, Germany: Vandenhoeck and Ruprecht, 1989), 40.

29. Cebeci, *Die deutsch-türkischen Beziehungen,* 71, 267.

30. Ibid., 267–269.

31. Bismarck to Radowitz, 12 October 1883, as quoted in Norbert Saupp, "Das Deutsche Reich und die Armenische Frage, 1878–1914" (PhD dissertation, University of Cologne, 1990), 29–30.

32. Bismarck to Kaiser Wilhelm I, 26 November 1879, as quoted in Saupp, "Das Deutsche Reich," 18.

33. Saupp, "Das Deutsche Reich," 15, 19.

34. Hatzfeldt to Bismarck, 23 April 1880, as quoted in Saupp, "Das Deutsche Reich," 19.

35. For example, Bismarck to Münster, 10 July 1883, as quoted in Saupp, "Das Deutsche Reich," 29; Cebeci, *Die deutsch-türkischen Beziehungen,* 270.

36. Scherer, *Adler und Halbmond,* 155.

37. Ibid., 306.

38. Bismarck to Hatzfeldt, 4 May 1888, as quoted in Saupp, "Das Deutsche Reich," 32.

39. Scherer, *Adler und Halbmond,* 308.

40. Ibid., xi–xii.

41. Vahakn N. Dadrian, *German Responsibility in the Armenian Genocide: A Review of the Historical Evidence of German Complicity* (Watertown, MA: Blue Crane Books, 1996), 14.

42. As quoted in Cebeci, *Die deutsch-türkischen Beziehungen,* 266.

43. Ibid., 233.

2. Germany and the Armenian Horrors of the 1890s

1. Malte Fuhrmann, *Der Traum vom deutschen Orient: Zwei deutsche Kolonien im Osmanischen Reich, 1851–1918* (Frankfurt am Main: Campus, 2006).

2. Some claim that, already by the end of Bismarck's time in office, Germany had no longer any alternative to its commitment to upholding the empire's integrity: Hans-Walter Schmuhl, "Friedrich Naumann und die 'armenische Frage'—Die deutsche Öffentlichkeit und die Verfolgung der Armenier vor 1915," in Hans-Lukas Kieser and Dominik J. Schaller, eds., *Der Völkermord an den Armeniern und die Shoah,* 503–516 (Zurich: Chronos, 2002), 506.

3. As quoted in Norbert Saupp, "Das Deutsche Reich und die Armenische Frage, 1878–1914" (PhD dissertation, University of Cologne, 1990), 32.

4. As quoted in ibid., 41.

5. Marschall commented in 1893 that the "partially justified complaints of the Armenians" were due to structural weakness in the Ottoman administrative system and would not be remedied as long as the empire existed. Marschall to Hatzfeldt, 10 October 1893, in Johannes Lepsius et al., eds., *Die große Politik der Europäischen Kabinette, 1871–1914,* vol. 9, *Der nahe und der ferne Osten* (Berlin: Deutsche Verlagsgesellschaft für Politik und Geschichte, 1924), 200.

6. Saupp, "Das Deutsche Reich," 54.

7. Vahakn N. Dadrian, *German Responsibility in the Armenian Genocide: A Review of the Historical Evidence of German Complicity* (Watertown, MA: Blue Crane Books, 1996), 8–9.

8. As quoted in Andreas Meier, ed., *Armin T. Wegner: Die Austreibung des armenischen Volkes in die Wüste—Ein Lichtbildvortrag* (Göttingen, Germany: Wallstein, 2011), 187.

9. For the reaction in the United States, see Ann Marie Wilson, "In the Name of God, Civilization, and Humanity: The United States and the Armenian Massacres of the 1890s," *Le mouvement social* 227 (2009): 27–44.

10. Radolin to Caprivi, 15 March 1894, as quoted in Saupp, "Das Deutsche Reich," 43.

11. Radolin to Caprivi, 27 March 1894, as quoted in ibid., 44.

12. On Sason see Vahakn N. Dadrian, *The History of the Armenian Genocide* (New York: Berghahn, 2004 [1995]), 116–119.

13. Radolin to Caprivi, 5 October 1894, as quoted in Saupp, "Das Deutsche Reich," 46.

14. Radolin to Hohenlohe, 17 December 1894, as quoted in ibid., 48.

15. Radolin to Hatzfeldt, as quoted in ibid., 52.

16. Uwe Feigel, *Das evangelische Deutschland und Armenien: Die Armenierhilfe deutscher evangelischer Christen seit dem Ende des 19. Jahrhunderts im Kontext der deutsch-türkischen Beziehungen* (Göttingen, Germany: Vandenhoeck and Ruprecht, 1989), 26–27.

17. Axel Meissner, *Martin Rades "Christliche Welt" und Armenien: Bausteine für eine internationale Ethik des Protestantismus* (Berlin: LIT Verlag, 2010), 27; Mehmet Cebeci, *Die deutsch-türkischen Beziehungen in der Epoche Abdülhamids II. (1876–1908): Die Rolle Deutschlands in der türkischen Außenpolitik* (Marburg, Germany: Tectum, 2010), 290–291.

18. Cebeci, *Die deutsch-türkischen Beziehungen*, 291.

19. Ibid., 286–290. The theme of bad administrators was also present in the press; see Necmettin Alkan, *Die deutsche Weltpolitik und die Konkurrenz der Mächte um das osmanische Erbe: Die deutsch-osmanischen Beziehungen in der deutschen Presse, 1890–1909* (Münster: LIT, 2003), 111.

20. Cebeci, *Die deutsch-türkischen Beziehungen*, 308.

21. Meissner, *Martin Rades "Christliche Welt,"* 31.

22. Saurma to Hohenlohe, 1 October 1895, as quoted in Saupp, "Das Deutsche Reich," 60; see also Saurma to Hohenlohe, 4 October 1895, in Johannes Lepsius et al., eds., *Die große Politik der Europäischen Kabinette, 1871–1914*, vol. 10, *Das türkische Problem, 1895* (Berlin: Deutsche Verlagsgesellschaft für Politik und Geschichte, 1923), 67.

23. Marschall to Kaiser Wilhelm II, 9 October 1895, in Lepsius et al., *Die große Politik*, vol. 10, 71; Gregor Schöllgen, *Imperialismus und Gleichgewicht: Deutschland, England und die orientalische Frage* (Munich: R. Oldenbourg, 1984), 70.

24. Hatzfeldt to the Foreign Office, 25 October 1895, in Lepsius et al., *Die große Politik*, vol. 10, 81.

25. "Roseberys diplomatischer Erfolg in Armenien," *Kladderadatsch*, January 1895.

26. Meissner, *Martin Rades "Christliche Welt,"* 32; Cebeci, *Die deutsch-türkischen Beziehungen*, 310–311.

27. Saurma to Hohenlohe, 11 November 1895, in Lepsius et al., *Die große Politik*, vol. 10, 102.

28. Saurma to Hohenlohe, 13 November 1895, in ibid., 104.

29. Cebeci, *Die deutsch-türkischen Beziehungen*, 313.

30. Saurma to Foreign Office, 23 December 1895, in Lepsius et al., eds., *Die große Politik*, vol. 10, 133–134.

31. Saupp, "Das Deutsche Reich," 72–76; Cebeci, *Die deutsch-türkischen Beziehungen*, 314; Saurma to Hohenlohe, 18 April 1896, in Lepsius et al., *Die große Politik*, vol. 10, 135.

32. Cebeci, *Die deutsch-türkischen Beziehungen*, 316; Saupp, "Das Deutsche Reich," 75.

33. Cebeci, *Die deutsch-türkischen Beziehungen*, 311.

34. Saurma to Hohenlohe, 26 October 1895, in Lepsius et al., *Die große Politik*, vol. 10, 84–85.

35. Saurma to Hohenlohe, 11 November 1895, in ibid., 102.

36. Saupp, "Das Deutsche Reich," 73.

37. Saurma to Hohenlohe, 11 December 1895, in Lepsius et al., *Die große Politik,* vol. 10, 118–119; similarly, see a second report from the same day, ibid., 119–120.

38. Feigel, *Das evangelische Deutschland,* 41.

39. A. S. Jerussalimski, *Die Aussenpolitik und die Diplomatie des deutschen Imperialismus Ende des 19. Jahrhunderts* (Stuttgart, Germany: Verlag Das Neue Wort, 1954), 190.

40. Saurma to Hohenlohe, 29 July 1896, as quoted in Saupp, "Das Deutsche Reich," 89–90.

41. Saupp, "Das Deutsche Reich," 79.

42. Meissner compares its effect to that of the Reichstag fire for the Nazis: Meissner, *Martin Rades "Christliche Welt,"* 129. See, for example, "Der Plan der Verschwörer," *Kölnische Zeitung,* 20 September 1896, as quoted in Alkan, *Die deutsche Weltpolitik,* 110–111; for more examples from the *Kölnische Zeitung,* see Alkan, *Die deutsche Weltpolitik,* 117; Meissner, *Martin Rades "Christliche Welt,"* 127.

43. *Allgemeine Evangelisch-Lutherische Kirchenzeitung* 30 (1896): 617, 809, as cited in Feigel, *Das evangelische Deutschland,* 50.

44. *Frankfurter Zeitung,* 23 August 1896, as quoted in Saupp, "Das Deutsche Reich," 120–121.

45. See Meissner, *Martin Rades "Christliche Welt,"* 127.

46. Saupp, "Das Deutsche Reich," 84–85.

47. Ibid., 91.

48. Meissner, *Martin Rades "Christliche Welt,"* 128.

49. Saupp, "Das Deutsche Reich," 91.

50. Cebeci, *Die deutsch-türkischen Beziehungen,* 317.

51. Marschall to Wilhelm II, 29 August 1896, in Johannes Lepsius et al., *Die große Politik der Europäischen Kabinette, 1871–1914,* vol. 12, bk. 1, *Alte und neue Balkanhändel, 1896–1899* (Berlin: Deutsche Verlagsgesellschaft für Politik und Geschichte, 1923), 21–22.

52. Feigel, *Das evangelische Deutschland,* 31.

53. For an often somewhat problematic analysis see also Alkan, *Die deutsche Weltpolitik,* 102–111.

54. Johannes Lepsius, *Armenien und Europa: Eine Anklageschrift,* 3rd ed. (Berlin: Verlag der Akademischen Buchhandlung W. Faber and Co., 1897), 9.

55. Meissner, *Martin Rades "Christliche Welt,"* 38–39, 42.

56. Wilhelm van Kampen, "Studien zur deutschen Türkeipolitik in der Zeit Wilhelms II." (PhD dissertation, University of Kiel, 1968), 117.

57. *Frankfurter Zeitung,* 15 November 1895, as quoted in Meissner, *Martin Rades "Christliche Welt,"* 40.

58. *Frankfurter Zeitung,* 8 November 1895, as quoted in ibid., 40–41.

59. *Frankfurter Zeitung,* 7 November 1895, as quoted in ibid., 39.

60. *Frankfurter Zeitung,* 9 November 1895, as quoted in ibid., 41, 109.

61. Meissner, *Martin Rades "Christliche Welt,"* 42.

62. Colmar von der Goltz, "Die Ereignisse von Talory," *Kölnische Zeitung,* 24 February 1895, as quoted in Saupp, "Das Deutsche Reich," 51, and Cebeci, *Die deutsch-türkischen Beziehungen,* 291.

63. "Das Gemetzel von Trapezunt," *Kölnische Zeitung,* 26 October 1895, as quoted in Meissner, *Martin Rades "Christliche Welt,"* 43.

64. Meissner, *Martin Rades "Christliche Welt,"* 43.

65. Ibid., 61.

66. Alkan, *Die deutsche Weltpolitik,* 111, 117; Meissner, *Martin Rades "Christliche Welt,"* 62.

67. "Armenische Greuel," *Vorwärts,* 11 June 1893; "Armenische Greuel," *Vorwärts,* 18 November 1894; "Armenische Greuel," *Vorwärts,* 12 February 1895, all as quoted in Alkan, *Die deutsche Weltpolitik,* 119–120.

68. "Zur orientalischen Frage," *Vorwärts,* 25 December 1895, as quoted in Alkan, *Die deutsche Weltpolitik,* 113; see also "Blaubuch über Armenien," *Vorwärts,* 31 January 1896, as quoted in ibid., 113–114; "Nachrichten aus der Türkei," *Vorwärts,* 2 July 1896, as quoted in ibid., 114.

69. Meissner, *Martin Rades "Christliche Welt,"* 57.

70. "Armenien," *Frankfurter Zeitung,* 28 August 1896, as quoted in Saupp, "Das Deutsche Reich," 125.

71. Meissner, *Martin Rades "Christliche Welt,"* 57.

72. Ibid., 122.

73. *Die Post,* 8 October 1896, as quoted in Saupp, "Das Deutsche Reich," 141; on Körte see Hilmar Kaiser, *Imperialism, Racism, and Development Theories: The Construction of a Dominant Paradigm on Ottoman Armenians* (Ann Arbor: Gomidas Institute, 1997), 10–13.

74. In the same article the paper also stressed that as long as there was suffering in Germany in any way, it was inexcusable to "export charity" to other countries. "Nochmals die armenische Frage," *Die Post,* 29 October 1896, as quoted in Saupp, "Das Deutsche Reich," 142, and van Kampen, "Studien," 118. Anderson claims that the Catholic papers were more sympathetic to the Armenians; Alkan finds that the *Germania* distinguished between "good" Catholic Christians and "bad" other Armenians. Margaret Lavinia Anderson, " 'Down in Turkey, Far Away'—Human Rights, the Armenian Massacres, and Orientalism in Wilhelmine Germany," *Journal of Modern History* 1 (2007): 80–111, here 91; Alkan, *Die deutsche Weltpolitik,* 115.

75. As quoted in Meissner, *Martin Rades "Christliche Welt,"* 79.

76. *Kölnische Zeitung,* 8 September 1896, as quoted in Saupp, "Das Deutsche Reich," 128.

77. *Neue Preussische (Kreuz-)Zeitung,* 10 September 1896, as quoted in Saupp, "Das Deutsche Reich," 130.

78. *Hannoverscher Courier,* 10 September 1896, as quoted in Saupp, "Das Deutsche Reich," 132.

79. Meissner, *Martin Rades "Christliche Welt,"* 104.
80. Feigel, *Das evangelische Deutschland,* 73–74; Meissner, *Martin Rades "Christliche Welt,"* 104–105.
81. Rolf Hosfeld, *Operation Nemesis: Die Türkei, Deutschland und der Völkermord an den Armeniern* (Cologne: Kiepenheuer and Witsch, 2005), 33.
82. Meissner, *Martin Rades "Christliche Welt,"* 105.
83. Feigel, *Das evangelische Deutschland,* 76–77; Anderson, "'Down in Turkey, Far Away,'" 103. Meissner illustrates this with the case of Garabed Thoumajan, who was forbidden to speak at Lepsius-organized events. Meissner, *Martin Rades "Christliche Welt,"* 105, 132–138.
84. Johannes Lepsius, "Die Wahrheit über Armenien," *Reichsbote,* pt. 1: 12 August 1896; pt. 2: 15 August; pt. 3: 16 August; pt. 4: 18 August; pt. 5: 19 August; pt. 6: 21 August; pt. 7: 22 August; pt. 8: 23 August; pt. 9: 25 August; pt. 10: 26 August; pt. 11: 27 August; pt. 12: 28 August; pt. 13: 29 August; pt. 14: 30 August; pt. 15: 1 September; pt. 16: 3 September; as cited in Meissner, *Martin Rades "Christliche Welt,"* 105, 106.
85. *Frankfurter Zeitung,* 25 August 1896, as quoted in Saupp, "Das Deutsche Reich," 123.
86. Feigel, *Das evangelische Deutschland,* 75. For reactions, see Kampen, "Studien," 116.
87. Feigel, *Das evangelische Deutschland,* 33; Rolf Hosfeld, "Johannes Lepsius: Eine deutsche Ausnahme," in Rolf Hosfeld, ed., *Johannes Lepsius: Eine deutsche Ausnahme,* 9–26 (Göttingen, Germany: Wallstein, 2013), 13; Meissner, *Martin Rades "Christliche Welt,"* 107.
88. Meissner, *Martin Rades "Christliche Welt,"* 107.
89. Lepsius, *Armenien und Europa,* 20–21.
90. Ibid., 5–6.
91. Ibid., 11, 68.
92. Ibid., 23–30.
93. Ibid., 123–158.
94. Ibid., 192.
95. Ibid., 197–210.
96. For example, see ibid., 83.
97. Ibid., 72.
98. Ibid., 83.
99. Ibid., 41.
100. Ibid., 69.
101. Ibid., 68.
102. Ibid., 83–84.
103. Ibid., 115.
104. Quoted in Meissner, *Martin Rades "Christliche Welt,"* 112.
105. Meissner, *Martin Rades "Christliche Welt,"* 112–113.
106. Ibid., 113.
107. Ibid.

108. For example, by Rade in his *Christliche Welt;* see ibid., 114–115.
109. Walter Siehe, "Aus dem Lande der armenischen Unruhen," *Die Post,* pt. 1: 16 January 1897; pt. 2: 20 January 1897; as quoted in Meissner, *Martin Rades "Christliche Welt,"* 116.
110. Meissner, *Martin Rades "Christliche Welt,"* 117.
111. Radolin to Hohenlohe, 17 April 1895, in Lepsius et al., *Die große Politik,* vol. 9, 225; Schöllgen, *Imperialismus und Gleichgewicht,* 69.
112. Saurma to Hohenlohe, 19 September 1896, as quoted in Schöllgen, *Imperialismus und Gleichgewicht,* 71.
113. Jerussalimski, *Die Aussenpolitik,* 276–277.
114. Mumm, 26 November 1896, as quoted in Saupp, "Das Deutsche Reich," 111–112; Meissner, *Martin Rades "Christliche Welt,"* 122.
115. Willibald Beyschlag, "Die armenischen Greuel," *Deutsch-evangelische Blätter* 21 (1896): 210, cited according to Meissner. There were at least two uses in political poetry. One in 1832 by August Graf von Platen in relation to the treatment of the Poles by Russia, and another by a fan of Platen's, Moritz Count von Strachwitz, not much later; see Meissner, *Martin Rades "Christliche Welt,"* 53–54.
116. As quoted in Helmut Donat, "Die Armeniermassaker im Spiegel der deutschen und der internationalen Friedensbewegung, 1895–1933," in Heinrich Vierbücher, *Armenien 1915: Was die kaiserliche Regierung den deutschen Untertanen verschwiegen hat,* 77–103 (Bremen: Donat Verlag, 2004 [1930]), 82.
117. As cited in Feigel, *Das evangelische Deutschland,* 37.
118. Otto Umfrid, "Die armenischen Greuel und die Friedfertigung des Orients," in Helmut Donat, ed., *Armenien, die Türkei und die Pflichten Europas,* 57–74 (Bremen: Donat Verlag, 2005), 62.
119. Meissner, *Martin Rades "Christliche Welt,"* 72–73.
120. *Frankfurter Zeitung,* 27 August 1896, as quote in Saupp, "Das Deutsche Reich," 124.
121. For example, also M. Kronenberg, "Ein unglückliches Volk," *Ethische Kultur—Wochenschrift für sozial-ethische Reformen* 32 (9 August 1902), as quoted in Donat, "Die Armeniermassaker," 83.
122. See the press discussion in Feigel, *Das evangelische Deutschland,* 43.
123. As quoted in Wolfgang Gust, *Der Völkermord an den Armeniern: Die Tragödie des ältesten Christenvolkes der Welt* (Munich: Carl Hanser Verlag, 1993), 110.
124. Feigel, *Das evangelische Deutschland,* 43; similarly in a book review in 1897 in the *Christliche Welt:* Meissner, *Martin Rades "Christliche Welt,"* 138; similarly, Paul Rohrbach, "Deutschland unter den Armeniern," *Preussische Jahrbücher* 96 (1899), as quoted in Alkan, *Die deutsche Weltpolitik,* 118.
125. Meissner, *Martin Rades "Christliche Welt,"* 49–50.
126. Saupp, "Das Deutsche Reich," 127.
127. See Scherer on an article critical of Abdul Hamid in the *Nationalzeitung* in 1886: Friedrich Scherer, *Adler und Halbmond: Bismarck und der Orient,*

384 Notes to Pages 57–60

1878–1890 (Paderborn, Germany: Ferdinand Schöningh, 2001), 374; on Bismarck, 516.

128. Anderson, "'Down in Turkey, Far Away,'" 102; also, Feigel, *Das evangelische Deutschland,* 61–62; Meissner, *Martin Rades "Christliche Welt,"* 36–37.

129. As, for example, at the assembly of the Protestant churches of Brandenburg: Meissner, *Martin Rades "Christliche Welt,"* 74–75.

130. Eugen Baumann, "In Sachen der Kirchenkollekte für die Armenier," *Reichsbote,* 6 November 1896, as quoted in Meissner, *Martin Rades "Christliche Welt,"* 76.

131. Meissner, *Martin Rades "Christliche Welt,"* 77.

132. As quoted in Feigel, *Das evangelische Deutschland,* 52.

133. See ibid., 78; Meissner, *Martin Rades "Christliche Welt,"* 111.

134. Kampen, "Studien," 118.

135. Hans Delbrück, "Politische Korrespondenz," *Preussische Jahrbücher* 86 (1896): 211–223, as cited in Meissner, *Martin Rades "Christliche Welt,"* 99; also in Kampen, "Studien," 118–119.

136. The claim in some parts of the literature that there was general outrage in the German press bears no relation to the reality as Feigel and Meissner have excavated it. Examples for such a misreading: Donald Bloxham, *The Great Game of Genocide: Imperialism, Nationalism, and the Destruction of the Ottoman Armenians* (Oxford: Oxford University Press, 2005), 54; Kampen, "Studien," 131.

137. Saupp, "Das Deutsche Reich," 142.

138. For a recent discussion of the how and why of the "nonintervention for the Armenians" stance, see Davide Rodogno, *Against Massacre: Humanitarian Interventions in the Ottoman Empire, 1815–1914: The Emergence of a European Concept and International Practice* (Princeton, NJ: Princeton University Press, 2012), 185–211.

139. Meissner, *Martin Rades "Christliche Welt,"* 80.

3. The Triumph of German Anti-Armenianism

1. See the discussion in Sigurd Sverre Stangeland, *Die Rolle Deutschlands im Völkermord an den Armeniern, 1915–1916* (Trondheim, Norway: NTNU, 2013), 320–325.

2. Compare on that point and interpretation: Hans-Walter Schmuhl, "Friedrich Naumann und die 'armenische Frage'—Die deutsche Öffentlichkeit und die Verfolgung der Armenier vor 1915," in Hans-Lukas Kieser and Dominik J. Schaller, eds., *Der Völkermord an den Armeniern und die Shoah,* 503–516 (Zurich: Chronos, 2002), 507.

3. See, for example, Richard Levy, "Political Antisemitism in Germany and Austria, 1848–1914," in Albert S. Lindemann and Richard S. Levy, eds., *Antisemitism: A History* (Oxford: Oxford University Press, 2010), 121–135; Jocelyn Hellig, *The Holocaust and Antisemitism: A Short History* (Oxford: Oneworld,

2003), 272–285; Shulamit Volkov, *Antisemitismus als kultureller Code* (Munich: Beck, 2000 [1990]), 37–53, 54–75.

4. Malte Fuhrmann, "Germany's Adventures in the Orient: A History of Ambivalent Semicolonial Encounters," in Volker Langbehn and Mohammad Salama, eds., *German Colonialism—Race, the Holocaust, and Postwar Germany*, 123–145 (New York: Columbia University Press, 2011), 126–127, 132.

5. For example, Uwe Feigel, *Das evangelische Deutschland und Armenien: Die Armenierhilfe deutscher evangelischer Christen seit dem Ende des 19. Jahrhunderts im Kontext der deutsch-türkischen Beziehungen* (Göttingen, Germany: Vandenhoeck and Ruprecht, 1989), 14; Mehmet Cebeci, *Die deutsch-türkischen Beziehungen in der Epoche Abdülhamids II. (1876–1908): Die Rolle Deutschlands in der türkischen Außenpolitik* (Marburg, Germany: Tectum, 2010), 269–270; Norbert Saupp, "Das Deutsche Reich und die Armenische Frage, 1878–1914" (PhD dissertation, University of Cologne, 1990), 29.

6. See Vahakn N. Dadrian, *The History of the Armenian Genocide* (New York: Berghahn, 2004 [1995]), 91.

7. Cebeci, *Die deutsch-türkischen Beziehungen*, 471.

8. For example, Sean McMeekin, *The Berlin-Baghdad Express: The Ottoman Empire and Germany's Bid for World Power, 1898–1918* (London: Penguin, 2011); see also, Wolfgang G. Schwanitz, " 'A Most Favourable Impression upon All Classes'—Wilhelm II., Sozialdemokraten, Muslime und Nordamerikaner, 1898," in Klaus Jaschinski and Julius Waldschmidt, eds., *Des Kaisers Reise in den Orient 1898* (Berlin: Trafo Verlag, 2002), 37–59; Klaus Jaschinski, "Des Kaisers Reise in den Vorderen Orient 1898, ihr historischer Platz und ihre Dimensionen," in Jaschinski and Waldschmidt, *Des Kaisers Reise*, 17–36.

9. As quoted in Axel Meissner, *Martin Rades "Christliche Welt" und Armenien: Bausteine für eine internationale Ethik des Protestantismus* (Berlin: LIT Verlag, 2010), 140–141.

10. Wilhelm van Kampen, "Studien zur deutschen Türkeipolitik in der Zeit Wilhelms II." (PhD dissertation, University of Kiel, 1968), 121.

11. "Auf der Fahrt nach Palästina," *Kladderadatsch*, 9 October 1898.

12. Meissner, *Martin Rades "Christliche Welt*," 123; Feigel, *Das evangelische Deutschland*, 87.

13. Meissner, *Martin Rades "Christliche Welt*," 150, 155.

14. Malte Fuhrmann, *Der Traum vom deutschen Orient: Zwei deutsche Kolonien im Osmanischen Reich, 1851–1918* (Frankfurt am Main: Campus, 2006); Malte Fuhrmann, "Den Orient deutsch machen—Imperiale Diskurse des Kaiserreiches über das Osmanische Reich," Kakanien Revisited, 28 July 2002, online at www.kakanien.ac.at/beitr/fallstudie/MFuhrmann1.pdf.

15. For example, Friedrich Naumann, *"Asia": Athen, Konstantinopel, Baalbek, Damaskus, Nazaret, Jerusalem, Kairo, Neapel*, 3rd ed. (Berlin: Verlag der Hilfe, 1900), 78.

16. Ibid., 31–32.

17. Meissner, *Martin Rades "Christliche Welt,"* 151; Schmuhl, "Friedrich Naumann," 503.
18. Naumann, *Asia,* 32.
19. Ibid., 135–136.
20. Ibid., 137.
21. Ibid., 137–138.
22. Ibid., 138.
23. Ibid., 139–140.
24. Ibid., 123.
25. Ibid., 141, 156.
26. Ibid., 141.
27. Ibid., 145.
28. Ibid., 147.
29. Ibid., 149.
30. Ibid., 139–140.
31. Paul Rohrbach, "Die deutsche Politik und die Tatsachen," *Christliche Welt* 12 (1898), as quoted in Schmuhl, "Friedrich Naumann," 513; Feigel, *Das evangelische Deutschland,* 88–89.
32. Feigel, *Das evangelische Deutschland,* 89.
33. Friedrich Naumann, "Zur Armenierfrage," *Christliche Welt* 12 (1898), 1187, as quoted in Meissner, *Martin Rades "Christliche Welt,"* 152–153.
34. As quoted in Feigel, *Das evangelische Deutschland,* 90; Schmuhl, "Friedrich Naumann," 509–510.
35. Heinrich Vierbücher, *Armenien 1915: Was die kaiserliche Regierung den deutschen Untertanen verschwiegen hat* (Bremen: Donat Verlag, 2004 [1930]), 36. On his service in the Ottoman Empire: Helmut Donat, "Die Armeniermassaker im Spiegel der deutschen und der internationalen Friedensbewegung, 1895–1933," in Vierbücher, *Armenien,* 77–103, here 81.
36. Naumann, *Asia,* 132.
37. See Alkan's analysis of the reform topic in the German press in the 1890s, Necmettin Alkan, *Die deutsche Weltpolitik und die Konkurrenz der Mächte um das osmanische Erbe: Die deutsch-osmanischen Beziehungen in der deutschen Presse, 1890–1909* (Münster: LIT, 2003), 96–102, 116.
38. Kampen, "Studien," 129.
39. Bülow to Marschall, 14 February 1898, as quoted in Saupp, "Das Deutsche Reich," 161.
40. Marschall to Bülow, 5 March 1898, as quoted in ibid., 162; also Marschall to Hohenlohe, 26 February 1898, as quoted in Gregor Schöllgen, *Imperialismus und Gleichgewicht: Deutschland, England und die orientalische Frage* (Munich: R. Oldenbourg, 1984), 114–115; see also commentary of Wilhelm II on the Macedonian reform plans, Marschall to Bülow, 7 October 1902, as quoted in Schöllgen, *Imperialismus und Gleichgewicht,* 134–135.
41. Marschall to Hohenlohe-Schillingsfürst, 26 December 1899, as quoted in Eric D. Weitz, *A Century of Genocide: Utopias of Race and Nation* (Princeton, NJ: Princeton University Press, 2005), 175, 181.

42. Marschall to Bülow, 7 October 1902, as quoted in Saupp, "Das Deutsche Reich," 165.

43. Wangenheim as quoted in Donald Bloxham, *The Great Game of Genocide: Imperialism, Nationalism, and the Destruction of the Ottoman Armenians* (Oxford: Oxford University Press, 2005), 8–9.

44. Marschall to Bethmann-Hollweg, 13 May 1911, as quoted in Weitz, *A Century of Genocide,* 189.

45. See, for more examples, Stangeland, *Die Rolle Deutschlands,* 302–311.

46. Hermann Esser, *Die jüdische Weltpest: Judendämmerung auf dem Erdball* (Munich: Franz Eher Nachfolger, 1939); Theodor Fritsch, *Handbuch der Judenfrage: Die wichtigsten Tatsachen zur Beurteilung des jüdischen Volkes,* 49th ed. (Leipzig: Hammer-Verlag, 1944), 270.

47. See also Dominik J. Schaller, "Die Rezeption des Völkermordes an den Armeniern in Deutschland, 1915–1945," in Kieser and Schaller, eds., *Der Völkermord,* 517–555; see also Stangeland, *Die Rolle Deutschlands,* 302–308; see also, for example, the *Allgemeine Konservative Monatsschrift* (1896) as quoted in Alkan, *Die deutsche Weltpolitik,* 94–95; Ewald Banse, "Fünf Landschaftstypen aus dem Orient," *Geographische Zeitschrift* 7 (1908): 361–372, here 376 (comparison to the Jews of Northern Africa); N. Honig, "Der Handel Konstantinopels," *Weltwirtschaftliches Archiv* 11 (1917): 41–67; Eugen Oberhummer, "Die Türken und das osmanische Reich," *Geographische Zeitschrift* 3 (1917): 133–162, here 157.

48. F. Roderich-Stoltheim, *Das Rätsel des jüdischen Erfolges,* 7th ed. (Leipzig: Hammer, 1928), 181.

49. See, for example, Feigel, *Das evangelische Deutschland,* 70; Margaret Lavinia Anderson, "'Down in Turkey, Far Away'—Human Rights, the Armenian Massacres, and Orientalism in Wilhelmine Germany," *Journal of Modern History* 1 (2007): 80–111, here 102.

50. Feigel, *Das evangelische Deutschland,* 70.

51. Ibid. See, for example, "Die Beurteilung der Lage in der Türkei," *Kölnische Zeitung,* 18 December 1895, as quoted in Alkan, *Die deutsche Weltpolitik,* 112–113.

52. Feigel, *Das evangelische Deutschland,* 86–87.

53. As quoted in Meissner, *Martin Rades "Christliche Welt,"* 149.

54. For example, "Armenien und seine Feinde," *Deutsche Reichspost,* 14 July 1905.

55. Marschall to Bülow, 17 November 1900, as quoted in Saupp, "Das Deutsche Reich," 165.

56. For example, "Die armenische Frage—Ergebnisse einer Studienfahrt," *Der Tag,* pt. 1: 23 November 1913; pt. II: 27 November 1913.

57. See Schmuhl, "Friedrich Naumann"; Melzig, *Der "kranke Mann,"* 70–79; Nina Berman, *Orientalismus, Kolonialismus und Moderne: Zum Bild des Orients in der deutschsprachigen Kultur um 1900* (Stuttgart, Germany: Metzler, 1997).

58. Karl May, *Im Reiche des silbernen Löwen,* vol. 2 (Radebeul, Germany: Karl-May-Verlag, 1897), 476–478. See also Dominik Melzig, *Der "kranke Mann"*

und sein Freund: Karl Mays Stereotypen als Beitrag zum Orientalismus (Husum, Germany: Hansa Verlag, 2003), 76–77; Schmuhl, "Friedrich Naumann," 503.

59. From Karl May's *Der Kys-Kaptschiji* (1896), cited according to Schmuhl, "Friedrich Naumann," 508; this saying was repeated, for example, in "Summarische 'Lösungen,'" *Germania,* 13 December 1922.

60. Melzig, *Der "kranke Mann,"* 70–79.

61. See Schmuhl, "Friedrich Naumann"; Hans-Walter Schmuhl, "Deutschland, Armenien und die Türkei—Anregungen zu einem kritischen Trialog unter Historikern," in Ischchan Tschiftdschjan, ed., *Stimmen aus Deutschland: Zum 90. Gedenkjahr des Völkermordes an den Armeniern, 1915–2005,* 158–166 (Antelias, Lebanon: Armenian Patriarchate, 2005), 161–162; Kampen, "Studien," xv.

62. Feigel, *Das evangelische Deutschland,* 70.

63. Anderson assumes that he was paid by the Ottomans to write it. His book was also republished in both the Federal Republic of Germany and in the German Democratic Republic. Anderson, "'Down in Turkey,'" 103; Feigel, *Das evangelische Deutschland,* 61. Hans Barth, *Ey Turk Uyan!* (Istanbul: Tarih Encumeni, 2003).

64. Hans Barth, *Türke, wehre Dich!,* 2nd ed. (Leipzig: Rengersche Buchhandlung, 1898), for example, 52; see Feigel, *Das evangelische Deutschland,* 62–63; Meissner, *Martin Rades "Christliche Welt,"* 119.

65. See the following chapters as well as Anderson, "'Down in Turkey,'" 97.

66. Barth, *Türke, wehre Dich!,* iii.

67. Ibid., 18, 20, 59, 68, 70, 71, 148, 152.

68. Ibid., 60, 151–152.

69. Barth, *Türke, wehre Dich!,* 13–14.

70. Ibid., 21.

71. Ibid., 273; Adolf Hitler, "Politik der Woche," *Illustrierter Beobachter,* 24 May 1930, reprinted in Institut für Zeitgeschichte, ed., *Hitler: Reden, Schriften, Anordnungen, Februar 1925 bis Januar 1933,* vol. 2, pt. 1, 202–206 (Munich: K. G. Saur, 1992), 203.

72. Barth, *Türke, wehre Dich!,* 60.

73. Ibid., 35–36.

74. Ibid., 3–4, 28.

75. Ibid., 4.

76. Ibid., 43, similarly 72.

77. Ibid., 34.

78. Ibid., 67.

79. Ibid., 25.

80. Ibid., 26.

81. Meissner, *Martin Rades "Christliche Welt,"* 120.

82. Ibid. In 1913, Barth published yet another article on the topic: Hans Barth, "Die große Türkenhetze," *Militärwochenblatt,* 8 February 1913.

83. Eduard Bernstein, "Die Leiden des armenischen Volkes und die Pflichten Europas," in Helmut Donat, ed., *Armenien, die Türkei und die Pflichten Europas,* 19–55 (Bremen: Donat Verlag, 2005), 21.

84. Bernstein, "Die Leiden," 33; Feigel, *Das evangelische Deutschland,* 97.

85. Bernstein, "Die Leiden," 25–26, 34.

86. Paul Rohrbach, "Deutschland unter den Armeniern," *Preußische Jahrbücher* 96 (1899): 308–329, as quoted in Elizabeth Khorikian, "Die Behandlung des Völkermordes an den Armeniern in der deutschen Presse und Literatur um 1915–1925," in Armenuhi Drost-Abgarjan, ed., *Armenologie in Deutschland,* 159–172 (Münster: LIT Verlag, 2005), 161.

87. Marschall to Hohenlohe, 14 September 1899, as quoted in Saupp, "Das Deutsche Reich," 163.

88. Bülow to Wangenheim, 24 July 1902, as quoted in ibid., 164.

89. "Es anti-pogromelt wieder," *Deutsche Zeitung,* 6 August 1906.

90. Meissner, *Martin Rades "Christliche Welt,"* 172.

4. From Revolution to Abyss

1. Norbert Saupp, "Das Deutsche Reich und die Armenische Frage, 1878–1914" (PhD dissertation, University of Cologne, 1990), 167–172; John C. G. Röhl, *Wilhelm II: Der Weg in den Abgrund, 1900–1941* (Munich: C. H. Beck, 2008), 742–743; Eric D. Weitz, *A Century of Genocide: Utopias of Race and Nation* (Princeton, NJ: Princeton University Press, 2005), 182–188.

2. As quoted in Uwe Feigel, *Das evangelische Deutschland und Armenien: Die Armenierhilfe deutscher evangelischer Christen seit dem Ende des 19. Jahrhunderts im Kontext der deutsch-türkischen Beziehungen* (Göttingen, Germany: Vandenhoeck and Ruprecht, 1989), 142; Peter Balakian, *The Burning Tigris: The Armenian Genocide and America's Response* (New York: Harper Perennial, 2004), 144.

3. Raymond Kévorkian, *The Armenian Genocide: A Complete History* (London: IB Tauris, 2012 [2006]), 59.

4. For example, Ernst Jäckh, *Der aufsteigende Halbmond* (Berlin: Die Hilfe, 1911) 141–142; Saupp, "Das Deutsche Reich," 193; Donald Bloxham, *The Great Game of Genocide: Imperialism, Nationalism, and the Destruction of the Ottoman Armenians* (Oxford: Oxford University Press, 2005), 60–61.

5. See the discussion in Kévorkian, *The Armenian Genocide,* 71–117; Vahakn N. Dadrian, *The History of the Armenian Genocide* (New York: Berghahn, 2004 [1995]), 179–183.

6. Feigel, *Das evangelische Deutschland,* 142–143.

7. Marschall to Foreign Office, 19 April 1909, as quoted in Saupp, "Das Deutsche Reich," 184.

8. Saupp, "Das Deutsche Reich," 192.

9. Marschall to Bülow, 31 May 1909, as quoted in ibid., 196.

10. Baudissin to Schoen, 28 April 1909, as quoted in ibid., 187.

11. Axel Meissner, *Martin Rades "Christliche Welt" und Armenien: Bausteine für eine internationale Ethik des Protestantismus* (Berlin: LIT Verlag, 2010) 183.

12. Kévorkian, *The Armenian Genocide,* 105.

13. See Kampen for a discussion of *Die Hilfe* and the *Preussische Jahrbücher,* Wilhelm van Kampen, "Studien zur deutschen Türkeipolitik in der Zeit Wilhelms II." (PhD dissertation, University of Kiel, 1968), 267–279.

14. Saupp, "Das Deutsche Reich," 198–201.

15. Walter Siehe, "Das Gemetzel in Adana—Von einem Augenzeugen," *Reichpost,* 14 April 1909.

16. Kampen, "Studien," 285; Saupp, "Das Deutsche Reich," 178.

17. Jäckh, *Der aufsteigende Halbmond,* 133–134.

18. Ibid., 139.

19. Ibid., 139–140.

20. Albrecht Wirth, "Ein Freund der Türkei," *Der Tag,* 12 November 1909.

21. Hans-Walter Schmuhl, "Friedrich Naumann und die 'armenische Frage'—Die deutsche Öffentlichkeit und die Verfolgung der Armenier vor 1915," in Hans-Lukas Kieser and Dominik J. Schaller, eds., *Der Völkermord an den Armeniern und die Shoah,* 503–516 (Zurich: Chronos, 2002), 523 (quoting Wirth's *Türkei und Persien,* 1912); on Wirth see also Hilmar Kaiser, *Imperialism, Racism, and Development Theories: The Construction of a Dominant Paradigm on Ottoman Armenians* (Ann Arbor: Gomidas Institute, 1997), 17–18.

22. Donald Quataert, "The Age of Reforms," in Halil Inalcik and Donald Quataert, eds., *An Economic and Social History of the Ottoman Empire,* vol. 2, *1600–1914* (Cambridge: Cambridge University Press, 1997), 793–795.

23. Taner Akçam, *The Young Turks' Crime against Humanity: The Armenian Genocide and Ethnic Cleansing in the Ottoman Empire* (Princeton, NJ: Princeton University Press, 2012), 87; Justin McCarthy, *Death and Exile: The Ethnic Cleansing of Ottoman Muslims, 1821–1922* (Princeton, NJ: Darwin Press, 1995), 336.

24. McCarthy, *Death and Exile,* 336.

25. Bloxham, *The Great Game,* 42; McCarthy, *Death and Exile,* 36.

26. Quataert, "Age of Reforms," 69; Bloxham, *The Great Game,* 36; Kampen, "Studien," 7; Wolfgang Gust, *Der Völkermord an den Armeniern: Die Tragödie des ältesten Christenvolkes der Welt* (Munich: Carl Hanser Verlag, 1993), 143; Balakian, *The Burning Tigris,* 157; Davide Rodogno, *Against Massacre: Humanitarian Interventions in the Ottoman Empire, 1815–1914: The Emergence of a European Concept and International Practice* (Princeton, NJ: Princeton University Press, 2012).

27. Dadrian, *The History,* 190.

28. On Lepsius see Rolf Hosfeld, "Johannes Lepsius: Eine deutsche Ausnahme," in Rolf Hosfeld, ed., *Johannes Lepsius: Eine deutsche Ausnahme,* 9–26 (Göttingen, Germany: Wallstein, 2013), 16; M. Rainer Lepsius, "Johannes Lepsius'

politische Ansichten," in ibid., 27–58, here 33–36; Aschot Hayruni, "Johannes Lepsius' armenische Verbindungen," in ibid., 207–226; Kévorkian, *The Armenian Genocide,* 157–158; Hermann Goltz, "Die 'armenischen Reformen' im Osmanischen Reich: Johannes Lepsius und die Gründung der Deutsch-Armenischen Gesellschaft," in Deutsch-Armenische Gesellschaft, eds., *75 Jahre Deutsch-Armenische Gesellschaft* (Mainz: Deutsch-Armenische Gesellschaft, 1989), 4–76; the reforms were widely discussed in the German press; see the coverage reprinted in Yetvart Ficiciyan, ed., *Der Völkermord an den Armeniern im Spiegel der deutschsprachigen Tagespresse (1912–1922)* (Bremen: Donat Verlag, 2015), 21–172.

29. See also Roderic H. Davison, "The Armenian Crisis, 1912–1914," *The American Historical Review* 3 (1948): 481–505; "Die Zukunft der Türkei," *Berliner Tageblatt,* 3 May 1913.

30. As quoted in Gregor Schöllgen, *Imperialismus und Gleichgewicht: Deutschland, England und die orientalische Frage* (Munich: R. Oldenbourg, 1984), 360.

31. Dadrian, *The History,* 187.

32. Wangenheim to the chancellor (24 February 1913), German Foreign Office R 14078; Jagow to Wangenheim (22 April 1913), German Foreign Office R 14078, both in Wolfgang Gust, ed., *The Armenian Genocide—Evidence from the German Foreign Office Archives, 1915–1916* (New York: Berghahn, 2014), 135–139, 139–140.

33. Mustafa Aksakal, *The Ottoman Road to War in 1914: The Ottoman Empire and the First World War* (Cambridge: Cambridge University Press, 2010), 73–74.

34. Margaret Lavinia Anderson, "Who Still Talked about the Extermination of the Armenians?—German Talk and German Silences," in Ronald Grigor Suny, Fatma Müge Göcek, and Norman M. Naimark, eds., *A Question of Genocide: Armenians and Turks at the End of the Ottoman Empire,* 199–217 (Oxford: Oxford University Press, 2011), 201.

35. As quoted in Aksakal, *The Ottoman Road,* 75.

36. Wangenheim to Bethmann, 21 November 1913, as quoted in Norbert Saupp, "Das Deutsche Reich," 216; Kampen, "Studien," 48.

37. Saupp, "Das Deutsche Reich," 202; Kampen, "Studien," 43; see also the private correspondence between State Secretary Jagow and Wangenheim, as quoted in Wolfgang Gust, "Einführung und Leitfaden," in Wolfgang Gust, ed., *Der Völkermord an den Armeniern 1915/1916: Dokumente aud dem Politischen Archiv des deutschen Auswärtigen Amts,* 17–109 (Springe, Germany: Zu Klampen, 2005), 77; see also Aksakal, *The Ottoman Road,* 66–68.

38. Gust, *Die Tragödie,* 151.

39. Aksakal, *The Ottoman Road,* 80–83; Christopher Clark, *The Sleepwalkers: How Europe Went to War in 1914* (London: Allen Lane, 2012), 338–349.

40. Dadrian, *History,* 193.

41. Ibid., 194–195; Gust, *Die Tragödie,* 165.

5. Notions of Total War

1. As quoted in Raymond Kévorkian, *The Armenian Genocide: A Complete History* (London: IB Tauris, 2012 [2006]), 196.

2. See, for example, Wilhelm van Kampen, "Studien zur deutschen Türkeipolitik in der Zeit Wilhelms II." (PhD dissertation, University of Kiel, 1968), 265; Isabel V. Hull, *Absolute Destruction: Military Culture and the Practices of War in Imperial Germany* (Ithaca, NY: Cornell University Press, 2006), 207–208, 218; Eric D. Weitz, *A Century of Genocide: Utopias of Race and Nation* (Princeton, NJ: Princeton University Press, 2005), 4. For examples from the press, see "Die Abreise des französischen und englischen Botschafters auf Konstantinopel," *Neue Preussische (Kreuz-)Zeitung*, 2 November 1914; "Italien und die Türkei," *Neue Preussische (Kreuz-)Zeitung*, 5 November 1914; Wilhelm Bela, "Die Feuerprobe der neuen Türkei," *Königsberger Hartungsche Zeitung*, 8 November 1914; "Sasonows Dumarede: Eine Rechtfertigung der türkischen Politik," *Neue Preussische (Kreuz-)Zeitung*, 15 February 1915; "Englands Kampf gegen die Türkei," *Die Post*, 3 January 1915.

3. For example, "Die Vorbereitungen am Suezkanal," *Neue Preussische (Kreuz-)Zeitung*, 6 November 1914.

4. "Sieg oder Untergang," *Deutsche Tageszeitung*, 11 November 1914.

5. See Winter, "Under the Cover of War."

6. On the German officers in the Ottoman Empire before and during World War I see Eberhard Diehm, "Zwischen Kulturkonflikt und Akkulturation: Deutsche Offiziere im Osmanischen Reich," *Zeitschrift für Geschichtswissenschaft* 8 (2005): 691–715.

7. John Horne and Alan Kramer, *German Atrocities, 1914: A History of Denial* (New Haven, CT: Yale University Press, 2001), 141–145; Hull, *Absolute Destruction*, 117–118.

8. Christopher Clark, *Iron Kingdom: The Rise and Downfall of Prussia, 1600–1947* (London: Penguin, 2007), 579.

9. Horne and Kramer, *German Atrocities*, 89–174.

10. Ibid., 23.

11. Ibid., 95.

12. Ibid., 134–136.

13. Hull, *Absolute Destruction*, 119–120.

14. Colmar Freiherr von der Goltz, *Das Volk in Waffen*, 5th ed. (Berlin: R. v. Deckers Verlag, 1899).

15. Şükrü M. Hanioğlu, *Atatürk: An Intellectual Biography* (Princeton, NJ: Princeton University Press, 2011), 187; Hull, *Absolute Destruction*, 270–271; Hans-Lukas Kieser, "Germany and the Armenian Genocide of 1915–1917," in Jonathan C. Friedman, *The Routledge History of the Holocaust*, 30–44 (London: Routledge, 2012), 31.

16. Hull, *Absolute Destruction*, 121.

17. Ibid.

18. As quoted in ibid.

19. Ibid., 231.

20. Ibid., 211.

21. Wolfgang Gust, *Der Völkermord an den Armeniern: Die Tragödie des ältesten Christenvolkes der Welt* (Munich: Carl Hanser Verlag, 1993), 337.

22. See Wolfgang Gust, "Einführung und Leitfaden," in Wolfgang Gust, ed., *Der Völkermord an den Armeniern 1915/1916: Dokumente aud dem Politischen Archiv des deutschen Auswärtigen Amts,* 17–109 (Springe, Germany: Zu Klampen, 2005), 92.

23. Horne and Kramer, *German Atrocities,* 143–144.

24. Hull, *Absolute Destruction,* 166.

25. For example, ibid., 231.

26. Tilman Lüdke, *Jihad Made in Germany: Ottoman and German Propaganda and Intelligence Operations in the First World War* (Münster: LIT Verlag, 2005); Sean McMeekin, *The Berlin-Baghdad Express: The Ottoman Empire and Germany's Bid for World Power, 1898–1918* (London: Penguin, 2011); Wolfgang G. Schwanitz, "Djihad 'Made in Germany': Der Streit um den heiligen Krieg, 1914–1915," *Sozial. Geschichte* 18 (2003): 7–34, here 10–11; Donald M. McKale, *War by Revolution—Germany and Great Britain in the Middle East in the Era of World War I* (Kent, OH: Kent State University Press, 1998).

27. "Der Islam aus dem Schlaf erwacht," *Neue Preussische (Kreuz-)Zeitung,* 7 October 1914.

28. Here are but a few examples from the *Kreuzzeitung:* "Die asiatischen Muselmanen und der Krieg," *Neue Preussische (Kreuz-)Zeitung,* 13 November 1914; "Türkische Erfolge an der kaukasischen und persischen Grenze," *Neue Preussische (Kreuz-)Zeitung,* 16 November 1914; "Das Fetwa i Scherif," *Neue Preussische (Kreuz-)Zeitung,* 16 November 1914; "Der afghanische Aufmarsch gegen Indien," *Neue Preussische (Kreuz-)Zeitung,* 17 November 1914; "Verkündigung des Heiligen Krieges an der Kaaba," *Neue Preussische (Kreuz-)Zeitung,* 29 November 1914; "Der Eindruck des Dschihad an den heiligen Stätten des Islam," *Neue Preussische (Kreuz-)Zeitung,* 1 December 1914; "Russische Angriffe von den Türken zurückgewiesen," *Neue Preussische (Kreuz-)Zeitung,* 11 December 1914; "Afghanistan und der Sudan im Gefolge des Kalifen," *Neue Preussische (Kreuz-)Zeitung,* 12 December 1914; "Der Dschihad," *Neue Preussische (Kreuz-)Zeitung,* 15 December 1914; "Die Leistungen der türkischen Armee," *Neue Preussische (Kreuz-)Zeitung,* 17 December 1914; "Türkische Erfolge über die Russen," *Neue Preussische (Kreuz-)Zeitung,* 18 December 1914; "Die Furcht vor dem türkischen Einfall in Aegypten," *Neue Preussische (Kreuz-)Zeitung,* 22 January 1915; "Der Krieg im Orient," *Neue Preussische (Kreuz-)Zeitung,* 10 February 1915.

29. Bülow, 13 November 1905, as quoted in Gregor Schöllgen, *Imperialismus und Gleichgewicht: Deutschland, England und die orientalische Frage* (Munich: R. Oldenbourg, 1984), 199.

30. McMeekin, *The Berlin-Baghdad Express,* 125.

31. For example, "Die Türken im Kaukasus," *Neue Preussische (Kreuz-)Zeitung,* 14 December 1914; "Türkische Erfolge in Armenien und im Kaukasus," *Neue Preussische (Kreuz-)Zeitung,* 29 December 1914; "Die Türken im Kaukasus," *Neue Preussische (Kreuz-)Zeitung,* 1 January 1915; "Weitere türkische Erfolge," *Neue Preussische (Kreuz-)Zeitung,* 4 January 1915.

32. "Beschießung von Batum durch die türkische Flotte," *Neue Preussische (Kreuz-)Zeitung,* 12 December 1914.

33. Ibid.

34. For example, "Der Dschihad," *Neue Preussische (Kreuz-)Zeitung,* 15 December 1914; "Die Türken am Suezkanal," *Neue Preussische (Kreuz-)Zeitung,* 7 February 1915; "Neue Kämpfe an der russisch-persischen Grenze," *Neue Preussische (Kreuz-)Zeitung,* 12 February 1915.

35. Horne and Kramer, *German Atrocities,* 1, 229–261, 291–325.

36. Ibid., 291.

37. Helmut von Gerlach in his memoirs, as quoted in David Welch, *Germany, Propaganda and Total War, 1914–1918* (New Brunswick, NJ: Rutgers University Press, 2000), 61.

38. Welch, *Germany, Propaganda and Total War,* 61.

39. Ibid., 61–62.

40. For example: "Fortdauer der türkischen Offensive am Kaukasus," *Neue Preussische (Kreuz-)Zeitung,* 11 November 1914; "Russischer Überfall auf das türkische Konsulat in Urmia," *Neue Preussische (Kreuz-)Zeitung,* 11 December 1914; "Afghanistan und der Sudan im Gefolge des Kalifen," *Neue Preussische (Kreuz-)Zeitung,* 12 December 1914; "Die Türken im Kaukasus," *Neue Preussische (Kreuz-)Zeitung,* 14 December 1914; "Türkische Erfolge und russischer Völkerrechtsbruch," *Neue Preussische (Kreuz-)Zeitung,* 8 January 1915; "Rußlands Achtung vor dem Völkerrecht," *Neue Preussische (Kreuz-)Zeitung,* 18 January 1915; "Die türkische Offensive im Kaukasus," *Neue Preussische (Kreuz-)Zeitung,* 28 January 1915.

41. For example: "Der türkische Kampfbericht," *Neue Preussische (Kreuz-)Zeitung,* 15 October 1915; "Völkerrechtsverletzungen gegen die Türkei," *Neue Preussische (Kreuz-)Zeitung,* 26 October 1915; "Entente-Granaten auf türkische Spitäler," *Neue Preussische (Kreuz-)Zeitung,* 7 December 1915.

42. For example: "Der Dschihad," *Neue Preussische (Kreuz-)Zeitung,* 15 December 1914; "Türkische Vergeltungsmaßregeln," *Neue Preussische (Kreuz-)Zeitung,* 28 June 1915.

43. "Russengreuel in Armenien," *Neue Preussische (Kreuz-)Zeitung,* 21 March 1916.

44. Horne and Kramer, *German Atrocities,* 84; McMeekin, *The Berlin-Baghdad Express,* 346.

45. Margaret Lavinia Anderson, "Who Still Talked about the Extermination of the Armenians? Imperial Germany and the Armenian Genocide," *Bulletin of the German Historical Institute* 49 (2011): 9–29, here 16.

46. For example: "Drangsalierung der russischen Juden," *Neue Preussische (Kreuz-)Zeitung,* 12 January 1915; "30000 vertriebene Juden in Warschau," *Neue Preus-*

sische (Kreuz-)Zeitung, 9 March 1915; see also the *Münchner Neueste Nachrichten* on 28 May 1915, as cited in Welch, *Germany, Propaganda and Total War,* 62.

47. Welch, *Germany, Propaganda and Total War,* 62, 273–274.
48. Ibid., 62.
49. Here are but a few examples: "Haltlose Verleumdungen gegen die Türkei," *Neue Preussische (Kreuz-)Zeitung,* 15 December 1914; Georg Kleibömer, "Brief aus Konstantinopel," *Neue Preussische (Kreuz-)Zeitung,* 29 December 1914, also in the *Rheinisch-Westfälische Zeitung,* 5 December 1914; "Türkische Erfolge," *Neue Preussische (Kreuz-)Zeitung,* 2 February 1915; "Der Lügenfeldzug der Entente gegen die Türkei," *Neue Preussische (Kreuz-)Zeitung,* 15 January 1915; "Christen und Fremde in der Türkei," *Vossische Zeitung,* 15 January 1915; "Keine Griechenverhaftungen in Konstantinopel," *Neue Preussische (Kreuz-)Zeitung,* 17 March 1915; "Griechische Märchen," *Neue Preussische (Kreuz-)Zeitung,* 4 June 1915; "Keine Griechenverfolgungen in der Türkei," *Neue Preussische (Kreuz-)Zeitung,* 27 July 1915. For reference to Germany as a "protective shield," see Vahakn N. Dadrian, *The History of the Armenian Genocide* (New York: Berghahn, 2004 [1995]), 204.
50. "Der Dritte im Bunde," *Neue Preussische (Kreuz-)Zeitung,* 2 May 1915.
51. "Englischer Greuelschwindel," *Der Tag,* 6 July 1915.
52. McKale, *War by Revolution.*
53. Gust, *Die Tragödie,* 157; Johannes Lepsius, *Bericht über die Lage des Armenischen Volkes in der Türkei* (Potsdam, Germany: Tempelverlag, 1916; Bad Schussenried, Germany: Gerhard Hess Verlag, 2011), 178. Citations refer to the 2011 edition.
54. Gust, *Die Tragödie,* 211.
55. McMeekin, *The Berlin-Baghdad Express,* 90; McKale, *War by Revolution,* 6.
56. Gust, *Die Tragödie,* 162; McMeekin, *The Berlin-Baghdad Express,* 179.
57. Donald Bloxham, *The Great Game of Genocide: Imperialism, Nationalism, and the Destruction of the Ottoman Armenians* (Oxford: Oxford University Press, 2005), 75–76.
58. See, for example, Stephan H. Astourian, "The Silence of the Land: Agrarian Relations, Ethnicity, and Power," in Ronald Grigor Suny, Fatma Müge Göcek, and Norman M. Naimark, eds., *A Question of Genocide: Armenians and Turks at the End of the Ottoman Empire* (Oxford: Oxford University Press, 2011), 55–81.
59. On the Armenian parties, see Gerard J. Libaridian, "What Was Revolutionary about Armenian Revolutionary Parties in the Ottoman Empire?," in Suny et al., *A Question of Genocide,* 82–112.
60. Bloxham, *The Great Game,* 80, 90–91.
61. Ibid., 17; on the so-called provocation thesis, see Ronald Grigor Suny, "Writing Genocide: The Fate of the Ottoman Armenians," in Suny et al., *A Question of Genocide,* 15–41, here 24–28.

62. See, for example, Axel Meissner, *Martin Rades "Christliche Welt" und Armenien: Bausteine für eine internationale Ethik des Protestantismus* (Berlin: LIT Verlag, 2010), 157–162.

63. Friedrich Scherer, *Adler und Halbmond: Bismarck und der Orient, 1878–1890* (Paderborn, Germany: Ferdinand Schöningh, 2001), 380–381.

64. Hull, *Absolute Destruction,* 214.

65. Bloxham, *The Great Game,* 208.

66. For example, Mehmet Cebeci, *Die deutsch-türkischen Beziehungen in der Epoche Abdülhamids II. (1876–1908): Die Rolle Deutschlands in der türkischen Außenpolitik* (Marburg, Germany: Tectum, 2010), 259–261, 266, 269.

67. Dadrian, *History,* 105.

68. Cebeci, *Die deutsch-türkischen Beziehungen,* 299.

69. Taner Akçam, *The Young Turks' Crime against Humanity: The Armenian Genocide and Ethnic Cleansing in the Ottoman Empire* (Princeton, NJ: Princeton University Press, 2012), 48–50, 242–253.

70. See ibid., 254–255.

71. Christoph Dinkel, "German Officers and the Armenian Genocide," *The Armenian Review* 1 (1991): 77–132, here 115–116.

6. Dispatches from Erzurum

1. As quoted in Elizabeth Khorikian, "Die Behandlung des Völkermordes an den Armeniern in der deutschen Presse und Literatur um 1915–1925," in Armenuhi Drost-Abgarjan, ed., *Armenologie in Deutschland,* 159–172 (Münster: LIT Verlag, 2005), 170; Reinhard M. G. Nickisch, *Armin T. Wegner: Ein Dichter gegen die Macht* (Wuppertal, Germany: Hammer, 1982), 51–52.

2. According to Gust, it was only Consul Heinrich Bergfeld at Trebizond who did not protest and who approved of the deportations. Wolfgang Gust, "Einführung und Leitfaden," in Wolfgang Gust, ed., *Der Völkermord an den Armeniern 1915/1916: Dokumente aud dem Politischen Archiv des deutschen Auswärtigen Amts,* 17–109 (Springe, Germany: Zu Klampen, 2005), 78.

3. See Rouben Paul Adalian, "American Diplomatic Correspondence in the Age of Mass Murder: The Armenian Genocide in the US Archives," in Jay Winter, ed., *America and the Armenian Genocide* (Cambridge: Cambridge University Press, 2003), 146–184.

4. Gust, "Einführung und Leitfaden," 22.

5. Ibid.

6. On the controversy at the time, as well as in the historiography, see Sean McMeekin, *The Berlin-Baghdad Express: The Ottoman Empire and Germany's Bid for World Power, 1898–1918* (London: Penguin, 2011), 256; Isabel V. Hull, *Absolute Destruction: Military Culture and the Practices of War in Imperial Germany* (Ithaca, NY: Cornell University Press, 2006), 276, 279–280; Vahakn N. Dadrian, *German Responsibility in the Armenian Genocide* (Watertown, MA: Blue Crane Books, 1996), 131–133; for more allegations of Germany's

erasure of archival records from Turkey, see ibid., 153, 158–160; for the Ottoman side, see Wolfgang Gust, *Der Völkermord an den Armeniern: Die Tragödie des ältesten Christenvolkes der Welt* (Munich: Carl Hanser Verlag, 1993), 22; Taner Akçam, *The Young Turks' Crime against Humanity: The Armenian Genocide and Ethnic Cleansing in the Ottoman Empire* (Princeton, NJ: Princeton University Press, 2012), 1–27.

7. Paul Leverkuehn, *Posten auf ewiger Wache: Aus dem abenteurreichen Leben des Max von Scheubner-Richter* (Essen, Germany: Essener Verlagsanstalt, 1938), 21–22.

8. Hull, *Absolute Destruction,* 289. See also the recent biography of the other German consul who intensively lobbied his embassy for the Armenians: Kai Seyffarth, *Entscheidung in Aleppo: Walter Rössler (1871–1929), Helfer der verfolgten Armenier* (Bremen: Donat Verlag, 2015).

9. Wangenheim to chancellor (15 November 1913), German Foreign Office R 14082, in Wolfgang Gust, ed., *The Armenian Genocide—Evidence from the German Foreign Office Archives, 1915–1916* (New York: Berghahn, 2014), 135–139, 140–146.

10. Secretary of State of the Foreign Office (Jagow) to the embassy in Constantinople (15 January 1914), German Foreign Office R 14083, in Gust, ed., *Armenian Genocide,* 146–147.

11. Ibid.

12. Wangenheim to the chancellor (29 December 1914), German Foreign Office R 14085, in Gust, ed., *Armenian Genocide,* 149–150. My versions quoted here conform mostly to the German original. I have used and quoted the English version as published by Gust wherever possible, even where I have used my own translation, and thus the text reproduced here does not always conform to the cited English source. For the original consult the version in the German version of Gust's source edition. If the quoted documents are available in neither of the two published source collections but in the online portal also published by Wolfgang Gust, then this will be cited here. Only in the instances in which the document in question is published nowhere will the archival citation be given exclusively. Gust, ed., *Der Völkermord;* Wolfgang Gust, ed., *Armenocide: Documents from the State Archives,* online at www .armenocide.net.

13. See Kaiser's work on both Scheubner and Erzurum as well as on German diplomatic denial: Hilmar Kaiser, " 'A Scene from the Inferno': The Armenians of Erzerum and the Genocide, 1915–1916," in Hans-Lukas Kieser and Dominik J. Schaller, eds., *Der Völkermord an den Armeniern und die Shoah* (Zurich: Chronos, 2002), 129–186; Hilmar Kaiser, "Denying the Armenian Genocide: The German Connection," *Journal of the Society for Armenian Studies* 9 (1999): 37–53, here 49–50; Hilmar Kaiser, "Historical Introduction," in Gomidas Institute, ed., *Paul Leverkuehn: A German Officer during the Armenian Genocide* (London: Gomidas Institute, 2008), xv–cxiv.

14. See Scheubner to embassy (3 March 1915), German Foreign Office, Kon 168, in Gust, *Armenocide* (online).

15. Gust, *Die Tragödie*, 225.

16. Dadrian, *German Responsibility*, 29–34.

17. Ibid., 35.

18. Scheubner to embassy (24 April 1915), German Foreign Office, Kon 168, in Gust, *Armenocide* (online).

19. Note by Mordtmann (26 April 1915), German Foreign Office, Kon 168, in ibid.

20. Scheubner to embassy (26 April 1915), German Foreign Office, Kon 168, in ibid.

21. Scheubner to embassy (26 April 1915), German Foreign Office, Kon 168, in ibid.

22. Wangenheim to Consulate Erzerum (28 April 1915), German Foreign Office Kon 168, in Gust, *Armenian Genocide*, 174.

23. Wangenheim to Bethman-Hollweg (30 April 1915), German Foreign Office, R 14085, in Gust, *Armenocide* (online).

24. Scheubner-Richter to Wangenheim (15 May 1915), German Foreign Office Kon 168, in Gust, *Armenian Genocide*, 177–180.

25. Hull, *Absolute Destruction*, 288.

26. Scheubner-Richter to Wangenheim (15 May 1915), German Foreign Office Kon 168, in Gust, *Armenian Genocide*, 177–180.

27. Scheubner to embassy (15 May 1915), German Foreign Office, Kon 168, in Gust, *Armenocide* (online).

28. Scheubner to embassy (16 May 1915), German Foreign Office, Kon 168, in ibid.

29. Scheubner to embassy (17 May 1915), German Foreign Office, Kon 168, in ibid.

30. Scheubner to embassy (18 May 1915), German Foreign Office, Kon 168, in ibid.

31. Wangenheim to Scheubner (19 May 1915), German Foreign Office Kon 168, in Gust, *Armenian Genocide*, 183–184.

32. Scheubner-Richter to Wangenheim (20 May 1915), German Foreign Office Kon 169, in ibid., 184–185.

33. Ibid.

34. John Horne and Alan Kramer, *German Atrocities, 1914: A History of Denial* (New Haven, CT: Yale University Press, 2001), 33.

35. As quoted in Christoph Dinkel, "German Officers and the Armenian Genocide," *The Armenian Review* 1 (1991): 77–132, here 82; Dadrian, *German Responsibility*, 121–122.

36. Scheubner-Richter to Wangenheim (20 May 1915), German Foreign Office Kon 169, in Gust, *Armenian Genocide*, 184–185.

37. As quoted in Dinkel, "German Officers," 105.

38. Scheubner-Richter to Wangenheim (22 May 1915), German Foreign Office Kon 169, in Gust, *Armenian Genocide,* 186–188.

39. Wangenheim to chancellor (27 May 1915), German Foreign Office R 14086, in ibid., 188–193.

40. Wangenheim to Scheubner (29 May 1915), German Foreign Office, Kon 168, in Gust, *Armenocide* (online).

41. Buege to Wangenheim, and reply (18 May and 21 May 1915), German Foreign Office Kon 169, in Gust, *Armenian Genocide,* 183.

42. Scheubner to Wangenheim (24 May 1915), German Foreign Office, Kon 168, in Gust, *Armenocide* (online).

43. Scheubner-Richter to embassy (4 June 1915), German Foreign Office Kon 169, in Gust, *Der Völkermord,* 156.

44. Answer Wangenheim to Scheubner-Richter (4 June 1915), German Foreign Office Kon 169, in Gust, *Armenian Genocide,* 197.

45. Scheubner to Wangenheim (2 June 1915), German Foreign Office, Kon 169, in Gust, *Armenocide* (online).

46. Ibid.

47. Scheubner-Richter to embassy and reply (2 June 1915), German Foreign Office Kon 169, in Gust, *Armenian Genocide,* 195.

48. Ibid.

49. Scheubner to Wangenheim (10 June 1915), German Foreign Office, Kon 169, in Gust, *Armenocide* (online).

50. Scheubner to Wangenheim (18 June 1915), German Foreign Office, Kon 169, in ibid.

51. Wangenheim to Scheubner-Richter (21 June 1915), German Foreign Office Kon 169, in Gust, *Armenian Genocide,* 212.

52. Note by Mordtmann (6 June 1915), German Foreign Office, Kon 169, in Gust, *Armenian Genocide,* 205.

53. Note by Mordtmann (30 June 1915), German Foreign Office, Kon 169, in ibid., 225–226.

54. Wangenheim to Foreign Office (2 July 1915), German Foreign Office, R 14086, in ibid., 229; Wangenheim to chancellor (7 July 1915), German Foreign Office, R 14086, in ibid., 230.

55. Scheubner to Wangenheim (26 June 1915), German Foreign Office, Kon 169, in Gust, *Armenocide* (online).

56. Scheubner to Wangenheim (30 June 1915), German Foreign Office, Kon 169, in ibid.

57. Scheubner to Wangenheim (30 June 1915), German Foreign Office, Kon 169, in ibid.

58. Scheubner to Wangenheim and reply (1 July 1915), German Foreign Office, Kon 169, in ibid.

59. Scheubner to Wangenheim (7 July 1915), German Foreign Office, Kon 169, in ibid.

60. Scheubner to Wangenheim and reply (5 July 1915), German Foreign Office, Kon 169, in ibid.

61. Scheubner to Wangenheim and replies (8 July 1915), German Foreign Office, Kon 169, in ibid.

62. Scheubner to Wangenheim and replies (7/14 July 1915), German Foreign Office, Kon 169, in ibid.

63. Scheubner to Wangenheim and replies (27 July 1915), German Foreign Office, Kon 170, in ibid.

64. Scheubner to Wangenheim (28 July 1915), German Foreign Office Kon 170, in Gust, *Armenian Genocide,* 272–273.

65. Scheubner-Richter to Hohenlohe-Langenburg (5 August 1915), German Foreign Office R 14088, in ibid., 278–285.

66. Ibid.

67. Scheubner-Richter to chancellor (10 August 1915), German Foreign Office, R 14088, in Gust, *Armenian Genocide,* 295–298.

68. Ibid.

69. Ibid.

70. Ibid.

71. Neurath to chancellor (9 November 1915), German Foreign Office Kon 171, in ibid., 445–446.

72. Scheubner to chancellor (4 December 1916), German Foreign Office R 14094, in Gust, *Armenian Genocide,* 691–695.

73. Ibid.

74. Rolf Hosfeld, *Operation Nemesis: Die Türkei, Deutschland und der Völkermord an den Armeniern* (Cologne: Kiepenheuer and Witsch, 2005), 254–255.

75. Ibid., 255.

76. Ibid.

77. Viscount d'Abernon, *An Ambassador of Peace,* vol. 1, *From Spa (1920) to Rapallo (1922)* (London: Hodder and Stoughton, 1929), 174.

78. Wangenheim to chancellor (7 July 1915), German Foreign Office R 14086, in Gust, *Armenian Genocide,* 229–231.

79. Ibid.

80. Rössler to chancellor (29 June 1915), German Foreign Office R 14086, in ibid., 217–221.

81. Wangenheim to chancellor (9 July 1915), German Foreign Office R 14086, in ibid., 239–240.

82. Correspondent of the *Kölnische Zeitung* to Foreign Office (5 September 1915), German Foreign Office R 14086, in Gust, *Armenian Genocide,* 361–372; Gust, "Einführung und Leitfaden," 35.

83. Jäckh to Zimmermann, 17 October 1915, as quoted in Norbert Saupp, "Das Deutsche Reich und die Armenische Frage, 1878–1914" (PhD dissertation, University of Cologne, 1990), 225.

84. Dadrian, *German Responsibility,* 83; Margaret Lavinia Anderson, "Who Still Talked about the Extermination of the Armenians?—German Talk and

German Silences," in Ronald Grigor Suny, Fatma Müge Göcek, and Norman M. Naimark, eds., *A Question of Genocide: Armenians and Turks at the End of the Ottoman Empire* (Oxford: Oxford University Press, 2011), 212.

85. Neurath to chancellor (12 November 1915), German Foreign Office R 14089, in Gust, *Armenian Genocide*, 455–458.

86. Kaiser also mentioned other Germans who put their own lives in jeopardy in order to help the Armenians (like an employee of the Vacuum Oil Company), Hilmar Kaiser, "Die deutsche Diplomatie und der armenische Völkermord," in Fikret Adanir and Bernd Bonwetsch, eds., *Osmanismus, Nationalismus und der Kaukasus*, 203–235 (Wiesbaden, Germany: Reichert Verlag, 2005), 208.

87. Dadrian, *German Responsibility*, 148; Hull, *Absolute Destruction*, 265.

88. Though Dadrian depicts him as an Armenian hater and coinstigator of the genocide. Liman had also deported Greeks from the vicinity of the Gallipoli front, but then had the survivors return. Dadrian, *German Responsibility*, 125–126; Hull, *Absolute Destruction*, 286–287.

89. Hull, *Absolute Destruction*, 287.

90. McMeekin, *The Berlin-Baghdad Express*, 256–257.

91. For his letters home, see Hilmar Kaiser, ed., *Eberhard Count Wolfskeel von Reichenberg: Zeitoun, Mousa Dagh, Ourfa—Letters on the Armenian Genocide* (Princeton, NJ: Gomidas Institute, 2001).

92. Padel to embassy (30 March 1915), German Foreign Office Kon 168, in Gust, *Armenian Genocide*, 160.

93. Dadrian, *German Responsibility*, 58; Gust, "Einführung und Leitfaden," 89.

94. This is the title of chapter 3 of Donald Bloxham, *The Great Game of Genocide: Imperialism, Nationalism, and the Destruction of the Ottoman Armenians* (Oxford: Oxford University Press, 2005), 115–133.

95. See also Weitz's analysis of the thesis of German responsibility, Eric D. Weitz, "Germany and the Young Turks: Revolutionaries into Statesmen," in Suny et al., *A Question of Genocide*, 175–198, especially 176–177.

96. See discussion by Weitz, "Germany and the Young Turks," 371n53.

97. Gust, *Die Tragödie*, 268.

98. Saupp, "Das Deutsche Reich," 228.

99. Bloxham, *The Great Game of Genocide*, 115–116.

100. Ulrich Trumpener, *Germany and the Ottoman Empire, 1914–1918* (Princeton, NJ: Princeton University Press, 1968), 269.

101. Bloxham, *The Great Game*, 125–126.

102. Grigoris Balakian, *Armenian Golgotha: A Memoir of the Armenian Genocide, 1915–1918*, translated by Peter Balakian with Aris Sevag (New York: Vintage Books, 2010), 271, 279–281.

103. Gust, *Die Tragödie*, 272; Dadrian, *German Responsibility*, 146; for general information on Humann: Frank G. Weber, *Eagles on the Crescent: Germany, Austria, and the Diplomacy of the Turkish Alliance* (Ithaca, NY: Cornell University Press, 1970), 25–26; Franz von Papen, *Der Wahrheit eine Gasse*

(Munich: List, 1952), 89; Gust, "Einführung und Leitfaden," 93; also, Anderson, "Who Still Talked," 199–217, here 204.

104. Dinkel, "German Officers," 113; Dadrian, *German Responsibility,* 147; Bloxham, *The Great Game,* 116.

105. Dinkel, "German Officers," 114–115.

106. McMeekin, *The Berlin-Baghdad Express,* 260.

107. Hull, *Absolute Destruction,* 276; Dinkel, "German Officers," 96; Otto von Feldmann, "Zum Talaatprozess," *Deutsche Allgemeine Zeitung,* 30 June 1921.

108. Maximilian Pfeiffer to Foreign Office and notes and answers (22 February–6 June 1918), German Foreign Office, R 13200, in Gust, *Armenian Genocide,* 719–722.

7. "Interlude of the Gods"

1. See, on Lepsius's trip, Zimmermann to Wangenheim (6 June 1915), German Foreign Office, R 14086, in Wolfgang Gust, ed., *The Armenian Genocide—Evidence from the German Foreign Office Archives, 1915–1916* (New York: Berghahn, 2014), 165.

2. Ambassador in Constantinople (Wangenheim) to the Foreign Office, 2 July 1915, plus answer by Zimmermann, 4 July 1915, in ibid., 229.

3. See Lepsius's published account: Johannes Lepsius, "Mein Besuch in Konstantinopel Juli/August 1915," *Der Orient* 1, no. 3 (1919): 21–33. The following is my own translation of the German original, but I have used the English translation (1934) as a guideline: Franz Werfel, *Die vierzig Tage des Musa Dagh* (Berlin: Aufbau-Verlag, 1987 [1933]), 127–149; Franz Werfel, *The Forty Days of Musa Dagh* (New York: Viking Press, 1934), 123–146. See also Hermann Goltz, "Bericht zum Abschluss der durch die Volkswagenstiftung geförderten Edition," in Armenuhi Drost-Abgarjan, ed., *Armenologie in Deutschland,* 77–172 (Münster: LIT Verlag, 2005), 91; Uwe Feigel, *Das evangelische Deutschland und Armenien: Die Armenierhilfe deutscher evangelischer Christen seit dem Ende des 19. Jahrhunderts im Kontext der deutsch-türkischen Beziehungen* (Göttingen, Germany: Vandenhoeck and Ruprecht, 1989), 212–213.

4. Lepsius's published account does not mention the statement about Morgenthau. It also does not discuss much the allegations of treason. Lepsius seems to have given up even faster in reality than his fictionalized self did. He remarks on the alleged rebellions that "not even under a magnifying glass [did they amount] to anything." Lepsius, "Mein Besuch," 26.

5. Christoph Dinkel, "German Officers and the Armenian Genocide," *The Armenian Review* 1 (1991): 77–132, here 82; Vahakn N. Dadrian, *German Responsibility in the Armenian Genocide: A Review of the Historical Evidence of German Complicity* (Watertown, MA: Blue Crane Books, 1996), 121–122, here 85.

6. Rolf Hosfeld, *Operation Nemesis: Die Türkei, Deutschland und der Völkermord an den Armeniern* (Cologne: Kiepenheuer and Witsch, 2005), 254.

7. Ibid.

8. Ibid.

9. Ibid.

10. Lepsius's Armenian Society had withdrawn funding at the last minute and it was up to him and Paul Rohrbach to fund and organize its publication. The report was also published in French already in 1918, translated by Agathon Bey, the secretary of Boghos Nubar Pasha in Paris, as well as in Dutch, also during the war. Hosfeld, *Operation Nemesis*, 257–258; Feigel, *Das evangelische Deutschland*, 219–220; Johannes Lepsius, *Bericht über die Lage des Armenischen Volkes in der Türkei* (Potsdam, Germany: Tempelverlag, 1916; Bad Schussenried, Germany: Gerhard Hess Verlag, 2011). Citations refer to the 2011 edition.

11. Apparently, of those intended for the parliamentarians, 191 copies had been confiscated by the Berlin police. Axel Meissner, *Martin Rades "Christliche Welt" und Armenien: Bausteine für eine internationale Ethik des Protestantismus* (Berlin: LIT Verlag, 2010), 231; Margaret Lavinia Anderson, "Who Still Talked about the Extermination of the Armenians?—German Talk and German Silences," in Ronald Grigor Suny, Fatma Müge Göcek, and Norman M. Naimark, eds., *A Question of Genocide: Armenians and Turks at the End of the Ottoman Empire*, 199–217 (Oxford: Oxford University Press, 2011), 214; Elizabeth Khorikian, "Die Behandlung des Völkermordes an den Armeniern in der deutschen Presse und Literatur um 1915–1925," in Drost-Abgarjan, ed., *Armenologie in Deutschland*, 159–172, here 167.

12. Mike Joseph, "Max Erwin von Scheubner-Richter: The Personal Link from Genocide to Hitler," in Hans-Lukas Kieser and Elmar Plozza, eds., *Der Völkermord an den Armeniern, die Türkei und Europa*, 147–165 (Zurich: Chronos, 2006), 152.

13. Johannes Lepsius, "Was hat man den Armeniern getan? Die Zeit zu reden ist gekommen," *Aus der Arbeit von Dr. Johannes Lepsius* 11, no. 12 (September/December 1918): 113–118, here 115.

14. See, for example, ibid.

15. Ibid., 134–135.

16. Ibid., 157.

17. Ibid., 98, 156, 244–245.

18. Already before the war was over, Wegner gave his first slideshow lectures on what he had seen in the Ottoman Empire. His "With von der Goltz in Mesopotamia" slideshow lecture was first delivered in front of officers of the Silesian branch of the German-Turkish Association on 9 February 1918, thus when the Great War was still raging on and censorship was still in full force. In it, Wegner had already alluded to Armenian suffering during the "deportations." His biographers were to assert that this lecture, sponsored by Goltz's widow, was not a "brave" one, as Wegner presented pro-Turkish justifications of the genocide as his own. They, however, also assert that Wegner did that in order not to share the fate of Lepsius, who had to flee to the Netherlands after his

clandestine report on the Armenians had been published. Andreas Meier, "Nachwort," in Andreas Meier, ed., *Armin T. Wegner: Die Austreibung des armenischen Volkes in die Wüste—Ein Lichtbildvortrag,* 153–192 (Göttingen, Germany: Wallstein, 2011), 154–156, 160–163; Feigel, *Das evangelische Deutschland,* 208–209.

19. Andreas Meier, "Kommentar," in Meier, ed., *Armin T. Wegner,* 93–105, here 104.

20. However, Gerlach was moved by Wegner's account and tried to get more information from other sources. Helmut Donat, "Die Armeniermassaker im Spiegel der deutschen und der internationalen Friedensbewegung, 1895–1933," in Heinrich Vierbücher, *Armenien 1915: Was die kaiserliche Regierung den deutschen Untertanen verschwiegen hat,* 77–103 (Bremen: Donat Verlag, 2004 [1930]), 86–87.

21. Khorikian, "Die Behandlung," 166; Feigel, *Das evangelische Deutschland,* 227.

22. Meier, "Nachwort," 157.

23. Norbert Saupp, "Das Deutsche Reich und die Armenische Frage, 1878–1914" (PhD dissertation, University of Cologne, 1990), 226.

24. Martin Niepage, *The Horrors of Aleppo . . . Seen by a German Eyewitness* (London: T. Fisher Unwin, 1917), 9–10.

25. Martin Niepage, *Ein Wort an die berufenen Vertreter des deutschen Volkes: Eindrücke eines deutschen Oberlehrers aus der Türkei* (Berlin: private manuscript, 1916), as quoted in Meissner, 235; I used the English version here: Niepage, *The Horrors,* 3.

26. Niepage, *The Horrors,* 4, 15.

27. Ibid., 7.

28. Ibid., 14.

29. Ibid., 19.

30. Ibid., 17–18.

31. Meissner, *Martin Rades "Christliche Welt,"* 235.

32. Wolfgang Gust, *Der Völkermord an den Armeniern: Die Tragödie des ältesten Christenvolkes der Welt* (Munich: Carl Hanser Verlag, 1993), 483.

33. "Widmungen für Herrn Wilson," *Kölnische Zeitung,* 23 January 1917.

34. The Foreign Office was anxious about the possible propagandistic value of the book. Stürmer was also put under surveillance. Hilmar Kaiser, "Denying the Armenian Genocide: The German Connection," *Journal of the Society for Armenian Studies* 9 (1999): 37–53, here 49–50.

35. Harry Stürmer, *Zwei Kriegsjahre in Konstantinopel* (Lausanne, Switzerland: Payot and Co., 1917), 22.

36. Ibid., 36.

37. Ibid., 38.

38. Ibid., 52.

39. Ibid., 42.

40. Ibid., 36.

41. For example, ibid., 59–60.

42. See Martin Niepage, *Quelques documents sur le sort des Arméniens en 1915–16* (Geneva: A. Eggimann, 1916); Martin Niepage, *Rædslerne i Aleppo* (London: Eyre and Spottiswoode, 1917); Martin Niepage, *Material zur Beurteilung des Schicksals der Armenier im Jahre 1915/16* (Basle, Switzerland: Schweizerisches Hilfswerk für Armenien, 1916).

43. C. A. Bratter, *Die armenische Frage* (Berlin: Concordia Deutsche Verlags-Anstalt, 1915), 20–21.

44. Ibid., 4.

45. Taner Akçam, *The Young Turks' Crime against Humanity: The Armenian Genocide and Ethnic Cleansing in the Ottoman Empire* (Princeton, NJ: Princeton University Press, 2012), 400; Eric D. Weitz, *A Century of Genocide: Utopias of Race and Nation* (Princeton, NJ: Princeton University Press, 2005), 195; Feigel, *Das evangelische Deutschland,* 226. Apparently Erzberger was especially vocal about Germany's disgust and outrage at the Armenian Genocide and had even claimed that the kaiser was ready to "shake the Turkish alliance." Frank G. Weber, *Eagles on the Crescent: Germany, Austria, and the Diplomacy of the Turkish Alliance* (Ithaca, NY: Cornell University Press, 1970), 184–186.

46. Anderson, "Who Still Talked," 208–209.

47. Lepsius, *Bericht über die Lage,* preface (unpaginated).

48. See, for example, "Der Reichskanzler zur Armenierfrage," *Neue Preussische (Kreuz-)Zeitung,* 27 November 1915.

49. Rolf Hosfeld, "Johannes Lepsius: Eine deutsche Ausnahme," in Rolf Hosfeld, ed., *Johannes Lepsius: Eine deutsche Ausnahme,* 9–26 (Göttingen, Germany: Wallstein, 2013), 21.

50. 26th session, 11 January 1916, in *Verhandlungen des Reichstags: Anlagen zu den stenographischen Berichten* (Berlin: Julius Sittenfeld, 1918), 512–513.

51. Wolff-Metternich to chancellor, note Bethmann-Hollweg (7/17 December 1915), German Foreign Office, R 14089, in Gust, *Armenian Genocide,* 490–493.

52. 26th session, 11 January 1916, in *Verhandlungen des Reichstags,* 512–513.

53. Note that in 1896 Rosa Luxemburg had written an article for the *Vorwärts* in order to get the SPD to "declare itself without reserve for the Armenian cause," which had been rejected by Wilhelm Liebknecht, Karl's father, then the editor of the *Vorwärts.* Margaret Lavinia Anderson, " 'Down in Turkey, Far Away'—Human Rights, the Armenian Massacres, and Orientalism in Wilhelmine Germany," *Journal of Modern History* 1 (2007): 80–111, here 86.

54. Quoted in Meissner, *Martin Rades "Christliche Welt,"* 257.

55. Scheidemann to chancellor (2 August 1916), German Foreign Office, R 14092, in Gust, *Armenian Genocide,* 614–615.

56. Aktenstücke, question no. 156, in *Verhandlungen des Reichstags,* 1604.

57. Hans-Walter Schmuhl, "Friedrich Naumann und die 'armenische Frage'—Die deutsche Öffentlichkeit und die Verfolgung der Armenier vor 1915," in Hans-Lukas Kieser and Dominik J. Schaller, eds., *Der Völkermord an den*

Armeniern und die Shoah, 503–516 (Zurich: Chronos, 2002), 511–512. Naumann had already mentioned the "violent transplant" of the Armenians to Mesopotamia in his journal *Die Hilfe:* "Kriegschronik," *Die Hilfe,* 28 September 1915, 606–607, as quoted in Anderson, "Who Still Talked," 206–207. Meissner claims that Naumann asked in the Reichstag about the Armenians on 1 March 1918 and on 6 May 1918; Meissner, *Martin Rades "Christliche Welt,"* 242.

58. See Ulrich Trumpener, *Germany and the Ottoman Empire, 1914–1918* (Princeton, NJ: Princeton University Press, 1968), 252.

59. 143rd session, 19 March 1918, in *Verhandlungen des Reichstags,* 4483.

60. 145th session, 22 March 1918, in ibid., 4543.

61. 145th session, 22 March 1918, in ibid., 4545.

62. 145th session, 22 March 1918, in ibid., 4552–4553.

63. 179th session, 24 June 1918, in ibid., 5607.

64. 180th session, 25 June 1918, in ibid., 5655.

65. 180th session, 25 June 1918, in ibid., 5665.

66. Weber, *Eagles on the Crescent,* 42. For an analysis of German foreign policy in relation to the Armenians in 1918, see Aschot Hayruni, "Die Armenische Frage in der deutschen Außenpolitik vom März bis Juni 1918," *Armenisch-Deutsche Korrespondenz* 4 (2007): part I, 18–23, and part II, 23–29; Aschot Hayruni, "Die Armenische Frage in der deutschen Außenpolitik im August 1918," part I: *Armenisch-Deutsche Korrespondenz* 2 (2009): 23–27; part II: *Armenisch-Deutsche Korrespondenz* 3 (2009): 29–33; part III: *Armenisch-Deutsche Korrespondenz* 4 (2009): 20–22.

67. Stürmer, *Zwei Kriegsjahre,* 256; see, for example, Paul Rohrbach, *Aus Südwest-Afrikas schweren Tagen* (Berlin: Weicher, 1909).

68. Stürmer, *Zwei Kriegsjahre,* 145.

69. Schmuhl, "Friedrich Naumann," 510; Feigel, *Das evangelische Deutschland,* 207.

8. What Germany Could Have Known

1. So far, opinion has been divided: Elizabeth Khorikian, the only researcher who has carried out an analysis of the wartime German press, though only for the year 1915, claims that just as Germany did not hear of the lost Battle of the Marne, it did not hear of the Armenian massacres, which is, as we shall see, wrong. Elizabeth Khorikian, "Die Behandlung des Völkermordes an den Armeniern in der deutschen Presse und Literatur um 1915–1925," in Armenuhi Drost-Abgarjan, ed., *Armenologie in Deutschland,* 159–172 (Münster: LIT Verlag, 2005), 161. Yet, Schaller claims that censorship in relation to the Armenian topic was not very tight: Dominik J. Schaller, "Die Rezeption des Völkermordes an den Armeniern in Deutschland, 1915–1945," in Hans-Lukas Kieser and Dominik J. Schaller, eds., *Der Völkermord an den Armeniern und die Shoah,* 517–555 (Zurich: Chronos, 2002), 524–525. The

German papers in 1919 had also stressed the previous censorship on the topic: untitled commentary, *Berliner Tageblatt,* 28 July 1919, 1–2; see also, Friedrich Dahlhaus, *Möglichkeiten und Grenzen auswärtiger Kultur- und Pressepolitik dargestellt am Beispiel der deutsch-türkischen Beziehungen, 1914–1928* (Frankfurt am Main: Peter Lang, 1990), 221–238; Margaret Lavinia Anderson, "Who Still Talked about the Extermination of the Armenians?— German Talk and German Silences," in Ronald Grigor Suny, Fatma Müge Göcek, and Norman M. Naimark, eds., *A Question of Genocide: Armenians and Turks at the End of the Ottoman Empire* (Oxford: Oxford University Press, 2011), 206–214. Gust claims that only the *Chemnitzer Volksstimme* and the *Leipziger Volkzeitung* really featured more extensive reporting on the Armenian topic; Wolfgang Gust, *Der Völkermord an den Armeniern: Die Tragödie des ältesten Christenvolkes der Welt* (Munich: Carl Hanser Verlag, 1993), 262; Uwe Feigel, *Das evangelische Deutschland und Armenien: Die Armenierhilfe deutscher evangelischer Christen seit dem Ende des 19. Jahrhunderts im Kontext der deutsch-türkischen Beziehungen* (Göttingen, Germany: Vandenhoeck and Ruprecht, 1989), 229–240.

2. Khorikian, "Die Behandlung," 162.

3. Maximilian Harden, "Zwischen Ost und West: Armenien in Moabit," *Die Zukunft,* 11 June 1921, 301, as quoted in Vahakn N. Dadrian, *German Responsibility in the Armenian Genocide* (Watertown, MA: Blue Crane Books, 1996), 157; Khorikian, "Die Behandlung," 169.

4. *Nachschlagebuch für die Pressezensur,* as quoted in Khorikian, "Die Behandlung," 162; see also similar entries for the Armenians and Turkey in "Kommunikationsüberwachende Vorschriften des Jahres 1917," in Heinz-Dietrich Fischer, ed., *Pressekonzentration und Zensurpraxis im Ersten Weltkrieg: Texte und Quellen* (Berlin: Volker Spiess, 1973), 199, 266–267.

5. Tilman Lüdke, *Jihad Made in Germany: Ottoman and German Propaganda and Intelligence Operations in the First World War* (Münster: LIT Verlag, 2005).

6. "Der Kriegsschauplatz im russisch-türkischen Landkriege," *Neue Preussische (Kreuz-)Zeitung,* 4 November 1914.

7. See the map in ibid.

8. "Der Kriegsschauplatz im russisch-türkischen Landkriege," *Neue Preussische (Kreuz-)Zeitung,* 4 November 1914; "Die russische Kaukasusarmee geschlagen," *Neue Preussische (Kreuz-)Zeitung,* 9 November 1914; "Das russisch-türkische Gefecht bei Keprikoei," *Neue Preussische (Kreuz-)Zeitung,* 11 November 1914; "Die Kriegserklärung der Türkei," *Neue Preussische (Kreuz-) Zeitung,* 13 November 1914; "Der türkische Kreuzer 'Hamidije' vor Tuapse," *Neue Preussische (Kreuz-)Zeitung,* 23 November 1914.

9. For example, "Die Erbitterung der Türken," *Berliner Neueste Nachrichten,* 31 October 1914; see also, "Der Freiheitskampf der Türken," *Deutsche Tageszeitung,* 30 October 1914; (without title) *Berliner Tageblatt,* 30 October 1914; "Rußland und die Türkei," *Vossische Zeitung,* 31 October 1914.

10. Paul Rohrbach, "Die Türkei im Kriege," in subsection "Die Türkei in ihrem Gegensatz zu Rußland und England," *Kölnische Zeitung,* 4 November 1914.

11. "Armenien im Weltkriege," *Vorwärts,* 20 November 1914.

12. For example, "Der Siegespreis der Türkei," *Vossische Zeitung,* 4 November 1914; Freiherr von Richthofen, "Deutschland und die Türkei," *Hannoverscher Kurier,* 7 November 1914; "Das französische Protektorat über die Katholiken des Orients," *Der Tag,* 14 January 1915.

13. "Die asiatische Türkei," *Vossische Zeitung,* 22 March 1915.

14. "Der Krieg und die große Politik," *Neue Preussische (Kreuz-)Zeitung,* 3 March 1915; also, Otto Hoesch, "Der Krieg und die große Politik," *Neue Preussische (Kreuz-)Zeitung,* 31 March 1915.

15. Articles in this month also continued to emphasize Armenian treachery. See, for example, "Verschwörung gegen die Türkei," *Vossische Zeitung,* 10 May 1915.

16. Wilhelm Feldmann, "Unterredung mit Talaat Bei: Die Völker des türkischen Reiches im Kriege," *Berliner Tageblatt,* 4 May 1915. The paper regularly printed interviews with leading Ottoman statesmen. See also, "Unterredung mit dem Sultan," *Berliner Tageblatt,* 7 April 1915; "Zwei Audienzen: Beim Großwesir, bei Talaat Bei," *Berliner Tageblatt,* 21 April 1915; "Unterredung mit Enver Pascha," *Berliner Tageblatt,* 18 September 1915; "Unterredung mit dem türkischen Kammerpräsidenten," *Berliner Tageblatt,* 23 October 1915.

17. See Khorikian, "Die Behandlung," 165.

18. Though Welch only mentions army reports, this seems to have applied to other kinds of enemy statements as well, as the Armenian topic in the press illustrates. David Welch, *Germany, Propaganda and Total War, 1914–1918* (New Brunswick, NJ: Rutgers University Press, 2000), 39–40.

19. "Eine armenische Revolution unter Leitung der Tripleentente: Offizielle türkische Erklärung," *Berliner Tageblatt,* 7 June 1915; "Eine Armenier-Verschwörung," *Neue Preussische (Kreuz-)Zeitung,* 7 June 1915.

20. "Eine Armenier-Verschwörung," *Neue Preussische (Kreuz-)Zeitung,* 7 June 1915.

21. "Eine armenische Revolution unter Leitung der Tripleentente: Offizielle türkische Erklärung," *Berliner Tageblatt,* 7 June 1915; the papers copied much of this verbatim from the news services: "Nichtamtlich," *Wolff's Telegraphisches Büro,* 7 June 1915.

22. "Eine Armenier-Verschwörung," *Neue Preussische (Kreuz-)Zeitung,* 7 June 1915.

23. Rössler to chancellor (27 July 1915), German Foreign Office, R 14087, in Wolfgang Gust, ed., *The Armenian Genocide—Evidence from the German Foreign Office Archives, 1915-1916* (New York: Berghahn, 2014), 265–269.

24. Freiherr von Mackay, "Armenien und orientalische Ententepolitik," *Magdeburger Zeitung,* 17 June 1915.

25. Franz Carl Endres, "Die armenischen Revolten," *Münchner Neueste Nachrichten,* 23 June 1915. The article also back-referenced an article in the

Münchner Neueste Nachrichten that had included the reply by the Ottomans (no. 286).

26. Johannes Lepsius, *Bericht über die Lage des Armenischen Volkes in der Türkei* (Potsdam, Germany: Tempelverlag, 1916; Bad Schussenried, Germany: Gerhard Hess Verlag, 2011), 210–211. Citations refer to the 2011 edition.

27. "Der Hochverrat der armenischen Revolutionäre," *Berliner Tageblatt*, 14 July 1915.

28. Ibid.

29. "Türkisches Erwachen," *Rheinisch-Westfälische Zeitung*, 14 July 1915; see also, "Die armenische Aufstandsbewegung," *Reichspost*, 15 July 1915.

30. "Die Wahrheit über die armenischen Rebellen," *Neue Preussische (Kreuz-)Zeitung*, 16 July 1915; "Die aufrührerischen Armenier," *Deutsche Tageszeitung*, 16 July 1915.

31. Halil Halid Bey, "'Auf das falsche Pferd,'" *Berliner Tageblatt*, 7 September 1915.

32. "Amerika und die Armenier," *Neue Preussische (Kreuz-)Zeitung*, 5 October 1915; see also, "Deutschland soll sich zugunsten der Armenier verwenden," *Neue Preussische (Kreuz-)Zeitung*, 2 October 1915.

33. "Für die Armenier?," *Deutsche Tageszeitung*, 4 October 1915.

34. Khorikian, "Die Behandlung," 162.

35. Davide Rodogno, *Against Massacre: Humanitarian Interventions in the Ottoman Empire, 1815–1914: The Emergence of a European Concept and International Practice* (Princeton, NJ: Princeton University Press, 2012), 205, 247.

36. "Armenierdebatte im englischen Oberhause," *Neue Preussische (Kreuz-)Zeitung*, 8 October 1915.

37. "Vierverbandslügen," *Neue Preussische (Kreuz-)Zeitung*, 9 October 1915.

38. "Der 'Armeniergreuel'-Rummel beginnt," *Deutsche Tageszeitung*, 9 October 1915; see also "Englands Armenier-Bluff," *Hamburger Nachrichteen*, 9 October 1915, and "Die 'Armeniernot,'" *Leipziger Tageblatt*, 15 October 1915, both reprinted in Yetvart Ficiciyan, ed., *Der Völkermord an den Armeniern im Spiegel der deutschsprachigen Tagespresse (1912–1922)* (Bremen: Donat Verlag, 2015), 204–209.

39. "Die Armenierfrage in der Türkei," *Frankfurter Zeitung*, 12 October 1915. Another article appeared that same day in the same paper (page 2), as reprinted in Wolfgang Gust, ed., *Der Völkermord an den Armeniern 1915/1916: Dokumente aud dem Politischen Archiv des deutschen Auswärtigen Amts* (Springe, Germany: Zu Klampen, 2005), 399–400.

40. "Niedriger hängen," *Pfälzischer Volksbote*, 12 October 1915.

41. "Die amerikanische Humanitätspolitik und die Armenier-Morde," *Pfälzische Volkszeitung*, 12 October 1915.

42. "Die Armenier-Lügen der englischen Presse," *Neue Preussische (Kreuz-)Zeitung*, 14 October 1915.

43. This interview is also discussed by Lepsius in his report, Lepsius, *Bericht über die Lage*, 160.

44. "Die Verschwörung der Armenier," *Vossische Zeitung,* 15 October 1915; "Die Verschwörung der Armenier," *Neue Preussische (Kreuz-)Zeitung,* 15 October 1915.

45. "Deutschland und die christlichen Völker der Türkei," *Kölnische Volkszeitung,* 18 October 1915.

46. For example, "Völkerrechtsverletzungen gegen die Türkei," *Neue Preussische (Kreuz-)Zeitung,* 26 October 1915. See also, "Die 'Armeniergreuel,'" *Neue Preussische (Kreuz-)Zeitung,* 24 October 1915.

47. "Der wahre Zweck der Armenier-Unruhen," *Neue Preussische (Kreuz-) Zeitung,* 28 October 1915; similarly in the *Norddeutsche Allgemeine Zeitung* on 27 October 1915, as reprinted in Gust, *Völkermord,* 365; see also, "'Greuel-taten,'" *Neue Preussische (Kreuz-)Zeitung,* 29 October 1915.

48. "Unterredung mit dem türkischen Kammerpräsidenten," *Berliner Tageblatt,* 23 October 1915.

49. Lepsius, *Bericht über die Lage,* preface (unpaginated).

50. "Der Reichskanzler zur Armenierfrage," *Neue Preussische (Kreuz-)Zeitung,* 27 November 1915.

51. "Das Wesen der 'armenischen Greuel,'" *Deutsche Tageszeitung,* 19 December 1915; see also "Die Armenier," *Rheinisch-Westfälische Zeitung,* 11 December 1915, reprinted in Ficiciyan, *Der Völkermord an den Armeniern,* 218–219.

52. "'Armeniergreuel,'" *Berliner Volkszeitung,* 29 January 1916.

53. "Die Türkei und die Armenier," *Neue Preussische (Kreuz-)Zeitung,* 25 February 1916.

54. Though there were occasional articles highlighting alleged Entente machinations in relation to the Christians, Jews, and Arabs in the Ottoman Empire, as well as reports on massacres carried out by Armenians. For example, "Russengreuel in Armenien," *Neue Preussische (Kreuz-)Zeitung,* 14 June 1916; "Die englische Politik in Armenien," *Kölnische Volkszeitung,* 16 June 1916, reprinted in Ficiciyan, *Der Völkermord an den Armeniern,* 228–229; "Vierverbandswühlereien in Syrien," *Neue Preussische (Kreuz-)Zeitung,* 13 July 1916; "Russengreuel in Armenien," *Neue Preussische (Kreuz-)Zeitung,* 21 March 1917; "England's Greuelfeldzug gegen die Türkei," *Neue Preussische (Kreuz-)Zeitung,* 7 July 1917; "Neue Greueltaten der Armenier," *Vossische Zeitung,* 6 February 1918; also, "Die Vernichtung der Mohammedaner in den besetzten Teilen Anatoliens," *Deutsche Tageszeitung,* 17 January 1917, as cited in Wolfgang Gust, "Das kaiserliche Deutschland und der Völkermord an den Armeniern 1915/1916," in Drost-Abgarjan, *Armenologie in Deutschland,* 153–158, here 154.

55. Hilmar Kaiser, "Die deutsche Diplomatie und der armenische Völkermord," in Fikret Adanir and Bernd Bonwetsch, eds., *Osmanismus, Nationalismus und der Kaukasus,* 203–235 (Wiesbaden, Germany: Reichert Verlag, 2005), 215; Margaret Lavinia Anderson, "Helden in der Zeit des Völkermords? Armin T. Wegner, Ernst Jäckh, Henry Morgenthau," in Rolf Hosfeld, ed., *Johannes*

Lepsius: Eine deutsche Ausnahme, 126–159 (Göttingen, Germany: Wallstein, 2013), 145.

56. For example, "Verurteilung armenischer Verschwörer," *Neue Preussische (Kreuz-)Zeitung*, 16 March 1916; "Die Türkei und der Weltkrieg," *Neue Preussische (Kreuz-)Zeitung*, 2 October 1916; see also, "Die Türken schaffen im Kaukasus Ordnung," *Neue Preussische (Kreuz-)Zeitung*, 14 February 1918.

57. "Widmungen für Herrn Wilson," *Kölnische Zeitung*, 23 January 1917; in a similar vein, see "Zum Verständnis der armenischen Frage," *Rheinisch-Westfälische Zeitung*, 22 May 1917, reprinted in Ficiciyan, *Der Völkermord an den Armeniern*, 256–258.

58. "Talaat Pascha über Entente-Verleumdungen und das Kriegsziel der Türkei," *Neue Preussische (Kreuz-)Zeitung*, 28 September 1917.

59. "Neue Greueltaten der Armenier," *Vossische Zeitung*, 6 February 1918; similar articles also in the *Tägliche Rundschau* and the *Weser Zeitung*, for example, as reprinted in Ficiciyan, *Der Völkermord an den Armeniern*, 262–263; see also "Die armenischen Gräuel im Kaukasus," *Norddeutsche Allgemeine Zeitung*, 12 February 1918, reprinted in ibid., 264–265; "Die furchtbaren Armeniergreuel," *Neue Preussische (Kreuz-)Zeitung*, 20 February 1918; "Trapezunt wieder in türkischer Hand," *Neue Preussische (Kreuz-)Zeitung*, 26 February 1918.

60. "Eine Anklage gegen die Armenier," *Internationale Korrespondenz*, 11 April 1918.

61. "Türken und Armenier," *Tägliche Rundschau*, 9 April 1918.

62. For example: Ernst Fischer, "Türkei und Kaukasus," *Berliner Neueste Nachrichten*, 13 April 1918; "Transkaukasien," *Hannoverscher Courier*, 28 May 1918.

63. For example, Achmed Emin, "Die Kaukasusfrage und die Türkei," *Vossische Zeitung*, 15 July 1918.

64. Count Reventlow, for example, had regurgitated Barth's discourse in the *Deutsche Tageszeitung* during the war; Lepsius, *Bericht über die Lage*, 155–156. On the Christian (internal) journals and the Armenians during the war, see Feigel, *Das evangelische Deutschland*, 230–238; Axel Meissner, *Martin Rades "Christliche Welt" und Armenien: Bausteine für eine internationale Ethik des Protestantismus* (Berlin: LIT Verlag, 2010), 216–228.

65. Joseph Wohlgemuth, *Der Weltkrieg im Lichte des Judentums* (Berlin: Jeschurun, 1915), 30–31.

66. Ibid., 80–81.

67. Felix A. Theilhaber, *Die Juden im Weltkriege: Mit besonderer Berücksichtigung der Verhältnisse für Deutschland* (Berlin: Weltverlag, 1916), 51.

68. Poale Zion, *Die Juden im Kriege: Denkschrift des jüdisch-sozialistischen Arbeiterverbandes Poale-Zion an das internationale sozialistische Bureau*, 2nd ed. (The Hague: Poale Zion, 1917), 41.

69. As one of many possible further examples of articles peddling anti-Armenian stereotypes, such as their alleged treacherousness, see Eugen Oberhummer,

"Die Türken und das osmanische Reich," *Geographische Zeitschrift* 3 (1917): 133–162, here 157.

70. Khorikian, "Die Behandlung," 163.

71. Ewald Banse, *Die Türkei* (Brunswick, Germany: Westermann, 1916); Ewald Banse, *Die Türken und Wir* (Weimar, Germany: Duncker, 1917); Feigel, *Das evangelische Deutschland*, 246–247. See also Vierbücher's 1930 critique: Heinrich Vierbücher, *Armenien 1915: Was die kaiserliche Regierung den deutschen Untertanen verschwiegen hat* (Bremen: Donat Verlag, 2004 [1930]), 46.

72. "Deutscher Frühling an der Bagdadbahn," *Kladderadatsch*, 28 May 1916.

73. Welch, *Germany, Propaganda and Total War*, 243, 253; Isabel V. Hull, *Absolute Destruction: Military Culture and the Practices of War in Imperial Germany* (Ithaca, NY: Cornell University Press, 2006), 312, 314; John Horne and Alan Kramer, *German Atrocities, 1914: A History of Denial* (New Haven, CT: Yale University Press, 2001), 339.

74. As quoted in Helmut Donat, "Die Armeniermassaker im Spiegel der deutschen und der internationalen Friedensbewegung, 1895–1933," in Vierbücher, *Armenien*, 77–103, here 87.

75. Karl Otten, as cited in Khorikian, "Die Behandlung," 163.

76. As quoted in ibid.

77. Maximilian Harden as quoted in ibid., 169.

78. See, for example, the front-page-filling "Türken und Armenier," *Neue Zürcher Zeitung*, 13 May 1916.

79. Anderson, "Who Still Talked," 207.

9. War Crimes, War Guilt, and Whitewashing

1. See Chapter 8, n. 1.

2. Johannes Lepsius, "Was hat man den Armeniern getan? Die Zeit zu reden ist gekommen," *Aus der Arbeit von Dr. Johannes Lepsius* 11, no. 12 (September–December 1918): 113–118, here 116.

3. Ibid., 115.

4. Stier's article seems to have been published at the request of the Foreign Office. Ewald Stier, "Armenien," *Frankfurter Zeitung*, 21 January 1919; Uwe Feigel, *Das evangelische Deutschland und Armenien: Die Armenierhilfe deutscher evangelischer Christen seit dem Ende des 19. Jahrhunderts im Kontext der deutsch-türkischen Beziehungen* (Göttingen, Germany: Vandenhoeck and Ruprecht, 1989), 276.

5. Stier to Solf (24 October 1914) German Foreign Office, R 14014, in Wolfgang Gust, ed., *Armenocide: Documents from the State Archives*, online at www.armenocide.net; Axel Meissner, *Martin Rades "Christliche Welt" und Armenien: Bausteine für eine internationale Ethik des Protestantismus* (Berlin: LIT Verlag, 2010), 2.

6. "Armenien," *Frankfurter Zeitung*, 21 January 1919.

7. Julius Richter, "Die deutschen evangelischen Missionskreise und das armenische Volk," *Allgemeine Missionszeitschrift*, 6 February 1919, in Gust, *Armenocide* (online).

8. See Meissner, *Martin Rades "Christliche Welt,"* 258–260.

9. Richter, "Die deutschen evangelischen Missionskreise."

10. Reprinted in Peter von Feldmann, *Otto von Feldmann—Türkei, Weimar, Hitler* (Borsdorf, Germany: Edition Winterwork, 2013), 139–140.

11. German Foreign Office to Schellendorf, 7 February 1919, PA R14105, in Gust, *Armenocide* (online); Christoph Dinkel, "German Officers and the Armenian Genocide," *The Armenian Review* 1 (1991), 77–132, here 82–83.

12. Feldmann, *Otto von Feldmann*, 140.

13. Parts of the German original, in a rather inaccurate English translation, in Vahakn N. Dadrian, *German Responsibility in the Armenian Genocide: A Review of the Historical Evidence of German Complicity* (Watertown, MA: Blue Crane Books, 1996), 263–271. The translation used is my own.

14. Apparently Wegner had tried to publish a similar open letter already after his return from the Ottoman Empire during the war, but was only able to get it published in the rather peripheral journal *Die Frau der Gegenwart* (Woman of Today). Armin T. Wegner, "Offener Brief an den Präsidenten der Vereinigten Staaten," *Berliner Tageblatt,* 23 February 1919; Armin T. Wegner, "Brief an den Präsidenten der Vereinigten Staaten," *Die Frau der Gegenwart* 9, no. 2 (1917): 11–14. Apparently Wegner also published another article the very same day in the *Frankfurter Zeitung*: Armin T. Wegner, "Eine armenische Mutter: Erinnerung an den türkischen Feldzug," *Frankfurter Zeitung*, 23 February 1919, as quoted in Andreas Meier, "Nachwort," in Andreas Meier, ed., *Armin T. Wegner: Die Austreibung des armenischen Volkes in die Wüste—Ein Lichtbildvortrag*, 153–192 (Göttingen, Germany: Wallstein, 2011), 173.

15. Published, for example, as "Die Greuel in Armenien," *Bayrischer Kurier,* 1 March 1919, as cited in Meissner, *Martin Rades "Christliche Welt,"* 248.

16. See also Vierbücher in his 1930 book, Heinrich Vierbücher, *Armenien 1915: Was die kaiserliche Regierung den deutschen Untertanen verschwiegen hat* (Bremen: Donat Verlag, 2004 [1930]), 73.

17. "Türkisch-armenische Konflikte in der Urania," *BZ am Mittag*, 20 March 1919; "Tumulte in der Urania," *Vossische Zeitung*, 20 March 1919.

18. "Ein stürmischer Vortragabend in der Urania," *Berliner Abendzeitung*, 20 March 1919.

19. Memorandum, Rössler (24 March 1919), German Foreign Office, R 14105, in Gust, *Armenocide* (online); Dinkel, "German Officers," 84–85.

20. Note that a version of one of his later and similar slideshow lectures was recently published as a book: Armin T. Wegner, "Die Austreibung des armenischen Volkes in die Wüste," in Meier, *Armin T. Wegner*, 11–89, here 32.

21. Ibid., 36–37.

22. Here, Wegner talks of pregnant women, even though he was talking about orphan girls and showing their picture. Perhaps this was merely a stylistic tool, or perhaps it reflected something he saw. Ibid., 37–38.

23. Andreas Meier, "Anhang," in Meier, *Armin T. Wegner*, 93–152, here 95.

24. Ibid., 104.

25. See the coverage in "Die Austreibung des armenischen Volkes in die Wüste," *Breslauer Zeitung*, 24 April 1919; "Die Austreibung des armenischen Volkes in die Wüste," *Schlesische Tagespost*, 24 April 1919; "Die Austreibung des armenischen Volkes in die Wüste," *Breslauer Morgenzeitung*, 25 April 1919; as cited in Meier, "Anhang," 94.

26. Armin T. Wegner, "Der Schrei vom Ararat: An die Regierungen der siegreichen Völker," *Die Weltbühne* 5 (1923): 122–126. Similarly in *Die Neue Generation* 18 (1922), 348–355; and in *Erkenntnis und Befreiung* 7 (1923), as quoted in Andreas Meier, "Nachwort," in Meier, *Armin T. Wegner*, 153–192, here 177.

27. As quoted in Elizabeth Khorikian, "Die Behandlung des Völkermordes an den Armeniern in der deutschen Presse und Literatur um 1915–1925," in Armenuhi Drost-Abgarjan, ed., *Armenologie in Deutschland*, 159–172 (Münster: LIT Verlag, 2005), 171.

28. "Die Probleme des näheren Orients," *Weimarsche Zeitung*, 4 March 1919.

29. Christopher Clark, *The Sleepwalkers: How Europe Went to War in 1914* (London: Allen Lane, 2012), 338–349.

30. "Anklagen gegen Liman von Sanders," *Vossische Zeitung*, 22 February 1919.

31. "Enver und Dschemal degradiert," *Vossische Zeitung*, 15 January 1919; "Kleine Nachrichten aus dem Auslande," *Neue Preussische (Kreuz-)Zeitung*, 16 January 1919.

32. For example, "Letzte Nachrichten," *Neue Preussische (Kreuz-)Zeitung*, 14 February 1919.

33. For example, "Die Hetze gegen Liman von Sanders," *Deutsche Allgemeine Zeitung*, 28 February 1919; "Ententehetze gegen Liman von Sanders," *Neue Preussische (Kreuz-)Zeitung*, 28 February 1919; "Liman von Sanders und die Armeniergreuel," *Vossische Zeitung*, 28 February 1919.

34. "Liman von Sanders verhaftet," *Vossische Zeitung*, 10 March 1919.

35. "Kein Kriegsgericht gegen Liman von Sanders," *Vossische Zeitung*, 31 March 1919.

36. Pierre Loti, "Pladoyer suprême pour les condamnés à mort," *Le Figaro*, 3 April 1919, in Gust, *Armenocide* (online).

37. See, for example, "Letzte Nachrichten," *Neue Preussische (Kreuz-)Zeitung*, 14 April 1919; for further, similar news, see, for example, "Kleine Nachrichten aus dem Auslande," *Neue Preussische (Kreuz-)Zeitung*, 23 April 1919; "Letzte Nachrichten," *Neue Preussische (Kreuz-)Zeitung*, 15 August 1919.

38. "Sühne für die Armeniermassakers—Kiamil Pascha gehängt," *Vorwärts*, 15 April 1919.

39. "Kiamil Pascha gehängt," *Rote Fahne*, 17 April 1919.

40. "Deutschland und die Armenier," *Berliner Lokal-Anzeiger,* 24 April 1919; Otto Liman von Sanders, "Deutschland und Armenien," *20. Jahrhundert: Dokumente zur Zeitgeschichte* 9 (1919), as quoted in Dinkel, "German Officers," 91.

41. Otto Liman von Sanders, *Fünf Jahre Türkei* (Berlin: A. Scherl, 1920), also in English: Liman von Sanders, *Five Years in Turkey* (Annapolis: US Naval Institute, 1927).

42. "Die Heimsendung des Liman von Sanders," *Heidelberger Zeitung,* 14 August 1919. Two weeks later, the papers reported of his imminent arrival. "Kurzmeldungen," *Vossische Zeitung,* 29 August 1919. On 3 September, the provincial press (again) debated the Entente allegations against Sanders, following the commentary of the national papers and their notions that all claims as to his participation in the Armenian massacres were "a pack of [Entente] lies." "Liman von Sanders Schicksal," *Badische Post,* 3 September 1919; "Liman von Sanders Schicksal," *Heidelberger Zeitung,* 3 September 1919.

43. H. Pfisterer, "Deutschland und die Armenierpolitik der Türkei," *Schwäbischer Merkur,* 29 April 1919.

44. Hermann Goltz, "Bericht zum Abschluss der durch die Volkswagenstiftung geförderten Edition," in Drost-Abgarjan, ed., *Armenologie,* 77–172, here 95.

45. In the *Schwäbischer Kurier,* 20 May 1919, and *Hannoverscher Courier,* 2 June 1919, as cited in Feigel, *Das evangelische Deutschland,* 277.

46. Johannes Lepsius, *Deutschland und Armenien, 1914–1918: Sammlung diplomatischer Aktenstücke* (Potsdam, Germany: Tempel-Verlag, 1919). Many, like Wolfgang Gust and Hilmar Kaiser, have studied Lepsius's editorial work and criticized the manipulation herein. The most thorough work has been carried out by Wolfgang Gust. Gust has written extensively on the Armenian Genocide as well as the German dimension of it, and he published a new edited volume with all the important existing German Foreign Office documents from 1915/1916. He thus, in a way, redid Lepsius's work. On Gust's website, where these documents plus a range of others are published (in German, English, and Turkish), one also finds an extensive analysis and documentation of the "manipulations" carried out in the Lepsius volume. Though some still dispute that it was actually Lepsius himself who manipulated these documents, his silence about the manipulation afterward is striking, also because in the preface he claims full responsibility for the publication and states he had been given full freedom. Also see Dadrian, *German Responsibility,* 154–156; Dinkel, "German Officers," 85–86. Gust stresses that the Foreign Office had already manipulated the copies of the materials it had given Lepsius. Wolfgang Gust, "Einführung und Leitfaden," in Wolfgang Gust, ed., *Der Völkermord an den Armeniern 1915/1916: Dokumente aud dem Politischen Archiv des deutschen Auswärtigen Amts,* 17–109 (Springe, Germany: Zu Klampen, 2005), 107–108; Hilmar Kaiser, "Denying the Armenian Genocide: The German Connection," *Journal of the Society for Armenian Studies* 9 (1999): 37–53, here 51–52.

47. Frank G. Weber, *Eagles on the Crescent: Germany, Austria, and the Diplomacy of the Turkish Alliance* (Ithaca, NY: Cornell University Press, 1970), 150–151.

48. Foreign Office to Lepsius (28 June 1919), German Foreign Office, R 14106, in Gust, *Armenocide* (online). For the trials, see Taner Akçam, *A Shameful Act: The Armenian Genocide and the Question of Turkish Responsibility* (London: Constable and Robinson, 2006).

49. Lepsius to Foreign Office (13 July 1919) and answer (26 July 1919), German Foreign Office, R 14106, in Gust, *Armenocide* (online).

50. On the broad reception, see also Ewald Stier, as quoted in Meissner, *Martin Rades "Christliche Welt,"* 258.

51. "Die Akten über die Armenierfrage," *Vorwärts,* 11 June 1919.

52. Lepsius to Foreign Office (13 July 1919) and answer (26 July 1919), German Foreign Office, R 14106, in Gust, *Armenocide* (online).

53. See, for example, the lead article in the *Berliner Volkszeitung:* "Die Armeniergreuel," *Berliner Volkszeitung,* 28 July 1919.

54. Rosen to Foreign Office (9 August 1919), German Foreign Office, PA R14106, in Gust, *Armenocide* (online).

55. Theodor Wolff, untitled daily commentary, *Berliner Tageblatt,* 28 July 1919, 1–2.

56. "Ein Dokument jungtürkischer Schande," *Braunschweiger Landeszeitung,* 29 July 1919.

57. "Die Ausrottung der türkischen Armenier," *Vossische Zeitung,* 30 July 1919. Strangely enough, this as well as the next article in the *Vossische Zeitung* on the Lepsius volume cannot be found in the scanned, online edition the *Staatsbibliothek zu Berlin* offers, yet they are found in various press-cutting collections (for example, the Reichslandbund collection at the Bundesarchiv).

58. "Der Massenmord am Armeniervolk," *Kölnische Volkszeitung,* 2 August 1919.

59. For more articles in these weeks see Yetvart Ficiciyan, ed., *Der Völkermord an den Armeniern im Spiegel der deutschsprachigen Tagespresse (1912–1922)* (Bremen: Donat Verlag, 2015), 302–318.

60. "Die Ausrottung der Armenier: Eine Entgegnung," *Vossische Zeitung,* 7 August 1919; Ficiciyan claims this article was printed in the *Berliner Tageblatt:* Ficiciyan, *Der Völkermord an den Armeniern,* 301.

61. "Zur Frage der Greuel in Armenien: Eine Rechtfertigungsschrift von A. Djemal Pascha," *Frankfurter Zeitung,* 3 September 1919.

62. The death sentence itself had also been reported. See, for example, "Todesurteil gegen Talaat und Enver," *Vossische Zeitung,* 14 July 1919.

63. "Zur Frage der Armeniergreuel," *Neue Preussische (Kreuz-)Zeitung,* 5 October 1919; "Eine Rechtfertigungsschrift Dschemal Paschas," *Deutsche Allgemeine Zeitung,* 5 October 1919.

64. Cemal Pascha, *Erinnerungen eines türkischen Staatsmanns* (Berlin: Drei Masken Verlag, 1922).

65. "Deutschlands Schuld an den armenischen Greueln," *Deutsche Orient-Korrespondenz,* 13 September 1919.

66. Johannes Lepsius, *Der Todesgang des armenischen Volkes: Bericht über das Schicksal des armenischen Volkes in der Türkei während des Weltkriege* (Potsdam, Germany: Tempelverlag, 1919).

67. "Der Todesgang des armenischen Volkes: Deutschlands Schuld?," *Essener Volkszeitung*, 2 January 1920.

68. See also "Die Schuldfrage für das Verbrechen an Armenien," *Kölnische Volkszeitung*, 13 January 1920.

69. "Germany and the Armenians," *New York Tribune*, 14 August 1919, in Gust, *Armenocide* (online).

70. "'Kultur' in Armenia," *(London) Times*, 27 August 1919, in Gust, *Armenocide* (online).

71. Stoedten to Foreign Office (21 August 1919) and answer (8 September 1919), German Foreign Office, PA R14106, in Gust, *Armenocide* (online).

72. For example Heinrich Vierbücher, "Opfer des Orients," *Vorwärts*, 10 August 1920, as cited in Helmut Donat, "Die Armeniermassaker im Spiegel der deutschen und der internationalen Friedensbewegung, 1895–1933," in Vierbücher, *Armenien*, 77–103, here 82; see also Alfred Kerr, "Armenisches Eiland," *Berliner Tageblatt*, 16 June 1920, reprinted in Ficiciyan, *Der Völkermord an den Armeniern*, 346–349; P. Joseph Kiera, "Der Todesgang des armenischen Volkes," *Kölnische Volkszeitung*, 16 August 1920, in ibid., 349–355.

73. "Die armenische Frage," *Neue Preussische (Kreuz-)Zeitung*, 2 January 1920.

74. Jeffrey Herf, *The Jewish Enemy—Nazi Propaganda during World War II and the Holocaust* (Cambridge, MA: Harvard University Press, 2006).

75. Ernst Paraquin, "Politik im Orient," *Berliner Tageblatt*, pt. 1: 24 January 1920; pt. 2: 28 January 1920, as quoted in Dadrian, *German Responsibility*, 60.

76. Serman, "Stichproben," *Berliner Lokal-Anzeiger*, 5 February 1920.

77. "Fortsetzung der Auslieferungsliste," *Neue Preussische (Kreuz-)Zeitung*, 12 February 1920; see also, "Talaat verhaftet?," *Vossische Zeitung*, 31 October 1919; "Auslieferungsbegehren auch an die ehemaligen Bundesgenossen?," *Neue Preussische (Kreuz-)Zeitung*, 7 February 1920; "Die Auslieferung türkische "Kriegsverbrecher," *Neue Preussische (Kreuz-)Zeitung*, 8 March 1920.

78. "Armenien und Amritsar," *Neue Preussische (Kreuz-)Zeitung*, 28 February 1920.

79. "Armeniergemetzel in Cilicien," *Berliner Tageblatt*, 1 March 1920.

80. See, for example, "Letzte Nachrichten," *Neue Preussische (Kreuz-)Zeitung*, 16 August 1919; "Das amerikanische Mandat über Armenien," *Neue Preussische (Kreuz-)Zeitung*, 17 August 1919; "Amerikanische Drohungen an die Türkei," *Neue Preussische (Kreuz-)Zeitung*, 28 August 1919; "Amerikas armenische Liebe," *Deutsche Tageszeitung*, 2 September 1919; "Die Grenzen Armenians," *Deutsche Allgemeine Zeitung*, 27 March 1920; "Amerikas Patenschaft über Armenien," *Deutsche Tageszeitung*, 7 April 1920; "Das Mandat über Armenien," *Deutsche Allgemeine Zeitung*, 9 April 1920; "Kleine Nachrichten aus dem Auslande," *Neue Preussische (Kreuz-)Zeitung*, 14 April 1920; "Das Mandat für Armenien," *Vossische Zeitung*, 26 May 1920; "Amerika lehnt Mandat über Armenian ab," *Neue Preussische (Kreuz-)Zeitung*, 3 June 1920.

81. "Das Ende der Türkei," *Deutsche Tageszeitung*, 23 April 1920.

82. "Armenier gegen Franzosen," *Neue Preussische (Kreuz-)Zeitung,* 28 April 1920; see the day before the report on atrocities against Armenians, "Letzte Nachrichten," *Neue Preussische (Kreuz-)Zeitung,* 27 April 1919.

83. "Mustafa Kemal Pascha," *Deutsche Zeitung,* 4 July 1920. For example, "Armenian und Russland," *Deutsche Allgemeine Zeitung,* 8 August 1920; Karl Roth, "Zwei Jahre armenische Republik," *Deutsche Allgemeine Zeitung,* 20 September 1920.

84. "Armeniergreuel," *Deutsche Zeitung,* 19 June 1920.

85. See, for example, "Angebot des Mandats über Armenien an Italien," *Neue Preussische (Kreuz-)Zeitung,* 2 November 1920.

86. See, for example, "Die armenische Frage," *Deutsche Allgemeine Zeitung,* 23 November 1920; "Armenien vor dem Völkerbunde," *Vossische Zeitung,* 23 November 1920; "Die Rettung Armeniens," *Deutsche Tageszeitung,* 24 November 1920; "Die äußere Politik der Woche," *Neue Preussische (Kreuz-)Zeitung,* 1 December 1920; "Moralische Unterstützung Armeniens durch Wilson," *Neue Preussische (Kreuz-)Zeitung,* 1 December 1920; "Die Völkerbundskonferenz in Genf: Angebot Wilsons zu 'persönlicher Vermittlung' in der armenischen Frage," *Berliner Tageblatt,* 3 December 1920; "Eine Lösung der armenischen Frage?," *Deutsche Allgemeine Zeitung,* 3 December 1920; "Armenische Friedensverhandlungen," *Deutsche Allgemeine Zeitung,* 4 December 1920; "Die armenische Frage," *Deutsche Allgemeine Zeitung,* 4 December 1920; "Aufnahme Armeniens in den Völkerbund," *Neue Preussische (Kreuz-)Zeitung,* 4 December 1920; "Die armenische Frage," *Neue Preussische (Kreuz-)Zeitung,* 4 December 1920; "Der Völkerbunds-Beschluß über die armenische Frage," *Neue Preussische (Kreuz-)Zeitung,* 6 December 1920; "Neu-Armenien," *Leipziger Nachrichten,* 9 December 1920.

87. "Die äußere Politik der Woche," *Neue Preussische (Kreuz-)Zeitung,* 15 December 1920.

88. Liman von Sanders, "Die Türkei von heute," *Der Tag,* 23 January 1921. The year of the denialists was not without opposition though. In 1920, a book was published in Berlin by Mehmed Zeki Bey with the telling title *Robber-Murderers as Guests of the German Republic (Raubmörder als Gäste der deutschen Republik).* It offered a strong condemnation of the Young Turk leadership. It featured a detailed analysis of the crimes committed by the Young Turk leaders. Mehmed Zeki Bey, *Raubmörder als Gäste der deutschen Republik* (Berlin: Verlag Die Verteidigung 1920); Rolf Hosfeld, *Operation Nemesis: Die Türkei, Deutschland und der Völkermord an den Armeniern* (Cologne: Kiepenheuer and Witsch, 2005), 17.

10. Assassination in Berlin, 1921

1. For an account of the assassination see the report in the *Vossische Zeitung* on 16 March 1921, reprinted in Şeref Ünal, *The Trial of Salomon Teilirian: Assassination of Talat Pasha, Berlin 2–3 June 1921* (New York: Okey, 2007), 2–3; also,

"Ein politischer Mord," *Freiheit,* 16 March 1921; A. Şerif Aksoy, *Jön Türkler Enver, Cemal ve Talat Paşaların Trajik Sonu* (Istanbul: Nokta Kitap, 2008), 194–196.

2. Wilhelm Feldmann, "Talaat Pascha in Berlin," *Berliner Tageblatt,* 23 April 1917.

3. Jacques Derogy, *Resistance and Revenge: The Armenian Assassination of the Turkish Leaders Responsible for the 1915 Massacres and Deportations* (New Brunswick, NJ: Transaction, 1990), 103–104; Rolf Hosfeld, *Operation Nemesis: Die Türkei, Deutschland und der Völkermord an den Armeniern* (Cologne: Kiepenheuer and Witsch, 2005), 25.

4. Bronsart von Schellendorff, "Ein Zeugnis für Talaat Pascha," *Deutsche Allgemeine Zeitung,* 24 July 1921.

5. Ernst Troeltsch, *Die Fehlgeburt einer Republik: Spektator in Berlin, 1918 bis 1922* (Frankfurt am Main: Eichborn, 1994), 128; Hosfeld, *Operation Nemesis,* 18.

6. All of the following on 15 March 1921: "Talaat Pascha ermordet?," *Vossische Zeitung;* "Talaat Pascha in Berlin ermordet," *Deutsche Zeitung;* "Talaat Pascha in Berlin ermordet," *Deutsche Allgemeine Zeitung.*

7. For example, "Mord auf offener Straße: Eifersuchtstat eines ausländischen Kandidaten," *Berliner Lokal-Anzeiger,* 15 March 1921.

8. "Talaat Pascha in Berlin ermordet," *Deutsche Allgemeine Zeitung,* 15 March 1921.

9. "Talaat Pascha ermordet," *Neue Preussische (Kreuz-)Zeitung,* 15 March 1921.

10. "Mord auf offener Straße: Eifersuchtstat eines ausländischen Kandidaten," *Berliner Lokal-Anzeiger,* 15 March 1921; "Ein Mord auf offener Straße," *Deutsche Tageszeitung,* 16 March 1921.

11. "Talaat Pascha ermordet," *Neue Preussische (Kreuz-)Zeitung,* 15 March 1921.

12. "Die Ermordung Talaat Paschas: Die Tat eines Armeniers," *Vossische Zeitung,* 16 March 1921.

13. Erwin Barth, "Talaat Pascha," *Vossische Zeitung,* 16 March 1921.

14. For example, "Die Ermordung Talaat Paschas," *Berliner Börsenzeitung,* 16 March 1921; "Zum Tode Talaat Paschas," *Kölnische Zeitung,* 16 March 1921.

15. "Die Ermordung Talaat Paschas," *Neue Preussische (Kreuz-)Zeitung,* 16 March 1921.

16. Other papers offered a bit more on the genocide itself. For example, "Die Vernehmung des Mörders von Talaat," *Berliner Morgenpost,* 17 March 1921.

17. "Talaat Pascha," *Neue Preussische (Kreuz-)Zeitung,* 16 March 1921; "Die Vernehmung des Mörders," *Neue Preussische (Kreuz-)Zeitung,* 16 March 1921; similarly in "Die Ermordung Talaat Paschas," *Kölnische Volkszeitung,* 16 March 1921.

18. See Stefan Ihrig, *Atatürk in the Nazi Imagination* (Cambridge, MA: Belknap, 2014), chapters 1 and 2.

19. "Die Ermordung Talaat Paschas," *Berliner Börsenzeitung,* 16 March 1921.

20. See also Hosfeld, who mentions the "anti-Armenian campaign" of the paper following the trial, Hosfeld, *Operation Nemesis*, 13.

21. Christoph Dinkel, "German Officers and the Armenian Genocide," *The Armenian Review* 1 (1991): 77–132, here 128.

22. Ibid., 112.

23. Margaret Lavinia Anderson, "Who Still Talked about the Extermination of the Armenians?—German Talk and German Silences," in Ronald Grigor Suny, Fatma Müge Göcek, and Norman M. Naimark, eds., *A Question of Genocide: Armenians and Turks at the End of the Ottoman Empire*, 206–217 (Oxford: Oxford University Press, 2011), 216.

24. "Die Ermordung Talaat Paschas," *Deutsche Allgemeine Zeitung*, 16 March 1921; "Talaat," *Deutsche Allgemeine Zeitung*, 16 March 1921; "Der armenische Mörder," *Deutsche Allgemeine Zeitung*, 16 March 1921; "Bedauerliche Entgleisungen," *Deutsche Allgemeine Zeitung*, 16 March 1921.

25. "Der armenische Mörder," *Deutsche Allgemeine Zeitung*, 16 March 1921.

26. "Bedauerliche Entgleisungen," *Deutsche Allgemeine Zeitung*, 16 March 1921.

27. "Der armenische Mörder," *Deutsche Allgemeine Zeitung*, 16 March 1921; see also, Ibn Insun, "Talaat," *Deutsche Allgemeine Zeitung*, 16 March 1921.

28. "Der Mord an Talaat Pascha," *Deutsche Zeitung*, 16 March 1921; see also, "Die Ermordung Talaat Paschas," *Deutsche Zeitung*, 16 March 1921; "Die letzte Unterredung mit Talaat Pascha," *Deutsche Zeitung*, 17 March 1921.

29. "Ein politischer Mord: Rache für die Armeniergreuel," *Freiheit*, 16 March 1921.

30. "Talaat Pascha, die Armeniergreuel und der 'Vorwärts,'" *Freiheit*, 16 March 1921; see also another article in the *Berliner Tageblatt*: "Talaat Pascha—Der Staatsmann des Komitees," *Berliner Tageblatt*, 16 March 1921.

31. "Talaat Pasha ermordet: Der Mord in der Hadenbergstrasse ein Nachwort für die Armeniermorde," *Germania*, 16 March 1921.

32. "Die Ermordung Talaat Paschas: Blutrache eines Armeniers," *Berliner Lokal-Anzeiger*, 16 March 1921.

33. Ibid.; "Die Ermordung Talaat Paschas: Eine armenische Verbindung als Mordanstifterin," *Berliner Lokal-Anzeiger*, 16 March 1921.

34. "Der frühere Großwesir Talaat Pascha in Berlin ermordet: Politischer Racheakt eines armenischen Studenten," *Berliner Morgenpost*, 16 March 1921; "Talaat Pascha," *Hamburger Nachrichten*, 18 March 1921; see also, "Erinnerungen an Talaat Pascha," *Danziger Zeitung*, 18 March 1921.

35. "Talaat und die Armenier," *Königsberger Hartungsche Zeitung*, 21 March 1921.

36. Hosfeld, *Operation Nemesis*, 12.

37. See, for example, "Bei den Armeniern in Genf," *Berliner Morgenpost*, 17 March 1921; "Der Mörder Talaat Paschas," *Vossische Zeitung*, 17 March 1921; "Talaats Mörder," *Berliner Lokalanzeiger*, 18 March 1921; Ernst von Reventlow, "Talaat Pascha: Englands Hand," *Der Reichswart*, 19 March 1921.

38. "Talaat Paschas Begräbnis," *Deutsche Allgemeine Zeitung*, 20 March 1921; for a pronounced pro-Armenian view, see the *Hessischer Volksfreund* on 19 March, as cited in Derogy, *Resistance and Revenge*, xxii–xxiii.

39. "Trauerfeier für Talaat Pascha," *Neue Preussische (Kreuz-)Zeitung,* 20 March 1921.

40. "Der wahre Talaat," *Deutsche Allgemeine Zeitung,* 20 March 1921; "Talaat Paschas Beisetzung," *Deutsche Allgemeine Zeitung,* 20 March 1921; "Talaat in englischer Beleuchtung," *Deutsche Allgemeine Zeitung,* 20 March 1921.

41. Kurt Kozyk, *Publizistik und politisches Engagement: Lebensbilder publizistischer Persönlichkeiten,* ed. W. Hömber and A. Kutsch (Münster: LIT Verlag, 1999), 465–467; Werner Stephan, *Joseph Goebbels: Dämon einer Diktatur* (Stuttgart, Germany: Union Deutsche Verlagsgesellschaft, 1949), 174–175.

42. Theodor Wolff, untitled daily commentary, *Berliner Tageblatt,* 28 July 1919, 1–2.

11. Trial in Berlin

1. See, for example, "Die Ermordung eines Volkes," *Deutsche Allgemeine Zeitung,* 12 April 1921.

2. "Die Ermordung Talaat Paschas," *Kölnische Volkszeitung,* 16 March 1921.

3. E. Stier, "Ein Volk, das nicht sterben kann," *Christliche Welt* 36 (1922): 148–153, as cited in Axel Meissner, *Martin Rades "Christliche Welt" und Armenien: Bausteine für eine internationale Ethik des Protestantismus* (Berlin: LIT Verlag, 2010), 264.

4. Alfred Rosenberg, "Mörder und Mörderschutz," *Der Weltkampf,* July 1926, 289–300.

5. "Der Großkriegsverbrecher," *Vorwärts,* 4 June 1921.

6. The excerpts from the court proceedings stem from Armin T. Wegner, ed., *Der Prozess Talaat Pascha* (Berlin: Deutsche Verlagsgesellschaft fuer Politik und Geschichte, 1921; facsimile repr., Tessa Hoffmann, ed., *Der Voelkermord vor Gericht* [Göttingen, Germany: Gesellschaft fuer bedrohte Voelker, 1980]). The published English translation was used as well; however, given the various, serious shortcomings of this version, most of the following is my own translation of the German original. Zoryan Institute, ed., *The Case of Soghomon Tehlirian,* translated by Vartkes Yeghiayan (Los Angeles: Varantian Gomideh, 1985).

7. Balakian's memoirs have recently been published in English: Grigoris Balakian, *Armenian Golgotha: A Memoir of the Armenian Genocide, 1915–1918,* translated by Peter Balakian with Aris Sevag (New York: Vintage Books, 2010); see also Valentina Calzolari, "1915 dans la littérature arménienne: Le Golgotha arménien de Grigoris Balakian," in Hans-Lukas Kieser and Elmar Plozza, eds., *Der Völkermord an den Armeniern, die Türkei und Europa* (Zurich: Chronos, 2006), 91–106.

8. A more extensive account of what Captain Shükrü had allegedly told Balakian can be found in Balakian's chapter, "The Confessions of a Slayer Captain," Balakian, *Armenian Golgotha,* 139–150 and 151–161.

9. Jan Armbruster, "Die Beziehung des Psychiaters Edmund Forster (1878–1933) zu Adolf Hitler (1889–1945)," *Schriftenreihe der Deutschen Gesellschaft für Geschichte der Nervenheilkunde* 7 (2009): 159–185.

10. Rolf Hosfeld, *Operation Nemesis: Die Türkei, Deutschland und der Völkermord an den Armeniern* (Cologne: Kiepenheuer and Witsch, 2005), 17–18; "Talaat verhaftet?," *Vossische Zeitung*, 30 October 1919.

11. This interpretation goes as far back as Raphael Lemkin and Alfred Rosenberg: Raphael Lemkin, *Totally Unofficial: The Autobiography of Raphael Lemkin*, Donna-Lee Frieze, ed. (New Haven, CT: Yale University Press, 2013), 20–21; Rosenberg, "Mörder und Mörderschutz"; also, for example, Michael Bobelian, *Children of Armenia: A Forgotten Genocide and the Century-Long Struggle for Justice* (New York: Simon and Schuster, 2009), 64; Aschot Hayruni, "Johannes Lepsius' armenische Verbindungen," in Rolf Hosfeld, ed., *Johannes Lepsius: Eine deutsche Ausnahme*, 207–226 (Göttingen, Germany: Wallstein, 2013), 224–225.

12. Christoph Dinkel, "German Officers and the Armenian Genocide," *The Armenian Review* 1 (1991): 77–132, here 94.

13. Gordon to Rössler (24 May 1921), German Foreign Office, NL Rössler, vol. 2, in Wolfgang Gust, ed., *Armenocide: Documents from the State Archives*, online at www.armenocide.net.

14. Rössler, draft (end of May 1921); Haimhausen to Gordon (1 June 1921); German Foreign Office, NL Rössler, vol. 2, in ibid.

15. Rössler to Lepsius (20 April 1921) German Foreign Office, NL Rössler, vol. 1, in ibid.

16. Rolf Hosfeld, "Ein Völkermordprozess wider willen," in Hosfeld, *Johannes Lepsius*, 248–257, here 255; Jacques Derogy, *Resistance and Revenge: The Armenian Assassination of the Turkish Leaders Responsible for the 1915 Massacres and Deportations* (New Brunswick, NJ: Transaction, 1990), xxv–xxvi.

17. "Kleine Nachrichten," *Staufener Tagblatt*, 4 June 1921.

18. "Die Ermordung Talaat Paschas," *Deutsche Allgemeine Zeitung*, 2 June 1921.

19. Fol. 030-03/198B, No. 1182, *State Archives Berlin*, 300–327.

20. "Die Ermordung Talaat Paschas," *Neue Preussische (Kreuz-)Zeitung*, 2 June 1921; "Der Mord an Talaat Paschas vor dem Schwurgericht: Die Vernehmung des Angeklagten," *Berliner Tageblatt*, 2 June 1921; "Die Ermordung Talaat Paschas," *Deutsche Tageszeitung*, 2 June 1921; "Die Ermordung Talaat Paschas," *Vossische Zeitung*, 2 June 1921.

21. See, for example, "Die Ermordung Talaat Paschas," *Berliner Börsenzeitung*, 2 June 1921; "Die Ermordung Talaat Paschas: Das gerichtliche Nachspiel," *Berliner Lokal-Anzeiger*, 2 June 1921; "Die Törung Talaats vor Gericht—Die Vernehmung des Armeniers Teilirian," *Berliner Volkszeitung*, 2 June 1921.

22. "Die Ermordung Talaat Paschas," *Deutsche Allgemeine Zeitung*, 2 June 1921.

23. "Die Ermordung Talaat Paschas," *Deutsche Zeitung*, 2 June 1921.

24. See, for example, "Die Ermordung Talaat Paschas," *Berliner Börsenzeitung*, 2 June 1921; "Die Ermordung Talaat Paschas," *Deutsche Tageszeitung*, 2 June

1921; "Der Mord an Talaat Pascha vor dem Schwurgericht: Die Vernehmung des Angeklagten," *Berliner Tageblatt,* 2 June 1921; in some papers, only the next day: "Die Ermordung Talaat Paschas," *Neue Preussische (Kreuz-)Zeitung,* 3 June 1921; "Der Mord an Talaat Pascha," *Kölnische Volkszeitung,* 3 June 1921.

25. "Die Ermordung Talaat Paschas vor Gericht: Die Vernehmung des Angeklagten," *Berliner Börsenzeitung,* 3 June 1921.

26. Similarly in "Das Attentat auf Talaat Pascha: Der Armenier Teilirian vor den Geschworenen," *Berliner Morgenpost,* 3 June 1921; "Die Ermordung Talaat Paschas: Berichte der Zeugen über die Armenier-Greuel," *Berliner Lokal-Anzeiger,* 3 June 1921.

27. See also, "Die Ermordung Talaat Paschas vor Gericht," *Kölnische Volkszeitung,* 3 June 1921.

28. See "Der frühere Großwesir Talaat Pascha in Berlin ermordet: Politischer Racheakt eines armenischen Studenten," *Berliner Morgenpost,* 16 March 1921; "Die Vernehmung des Mörders von Talaat," *Berliner Morgenpost,* 17 March 1921; "Bei den Armeniern in Genf," *Berliner Morgenpost,* 17 March 1921.

29. "Das Attentat auf Talaat Pascha: Der Armenier Teilirian vor den Geschworenen," *Berliner Morgenpost,* 3 June 1921.

30. "Die Ermordung Talaat Paschas," *Deutsche Zeitung,* 3 June 1921.

31. "Das Attentat auf Talaat Pascha: Der Armenier Teilirian vor den Geschworenen," *Berliner Morgenpost,* 3 June 1921; "Die Ermordung Talaat Paschas," *Deutsche Zeitung,* 3 June 1921; Ernst Feder, "Die Lehre des Talaat-Prozesses: Zur Freisprechung Teilirians," *Berliner Tageblatt,* 4 June 1921; "Die Armenischen Greuel: Die Tötung Talaats vor Gericht—Sensationelle Bekundungen der Sachverständigen," *Berliner Volkszeitung,* 3 June 1921.

32. Verbatim the same quotes, for example in "Die Ermordung Talaat Paschas vor Gericht: Die Vernehmung des Angeklagten," *Berliner Börsenzeitung,* 3 June 1921; "Die Ermordung Talaat Paschas: Berichte der Zeugen über die Armenier-Greuel," *Berliner Lokal-Anzeiger,* 3 June 1921; "Der Mörder Talaat Paschas vor Gericht: Die armenischen Greuel," *Germania,* 3 June 1921; "Das Attentat auf Talaat Pascha: Der Armenier Teilirian vor den Geschworenen," *Berliner Morgenpost,* 3 June 1921; "Die Ermordung Talaat Paschas," *Deutsche Zeitung,* 3 June 1921.

33. "Der Mörder Talaat Paschas vor Gericht: Die armenischen Greuel," *Germania,* 3 June 1921; "Die Ermordung Talaat Paschas: Beginn der Beweisaufnahme," *Vossische Zeitung,* 3 June 1921; "Der Mord an Talaat Pascha vor dem Schwurgericht: Beginn der Beweisaufnahme," *Berliner Tageblatt,* 3 June 1921.

34. "Die Ermordung Talaat Paschas," *Neue Preussische (Kreuz-)Zeitung,* 3 June 1921 (morning).

35. "Die Ermordung Talaat Paschas," *Neue Preussische (Kreuz-)Zeitung,* 3 June 1921 (evening); "Tötung des ehemaligen Großweziers Talaat Pascha vor dem Schwurgericht," *Deutsche Tageszeitung,* 3 June 1921; see also, "Talaats Mörder freigesprochen," *Deutsche Zeitung,* 4 June 1921; "Die Ermordung Talaat Paschas—Die Plädoyers," *Vossische Zeitung,* 3 June 1921.

36. See, for example, "Die Ermordung Talaat Paschas vor Gericht," *Kölnische Volks-zeitung*, 3 June 1921.

37. "Der Großkriegsverbrecher," *Vorwärts*, 4 June 1921.

38. The *Berliner Volkszeitung*, in most of the copies of its evening edition, for ex-ample, had ended its coverage abruptly with the jury retreating to discuss their verdict. The next day, it mentioned that only some of the copies of its evening edition had actually announced the verdict. "Die Plädoyers im Talaatprozeß," *Berliner Volskzeitung*, 3 June 1921; "Der Freispruch im Talaat-Prozeß—Die Tragödie eines Volkes," *Berliner Volkzeitung*, 4 June 1921; see also, "Die Ermordung Talaat Paschas vor Gericht—Die armenischen Greuel," *Kölnische Volkszeitung*, 4 June 1921; "Freispruch im Talaat-Pascha-Prozeß," *Germania*, 4 June 1921.

39. "Die Ermordung Talaat Paschas vor Gericht: Das Plädoyer des Staatsanwalts," *Berliner Börsenzeitung*, 4 June 1921.

40. "Der Freispruch Teilerians," *Berliner Lokal-Anzeiger*, 4 June 1921.

41. Emil Ludwig, "Ein weltgeschichtliches Urteil," *Die Weltbühne* 29 (1921): 62–65.

42. "Der Freispruch im Talaat-Prozeß," *Berliner Volkszeitung*, 4 June 1921; see also, "Teilirian," *Berliner Morgenpost*, 4 June 1921.

43. Sabine Mangold-Will, *Begrenzte Freundschaft: Deutschland und die Türkei, 1918–1933* (Göttingen, Germany: Wallstein, 2013), 166.

44. As quoted in Wolfgang Schwanitz, "Immer guter Laune: Gutmann und die Deutsche Orientbank," in Vivian J. Reinheimer, ed., *Herbert M. Gutmann: Bankier in Berlin, Bauherr in Potsdam, Kunstsammler*, 61–77 (Leipzig: Koehler and Amelang, 2007), 61.

45. See "Ein grosser Patriot in heimatlischer Erde beigesetzt," *Türkische Post*, 26 February 1943.

12. The Victory of Justificationalism

1. "Der Großkriegsverbrecher," *Vorwärts*, 4 June 1921; "Die Armeniergreuel: Ein Versuch der Ehrenrettung Talaat Paschas," *Neue Preussische (Kreuz-) Zeitung*, 24 June 1921; "Teilirian," *Berliner Morgenpost*, 4 June 1921; "Teilirian," *Frankfurter Zeitung*, 7 June 1921; Professor Moritz, "Türken und Armenier: Zur Ermordung Talaat Paschas (I)," *Berliner Lokal-Anzeiger*, 7 June 1921.

2. "Der Freispruch im Talaat-Prozeß," *Berliner Volkszeitung*, 4 June 1921.

3. "Die Ermordung Talaat Paschas," *Neue Preussische (Kreuz-)Zeitung*, 3 June 1921; similarly "Die Ermordung Talaat Paschas vor Gericht: Das Plädoyer des Staatsanwalts," *Berliner Börsenzeitung*, 4 June 1921.

4. See, for example, the readers' letters on the topic of the acquittal: Major Schmid, "Talaat und die Armenier," *Vossische Zeitung*, 12 June 1921; Dr. Gutt-mann, "Talaat und die Armenier," *Vossische Zeitung*, 19 June 1921.

5. See Heinrich Vierbücher, *Armenien 1915: Was die kaiserliche Regierung den deutschen Untertanen verschwiegen hat—Die Abschlachtung eines Kulturvolkes*

durch die Türkei (Hamburg: Fackelreiter-Verlag, 1930; Bremen: Donat Verlag, 2004); Alfred Rosenberg, "Mörder und Mörderschutz," *Der Weltkampf* (July 1926): 289–300.

6. B. Elfers, "Stinnes und die D. A. Z.," *Die Weltbühne* 34 (1922): 203–204, here 203.

7. "Zum Talaat-Prozeß," *Deutsche Allgemeine Zeitung*, 3 June 1921.

8. "Der Freispruch des Mörders," *Deutsche Allgemeine Zeitung*, 4 June 1921; see also another article on the same day, "Nachklänge zum Talaat-Prozeß," *Deutsche Allgemeine Zeitung*, 4 June 1921.

9. On the logic of (Armenian) genocide denial: Fatma Müge Göcek, "Reading Genocide: Turkish Historiography on 1915," in Ronald Grigor Suny, Fatma Müge Göcek, and Norman M. Naimark, eds., *A Question of Genocide: Armenians and Turks at the End of the Ottoman Empire* (Oxford: Oxford University Press, 2011), 42–52; Erik Jan Zürcher, "Renewal and Silence: Postwar Unionist and Kemalist Rhetoric on the Armenian Genocide," in ibid., 306–316.

10. "Der Freispruch," *Deutsche Zeitung*, 4 June 1921.

11. "Zum Freispruch des Mörders Talaat Paschas," *Deutsche Tageszeitung*, 4 June 1921.

12. Şefik Arslan, "Offener Brief an Johannes Lepsius," *Vossische Zeitung*, 6 June 1921.

13. "Teilirian," *Frankfurter Zeitung*, 7 June 1921.

14. Moritz, "Türken und Armenier: Zur Ermordung Talaat Paschas (I)," *Berliner Lokal-Anzeiger*, 7 June 1921; Moritz, "Türken und Armenier: Zur Ermordung Talaat Paschas (II)," *Berliner Lokal-Anzeiger*, 8 June 1921.

15. See, for example, an article in the *Deutsche Tageszeitung* as referenced and discussed in the following article: "Verherrlichung der Armeniergreuel," *Freiheit*, 6 June 1921.

16. It had printed an open letter to the German president by Mansur Rifat, a prominent Muslim politician in Berlin, part of the Ottoman exile community. He expressed the outrage of the Turkish community about the trial. He claimed Liman von Sanders had stated that he had not been able to speak in favor of the Turkish side as he had wanted. Why he could not does not become clear; he had been neither interrupted nor (openly) guided in his testimony. Similarly, Rifat complained that the trial treated the whole subject through a religious lens, which he condemned, but which also had not been the case. "Das beleidigte Rechtsgefühl der Türken: Ein türkischer Protestbrief an den Reichspräsidenten," *Neue Preussische (Kreuz-)Zeitung*, 18 June 1921; see also, Mansur Rifaat, "Der einseitige Prozeß," *Deutsche Zeitung*, 7 June 1921; "Zur Freisprechung Teilirians: Ein türkischer Protest," *Berliner Tageblatt*, 9 June 1921.

17. "Die Armeniergreuel: Ein Versuch der Ehrenrettung Talaat Paschas," *Neue Preussische (Kreuz-)Zeitung*, 24 June 1921.

18. "Teilirian," *Deutsche Allgemeine Zeitung*, 8 June 1921. Dinkel mentions that Humann thought Guse's was a "good article" while the one by Feldmann was

"unfortunately of lesser quality." Felix Guse, "Zum Talaatprozess," *Deutsche Allgemeine Zeitung,* 28 June 1921; Christoph Dinkel, "German Officers and the Armenian Genocide," *The Armenian Review* 1 (1991): 77–132, here 94–95; on Guse: 99–100.

19. Otto von Feldmann, "Zum Talaatprozess," *Deutsche Allgemeine Zeitung,* 30 June 1921; Otto von Feldmann, "Zum Talaatprozess," *Weser Zeitung,* 4 July 1921. Feldmann's name seems to have been still of some import in Turkey. President İsmet İnönü answered his condolence letter on Atatürk's death and his congratulations for having been named his successor relatively fast and in German, in December 1938. As reprinted in Peter von Feldmann, *Otto von Feldmann—Türkei, Weimar, Hitler* (Borsdorf, Germany: Edition Winterwork, 2013), 304.

20. Already in a letter in 1919 to a German diplomat who had served in Constantinople, Feldmann justified all that had happened to the Armenians—and he was clearly in a position to know the full extent of it—out of military necessity, but also making note of the Armenians' treacherous character and the impossibility of maintaining "such a people" in the rear of an army. Reprinted in Feldmann, *Otto von Feldmann,* 140–143, here 142.

21. Bronsart von Schellendorff, "Ein Zeugnis für Talaat Pascha," *Deutsche Allgemeine Zeitung,* 24 July 1921.

22. Vahakn N. Dadrian, *German Responsibility in the Armenian Genocide: A Review of the Historical Evidence of German Complicity* (Watertown, MA: Blue Crane Books, 1996), 90, 92–93, 116–118, 121–126, 146.

23. "Der Armenier-Schlächter," *Welt am Montag,* 12 September 1921.

24. "Ein Wort für die Türkei," *Deutsche Zeitung,* 15 September 1921.

25. Armin T. Wegner, "Vorwort," in Armin T. Wegner, ed., *Der Prozess Talaat Pascha* (Berlin: Deutsche Verlagsgesellschaft fuer Politik und Geschichte, 1921; facsimile repr., Tessa Hoffmann, ed., *Der Voelkermord vor Gericht* [Göttingen, Germany: Gesellschaft fuer bedrohte Voelker, 1980]), vii–xi, here viii.

26. Ibid., ix.

27. Ibid.

28. Ibid.

29. Ibid.

30. "Der Prozeß Talaat Pascha," *Westdeutsche Zeitung,* 13 October 1921.

31. Willy Meyer, "Der Prozess Talaat Pascha (I)," *Germania,* 11 November 1921; Willy Meyer, "Der Prozess Talaat Pascha (II)," *Germania,* 11 November 1921.

32. Jürgen Schmidt and Bernd Ulrich, "Pragmatischer Pazifist und Demokrat, Hauptmann a.D. Willy Meyer (1885-1945)," in Wolfram Wette and Helmut Donat, eds., *Pazifistische Offiziere in Deutschland, 1871–1933* (Bremen: Donat Verlag, 1999), 303–317; see Willy Meyer, "Berufssoldat und Pazifismus," *Die Weltbühne,* 10 March 1921, 271–273.

33. "Die Christen im Orient," *Deutsche Allgemeine Zeitung,* 22 December 1921.

34. "Die Memoiren Talaat Paschas," *Deutsche Allgemeine Zeitung,* 12 February 1922; "Talaat Paschas Memoiren," *Deutsche Allgemeine Zeitung,* 9 March 1922.

35. "Wieder einmal Stoff zur Hetze," *Deutsche Tageszeitung*, 15 March 1922; "Talaat Paschas Erinnerungen," *Neue Preussische (Kreuz-)Zeitung*, 11 April 1922.

36. Prozessakte Tehlirian, PrBr 030–03/198B, no. 1799, *State Archive Berlin*.

37. "Die Außenministerkonferenz," *Neue Preussische (Kreuz-)Zeitung*, 25 March 1922.

38. "Einseitigkeit," *Deutsche Allgemeine Zeitung*, 5 April 1922.

39. Isabel V. Hull, *Absolute Destruction: Military Culture and the Practices of War in Imperial Germany* (Ithaca, NY: Cornell University Press, 2006), 273.

40. "Wieder eine politische Mordtat: Zwei Türken heute nacht erschossen," *Vossische Zeitung*, 18 April 1922.

41. "Ein politischer Doppelmord," *Germania*, 18 April 1922.

42. "Die armenische Mörder-Organisation," *Deutsche Zeitung*, 19 April 1922; see also, "Politischer Doppelmord in Berlin," *Deutsche Zeitung*, 18 April 1922; "Der politische Doppelmord," *Deutsche Zeitung*, 19 April 1922; "Die Untersuchung des Türkenmordes," *Deutsche Zeitung*, 20 April 1922; "Armenische Geheimbünde," *Deutsche Allgemeine Zeitung*, 22 April 1922.

43. See "Der Doppelmord an den Türken," *Vossische Zeitung*, 19 April 1922; see also, "Der politische Doppelmord: Noch keine Spur von den Tätern," *Vossische Zeitung*, 19 April 1922; similarly, "Der politische Doppelmord," *Germania*, 19 April 1922.

44. "Die Türkenmorde," *Neue Preussische (Kreuz-)Zeitung*, 20 April 1922.

45. See the reactions to the tweet by Rupert Murdoch after the Charlie Hebdo attack in January 2014 by J. K. Rowling and Aziz Ansari: "J. K. Rowling Attacks Murdoch for Tweet Blaming All Muslims for Charlie Hebdo Deaths," *The Guardian*, 11 January 2015; "US Comedian Aziz Ansari Condemns Rupert Murdoch 'Jihadist Cancer' Tweet," *The Guardian*, 12 January 2015.

46. "Der Freispruch des Mörders," *Deutsche Allgemeine Zeitung*, 4 June 1921.

47. "Zum Türkenmorde," *Deutsche Zeitung*, 20 April 1922.

48. "Die Türkenmorde," *Germania*, 20 April 1922.

49. See, for example, "Der Türkenmord," *Neue Preussische (Kreuz-)Zeitung*, 21 April 1922; "Die beiden verhafteten Armenier," *Neue Preussische (Kreuz-)Zeitung*, 21 April 1922; "Auf der Spur der Mörder?—Zwei Verhaftungen in Leipzig," *Vossische Zeitung*, 21 April 1922.

50. "Der Türkenmord in der Uhlandstraße," *Berliner Lokal-Anzeiger*, 19 April 1922; "Die Ausländer in Berlin," *Berliner Lokal-Anzeiger*, 19 April 1922.

51. "Schuldlose Opfer," *Berliner Lokal-Anzeiger*, 22 April 1922.

52. "Die Totenfeier auf dem Türkenfriedhof," *Berliner Lokal-Anzeiger*, 24 April 1922.

53. "Politik der Woche," *Deutsche Zeitung*, 22 April 1922.

54. "Die Ermordung Djemal Paschas," *Neue Preussische (Kreuz-)Zeitung*, 26 July 1922.

55. "Die Agitation der Armenier," *Berliner Tageblatt*, 16 August 1922; "Die Ermordung Djemal Paschas," *Neue Preussische (Kreuz-)Zeitung*, 17 August 1922;

see also "Djemals Ermordung," *Vossische Zeitung,* 17 August 1922; "Mord-prozeß Djemal Pascha," *BZ am Mittag,* 19 August 1922.

56. "Enver Pascha gefallen," *Vossische Zeitung,* 18 August 1922; "Enver Pascha ge-fallen," *Neue Preussische (Kreuz-)Zeitung,* 18 August 1922.

57. For example, "Rundschau im Auslande: Der Prozeß gegen die Mörder Djemal Paschas," *Neue Preussische (Kreuz-)Zeitung,* 19 August 1922.

58. F. S. Nitti, "Die Türkei und Griechenland," *Berliner Tageblatt,* 28 October 1922.

59. "Die letzten Jahre Dschemal Paschas," *Der Reichswart,* 2 December 1922.

60. "Summarische 'Lösungen,'" *Germania,* 13 December 1922.

61. "Eine Protestnote des Papstes gegen die Türkei," *Neue Preussische (Kreuz-)Zei-tung,* 6 December 1922.

62. "Summarische 'Lösungen,'" *Germania,* 13 December 1922.

63. "Lösung in Lausanne," *Deutsche Allgemeine Zeitung,* 28 December 1922.

64. "Die türkischen Minderheiten," *Deutsche Tageszeitung,* 29 December 1922.

65. The *Kreuzzeitung,* inadvertently probably, gave the highest number of vic-tims of the Armenian Genocide yet—2.7 million: "Minderheitenschutz und Bevölkerungsaustausch," *Neue Preussische (Kreuz-)Zeitung,* 13 December 1922.

66. "Aufstand im Mossulgebiet: Amerika und die armenische Frage," *Neue Preus-sische (Kreuz-)Zeitung,* 2 January 1923; "Ergebnislose Beratungen in Lau-sanne," *Neue Preussische (Kreuz-)Zeitung,* 5 January 1923; "Ausschusssitzungen in Lausanne," *Neue Preussische (Kreuz-)Zeitung,* 28 January 1923.

67. "Der Konflikt in Lausanne," *Neue Preussische (Kreuz-)Zeitung,* 9 January 1923.

68. "Die entscheidende Woche der Lausanner Konferenz," *Neue Preussische (Kreuz-)Zeitung,* 14 May 1923; "Pessimistische Stimmung in Lausanne," *Neue Preussische (Kreuz-)Zeitung,* 22 May 1923.

69. "Die Schlusssitzung in Lausanne," *Neue Preussische (Kreuz-)Zeitung,* 18 July 1923.

70. For example, "Mustafa Kemal Pascha," *Deutsche Zeitung,* 4 July 1920.

71. "Der Frieden von Lausanne," *Neue Preussische (Kreuz-)Zeitung,* 25 July 1923.

72. "Türkische Möglichkeiten," *Deutsche Allgemeine Zeitung,* 16 October 1923.

73. For example, "Frankfurt, 25. Juli" (commentary), *Frankfurter Zeitung,* 25 July 1923; "Die neue Türkei," *Deutsche Allgemeine Zeitung,* 28 June 1923; see also, "Der Konflikt in Lausanne," *Neue Preussische (Kreuz-)Zeitung,* 9 January 1923; also, Hans H. Mulzer, "Die Wiedergeburt der Türkei: Vom Waffenstillstand von Mudros zum Frieden von Lausanne," *Zwischen Kaukasus und Sinai–Jahrbuch des Bundes der Asienkämpfer* 4 (1924): 9–34, here 33.

74. See, inter alia, "Kleine Nachrichten aus dem Ausland," *Neue Preussische (Kreuz-)Zeitung,* 8 August 1919; "Letzte Nachrichten," *Neue Preussische (Kreuz-)Zeitung,* 15 August 1919; "Das amerikanische Mandat über Arme-nien," *Neue Preussische (Kreuz-)Zeitung,* 17 August 1919; "Amerikanische Drohung an die Türkei," *Neue Preussische (Kreuz-)Zeitung,* 17 August 1919; "Amerikanische Truppen für Armenien," *Neue Preussische (Kreuz-)Zeitung,*

6 October 1919; "Die nationale Selbsthilfe des 'kranken Mannes' (I)," *Heimatland*, 18 June 1921; Hauptmann Tröbst, "Mustafa Kemal Pascha und sein Werk (I)," *Heimatland*, 1 September 1923; "Die äußere Politik der Woche," *Neue Preussische (Kreuz-)Zeitung*, 28 January 1920; "'Armeniergreuel,'" *Deutsche Zeitung*, 19 June 1920; "Mustafa Kemal Pascha," *Deutsche Zeitung*, 4 July 1920; "Niederlage der türkischen Nationalisten," *Neue Preussische (Kreuz-)Zeitung*, 14 August 1920; "Blutige Unruhen in Armenien: Die Folgen der Freisprechung des Mörders Talaat Paschas," *Deutsche Tageszeitung*, 23 June 1921; "Talaat Paschas Erinnerungen," *Neue Preussische (Kreuz-)Zeitung*, 11 April 1922; "Lösung in Lausanne," *Deutsche Allgemeine Zeitung*, 28 December 1922; "Deutsch-türkische Beziehungen," *Deutsche Allgemeine Zeitung*, 22 June 1923.

75. Ernst von Reventlow, "Talaat Pascha: Englands Hand," *Der Reichswart*, 19 March 1921.

76. For example, "Talaat Pascha, die Armeniergreuel und der 'Vorwärts,'" *Freiheit*, 16 March 1921; "Vergeltung und Verantwortung," *Freiheit*, 6 June 1921.

77. "Verherrlichung der Armeniergreuel," *Freiheit*, 6 June 1921.

78. Major Schmid, "Talaat und die Armenier," *Vossische Zeitung*, 12 June 1921.

79. For example of Tamcke, as cited in Andreas Meier, "Nachwort," in Andreas Meier, ed., *Armin T. Wegner: Die Austreibung des armenischen Volkes in die Wüste—Ein Lichtbildvortrag*, 153–192 (Göttingen, Germany: Wallstein, 2011), 177–178.

80. Jeffrey Herf, *The Jewish Enemy—Nazi Propaganda during World War II and the Holocaust* (Cambridge, MA: Belknap Press, 2006), for example, 51, 64, 110–111, 154–155.

81. See, for example, Armenag S. Baronigian, *Armenien und die Türkei: Erzählungen und Erlebnisse aus Armeniens jüngster Martyriumsgeschichte* (Lößnitzgrund: Armenisches Hilfskomitee, 1927 [1916]); Melkon Krischtschian, *Deutschland und die Ausrottung der Armenier in der Türkei: Ein Rückblick* (Potsdam, Germany: Missionsbuchhandlung, 1930); A. Hopf, *Unter Verfolgung und Trübsal: Missions- und Kulturbilder aus dem Orient gesammelt auf meiner Reise zu den armenischen Flüchtlingen* (Meiringen, Switzerland: W. Loepthien, 1928); Bruno Eckart, *Meine Erlebnisse in Urfa* (Potsdam, Germany: Tempel-Verlag, 1922); Fritjof Nansen, *Betrogenes Volk: Eine Studienreise durch Georgien und Armenien als Oberkommissar des Völkerbundes* (Leipzig: Brockhaus, 1928). Furthermore, see Rafael de Nogales, *Vier Jahre unter dem Halbmond* (Berlin: Hobbing, 1925); see also the controversy preceding its publication within the German Foreign Office: R 78 484, *Political Archives of the German Foreign Office*. See also the timid mentioning of the massive loss of life in a geography textbook: Walther Vogel, *Das neue Europa und seine historisch-geographischen Grundlagen*, 2nd ed. (Bonn, Germany: K. Schroeder, 1923), 239.

82. Heinrich Vierbücher, *Armenien 1915: Was die kaiserliche Regierung den deutschen Untertanen verschwiegen hat* (Bremen: Donat Verlag, 2004 [1930]).

83. Helmut Donat, "Die Armeniermassaker im Spiegel der deutschen und der internationalen Friedensbewegung, 1895–1933," in Vierbücher, *Armenien,* 77–103, 88–89.

84. Interestingly, the *Reichswart* published an article in 1931 reminding Turkophiles of the Armenian massacres: "Armenier," *Der Reichswart,* 24 January 1931; similarly, the *Germania* restated claims about a large-scale Armenian rebellion at the behest of Russia and Britain: "Volk ohne Land und Recht: Armenier-Elend," *Germania,* 16 January 1931, as quoted in Donat, "Die Armeniermassaker," 89.

85. "Kurden, Armenier und Griechen: Der Aufstieg der Türkei," *Berliner Tageblatt,* 24 June 1925.

86. See, for example, "Wilhelm II. und Abdulhamid," *Hamburger Fremdenblatt,* 27 November 1923; "Deutschland und die Türkei," *Hamburgischer Correspondent,* 5 March 1924; "Kurden, Armenier und Griechen: Der Aufstieg der Türkei," *Berliner Tageblatt,* 24 June 1925; "Der nationale Aufstieg der Türkei," *Neue Preussische (Kreuz-)Zeitung,* 14 December 1928; O. Welsch, "Führer zur türkischen Freiheit: Eine deutsche Biographie Mustafa Kemals," *Deutsche Tageszeitung,* 25 March 1929.

87. See, for example, Bernhard Kunsteller et al., *Geschichtsschulbuch für die deutsche Jugend—Dritter Teil* (Leipzig: K. Schroeder, 1927), 83; see also, Kurt Ziemke, *Die neue Türkei: Politische Entwicklung 1914–1929* (Stuttgart, Germany: Deutsche Verlags-Anstalt, 1930), 11, 87, 89, 96, 98, 130, 271–285, 437.

88. Richard Hartmann, "Die neue Türkei," in Ausschuß zur Förderung des Ausslandsstudiums an der Universität Königsberg, ed., *Der vordere Orient,* 88–115 (Königsberg: Gräfe and Unzer, 1929), 106.

89. Felix Guse, "Der Armenieraufstand 1915 und seine Folgen," *Wissen und Wehr* 10 (1925), as quoted in Dinkel, "German Officers," 100; Felix Guse, *Die Kaukasusfront im Weltkrieg bis zum Frieden von Brest* (Leipzig: Koehler and Amelang, 1940).

90. Dominik J. Schaller, "Die Rezeption des Völkermordes an den Armeniern in Deutschland, 1915–1945," in Hans-Lukas Kieser and Dominik J. Schaller, eds., *Der Völkermord an den Armeniern und die Shoah* (Zurich: Chronos, 2002), 517–555.

13. Racial Discourse and the Armenians

1. Hutton discusses how discourses on race and *Volk* conflicted and merged in the Third Reich. Christopher M. Hutton, *Race and the Third Reich: Linguistics, Racial Anthropology and Genetics in the Dialectic of Volk* (Cambridge, UK: Polity, 2005); see Evans on the time before: Andrew D. Evans, *Anthropology at War: World War I and the Science of Race in Germany* (Chicago: Chicago University Press, 2010), 68–80, 201–207.

2. See also, Evans, *Anthropology at War,* 13, 189–221.

3. Ibid., 26–31, 57–96.

4. Ibid., 43–44, 198.
5. Felix von Luschan, *The Early Inhabitants of Western Asia: The Huxley Memorial Lecture for 1911* (London: Royal Anthropological Institute, 1911), 242.
6. Felix von Luschan, "Book Review of 'America's Greatest Problem: The Negro,'" *American Anthropologist* 17 (1915): 573–574.
7. On the Aryan theory and its influence on the Nazis, see, Hutton, *Race and the Third Reich*, 80–100.
8. Felix von Luschan, *Völker, Rassen, Sprachen* (Berlin: Welt-Verlag, 1922), 53, 62.
9. See Carl Helm, *Arier, Wilde und Juden* (Leipzig: C. W. Stern, 1923), 31–32.
10. Ibid., 48–49.
11. Ibid., 36.
12. Luschan, *Völker*, 165.
13. Ibid., 168.
14. On Günther see also Hutton, *Race and the Third Reich*, 35–63.
15. See Reichsführer SS and SS-Hauptamt, eds., *Rassenpolitik* (Berlin: SS-Hauptamt, 1943), 15.
16. Hutton, *Race and the Third Reich*, 63.
17. Hans F. R. Günther, *Herkunft und Rassengeschichte der Germanen* (Munich: Lehmanns Verlag, 1939), backmatter.
18. Hans F. R. Günther, *Rassenkunde des deutschen Volkes*, 16th ed. (Munich: Lehmanns Verlag, 1939).
19. See Günther, *Herkunft und Rassengeschichte*, backmatter.
20. Günther, *Rassenkunde des deutschen Volkes*, 227.
21. Hans F. R. Günther, *Rassenkunde des jüdischen Volkes*, 2nd ed. (Munich: J. F. Lehmanns Verlag, 1930), 30.
22. Hans F. R. Günther, *Kleine Rassenkunde des deutschen Volkes* (Munich: J. F. Lehmanns Verlag, 1934 [1929]), 52.
23. Hans F. R. Günther, *Rassenkunde Europas mit besonderer Berücksichtigung der Rassengeschichte der Hauptvölker indogermanischer Sprache*, 3rd ed. (Munich: J. F. Lehmanns Verlag, 1929), 180.
24. Ibid., 92–95.
25. Hans F. R. Günther, *Die nordische Rasse bei den Indogermanen Asiens* (Munich: J. F. Lehmanns Verlag, 1934), 223, as quoted in Dominik J. Schaller, "Die Rezeption des Völkermordes an den Armeniern in Deutschland, 1915–1945," in Hans-Lukas Kieser and Dominik J. Schaller, eds., *Der Völkermord an den Armeniern und die Shoah*, 517–555 (Zurich: Chronos, 2002), 555n219.
26. Theodor Fritsch, *Handbuch der Judenfrage: Die wichtigsten Tatsachen zur Beurteilung des jüdischen Volkes*, 49th ed. (Leipzig: Hammer-Verlag, 1944), 12.
27. Ibid. For Hitler's blurb, see, for example, Theodor Fritsch, ed., *Die Zionistischen Protokolle: Das Programm der internationalen Geheimregierung* (Leipzig: Hammer-Verlag, 1933).
28. Fritsch, *Handbuch der Judenfrage*, 13.
29. Ibid., 15.

30. Ibid.
31. Ibid.
32. Richard Lewinsohn, "Anti-Spengler," *Weltbühne* 24 (June 1921): 664–665.
33. Houston Chamberlain, *Die Grundlagen des Neunzehnten Jahrhunderts,* 3rd. ed. (Munich: Verlagsanstalt F. Bruckmann, 1901), 44.
34. Ibid., 44–45.
35. Ibid., 357, 359, 361, 590.
36. Albrecht Wirth, *Volkstum und Weltmacht in der Geschichte* (Munich: Verlagsanstalt F. Bruckmann, 1901), 25.
37. Ibid., 43, 132.
38. For example in the third edition: Chamberlain, *Die Grundlagen,* 29.
39. Albrecht Wirth, *Männer, Völker, und Zeiten: Eine Weltgeschichte in einem Bande* (Hamburg Alfred Jansen, 1917), 69; Albrecht Wirth, *Der Balkan: Seine Länder und Völker in Geschichte, Kultur, Politik, Volkswirtschaft und Weltverkehr* (Stuttgart, Germany: Unions Deutsche Verlagsgesellschaft, 1914), 287.
40. Albrecht Wirth, *Deutschtum und die Türkei* (Vienna: Osterwieck 1910); Albrecht Wirth, *Türkei, Österreich, Deutschland* (Stuttgart, Germany: Dolge, 1912).
41. Albrecht Wirth, *Geschichte der Türkei* (Stuttgart, Germany: Franckh, 1912), 5.
42. Ibid., 70.
43. Wirth, *Türkei,* 70.
44. Constantin Brunner, *Judenhass und die Juden* (Berlin: Oesterheld and Co. Verlag, 1918), 304–305.
45. S. Weissberg, *Die südrussischen Juden: Eine anthropometrische Studie* (Brunswick: Friedrich Vieweg und Sohn, 1895), 123.
46. Arthur Ruppin, *Die Juden der Gegenwart: Eine sozialwissenschaftliche Studie,* 3rd ed. (Berlin: Jüdischer Verlag, 1920), 189; on Ruppin, see Amos Morris-Reich, "Arthur Ruppin's Concept of Race," *Israel Studies* 3 (2006): 1–30.
47. Ruppin, *Die Juden,* 41.
48. Ibid., 181.
49. Ibid., 189; on the similarity between Jews and Armenians see Arthur Ruppin, "Juden und Armenier," *Zeitschrift für Demographie und Statistik der Juden* 2 (1916): 177–181, as quoted in Morris-Reich, "Arthur Ruppin's," 30.
50. Fritz Kahn, *Die Juden als Rasse und Kulturvolk,* 3rd ed. (Berlin: Welt-Verlag, 1922).
51. Ibid., 74–75, 80–82.
52. Alexander Schüler, *Der Rassenadel der Juden: Der Schlüssel zur Judenfrage* (Berlin: Jüdischer Verlag, 1912).
53. Friedrich Hertz, *Rasse und Kultur* (Leipzig: Alfred Kröner, 1915), 297.
54. Maurice Fishberg, *Die Rassenmerkmale der Juden: Eine Einführung in ihre Anthropologie* (Munich: Ernst Reinhard, 1913), 228.
55. Ibid., 233, similarly 234.

56. Ibid., 262.

57. Further examples: Albert Drexel, *Grundriss der Rassenkunde* (Freiburg, Switzerland: Universitätsverlag, 1941), 81, as quoted in Schaller, "Die Rezeption," 543. See also, for example, books on Eastern European history: In *History of the Jews in Poland and Russia* by Josef Meisl, the Jews and the Armenians were equally stressed to have been very successful in trade in fourteenth-century Poland, for example. Josef Meisl, *Geschichte der Juden in Polen und Russland* (Berlin: C. A. Schwetschke und Sohn, 1921), 75, 104.

58. See Siegfried Passarge, *Das Judenthum als landschaftskundlich-ethnologisches Problem* (Munich: J. F. Lehmanns Verlag, 1929), 86, 87, 88, 91, 93, 96.

59. Henry Ford, *Der Internationale Jude,* 33rd ed. (Leipzig: Hammer-Verlag, 1937), 416.

60. Armin Pfahl-Traughber, *Der antisemitisch-antifreimaurerische Verschwörungsmythos in der Weimarer Republik und im NS-Staat* (Vienna: Braumüller, 1993), 39; see "Ford and GM Scrutinized for Alleged Nazi Collaboration," *Washington Post,* 30 November 1998.

61. Alfred Rosenberg, *Der Mythus des 20. Jahrhunderts* (Munich: Hoheneichen-Verlag, 1934 [1930]), 213.

62. Hermann Esser, *Die jüdische Weltpest: Judendämmerung auf dem Erdball* (Munich: Franz Eher Nachfolger, 1939); Fritsch, *Handbuch,* 270.

63. Karl Baumböck, *Juden machen Weltpolitik,* Nationalpolitische Aufklärungsschriften 16 (Berlin: Paul Hochmuth, 1942), 7; Karl Georg Kuhn, *Die Juden als weltgeschichtliches Problem* (Hamburg: Hanseatische Verlagsanstalt, 1939), 18–19; Martin Staemmler, *Rassenpflege im völkischen Staat* (Munich: J. F. Lehmanns Verlag, 1933), as quoted in Uwe Feigel, *Das evangelische Deutschland und Armenien: Die Armenierhilfe deutscher evangelischer Christen seit dem Ende des 19. Jahrhunderts im Kontext der deutsch-türkischen Beziehungen* (Göttingen, Germany: Vandenhoeck and Ruprecht, 1989), 292, and in Axel Meissner, *Martin Rades "Christliche Welt" und Armenien: Bausteine für eine internationale Ethik des Protestantismus* (Berlin: LIT Verlag, 2010), 287.

64. For example, Egon Freiherr von Eickstedt, *Rassenkunde und Rassengeschichte der Menschheit* (Stuttgart, Germany: Enke, 1934), 163, as quoted in Schaller, "Die Rezeption," 555n217; on racial relatedness to Jews, see Dieter Gerhardt, *Kurzer Abriss der Rassenkunde* (Munich: J. F. Lehmanns Verlag, 1938), 5; Schaller, "Die Rezeption," 555n217; also in Hans Weinert, *Die Rassen der Menschheit* (Leipzig: B. G. Teubner, 1938 [1935]), 166; K. Saller, "Beitrag zur Anthropologie der Ostjuden," *Zeitschrift für Morphologie und Anthropologie* 1/2 (1933): 125–131, here 126–127.

65. Johann von Leers, *Adolf Hitler* (Berlin: R. Kittler, 1934 [1932]); Gregory Wegner claims that Leers later changed his name to Omar Amin von Leers and became a Muslim, to be buried in 1965 according to Islamic rites; Gregory Wegner, *Anti-Semitism and Schooling under the Third Reich* (New York: Routledge, 2002), 22 (adviser to Goebbels, 208).

66. Wegner, *Anti-Semitism*, 22; see Jeffrey Herf, *Nazi Propaganda in the Arab World* (New Haven, CT: Yale University Press, 2009), 265; Robert S. Wistrich, *Who Is Who in Nazi Germany* (London: Routledge, 1995 [1982]), 152–153.

67. Johann von Leers, *Forderung der Stunde: Juden raus!*, 2nd ed. (Berlin: Propaganda Verlag, 1933 [1928]), 4.

68. Ibid., 4–5.

69. Ibid.

70. Ibid., 21.

71. Ibid., 22.

72. Johannes von Leers, *Rassen, Völker und Volkstümer* (Langensalza, Germany: Beltz, 1938), 127, as quoted in Schaller, "Die Rezeption," 555n219. Apparently, however, Leers had also published an essay in a book edited by the German-Armenian Society in 1934 in which he attested to the Armenians' "Aryan character"—apparently he had changed his mind later on again. Schaller, "Die Rezeption," 543–544.

73. Leers, *Forderung der Stunde*, 20; Leers, *Adolf Hitler*, 5.

74. For example, Werner Sombart, *Die Juden und das Wirtschaftsleben* (Leipzig: Duncker und Humblot, 1911), viii; Max Biehl, *England als Wucherbankier* (Berlin: Junker und Dünnhaupt Verlag, 1940), 20.

75. Press directive ZSg. 101/7/83/No. 119 (4 February 1936), in Hans Bohrmann, ed., *NS-Presseanweisungen der Vorkriegszeit*, vol. 4, part 1 (Munich: K. G. Saur, 1993), 114.

76. "Rede auf Generalmitgliederversammlung der NSDAP/NSDAV e.V. in München," Document no. 159 (30 July 1927), in Institut für Zeitgeschichte, ed., *Hitler: Reden, Schriften, Anordnungen, Februar 1925 bis Januar 1933*, vol. 2, part 2 (Munich: K. G. Saur, 1992), 429.

77. Adolf Hitler, "Politik der Woche," *Illustrierter Beobachter*, 7 September 1929, reprinted in Institut für Zeitgeschichte, *Hitler: Reden, Schriften, Anordnungen*, vol. 2, part 1, 374–378, here 378.

78. F. Roderich-Stoltheim, *Das Rätsel des jüdischen Erfolges*, 7th ed. (Leipzig: Hammer, 1928), 181.

79. Adolf Hitler, "'Young Plan' und Parlamentswirtschaft," *Illustrierter Beobachter*, 5 October 1929, reprinted in Institut für Zeitgeschichte, *Hitler: Reden, Schriften, Anordnungen*, vol. 2, part 1, 395–399, here 397.

80. "Rede auf NSDAP-Versammlung in Nürnberg," Document no. 61 (3 December 1928), in Institut für Zeitgeschichte, ed., *Hitler: Reden, Schriften, Anordnungen*, vol. 2, part 1, 297–316, here 310.

81. Hans-Lukas Kieser, "Germany and the Armenian Genocide of 1915–1917," in Jonathan C. Friedman, *The Routledge History of the Holocaust*, 30–44 (London: Routledge, 2012), 39.

82. At the Klessheim Conference, 17 April 1943, Vahakn N. Dadrian, *The History of the Armenian Genocide* (New York: Berghahn, 2004 [1995]), 402.

83. Adolf Hitler, "Politik der Woche," *Illustrierter Beobachter*, 24 May 1930, reprinted in Institut für Zeitgeschichte, ed., *Hitler: Reden, Schriften, Anordnungen*, vol. 2, pt. 1, 202–206, here 203.

84. Henry Picker, ed., *Hitlers Tischgespräche im Führerhauptquartier: Hitler wie er wirklich war* (Stuttgart, Germany: Busse-Seewald, 1977 [1963]), 422; Kevork B. Bardakjian, *Hitler and the Armenian Genocide* (Cambridge, MA: Zoryan Institute, 1985), 30.

85. Aschot Hayruni, "Die deutsche Orient-Mission—Ihre publizistische und organisatorische Tätigkeit für Armenien unter dem nationalsozialistischen Regime," *Armenisch-Deutsche Korrespondenz* 140 (2008): 23–28.

86. In the literature there exists the claim that the intense lobbying of pro-Armenian circles resulted in the official recognition of Third Reich authorities of the Armenians as "Aryans" in the year 1933 already (though such things would have only mattered after the Nuremberg Laws [1935] anyway), as protection for the very small group of Armenian foreign nationals living in Germany. In any case, the term "Aryan," according to the Nuremberg Laws, was to apply only for Germany and not to nations and peoples abroad. Feigel, *Das evangelische Deutschland*, 292; Meissner, *Martin Rades "Christliche Welt,"* 288; Joachim Hoffmann, *Kaukasien 1942/43: Das deutsche Heer und die Orientvölker der Sowjetunion* (Freiburg, Germany: Rombach, 1991), 315–316.

14. The Nazis' New Turkey

1. For more details on the following, see Stefan Ihrig, *Atatürk in the Nazi Imagination* (Cambridge, MA: Belknap Press, 2014).

2. See ibid., chapters 1, 2, 4, and 5; also see Dominik J. Schaller, "Die Rezeption des Völkermordes an den Armeniern in Deutschland, 1915–1945," in Hans-Lukas Kieser and Dominik J. Schaller, eds., *Der Völkermord an den Armeniern und die Shoah,* 517–555 (Zurich: Chronos, 2002), 539. (In addition to those mentioned here, he also discusses Richard Hartmann's concurrent views of the "racial war" against the Armenians and their destruction as a precondition, 539–540.)

3. See, for example, "Betrogene Betrüger," *Freiheit,* 20 July 1921.

4. Ihrig, *Atatürk,* chapters 1 and 2.

5. Ibid., chapter 2.

6. "Außenpolitische Rundschau: Die heldenhafte Türkei," *Völkischer Beobachter,* 1 January 1921; "Die Türkei: Der Vorkämpfer," *Völkischer Beobachter,* 6 February 1921.

7. "Die Türkei und Moskau," *Völkischer Beobachter,* 22 February 1921.

8. "Die Entente und die Türkei," *Völkischer Beobachter,* 10 March 1921.

9. "Die nationale Selbsthilfe des 'kranken Mannes,'" *Heimatland,* part I: 18 June 1921; part II: 25 June.

10. "Die deutsche 'Erfüllungspolitik' im neutralen Urteil," *Heimatland* (no date, probably 1 April) 1922; A. Steinitzer, "Deutschland, Italien, Türkei: Geschichtliche Parallelen VI," *Heimatland* (no date, probably 23 September), 1922.

11. Hauptmann Hans Tröbst, "Mustafa Kemal Pascha und sein Werk (VI)," *Heimatland,* 15 October 1923.

12. Ibid.

13. Ibid.
14. Ibid.
15. Ibid.
16. As quoted in Götz Aly, *Why the Germans? Why the Jews? Envy, Race Hatred, and the Prehistory of the Holocaust* (New York: Metropolitan Books, 2014 [2011]), 209–211.
17. "Letter from 7 September 1923, by secretary Fritz Lauböck," no. 47, folder C, *Tröbst Papers*, at the Institute for Press Research, University of Bremen; see also Hartwig Gebhardt, *Mir fehlt eben ein anständiger Beruf: Leben und Arbeit des Auslandskorrespondenten Hans Tröbst, 1891–1939* (Bremen: Edition Lumière, 2007), 20.
18. Hans Tröbst, "Der 'Unsinn' der Angora-Regierung," *Völkischer Kurier*, 13 March 1924; see further for Tröbst's views on ethnic purity: Hans Tröbst, "Mustafa Kemal Pascha und sein Werk (I)," *Heimatland*, 1 September 1923; Hans Tröbst, "Mustafa Kemal Pascha und sein Werk (II)," *Heimatland*, 9 September 1923; Hans Tröbst, *Soldatenblut: Vom Baltikum zu Kemal Pascha* (Leipzig: Koehler, 1925), 329.
19. Ihrig, *Atatürk*, chapter 3.
20. Falih Rıfkı Atay, *Mustafa Kemal'in Mütareke Defteri* (Ankara: Kültür Bakanlığı, 1981), 79; also somewhat incorrectly cited in Halil Gülbeyaz, *Mustafa Kemal Atatürk: Vom Staatsgründer zum Mythos* (Berlin: Parthas, 2003), 228.
21. Heinrich Hoffmann, *Hitler Was My Friend* (London: Burke, 1955), 88.
22. R. Hüsrev Gerede, *Harb İçinde Almanya, 1939–1942*, ed. H. Turgut and S. Y. Cebeci (Istanbul: ABC, 1994), 32.
23. Johann von Leers, *Adolf Hitler* (Berlin: R. Kittler, 1934 [1932]), 5.
24. Ihrig, *Atatürk*, chapter 4.
25. Ibid., 187–195.
26. For example, "Das Echo der Türkei-Feiern," *Völkischer Beobachter*, 7 November 1933; "Papen an seine Waffenbrüder," *Kölnische Zeitung*, 1 November 1933; "Aus Not und Hoffnungslosigkeit zu neuem Leben," *Deutsche Zeitung*, 1 November 1933.
27. See, for example, W. v. Lojewski, *Aufmarsch im Orient* (Leipzig: W. Goldmann, 1941), 118; Norbert von Bischoff, *Ankara: Eine Deutung des neuen Werdens in der Türkei* (Vienna: Holzhausens Nachfolger, 1935), 33, 95–96, 124, 155–156; Herbert Melzig, *Kamâl Atatürk: Untergang und Aufstieg der Türkei* (Frankfurt am Main: Societäts Verlag, 1937), 71–72, 93–94, 210; Hanns Froembgen, *Kamal Atatürk: Soldat und Führer*, 7th ed. (Stuttgart, Germany: Franckhsche Verlagsbuchhandlung, 1935), 101–102; Dagobert von Mikusch, *Gasi Mustafa Kemal: Zwischen Europa und Asien*, 10th ed. (Leipzig: List, 1935 [1929]), 72, 80–81, 156, 272, 311; August von Kral, *Das Land Kamal Atatürks: Der Werdegang der modernen Türkei* (Vienna: Wilhelm Braumüller, 1935), 173; Martin Bethke, *Im Lande Ismet Inönüs: Beobachtungen und Streiflichter aus der Türkei* (Berlin: Deutscher Verlag, 1944), 60, 93, 169–173; Roedenbeck mentions only

that two million Armenians had been "resettled to Syria and Russian Armenia": Georg Roedenbeck, *Das Türkische Reich: Ein Brennpunkt politischen Geschehens* (Berlin: Otto Stollberg, 1939), 28, also on the massacres: 57. See also Kurt Ziemke, *Die neue Türkei: Politische Entwicklung, 1914–1929* (Stuttgart, Germany: Deutsche Verlags-Anstalt, 1930), 271–285. Some texts, however, very explicitly fail to mention the Armenians, even though they praise the fact that the New Turkey was purely *völkisch* and had rid itself of its minorities. In an exemplary fashion: H. von Engelmann, "Köpfe der Weltpolitik: Ghasi Mustafa Kemal Pascha," *Münchner Neueste Nachrichten,* 18 January 1934; Wilhelm Koppen, "Atatürks Erbe," *Völkischer Beobachter,* 22 November 1938.

28. This was the central theme of a 1923 article, "Die äußere Politik der Woche: Der Frieden von Lausanne," *Neue Preussische (Kreuz-)Zeitung,* 25 July 1923.

29. "Ankara: Herz und Hirn der neuen Türkei," *Berliner Börsenzeitung,* 15 August 1936; see also, Karl Klinghardt, *Angora: Konstantinopel, Ringende Gewalten* (Frankfurt am Main: Frankfurter Societäts-Druckerei, 1924), 158.

30. See Brigitte Hamann, *Hitlers Wien: Lehrjahre eines Diktators* (Munich: Piper, 1997).

31. Froembgen, *Kamal Atatürk,* 9.

32. Ibid.

33. For example, very obvious in "Kamal Atatürk," *Dresdner Neueste Nachrichten,* 10 November 1938; Reinhard Hüber, *Die Türkei: Ein Weg nach Europa* (Berlin: Volk und Reich Verlag, 1942), 37; Heinz Mundhenke, "Die türkische Hauptstadt: Einst und jetzt," in ed. unnamed, *Die neue Türkei* (Istanbul: Universum, 1936), 1–3.

34. Karl Klinghardt, *Türkün Jordu: Der Türken Heimatland—Eine geographisch-politische Landesschilderung* (Hamburg: Friederichsen, 1925), 126; Bischoff, *Ankara,* 155–157; Theodor Böttiger, *Führer der Völker* (Berlin: Junge Generation, 1935), 75–76; Felix Guse, *Die Türkei* (Leipzig: Koehler and Amelang, 1943), 108–109; Roedenbeck, *Das Türkische Reich,* 24, 28–29; also, "'Vater der Türken'—Der Schöpfer der neuen Türkei,'" *Münchner Neueste Nachrichten,* 11 November 1938; "Das Werk des Befreiers," *Neues Wiener Journal,* 11 November 1938; also in 1929: Richard Hartmann, "Die neue Türkei," in Ausschuß zur Förderung des Ausslandsstudiums an der Universität Königsberg, ed., *Der vordere Orient,* 88–115 (Königsberg: Gräfe and Unzer, 1929), 106–112; see also Schaller, "Die Rezeption," 539. Even Rohrbach makes this point, though rather masked: Paul Rohrbach, *Balkan, Türkei: Eine Schicksalszone Europas* (Hamburg: Hoffmann and Campe, 1941), 54.

35. Mikusch, *Gasi Mustafa Kemal,* 81.

36. Ibid.; similarly in Bischoff, *Ankara,* 225; for the Indian metaphor used by Hitler in conversation with Fritz Sauckel and Fritz Todt regarding the Germanization of the East, see Christopher Browning, *The Origins of the Final Solution: The Evolution of Nazi Jewish Policy, September 1939–*

March 1942, with contributions by Jürgen Matthäus (London: Arrow Books, 2005), 370.

37. Fritz Rössler, *Kemal Pascha* (Berlin: R. Kittler, 1934), 79; similarly, see Bischoff, *Ankara*, 63.

38. Rössler, *Kemal Pascha*, 78–80; similar phrasing in Bischoff, *Ankara*, 106.

39. Klinghardt, *Türkün Jordu*, 29; see also Froembgen, *Kamal Atatürk*, 100; Bethke, *Im Lande Ismet Inönüs*, 145; Guse, *Die Türkei*, 108–109.

40. Froembgen, *Kamal Atatürk*, 100–101, 142, 155; Rössler, *Kemal Pascha*, 79; Kral, *Das Land Kamal Atatürks*, 5; Gotthard Jäschke, *Türkei* (Berlin: Junker and Dünnhaupt, 1941), 27; Bethke, *Im Lande Ismet Inönüs*, 193, 201, 206, 218; Guse, *Die Türkei*, 55–56, 74–75; Egon Heymann, "Zehn Jahre neue Türkei," *Berliner Börsenzeitung*, 28 October 1933; Wilhelm von Kries, "Der gesunde Staat am Bosporus: Zehn Jahre neue Türkei," *Berliner Lokal-Anzeiger*, 31 October 1933; "Mustafa Kemal und der moderne Orient," *Deutsche Zeitung*, 27 September 1934; "Der Weg der Türkei," *Völkischer Beobachter*, 22 June 1941; "Kemal Atatürk: Der Schöpfer der neuen Türkei," *Neue Preussische (Kreuz-)Zeitung*, 10 January 1937; Wilhelm Renner, "Der Vater der Türken," *Berliner Tageblatt*, 11 November 1938; W. Koppen, "Kamal Atatürk," *Hannoverscher Kurier*, 1 December 1938.

41. See, for example, Bischoff, *Ankara*, 63, 72, 95–96, 202; see also, Hartmann, "Die neue Türkei," 102; Melzig, *Kamâl Atatürk*, 94, 149; Froembgen, *Kamal Atatürk*, 9–10, 16, 66, 87–92, 100–101, 107–109, 137–142; Mikusch, *Gasi Mustafa Kemal*, 9, 22–24, 63–64, 80–81; Rössler, *Kemal Pascha*, 61, 78–79; Jäschke, *Türkei*, 39; Bethke, *Im Lande Ismet Inönüs*, 60, 169, 172–173; Roedenbeck, *Das Türkische Reich*, 57; Guse, *Die Türkei*, 50–51, 142; "'Nun, die Steuerpächter seid ihr los . . . !'—Kemal Atatürk, der Befreier des türkischen Bauern," *Nationalsozialistische Landpost*, 12 November 1938.

42. "Die Stellung der neuen Türkei," *Hamburger Tageblatt*, 5 May 1935. For examples of negative discussions of the Greeks, see "Kamal Atatürk," *(Linzer) Tages-Post*, 10 November 1938; H. von Engelmann, "Köpfe der Weltpolitik: Ghasi Mustafa Kemal Pascha," *Münchner Neueste Nachrichten*, 18 January 1934; Rössler, *Kemal Pascha*, 104; Schaller, "Die Rezeption," 539.

43. "Lausanne und wir," *Deutsch Allgemeine Zeitung*, 19 December 1922; "Summarische 'Lösungen,'" *Germania*, 13 December 1922; Mikusch, *Gasi Mustafa Kemal*, 338; similarly, Kral, *Das Land Kamal Atatürks*, 170; Bethke, *Im Lande Ismet Inönüs*, 169–170, 220.

44. "Die neuen Völkerwanderungen auf dem Balkan," *Neue Preussische (Kreuz-)Zeitung*, 2 December (evening) 1922.

45. "Der Umbau einer Nation: 10 Jahre staatsmännische Arbeit in der Türkei," *Nationalsozialistische Partei-Korrespondenz*, 28 October 1933.

46. "Die griechisch-türkischen Beziehungen," *Völkischer Beobachter*, 14 September 1933; similarly, for example, Roedenbeck, *Das Türkische Reich*, 26; Fritz Rössler, 'Die Außenpolitik der türkischen Republik,' *Der Reichswart*, 31 October 1936.

47. Melzig, *Kamâl Atatürk*, 210.

48. Bischoff, *Ankara*, 157, also 155, 159–160, 225; similarly in Rohrbach, *Balkan, Türkei*, 54.

49. Klinghardt, *Türkün Jordu*, 114; see also Froembgen, *Kamal Atatürk*, 189–191.

50. For example, Bischoff, *Ankara*, 155; Hüber, *Die Türkei*, 11; Jäschke, *Türkei*, 12; Mikusch, *Gasi Mustafa Kemal*, 22–25; Bethke's book even included a chapter on the topic with the telling title "The Solved Problem": Bethke, *Im Lande Ismet Inönüs*, 169–173, see also 60; "Papen an seine Waffenbrüder: Eine Rede zum Jubelfest der Türkei," *Kölnische Zeitung*, 1 November 1933; Hans Rabe, "30 Jahre Freund der Türkei: Ein Nachwort zum türkischen Jubiläum," *Neue Preussische (Kreuz-)Zeitung*, 1 November 1933; Mümtaz Fazil Bey, "Wirtschaftsentwicklung unter nationalem Führertum," *Berliner Börsenzeitung*, 28 October 1933; Wilhelm von Kries, "Der gesunde Staat am Bosporus: Zehn Jahre neue Türkei," *Berliner Lokal-Anzeiger*, 31 October 1933; "Das Werk des Befreiers," *Neues Wiener Journal*, 11 November 1938.

51. Joseph B. Schechtman, *European Population Transfers, 1939–1945* (New York: Russell and Russell, 1946), 22.

52. Holm Sundhaussen, "Lausanner Konferenz," in Detlef Brandes, Holm Sundhaussen, and Stefan Troebst, eds., *Lexikon der Vertreibungen: Deportation, Zwangsaussiedlung und ethnische Säuberung im Europa des 20. Jahrhunderts*, 387–388 (Vienna: Böhlau, 2010), 388; also, Michael Barutciski, "Lausanne Revisited: Population Exchanges in International Law and Policy," in Renée Hirschon, ed., *Crossing the Aegean: An Appraisal of the 1923 Compulsory Population Exchange between Greece and Turkey*, 23–37 (New York: Berghahn, 2004), 25; Eric D. Weitz, *A Century of Genocide: Utopias of Race and Nation* (Princeton, NJ: Princeton University Press, 2005), 51; see also Richard J. Evans, *The Third Reich at War, 1939–1945* (London: Allen Lane, 2008), 28.

53. Browning, *The Origins*.

15. No Smoking Gun

1. Hermann Wygoda, *In the Shadow of the Swastika*, ed. Mark Wygoda (Urbana: University of Illinois Press, 2003), 31.

2. "A78: Die Judenverfolgungen," in Sopade, *Deutschland-Berichte der Sozialdemokratischen Partei Deutschlands (Sopade), 1934–1940, Sechster Jahrgang 1939* (Frankfurt am Main: Verlag Petra Nettelbeck und Zweitausendeins, 1980), 201–202.

3. See, for example, Peter Longerich, *The Unwritten Order—Hitler's Role in the Final Solution* (Stroud, UK: Tempus, 2001).

4. Christoph Dinkel, "German Officers and the Armenian Genocide," *The Armenian Review* 1 (1991): 77–132, here 108; Mike Joseph, "Max Erwin von Scheubner-Richter: The Personal Link from Genocide to Hitler," in Hans-Lukas Kieser and Elmar Plozza, eds., *Der Völkermord an den Armeniern, die*

Türkei und Europa, 147–165 (Zurich: Chronos, 2006), 154; Erich F. Sommer, *Botschafter Graf Schulenburg: Der letzte Vertreter des deutschen Reiches in Moskau* (Asendorf, Germany: Mut Verlag, 1989), 28–36; Tessa Hoffmann, "New Aspects of the Talat Pasha Court Case: Unknown Archival Documents on the Background and Procedure of an Unintended Political Trial," *Armenian Review* 4 (1989): 41–53, here 45.

5. Rohrbach is an exceedingly difficult person to characterize in this context. He was, in fact, another of our protagonists, intervening for the Armenians, as a pro-Armenian activist. Yet, at the same time, he was a major thinker of German aggressive expansionism and imperialism. See, for example, Isabel V. Hull, *Absolute Destruction: Military Culture and the Practices of War in Imperial Germany* (Ithaca, NY: Cornell University Press, 2006), 330–331.

6. See Armin T. Wegner, "Vorwort," in Armin T. Wegner, ed., *Der Prozess Talaat Pascha* (Berlin: Deutsche Verlagsgesellschaft fuer Politik und Geschichte, 1921; facsimile repr., Tessa Hoffmann, ed., *Der Voelkermord vor Gericht* [Göttingen, Germany: Gesellschaft fuer bedrohte Voelker, 1980]), vii–xi, here viii.

7. Robert M. W. Kempner, "Vor sechzig Jahren vor einem deutschen Schwurgericht: Der Völkermord an den Armeniern," *Recht und Politik* 3 (1980): 167–169.

8. Joseph, "Scheubner-Richter," 153.

9. Michael Kellogg, *The Russian Roots of Nazism: White Émigrés and the Making of National Socialism, 1917–1945* (Cambridge: Cambridge University Press, 2005), 106.

10. Malte Fuhrmann, *Der Traum vom deutschen Orient: Zwei deutsche Kolonien im Osmanischen Reich, 1851–1918* (Frankfurt am Main: Campus, 2006), 362.

11. Karl Helfferich, *Die deutsche Türkenpolitik* (Berlin: Vossische Buchhandlung, 1921), 12.

12. Rudolf Hoess, *Commandant of Auschwitz: The Autobiography of Rudolf Hoess* (London: Phoenix Press, 2000 [1959]).

13. Sylvia Taschka, *Diplomat ohne Eigenschaften?—Die Karriere des Hans Heinrich Dieckoff, 1884–1952* (Stuttgart, Germany: Steiner, 2006), 42–46.

14. Kellogg, *Russian Roots,* 140. His role is still somewhat disputed. Fest claims that "his influence on Hitler was considerable," as quoted in Vahakn N. Dadrian, *The History of the Armenian Genocide* (New York: Berghahn, 2004 [1995]), 412.

15. Kellogg, *Russian Roots,* 197.

16. As quoted in Dadrian, *History,* 412.

17. This at least was the version as told by Scheubner's widow; Kellogg, *Russian Roots,* 211.

18. Paul Leverkuehn, *Posten auf ewiger Wache: Aus dem abenteurreichen Leben des Max von Scheubner-Richter* (Essen, Germany: Essener Verlagsanstalt, 1938), 9. An English translation is available: Paul Leverkuehn, *A German Officer during the Armenian Genocide: A Biography of Max von Scheubner-*

Richter (London: Taderon Press, 2008), though the German version was used here. Nolte claims that somebody else wrote this book, a ghostwriter, apparently, by the name of Erik Reger. Ernst Nolte, *Der europäische Bürgerkrieg, 1917–1945: Nationalsozialismus und Bolschewismus* (Frankfurt am Main: Propyläen Verlag, 1987), 114n22.

19. Joseph claims that this was indeed a warning of genocide and that Leverkuehn also tried to warn his colleagues in Hitler's Wehrmacht directly about the Holocaust. Joseph, "Scheubner-Richter," 155.

20. Leverkuehn, *Posten*, 32.

21. Ibid., 33.

22. Ibid., 34.

23. Ibid., 35.

24. Ibid., 40–41.

25. Ibid., 44.

26. Ibid., 45.

27. Ibid., 45–46.

28. Ibid., 46.

29. Ibid.

30. Ibid., 49, 51.

31. Ibid., 64–65.

32. Ibid., 66.

33. Ibid., 67–68.

34. Ibid., 83, 102.

35. Ibid., 158–159.

36. Ibid., 186–187.

37. Ibid., 190–191, see also 192–193.

38. Friedrich Kress von Kressenstein, *Mit den Türken zum Suezkanal* (Berlin: 1938), 138.

39. "Besuch bei Frau Mathilde von Scheubner-Richter am 3 April 1936 (Bericht vom 4. April 1936)," NS 26–2537, *Bundesarchiv Berlin;* the report speaks of one and a half years to two years.

40. See "Letter Mathilde von Scheubner-Richter to Heinrich Himmler, 17 April 1935," NS 26–1263 Scheubner-Richter, *Bundesarchiv Berlin.*

41. Compare: "Allgemeine Korrespondenz/Himmler," N 1126/17 (especially the letter by Haji Mazar from 18 September 1923), *Bundesarchiv Koblenz;* Peter Longerich, *Heinrich Himmler: Biographie* (Munich: Pantheon, 2008), 60–61.

42. An article in the *Deutsche Allgemeine Zeitung* on 9 February 1941 that glossed over the fate of the Armenians during World War I provoked protest from the German consul in Trabzon, Hermann Hoffmann-Fölkersamb. He felt he had to speak against this whitewashing of the Armenian genocidal past and cited the Lepsius volume as well as Werfel's *The Forty Days of Musa Dagh* as establishing the truth about what had happened to the Armenians in a report to his superiors. Hermann Hoffmann-Fölkersamb, "Politisches," 11 April 1941, Ankara 442, *Political Archives of the German Foreign Office.*

43. Max Biehl, *England als Wucherbankier* (Berlin: Junker und Dünnhaupt Verlag, 1940), 25.

44. See, for example, Carl Mühlmann, "Unsere türkischen Bundesgenossen," *Völkischer Beobachter*, 31 October 1934; Carl Mühlmann, "Die Landung an den Dardanellen," *Völkischer Beobachter*, 25 April 1935; Gustav Goes, "Der militärische Zusammenbruch der alten Türkei," *Völkischer Beobachter*, 15 November 1938.

45. Hermann Wanderscheck, *Englische Lügenpropaganda im Weltkrieg und heute* (Berlin: Junker and Dünnhaupt, 1940), 41; a book by the same author in 1936 had at least mentioned Toynbee's book on the Armenian atrocities (however, mainly to introduce the Lord Bryce, who was featured extensively in Toynbee's book) in a list of "horrors propaganda" literature, Hermann Wanderscheck, *Weltkrieg und Propaganda* (Berlin: Mittler, 1936), 135.

46. "*Life* Presents This War's First Great Memoirs "Failure of a Mission" by the Right Honourable Sir Nevile Henderson," *Life*, 25 March 1940, 89–99, here 89.

47. Louis P. Lochner, *What About Germany?* (London: Hodder and Stoughton, 1943), 12; see also, "Document L-3," in Office of the United States Chief of Counsel for Prosecution of Axis Criminality, ed., *Nazi Conspiracy and Aggression*, vol. 7 (Washington, DC: Government Printing Office, 1946), 753.

48. See Eric D. Weitz, *A Century of Genocide: Utopias of Race and Nation* (Princeton, NJ: Princeton University Press, 2005), 240–241.

49. See Winfried Baumgart, "Zur Ansprache Hitlers vor den Führern der Wehrmacht am 22. August 1939: Eine quellenkritische Untersuchung," *Vierteljahrshefte für Zeitgeschichte* 2 (1968): 120–149; Margaret Lavinia Anderson, "'Down in Turkey, Far Away'—Human Rights, the Armenian Massacres, and Orientalism in Wilhelmine Germany," *Journal of Modern History* 1 (2007): 80–111; here 110–111.

50. See, for example, Kevork B. Bardakjian, *Hitler and the Armenian Genocide* (Cambridge, MA: Zoryan Institute, 1985). For Turkish historiography on the topic see Fatma Müge Göçek, "Reading Genocide: Turkish Historiography on 1915," in Ronald Grigor Suny, Fatma Müge Göcek, and Norman M. Naimark, eds., *A Question of Genocide: Armenians and Turks at the End of the Ottoman Empire* (Oxford: Oxford University Press, 2011), 42–52; and Erik Jan Zürcher, "Renewal and Silence: Postwar Unionist and Kemalist Rhetoric on the Armenian Genocide," in ibid., 306–316. See also, Uğur Ümit Üngör, *The Making of Modern Turkey: Nation and State in Eastern Anatolia, 1913–1950* (Oxford: Oxford University Press, 2011), 218–250.

51. Heath W. Lowry, "The US Congress and Adolf Hitler on the Armenians," *Political Communication and Persuasion* 2 (1985), online at www.ataa.org /reference/hitler-lowry.html (accessed July 2011). On Lowry's role in the denial of the Armenian genocide see Ronald Grigor Suny, "Writing Genocide: The Fate of the Ottoman Armenians," in Suny et al., eds., *A Question of Genocide*, 15–41, especially 15, 23–24; see also, Heath W. Lowry, *The Story behind Ambassador Morgenthau's Story* (Istanbul: Isis, 1990).

52. Bardakjian, *Hitler and the Armenian Genocide,* 28.

53. Dominik J. Schaller, "Der Völkermord an den Armeniern und der Holocaust: Grenzen und Möglichkeiten eines Vergleichs," in Ischchan Tschiftdschjan, ed., *Stimmen aus Deutschland: Zum 90. Gedenkjahr des Völkermordes an den Armeniern, 1915–2005,* 196–201 (Antelias, Lebanon: Armenian Patriarchate, 2005), 200.

54. As others argue as well; see, for example, Margaret Lavinia Anderson, "Who Still Talked about the Extermination of the Armenians?—German Talk and German Silences," in Suny et al., *A Question of Genocide;* Norman M. Naimark, *Fires of Hatred: Ethnic Cleansing in Twentieth-Century Europe* (Cambridge, MA: Harvard University Press, 2001), 57–58; see also Gruner, who shows through an analysis of encyclopedias of the time that knowledge about the Armenian Genocide was expected to be commonplace: Wolf Gruner, "'Armenier-Greuel': Was wussten jüdische und nichtjüdische Deutsche im NS-Staat über den Völkermord von 1915/16?," in Fritz Bauer Institut and Sybille Steinbacher, eds., *Holocaust und Völkermorde: Die Reichweite des Vergleichs* (Frankfurt am Main: Campus, 2012), 31–54.

55. *Grundfragen einer deutschen Grossraumverwaltung: Festgabe für Heinrich Himmler* (Darmstadt, Germany: Wittich, 1941); excerpts published in *Zeitschrift für Politik* (June 1942), as reprinted in "The Criminal Conspiracy against the Jewish People: The Preconceived Plan to Annihilate the Jewish People," fol. 22, Weizmann Archive, WA 1: Dokumente zur Rettung europäischer Juden, *Max Kreutzberger Collection.*

56. Joachim Fest, *Speer: Eine Biographie* (Berlin: Fest, 1999), 77; see also, Ian Kershaw, *Hitler, 1889–1936: Hubris* (London: Penguin, 2001 [1998]), 15.

57. Karl Gustav Ossiannilsson, *Sven Hedin, Nobleman: An Open Letter* (London: T. Fisher Unwin, 1917), for example 157, 215–217; Sarah K. Danielsson, *The Explorer's Roadmap to National-Socialism: Sven Hedin, Geography and the Path to Genocide* (Farnham, UK: Ashgate, 2012), 99–100.

58. For this and more see Danielsson, *The Explorer's Roadmap,* 157–159.

59. Ibid., 171.

60. Karsten Brüggemann: "Max Erwin von Scheubner-Richter (1884–1923): Der 'Führer des Führers'?," in Michael Garleff, ed., *Deutschbalten, Weimarer Republik und Drittes Reich,* vol. 1, 119–145 (Cologne: Böhlau, 2001), 131; Stangeland claims that Scheubner was merely one of hundreds of Nazis and that he had no special place in Nazi history: Sigurd Sverre Stangeland, *Die Rolle Deutschlands im Völkermord an den Armeniern, 1915–1916* (Trondheim, Norway: NTNU, 2013), 175.

61. Nolte claimed that for Scheubner the Armenian Genocide was objectionable because it was "Asian." Such a claim cannot at all be substantiated by what we discussed in Chapter 6. Nolte, *Der europäische Bürgerkrieg,* 114.

62. Joseph, "Scheubner-Richter." Stangeland makes a similar argument, but does not even acknowledge the possibility of Scheubner transmitting "Armenian knowledge." Stangeland, *Die Rolle Deutschlands,* 175.

63. Schaller thinks Scheubner and Hitler talking about the Armenians is "improbable," but makes no argument for this. Dominik J. Schaller, "Die Rezeption des Völkermordes an den Armeniern in Deutschland, 1915–1945," in Hans-Lukas Kieser and Dominik J. Schaller, eds., *Der Völkermord an den Armeniern und die Shoah*, 517–555 (Zurich: Chronos, 2002), 542.

64. Jay Winter, "Under the Cover of War: The Armenian Genocide in the Context of Total War," in Jay Winter, ed., *America and the Armenian Genocide*, 37–51 (Cambridge: Cambridge University Press, 2003), 39; Robert Fisk, *The Great War for Civilization: The Conquest of the Middle East* (London: Harper Perennial, 2006), 406. Bloxham criticizes such arguments as too simplistic, but the fact remains that it had gone unpunished and it had unfolded a strong attraction as a means of solving minority questions. Donald Bloxham, *The Great Game of Genocide: Imperialism, Nationalism, and the Destruction of the Ottoman Armenians* (Oxford: Oxford University Press, 2005), 217.

65. Julius Richter, "Die deutschen evangelischen Missionskreise und das armenische Volk," *Allgemeine Missionszeitschrift*, 6 February 1919, in Wolfgang Gust, ed., *Armenocide: Documents from the State Archives*, online at www.armenocide.net.

66. Raphael Lemkin, *Totally Unofficial: The Autobiography of Raphael Lemkin*, Donna-Lee Frieze, ed. (New Haven, CT: Yale University Press, 2013), 113; see also, Yehuda Bauer, *Rethinking the Holocaust* (New Haven, CT: Yale University Press, 2002), 223.

67. " 'Greueltaten,' " *Neue Preussische (Kreuz-)Zeitung*, 29 October 1915.

68. See, for example, Medardus Brehl, " 'Diese Schwarzen haben vor Gott und den Menschen den Tod verdient'—Der Völkermord an den Herero 1904 und seine zeitgenössische Legitimation," in Fritz Bauer Institut, ed., *Völkermord und Kriegsverbrechen in der ersten Hälfte des 20. Jahrhunderts* (Frankfurt: Campus, 2004), 77–97.

69. Gust stresses that conversion as an exit was not approved by Talât; Wolfgang Gust, *Der Völkermord an den Armeniern: Die Tragödie des ältesten Christenvolkes der Welt* (Munich: Carl Hanser Verlag, 1993), 235; Taner Akçam, *The Young Turks' Crime against Humanity: The Armenian Genocide and Ethnic Cleansing in the Ottoman Empire* (Princeton, NJ: Princeton University Press, 2012), xxx; further on the comparison, see Vahakn N. Dadrian, "The Prefiguration of Some Aspects of the Holocaust in the Armenian Genocide: Revisiting the Comparative Perspective," *Genocide Studies and Prevention* 1 (2008): 99–109; Hans-Walter Schmuhl, "Der Völkermord an den Armeniern, 1915–1917, in vergleichender Perspektive," in Fikret Adanir and Bernd Bonwetsch, eds., *Osmanismus, Nationalismus und der Kaukasus* (Wiesbaden, Germany: Ludwig Reichert Verlag, 2005), 271–299; Norman Naimark, *Ethnic Cleansing in Twentieth-Century Europe* (Cambridge, MA: Harvard University Press, 2002), 35–36.

70. See, for example, Christopher Browning, *The Origins of the Final Solution: The Evolution of Nazi Jewish Policy, September 1939–March 1942*, with con-

tributions by Jürgen Matthäus (London: Arrow Books, 2005); on the comparison see also, for example, Robert Melson, "Paradigms of Genocide: The Holocaust, the Armenian Genocide, and Contemporary Mass Destructions," in "The Holocaust: Remembering for the Future," special issue, *Annals of the American Academy of Political and Social Science* 548 (1996): 156–168.

Epilogue: Armenian Writings on the Wall

1. Andreas Meier, "Nachwort," in Andreas Meier, ed., *Armin T. Wegner: Die Austreibung des armenischen Volkes in die Wüste—Ein Lichtbildvortrag*, 153–192 (Göttingen, Germany: Wallstein, 2011), 182–183; for a critical assessment of Wegner see Margaret Lavinia Anderson, "Helden in der Zeit des Völkermords? Armin T. Wegner, Ernst Jäckh, Henry Morgenthau," in Rolf Hosfeld, ed., *Johannes Lepsius: Eine deutsche Ausnahme*, 126–159 (Göttingen, Germany: Wallstein, 2013), 129–130.
2. Meier, "Nachwort," 183–184.
3. Ibid.
4. As quoted in Elizabeth Khorikian, "Die Behandlung des Völkermordes an den Armeniern in der deutschen Presse und Literatur um 1915–1925," in Armenuhi Drost-Abgarjan, ed., *Armenologie in Deutschland*, 159–172 (Münster: LIT Verlag, 2005), 171.
5. Anderson, "Helden," 129–130.
6. Johanna Wernicke-Rothmayer, *Armin T. Wegner: Gesellschaftserfahrung und literarisches Werk* (Frankfurt am Main: Peter Lang, 1982), 190, 193.
7. Margaret Lavinia Anderson tries to demolish all of Wegner's heroism and criticizes him for the lenient treatment he experienced in the concentration camp, as well as for the fact that the letter was not a public one but rather a "private" one, as it was sent to Hitler directly and not published anywhere else. Yet, this critique glosses over the fact that it would seem improbable that a Third Reich paper would reprint such an open letter at all—note how difficult it had been to find a paper for his open letter to President Wilson. Anderson, "Helden," 126–159.
8. A version of the letter is reprinted in Wernicke-Rothmayer, *Armin T. Wegner*, 321–328.
9. Wernicke speaks of his "pacifism" as a reason, but that would, as a term and indictment, not exclude the open letter to Hitler; perhaps it was a pretext so that the open letter did not need to be mentioned in official documents. Wernicke-Rothmayer, *Armin T. Wegner*, 194.
10. Anderson, "Helden," 127.
11. "Armin T. Wegner," Yad Vashem website, www.yadvashem.org/yv/en/righteous/stories/wegner.asp.
12. Anderson criticizes Wegner for not having criticized Italian fascism and for having lived in a comfortable state of exile there. Anderson, "Helden," 129.

13. Jonathan Kreutner, "Die Reaktion der deutschen Juden auf die Verfolgung der Armenier von 1896 bis 1939," in Hans-Lukas Kieser and Elmar Plozza, eds., *Der Völkermord an den Armeniern, die Türkei und Europa,* 133–146 (Zurich: Chronos, 2006), 142.

14. "Vorlesung von Franz Werfel in der Akademie," *Deutsche Allgemeine Zeitung,* 9 December 1932.

15. The novel was not among Werfel's books that were burned by the Nazis in early 1933, as Auron claims; it was only published months later. Yair Auron, *The Banality of Indifference: Zionism and the Armenian Genocide* (New Brunswick, NJ: Transaction, 2000), 294.

16. As, for example, the actress Adrienne Barbeau relates that *The Forty Days* was an essential, if not expected, part of exploring her (or one's) Armenian identity. Adrienne Barbeau, *There Are Worse Things I Could Do* (New York: Carroll and Graf Publishers, 2007), 6.

17. Ferda Balancar, ed., *The Sounds of Silence: Turkey's Armenians Speak* (Istanbul: International Hrant Dink Foundation Publications, 2012), 37–43.

18. Matthew C. Roudané, *Conversations with Arthur Miller* (Jackson: University Press of Mississippi, 1987), 324.

19. Anthony Summers and Robbyn Swan, *Sinatra: The Life* (London: Corgi, 2006), 123.

20. Edward Said, *Out of Place: A Memoir* (London: Granta Books, 1999), 206.

21. Vaclav Havel, *Letters to Olga, June 1979–September 1982,* trans. Paul Wilson (London: Faber and Faber, 1990), 32.

22. Michael Bobelian, *Children of Armenia: A Forgotten Genocide and the Century-Long Struggle for Justice* (New York: Simon and Schuster, 2009), 83.

23. Karl H. Schlesier, *Flakhelfer to Grenadier: Memoir of a Boy Soldier, 1943–1945* (Solihull, UK: Helion and Company, 2014), 102.

24. Robert Leonard, *Von Neumann, Morgenstern, and the Creation of Game Theory: From Chess to Social Science, 1900–1960* (Cambridge: Cambridge University Press, 2012), 205.

25. On the Jewish knowledge of the Armenian Genocide, see also, Wolf Gruner, "'Peregrinations into the Void?' German Jews and Their Knowledge about the Armenian Genocide during the Third Reich," *Central European History* 1 (2012): 1–26.

26. Auron, *The Banality of Indifference,* 294.

27. The following account is deeply indebted to Auron's work on the subject: Yair Auron, *The Banality of Denial: Israel and the Armenian Genocide* (New Brunswick, NJ: Transaction, 2003); Auron, *The Banality of Indifference.*

28. Marcel Reich-Ranicki, *The Author of Himself: The Life of Marcel Reich-Ranicki* (London: Phoenix, 2002), 25.

29. William W. Mishell, *A Kaddish for Kovno: Life and Death in a Lithuanian Ghetto, 1941–1945* (Chicago: Chicago Review Press, 1998), 141.

30. Dina Abramowicz, "The Library in the Vilna Ghetto," in Jonathan Rose, ed., *The Holocaust and the Book: Destruction and Preservation,* 165–171 (Amherst, MA: University of Massachusetts Press, 2008), 168.

31. Rachel Margolis, *A Partisan from Vilna* (Brighton, MA: Academic Studies Press, 2010), 295.
32. As quoted in Sara Bender, *The Jews of Bialystok during World War II and the Holocaust* (Lebanon, NH: University Press of New England, 2008), 162.
33. As quoted in Auron, *The Banality of Indifference*, 302.
34. As quoted in ibid.
35. As quoted in ibid., 303.
36. Auron, *The Banality of Indifference*, 306.
37. Ibid., 304–305.
38. Ibid., 307; on the Warsaw Ghetto see also, Jonathan Kreutner, "Die vierzig Tage des Musa Dagh: Zur jüdischen Rezeption von Werfels Roman während der NS-Herrschaft," in Dan Diner, ed., *Leipziger Beiträge zur jüdischen Geschichte und Kultur*, vol. 3, 199–213 (Leipzig: Universitätsverlag, 2005), 211.
39. Auron, *The Banality of Indifference*, 306.
40. Ibid., 294.
41. Ibid., 295.
42. Ibid., 296; a different translation is also in Na'ama Sheffi, "The Hebrew Absorption of German Literature in the Yishuv," in Efraim Karsh, ed., *Israel: The First Hundred Years*, vol. 1, *Israel's Transition from Community to State*, 158–171 (London: Routledge, 2013 [2000]), 168, 171.
43. Auron, *The Banality of Indifference*, 298.
44. Ibid., 300.
45. Yoram Kaniuk, *Commander of the Exodus* (New York: Grove Press, 2001), 5.
46. Ibid., 49.
47. The chicken quote: Vartkes Yeghiayan, *Pro Armenia: Jewish Responses to the Armenian Genocide* (Glendale, CA: Center for Armenian Remembrance, 2011), 204.
48. Steven L. Jacobs, "Raphael Lemkin and the Armenian Genocide," in Richard G. Hovannisian, *Looking Backward, Moving Forward: Confronting the Armenian Genocide* (New Brunswick, NJ: Transaction, 2003), 125–135. A shorter comment on the matter is included in the version of Lemkin's memoirs recently published: Raphael Lemkin, *Totally Unofficial: The Autobiography of Raphael Lemkin*, Donna-Lee Frieze, ed. (New Haven, CT: Yale University Press, 2013), 20; Rolf Hosfeld, *Operation Nemesis: Die Türkei, Deutschland und der Völkermord an den Armeniern* (Cologne: Kiepenheuer and Witsch, 2005), 7.

Acknowledgments

First and foremost, this book and its author are deeply indebted to many researchers, most of whom I never had the pleasure of meeting, but all of whom I have to thank for their work on the topic. Most of this book's core chapters rely on my own research, but without the previous research of many others, this book would not have been possible.

The topic—Germany and the Armenians—has seen a number of significant contributions in German-language publications in the recent years, many of which have not received adequate attention so far. Out of all the texts cited in the previous chapters, a few deserve special mention here: Two edited volumes, one by Hans-Lukas Kieser and Dominik J. Schaller, the other by Kieser and Elmar Plozza, have contributed much to the further exploration of the nexus and the comparison of the Armenian Genocide and the Holocaust. Here especially the essays by Dominik J. Schaller and Hans-Walter Schmuhl opened up new perspectives on the German reception of the Armenian Genocide, as did Rolf Hosfeld's book on the German-Armenian connections. Previous studies and unpublished PhD theses, especially those by Norbert Saupp, Friedrich Scherer, Gregor Schöllgen, and Wilhem van Kampen, have done much of the ground work for the time up until 1914. Mehmet Cebeci's recent book on Abdul Hamid and Germany, focusing especially on the various national questions, among them the Armenian question, has been a welcome addition to the field. The books by Uwe Feigel and Axel Meissner on German pro-Armenian circles have meticulously excavated an otherwise neglected topic. Yair Auron's work was crucial for exploring how the Armenian Genocide has influenced Jews in Europe and in Israel/Palestine.

Of great importance has been Wolfgang Gust's work on the German sources. His collection of documents from the German Foreign Office, now also available in English, has made the topic much more accessible and will certainly (further) revolutionize how the Armenian Genocide is discussed. Here, I honor his work— as well as the wonderful students of my source-focused course at the University of Regensburg (2010/2011) in which we worked with Gust's source edition extensively—by citing mainly documents directly from his source collections so that others may discover and use them as well.

Much of this book reconstructs published public opinion in the form of press discourse. This was done for the three key periods—1914–1918, 1919–1923, and 1933–1945—through a mix of complete analysis of key newspapers (here availability and importance were selection criteria), cross-paper checks, as well as extensive use of press clipping collections. I am deeply grateful to the unnamed and unknown people of the Reichslandbund who, beginning well over a hundred years ago, started cutting and collecting newspaper clippings on various topics of German and international politics. Their collection at the German Federal Archives in Berlin is a treasure for all who work on the history of the discursive sphere. As always, I am also indebted to the various libraries, librarians, archivists, and institutions around the world supporting such a project, especially those at the German Federal Archives, the German Foreign Office Political Archive, Heidelberg University Library, and the Institute Deutsche Presseforschung at Bremen University.

It would have been impossible to write this book without the fantastic support, collegial atmosphere, and inspired discussions at the Van Leer Institute and the Polonsky Academy. I especially thank Leonard Polonsky and Gabriel Motzkin for their generous support. I also thank the other institutions that have enabled my travels along this difficult path, especially the Gulbenkian Foundation in Lisboa and the Zentrum für Literatur- und Kulturforschung in Berlin.

Ronen Mandelkern, Pascal Firges, and Tobias Graf read the script and helped me improve it in many ways. Allison Dawe and Ashley Moore were vigilant, critical, and inspired copyeditors. I also thank the two anonymous reviewers for helping me shape my arguments further and avoid mistakes. Both author and book are especially indebted to our editor, Ian Malcolm, and the team at Harvard University Press, and here especially Joy Deng, for making this book possible and for having fun with it in the process.

It is impossible to name everybody, but I am very grateful for and happy about all the helping hands and constructive comments offered to me, first and foremost by Sir Richard J. Evans, but also by Christopher Clark, Mariana Hausleitner, Ulf Brunnbauer, Raymond Kevorkian, Lewis Enim, Nathan Marcus, Amos Morris-Reich, Rolf Hosfeld, Erdal Kaynar, Corry Guttstadt, Nazan Maksudyan, Mehmet Yercil, David Motadel, Bedross Der Matossian, Amos Goldberg, Margaret Lavinia Anderson, Yehuda Bauer, Moshe Zimmermann, Holger Böning, Yair Auron, Nathan Gardels, Michelle Tusan, George Hintlian, Merav Mack, Medi Nahmiyaz, Silvia Jonas, Tal Kohavi, Shimon Alon, Miriam Ben David, and Stella Khalafyan.

My greatest thanks go out to those closest to me who had to suffer under the weight of this project. Especially my wife, Roni, our families and friends, and especially my parents, Beate and Johann, who, as always, supported me and my work. As always, this book is also dedicated to them.

Index

Abdul Aziz, 20

Abdul Hamid II, 14, 20–21, 60, 85, 87, 160, 166; relationship with Bismarck and Germany, 24, 26–29, 33, 38; Armenian reforms, 35, 103–104, 245; events of 1896, 40–41, 248; Hamidiye, 40; influence on German media, 43, 56; Naumann's support, 69; revolution, end of reign, 82, 85, 87, 88, 246. *See also* Young Turks

Abramowicz, Dina, 366

Adana: Lepsius visit, 49; massacre of 1909, 83–84, 232, 239; consuls in, 116, 130, 352; rebellion in, 165

Agence Havas, 167, 170

Agence Milli, 168

Akçam, Taner, 104

Albania, 24

Aleppo: consuls in, 113, 130; Walter Rössler, 131, 133, 166, 199, 262–263; Martin Niepage, 146–147, 297; Young Turks, 280

Alexander Karatheodori Pasha, 21

Algeria, 97

Allgemeine Evangelisch-Lutherische Kirchenzeitung, 40

Allgemeine Missionszeitschrift, 195

Ankara, 352; attacks on deportees, 131, 248; New Turkey, 294, 322, 327, 329; the Ankara solution, 325–326

anti-Semitism: and anti-Armenianism, 2, 3, 57, 60–61, 74–77, 81, 123–124, 145, 161, 188, 221, 260, 293–294, 296, 301–310; Jewish question, 14, 288, 294, 301, 319, 350–351; and racialism, 60, 296, 302, 310–312; Naumann, 64; and the Nazis, 187, 220, 301–302, 312, 315–318; Hans Humann, 293–294; Hitler, 335, 346, 361

Arco-Valley, Anton, 198

Ardahan, 22, 153

Armenian Triple Entente (Great Britain, France, and Russia), 33, 40, 165

Armenian Horrors (1894–1896), 7, 29, 33–34, 53, 59; and the press, 41–47, 55–56, 61, 69, 173; Johannes Lepsius lectures, 47–49, 53; Martin Rade, 58

Arslan, Şefik, 274

Aryan, 220, 303–305, 308–311, 317–319, 325, 334, 349

Asaf Bey, 249

Assyrians, 98, 126

Atatürk, Mustafa Kemal, 86, 95, 291; Leer's biography of Hitler, 316; Turkish War of Independence, 320–322; Nazi admiration, 326–329, 346–347; Hitler's Putsch, 349, 352. *See also* Hitler; Turkish War of Independence

Auf gut Deutsch, 85

Auschwitz, 107, 298, 338, 351, 352, 367

Austria-Hungary, 7, 24, 66, 107, 135; Berlin Treaty, 26–27

Axenfeld, Karl, 196

Azmi, Cemal, 284

451